About the Author

Matthew Sparke is Professor of Geography and International Studies at the University of Washington, where he also serves as the Director of the undergraduate program in Global Health. He has authored over 60 scholarly publications, including the book *In the Space of Theory* (2005), but he is also dedicated to teaching about globalization as well as writing about it. He has multiple awards for his work as a teacher, including the lifetime Distinguished Teaching award from the University of Washington.

INTRODUCING GLOBALIZATION

Ties, Tensions, and Uneven Integration

Matthew Sparke

A John Wiley & Sons, Ltd., Publication

Blackwell Publishing was acquired by John Wiley & Sons in February 2007. Blackwell's publishing program
has been merged with Wiley's global Scientific, Technical, and Medical business to form Wiley-Blackwell.

Registered Office
John Wiley & Sons, Ltd, The Atrium, Southern Gate, Chichester, West Sussex, PO19 8SQ, UK

Editorial Offices
350 Main Street, Malden, MA 02148-5020, USA
9600 Garsington Road, Oxford, OX4 2DQ, UK
The Atrium, Southern Gate, Chichester, West Sussex, PO19 8SQ, UK

For details of our global editorial offices, for customer services, and for information about how
to apply for permission to reuse the copyright material in this book please see our website at
www.wiley.com/wiley-blackwell.

Library of Congress Cataloging-in-Publication Data

Sparke, Matthew.
  Introducing globalization : ties, tensions, and uneven integration / Matthew Sparke.
     pages   cm
  Includes bibliographical references and index.
  ISBN 978-0-631-23128-8 (hbk.) – ISBN 978-0-631-23129-5 (pbk.)
 1. International economic integration.   2. Globalization.   I. Title.
  HF1418.5.S685 2013
  303.48′2–dc23
                                        2012031790

A catalogue record for this book is available from the British Library.

Cover image: Morocco © GavinD/iStockphoto; forest © Stephen Rees/iStockphoto; ship © james steidl/
iStockphoto; Times Square © Terraxplorer; monk © Glen Allison/Getty; concrete wall © AFP/Getty Images
Cover design by www.cyandesign.co.uk

Set in 10.5/13pt Minion by SPi Publisher Services, Pondicherry, India
Printed in The USA by Sheridan Books, Inc.

3   2014

Contents

Figures

Tables

Preface

This is a preface to a textbook on globalization, written in Seattle, on a Chinese-made computer, by an American citizen, who grew up in England, who first became interested in global ties thanks to a children's book about the British empire (Figure 0.1), who went on to be taught global geography at Oxford by critics of imperialism, where he was told he should get a "more global" post-graduate education by leaving the United Kingdom, who then earned a PhD from a Canadian university, who is now a professor at a US university, teaching about globalization to classes filled with a new generation of international students, who have themselves been promised a "global education," which is now measured by rankings of the world's "most global universities," which are listed like the ratings used to guide global investments in global corporations, which have created the globally competitive job market for which students seek globally valued knowledge, which is offered in globally circulated articles and books which, like this textbook, are written on computers made in low-wage factories, by young workers who never go to university, who as migrants from rural areas are often denied citizenship rights in the factory zones, whose exploitation is a major concern of global anti-sweatshop activism, which, ever since the protests against the World Trade Organization in Seattle in 1999, has made globalization the contentious issue that it remains today, and as such, a major focus of public debate, analysis, and, as this textbook also exemplifies, education.

One of the most common protestor slogans seen in Seattle back in 1999 was: "NO GLOBALIZATION WITHOUT REPRESENTATION" (Figures 0.2 and 0.3). The simple point here was to say that economic forms of globalization, like transnational trade, ought to come with new political forms of global participation, that they should provide workers, environmentalists, and human rights activists as well as trade ministers with a democratic voice in the global rule-making process. Recalling the language of the American revolution – "NO TAXATION WITHOUT REPRESENTATION" – this was a demand for political representation and

Figure 0.1 Front cover of *The Wonder Book of Empire for Boys and Girls*, ed. Harry Golding (London: Ward, Lock & Co, Ltd, 1939).

Figure 0.2 "No Globalization Without Representation." Photograph by Matthew Sparke.

democratic participation on a new transnational scale. Intentionally or not, however, the slogan also underlined the fact that representations of globalization – of what it involves, who it effects and how it reorders societies – are just as much part of the globalization story as the processes of global economic integration. In other

Figure 0.3   "No Globalization Without Representation." Photograph by Matthew Sparke.

words, how we represent globalization makes a difference because it shapes how global ties and tensions are understood, managed, and contested. This obviously makes writing a textbook on globalization a particular challenge. There is a need to represent the story of growing global integration as clearly as possible, but it has to be done in a way that also allows for reflection on the story-telling process itself – its interests, influences, and impacts all included.

Starting this preface with one long run-on sentence about the background of writing the book is just one way of provoking reflection on the story-telling process. Hopefully, it has already helped to make you reflect on how it is that you have come to be reading a textbook about globalization, and, perhaps, on how your ties to the technologies involved may link your own life with the lives of workers in far away factories. Maybe it has also raised questions in your mind about how your own perspective on globalization might be different from the perspectives of those workers. And maybe the information about my own background as the book's author may have in turn made you wonder about how the imperial perspective indicated by that other older book – the one about the wonder of the British empire that was given to me by my grandfather – may have shaped this one.

None of the sentences in the pages that follow are as long and convoluted as the one at the start of this preface. The aim instead is to keep the writing simple so that the facts, theories, and debates about globalization are as easy to understand as possible. No assumptions are made about theoretical jargon that students are already supposed to know (and there is also a glossary at the end of the book that provides definitions of all the key terms that are introduced in bold in the main chapters). Moreover, the distinct disciplinary frameworks, models, and assumptions of particular academic fields of study are avoided as much as possible in the hope that the writing will therefore prove more open and accessible to all. Nevertheless, none of this means that the expectations for student learning are somehow set low or that complex ideas and arguments are ignored. Thanks to the example and inspiration of my students at the University of Washington, I believe it is perfectly possible for undergraduates to grasp the complexity of globalization in ways that allow them to become active participants themselves in the debates over how it *should* be represented. Again and again, students taking my *Introduction to Globalization* class have shown me that they can understand and engage in some of the most complicated, challenging, and politically fraught debates over globalization just as long as the course material is introduced in a way that builds a structure for new knowledge as it moves forward. Inspired by the achievements of these students over a decade of teaching this course, I have tried to create a learning "scaffolding" in the same way here in this book: assuming no specialist knowledge at the start, but trying to enable increasing intellectual engagement and critical reflection as the chapters of analysis and argument proceed.

In what follows, each chapter builds on the one that comes before with a view to supporting increasingly sophisticated understanding and explanation. As a result, the chapters towards the end of the book (the chapters on governance, space, and health) are longer than those that come before, and they address some of the most complex ways in which globalization creates new tensions and divisions as well as new forms of global integration. The final chapter builds in turn on all of this analysis to present one of the most difficult learning challenges of all: namely, the challenge of what is to be done, of working out how we should best respond as students and scholars to the current forms of globalization. Here, we return to the question of representation once more, rethinking it in terms of how our ability to respond to globalization – our response-ability – relates back to how we represent our ties to the processes of global integration and how we therefore understand (or ignore) our global responsibilities.

In order to approach the complexities of globalization in a way that makes room for reflection on responses, it is vital to remember at least three key points. The first is that globalization has a long global history of antecedents that structure what different individuals and institutions can do. These antecedents of contemporary globalization clearly include the sorts of global integration (and division) associated with earlier eras of empire. The second is that today's processes of global integration are by no means inevitable or unstoppable; that they can instead be reversed or reorganized and re-regulated, too. And the third key point (one that remains as prominent through this book as it is in the title) is that globalization has not simply created a single "level playing field," or "flat world" or "one world" as some of the more gung-ho commentators have tended to suggest. To be sure, this is a very common representation of globalization, and it is also a very influential representation in shaping global policy-making. However, it ignores far too much of what is happening. The new global interconnections of our world come with all sorts of inequalities and asymmetries of wealth and power. The ties have created tremendous global opportunities for connection, communication, and shared knowledge. They have made possible extraordinary growth in some places and amazing forms of global coordination between such places, too. Just visit a big global shipping port such as Singapore or Hong Kong, or spend some time in any global airport, and the sheer scale of global coordination is overwhelming. But this stunning world of connection and coordination has been built in such a way as to create terrible suffering, exclusion, waste, and violence at the same time. To play off the spatial metaphors in the titles of two books about globalization that have been popular among my students over the last few years, Thomas Friedman's assertion that *The World is Flat* needs therefore to be constantly contrasted with the observations about *Mountains Beyond Mountains* in Tracy Kidder's account of the obstacles facing the global struggle for global health.[1]

Kidder's book is about the work of the physician and anthropologist, Paul Farmer, whose own writing about globalization and the recriminations of the world's poor and sick is especially inspiring to me. As the alliterations in his books' titles indicate – for example, *Infections and Inequalities* and *Pathologies of Power* – Farmer continually asks his audiences to remember how global health interconnections and global inequalities are related to one another; that they shape one another at the very same time.[2] He thereby draws on the arguments of his patients in poor countries such as Haiti to make the case that the whole history of global integration from the age of plantation slavery and empire through to today's era of debt, credit downgrades, and austerity has repeatedly involved division and dispossession, too. In this regard, another important inspiration for me in writing this book is a wonderful geographic history of globalization sketched by the Mexican cartoonist Rafael Barajas. Published under his newspaper name, *El Fisgón, the book is* entitled: *How to Succeed at Globalization: A Primer for the Roadside Vendor.*[3] The point of this subversive title is to remind us once more that *history, power*, and, most of all, *location* matter a great deal in shaping who ends up "succeeding" at globalization. Against the view that the world is flat, we here are therefore again confronted with a critical commentary from the perspective of those who – like a roadside vendor in a poor country – find themselves on the impoverished sidelines of the so-called global level playing field.

Following Farmer and El Fisgón, this is a textbook on globalization that seeks to explain how we have come to live in a world defined by global integration and inequality at the same time. For the same reason, the book cover features no single satellite photo, global image, or abstract sphere representing a globalized globe, and the pages that follow offer no simple sound bites about a "borderless world." The book spends much time addressing the increasing global influence of market competition on people's lives, communities, and governments, but it avoids suggesting that there is a single liberal-capitalist or market-based "end state" of globalization to which we are all inevitably heading. My hope is that the book will therefore better enable and encourage your own critical thinking rather than offer the final word on whether globalization is good, bad, or ugly. It is a book that is meant to help you think and ask questions about connections and contradictions as well as learn facts. It is meant to help you become a knowledgeable participant in public debates over globalization. And it is also meant to show why the representation of globalization within these debates matters.

Of course, many people debate globalization simply because it is a fascinating focus for study and conversation. But, in the end, this book is written in the hope that it will help you to go beyond study, student conversations, and academic debates. Ideally, it will also allow you to join efforts to redefine and remake globalization in the world beyond the university. My own big hope as an author therefore is that by avoiding the language of inevitability, I have represented globalization in a way that makes such change seem possible. This is a much more wonderful global prospect than the children's book I was given about the wonder of empire. And, in the same way, I hope it leads to personal journeys for readers that are still more global and transformative than my own.

Matthew Sparke, Seattle

Notes

1   Thomas L. Friedman, *The World Is Flat: A Brief History of the Twenty-First Century* (New York: Farrar, Straus and Giroux, 2005); and Tracy Kidder, *Mountains Beyond Mountains* (New York: Random House, 2003).

2   Paul Farmer, *AIDS and Accusation: Haiti and the Geography of Blame* (Berkeley: University of California Press, 2009); Paul Farmer, *Infections and Inequalities: The Modern Plagues* (Berkeley: University of California Press, 1999); Paul Farmer, *Pathologies of Power: Health, Human Rights, and the New War on the Poor* (Berkeley: University of California Press, 2003).

3   El Fisgón. *How to Succeed at Globalization: A Primer for the Roadside Vendor* (New York: Metropolitan, 2004).

1

Globalization

Chapter Contents

Chapter Concepts

Globalization needs to be understood on two levels:

- as a name for increasing global interdependencies
- as an influential key term in political speech.

Key Concept

The two main ways of understanding globalization need to be carefully distinguished. On the one hand, it is used by scholars to name the compound effects of intensifying and increasingly consequential global interconnections. By exploring these interconnections – including their component economic, political, legal, and ecological interrelationships – it is possible to understand how globalization has created global interdependencies that link the fates of people around the planet. On the other hand, we additionally need to understand how "Globalization" is simultaneously put to work as an influential codeword in political speech, a codeword that shapes policy-making and thus also alters the ways in which lives are actually lived globally.

1.1   Introducing a World of Interdependency and a Word

Why are you reading this book? It seems a simple question, and answers come easily to mind. It was recommended to you or is required reading for a class. It is about a topic that seems relevant, interesting or, at least, socially important. And, of course, you bought it. But think again. What actually enabled that simple purchase to happen? When you bought it, did you consider where and how the book was made: where the paper was made (China), where the typesetting took place (India), where the inks were manufactured (Switzerland), where the book was printed (Singapore), or who made the printing presses (Germans and Japanese)? You probably did not think of these things because the simple act of buying something usually conceals all this work. Likewise, when you buy a book you do not normally think about the global networks of air, sea, rail, and road transportation that put it in the bookshops; the oil and other forms of energy used in the process of transportation; or the global systems of electronic funds transfer that allow money to move from your account to the bookstore's account to the accounts of the publisher, to the pension plans, and the stocks and bonds into which people working for the publisher might be putting the profits.

As if the globalized ramifications of all the book-publishing economic links are not already hard enough to track, think about the still more complex political and cultural phenomena that have come together to make the *idea* of globalization seem relevant, interesting, and important. When did you first hear the word or some related term like the global economy, global system, or globalism? How many times a day do you see adverts and promotional publications that use images of the globe to sell things? Why do so many activists, economists, reporters, and politicians repeat the word "globalization" as if it is some sort of common-sense code-word that everyone just understands? What has made it the focus of street protests and widespread controversy across the planet? And on top of all that, have you thought about why your university or college has come round to the view that it is worth having a course that introduces globalization at a level that demands reading a book that is entirely focused on the subject? What has put globalization onto the academic radar screen? Why has it become relevant and interesting? What makes it important? And what, you should hopefully be asking yourself at this point, *is* it exactly?

In starting with this set of questions, these first paragraphs have already given a clue as to the way the rest of the book sets about defining and explaining globalization. Global interconnections of production, commerce, and finance like those that made your book purchase possible are key, but so, too, are the political and cultural controversies that have made globalization the latest big buzzword. Other academic surveys of globalization generally prefer to focus only on the interconnections themselves. Most scholars are wary of the way in which globalization has become so fashionable as an idea and so blurred as a concept (even if putting it in the title of a book or article helps draw attention to their work). For usually good reasons, academics therefore tend to be suspicious about all the hype surrounding the term. One problem with this tendency, however, is that it treats the slogans, myths, and exaggerations about globalization as just irritants. By contrast, this book pays attention to the hype as more than a mere annoyance. The account that follows is still fundamentally organized around an analysis of real global interconnections. Each chapter is therefore focused on particular types of interconnection ranging from those of world trade and finance to those of law, politics, and health. However, along the way, the book also critically examines the buzz about globalization in order to underline how, as a dominant way of talking about and thinking about the world, the term has had its own global effects. The book as a whole, therefore, works with a double definition of globalization, a definition that addresses both (1) the actual networks of global integration and (2) the political and cultural concerns that have made "Globalization" a buzzword.

1.1.1 Globalization as integration

First of all, globalization refers to (processes of economic, political, and social integration that have collectively created ties that make a difference to lives around the planet.) Another way of saying this is that *globalization is the extension, acceleration, and intensification of consequential worldwide interconnections*. These are interconnections that mean that what happens "here" (like you buying and reading this book) affects things over "there" (like the logging of trees in faraway forests). Reciprocally, the interconnections can work the other way round with events over "there" (like an environmental group's campaign against deforestation) leading to effects "here" (like you wishing that the book was made out of recycled paper or available on the Internet). These sorts of two-way ties are often referred to by social scientists as "interdependencies." It means that the lines of dependency run in both directions, even if, as is most common, the dependency is felt more strongly at one end of the connection (for example, amongst the different parties to disputes over logging) than at the other (amongst readers of a single book). Whether or not they are felt or even noticed, though, these sorts of interdependencies are creating a world where, despite huge inequalities in life chances, people's lives are being increasingly bound together.

As we shall see in Chapter 3, the capitalist system of economic development has always depended from the sixteenth century onwards on forms of long-distance interdependency. Indeed, capitalism is generally understood to have begun through the gradual incorporation and capitalization of extensive pre-capitalist trading networks. From these early developments in the sixteenth century, the webs of economic interconnection have grown widely and deeply in terms of both their geographical scope and societal significance. The linkages have nevertheless always expanded *unevenly*, initially leading to economic growth in just one part of the world (Europe during the sixteenth, seventeenth, and eighteenth centuries) and then in others (the United States in the nineteenth and twentieth centuries, but also parts of Asia, the Middle East, and Latin America, too). Sometimes, most notably in the period of European empire building in the late nineteenth century, the global ties were very strong and had huge day-to-day impacts. Indeed, by the start of the twentieth century, global trade was so extensive that at its epicenter in London, England, most features of daily life – from the cotton people wore, to the sugared tea they drank, to the companies they worked for, to the banks where they deposited their money – were intimately tied to everyday life in places as far apart as Central Africa, the Caribbean, India, North America, and Latin America. At other times, both before and after the height of European imperialism, the consequences of the long-distance ties were less significant in terms of linking and shaping daily life in different parts of the world. Despite this episodic and uneven process of development, though, the important point is that global ties are not new. What *is* new, and what is quite remarkable in this regard, is the rise of a widely shared sense of the importance of something called "Globalization." This really only happened in the late twentieth century, starting in the 1960s and becoming increasingly omnipresent as a focus of debate and concern in the periods from the 1990s to today.

One reason for the rising concern with globalization over the last two decades is that it was only after key industrial, financial, and technological shifts in the 1960s and 1970s that the door was opened for different forms of global interdependency to *come together* to have a collective globalizing impact. Economic, political, and social networks – networks of commodity production, of finance, of trade, of migrants, of communication, of media, of political organizing, and even of new disease vectors – all came together in the sense of accelerating and intensifying one another. In doing so, they linked more and more countries and communities to create an interdependent global whole that was greater than the sum of all the particular component network parts. No longer was it just trade, or money flows, or political systems, or the movements of migrants that linked different regions. Now, global interconnection was characterized by an evermore dense integration of *all* these different transnational ties into a larger interdependent system in which the spatial reach of the ties, the speed of the relays and reverberations through the ties, and the capacity of the ties to lead to significant impacts were all much greater. These comprehensive integrative effects also had powerful political consequences with governments around the world increasingly tying national policies to an acceptance of the idea that economic growth and development are dependent on integrating with global markets and liberalizing business from national regulation.

A key sign of this novel late twentieth-century interdependency and market-based integration was the invention of the actual word "globalization" itself. Despite all the global connections of nineteenth-century European imperialism, a word like globalization had never been used before. It only first appeared in a dictionary in Merriam Webster's *New International Dictionary* in 1961. Around this time, it was often used in its English spelling (i.e. "globalisation" with an "s") in British journals and papers such as *The Spectator* and *The Sunday Times* (to be followed by its first of many uses in *The Economist* in 1965). French academics were also early to start using the term (although in France, it came to be replaced by *mondialisation*). This emergence of the word globalization into popular usage in the 1960s was a sign of the wider developments in the interconnectedness of global networks and their increasingly influential impact on policy making. Reciprocally, however, the subsequent explosion of debate and dispute over globalization also reflected the various ways in which politicians, activists, journalists, and other opinion leaders began to load the word with more and more political meaning based on their political perspectives on market freedom, market integration and the influence of market forces over much of social life. This process of politicization really only took off two decades later in the 1980s, and to understand it most effectively it is useful to introduce the second definition of globalization.

1.1.2   Globalization as buzzword

In a context where political leaders and polemicists from both the right and the left have increasingly used the term to pursue political goals, Globalization has become *an instrumental term put to work in shaping as well as representing the growth of global interdependency.* Some scholars refer to such politicized discourse on Globalization as "Globaloney" or "hyper-globalization," while others view it as a reflection of a cultural common-sense they call "Globalism."[2] Here, however, in this book, such political use of the term is indicated by simply spelling "Globalization" with a capital "G." The key era for the development of this kind of politicized discourse about capital "G" Globalization was the 1980s. In this decade, influential politicians in the West – most notably, Prime Minister Margaret Thatcher in the United Kingdom and President Ronald Reagan in the United States – made the political argument that a huge range of trade, labor, finance, welfare, and social policies had to be radically reformed to make states more competitive and more open to integration in the context of a globalizing capitalist market economy. Free trade, privatization, tax cuts, welfare reform, low inflation, and the general deregulation of business and finance were all necessary, went the argument, if nation-states were to stand a chance of surviving the onrush of global competition.

Although this familiar package of political policies was originally promoted in the United States and United Kingdom by conservative politicians, it was quickly adopted by more liberal governments in wealthy democracies such as Canada and New Zealand. In other countries such as Chile, it was a policy package that was introduced and enforced using military violence, while elsewhere, particularly in Asian countries such as Singapore, Taiwan, South Korea, and, subsequently, China, it was adapted in ways that combined the commitments to export-led development and market integration with often authoritarian approaches to managing social and political life. In yet other developing countries in Latin America, Asia, the Middle East, and Africa, it was imposed in order to comply with conditions issued by international lending agencies – most importantly, the International Monetary Fund (IMF) and World Bank – and western-trained pro-market economists. The result has been the rise of a form of global political common-sense about the need for pro-market policy-making, economic liberalization, and global market integration, a common-sense that is referred to variously as "market fundamentalism," "neoliberalism," the "Washington Consensus," "*laissez-faire* market capitalism" or simply just "Globalization." In other words, the buzzword usage of Globalization has effectively made the word a synonym for a suite of pro-market policy norms and the wider influence of market-forces in political, social, and personal relations. Being pro-Globalization has therefore come to mean being pro-market, and being anti-Globalization has reciprocally become a simplistic description for activists who contest the benefits and highlight the suffering caused by global market forces. Similarly, whether used thus by earnest advocates in books with titles such as *Why Globalization Works* and *In Defence of Globalization,* or instead used by trenchant critics in books with titles such as *The Endgame of Globalization* and *Globalization and Its Terrors,* the association with pro-market policy norms remains constant.[3] For this reason, we have to take a moment here to examine what exactly these norms look like and what capital "G" Globalization and its synonyms therefore seek to name.

The pro-market policy norms associated with Globalization are now so common and widespread that they sometimes seem like they are the only options available. Indeed, a very wide range of politicians – including most Democrats as well as Republicans in the United States, most Labour MPs as well as Conservatives in the United Kingdom, most Liberals and Socialists as well as right-wing politicians in Japan, Canada, France, Germany, Australia, New Zealand, and Sweden, and most democrats as well as autocrats in the poorer parts of the world – have all at various moments come to the same so-called "**TINA**" conclusion that Margaret Thatcher reached in the 1980s: namely, that in the context of global market integration, "*There Is No Alternative*" to pro-market policies. What then do these policies look like? The top 10 are well known, and for each there is also a sound-bite slogan that is also very familiar from everyday political speech:

1.   trade liberalization – "adopt free trade"
2.   privatize public services – "use business efficiency"
3.   deregulate business and finance – "cut red tape"
4.   cut public spending – "shrink government"
5.   reduce and flatten taxes – "be business friendly"
6.   encourage foreign investment – "reduce capital controls"
7.   de-unionize – "respect rights to work & labor flexibility"
8.   export led development – "trade not aid"
9.   reduce inflation – "price stability & savings protection"
10. enforce property rights – "patent protection" & "titling."

Throughout this book, and especially in Chapter 7, where we examine how these policy norms have come to shape practices of government around the world, the more historically accurate and theoretically nuanced term **neoliberalism** is used instead of Globalization to describe the resulting policy package (this also helps avoid confusion with lower-case-"g" "globalization"). Like other terms shown in bold in the book, you can look up a longer definition of neoliberalism in the glossary. But because understanding this key term is also key to understanding the popular usage of synonyms such as Globalization, and because neoliberalism is counter-intuitive for many students (especially those in the United States who have grown up thinking that liberals are more inclined to regulate the market and impose taxes on business), a few more things must be noted about why scholars find this particular neologism (i.e. term of social science jargon) useful.

In a nutshell, the liberal in "neoliberal" refers to the liberal market (or "free market") arguments of late eighteenth-century and nineteenth-century economists such as Adam Smith and David Ricardo who were arguing, amongst other things, for the liberalization of economic activity from control by the aristocracy. However, coming after the welfare-state liberalism of the mid-twentieth century, *neo*liberalism names a new return to these historical ideas that also comes with a political repudiation of liberal welfare-state policies (also known as "liberal Keynesian," "New Deal," or "Great Society" policies) about redistributing wealth and using government investments and regulations to generate and guide national growth. Instead, the top 10 neoliberal policy norms – the "10 commandments of neoliberalism," if you will – are based on the idea that the best way to generate the greatest growth in the context of increasing global interdependency is by shrinking government (making it "smaller," "more efficient," or "leaner and meaner" in the sound bites we hear most often), while simultaneously liberating business and market forces from governmental control. Even after the financial crises of 2008–2012, no major reforms were made to neoliberal norms, and the influence of global market forces over social life continued to expand everywhere unabated. There were some major misgivings articulated by pro-business commentators who feared that unemployment, debt problems, and banking excesses would undermine the global future for capitalism.[4] But instead of heeding these warnings, advocates of pro-market policy-making effectively used the crisis to further expand and entrench neoliberal norms with calls for more privatization, more tax reductions for the wealthy, and more cuts to liberal welfare-state protections.[5]

While supporters of neoliberalism often prefer alternative terms such as "free market capitalism," both they and critics alike agree that there have been some fairly consistent results.[6] Twentieth-century ideas about comprehensive government control over national economies have been abandoned or at least eclipsed by the new emphasis on minimalist and market-friendly government. The class interests of business elites have also been consistently advanced. Inequalities within populations have become more pervasive globally. All sorts of social institutions and relations – citizenship, education, dating, and even lining up in queues – have been marketized. And almost everywhere, policies of social redistribution and nationally inclusive health, welfare, and environmental protection have been subordinated to the competitive pressures of the global market. In place of the plural "freedoms" once celebrated by twentieth-century liberal leaders such as the President Franklin Roosevelt – whose famous "Four Freedoms" included "Freedom From Want" and

"Freedom from Fear" – neoliberalism has substituted the singular freedom of the "Free-market." To be sure, neoliberalism still only names a set of policy norms and governmental tendencies. In practice, the ability of its advocates to achieve their idealized utopia of total market freedom has been globally uneven. They have often met with resistance, and where they have made progress towards their free-market ideals, the direction of reform has been shaped by local and national conditions. In reality, therefore, we do not see a single one-size-fits-all neoliberalism globally, but rather a patchwork of variegated and path-dependent neoliberalization processes.

Some of the variety in macro-scale forms of neoliberalization across countries and regions has been associated in turn with micro-scale variations in how individuals have been personally enlisted into new market-based behaviors. Scholars studying the social relations of neoliberalism also therefore sometimes use the term to describe market-based behavioral norms of competition and individualism, including speculative, entrepreneurial, or actuarial ideas about how to manage risk in one's personal life.[7] These accounts of the so-called "responsibilization" of individuals in neoliberal societies and the cultivation of "enterprising subjects" are not necessarily critical of the associated emphasis on personal accountability. Some point to the problems and inequalities introduced by taking aggressively individualistic approaches to allocating incentives and punishments, but others are simply interested in how the new market-oriented forms of individualism change older ideas of citizenship and social solidarity. By contrast, social justice campaigners in the so-called "Anti-Globalization" movement have frequently linked their arguments against neoliberal policy reforms (such as privatization) with equally damning criticisms of the ways personal freedom and creativity become targets of commercialization (such as Apple ads inviting wealthy consumers to think differently by buying a Mac).[8] For the same reason, "Anti-Globalization" activism is generally better understood as "anti-neoliberal" activism. What brings the activists together on the streets and on the Internet is a shared opposition to both neoliberal policies and the neoliberal refashioning of responsibility as always and everywhere individualistic. This in turn helps explain better why it is an activism that has traveled across borders, too, thereby leading to a global movement against neoliberalism that is not at all opposed to the globalization of social justice and solidarity amongst those who feel alienated from global competition.

While "Anti-Globalization" does not really work very well as a label for the anti-neoliberal critics, for pro-market advocates of neoliberalization the term "Globalization" has often proved very useful, allowing them to shift easily from observations about global changes to arguments that neoliberal policies are the only ones that make sense in a globalizing world. This brings us back to the example of the TINA argument. One reason for the TINA-touts' early success in selling the idea there was no alternative to neoliberal reforms was that with the fall of the Berlin Wall in 1989 and the subsequent collapse of the Soviet Union in 1990, there really were no significant alternatives to market capitalism anymore. Overnight, these changes brought 30 former communist countries and over 400 million people into the global market economy. Communist China had also started to go capitalist with a vengeance during this period, and with the very small and partial exceptions of countries such as Cuba noted, few governments in the world actively tried to foster non-capitalist economic organization. Yet, in addition to the dearth of counter-capitalist examples, the second basis for TINA-tout arguments has been their successful association of the need for neoliberal reforms with simplistic claims about globalization. (In other words, what helped make neoliberalism seem like the only policy-making alternative after communism was the successful conflation of globalization with Globalization.) Instead of a complex interplay of interdependencies, Globalization was thereby represented as a simple sort of natural phenomenon like the morning sunrise: something that was sweeping the world and was basically a good thing, but something, too, that was also unstoppable and unchangeable. The only response to the ties that bind, said the TINA touts, was to tie them more strongly by implementing pro-market reforms.

Not surprisingly, these sorts of associations and claims have subsequently been widely contested by anti-neoliberals. Groups as diverse as unions, environmentalists, feminists, landless peasants, and AIDS activists have all rejected the argument that globalization is unchangeable. They also therefore question the claim that it necessitates a single neoliberal rule-set for policy-making. For them, globalization does not equate with neoliberal Globalization. Instead, and despite their great diversity, the critics argue that there are real achievable alternatives to neoliberal policies (see Chapter 10). Other forms of more just, equitable, environmentally sustainable and democratic globalization are possible, they say. In doing so, they have also obviously questioned the meaning and definition of Globalization, too. The result has been a storm of debate involving all kinds of clashing definitions, data, interpretations, slogans, myths, and exaggerations. And it has been in the midst of all this controversy that Globalization has become the contested buzzword we know it as today.

As will become clear in the chapters that follow, it is not always as easy to distinguish between globalization (the name for heightened global interdependency) and Globalization (the politically loaded buzzword) as the spelling with the lower-case and upper-case "G"s implies. The two-way relationships between the different uses instead repeatedly blur the distinction between them. The instrumental political uses of the term, for example, are at least to some extent the political outcome of pressures created by basic shifts in the organization of global capitalist networks. In turn, the pro-market policies that have been put in place by politicians appealing to the TINA take on Globalization have enabled yet more global economic linkages to develop. These additional linkages really have generated market forces that are hard to change, and these have in turn led to the still more widespread political description of Globalization as an unstoppable juggernaut that necessitates neoliberalism. However, for the purposes of making academic sense of all these relays and relationships, the distinction remains a useful starting-point. The rest of this introductory chapter is therefore organized around a deeper examination of globalization in terms of the overlapping global interdependencies it brings together. All the more politically loaded questions about the use and abuse of

Globalization as a term of political discourse are deferred to Chapter 2, and it is there that you will discover more about why the term has become so significant and so fraught with controversy. The rest of this chapter, by contrast, outlines the main forms of global interdependency – commodity ties, labor ties, money ties, legal ties, governmental ties, ecological ties, health ties, and the ties of social and political response – which are used as the organizing themes for the subsequent chapters of this book (Chapters 3–10).

1.2   The Networks of Global Interdependency

Part of what social scientists always do when trying to make sense of complicated social phenomena is to make classificatory distinctions that "unpack" the phenomena in question into various component parts. With topics such as globalization, this is rather difficult. Indeed, the problems presented by globalization are a little like the challenge presented by the fabled elephant in the story about the six blind men. This traditional oral fable about the blind men and the elephant is itself something of a global legend, having been retold right across Asia from Han Dynasty China, to India, through retellings in the Buddhist Sutra, to more recent renditions as an exercise for US Peace Corps volunteers to practice in places as far apart as Lesotho and Lithuania! In any event, the story is a good allegory of the dangers of only looking at parts of a larger whole. In the story, the first blind man feels the side of the elephant and concludes that it is a wall. The second feels the trunk and thinks it is a snake. The third feels the tusk and says it is a spear. The fourth feels the knee and argues it is a tree. The fifth feels the ear and thinks it is a fan. And the sixth feels the tail and believes it is just a rope. Religious retellings of this story often suggest that the elephant represents a god that ordinary mortals cannot fully understand. To some extent, this is a good metaphor for the way Globalization is repeated like a holy mantra in political speech. However, here the main point of using this allegory is to make a more practical point about academic interpretations of the interconnections comprising globalization.

The way scholars have approached globalization through the questions and concerns of their own particular disciplines sometimes makes their preoccupations seem a little like the arguments of the six blind men. Political scientists, for example, often meet something like a wall in so far as their focus on the ways that national governments act in the context of global interdependency can obscure other forms of government that operate at other scales or that work through the market. Communications theorists discover a trunk in new networks like the Internet, but may not always see the economic and political projects, including older national projects, that such new media support. Economists, ever focused on the financial flows and market mechanisms of global commerce, seem to see the spear of globalization but only a fraction of its larger political and cultural consequences. Geographers (of which this author is one) are fascinated with the spatial connections and transformations brought about by globalization, but in exploring these routes, they do not always adequately examine globalization's historical roots. Anthropologists find an ear of sorts in studying the ways in which new hybrid cultural practices like world music or patient–doctor relations are changing amidst global ties to the Internet. However, they do not so often investigate the commercial connections and political transformations that shape and confine cultural creativity. And sociologists, to pick one last example, chart all kinds of demographic outcomes of globalization, particularly in terms of the impact of migration, but sometimes allow long lines of numbers to obscure political and economic forces that put populations in motion in the first place. In all these disciplines, there are scholars who can readily claim that their work serves as a counter-example to such tendencies, but the point surely is clear. Disciplinary traditions can often elide the full complexity of globalization. Even as we develop specialist thematic analyses, therefore, we also need to constantly keep in mind the way in which globalization has developed as a complex tapestry of ties that exceed any simple disciplinary purview.

There is one more lesson in the fable of the blind men and the elephant that we can draw on as a guide to analyzing the complex tapestry of globalization. It is a lesson about collaboration. In this sense, the problem with the six blind men was not their blindness so much as their inability to share their experiences and information. The academic corollary of this is simple. To avoid the dangers of disciplinary division and elision, we need a more interdisciplinary approach. Ideally, this is exactly what a university education provides, and it is also what good scholarship provides in so far as it draws on ideas, arguments, and evidence developed in a wide range of disciplines. The chapters that follow are written in the spirit of this ideal. Each chapter still seeks to focus on a particular thematic focus, but the overall aim is to assemble an interdisciplinary assessment of globalization on which more specialist and advanced work can subsequently be built.

Of course, no one book, least of all one authored by a single scholar, can hope to address every single disciplinary contribution to our understanding of global interconnections. So, while the ideal here is unabashedly interdisciplinary, the account of globalization that follows still has a thematic focus that reflects this author's academic home in the social sciences. After all, it would be perfectly possible to introduce globalization with a natural science focus on global ecosystem interconnections, global climate change dynamics, and the planetary movements of microbes. Chapter 9 does in fact attempt to address some of these ecological ties, too. But, just like most other treatments of globalization by economists, political scientists, sociologists, anthropologists, and other geographers, the substantive focus running through the book as a whole is on the social system of capitalism. Thus, a little justification is needed now of what this basic focus brings into view and why it matters.

Without a doubt, the driving force of global social interdependency from the sixteenth century onwards has been the development and expansion of the economic system of capitalism. Capitalism has at least four innate economic characteristics that help explain the ways in which it has led to more and more global interconnection. It is an economic system that depends first of all on *growth*. Capitalists have to keep on making profits to stay in business, and the sum of all these profits adds up to growth (which can be measured on a regional, national, or global basis over varying lengths of time). Second, in this ceaseless pursuit of profit, capitalists are constantly searching for *new markets* into which they can expand and sell their commodities. Third, in competing with one another to survive and make higher profits, capitalists are also always seeking ways to cut costs by finding *cheaper inputs* including cheaper raw materials and cheaper labor. And fourth, capitalists are also always driven by competition to *speed up* the production and sales process so that they can produce profits faster. These needs lead in turn to system-wide imperatives to (accelerate transportation) and overcome distance while also simultaneously creating a remarkable system of market-based coordination of the resulting ties. Just as Adam Smith and Karl Marx were both fascinated by these invisible effects of integration in early capitalism, contemporary commentators from radically different political perspectives also tend to agree that the main characteristics of capitalism (create ties that bind and coordinate across the whole planet.[9])

It is quite easy to see how pressures that emerge from the basic forces of capitalism have led to key developments that are now associated with globalization. From the nineteenth-century railways that imperialists built across Africa, India, and Latin America to today's dense air transportation networks, we can chart many ways in which the capitalist need to overcome spatial barriers has revolutionized transportation. Between 1920 and 1990, for example, the cost of ocean freight transport was reduced by 70%. Likewise, from the early use of the telegram to today's use of the Internet and satellites, the need for companies and investors to do business across ever larger distances has led to the radical transformation of global communications. The cost of a 3 min phone call from New York to London, for instance, fell to $0.20 in 2012 from the equivalent of $60.42 in 1960.

Data like these on what is sometimes called the "destruction of distance" or "the annihilation of space" are remarkable and can be easily multiplied. Ironically, however, journalistic commentaries on globalization often tend to downplay the capitalist causes of such transportation and communication developments. They tend to focus too much on the technological innovations themselves as the primary causes and defining features of global integration. Here, by contrast, the emphasis is placed on examining the ways in which these technologies work *through* capitalism to connect lives across the planet. To do this most effectively, we must therefore examine how the interdependencies of capitalist networks organize and coordinate the global connections of commodities, labor, money, laws, government, spaces, and health. In other words, how can we trace the coordinating effects of capitalism through the main forms of global interdependency explored in the rest of the book?

1.2.1   The interdependencies of commodities

The economic interconnections of globalization present themselves first and foremost as an immense collection of commodities. From cars, coffee, and computers to wheat, water, and Windows' software, practically everything that is bought and sold today represents the coming together of global economic ties. As soon as you stop to think about how cars are made, where your coffee has come from, or what goes into a computer, your mind immediately has to start making a global journey. Car buyers can sometimes do this when they read the stickers on new cars. Below the price, another shock on a car price sticker may well be the long list in small print of all the countries from which the car's components have come. Likewise, in walking into a Starbucks coffee shop, you not only walk into a global retail chain; you also come face to face with an emporium of global coffee production. Beans from Guatemala, from Hawaii, from Ethiopia, from Vietnam, and from Colombia are all available on the same shelves, not to mention the global brand design of the shops and wooden shelves, the global music, and the "made in China" global mugs. And in opening up a computer, one is similarly confronted with the global scope of high-tech production, the microchips often being inscribed with their country of origin. Sometimes, it is easy to trace these networks of commodity production, not least of all on university campuses where student activism has led to efforts like the Workers Rights Consortium database detailing all the factories where university apparel is made.[10] At other times, especially with basic staple products like paper, petroleum, and plastic, it is very hard. Try as they might, fair trade activists are unlikely to be able to pressure companies to offer consumers fair trade plastic even to wrap-up certified and transparently sourced fair-trade food. But easy or hard, tracing where everyday products come from is nearly always an exercise that leads towards some sort of global exploration.

Chapter 3 invites readers to embark on some of these global explorations by investigating how capitalist commodity networks are put together. In order to explain the complexity of the global production networks that produce what consumers buy, the chapter introduces the concept of **commodity chains**. These are basically the chains of economic links that lead from the production and processing of raw materials all the way through to the manufacturing of sub-components to the work of assembly or packaging to the final sale of a product in the market. The chapter introduces some key features distinguishing different types of commodity chain and highlights their consequences in terms of different patterns of globalization in different economic sectors. This leads in turn to a survey of such divergent global business strategies as foreign direct investment, joint ventures, outsourcing, and subcontracting. The final part of Chapter 3 proceeds to introduce the ways in which transnational corporations (otherwise known as **TNCs**) have been instrumental in developing global commercial ties in the last 30 years. While this analysis underlines the importance of TNCs as key actors in the development of global economic interdependency, it also makes clear that the notion of a completely rootless and placeless global corporation remains more a fantasy of global business gurus and politicians than an economic reality. Instead, most TNCs remain very much tied to particular places, and to show how Chapter 3 concludes by surveying the important influences of national foreign policy, national economic policy and national culture on TNC development.

1.2.2   The interdependencies of workers

A key common denominator of any commodity chain is that it involves the employment of a whole range of different workers in different parts of the planet. Thus, behind the commodity chains that are the commercial face of globalization, we need to investigate the interdependent worlds of workers themselves. Workers are tied to commodity chains in two key ways. First and foremost, they are the producers of the profit that business needs to survive, but second, they are the consumers that – at some point, in some part of the world – must purchase the goods that businesses produce in order for profits to be realized. If a market for a commodity cannot be found, if no one anywhere can afford to buy it or wants to buy it, then, however much work has gone into its production, the commodity is effectively worthless in capitalist terms. Historically, this double dependency of capitalism on workers has led to a number of different social and political outcomes.

In the years after World War II, most of the richer western nation-states including the United States, the United Kingdom, Germany, and France, developed national economic strategies that fundamentally depended on the idea that the majority of workers in a country would also double as the core consumer base for buying commodities produced in that country. This meant that the workers in question had to be paid enough to be able to consume domestically manufactured products. In some wealthy countries that especially depended on exports of raw materials – countries such as Canada, Australia, and New Zealand – this strategy had to be modified (with the fate of workers in a country like Canada becoming connected very closely to the consumption of their exports in the United States). In most of the poorer countries of the world where dependency on the exports of raw materials was even higher, it eventually proved impossible to combine such dependency with any kind of sustained domestic development. However, in the core capitalist countries of northern Europe and America, national development in the mid twentieth century centrally depended on harmonizing national mass production with national mass consumption. This social and economic effort at harmonization regulated by the state is sometimes referred to as **Fordism**, because it is based on the same economic idea Henry Ford used in his giant car plant in Detroit in the early twentieth century. The idea was that if workers were paid enough, they could afford to buy the products they made (so long as they also behaved properly and bought into a consumer lifestyle – something that Ford himself sought to foster with the use of education programs and social workers).

In the 1960s, as international trade increased, and the once war-ruined economies of Japan and Germany were up and running again, the Fordist system of balancing national production with national consumption began to change. Not just American businesses, but increasingly businesses everywhere, looked to foreign consumers for new markets. Global trade offered them an escape from their dependency on domestic consumer markets. In this context, the need to pay domestic workers at levels that enabled them to consume domestic products began to decrease at the very same time as new transportation and logistics technologies increasingly allowed for the development of overseas factories. These changes have led to a significant realignment of the interdependencies between businesses and workers on a global scale. In the wealthier countries, new pressures on workers to be ever more adjustable and flexible have heightened at the same time as wages and benefits have been pushed downwards. Meanwhile, manufacturing work and increasingly **services** work, too, have been shifted to the poorer parts of the global economy where workers tend to be paid much less. In this new context of post-Fordism, the freedoms of business to search out and employ low-paid workers have come together with the abandonment of state commitments to universal national welfare, education, and healthcare services.

Outlining the collapse of Fordism, Chapter 4 describes the interdependent experiences of workers in the post-Fordist global economy in terms of changing geographical and social divisions of labor. The geographical changes reflect the ways in which the double dependency of business on workers has been fundamentally reorganized by global commodity chains. Gone are the territorialized two-way ties between national workers and national business, and in their place have emerged multi-faceted transnational networks of production and consumption. In concert with these geographical shifts, the end of Fordism has also been characterized by a complex recalibration of social divisions of labor. Class polarization and inequality have increased within nation-states, creating a highly mobile transnational business class at the same time as relegating unemployed and underemployed workers to communities of increased isolation and alienation. Despite the fact that the transnational business class has been joined by increasing numbers of women, economic globalization has not transcended traditional gendered divisions of labor and done away with the second shift of domestic work undertaken by the vast majority of women around the world. Instead, it has led to tighter transnational ties between the gendering of work in different places. Indicative of these new ties are the global "care chains" represented by migrant nannies and nurses. By examining these specific chains, Chapter 4 provides examples of how gendered work roles for women from poor nation-states are implicated in the professionalization of women's work in rich countries. Racialized divisions of labor have also been remade in similar ways. However, even as transnational migrants of color have been incorporated into especially precarious work-roles in rich countries (e.g. garden work, fast-food work, and cleaning work), divisions between rich-country and poor-country workers continue to be marked by racializing assumptions and assertions (e.g. "Asians have nimble fingers"). Like class divisions and gender divisions, such racialization of the transnational division of labor represents a significant challenge for organized labor, and, for all these reasons, the final section of Chapter 4 addresses the ways in which unions have begun to transform their approach to organizing and building links between workers in the context of globalization. It describes how the new global commodity chains have led to a reapplication of old ideas about international solidarity. But, at the same time as outlining the factors that enable and shape transnational solidarity efforts by unions, the chapter notes some of the limits of language and nationalist politics that still curtail worker organization on a global scale.

1.2.3   The interdependencies of money

In contrast to the obstacles that continue to frustrate the transnational organization of labor, the instantaneous movement of money around the world has become the most powerful example of globalization's economic interdependencies. Money is an abstract representation of the value produced by human work. However, it is infinitely more mobile than workers themselves, and it moves around today's world at the speed of light in fiber-optic cables. According to data from the Bank of International Settlements, global foreign-exchange markets saw the equivalent of about $4 trillion of money bought and sold *daily* in 2010.[11] While the "borderless world" idea that is so often referred to in political soundbites about Globalization is something of a myth, in the case of these deregulated and computer-facilitated money movements, the vision comes close to reality. In particular, global finance – the networked world of banks, investment houses, stock markets, currency markets, and so on – has become a kind of borderless nerve center for global capitalism (and, many commentators note, a very nervous center, too, following the global debt and credit crises of 2008–2012). Financial movements are still directed from fixed command and control sites such as New York, London, and Tokyo (and these sorts of Global Cities are discussed further in Chapter 8), but within the flows of money, all the transnational ties of production and consumption, all the tensions produced by uneven development, and all the contradictions ultimately come together in an integrated and extraordinarily complex world of border-transcending financial interdependence. Chapter 5 introduces this world and seeks to demystify as much of its complexity as possible.

To understand the emergence to today's global financial system, we have to go back to the Bretton Woods agreements orchestrated by the United States in 1944. Not only did these set up the **IMF** and establish the basis for the **World Bank**, but also they turned the US dollar into the world's reserve currency by formally pegging it to the value of gold. All the while the United States was the leading world exporter through the late 1940s, 1950s, and early 1960s, this dollar–gold peg was sustainable, but in the late 1960s it came under stress from global competition, America's faltering export performance, and the costs on the US treasury of fighting the Vietnam War and the Cold War more generally. As a result, in 1971 President Nixon abandoned the fixed dollar–gold peg. From that point on, the world entered into a system of floating exchange rates that have led over the last three decades to today's system of non-stop foreign-exchange trading and the associated rise of complex derivatives markets. Chapter 5 explains these developments and describes the workings of the most common forms of financial credit including stocks and bonds, as well as derivatives such as futures, swaps, and options. Arguing that the increasing proliferation of complex financial instruments has to be understood in the context of the increasing deregulation of financial markets, the chapter also explores how financial deregulation has reduced the influence of even wealthy nation-states *vis-à-vis* money markets. In this respect, the influence of the United States requires special attention because of the system of dollar dominance established at Bretton Woods. Section 2 of Chapter 5 closes with some reflections on how the status of the dollar as a reserve currency has been increasingly undermined by US indebtedness and the huge global imbalances in trade and finance American borrowing represents.

The way the United States and other wealthy nation-states are coming to depend more on the decisions of global financial players such as investment banks, risk ratings firms, and accounting companies means that their relationship to global finance is gradually becoming more like the tortured ties of financial dependency that have been familiar to poorer nation-states in the **global south** or so-called developing countries for well over a century. These similarities and the increasing difficulties of extremely indebted countries in the Global South make it vital to examine the painful underside of the fast and integrated world of finance, namely the slow and often disintegrating world of **debt**. Chapter 5 describes the development of the Global South debt crisis in the 1970s and 1980s, and its links to the ups and downs of foreign currency trading in dollars. It also outlines some of the major global responses to date, including debt rescheduling and the ways in which this has increased the power of the World Bank and IMF to impose neoliberal development policies on indebted countries through so-called structural adjustment plans (**SAP**s). In the aftermath of the failures of structural adjustment to produce sustainable development, there have been calls for debt relief and new microcredit initiatives at the very same time. Chapter 5 concludes with an assessment of the progress and pitfalls of both debt relief and microcredit, documenting how, despite their differences in approach, both have become mechanisms of poverty management that operate on the basis of similar neoliberal codes of conduct as structural adjustment.

1.2.4   The interdependencies of the law

While systems of poverty management through debt have achieved a *de facto* law-like status in practice, there are also a wide variety of codified *de jure* laws that have developed in concert with the rise of global economic interdependencies. In order to understand how the worlds of commodities, labor, and money come together in a relatively ordered manner on a global scale, it is necessary therefore to turn directly to the theme of globe-spanning laws and legal institutions. This is a relatively neglected category in wider discussions of globalization, because the neoliberal vision of a "*laissez-faire*" free market order is dominated by the idea of deregulation. This vision is misleading, because even free trade requires laws to make it work in practice. Indeed, the huge policy-making changes undertaken in the name of liberalizing business since the 1970s onwards are best understood as *re-regulation* rather than deregulation. Not surprisingly, they have therefore depended on all sorts of new laws. In the shape of new free-trade agreements and the binding legislation and arbitration they have established, such laws have had an increasingly global reach as well as an ever-deeper local influence. Despite the significance of these new legal regimes, their many acronyms and complex interrelations commonly defy easy comprehension. Chapter 6 therefore sorts through the alphabet soup of trade agreements with a view to making clear their underlying legal implications as well as explaining their basic enforcement mechanisms and relevance to the wider development of global economic interdependency.

The analysis begins at the global scale with an account of the development of the General Agreement on Tariffs and Trade (the **GATT**). The culmination of the Uruguay round of GATT talks is outlined as a way of introducing the emergence of the World Trade Organization (**WTO**) and the legal significance of its acronym-heavy agreements. In this way, the major controversies surrounding WTO policy are introduced, including the failure of the Seattle, Doha, and Cancun WTO meetings and the fierce debates over Trade Related Investment Measures (TRIMS), Trade Related Intellectual Property protections (TRIPs), and a new General Agreement on Trade in Services (**GATS**). In Section 2 of Chapter 6, the relationship between these global free trade laws and regional free trade laws is examined in more detail. Their similarities are examined through a discussion of the ways in which they both circumscribe national democracy. But their differences are also addressed through an analysis of the divergences in regional free-trade agreements. The North American Free Trade Agreement (**NAFTA**) is thus compared with the rather different European Union (**EU**) model of legislating trade law. This comparison leads in turn into a wider discussion of the debate over whether regional free trade can be made into a more democratically accountable system of regulation. The final section of Chapter 6 moves on to consider other much more radical alternative models for regulating trade and investment. It examines transnational lawsuits that have been filed against TNCs as well as other efforts by transnational advocacy networks (TANs) to use both existing national legal tools and transnational consumer pressure to improve protections for workers and raise environmental standards. Throughout this discussion, attention is paid to the ways in which the tapestry of transnational connections woven by economic interdependency has led to the development of global legal actions and plans that far exceed the narrow concerns of trading freedom and property rights protection afforded by free-trade agreements.

1.2.5   The interdependencies of governance

All the questions surrounding transnational legal regulations lead in turn to the broader topic of political globalization. In political speech about Globalization as well as in many academic analyses of global interdependency, it is quite common to read that a defining political feature of today's global system is the end of geography or the so-called deterritorialization created by borderless global networks. These arguments, whether implicitly or explicitly, make the parallel suggestion that what we are witnessing today is the looming end of the nation-state. National-state regulation over clearly demarcated territorial space is, so the argument goes, becoming overtaken by the transnational forces of market regulation and coordination. In these ways, claims about the political implications of globalization are woven closely together with claims about geography. Despite their appealing simplicity, however, there are two big problems with these sorts of interwoven arguments. The first is that they rest on too much hype and exaggeration. Ask anyone in any part of the world today about who they pay taxes to, about who regulates their road system, or who controls their army, and they will most often point to their national government. The nation-state is obviously not dead, and, in fact, some of the most significant forms of transnational re-regulation that have developed alongside economic interdependency – ranging from Intellectual Property Rights protection to trade agreements such as NAFTA – fundamentally depend upon nation-states for their operational implementation. The second big problem with the deterritorialization and "end of the nation-state" claims is that they tend to ignore important forms of **reterritorialization** that involve new forms of governance, too.

Governance is a collective catch-all term for the many different forms of political organization that have a capacity to regulate human life. Historically, this has tended to refer to just formal political entities such as monarchs, dictatorships, elected governments, and their bureaucracies. However, with increasing interest in the informal and social ways we are disciplined by market forces (what scholars of neo-liberalism call **governmentality**), including all the ways in which institutions such as schools and universities cultivate enterprising approaches to investing in your "self," governance has come to mean any kind of systematic power dynamic including both formal governmental and informal social types of regulation. In the context of globalization, this broad approach to political power is important, because while nation-states have not by any means come to an end, their regulative capacities have undoubtedly been transformed and augmented by new kinds of governance. This is the approach taken in Chapter 7 to assessing the debate over the supposed end of the nation-state. The chapter begins by evaluating some of the exaggerations about the death of the nation-state and eclipse of national sovereignty. Focusing on the ways in which global ties are transforming traditional forms of state sovereignty, authority, and hegemony, this section proceeds to explore how advocates of neoliberalism have sought to harness the national state to the project of securing transnational conditions for market rule. Such "facilitative" state making often remains national and yet it clearly also facilitates a form of transnational market discipline at the same time. And whether this happens through peaceful transna-tional agreements on cross-border development, or through draconian national reforms, or through violent military interventions, we repeatedly see national governments enabling market forces to govern through the extension and entrenchment of neoliberal policies.

Beyond the role played by national states, the politics of globalization nevertheless still also involve additional forms of transnational governance from above. In this respect, it is important to consider the increasing authority of institu-tions such as the **IMF**, the **World Bank**, the **WTO**, and, though to a much lesser extent, the **G8** and **G20**. Much of the authority of these institutions rests on the ways in which they serve as key switching points for broader market calculations of the sort introduced in Chapters 3 and 5. The controversies over the IMF, the World

Bank, and the WTO need in particular to be evaluated with this in mind. Moralistic depictions of the institutions as variously good, bad, heroic, and evil do little to draw out the ways in which they represent institutional and thus political embodiments of highly unstable, uneven, and unaccountable economic ties. For the same reason, this section also emphasizes the importance of assessing the power of these international institutions in terms of how they internalize and thereby institutionalize the influence of global market relations.

The third section of Chapter 7 takes up in turn the question of what is sometimes called "transnational governance from below." To some extent, this label is unhelpful because the ways in which transnational governance by institutions such as the IMF works involves all kinds of highly localized micro-practices such as accountancy that also represent a form of governance from below. However, what is normally meant by transnational governance from below is instead the development of transnational political campaigns by grassroots roots organization such as environmentalists, feminists, human rights campaigners, unions, and aid groups. These so-called non-governmental organizations (**NGOs**) play an important role in the politics of globalization. They have been the groups who have campaigned hardest against the narrow neoliberal interests and exclusionary economic focus of organizations such as the WTO. They have also often been held up as examples of the more inclusive rainbow politics that global interdependency makes possible. They are frequently described in this respect as the representatives of global civil society. However, critics contend that NGOs often operate as Trojan Horses for neoliberalism, and serious questions remain about how representative they actually are of the diversity of global civil society. These are vital questions, given that NGOs do actually end up shaping global governance despite being grouped together under an acronym that announces their supposedly non-governmental nature. Exploring these governmental effects of non-governmental institutions still further, the final part of the chapter explores how the same rankings and accountability metrics used to measure and manage NGO performance now also operate in deeply influential ways to govern personal behavior, too.

1.2.6   The interdependencies of space

Chapter 8 examines the uneven development outcomes of global interdependency in closer detail, the central aim being to offer a more realistic account of globalization's geography than provided in popular visions of a borderless and flattened world. The first section addresses the ways in which uneven development plays out at a global scale. Based on the enduring tension between spatial fixity and geographical expansion that lies at the very heart of capitalist growth, global struggles over territory go through repeated cycles of consolidation, expansion, and reconsolidation of capitalist state-making and state control. Growth and expansion led by powerful states leads to new forms of spatial control and integration, but it can also lead to geopolitical conflict with other states along the way. The resulting tensions lead in turn to competing geostrategic discourses that pit geopolitical claims to consolidated territory with expansionary geoeconomic visions of integrating new spaces into global economic ties.

Having explored the tensions between spatial fixity and geographical expansion at a transnational scale, the chapter turns next to how they play out in urban contexts. Focusing particularly on contemporary global cities, we review the ways in which they compete with one another in global business rankings of best cities, and how this in turn subjects cities to the disciplinary and often volatile effects of speculative urbanism. We then consider the destructive underside of speculative urban growth and competition: namely, the splintered urbanism that has led to local landscapes of stark inequality where enclaves of privilege and possessive individualism exist right beside slums and communal spaces of dispossession.

1.2.7   The interdependencies of health

Global health is the ultimate way in which the interdependencies of globalization come together to shape destinies. They are also the most longstanding in the sense that they are vitally linked with the global ecologies of interdependence created by the Earth as a shared global environment. Chapter 9 therefore begins by reflecting on how global environmental change, and climate change in particular, has intensified and further integrated these ties of ecological interdependence. It reflects on how this has created a new geological–ecological era that is increasingly referred to as the anthropocene, and then turns to how the simultaneous biomedical innovations of this era promise to provide coping solutions for the ill-effects of changes such as global warming. While the global ties involved are inescapable, they are embodied in radically different and unequal experiences of interdependency. Exploring this pattern of interdependency plus inequality, the chapter then examines how the global ties of biomedicine mean that the improved health and global biological citizenship of some are often dependent on the sub-citizenship and exploitation of others. We then turn to consider the many global health initiatives that have been launched to reach out to those whose health has been undermined by global market ties, and we explore how the resulting development of disease-specific donor-driven vertical programs and grant competitions remains profoundly shaped by market forces.

The reflections on ways in which global market forces shape approaches to global health intervention lead to the concluding chapter of the book and to a review of the ways in which neoliberalization processes more generally both provoke and shape responses to the exclusions and asymmetries created by global market ties. Some of the responses represent conservative and often nationalistic reactions to the perceived threats of the meta-Globalization juggernaut. Others by contrast tend towards forms of resistance based on ideas about global justice. As such, they generally seek to suggest that other non-neoliberal approaches to global integration are possible. In between, are diverse forms of resilience, many of which can be found in contemporary universities. It is thus with a final focus on the university as a venue caught at the intersection of neoliberalization, resilience, and resistance that the book ends.

To summarize the arguments of this overview of the book, the basic point is that (globalization fundamentally involves increasing global interdependency. We have seen how these ties can be picked apart, too. But as you go forward in the chapters that follow, it is important to track the ties *between* the different types of global interconnection. Likewise, it is also important to remember that there are other global ties which are not given chapter-length attention in what follows – the transnational movements of migrants, of Internet-enabled communications, and of religious practices, for example – but which nevertheless also influence the overall movement towards greater global interdependency. Global climate change and global terrorism ties are two especially significant forces shaping globalization in this way, and they will keep forcing their way into our interconnected lives whether we acknowledge them or not. This means we are faced with a very complicated picture of global interconnection that demands the same sort of open-ended analysis that has come with the global spread of science itself: analysis that, like scientific best practice, repeatedly opens itself up for deliberative review on an increasingly global and critical but collaborative basis. Another way of putting this is that we need to avoid the dangers of acting like the blind villagers. We must work deliberatively and collaboratively in an open-ended way in order to avoid confusing the overall elephant of globalization with any one component part. In addition, though, the goal of the rest of the book is also to avoid treating globalization as some sort of ungraspable and unknowable spirit. The elephant is more than the sum of its parts, but it is not a god! In other words, the chapters that follow also aim to avoid confusing globalization with the often religious-like myths that circulate around Globalization. In Chapter 2, we consider some of these myths in more detail and identify some of the best tactics for avoiding their misleading depictions while still tracking their influence.

Student Exercises

Individual:
1. Pick something you ate for breakfast and try to brainstorm on all the different sorts of global networks that made it possible for you to eat. Draw a global sketch map diagramming these connections in one color. Then, draw on the same sketch map in a different color where you imagine the money you have spent on your breakfast has gone. Students can draw their own sketch-maps or work as a group, but either way, it is useful at the end to reflect with others on the disjunctions between the map of money flows and the map of commodity connections.

Group:
2. Pick a street, office, factory, shop, building, or public space in your city. Visit it as a group and collectively consider the ways in which it is unique and the ways

in which it is similar to other places in other cities and other countries. Think about what signs of global interdependency are revealed by the site, and discuss the ways in which members of the group normally take these signs for granted without thinking about the ties to other people.

Notes

1   Some of the most thorough and thoughtful analyses of globalization that inspire the approaches taken here include: John Agnew, *Hegemony: The New Shape of Global Power* (Philadelphia: Temple University Press, 2005); Manuel Castells, *The Rise of the Network Society* (Cambridge, MA: Blackwell Publishers, 1996); Robin Cohen and Paul Kennedy, *Global Sociology* (London: Macmillan, 2000); Peter Dicken, *Global Shift: Reshaping the Global Economic Map in the 21st Century* (New York: Guilford Press, 2007); Barbara Ehrenreich and Arlie Russell Hochschild, eds., *Global Woman: Nannies, Maids, and Sex Workers in the New Economy* (New York: Metropolitan Books, 2003); David Held, Anthony McGrew, David Goldblatt, and Jonathan Perraton, *Global Transformations: Politics, Economics and Culture* (Stanford, CA: Stanford University Press, 1999); Andrew Herod, *Geographies Of Globalization: A Critical Introduction* (Oxford: Wiley-Blackwell, 2009); James H. Mittelman, *The Globalization Syndrome* (Princeton, NJ: Princeton University Press, 2000); Saskia Sassen, *Territory, Authority, Rights: From Medieval to Global Assemblages* (Princeton, NJ: Princeton University Press, 2006); Jan Aart Scholte, *Globalization: A Critical Introduction* (New York: Palgrave, 2000); Leslie Sklair, *Globalization: Capitalism and Its Alternatives* (Oxford: Oxford University Press, 2002); William Tabb, *Economic Governance in the Age of Globalization* (New York: Columbia University Press, 2004); and Göran Therborn, *The World: A Beginner's Guide* (Cambridge: Polity Press, 2011).
2   Manfred Steger, *Globalisms: The Great Ideological Struggle of the 21st Century* (Lanham, MD: Rowman & Littlefield, 2009); Michael Veseth, *Globaloney: Unraveling the Myths of Globalization* (Lanham, MD: Rowman & Littlefield, 2005).
3   Jagdish Bhagwati, *In Defense of Globalization* (Oxford: Oxford University Press, 2004); Teresa Brennan, *Globalization and Its Terrors: Daily Life in the West* (New York: Routledge, 2003); Neil Smith, *The Endgame of Globalization* (New York: Routledge, 2005); Martin Wolf, *Why Globalization Works* (New Haven, CT: Yale University Press, 2004).
4   *The Economist*, "Market Fatigue: The Anglo-Saxon Model Has Taken a Knock," *The Economist*, October 3 (2009); Michael Lewis, *The Big Short: Inside the Doomsday Machine* (New York: W.W. Norton & Co., 2010); Gillian Tett, *Fool's Gold: How the Bold Dream of a Small Tribe at J.P. Morgan Was Corrupted by Wall Street Greed and Unleashed a Catastrophe* (New York: Free Press, 2009); Martin Wolf, "Why a new Bretton Woods is vital – and so hard," *Financial Times*, November 5 (2008); and Martin Wolf, *Fixing Global Finance* (Baltimore, MD: Johns Hopkins University Press, 2010).
5   For discussion of how neoliberal norms (and associated forms of financialization) remain remarkably dominant despite the 2008–2009 financial crisis and subsequent depression, see: John Bellamy Foster and Robert W. McChesney, "The Endless Crisis," *Monthly Review* 64, no. 1 (May, 2012): http://monthlyreview.org/2012/05/01/the-endless-crisis, Paul Krugman, *End this Depression Now!* (New York: W. W. Norton, 2012); Jamie Peck,

Nik Theodore, and Neil Brenner, "Neoliberalism Resurgent? Market Rule after the Great Recession," *South Atlantic Quarterly* 111, no. 2 (2012): 265–88; Joseph E. Stiglitz, *Freefall: America, Free Markets, and the Sinking of the World Economy* (New York: W.W. Norton & Co., 2010); and William Tabb, *The Restructuring of Capitalism in Our Time* (New York: Columbia University Press, 2012).

6   Further details about the historical–geographical evolution of neoliberalism are provided in Chapter 7, but useful overviews are provided by both advocates and critics. For a particularly accessible online overview that is enthusiastic about neoliberalism, see the PBS materials associated with its series *Commanding Heights* http://www.pbs.org/wgbh/commandingheights/. For a clear and influential account from a widely respected critic, see David Harvey, *A Brief History of Neoliberalism* (Oxford: Oxford University Press, 2005).

7   Andrew Barry, Thomas Osborne, and Nikolas Rose, eds., *Foucault and Political Reason: Liberalism, Neo-liberalism and Rationalities of Government* (Chicago: University of Chicago Press, 1996); Lisa Duggan, *The Twilight of Equality: Neoliberalism, Cultural Politics and the Attack on Democracy* (Boston: Beacon Press, 2003); Michel Foucault, *The Birth of Biopolitics* (New York: Palgrave Macmillan, 2008); Ian Hacking, "Making Up People," in *Reconstructing Individualism: Autonomy, Individuality, and the Self in Western Thought*, ed. Sosna Weller (Palo Alto, CA: Stanford University Press, 1986); Barry Hindess, Neo-liberal citizenship. *Citizenship Studies* 6 (2002): 127–43; Jamie Peck, *Constructions of neoliberal reason* (Oxford: Oxford University Press, 2010); Wendy Larner, and William Walters, editors, *Global Governmentality: New Perspectives on International Rule* (New York: Routledge, 2004); Simon Springer, "Neoliberalism as discourse," *Critical Discourse Studies* 9, no. 2 (2012): 23–46; and Jason Read, "A Genealogy of Homo-Economicus: Neoliberalism and the Production of Subjectivity," *Foucault Studies* 6 (2009): 25–36.

8   Most powerfully, this was the argument of Naomi Klein, *No Logo: No Space, No Choice, No Jobs, No Logo* (New York: Picador, 2002). For all her ongoing reports, videos, and interviews on anti-neoliberal organizing, see http://www.naomiklein.org/no-logo.

9   From a decidedly pro-market point of view, the economist Donald Boudreaux writes thus about how capitalist ties now coordinate production and consumption across global distances and multitudes of people: "This beneficial coordination of the plans and actions of millions of different people from around the world is a system of global cooperation – each person doing a specific task, that, when combined with the tasks performed by others, results in a steady output of vast quantities of valuable goods and services." Donald Boudreaux, *Globalization* (Westport, CT: Greenwood Press, 2008) at page 3. Meanwhile, Marxian critics highlight how this coordination across distance benefits capitalist class interests in particular: "What we now call 'globalisation' has been in the sights of the capitalist class all along," says David Harvey. "The conquest of space and time, along with the ceaseless quest to dominate nature, have long taken centre stage in the collective psyche of capitalist societies. The result has been an inexorable trend for the world of capital to produce what I call 'time–space compression' – a world in which capital moves faster and faster and where distances of interaction are compressed." David Harvey, *The Enigma of Capital and the Crises of Capitalism* (Oxford: Oxford University Press, 2010).

10   http://www.workersrights.org/.

11   Bank of International Settlements, *Triennial Central Bank Survey of Foreign Exchange and Derivatives Market Activity in 2010 – Final Results* http://www.bis.org/publ/rpfxf10t.htm.

Keywords

commodity chains	GATT	reterritorialization
debt	global south	SAP
EU	governmentality	services
Fordism	IMF	TINA
G20	NAFTA	TNCs
G8	neoliberalism	World Bank
GATS	NGOs	WTO

2

Discourse

Chapter Contents

Chapter Concepts

1. The dominant discourse on globalization draws on and reproduces three main myths:
    a.   the myth of newness
    b.   the myth of inevitability
    c.   the myth of leveling.
2. These myths make neoliberal policies of free trade, privatization, tax reduction, and so on seem like the only viable governmental response.
3. Dissident discourse challenges the idea that there is no alternative to neo-liberalism and interprets the implications and opportunities of globalization in other ways.

Key Concept

The power of discourse about globalization is considerable. This accounts for much of the interest and buzz about the term. But it also makes it vital to explore the relationship between myths about globalization and what is really happening in the world at large.

Introducing Globalization: Ties, Tensions, and Uneven Integration, First Edition. Matthew Sparke.
© 2013 Matthew Sparke. Published 2013 by Blackwell Publishing Ltd.

2.1   Globalization as Dominant Discourse

The buzzword Globalization is much more than just a single word. It is a key term for a powerful script about the implications of growing global interdependency and integration, a term that is therefore closely tied to a whole suite of claims about what such interdependency and integration both mean and necessitate. We have all heard the resulting sorts of sound bites:

> *Globalization means we now compete with everyone everywhere for everything*
> *Globalization demands that we adjust our laws and education for competition*
> *Globalization means that governments must strive to win market approval*
> *Globalization is a juggernaut of change to which we can only adapt*
> *Globalization is not something we can hold off or turn off*
> *Globalization is bringing the end of the nation-state*
> *Globalization is leveling a global playing field*
> *Globalization means that resistance is useless*
> *Globalization presents a new world order*
> *Globalization creates a borderless world*
> *Globalization means the world is flat*
> *Globalization is unstoppable.*

In addition to hearing such soundbites, we have all also seen pundits and politicians reading from the overarching Globalization script as if it is something both commonsensical and legally binding at the very same time. Often times, it seems they hope to tap into the power they ascribe to Globalization so as to better increase their own influence. Meanwhile, their opponents play the same game in reverse, denying the scope of global interdependency so as to oppose the policies that Globalization supposedly demands. Not surprisingly, the result fast becomes a confusing buzzword battle over the key-term itself with hype from all sides loading the one word "globalization" with multiple meanings it can neither carry nor contain.

In the scholarly version of the buzzword battle, there are exaggerators and skeptics, too. However, many academics adopt a three-step dance around all the political debate: first, criticizing the exaggerations about Globalization the unstoppable juggernaut; second, saying the skeptics are wrong to deny the sweeping scope of global change; and third, offering their own middle way through the debate between the pitfalls of exaggeration and skepticism.[1] This sort of three-step is undoubtedly a useful prelude to comparing the bold claims about Globalization with the real-world realities of global interdependency (and in this sense it also guides the approach taken in the rest of this book). However, the three-step dance is unhelpful to the extent that it obscures the politically motivated myth-making around the contested key-term at the center of the debate. Thus, here, rather than recoiling from all the political use and abuse of the term, the aim of this chapter is to study how Globalization operates as an important and influential global phenomenon in its own right. At the heart of this phenomenon are a set of myths about Globalization that enable its users to fight and win political arguments. As we shall now explore in more detail, the reason why the political instrumentalization of these myths has proved so effective is that together they create a common-sense discourse about the facts of the world. We need to begin therefore by considering how Globalization operates as a discourse.

A discourse is *a set of terms and arguments about the nature of reality that are tied together in a narrative that systematically shapes the reality it purports to describe.* Like other powerful political discourses such as "patriotism," the Globalization narrative is based at least partially on facts. Just as there are people who feel strongly attached to what they see as their homeland, and just as they feel and show such patriotic attachment in multiple ways, there clearly are multiple global interdependencies that today link people's fates together around the world. However, in the same way as the labels "patriotic" and "unpatriotic" are used in partisan ways to make citizens accept particular national policies like war, so too is the discourse of Globalization used to turn the facts about global interdependency into much more biased lessons about what we should do in response. As we shall see, anti-neoliberal activists can engage in the myth-making and myth recycling at times, but by far the most common use of Globalization myths has been by advocates of neoliberal reform: politicians and pundits who argue that trade **liberalization**, privatization, tax cuts, and other pro-market reforms are necessary because of Globalization.

The political discourse of Globalization actively shapes the world it represents using oversimplified and ideologically biased myths about globalization. There are in this sense at least three main myths that lie at the heart of Globalization discourse:

1. that Globalization is new
2. that Globalization is inevitable and
3. that Globalization is a leveler.

a radical who advocates the abolition of political or economic or social inequalities

In the case of each myth we need to examine both what it ignores about globalization and what it accomplishes politically in the interests of advancing neoliberal policy reforms. How, in other words, do certain sorts of silences in depictions of a new, inevitable, and globally leveling Globalization serve to support the promotion of free market reforms?

Before we look into each myth in more detail, it is also important to remember three broader socio-political aspects of the discourse of Globalization. The first is that the actual term Globalization lies at the heart of a web of synonyms – including terms like "global competition," "global change," "global opportunity," and "new world order" – that can all be used interchangeably in the same basic discourse linking interdependency with the need for neoliberal reform. The second is that it is not just the particular words and slogans surrounding Globalization that do the political work. It is instead the wider common-sense vision of the world that the Globalization story conjures up: a vision of a world market, of unfettered global opportunities, and of intense and unending competition. Sometimes this hyper-competitive vision of Globalization is linked to rankings of global competitiveness which are presented and used as indices of Globalization.[2] But whether used to construct a ranked Globalization Index or not, there is no doubt that these market-based ideas about Globalization are interlinked with assumptions about a competitive market-mediated struggle for survival of the fittest on a planetary scale. In turn, and in response to this Darwinian vision of Globalization, there is a third feature of the political use of the term that we also need to remember. This is (the way in which critics of the failures, crises, destruction, and suffering that come with global capitalism reuse and rework the word Globalization as they seek to develop different discourses about other worlds being possible.) Thus, after examining the three main neoliberal myths about newness, inevitability, and leveling, the chapter ends by considering how neoliberalism's critics have sought to retell the big Globalization narrative by imagining a different plot with additional characters and another ending.

2.1.1   The myth of newness

The suggestion that Globalization is new can take many different forms. It can be based on a nerdish fascination with new technologies and the ways in which they have revolutionized global communication. It can be based on exaggerated arguments about the novelty and power of transnational corporations. It can be based on excited accounts about supposedly innovative global business strategies and the books designed to promote them.[3] Or, as is perhaps most common, it can reflect a purely political need to promote a new policy or new reform in the name of adjusting to supposedly new global circumstances. However, what links all these sorts of appeals to the newness of Globalization is a classic capitalist fascination with the so-called "brand new." Capitalist societies have been excited by new commodities since the origins of capitalism. In this sense, what the newness of the brand-name Globalization obviously and ironically ignores are the long historical roots of today's globalized routes. Capitalism may have never before involved the intense planetary interdependencies it involves today, but it has long been shaped by the need to conquer distance, find new markets, access new inputs, and speed up the connections between production and consumption. The basic imperatives remain the same, and the basic challenges have only increased, but the brand-name Globalization helps repackage them as something as new and as exciting as, for example, sugar once seemed. So, if the supposed newness of Globalization ignores the history of global capitalist connections and their causes, how does this serve the interests of promoting **neoliberalism**?

Within the world of business development itself, the links between the newness myth and political lobbying are often quite clear. "We face a new world of global competition," goes the normal argument, "so we need tax cuts and less red tape in order to beat our foreign competitors and make the most of the new opportunities." For corporate lobbyists all over the world, this is a common refrain. Politicians in turn repeat the same sorts of arguments. However, in their hands, the hype about a new world market becomes more clearly linked to neoliberal commitments to governmental reform and the creation of a so-called "business-friendly" economic environment. Here, for example, is the former British prime minister Tony Blair justifying his Labor Party's commitments to continuing the policies of tax cuts, fiscal austerity, and financial deregulation initiated by Margaret Thatcher's Conservatives.

> The new world market, which today is industrially and financially transformed, demands a new economics. . . . We must recognise that the UK is situated in the middle of an active global market for capital – a market which is less subject to regulation today than for several decades. . . . To that extent the room for manoeuvre of any government in Britain is already heavily circumscribed.[4]

This argument, which Blair repeated many more times in the years that followed, represents a classic example of how politicians appeal to the newness of globalization in order to advocate new policies. Such policies are implied in such ways to be rational responses to a new global situation. It is not the politician who is circumscribing old policies but, we are told, the new reality of Globalization itself. Moreover, it is not just a "new economics" that has been demanded in this way. The actual policy reforms that have been promoted in the name of adapting to the new global order have often gone way beyond fiscal and monetary policy to include welfare reform, penal reform, educational reform, and legal reform, too. The key point is that again and again, politicians have appealed to the argument that Globalization dictates an abandonment of older national policies that are said to be unfit for the new world order of global competition.

In the US context, the justification for reform based on appeals to Globalization discourse was made with particular force in the 1990s by the leader of the Republicans in the US House of Representatives, Newt Gingrich. A copy of one of his speeches printed in the book version of the Republicans' *Contract with America* rehearsed a typically excited example of the argument.

> [W]e need to recognize the objective reality of the world market, to realize that we create American jobs through world sales and that we need to make a conscious national decision that we want to have the highest value added jobs on the planet with greatest productivity so we can have the highest take-home pay and the greatest range of choices of lifestyles. In order to do that we have to literally rethink the assumptions that grew up in a self-indulgent national economy and we have to recognize that litigation, taxation, regulation, welfare, education, the very structure of government, the structure of health – all those things have to be reexamined from the standpoint of what will make us the most competitive society on the planet, the most desirable place to invest to create jobs, and the place with the best trained and most entrepreneurial workforce.[5]

Not only did Gingrich insist that the new policies were a necessary adaptation to the "objective reality" of the new world market, but also he clearly saw opportunities aplenty in abandoning the older policies of a "self-indulgent national economy." What such a picture of new opportunities ignored, however, was the whole history of how national economic management and national welfare, education, and legal policy were originally fashioned in the mid-twentieth-century period as *a response* to the crises of global capitalism in the 1930s – crises that led to the Great Depression when lay-offs caused by increasing global overproduction led in country after country to unemployment, underconsumption, declining profits, and more lay-offs in a savage spiral of economic decline. These were the crises that led ultimately into the horrors of World War II, and Gingrich as a former history teacher may well have known about this past period of global integration and crisis. But the newness of the Globalization story trumped all this. Policies of regulating business and trade in the interests of protecting citizens from capitalism's crises could thus become rhetorically repositioned as out of date and "self-indulgent."

Gingrich's dismissive use of the word self-indulgent may have also been meant as a jab at the poor personal self-control of President Bill Clinton. However, in his views on Globalization, Clinton shared much of the same common-sense vision as Gingrich. His speeches often invoked the newness of economic integration as a prelude to calling on Americans to adapt. Like Gingrich too, Clinton was fascinated with how technological change opened up new opportunities. And ever the captivating communicator, he was able even more than Gingrich to make Globalization seem profoundly exciting. Here, for example, is a small part of a speech he gave right near the end of his presidency while visiting Tony Blair in the United Kingdom.

> The intensifying process of economic integration and political interdependence that we know as globalization is clearly tearing down barriers and building new networks among nations, peoples, and cultures, at an astonishing and historically unprecedented rate. It has been fueled by an explosion of technology that enables information, ideas and money, people, products and services to move within and across the national borders at increasingly greater speeds and volumes. . . . This process, I believe, is irreversible.[6]

Clinton went on to discuss the ways in which he felt global interdependence could be managed more effectively on a global scale (something which Gingrich avoided by only talking about the self-interests of Americans), but a key prelude for Clinton's recommendations for global governance was his declaration that the new networks had created an "irreversible" global movement towards interdependency. This statement clearly connects to the second big myth running through the dominant political common-sense about Globalization, namely that it is inevitable.

2.1.2 The myth of inevitability

The assertions and assumptions about the inevitability of Globalization have in fact been repeated still more often than the arguments about its novelty. Typing "Globalization is inevitable" into Google at the time of writing this chapter, over 4 million pages came up, some critical, but most repeating the myth with repetitive zeal. Two typical examples came near the top of the list. The first was from the former Korean President Kim Dae Jung who was making the case for why Asia should "globalize." "Globalization is a historically inevitable path," he said. "Any nation will face defeat if it goes against globalization."[7] The second example was no less axiomatic. It came from a session of the 2002 World Economic Forum entitled "Is India Afraid of Globalization?" The summary of the session read: "Globalization is inevitable, and India can reap its benefits by proper policy measures."[8] Both of these Google examples used the word "inevitable" itself, but multiple alternatives are commonly put to work in order to activate the same basic myth about Globalization. "Unstoppable," "unchangeable," "irreversible," "inexorable," and "not an option" are all thus used as synonyms to convey the same basic sense of an impossible-to-stop force. The Australian prime minister, speaking in 1999, put it like this:

> We don't really have an option, globalization is with us. Nobody has an option of saying, well, I won't take globalization, I'll take something else because there isn't anything else. It's the paradigm under which the world operates now and we can't avoid it.[9]

Likewise, this was also the message Barack Obama brought to Flint Michigan when he was campaigning to be US president.

> Not only is it impossible to turn back the tide of globalization, but efforts to do so can actually make us worse off. So rather than fear the future, we have to embrace it.

Clearly, the exact word choice is less important than the general idea about inevitability that is connected to whatever process the particular commentator is trying to argue lies at the heart of Globalization. The point, of course, is that, whatever this process is said to be, it is meant by the commentator to be accepted as an unarguable self-evident truth about the world, as not an option. Moreover, the usual conclusion drawn by politicians is that this truth about the inevitability of Globalization implies in turn the self-evident importance of whatever *neoliberal* policy reform they happen to be recommending. You are not meant to argue with the policies being recommended because they are simply being offered as responses to something which, after all, has the obvious inevitability of an act of nature. This therefore is how the discourse of Globalization simultaneously excludes other options (depicting them as unnatural) while simultaneously making free trade, privatization, deregulation, and all the other neoliberal norms seem unquestionably normal.

The one–two political punch of an appeal to inevitability followed by the call for neoliberal reform has been articulated most powerfully in the US context by the *New York Times* columnist Thomas Friedman. Near the start of his first big book on Globalization, Friedman even repeats the inevitability argument in the form of a naturalizing metaphor. "I feel about globalization a lot like I feel about the dawn," he says.

Generally speaking, I think it's a good thing that the sun comes up every morning. It does more good than harm. But even if I didn't care that much there isn't much I could do about it. I didn't start globalization, I can't stop it – except at huge cost to human development – and I'm not going to waste time trying. All I want to think about is how I can get the best out of this new system, and cushion the worst for the most people.[10]

As he proceeds to explain how he thinks he can get the best out of the system and cushion the worst, Friedman's argument turns from this naturalization of Globalization into a full-blown promotion of neoliberalism. Indeed, while his book is innocuously entitled *The Lexus and the Olive Tree*, it might just as well be called a *Beginner's Guide to Neoliberalism*. Thus, in the pages that follow his salute to the dawn of Globalization, Friedman develops another catchy metaphor to explain the neoliberally correct policy response. The metaphor is of a "Golden Straitjacket," and Friedman's description of how to put it on reads like a neoliberal politician's teleprompter.

To fit into the Golden Straightjacket a country must either adopt, or be seen as moving toward, the following golden rules: making the private sector the primary engine of its economic growth, maintaining a low rate of inflation and price stability, shrinking the size of its state bureaucracy, maintaining as close to a balanced budget as possible, if not a surplus, eliminating and lowering tariffs on imported goods, removing restrictions on foreign investment, deregulating its economy to promote as much domestic competition as possible, eliminating government corruption, subsidies and kickbacks as much as possible, opening its banking and telecommunications systems to private ownership and competition, and allowing its citizens to choose from an array of competing pension options and foreign run pension and mutual funds. When you stitch all of these pieces together you have the Golden Straitjacket.[11]

The cleverness and appeal of Friedman's metaphor lie in its capacity to capture the controlling, which is to say the straitjacketing, characteristic of neoliberal reforms while still suggesting that they will ultimately bring golden riches. And the reason why the neoliberal straitjacket is said to bring such riches, of course, lies back in the inevitability myth. Because Globalization is supposed to be like the dawn, because it is supposed to do more good than harm, resisting it would be like killing the goose that lays the golden egg, or, to switch to another mythic metaphor, it would be like Jason and the Argonauts trampling the golden fleece in the mud. All we can do is don the straitjacket of neoliberal policy, adapt to the inevitable, cushion ourselves in a Lexus car if we can afford one (Friedman writes enthusiastically about his), and await the golden promise of the dawn. Thus are we presented with the **TINA** axiom in metaphors of inevitability that even a 10 year old can understand. Dawn! Golden Straitjacket! There Is No Alternative! Considered more carefully, however, three features of this kind of myth-making nevertheless enable one to draw rather different conclusions.

When you look at an argument about inevitability more closely, what you first find very often is a *logical paradox*. The process of Globalization is supposed to be inevitable, and yet what the politicians connect to it and what they want you to accept as an inevitably necessary reform is generally a policy aimed at making Globalization work more effectively. The ironic paradox in this is that it underlines how the free-market organization of global interdependency is far from inevitable and actually requires all sorts of governmental adjustments, adaptations, and reforms in order to work. Free trade needs new laws, deregulation needs re-regulation, new global consumption patterns require copious amounts of new advertising, and even welfare reform often necessitates increased policing and imprisonment as individuals and society adjust to life without a social safety net. Considered in their totality, all of the interdependencies comprising neoliberal globalization have required massive amounts of economic, political, and social organization. The process has hardly therefore been inevitable. However, it is easy to make it seem inevitable because it involves so many different sorts of linkages operating on so many different spatial scales that, at present, there exists no single political venue where the different processes can be made democratically accountable to all the people of the world. This is the second key feature of the inevitability myth. It reflects a deep-seated sense of lost political control. Repeating the myth only deepens and exaggerates the sense of loss, but there can be no doubting the fact that the myth itself is a symptom of a profound *political–geographical incongruity* between the global market and the threadbare patchwork of local, national, and global forms of governance that currently fail to render the intensified economic interdependencies democratically accountable.

In response to the sense of political loss, the third feature of the inevitability myth is that it is often accompanied by arguments that *Globalization can and should be moderated*. Here, for example, is President Clinton again making the inevitability argument, but adding a crucial coda concerning policies that he hoped might moderate Globalization's negative impacts. "Globalization is going to proceed and you can't stop it even if you want to," he told students and faculty members at a university in Brazil.

> But you cannot have a global economy unless you also have a global economic empowerment policy, a global health care policy, a global education policy, a global environmental policy, and a global security policy.[12]

It is not just Clinton by any means who has made these sorts of moderating policy recommendations on the back of arguments about inevitability. Another example is provided by UN Secretary General Kofi Annan. In 1999, he described Globalization as "an irreversible process, not an option." However, he also said the process was "blind and therefore needs to be carefully harnessed," and, in the interests of harnessing it, he launched a proposal to the world business community that he called the **Global Compact**.[13] The proposal largely proved a failure because of its dependence on voluntary corporate compliance. This, plus all of the controversies and protests over globalization that intensified after 1999, meant that by 2001, the Secretary General was sounding much more desperate. "If we cannot make globalization work for all," he told an audience at the World

Economic Forum, "in the end it will work for none." Trying hard to drum up new support for the Global Compact, he continued:

> The unequal distribution of benefits and the imbalances in global rule-making, which characterize globalization today, inevitably will produce backlash and protectionism. And that, in turn, threatens to undermine and ultimately unravel the open world economy that has been so painstakingly constructed over the course of the past half-century.[14]

Here clearly we see another kind of inevitability being introduced: the inevitability of the end of Globalization's supposed much touted inevitability! But for leaders like Annan, this is not a problem or contradiction because there is always the third main myth of the Globalization story to fall back on. Globalization will still prevail, goes the story, because, in the end, all of its imbalances and inequalities will be ameliorated by its deeper capacity to serve as a great global leveler.

2.1.3   The myth of global leveling

The myth that Globalization has a leveling effect is so strong because of the way in which it mixes theoretical convictions that economic interdependency is the best cure for global inequality with geographical visions of economic integration operating like some sort of market-mediated bull-dozer to, as the cliché has it, level the global playing field. As such, the myth has developed at the point where theoretical *assumptions* about the economic space of the capitalist market have come together with the *world-view* afforded by the spatial practices of capitalist elites, the world-view afforded, for example, by a business jet.

The assumptions behind the myth come down to the notion that economic competition is leading ever closer to the sort of competitive equilibrium of the kind envisaged in economics textbooks. Arguments in economics often begin with assumptions, and one of the key assumptions is about the space of economic interaction which generally, if not always, is imagined as flat and smooth or at least ultimately destined to become so. Before important recent developments in the field, economic geographers used to make the same assumptions more explicit when they located their models of economic organization on a level and perfectly even or so-called "isotropic plane." Whether they make such spatial assumptions clear or not, orthodox economists remain committed to the more substantive idea that international trade will ultimately produce global commonalities (such as an average global wage) by enabling competition to level out economic disparities on a global scale. Free trade in this economistic universe is considered a win–win opportunity, and institutions dominated by orthodox economists ranging from the **IMF** to the **World Bank** to business schools constantly relay and amplify the message that the global liberalization of trade and investment flows is the best possible solution to world poverty and inequality. In other words, a powerful combination of academic assumptions and institutional indoctrination systematically encourage people to think of Globalization as a leveler.

Even if corporate managers were not relentlessly instilled with economic arguments about the leveling effects of Globalization in college and business

Only Heathrow brings growth to our door.

The world's emerging markets are growing at over 8%. Heathrow is best placed to bring that growth home. Find out more at Heathrow.com/hub.

Figure 2.1　Remapping the world in Heathrow airport. Photograph by Matthew Sparke.

school, there is another way in which the practices of global capitalism would tend to encourage them to believe in the myth of global leveling. If you read the promotional literature of new start-up firms, for example, it is commonly filled with claims that they will beat entrenched competitors with new practices that "level the playing field." Internet firms in particular appeal in this way to the advantages of the distance-destroying practices made possible by the web. According to Atul Vashishtha, for example, an entrepreneur behind an Indian start-up called NeoIT: "it is important to recognize that globalization is not a fleeting phenomenon, it is a market reality." Describing the possibilities of off-shoring high-tech work, he notes it is at once "a great competitive weapon for some" and " a great equalizer."[15] These might seem very specific practices and visions, but on top of them, quite literally so, we should note the much more general way in which the world's corporate leadership have come to see the world from a sort of orbital distance. Their world is a world of fast borderless business flights, a world, of elite privilege, access, and influence, a world of commanding and long-distance vision. The resulting world-view of the planet seen from afar is illustrated in endless maps and images of the globe used in business magazines, in shareholder reports, and in practically every other corporate advertisement one sees today. It is a world-view that revisions the Earth as a space for borderless economic expansion. Turning countries into business opportunities and reducing national communities into target consumer markets, it is also a view on the world that reflects the easy cross-border mobility of the jet-setting business class travelers whose search for all new opportunities and customers sends them flying around the planet (e.g. Figure 2.1).

Given their high-in-the-sky jet-set perspective, it is not surprising that business elites, not to mention many consumers, come to see the globe without its wrinkles, asymmetries, and unevenness. Of course, business managers are acutely aware of all the differences that make particular locations preferable for particular types of business. Global accounting agencies such as Standard and Poor's, for example, are constantly providing rankings for the world's business elite that distinguish between high-risk and low-risk sites, and, as Chapter 3 shows, other intermediaries track all kinds of data on the regional differences that affect how TNCs globalize their operations. But, beyond these location-specific cost/benefit calculations, the world's business elite still see a single global level plain of competition. For them, the **level playing field** is therefore more than a cliché; it is a world-view for a worldwide game with world-changing consequences.[16] Thomas Friedman, himself the epitome of an elite player on this field, has done able service describing the result. In 1999, he said that Globalization had created "a single, integrated, open plain," explaining further that: "Today that plain grows wider, faster, and more open every day, as more walls get blown down and more countries get absorbed."[17] But subsequently in order to emphasize this planar vision still more, Friedman's recent best-seller is actually entitled: *The World is Flat*. One can understand why such a title might have appealed. The shock value of the concept no doubt helped with the marketing, while the simple declaration also clearly helps Friedman tell his tale as a story of a latterday Columbus making a discovery on the road back to Bangalore from the headquarters of India's leading outsourcing firm, Infosys. The fact that Nandan Nilekani, the CEO of Infosys, had said nothing about flatness but rather "Tom, the playing field is being leveled," is not allowed to interrupt Friedman's new world narrative. Neither is he put off from his discovery discourse by the fact that the actual road to the Infosys headquarters is pockmarked and bumpy. "As I left the Infosys campus that evening and bounced along the road back to Bangalore, I kept chewing on that phrase: "The playing field is being leveled." What Nandan is saying, I thought, is that the playing field is being flattened . . . Flattened? Flattened? My God, he's telling me the world is flat!"[18]

In the real world of unequal economic opportunity, Friedman's level plain does not look so flat, so open, or so playful. We will examine the far-from-level playing field for workers in the new international divisions of labor in Chapter 4, but here it is still worth underlining some of the starker inequalities that are obscured by the myth of leveling. In 1999 (the same year Friedman first published *The Lexus and the Olive Tree*), a United Nations Development Program study showed that the world's 200 richest people have a combined wealth of over $1 trillion, equal to the combined annual income of 41% of the world's people (2.5 billion). Moreover, the globe's three richest people have assets that exceed the combined GNP of all of the least developed countries put together. In the context of heightened global protests about these sorts of inequalities; in the context of the suffering and pain caused by the adjustments required by trade liberalization and privatization; and especially in the context of the far-from-level subsidies that rich countries continue to give their domestic agri-businesses, their military industries, and their developers of patented drugs and software, the flat world vision has come in for something of a beating. Writing from a much more grounded Indian perspective to that of Friedman's flying visit to Infosys, the critic Vandana Shiva summarizes how the blinders that make the flat world conceivable also help to cover-up its exclusionary impacts when used to justify neoliberal policy. "Friedman," she writes in a scathing review of *The World is Flat*,

> has reduced the world to the friends he visits, the CEOs he knows, and the golf courses he plays at. From this microcosm of privilege, exclusion, blindness, he shuts out both the beauty of diversity and the brutality of exploitation and inequality, he shuts out the social and ecological externalities of economic globalization and free trade, he shuts out the walls that globalization is building – walls of insecurity, hatred and fear – walls of "intellectual property," walls of privatization.[19]

Against these sorts of criticisms, though, the myth of leveling still does service in defense of neoliberalism. Reflecting on the aftermath of the 1999 anti-WTO protests in Seattle and the gathering concerns about free-market policy more generally, the *Financial Times* of London advised its readers in a 2002 editorial that business elites can only take on the criticisms by keeping to the story line of Globalization and continuing to make the case that neoliberal reform will ultimately allow free trade to deliver the greatest benefit to the greatest number. "Those who believe in the benefits of globalization," it declared, "must make the arguments to prove that more liberalization can spread the benefits."[20] This call to the faithful to remember the leveling myth was made yet more urgently in the United States after the terrorist attacks of 9/11 2001. "In the wake of September 11, the defenders of globalization need to speak with an even louder, more confident voice," wrote David Komansky, chairman of Merrill Lynch. "We should use our resources and reputations to promote a vision of global prosperity and freedom wherever we can." Likewise, in the same New York Stock Exchange magazine, Michael Eskew, chairman of United Parcel Service, intoned that "Globalization and expanded trade is a great equalizer."[21] The big problem for these kinds of advocates of neoliberalism, however, is that globalization in the real world is not panning out in the new, inevitable, and leveling way it does in the great Globalization story. So far, at least, global inequality has only increased (especially when measured *within* countries). In the year 2001, 85% of the world's population earned 20% of gross world income, and 15% percent of the rich nations' people made 80% of gross world income. Or, to use a still more striking statistic for the same year, the top 1% of the world had the same combined income as the bottom 57%. The resulting tensions and discontent about the injustice of the global system – both the uneven spread of its costs and benefits and the unfair ways in which free trade is forced on the poor while rich countries continue to protect key sectors – are creating growing anger and organized opposition.

One response, the response that Friedman ultimately turns to near the end of his 1999 book, is to temporarily give up on the whole myth of the inevitable level playing field. In this sort of revisionist narrative, Globalization is reframed as a fragile development that needs the strong force of the state, in particular the United States, to back it up, to fend off the dissenters, and to make the world safe for the Globalizers. Reworking the "hidden hand" metaphor used by the famous eighteenth-century economist Adam Smith to characterize the anonymous organizational work of the market, Friedman suggests the free market of globalization also needs a "hidden fist."

> The hidden hand of the market will never work without a hidden fist. McDonald's cannot flourish without McDonnel Douglas, the designer of the US Air Force F-15. And the hidden fist that keeps the world safe for Silicon Valley's technologies to flourish is called the US Army, Air Force, Navy and Marine Corps. And these fighting forces and institutions are paid for by American taxpayer dollars.[22]

Smith himself, the author of *The Wealth of Nations*, may not have found these militaristic propositions as strange as they may sound to some of our contemporary "market knows best" devotees. While he is now celebrated as the ultimate authority on the economic expediency of free trade, he was himself no stranger to the violence through which British imperialists began to impose free trade on the world. But while Friedman may not therefore be contradicting the first theorist of free trade, his argument about the need for military intervention certainly contradicts both the inevitability myth and the leveling myth head on. A social and economic process cannot be called "inevitable" if you need the largest military force the world has ever known to keep it on track; and it cannot be called a "leveler" if: (1) it has created so much discontent that you need a hidden fist to reincorporate rebels; and (2) it functionally depends on having a global hyper-power whose dominance itself represents a complete contradiction of the vision of a global level playing field.

None of the contradictions seem to stop Friedman himself. He and those for whom he serves as a teleprompter already have an answer. They are convinced that

> there is no more First World, Second World or Third World. There's just the Fast World – the world of the wide open plain – and the Slow World – the world of those who either fall by the way-side or choose to live away from the plain in some artificially walled-off valley of their own.[23]

The great advantage of this sort of storyline is that any problems, crises, and suffering of the poor and marginalized can never be blamed on Globalization. They are caused only by the slowness of the victims themselves, the supposedly unconnected communities who will never earn enough to buy a Lexus or to see the world from a jet. The prescription that follows from this diagnosis, of course, is simply more Globalization and thus more neoliberalism. However, from the perspective of critics, Friedman's picture, and the picture conjured up by the larger Globalization story, is as wrong as it is bold.

In summary, it needs underlining that the three myths about Globalization are not only flawed, but biased in the interests of promoting free-market reform. Each has a basis in reality, but each has in turn been instrumentalized and simplified to tell a story about Globalization that is skewed in the interests of legitimating neoliberalism. While today's global economic interdependencies are new in their scale and scope, they grow out of patterns of global capitalist development that have very long histories and world-encompassing geographies, too. These histories have involved various periods of spatial expansion followed by crisis, including the huge crisis that engulfed the world with the end of imperialism in the first part of the twentieth century. By ignoring these historic crises, and by talking instead about Globalization's newness, advocates of neoliberalism fashion an argument for market reform. More than this, they also ignore the ways in which non-neoliberal policies such as public welfare programs were developed in the past in response to the crises of global capitalism. This way, they can make their pro-market agenda seem more like a bold new plan rather than a retreat to the *laissez-faire* policies of late imperialism (with their often unpleasant associations with imperial violence, workhouses, debtors' prisons, child labor, industrial accidents, mass poverty, ill-health, rural enclosures, and urban squalor).

While today's global integration imperatives are immensely powerful, they are not the inexorable and unstoppable forces that the inevitability myth makes one imagine. The logical paradox of this myth – namely, that something is not inevitable if so many people have to keep arguing it is inevitable to make it happen – also reflects its basic inaccuracy. Neoliberalism itself has had to be repeatedly enforced. Far from inexorable and automatic, it has had to be planned and implemented with great effort. And contrary to the idea that it is the only option in the context of Globalization, there are clearly many viable alternatives to the one-size-fits-all free market agenda. While global competition is real, it does not mean that a minimalist and market-oriented model of government is the only option. Such myth-making obscures the many possibilities that exist for governing economic forces and harnessing them to pursue more just, sustainable, and redistributive ends. Yet such possibilities are only further obscured by the third myth that market forces left to their own will level the global playing field all on their own. This myth captures capitalism's bull-dozing and incorporative effects transnationally, but, far from creating a level or flat world, the combination of global market forces and neoliberal reform has thus far exacerbated uneven development patterns globally, increasing inequalities within countries, unleashing diverse political, cultural, and religious reactions, and precipitating all sorts of unilateral interventions by the United States on the international stage. None of these developments have so far stopped the story-telling about Globalization, but they have led a wider variety of critics from all over the world to begin to tell different, dissident stories of Globalization. It is to these that we now turn.

2.2 Dissident Discourse on Globalization

To begin with, critics such as Vandana Shiva point out that the sorts of
Friedman calls "slow" (his "olive tree" places such as Iran, Saudi Arabia,
are hardly disconnected from the global economic system. The

profoundly integrated, either historically as producers of key raw materials or, more recently, as zones of intensive export production through resource extraction, agri-business, or sweatshop manufacturing. Moreover, it has been precisely these extractive and exploitative modes of integration into the global economy that are the key causes of political instability, foreign meddling, authoritarian government, poor education, and religious fundamentalism. Britain, France, and the United States, for example, have historically helped to install traditionalist, tribalist, and tyrannical leaders in many Middle Eastern countries in order to secure a steady supply of oil. Moreover, while many workers in the poorer parts of today's world may seem slow and immobile to the likes of Friedman, this is rarely out of choice and does not mean they are disconnected from the fast world. Indeed, they or one of their relatives may have been devastated by the effects of wars fought to keep the oil flowing fast. Or, if they live in an export-processing zone, they may have helped build a component for a jet or a Lexus, even if flying or riding in such vehicles remains an impossible dream. In other words, the "slow world/fast world" distinction does not make much sense when compared with the real economic interdependencies linking real lives across the planet. In the same way, the three main myths about Globalization are equally vulnerable to real-world criticisms.

Against the myth of newness, many residents of poorer African, Middle Eastern, Asian, and Latin American countries see only parallels and connections with their past experiences under European imperialism. Although these countries may not nowadays be bombed from the sea (the exceptions of Afghanistan and Iraq noted), they are still nonetheless subject to forms of long-distance control. Instead of the colonial bureaucrats and soldiers that the British, French, and other imperial European states used to send abroad, today poor countries now see IMF officials and attendant armies of accountants and executives busily imposing what is called **structural adjustment** in the name of integrating them more effectively into the world of market states. While the days of formal empire are largely over, therefore, there remain a whole set of similarities ranging from the basic bureaucracy of long-distance control, to the projects of resource and value extraction, to the accompanying assumptions among the foreigners that they are really doing good.[24] Thus, when the *World Commission on the Social Dimension of Globalization* asked African representatives what they thought about globalization, it was perhaps not very surpri͏   ikened it to "the recolonization of our countries," another called it
                    ʼch would lead to certain death," and yet another said that Africa
                    ılture of resistance."[25] From this anti-colonial perspective, today's
                    interconnection is not so very new. It may take the form of
                    ʼnvolve the hidden hand of the free market in privatizing and
                    , but, for the critics in the **Global South**, it is also a form of
                    ʼuch, it remains powerfully resonant with previous rounds
                    control. The arrival of the not-so-hidden fist of American
                    and Iraq only serves to make this clearer.
                    vitability, another group of Globalization's critics are
                    ʼnvironmentalists. Carl Pope, executive director of the

US environmentalist group, the Sierra Club, thus makes the argument against the paradox of inevitability very clear indeed:

> Inevitable forces in society do not require 3,000 page treaties to make them happen. Inevitable forces do not depend on suppressed public dialogue and parliamentary tricks to move them along. They don't depend on elaborate exemptions from the normal rules of social life to take place.[26]

Likewise, whether they be local conservationists or globally engaged organizations such as Greenpeace, environmentalists refuse to accept that environmental destruction and environmental changes such as global warming and ocean pollution represent the inevitable outcomes of global interdependency. Global connections, they argue, can be organized in other ways so that a more sustainable, long-term approach to living in an integrated planetary ecosystem can be developed. It is true that some environmental groups sometimes mobilize apocalyptic language about looming global devastation. In other words, they also rework visions of a new endstate for the world. But this needs to be seen itself as a rewriting of the inevitability myth: a rewriting aimed at mobilizing people to think of what the end of the big Globalization story might mean environmentally, but a rewriting too made as part of a campaign to stop the supposedly inevitable.

More generally, this campaign has been joined by other critics of neoliberalism whose concerns are not just environmental. Arundhati Roy, for example, an Indian activist who has campaigned against river damming in India, but who has also been an eloquent critic of global privatization trends and the invasion of Iraq, concluded her address to fellow critics in Brazil with the following call to resistance:

> The corporate revolution will collapse if we refuse to buy what they are selling – their ideas, their version of history, their wars, their weapons, their notion of inevitability.[27]

Others argue in the same way that refusing to buy into the myth of inevitable Globalization is not a simple consumer choice, but rather about politics and social struggle, too. David Korten, the president of the People-Centered Development Forum, turns the argument thus into a call for action. "Economic globalization will be inevitable as long as we allow corporations to elect our leaders and write our laws," he says.

> It took decades of bold and dedicated effort by legions of economists, lawyers, and politicians on the payrolls of powerful monied interests to design and implement such a perversely life destroying system. It required a radical altering of long established and deeply imbedded cultural values, the restructuring of many important institutions, and the creation of the International Monetary Fund, the World Bank, the GATT and the World Trade Organization – all structured to place economic policy beyond the reach of global accountability. It will take a similarly bold and committed effort on the part of civil society to restore democratic accountability, rebuild cultures that honor cooperation and compassion, and create a planetary system of locally rooted economic justice and environmental sustainability.[28]

Third, against the leveling myth, some of the strongest critics have been women's groups. So often the advocates of neoliberalism use the plight of women around the world to defend the model of free-market-led development. According to this popular sub-plot of the Globalization story, the oppression of women – including their exclusion from education, the violence they face in the home, and their economic exploitation – will all diminish as countries adopt the neoliberal model and become more tightly integrated into global commodity chains. However, as many women's groups point out, this has hardly ever happened in practice. Moreover, in the words of the American feminist scholar, Teresa Brennan:

> Wherever globalization has a negative effect on human beings, whether it is increasing the time they have to work, or the time they have to spend in domestic work, or the time they have to spend in consumption, women are hit worse than men. . . . In all regions of the world, women work longer hours for less pay than their male counterparts, and there are no signs that this situation is improving.

Backing up this claim with data, Brennan goes on to describe how globally women still earn only between 50 and 80% of male wages for the same work (outside of agriculture); that they hold less than 6% of senior management posts; and that they work 10–25 h more per week than men in paid and unpaid employment.[29] Aside from such statistical trends, feminist critics often point out that women also tend to have a more grounded understanding of globalization that serves to contradict the level-playing-field vision seen from business jets. Christa Wichterich, the author of *The Globalized Woman*, puts it like this:

> For women around the world . . . globalization is not an abstract process unfolding on an elevated stage. It is concrete and actual. Female textile workers from . . . Eastern Germany are losing their jobs to women in Bangladesh; Filipinas clean vegetables and kitchens in Kuwait; Brazilian prostitutes offer their services around Frankfurt's main railway station; and Polish women look after old people at rock-bottom prices in . . . Germany.[30]

Thus, whether considered from the perspective of data on women's labor or the actual practices through which women's lives are integrated into globalization, the idea of global leveling looks much more mythical than real.

To make these sorts of critical arguments is clearly a criticism of Globalization, its myths and myth-makers, but it is not a rejection of globalization in the substantive sense. The resistance movements of the various critics are certainly anti-neoliberal and often anti-corporate. Sometimes they also see themselves still more radically as anti-capitalist and anti-imperial. However, they are not anti-globalization in the sense of being against global networks and global collaboration. For example, the American doctor, Paul Farmer, who is a steadfast critic of global inequalities, neoliberalism, and the corporatization of medicine, is nevertheless simultaneously a strong supporter of global human rights efforts and, in particular, efforts to spread the benefits of medical science to everybody on the planet no matter where they live.[31] It is for these sorts of reasons that critics of neoliberal policies generally reject the "anti-globalization" label, preferring titles such as the "Global Justice Movement," "Globalization from Below," "Grassroots Globalization," "People's Globalization" and the "Alter-Globalization Movement," the latter being itself a globe-trotting and border-crossing *double entendre* based on the French term "*Alter-Mondialisation*."

The terminological nuances reflect the fact that some of the best-argued and well-researched critical arguments about the costs of neoliberalism come from activists and scholars who are committed to alternative kinds of political solidarity that reach around the world. They have been pioneers in using the Internet to organize globally; they strive to create alternative global media and trade networks; and they have generally, if not always successfully, placed great emphasis on integrating critics from the poorest parts of the world into the heart of shared strategies of resistance and action. Even the environmentalist groups that call for new economic development strategies of "localization" and the indigenous activists who call for aboriginal sovereignty do not promote political isolationism. They have instead sought to build global movements: environmental movements that share ideas about more ecologically accountable approaches to production and consumption; and, indigenous movements that strategize globally on how to win recognition of native land rights and place-based traditions.

At yet another distinct scale, critics such as the French group **ATTAC** that propose alternative forms of managing global finance – including the development of global taxes and the organization of systems of international redistribution – remain clearly committed to an alternative globalization, too. These sorts of projects, arguments, and political engagements vary greatly, but what all the critics nevertheless share is a rejection of the simple political equation that "Globalization = Neoliberalism." In order to suggest that another world is possible and that alternative forms of "grassroots globalization" can be organized, all of the critics thus endeavor in one way or another to sever the automatic link made in the dominant discourse of Globalization between increasing global interdependency and increasing need for neoliberal policies. However, they do this in very different ways, and the variations between these different critical positions pose a difficult analytical question: namely, what kind of political project are the critics creating? This chapter will therefore end with a brief consideration of three distinct approaches to conceptualizing the worldwide struggles against neoliberal Globalization.

The easiest and yet most inaccurate approach to describing the political movement of the critics is to describe them simply as "**anti-globalization** protesters."[32] This has been the approach of many mainstream advocates of neoliberalism such as Thomas Friedman. Ever since the so-called Battle in Seattle when street protests seriously disrupted the 1999 meetings of the World Trade Organization (**WTO**), Friedman has led the way in painting the political project of the critics as a simple-minded and reactively localist sort of struggle led by privileged American students with little knowledge of life and economic reality in the poorer parts of the world. In Friedman's one-dimensional world-view, there really is no alternative to neoliberal Globalization, and so anyone who is against neoliberalism is against globalization altogether. This broad brush form of dismissal is easy to learn and repeat, of course, and directed at events such as the Seattle protests, it appears at first blush to neatly erase all the complexities of the critics' arguments. Unfortunately for Friedman and the politicians for whom he speaks, however, his picture of the protesters was at odds with the facts. In Seattle, American students were certainly involved (many of them well educated about global economics by campus-based fair-trade and anti-sweatshop campaigns), but they were joined by thousands and thousands of other critics from other walks of life and from other parts of the world. More than 50 000 marchers led by American unions supported the direct action efforts to block access to the WTO convention. The march, which thus effectively took over the whole downtown core of Seattle, included a huge range of other critics ranging from Canadian, Mexican, Asian, and European union members to environmentalists, women's groups, border-region solidarity groups, peace groups, human rights groups, fair-trade groups, and farmers' groups, as well as representatives of Latin American landless peasants and the Zapatistas of Chiapas in Mexico. What was so remarkable about this gathering (and why the "anti-globalization" label was especially inaccurate) was that the vast majority of the messages and slogans used by these critics advocated alternative forms of global connection, global governance, and global solidarity (see Figure 2.2 – a collage of three photos from the protests). In other words, the protests were not a rejection of global interdependency but rather a representation of globe-spanning political solidarity by groups unwilling to accept that interdependency should be organized along the neoliberal lines dictated by the WTO.

If "anti-globalization" is such an unhelpful label, what are the other alternatives to conceptualizing the political project of the critics? A second notable approach that has received a great deal of attention in the last decade was outlined in 2000 by an American literary theorist Michael Hardt and an Italian philosopher Antonio Negri in a book entitled *Empire*. The thesis of this long and often arcane book is ultimately quite simple. Hardt and Negri argue that what they call the "Empire" of globalization is today digging its own grave by creating a new revolutionary subject on the world stage, a subject that they call "the multitude." This thesis builds on the old Marxist argument about capitalism creating a revolutionary working class on the world stage, but unlike Marx (who connected his political arguments to a much more extensive and detailed examination of capitalism's economic dynamics), Hardt and Negri's claims about "the multitude" are most often abstract and decontextualized. It is true that as a more philosophical term, "the multitude" is an improvement on the dismissive "anti-globalization" label. Rhetorically it sounds positively inclusive, and it evokes the plurality of the protest movements around the world. However, it does so in such an abstract and singular way – it is only after all *the* multitude, not multitudes, and certainly not particular protest movements in particular economic contexts that are discussed – that the book comes close to mirroring the same one-dimensional depictions of globalization and anti-globalization as those sketched by Friedman. Neoliberal policies are described by Hardt and Negri as creating Empire's globally networked "constitutional order," and, while they see this order as something of a

Figure 2.2   Examples of appeals for global solidarity in the Seattle protests of 1999.
Photographs by Matthew Sparke.

disciplinary straitjacket, they also (like Friedman with his vision of a golden strait-jacket) see the glint of golden promise in Empire's constitution in so far as the so-called multitude is said to be already in the midst of remaking the networked global order for the better. It is never clear who is a member of the multitude exactly, but this does not seem to matter because we can all sit back and watch the inevitable dawning of the new world order. This abstract idea of looming inevitability makes Hardt and Negri's argument about global change appear quite similar to Friedman's analogy of globalization with the dawn. Combined with their account of Empire's novelty and spatial "smoothness" – an account that therefore joins the myth of inevitability with the myths of newness and leveling – it all helps make the book more akin to *The Lexus and the Olive Tree* than its authors would probably like to admit. In any event, Hardt and Negri's vision of the multitude remains too abstruse to provide anything very practical to say about the political projects of the critics of neoliberal globalization.

A third and more adequate approach is suggested by the accounts of those who have been more intimately involved with protest movements themselves. These movements – and the plural is vital here – have been steadily increasing and diversifying in recent years. The Battle in Seattle after all inspired many other big urban protests. Between 2000 and 2005, cities all over the world saw demonstrations, including Washington DC, Quebec City, Prague, Chiang Mai, Gothenburg, Genoa, Barcelona, Cancun, London, and Evian. Most of these protests were ranged initially against the IMF, the World Bank, the G8, and the prospect of a Free Trade Area of the Americas, as well as against the WTO. Yet they were also tied to the much wider rejections of neoliberalism manifested in the hugely popular Argentinian and Bolivian uprisings of 2002, uprisings that followed the failure of neoliberal leaders to deliver two things they pride themselves on most: namely, jobs and economic stability. At the same time and at a smaller scale, activist organizations like the People's Global Action network helped organize protest projects like the Intercontinental Caravan (a joint anti-corporate resistance effort linking the Karnataka State Farmer's Union from India with British activists) by forging ties between critics from both poor and rich parts of the world in coordinated protest actions.[33] It is in the context of these worldly protest movements, and with a direct interest in how they change the casting and narrative of the Globalization story, that activists have also set about trying to develop clear proposals for alternative, socially, and environmentally responsible forms of globalization.

One of the many sites at which these efforts took place in the new millennium was the World Social Forum (WSF), an annual gathering of alter-globalization activists originally organized as a counterpoint to the annual meeting of neoliberal elites at the World Economic Forum in Davos, Switzerland. The first forum took place in January 2001 in Porto Alegre, Brazil, and has since been followed by more global meetings in Porto Alegre, Mumbai (India), Dakar (Senegal), and Belem (Brazil), and many more regional World Social Forums organized by local activists in contexts as diverse as Florence (Italy), Cape Town (South Africa), Linz (Austria), Bamako (Mali), Buenos Aires (Argentina), Conakry (Guinea), Lima (Peru), Addis Ababa (Ethiopia), Lahore (Pakistan), and Detroit (United States) (see Figure 2.3). Resisting the direction of mar-

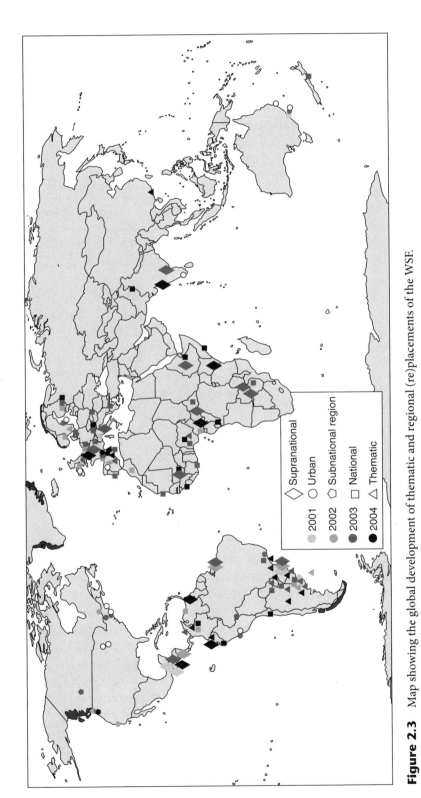

Figure 2.3 Map showing the global development of thematic and regional (re)placements of the WSF.

ket-led globalization, its inequalities and ill-effects, these events have all also been about imagining other better ways of organizing global ties. Thus, although neoliberals such as Friedman said the WSF was just another "anti-globalization protest," and although Michael Hardt suggested that it represented a massing of "the multitude," other commentators on this evolving convergence space of alter-globalization activism saw a much more complex and variegated form of grassroots globalization taking shape.[34] For example, the Brazilian and French intellectual, Michael Löwy, reported in this way that the WSF represented a movement involving:

> trade unions, feminists, Marxists, anarchists, ecologists, Christians for liberation, socialists of several colours and shades, peasant and indigenous movements, non-government organisations (NGOs), intellectuals, and many young people, women and workers without other affiliations, who wish to protest, march, fight and discuss with others.[35]

Also, emphasizing its heterogeneity, Nikhil Anand a student at Yale Univesity noted that:

> As a confluence of funders, mainstream development and environment organisations such as Oxfam, the World Wildlife Fund, indigenous people's organisations, small environmental groups, and more radical political units such as the PSTU of Brazil, the WSF confronts participants with encounters and meetings that challenge communicating within familiar discourses.[36]

Anand's point about the challenging quality of the often contradictory encounters at the WSF was an important one. It underlined not only the diversity of alter-globalization efforts but also the potential *democratic value* of the resulting arguments. Highlighting this achievement, Jai Sen, one of the organizers of the Mumbai Forum in India, wrote that:

> The real "success" of the Forum is that it is making possible a scale of talking across boundaries that has rarely been dreamt of before, and contributing to building a culture of open debate across conventional walls. The real "alternative" it offers is showing that it is possible to create, and to sustain, a non-directed space. In my understanding, helping to bridge old politics and the new is arguably one of the most crucial but most difficult challenges for the Forum, and quite possibly also one of its historically most important.[37]

For supporters such as Sen, this kind of boundary-crossing "democracy from below" was what made it possible for WSF attendees to claim that: "Another World Is Possible." In this way, the radical democracy of the WSF was also imagined as an alternative "beginning" to replace the normal neoliberal ending to the dominant Globalization narrative.[38] However, as Sen and other participants were also critically aware, it was an alternative that remained far from inevitable. Indeed, Sen worried that it remained overshadowed by forces that might turn the Forum itself into a form of commodity. "Even as I celebrate the fact of the Forum and what it is doing," he said, "I also believe that there are several tendencies taking shape within it that are deeply negative and contradictory to its very spirit. Most centrally, they include the Forum becoming a commodity and a brand name and its motto a logo and the beginning of a kind of worldwide franchising."[39] Ultimately, the worry here was that the WSF would degenerate into producing nothing but its own-dimensional discourse, railing against market fundamentalism only to end up being turned into just another commodity in the global political marketplace.

Towards the end of the first decade of the new millennium, it was not so much **commodification** as marginalization that seemed the bigger threat to the WSF. While the World Economic Forum in Davos continued to attract headlines, money, and world leaders, attention seemed to decline for the big annual World Social Forum events in January each year. Part of the problem, it appeared, was that in the context of the US War on Terror, arguments against global market dominance and the inevitability of market-led Globalization had been overshadowed by new concerns with unilateral American dominance and the Pentagon-led wars in Iraq and Afghanistan. As we shall explore further in Chapter 8, these US military interventions were often explained and justified in Washington DC in the geoeconomic terms of bringing freedom and free markets to countries described as being "disconnected" from globalization. But the unilateral geopolitical challenge of the wars that the United States used to pursue these goals nevertheless still distracted from the alter-globalization efforts because many global justice activists saw "American imperialism" or "American hegemony" as the most pressing global problem. Instead of inequality and exploitation in low-wage factory zones, it was torture and dehumanization in Guantánamo Bay and Abu Ghraib that suddenly seemed more urgent global issues.

Then, in 2008 with the collapse of Lehman Brothers and the crises in US stock and credit markets, the economic malaise facing Americans themselves increasingly put US hegemony into question. At the same time, the shared sense of global vulnerability to the market turmoil also brought activists back together globally to challenge the contradictions and convolutions of global finance and global capitalism more generally. It was in this way in turn that the longstanding WSF questions about inequality and the ill-effects of market dominance dramatically came back to the streets of America itself in late 2011. Taking form and literally taking place in what became known as the Occupy movement, this youth-led approach to direct action took off nationally while also both emulating and inspiring street protests in other countries badly affected by the global economic crises. American city centers came thus to look a lot like city centers in Greece and Spain, filled with encampments and protests by young people who might once have looked forward to six-digit salaries after college, but who now increasingly saw precarious part time jobs, chronic indebtedness, and diminished public services as their destiny.[40] The connections highlighted by the crisis between these debt-defined destinies in wealthy countries and ongoing experiences of debt-based market discipline in poorer countries also in turn made the relays and resonances between Occupy activism and other global protest movements in the Global South that much stronger, too. Thus, in a technologically telling sign of the times, a map of Occupy-related

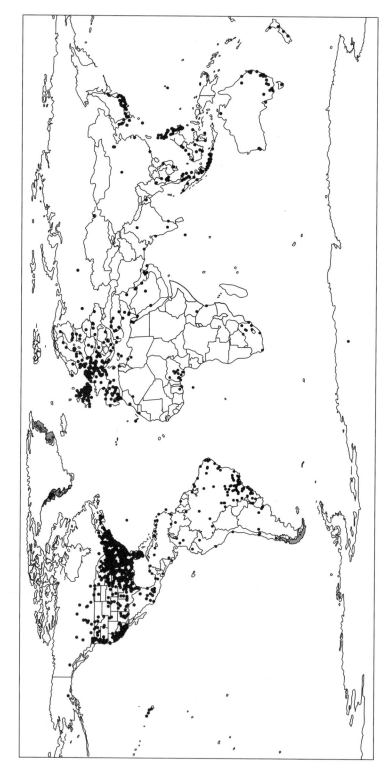

Figure 2.4 Map of Occupy-related, geolocated tweets from October 15 to November 5, 2011. *Source:* produced and formatted by Josef Eckert.

"tweets" in the fall of 2011 highlights how social media interest and engagement in the street occupations spread right around the world (Figure 2.4).

The global ties to other protests ranging from the *Indignados* in Europe to factory occupations in Latin America to the uprisings of the Arab Spring also meant that Occupy activism shared with WSF activism a form of "horizontalist" capacity to enable talking across boundaries. But just as Sen was worried by the commodification of the WSF, a concern haunting many Occupy activists in 2012 was that their leaderless efforts might become co-opted by national political leaders, or just disconnected from the original border-crossing criticisms of the debt, dispossession, and inequality imposed by global markets. Whether these concerns prove valid, and whether or not Occupy ideas are themselves commodified, franchised, and turned into empty logos can only be evaluated by future studies. But hopefully, having now come to terms with the implications of Globalization as a discourse, and having learned about how it has worked to legitimate the norms of neoliberalization, you, as a reader of this chapter, are in a better position to make such evaluations yourself. Perhaps, though, the concern with commodification simply leaves you perplexed. What, after all, is a commodity? And what does it have to do with globalization or, for that matter, with neoliberalism and Globalization? It is to these complex questions that we now turn in Chapter 3.

Student Exercises

Group:
1. Find a business article on globalization in a particular magazine or paper such as *Business Week, The Economist, Fortune,* the *Financial Times,* or the *Wall Street Journal.* Try to track which of the three main myths about Globalization it uses most and what policies or developments are recommended as a result.

Individual:
2. Use *Google* to go to the site of a progressive global NGO such as Oxfam, Greenpeace, Amnesty International, or Save the Children. Investigate their statements and reports about global development and examine whether they contest any of the three main myths about Globalization. If they do, what stories about Globalization or globalization do they offer as alternatives?

Notes

1   This three-step dance towards the moderate academic middle is best illustrated by David Held and Anthony McGrew, *Globalization/Anti-Globalization* (Oxford: Blackwell, 2002); David Held, Anthony McGrew, David Goldblatt, and Jonathan Perraton, *Global Transformations: Politics, Economics and Culture* (Palo Alto, CA: Stanford University Press, 1999); and Jan Aart Scholte, *Globalization: A Critical Introduction* (New York: Palgrave, 2000). For a questioning study of where this three step takes these sorts of

analyses conceptually, see Justin Rosenberg, *The Follies of Globalisation Theory* (London: Verso, 2000). To the extent that Rosenberg is right, and these scholars resort to spatial arguments about trans-territoriality to define what is really new and different about globalization, the three-step dance might also be said to replace attention to the space of discourse about Globalization with an uncritical approach to the spatial dynamics of globalization. Here instead in Chapter 8 on space, we explore the way globalization creates spatial ties that bind in ways that are profoundly political and economically consequential precisely because they are also uneven and asymmetrical.

2   Variations on such competitive global rankings – all of which tend to index globalization in terms of a neoliberal ideal type of Globalization – include: the World Economic Forum's "Global Competitiveness" ranking http://www.weforum.org/issues/global-competitiveness; *AT Kearney* and *Foreign Policy* magazine's "Globalization Index" http://www.atkearney.com/index.php/Publications/globalizationindex.html; the KOF "index of globalization" http://globalization.kof.ethz.ch/; and the Wikipedia version of KOF http://en.wikipedia.org/wiki/Globalization_Index. For further discussion of the real-world governmental effects of such rankings, including the ways in which they function like credit ratings to discipline policy makers, see Chapter 7.

3   Sometimes this also leads authors to invent new names for Globalization in order to repackage the brand and promote it afresh. See, for example, Harold L. Sirkin, James W. Hemerling, and Arindam K. Bhattacharya, *Globality: Competing with Everyone from Everywhere for Everything* (New York: Business Plus, 2008).

4   Tony Blair, "Blair Sets Out Framework to Cure Economic Ills: Mais lecture," *Financial Times* May 23, Tuesday (1995), A10.

5   Newt Gingrich cited in *Contract with America: The Bold Plan by Rep. Newt Gingrich, Rep. Dick Armey and the House Republicans to Change the Nation*, eds M. Fisher and T. Ponniah Gillespie and Bob Schellhas (New York: Times Books, 1994), 188.

6   Bill Clinton, "Remarks by the President to the Community of the University of Warwick," Coventry, Warwickshire, England, December 14, 2000, published on a now inoperative webpage of the University of Warwick.

7   Kim Dae Jung, "Why should Asia globalize?," *Asia Week*, http://www.asiaweek.com/asiaweek/magazine/2000/1124/ann.voices_kim.html.

8   World Economic Forum site, http://www.weforum.org/site/knowledgenavigator.nsf/Content/Is%20India%20Afraid%20of%20Globalization%3F_2002?open&country_id=.

9   The Australian Prime Minister John Howard to the Commonwealth Heads of Government Meeting (CHOGM) in 1999, quoted in *Sydney Morning Herald* 14th November 1999.

10   Thomas Friedman, *The Lexus and the Olive Tree: Understanding Globalization* (New York: Farrar Straus and Giroux, 1999).

11   Friedman, *Lexus and the Olive Tree*, 103.

12   Bill Clinton quoted in an Associated Press article "Clinton Addresses Brazil Students," August 29, 2001, http://www.rose-hulman.edu/~delacova/brazil/clinton.htm.

13   The quotations are taken from the website of the International Chamber of Commerce which foregrounds Annan's proposals, http://www.iccwbo.org/home/case_for_the_global_economy/globalization_is_irreversible.asp.

14   Kofi Annan, "Globalization: What Is At Stake?," on the World Economic Forum website http://www.weforum.org/site/knowledgenavigator.nsf/Content/Globalization:%20What%20Is%20At%20Stake%3F_2001?open&topic_id=.

15   Atul Vashishtha quoted on the website of Offshore Development.Com, http://www.
     offshoredev.com/jsp/features_detail.jsp?fid=176 on 2/08/04.

16   A funny definition of the "level playing field" in a dictionary of in-house business terms
     captures both the bias and the mystifying power of the term with wit. "level playing field
     1. My rules. 2. A theological construct, a happy hunting ground where the young
     knights of the business Round Table contend with each other and, when the joust is
     done, refresh themselves in waters drawn from the clear rills and crystalline runnels
     whence the cash doth flow; a condition not unlike heaven, where all is fair and no one
     loses." Nicholas von Hoffman, *Devil's Dictionary of Business; Monkey Business; High
     Finance and Low; Money, the Making, Losing and Printing Thereof; Commerce; Trade;
     Clever Tricks; Tours de Force; Globalism and Globaloney; Industry; Invention; the Stock Mar-
     ket; Marvelous Explanations and Clarifications; All Presented with Wit and Attitude . . .*
     (New York: Nation Books, 2004). Hoffman's entry for globaloney itself is equally irrever-
     ent: "globaloney The doctrine that unfettered world trade cures warts."

17   Friedman, 1999, *op. cit.* p. 41.

18   Thomas L. Friedman, *The World is Flat: A Brief History of the Twenty-First Century*
     (New York: Farrar, Straus and Giroux, 2005), 7.

19   V. Shiva, "The Polarised World of Globalisation" (2005), http://www.zmag.org/Sustain-
     ers/Content/2005-05/27shiva.cfm.

20   Quoted on the website of the International Chamber of Commerce, http://www.iccwbo.
     org/home/news_archives/2002/serious%20protestors.asp.

21   Quoted on the website of the New York Stock exchange, http://www.nyse.com/content/
     magazinearticles/1043269646002.html.

22   Friedman, *op. cit.* p. 373.

23   Hoffman, *Devil's Dictionary*, 41.

24   This is one of the main lessons of the brilliant graphic "primer" on the long history
     of globalization and its connections with colonization, El Fisgón, *How to Succeed at
     Globalization: A Primer for the Roadside Vendor* (New York: Metropolitan Books,
     2004).

25   Quoted in The International Labor Organization's report, *The World Commission on the
     Social Dimension of Globalization* (Geneva: ILO, 2004), 15.

26   Quoted on the website of the *International Forum on Globalization* on a useful page
     dedicated to arguments against inevitability, http://www.ifg.org/inevitable.html

27   Arundhati Roy, "Confronting Empire," in *The World Social Forum: Challenging Empires*,
     eds M. Fisher and T. Ponniah Jai Sen, Anita Anand, Arturo Escobar, and Peter Waterman
     (Viveka Foundation: New Delhi, 2004), 54.

28   Quoted in the website of the *International Forum on Globalization* at http://www.ifg.org/
     inevitable.html.

29   Teresa Brennan, *Globalization and Its Terrors: Daily Life in the West* (New York:
     Routledge, 2003), 26.

30   Quoted on the webpage of the Canada-based UN Platform for Action Committee,
     http://unpac.ca/economy/introglob.html.

31   Paul Farmer, *Pathologies of Power: Health, Human Rights, and the New War on the Poor*
     (Berkeley: University of California Press, 2005). Instead of offering us vistas of a Flat
     World, Farmer is at pains to point to the mountains beyond mountains of inequality
     created by neoliberalism and neocolonialism; see Tracy Kidder, *Mountains Beyond
     Mountains: The Quest of Dr. Paul Farmer, A Man Who Would Cure the World* (New York:
     Random House 2003).

32 Ironically, this is what another critic of Globalization mythology does who ascribes most of the myth-making to the protestors. Alan Shipman, *The Globalization Myth: Why the Protestors Have Got It Wrong* (Cambridge: Icon Books, 2002).

33 For useful studies of the Intercontinental Caravan and the Peoples Global Action network see David Featherstone, "Spatialities of Transnational Resistance to Globalization: the Maps of Grievance of the Inter-Continental Caravan," *Transactions of the Institute of British Geographers* NS 28 (2003): 404–21; and Paul Routledge, "Convergence space: process geographies of grassroots globalization networks," *Transactions of the Institute of British Geographers* NS 28 (2003): 333–49.

34 Michael Hardt, "Today's Bandung?" *New Left Review* 14 (2004): 112–18.

35 Michael Löwy, "Towards a New International?" in Jai Sen, Anita Anand, Arturo Escobar, and Peter Waterman, eds., *The World Social Forum: Challenging Empires* (New Delhi: Viveka Foundation, 2004), 21. Many contributors to this volume make similar points as do yet others in *Another World Is Possible: Popular Alternatives to Globalisation at the World Social Forum*, eds M. Fisher and T. Ponniah (London: Zed Books, 2003).

36 Nikhil Anand, "Bound to mobility? Identity and purpose at the WSF," in *The World Social Forum: Challenging Empires*, eds Jai Sen, Anita Anand, Arturo Escobar, and Peter Waterman (New Delhi: Viveka Foundation, 2004), 141–47, 143.

37 Jai Sen, "The Forum As Logo, the Forum As Religion: Skepticism of the Intellect, Optimism of the Will," in *The World Social Forum: Challenging Empires*, eds Jai Sen, Anita Anand, Arturo Escobar, Peter Waterman (New Delhi: Viveka Foundation, 2004), 210–27, at 212.

38 For further discussion of these democratizing possibilities in relation to economic theories of globalization see Matthew Sparke, Elizabeth Brown, Dominic Corva, Heather Day, Caroline Faria, Tony Sparks, and Kirsten Varg "The World Social Forum and the Lessons for Economic Geography," *Economic Geography* 81, 4 (2005): 359–80.

39 Sen, *Forum as Logo*, 210. By 2006, other scholars were arguing that Sen's fears had already come true, that the World Social Forum had become a an anti-logo logo. See Robert Huish, "Logos a Thing of the Past? Not So Fast, World Social Forum," *Antipode* 38, no. 1 (2006): 1–6.

40 David Harvey, *Rebel Cities: From the Right to the City to the Urban Revolution* (New York: Verso, 2012); and Matthew Sparke, "From Global Dispossession to Local Repossession: Towards a Worldly Cultural Geography of Occupy Activism," in *The New Companion to Cultural Geography*, eds Jamie Winders and Richard Schein (Oxford: Wiley-Blackwell, 2012).

Keywords

anti-globalization	Global South	neoliberalism
ATTAC	IMF	structural adjustment
commodification	level playing field	TINA
G8	liberalization	World Bank
global compact	neocolonialism	WTO

3

Commodities

Chapter Contents

Chapter Concepts

1. Networks of commodity trading form the heart of global economic interdependency.
2. We can examine global economic ties in terms of commodity chains, the globe-spanning links from commodity production to distribution to consumption.
3. Commodity chains are of five main types: (a) in house; (b) captive supplier; (c) modular; (d) relational; (e) marketized.
4. The main drivers that organize the integration of commodity chains are TNCs.
5. TNCs globalize in order to reach new markets or to create sourcing efficiencies (including cheap inputs of components and labor), or both.
6. TNCs can globalize their operations either directly through foreign direct investment or indirectly through outsourcing.

Key Concept

In order to understand the economic interdependencies of globalization today, we need to unpack global commodity chains and come to terms with the business

Introducing Globalization: Ties, Tensions, and Uneven Integration, First Edition. Matthew Sparke.
© 2013 Matthew Sparke. Published 2013 by Blackwell Publishing Ltd.

decisions inside TNCs that have led them to globalize their organization of commodity production, distribution, and sales.

3.1   What is a Commodity?

Commodities are things that are bought and sold for money. They include both material goods (known by trade statisticians as "merchandise") and services (known by the more practically minded as "commodities that you cannot drop on your foot"). Commodities therefore range widely: from Japanese TVs assembled in Mexico out of Indonesian components and discounted in Wal-Mart stores across America; to a *Manchester United* versus *Real Madrid* game featuring adverts for Bangladesh-made German-marketed sportswear and broadcast by a pay-per-view cable channel in a bar in Malaysia; to French-designed cookware made in China in a Taiwanese-owned factory on the shelves of a shop in a Canadian mall; to west African cocoa and genetically modified Kansas soy beans marketed as a chocolate soy milk drink in Singapore; to computer code jointly written by Seattle- and Bangalore-based programmers encrypted into operating systems pre-purchased on computers for sale everywhere; and so on. Such a list of globe-trotting commodities can be extended indefinitely, and as such makes clear that a great many commodities today are bought and sold *across* international borders. Their transnational travels and ubiquity make such commodities the most taken for granted, telling, and yet troubling examples we have of economic globalization. Taken for granted, because, despite all the purchases that are made everyday in every part of the world, consumers rarely think about, let alone explore, where commodities come from. Telling, because once one does start to explore where commodities come from a whole world of interdependence starts to come into view. And troubling because this economic interdependence raises far-reaching ethical and political questions about our responsibilities as consumers, workers, and managers with ties to commodity production in foreign countries.

The overall aim of this chapter is to introduce ways of deciphering the information about economic globalization provided by tracking commodities. It is worth remembering in this respect that key statistics used to measure commodity flows remain based on national data that are still gathered – as the root of the word *statistics* reminds us – by *states*. While also collected and compared by global agencies such as the World Trade Organization (WTO), they are mainly counted by national state governments with a focus on national economic activities. Gross domestic product (GDP), for example, is normally calculated by adding up the value of all the finished goods and services produced within a particular national economy in a particular year. Likewise, trade data measure imports and exports into and out of particular national economies. As we shall see, the relationship between these two key commodity metrics – the ratio of trade to GDP – can tell us a great deal about changes in the degree of economic globalization over time. But, by the same token, today's form of globalization is so intense and multilayered that it is also changing the meaning of the national statistics, too: making national GDP an inadequate tool for measuring and managing cross-border economic coordination; and sometimes overstating the ratio of trade to GDP because of how the latter does not include all the non-finished goods – the multiple components and intermediate products – that increasingly comprise such a big portion of cross-border commodity flows in the most globalized economies.[1]

Despite the changes, and sometimes clearly because of them too, commodity data still tell us important information about globalization. Thus, we begin Section 3.2 at the macro-economic level by discussing what world-trade history and trade data tell us about the uneven development of global economic integration. Then, in order to understand the dynamics lying behind the data, we turn in Section 3.3 to the concept of the **commodity chain**, a name for all the steps in the economic journey connecting the production of raw materials and components, to the assembly and packaging of commodities, to their distribution, marketing, sale, and consumption. Lastly, in Section 3.4, we will look at the ways in which the production, distribution, and consumption of commodities can be further explained at a more micro level by examining the coordination and management of specific commodity chains by corporations and, in particular, by examining the main reasons why transnational corporations (**TNCs**) have become transnational.

At the outset, it needs to be clarified that there are three special sorts of commodity that are crucial inputs into most commodity chains but which, because of their complexity and unique characteristics, need to be discussed in greater detail in later chapters. The first is labor, the fundamental source of the underlying value for which commodities are made and sold by business, but which is also itself a commodity traded for a price between workers and their employers (see Chapter 4). The second special initial input of capitalist commodity chains is the money that businesses use to purchase labor and other commodities at the start of the chain, and which they aim to recoup with an extra dividend when the commodities that are produced are bought by consumers (see Chapter 5). And the third special initial input is nature, the source of the many raw materials, the energy, and the space, out of which, through which, and in which commodities are made (see Chapter 8). In addition to these three special inputs, there are yet other, hybrid kinds of commodities that cannot be adequately discussed in this present chapter. These include previously public or naturally free things (such as education, DNA, and rivers) that have been transformed into private and thus tradable commodities (such as globally marketed degree programs, patented drugs, and hydroelectricity futures). Such processes of transformation, or **commodification** as it is often called, need to be understood in terms of the neoliberal approaches to policy reform, which we will discuss further in terms of governance in Chapter 7. Finally, there are diverse "alternative" commodities such as those bought and sold under the name of "Fair Trade." These include products such as fair-trade coffee and fair-trade cotton, which are often imagined by their consumers and vendors as the basis for a non-neoliberal or, at least, more just form of economic globalization. We will discuss these commodities further in the final chapter of the book on alternatives (Chapter 10). However, to understand their significance, and to adequately come to terms with the wider world of profit-driven commodity chains within which fair-trade networks remain embedded, we have to begin by understanding how historic forms of trade in commodities have become incorporated and radically reorganized over time by the networks of commodity production, distribution, and consumption under capitalism.

3.2   World Trade

Quinquireme of Nineveh from distant Ophir,
Rowing home to haven in sunny Palestine,
With a cargo of ivory,
And apes and peacocks,
Sandalwood, cedarwood, and sweet white wine.

Stately Spanish galleon coming from the Isthmus,
Dipping through the Tropics by the palm-green shores,
With a cargo of diamonds,
Emeralds, amethysts,
Topazes, and cinnamon, and gold moidores.

Dirty British coaster with a salt-caked smoke stack,
Butting through the Channel in the mad March days,
With a cargo of Tyne coal,
Road-rails, pig-lead,
Firewood, iron-ware, and cheap tin trays.

John Masefield, *Cargoes* (first published in 1902)

The early twentieth-century British poet John Masefield captured some of the complexity of world trade in his famous sea poem, *Cargoes*. Although it represents a romantic reflection on pre-capitalist trade networks, there is a way in which the rhythmic energy of the poem captures the continuities as well as the contrasts between ancient examples of world trade and the industrial goods – coal, rails, pig-lead, and so on – being traded as commodities at the peak of British imperialism. The poem reminds us in this way that long-distance, if not entirely globe-spanning, trade has been a constant feature of human life going back millennia. Spices and precious fabrics traded across Asia, African goods circulated in Europe, and semi-precious stones that can be geologically traced to areas that are now part of Canada were traded right down the Pacific coast to places now in Mexico. These sorts of trading ties ebbed and flowed in different world regions through the centuries, but they began to be reorganized on a global scale with the development of European colonialism in the sixteenth century. After this period, and especially after the development of more formal forms of European imperialism in the nineteenth century, global trade became more and more shaped by the profit-making imperatives of capitalism. This did not end pre-capitalist forms of trading – and in this sense the stark contrast drawn by Masefield between the romance and beauty of earlier epochs of sea-trading and the dirtiness of his own industrial age was misleading. Older forms of world trade were just as "dirty," and more significantly, they were not eclipsed so much as *incorporated* and exploited by industrial capitalists for the larger purpose of financial gain.

It was, for example, through incorporation and exploitation that slave trading in Africa was dramatically expanded and completely reorganized on a planetary scale under imperialism. There developed as a result complex new triangles of trade and interdependency transcending the world's oceans. Notably, the African slaves being brought to work on Caribbean plantations produced a new product – cheap sugar for the mass market – that, once transported to Britain and France, created a new sugar-filled diet for workers. The relative cheapness of this diet in comparison with other earlier sources of calories made it possible for European factory owners to pay lower wages, a cheapening of the cost of labor, which in turn made their products more competitive. These efficiencies were further complemented by the use of cheap raw cotton produced by yet other slaves in the American south. The cotton cloth and clothing that emerged from these global ties were not surprisingly very competitive on the emergent world market. This in turn meant that the reverberations and relays were not just limited to Africa, the Caribbean, the American South and the industrial cities of Europe. Other places such as India were affected as Britain began to pursue a new export-led, free-trade agenda. Britain's producers had previously protected their domestic market from Indian cotton exports, but as soon as their own exports were more competitive – and clearly slavery helped to ensure they were very competitive indeed – they converted to "free trade" and in this way turned India overnight from a cotton exporter to cotton importer. Overnight, too, thousands of former Indian textile makers lost their livelihoods, their dismal fate thereby becoming bound up through world trade networks and sugared tea with the still more dismal brutality of slavery on the other side of the planet.

The triangles of capitalist commodity production, slavery, and colonialism were just part of the world trade picture in the era of imperialism. At the same time, some of the industrial goods like the road-rails and pig iron in Masefield's "Dirty British coaster" were being used to extend economic ties into other previously unconnected corners of the globe. These new railroads and steam-ship interconnections were extraordinarily extensive – going far, for example, into the interiors of Argentina, Australia, and South Africa – but also allowed for much faster, and thus much more intensive, long-distance ties that could have much more immediate and transformative impacts. As these consequential ties continued to expand in the early years of the twentieth century, they involved increasingly larger movements of money and people, too, movements that allowed a new business class in the command centers of imperialism unprecedented global access and influence. The resulting interdependencies as they were felt in the heart of empire were sketched very well by the British economist John Maynard Keynes in his description of life for a businessman in London in August 1914.

> [He] could order by telephone, sipping his morning tea in bed, the various products of the whole earth, in such quantity as he might see fit, and reasonably expect their early delivery upon his doorstep; he could at the same moment and by the same means

adventure his wealth in the natural resources and new enterprises of any quarter of the world, and share, without exertion or even trouble, in their prospective fruits and advantages.[2]

Today, one of the most common concepts associated with globalization still remains the idea of wealthy consumers being able to bring the world to their doorsteps by buying things. For this reason, Keynes's reflections raise an obvious question about our own situation over a hundred years later: what is so new now? We might note in this regard that women and wealthy people outside of London and Europe can also now enjoy the privilege of making consumption choices and investment decisions with worldwide repercussions. A cynic might also note that in London today, "the various products of the whole earth" might get to one's doorstep rather more slowly because of the congestion that has resulted from the poor planning and disinvestment following Margaret Thatcher's free-market revolution; or that the adventuring of investment in foreign factories through today's complex financial products has become so risky that it entails quite a great deal of effort and trouble. However, contradictions aside, the basic image of global influence through the control of global commodity movements is still very similar. This similarity, though, is deceptive because it hides the changing ways in which commodities are made, distributed, and sold on a global basis. To better understand these changes, we need next to consider the changing patterns of world commodity flows through the twentieth century. This is where quantitative data on trade can help. By examining the statistics on changing trade flows from the heights of European imperialism to today, we can create a more accurate picture of the contrasts as well as the continuities with historical patterns of global trade.

What twentieth century trade data reveal most clearly are two forms of *unevenness*: (1) temporal unevenness; and (2) geographical unevenness. Starting with temporal unevenness, what the data show contradicts the common assumption that global trade has simply continued to expand at a steady and predictable pace from European imperialism onwards. What we see instead is an incredibly uneven, rollercoaster journey from the late imperial period to today. By graphing the changing ratio of trade to GDP for all trading countries (a ratio sometimes seen as an index of "openness" or even as a measure of economic globalization itself) we can trace the changing *relative* importance of trade amidst a growing global economy (see Figure 3.1). On this basis, it is clear that after both the later nineteenth-century peak and early twentieth-century peak in the importance of world trade, there was a huge dip during and after the Great Depression when producing things nationally for national consumers took precedence. It took almost until the 1980s to return to the levels of trade-to-GDP seen in imperial times.

After World War I and the economic melt-down at the end of the 1920s, the largest economies of the world became much more inwardly oriented or, to use the technical term, "autarchic" during the Great Depression of the 1930s. After World War II, this same autarchic pattern of economic organization persisted for almost another two decades. Although not quite as internally oriented as the Communist economies with which they were competing politically, the main capitalist economies

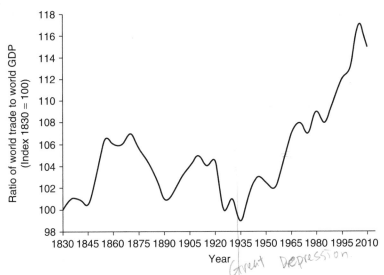

Figure 3.1   Indexed global ratio of trade to GDP. *Source*: based on recent data from the IMF for GDP, and from WTO for trade. Historical ratios before 1980 come from Christopher Chase-Dunn, Yukio Kawano, and Benjamin D. Brewer, 2000, "Trade Globalization Since 1795: Waves of Integration in the World-System," *American Sociological Review* 65 (1): 77–95.

still mainly produced commodities for their domestic markets. As a result, trade-to-GDP ratios fell significantly. Elsewhere, many of their former colonies – countries such as India, Ghana, and Indonesia that had won independence in the years following the World Wars – also set about creating similarly inward-oriented industrial policies based on the policy of "import substitution" (substituting domestically manufactured goods for the imports formally foisted on them by the imperial powers). Thus, only slowly did international commerce begin to pick up in the years after 1945, and it was not really until the mid-1960s, when the German and Japanese economies were fully rebuilt, that trade started to come close to pre-depression levels. Since the 1960s, the world has seen more and more trade liberalization, and with it, increasing absolute levels of trade as all kinds of new exporters, including most recently China, have begun to compete on the global market. These developments – combined with the collapse of the Communist bloc and the end of import-substitution policies in the Third World – have brought us to the new heights of intense economic interdependency we know today, although even these high levels of trade to GDP have not entirely emerged unscathed from the fall-out of the global financial crisis that hit in 2008. Thus, from the former peaks of imperial times to the autarchy of the mid-twentieth century, it has been something of a wild ride that has brought us to the contemporary period of trade-intensive globalization. It is a period in which the absolute numbers as well as the values of commodities trading around the globe are much larger than at any other previous point in world history, but it has by no means been steady escalation to this point.

While the historical development of international trade has clearly been episodic, its geography has been still more uneven. Unfortunately, the common spatial image associated with ideas about economic globalization – the Earth seen from orbit – tends to obscure this geographic unevenness. Indeed, instead of unevenness, the images associated with globe-spanning trade flows usually present us with a view of a smooth planet surface that has no apparent center. Partly as a result of this, when people start to think for the first time about all the global interconnections represented by today's everyday goods, they also often tend to imagine the world itself as a maze of interlinkages that shrink the planet and smooth over old borders and hierarchies. This is a problem because while our world is undoubtedly a maze of interlinkages, these have created a *lumpy* as opposed to a smooth system of interdependency. Even a brief review of the historical geography of trade in the twentieth century makes this unevenness clear.

At the height of imperialism, much of world trade consisted of raw materials coming from the colonies into the imperial homelands of countries such as Britain, the Netherlands, France, and Germany to be turned into finished goods. To the extent that the colonies could pay for them, the finished goods were also exported back around the world, but most of the commodities were consumed in the imperial centers, and it was mainly money that flowed abroad again in the form of investments, such as in railroads, aimed at extracting yet more raw materials from the colonies. After World War II, this geographical pattern of trade changed quite drastically. The old European imperial powers faced enormous debts, ruined infrastructure, and economic disarray. Only America survived the war as a dominant power, and, with its own factories and economy still in good shape, it was in a very strong position to set the terms of post-war economic development. Having become by far the largest exporter in the world, the United States sought, among other things, to open up foreign markets for its goods. This was the start of the trade-liberalization trend that is now associated so commonly in the public mind with globalization. It is important, nevertheless, to remember that it had its origins not in a multi-polar world system of center-less networks, but rather in the unipolar dominance of the world economy by America after World War II. Moreover, the resulting period of accelerated trade expansion in the 1950s was characterized by the further development and strengthening of this dominance as American businesses, and to a lesser extent, American workers enjoyed the benefits of being the world's leading exporters. This so-called "Golden Age," however, was not to last.

Another outcome of American economic dominance in the late 1940s and 1950s was the huge investment the US government made into the post-war rebuilding of the economies of Japan and, through the Marshall Plan, Germany. Part of the reason for these investments was to ward off the specter of Soviet Communism. But while thereby pre-empting a Cold War competitor, the United States created for itself two new and increasingly formidable capitalist competitors. Thus, by the late 1960s, the world market began to be flooded by the highly competitive exports (particularly of manufactured goods) coming out of Japan and Germany. As a result, during the 1970s, the United States lost its "workshop of the world" position as the dominant global exporter of manufactured commodities. From 1963, when it produced 17.4% of the world's merchandise, to 2002, when it produced only 10.7%, the United States saw its status as the leading global manufacturer steadily

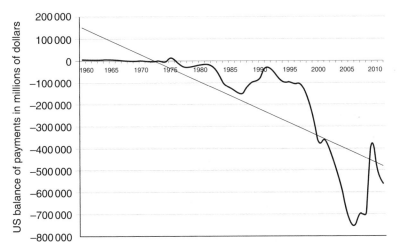

Figure 3.2   US balance of payments deficits (US$ million). *Source*: based on data from the US Census, http://www.census.gov/foreign-trade/statistics/historical/.

diminishing. By 2010, the US share of global merchandise exports (thus excluding services) was down to just 8.5%. Like Britain, the previously dominant manufacturing exporter of the nineteenth century, America became more dependent on the export of service commodities (such as management consultancy and advertising). However, in contrast to Britain (which by 2002 accounted for only 4.3% of world merchandise exports and 5.2% of merchandise imports), the United States nevertheless retained its role and, over this period, massively increased its significance as a global *importer*. In fact, by 2002, the US market accounted for 18% of all imports in the world economy. And by 2010, while still accounting for almost $1.3 trillion in merchandise exports, the US import bill for goods was close to $2 trillion, thereby creating a merchandise **trade deficit** (the value of merchandise exports minus the value of merchandise imports) of approximately $645 billion.[3] It is true that as a result of the financial crisis that erupted in 2008, US consumers significantly reduced the deficit by cutting back consumption and reducing imports. But due to financial forces that support (albeit unstably) America's ability to borrow globally in its own currency, it has continued as the world's number one consumer. We explore this increasingly precarious dependency on financial counter-flows in much greater length in Chapter 5. Here, it is enough to note that by the end of the twentieth century, the United States had shifted from being a huge net exporter to a huge net importer. Even including trade in services in which the country built a surplus in the 2000s (reaching almost + $180 billion in 2011), the United States still ended up the first decade of the twenty-first century with a record overall balance of payments deficit of $600 billion. Historically the clear trend in the country's balance of payments has therefore been into negative territory, with ever-larger deficits in the new millennium completely dwarfing the small net surpluses recorded in the 1960s and 1970s (Figure 3.2).

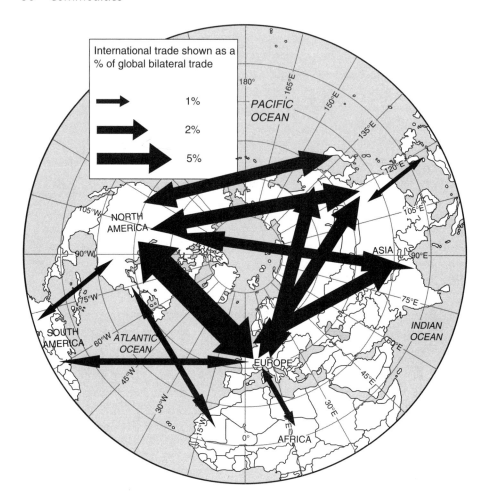

Figure 3.3 Map by author of global trade triad based on data from the European Spatial Planning Observation Network, http://www.espon.eu/main/Menu_Publications/Menu_MapsOfTheMonth/map0806.html.

America's transition from global producer to global consumer – from "work-shop of the world" to "Walmart of the world" – has by no means leveled the global playing field, but it has led to a more multi-polar kind of lumpiness in the map of world trade. Specifically, with the redevelopment of Europe and East Asia as export leaders, it has led to what analysts of world trade data call the global triad. This triad of North America, Europe, and Asia contributes to the unevenness of global commodity flows in two key ways. First, trade flows *between* these three regions are far larger than any bilateral trade between any other regions, creating a kind of cartographic triangle of trans-triad-trade when sketched on a world map that is centered on the north pole (Figure 3.3). Second, and still more significantly, transnational trade between countries *within* each triad completely dwarfs other kinds of global trade (Figure 3.4). Trade within the North American Free Trade

Figure 3.4 Global merchandise exports by region and destination in 2010 (US$ billion). *Source:* based on data from WTO, International Trade Statistics 2011, pp. 12–13, http://www.wto.org/english/res_e/statis_e/its2011_e/its11_toc_e.htm.

Agreement (NAFTA) region countries of Mexico, the United States, and Canada; trade between Asian countries, and most spectacularly, trade between European countries account thus for the largest share of total merchandise trade globally. Together the three regional economies of the global triad accounted in 2001 for more than 85% of world trade. A decade later in 2011, this dominance continued, with inter-regional trade *within* each of the three regions also becoming a still more notable feature of global trade statistics: 71% of exports from EU countries went to other EU countries; 53% of Asian exports went to other Asian countries; and almost 50% of the exports from United States, Canada, and Mexico went to each other.[4]

Figure 3.5 Ship carrying containers up the Rhine in Germany. Photograph by Matthew Sparke.

Given the massive populations of the three regions, their trading dominance might not seem so surprising, but think of the other massive population centers in the rest of world that are dwarfed by this triad of trade. Africa scarcely figures at all, and, with only 12% of African country merchandise exports going to other African countries in 2011, the continent also clearly remains highly dependent on exports to the triad, too. More complexly, the Middle East and Latin America are also highly dependent on triad markets for their exports of raw materials, food, and, of course, fuel. So, the world of global trade is hardly the inclusive and level space that it is depicted as in all the glossy global images featuring satellite pictures of a smooth planetary surface. Instead, most of the planet's supposedly center-less trade networks remain centered on the three key regional bases of the triad. As we shall explore further in Chapters 7 and 8, there is a complex political history behind this triadic trading geography. For this reason, it is worth remembering that age-old trading ties form the basis of some of the contemporary concentrations, most notably within Europe where commodity shipments moving down key arteries such as the Rhine pass by ancient castles that guarded the trading routes of the past (Figure 3.5). But notice that, today, these shipments within Europe include containers coming from and returning to Asia, too (Hanjin is a Korean-based shipping company, and Evergreen is headquartered in Taiwan). For the same reason, both aspects of the contemporary trading triad's unevenness – trade *between* the three transnational regions and trade *within* the three transnational regions – need to be kept in mind at the same time.

If the trade data evidence about unevenness cuts against some of the popular myths about the geography of globalization, a comparison of such data with basic production data nevertheless still clearly points towards growing global interdependency. As we saw in the changing global trade-to-GDP ratio (Figure 3.1), the overall importance of trade in relation to GDP has been increasing significantly from 1980 onwards. Over this period, more of the commodities that are bought and sold in the world have become traded internationally, and this in turn indicates that the basic level of integration in the global economy has been increasing, too. Indeed, this is why trade-to-GDP is one of the simplest and most significant measures we have of increasing global economic interdependency. This interdependency is not just a feature of higher quantitative levels of trade. It is also about a qualitative shift in the role played by trade in the organization of the global economy. Global trade now increasingly allows for the *functional integration* of production, distribution, and consumption on a world scale. In other words, the movement of goods around the world is no longer just trade in raw materials from some countries and finished goods from others. It is a much more complex mix of these sorts of commodities, with all sorts of other intermediate goods that are components and semi-finished products that need to be combined with yet other components and other semi-finished products before being sent onward through diverse marketing and sales operations to their multiple international points of consumption. Thus, in 2008, the share of intermediate manufactured products in world trade (excluding trade in fuel) was about 40%. Moreover, in the export-oriented and highly globalized manufacturing sectors of countries such as China and India, intermediate goods accounted for over 70% of their merchandise trade in 2005 (thereby also creating a form of statistical over-counting of the significance of trade over domestic production in these economies).[5]

The functional integration of the global economy is one of the main features of the contemporary period of globalization that distinguishes it from previous forms of trade-mediated interconnection. But, beyond the macro-statistical measures of trade vis-à-vis production, how can such functional integration be best investigated? Inspired by Masefield's vision of commodities on the move on boats, one approach might be to commandeer a container ship in a busy shipping lane like the Straits of Malacca between Singapore and Indonesia, and, after breaking open a thousand or so containers, come up with a contemporary portrait of the sorts of commodities moving around the world![6] Yet, given the risks of arrest that attend such piratical research efforts, another more academic strategy is to examine the interdependent chains of commodity production that account for all the commodities in the containers in the first place. It is to such work of commodity-chain analysis that we now turn.

3.3 Commodity Chains

The typical capitalist commodity chain comprises three main parts: (1) production, (2) distribution, and (3) consumption. To understand the global journey of something such as a TV, therefore, we have to start by examining how the three parts of the commodity chain are geographically organized. And to understand such geographical organization, we need to explore what factors account for where and how production, distribution, and consumption take place. In all three parts of the normal commodity chain, the three "special" commodities noted at the beginning – labor, money, and nature – all play a crucial role as controlling factors. Without workers, without money, and without raw materials, no commodity production could begin. Likewise, without workers, without money, and without basic natural inputs such as oil and water, most commodities would never get to their markets. And lastly, without a great deal of marketing and sales labor, without yet more money for advertising and retailing, and without the real and imagined needs of life, there would be little consumption. Money, moreover, and the very basic capitalist imperative to make more of it, accounts for why commodity chains keep growing and multiplying. Money is put in by business investors at the beginning, and when consumers exchange their money for the commodities at the other end of the chain, the investors' aim is always to make more money than they put in at the start. This is the very essence of economic growth. When this fails to happen, capitalist crises quickly ensue: businesses go bankrupt, workers are laid off, and the transformation of nature into commodities slows down. If the slow down is big and systemic – as happened in the Great Depression and in the 2008–2009 global crisis – then the wider societal and governmental contexts in which commodity chains are situated start to be shaken too, revealing in turn how the economic ties of commodity production, distribution, and consumption are also always deeply political.

Analytically, each of the three basic parts of any normal commodity chain has to be understood from the start as nested within the special processes that produce or affect the availability of labor, money, and nature, including the political systems of nation-states and all the inter-governmental agreements that shape international relations. Commodity chains are thus situated, among other things, within various governmental regimes that regulate the supply and use of labor, money, and nature. In addition, though, at the heart of most commodity chains today, there is yet another kind of nesting or interdependence within the chains of *other* commodities. One way to conceptualize this inter-commodity-chain interdependence is in terms of the multiple stages in which different commodities are combined before they are finally bought, consumed, recycled, and/or discarded. In early stages, all sorts of raw materials are prepared, purchased, and then combined to create sub-components and components for recombination in the later stages of assembly. All sorts of service sector inputs ranging from education and accounting to design and marketing are involved in further shaping commodities as they move through commodity chains. And making such movement possible, a long list of yet other commodities ranging from roads, railways, and energy to vehicles, computers, and buildings combine to provide vital infrastructural inputs too (Figure 3.6).

It is the increasing dependence of contemporary commodity chains on multiple inputs supplied by other commodity chains that accounts for much of the complexity and density of today's world trade flows. If we really did board a ship in the Straits of Malacca and starting hacking into containers, what we would find would not be simply hundreds of thousands of finished goods on their way to market. Alongside these would also be innumerable components made for other commodity chains,

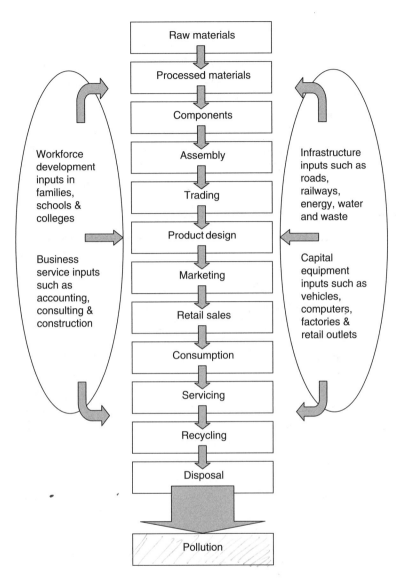

Figure 3.6 Normal commodity-chain stages and inputs.

too: component inputs ranging from semiconductors to gearboxes to plywood that are en route between different production, distribution, and consumption sites in extended global commodity chains spanning the world. This is one of the main differences between commodity movements today and the sorts of commodity movements that characterized world trade in 1900. Nowadays, the commodities on the move are often *functionally integrated* into the production (or distribution or sales) of other commodities in other parts of the world. This is why one of the most startling and significant statistical measures of contemporary economic interdependency is the fact that about 45% of world trade is *intra-corporate* trade: in other

Transnational Corporation

words, trade being conducted *within* a single TNC. Such trade is still international. It crosses national borders. But it remains within networks of production, distribution, and marketing controlled by particular TNCs. We shall turn in the next section to examine how TNCs have developed different sorts of commodity-chain management strategies. Before this, though, it is crucial to come to terms with the basic forces that bear upon and stem out of commodity chains themselves.

First of all, we need to consider what factors explain the core character of commodity chains under capitalism. As products ranging from Tang dynasty vases to Christian statues to ancient Hindu temples attest, pre-capitalist societies produced commodities in ways that relied on supply chains of other goods. Yet, while money often changed hands, and artisans (if not slaves) were frequently paid for their labor, the basic reasons for making the goods in these chains had more to do with the maintenance of royal and religious order and much less to do with profit for profit's own sake. With the rise of capitalism, by contrast, the profit motive rose to become the primary rationale for all commodity production. Under capitalism, the whole reason for producing commodities became more and more about selling them to consumers for a profit. And, of course, the purpose for making such profits became about reinvesting it (as opposed to hoarding it) and thereby using it to make more commodities and yet more profits. It needs emphasizing again, therefore, that this is the basic meaning of the economic "growth" that has become such a central preoccupation of our capitalist world. Without profits, and thus without growth, capitalism collapses. Slow growth, let alone economic contraction, in contemporary economies is considered a major problem. This is also why any normal commodity chain must have distribution and consumption as well as production. If a commodity is made but cannot for whatever reason be taken to market, it becomes worthless. Likewise, if a commodity is made, and it has no market, then, however much labor, effort, and invention have gone into its production, it is also worthless. All three steps of the chain have to be made for profits to be realized. And only by realizing such profits can a capitalist case be made for investing more money in a new round of production. There are, of course, certain short-term exceptions such as the underpriced goods sold by startup companies seeking to dislodge established competitors. But, in the end, all these exceptions have to come face to face with the iron rule of capitalism: profits are primary.

One of the immediate implications of the capitalist need for profits and growth is that in all capitalist commodity chains, there is a built-in imperative to try to reduce the time taken to move through the three steps of the chain, a period of time sometimes referred to as *turnover time*. The quicker companies can move from their initial outlay of money at the start of production to their profit-taking at the point of sale the quicker these profits can be reinvested in more production, more sales, and more profit making. Because time is therefore money, capitalism puts a great premium on moving commodities through commodity chains from the point of production to the point of sale as quickly as possible. This very basic capitalist need to reduce turnover time has created in turn one of the main forces driving the huge investments that have been made over the years to improve transportation and communication technologies. Space too, or, more precisely, its contraction, has also become critical to making money. Coming together with the needs of capitalists to seek out new markets and cheaper inputs, the need to reduce turnover time therefore helps us explain some of the impressive technological developments that have contributed to the so-called "shrinking" of the planet from the age of empire to today.

First came roads, railways, and steamship freighters, but these have now been complemented by the still-faster technologies provided by commercial jet airplanes (for light and/or perishable goods), the Internet (for non-physical commodities ranging from architectural designs to business services), and container ships (for more hefty goods that need not travel quite so fast but still have to shrink huge distances in very large volumes). Probably more than any other single technological innovation, it is the containerization of trans-oceanic shipping that has most significantly altered the scale and scope of world trade in the late twentieth century. The first container ship was American and was launched in 1956, the brainchild of a former North Carolinan truck driver called Malcolm McLean. It was his idea to move the fully loaded metal boxes from trucks onto ships saving the expensive and time-consuming job of loading and unloading cargo piece by piece. Before this, it had taken 24 000 person hours to load and unload a 40 000 ton vessel. After containerization, it takes today only about 750 person hours. Nowadays, too, standard containers can carry between 20 and 30 tons when fully loaded. They keep shipments together and protect them from bad weather and the risk of robbery (not to mention the prying eyes of researchers). As a result of the ease and enormous capacity of container shipping, it has grown steadily to become the main means of transportation for about 90% of world trade – excluding oil and bulk cargoes. Approximately 100 million containers traverse the world's oceans each year in over 5000 container ships. Moreover, the speed of the container ships has itself increased dramatically over these years, reducing the journey time, for example, of shipments from Hong Kong to New York from about 50 days in 1970 to about only 17 days in 2003. This speed, combined with the reliability of the system, has in turn made it possible for businesses to treat container ships almost as if they are warehouses. Instead of having to waste money and space in stockpiling huge inventories, companies can now order components and intermediary products so that they arrive "just in time" for their own production processes.

One notable result of today's global transportation capacity is a much more flexible, networked, and transnationally integrated form of manufacturing than the old "make it all in one place" approach exemplified at its early twentieth-century peak by Henry Ford's famous Rouge River plant in Detroit. This was a massive factory complex (the biggest in America at its time) where everything from the steel to the steering wheels was manufactured in the same place: a plant that retained large inventories of parts "just in case" there were shortages, and a plant which made nearly all its cars (including the famous Model T) for just the domestic American market. By contrast, a contemporary "world car" such as Fiat's *Palio* is built in over seven countries (including China, Morocco, Turkey, Brazil, Argentina, South Africa, and India), out of globally sourced components from over 100 suppliers, and is sold in 32 countries. Relatedly, the International Organization of Motor Vehicle Manufacturers (OICA) which collects data on annual car production provided an explanatory note with its 2011 list of top-ranking producer countries that made the following clarifications:

> National trade organisations make a distinction between production of completely built up (CBU) vehicles and assembly of completely knocked down (CKD) or semi-knocked down (SKD) sets when vehicle parts originate from another country.

The attached data showed that China was the top-ranked world producer in 2011 with over 18 million vehicles. At considerably less than half this number, the United States and Japan trailed in the second- and third-ranked positions with just over 8 million vehicles each. But with a large number of all these vehicles in the CKD and SKD categories, and with so many intermediate component car parts moving around the globe, the meaning of the overall country rankings remained unclear. What was clear, however, was that it would not be possible to organize vehicle production on such an extensive global basis without the availability of high-capacity, low-cost shipping.

More generally, one of the key results of the time–space shrinkage produced by containerization, air-freight transportation and the Internet, is that both the "Production" and "Consumption" stages of the normal commodity chain can be broken up and globally distributed. A single commodity can be made out of parts produced in multiple places all around the planet by many different companies and diverse workers. It also can in turn be marketed and sold in many different places, often using sales, logistics, advertising, and accountancy services of yet more companies and workers from a range of different countries. These developments are clearly quite novel developments in terms of their global scale, scope, and diversity. Before, at the start of the twentieth century, world trade mainly mediated just the "Distribution" part of most commodity chains. The production mainly happened in only one place from where finished goods were sent to their final site of consumption in another place. It is true that the colonies of Europe, America, and Japan produced many raw materials that were sent to the various colonial centers, where they served as basic inputs into manufacturing processes. But what one did not see in the 1900s were the massive movements we see today of all kinds of intermediate goods that represent component parts and semi-finished commodities on the move from one production site to another. Moreover, thanks to the communications revolution enabled by the Internet, cheap telephone calls, and fax machines, and thanks also to important logistic innovations such as bar-code tracking, today's incredibly complex movements of goods are much more globally integrated, predictable, and thus manageable. This global integration of the world trading system with its almost seamless ties between road, rail, air, and ocean transportation has had another two important integrative effects on commodity chains. First, it has allowed for the increasing integration of markets and thus competition on a global scale. Second, by integrating global markets, the worldwide networks of trade have in turn made possible much more market-based and market-managed forms of commodity-chain integration. In the remainder of this section, we will look at each of these integrative effects – the emergence of global competition, and the development of global management – along with their complex and often disintegrative reverberations for other social, political, and organizational institutions.

3.3.1 The emergence of global competition

In terms of market integration, there can be no doubting the huge transformations being wrought by the expansion of world trade networks. As the costs and time for moving goods around the world diminish, the more it becomes possible for producers who are thousands of miles apart to compete. There are other effects of integration too, of course, including the destabilizing ways in which a slowdown in demand in one part of the world (e.g. in the United States in 2008–2009) is immediately translated to other places through a contraction in global trade (which fell by a massive 13% in 2009). Whether it was Liberian rubber producers being hit by the fall-off in demand for cars in the United States or, more complexly, US semiconductor makers being hit by the decline in overseas computer production for the US market, the knock-on effects were both vast and fast in the ways they reverberated around the globe. Over the long-term, though, it is global competition unleashed by global trade that has the most systemic and enduring effects. In much older localized commodity markets, competition took place only between goods produced within a day's walk or donkey ride of the marketplace. Today, by contrast, the marketplace is often virtual, and the competition often takes place between goods made all over the world. To be sure, there remains lots of lumpiness within this field of competition. The costs of transportation are by no means nil; pricing is by no means transparent and consistent; government intervention such as US and EU agricultural subsidies distorts market relations; and all sorts of other local, national, and regional governmental regulations restrict and curtail the movements of many commodities. We live, therefore, in a very different economic space to the fantasy of a global "level playing field" assumed in the Globalization cliches and the abstract models of orthodox economics. Nevertheless, the integration of global transportation networks has still begun to unleash extremely powerful forms of competition across huge areas of the planet.

Global competition, distorted and uneven though it often is, forces prices downwards and pits producers and workers in different parts of the world against each other in repeated struggles for survival. Thus, as lower-priced commodities find their way to distant markets, they start to reshape economic geography quite dramatically. When cheap Chinese-made furniture started flowing into the United States, for example, it very quickly started to make domestically manufactured furniture uncompetitive. Workers in places like Kernersville, North Carolina soon lost their jobs as the Chinese goods took market share, and the American factories closed down. In effect, the low costs involved in transporting a relatively heavy and bulky cargo across the Pacific made it possible for Chinese producers to compete directly with American producers. Because the Chinese producers are able to employ workers at very low wages in factories that operate without meaningful health and environmental regulations, they won this competition handily. In cases like this, the integration of the marketplace makes possible competition between capitalists and workers living in very different contexts. For critics, this competition creates a **race to the bottom**, as workers in places with higher labor standards and better pay are effectively forced to compete with other workers who have never benefited from historic struggles for decent wages, benefits, health, and environmental protections. For capitalist proponents of global competition, such tendencies simply create **sourcing efficiencies**, providing consumers with cheaper choices and giving businesses the benefit of cheaper inputs (e.g. low-cost office furniture) into other commodity chains. Whatever we call these tendencies, though, there can be no doubting that the increasing global integration of commodity markets intensifies competition and, as we shall see in Chapter 4, forces enormous changes on to workers and their communities right around the world.

3.3.2   The development of global management

As well as creating heightened competition, another outcome of today's globally integrated trade networks concerns the way in which the integration and resulting competition come together to create a new context for business organization itself. No longer does a single company operating in a single place or even just a single company operating in multiple places need to control all of the production process. Instead, innumerable new forms of *intermediation* have developed in global commodity chains. Diverse intermediary actors ranging from component suppliers to buyer brokers to fast-freight forwarders to insurance companies are thus now involved in producing and moving all kinds of intermediate products. This gives big brand-name or lead firms the option of subcontracting or **outsourcing** much of the production process to other companies in other places based on basic criteria such as cost, quality, and reliability. Japanese TVs really can therefore be made in Mexico using Indonesian components and then marketed in the United States. Moreover, their distribution and sales can also be managerially disintegrated: tracked by separate shipping and logistics companies, and marketed by yet other advertising and retail firms. In turn, as buyers buy the TVs, and cashiers' scanners record the depletion of stocks, the whole system can immediately transmit information about the demand levels back down to the diverse points of production on different sides of the Pacific.

TVs are just one commodity in one economic sector, and as scholars of commodity chains have studied different chains in different sectors, they have begun to chart a whole range of approaches to global commodity chain management. Not all companies have globalized production through subcontracting and the market-mediated coordination of commodity chains. In other words, not all forms of **offshoring**

Table 3.1 Five models of commodity-chain organization

Name of model	Characteristics	Examples
1 In-house	Internalization of most of the commodity chain within one company	Boeing (before its recent move towards more outsourcing)
2 Captive-supplier	Lead firm strictly controls key suppliers through contract codification	IBM (before its more recent turn to outsourcing)
3 Modular	Lead firm sets standards for modular components but subcontracts out their production	Dell, Shimano, Fiat
4 Relational	Outsourcing coordinated by family networks and historic business groups	Cheung Kong Holdings (the business group of Li Ka-Shing)
5 Marketized	Outsourcing fully mediated by competitive open market bidding amongst vendors	Nike, Wal-Mart

Source: adapted from Gary Gereffi, John Humphrey, and Timothy Sturgeon, "The Governance of Global Value Chains," *Review of International Political Economy* 12, no. 1 (2005): 78–104.

involve outsourcing.[7] Some companies control foreign production directly by keeping the foreign factories under the ownership and control of the core company. This internalizing approach to managing transnational commodity chains is referred to as *vertical integration*. Other firms outsource everything to external producers and coordinate commodity chains as much as possible through market-based mechanisms. This externalized and market-based approach to coordinating commodity chains is referred to as *horizontal integration*. While research into global commodity chains suggests that horizontal integration through market-mediated links is in the ascendancy, there remain many companies that opt for various mixes of vertical and horizontal integration.[8] In order to come to terms with these variations, researchers have suggested that it is possible to identify a spectrum of at least five different approaches ranging from very low to very high levels of market mediation (see Table 3.1).[9] By outlining this spectrum of corporate strategies (1–5), it is therefore possible to disaggregate some of the factors that help explain why different commodity chains have different mixes of horizontal and vertical integration.

1.   At the lowest level of market mediation is the *in-house model* of commodity chain organization characterized by the vertical integration of production, distribution, and sales all within the same company. Traditionally, this vertically integrated in-house model has been characteristic of industries manufacturing especially complex products such as cars and aircraft. The complexity of the production processes, the extremely high levels of investment required, the desire to protect intellectual property, and the overwhelming need for coordination are all

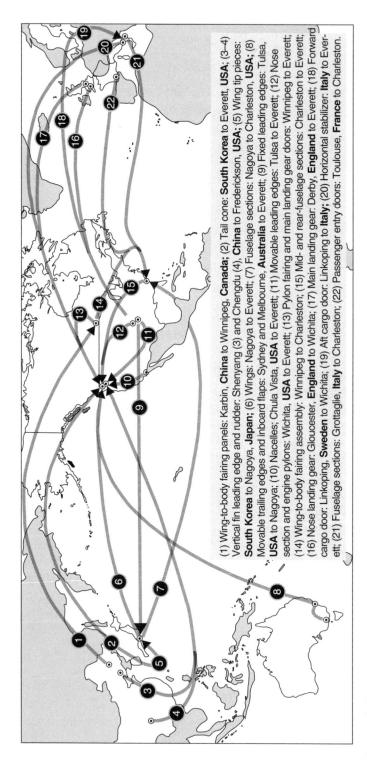

(1) Wing-to-body fairing panels: Karbin, **China** to Winnipeg, **Canada**; (2) Tail cone: **South Korea** to Everett, **USA**; (3–4) Vertical fin leading edge and rudder: Shenyang (3) and Chengdu (4), **China** to Frederickson, **USA**; (5) Wing tip pieces: **South Korea** to Nagoya, **Japan**; (6) Wings: Nagoya to Everett; (7) Fuselage sections: Nagoya to Charleston, **USA**; (8) Movable trailing edges and inboard flaps: Sydney and Melbourne, **Australia** to Everett; (9) Fixed leading edges: Tulsa, **USA** to Nagoya; (10) Nacelles; Chula Vista, **USA** to Everett; (11) Movable leading edges: Tulsa to Everett; (12) Nose section and engine pylons: Wichita, **USA** to Everett; (13) Pylon fairing and main landing gear doors: Winnipeg to Everett; (14) Wing-to-body fairing assembly: Winnipeg to Charleston; (15) Mid- and rear-fuselage sections: Charleston to Everett; (16) Nose landing gear: Gloucester, **England** to Wichita; (17) Main landing gear: Derby, **England** to Everett; (18) Forward cargo door: Linkoping, **Sweden** to Wichita; (19) Aft cargo door: Linkoping to **Italy**; (20) Horizontal stabilizer: **Italy** to Everett; (21) Fuselage sections: Grottaglie, **Italy** to Charleston; (22) Passenger entry doors: Toulouse, **France** to Charleston.

Figure 3.7 Map of the global commodity chains supplying component parts for the final assembly of the Boeing Dreamliner.

considered to have been key factors explaining high levels of vertical integration in these industries. Ford's Rouge River factory complex is again a good example in this respect, but, as other more contemporary auto manufacturing models illustrate, the auto sector has itself seen increasing levels of horizontal integration as companies such as Ford as well as Fiat have sought to outsource more and more. Commercial aircraft manufacturing by the Boeing company was until recently another good example of the in-house production with low market intermediation. But since the 1990s, facing stiff competition from the multi-firm commodity chains going into Airbus planes, Boeing has tried to source more and more component production outside of the company, thereby relying on market-based transactions, price signals, and competition to coordinate and manage the commodity chain. By 2003, 64% of the content of Boeing aircraft was coming from outside suppliers, with companies in Japan, Italy, and elsewhere shipping fuselage pieces and even entire wings to Seattle for final assembly. More recently, this global outsourcing has gone still further with the extraordinarily extensive commodity chains of components for the Boeing 787 Dreamliner (Figure 3.7). However, this globalization of Boeing's commodity chains has also hit snags. It may have gone further than the Airbus competition, and it may have also served to discipline Seattle region workers and unions with non-unionized competition, but the final assembly of the aircraft has not always gone smoothly because of errors made by suppliers. Instead, the Dreamliner has been turned into something of a nightmare-liner for Boeing by all the delays created by trying to remake in-house all the ill-fitting components made overseas. Elsewhere, in-house production continues for more strategic reasons despite the pressures for increased outsourcing. For example, although drug companies like Ely Lilly rely on outsourced inputs for parts of the product-development process (especially the huge subsidies provided by publically funded research universities), they nevertheless tend to manage most of the production, distribution, and sales of drugs on an in-house basis because of the high levels of technological sophistication involved and their desire to retain private monopoly claims on the intellectual property (see Chapter 9).

2.   One option for companies such as Boeing, as they seek to develop more outsourced commodity chains, is to create supply links with component makers who produce *only* for them (in other words, only for a *single* lead firm such as Boeing). This hierarchical *captive supplier model* of commodity chain organization clearly involves market mediation, but the lead firm retains a great deal of control over the production process. This can provide a way of protecting intellectual property, as well as ensuring high-quality output of technologically sophisticated components. As the "captive firm" only has the one customer, it is less likely to re-use or re-market the technological information it receives from the lead firm. However, while it thereby reduces the chances of opportunism by suppliers, the dependency created by the captive supplier model is not without its risks for lead firms. Captive suppliers do not develop very high levels of innovation capability, and because they are dependent on the lead firms for a market as well as for design and process technology development, they are therefore especially vulnerable to bankruptcy if

an economic downturn reduces demand from the lead firm. It is because of these risks that some lead firms – IBM in computing is a good example – demand that their suppliers depend on them only for 25% or lower of their sales. Such contractual practices tend in turn, though, to create other models of commodity-chain organization where suppliers are much less "captive."

3.   A third, more market-mediated, approach to managing commodity chains that has developed as an alternative to the captive supplier model involves breaking up the production process for complex products into more simple modules. The resulting *modular model* offers a way of combining the flexibility of market mediation with the complexity-handling capabilities of in-house and captive supplier approaches. It only works, however, if the design and composition of products can be broken down by lead firms into generic and standardized component specifications. In these commodity chains, the communication between buyers and suppliers clearly involves much more than price signals, but the costs for both parties of changing partners are kept quite low. Suppliers are thus much freer to innovate, both in terms of delivering a higher-quality or lower-priced product and in terms of finding other markets. This type of approach to commodity-chain development is becoming increasingly common in the auto sector as a replacement to former in-house strategies of vertical integration. The global production of the Fiat Palio car, for example, has been made possible precisely by such modularization. However, many other economic sectors are characterized by lead firms that have developed this sort of approach including Dell in computers, and Shimano in bicycles. In the electronics sector, the modular model has been especially influential, leading to new forms of transnational horizontal integration dominated by large so-called "contract manufacturers" that outsource production by defining product packages in terms of modules. Take, for example, the Californian contract manufacturer of electronic goods, Solectron. In 1988, it was a small Silicon Valley-based company with 3500 workers and $256 million in revenue. By 2000, it had become a global giant with over 80 000 employees in more than 50 locations and almost $20 billion in revenue. To achieve such startling global growth, Solectron introduced as many modules as possible into the commodity chains it managed. By creating bundles of technology and specifying highly standardized protocols for moving them through the chain, the company was able to extend its products beyond circuit-board assembly to include a whole set of other "deliverables" ranging from product design, test routine development, and final product assembly to component purchasing, inventory management, global logistics, distribution, and after-sales service and repair. It might not seem so surprising that the electronics sector has seen such extensive modularization. However, the modular model has also been taken up in more unlikely economic arenas, too. For example, it has increasingly become a feature of food commodity chains with big European supermarkets such as Tesco, Asda, and Sainsbury in the United Kingdom and Carrefour in France developing exactly the same sorts of codified but market-mediated ties involving pre-specified product bundles with exporters from African countries such as Kenya.

4.   The specifications for many commodities cannot be so easily codified and broken down into modules. For these, a fourth kind of commodity chain based on a *relational model* is more common. In these sorts of commodity chains, there is much more codependence between buyers and producers. Buyers rely on producers to take initiative in innovating, developing, and providing components, and suppliers rely on the loyalty and trust of buyers. Such mutual dependence is enabled through relational ties based on reputation, family, or ethnic connections, and it is maintained through repeated face-to-face interactions or at least interpersonal exchanges between members of dispersed family networks.[10] In these kinds of commodity chains, market mediations and messages are thus to some extent superceded by relational ties, even if the point of producing commodities for profit remains the basic constant. Many types of apparel, furniture, plastics, and home hardware are produced in these sorts of commodity chains that have become especially common in East and Southeast Asia. Most notably, ethnic Chinese family and village networks have organized production, distribution, and sales in such ways both between and within China, Taiwan, Malaysia, Indonesia, and Singapore. These networks have proved to be highly flexible and dynamic as well as financially enduring because of various forms of a family and kin-based credit pooling. Notably vis-à-vis other commodity chains, they have fostered a considerable degree of technological competency among producers, and, because they have established long distance trading ties, they have also in many cases laid the foundations for other more market-mediated networks, too. Such, is the case, for example, of Chung-Kong Holdings, the huge business empire of Hong Kong businessman, Li Ka-Shing. Some of the commodity-chain models of other large Asian conglomerates – including, the "Keiretsu" business groups of Japan (such as Mitsui), and the "Chaebol" business groups of Korea (such as Hyundai) – have likewise developed much more complex and market-mediated networks out of the kin and community ties that were key to their initial formation.

5.   The most market-mediated approach to commodity chain management is the "flexible network" or *marketized model*. In this model, most of the coordination and control of the commodity chain is relayed through market mechanisms and price signals all the way down from consumers through big retailers to buyers agents and trading companies to diverse independent producers. The production of apparel for the world's big retailers such as Wal-Mart, Carrefour, Metro, and Royal Ahold is most often organized in this highly market-mediated way. Likewise, the production of shoes for the big brand name companies like Nike, Adidas, and Reebok is based upon the same model. None of these companies actually own factories or pay factory workers directly. Instead, they are consumer-oriented corporations that manage marketing and brand development all the while they contract out as much of the rest of the commodity chain as possible. Such high levels of market mediation, however, are only possible for certain sorts of commodities. Like apparel and shoes, they have to be commodities that have simple product specifications and which suppliers can therefore make with minimal levels of buyer involvement. In the resulting forms of commodity chain, the buyers (i.e. the big retailers and brand

companies) respond to prices set by suppliers and exercise control chiefly by moving from one supplier to the next based on price and quality. At the same time, suppliers are free to seek out other buyers and are not necessarily trapped as clients of just one company.

In the case of a big retail company like Wal-Mart, it might be argued that the market mediation is not all that significant or new. After all, retailers have rarely been involved in production in the past. The point though is that while Wal-Mart is resolutely oriented towards its shoppers, their wants and price sensitivities, it and the other big retailers of today are also extraordinarily *big buyers* whose actions systematically control commodity chains that stretch right around the world. In other words, as the lead firms at the top of market-mediated commodity chains, the big retailers have helped create a system with extremely intense and consequential transnational ties. This is important for at least two critical reasons. First, it underlines the significance of retailers and brand-name firms in global economic development patterns. While economists have traditionally sought to explain the development of countries such as Taiwan and South Korea based on various endogenous or local factors such as state policy and macro-economic stability, other scholars studying commodity chains have shown that in fact another critical factor in explaining the rapid development in these countries in the late 1970s, 1980s, and 1990s were the ties between Taiwanese and Korean producers and the big retail buyers, and most especially the biggest of the big buyers in America such as Wal-Mart.[11] The same has been happening more recently with China's rapid development over the last decade. Indeed, if it were an independent country, Wal-Mart would have ranked in 2004 as China's eighth-largest trading partner. This means that it is hard to over-emphasize the importance of market-mediated commodity chains as important influences on economic development.

One last significant implication of the consequential ties running through the market-mediated commodity chains between big retail firms and producers in far-away countries concerns the status of the retailers as TNCs. As we shall now see in the third and final section of the chapter, TNCs have traditionally been seen as companies that buy up or set up operations abroad for reasons of market access or sourcing efficiency. But what the market-mediated commodity chains of Wal-Mart, Nike, and companies like The Gap show us is that a company does not have to establish itself physically abroad to have massive effects on foreign producers, workers, and their communities. This means that as we approach the problem of defining TNCs and as we seek to understand their role in globalization, we have to be mindful of horizontal as well as vertical forms of transnational business integration. Marketized, modular, and relational commodity chains, in other words, are now just as much part of transnational corporate development as was the old in-house model deployed by Henry Ford when he set up his first European factory in Manchester in 1911 to build cars for the British market.

3.4 TNCs

Given the variety of contemporary commodity chains, TNCs are best defined as *companies that have the capacity to coordinate and control operations in more than one country, even if they do not own the factories and pay foreign workers directly.* Nike is in this sense just as much a TNC as GE, Nestle, and Shell. Some commentators use a narrower definition that contrasts TNCs with MNCs or Multi-National Corporations. The latter term is thus sometimes used to describe the vertically integrated corporate internationalism of the mid-twentieth century (business strategies that offshored production without outsourcing). At this time, a relatively small set of companies operated in multiple countries yet without functionally integrating their whole sourcing, production, and marketing system on a global scale. MNCs are thus understood to have operated *multi-nationally*, but not by creating organizational networks of commodity chains *across* national boundaries: not, in other words, *trans-nationally*. With the rise today of companies that coordinate operations on a global basis, and with the staggering development of intracorporate transnational trade, it seems that the TNC term is more appropriate. The classic MNC model still survives, but it is increasingly being transformed by the new models of commodity chain that incorporate more horizontal, market-mediated integration strategies. These definitional nuances are worth noting simply as a way of better understanding the varying terms used in different books and articles. In addition, though, they also underline how the relationships between TNCs and globalization are more complex than the one word "transnational" would seem to imply. In order to cut through this complexity and identify the most important ways that TNCs are tied into increasing global economic interdependency, we need to answer four specific questions: *when, why, where, and how* have TNCs gone abroad?

3.4.1   When?

Given our broad working definition of a TNC, it might be suggested that these sorts of corporations can be traced back to the old sixteenth- and seventeenth-century imperial trading businesses such as the British East India Company, the Dutch East India company and the Hudson Bay Company. Even if we do not go back quite so far as this, there are clearly a subset of TNCs that are still in operation today that have had transnational dealings dating right back to the heights of imperialism. Oil companies, for instance, just as much as trading companies, have long been involved in foreign operations. To pick just two examples: the Standard Oil Company of New Jersey was involved in Mexican oil production (and, for the same reason, Mexican politics) from the early 1900s onwards, and British Petroleum's historic role in Iran goes back to 1901, when William Knox D'Arcy obtained a concession from the Shah of Persia to exploit the area's oil deposits. All kinds of other businesses involved in the extraction and processing of raw materials – mining companies, logging companies, fishing companies, rubber companies, and so on – have all also been TNCs for well over a century. In another more mobile sense, so too have been the big transportation companies such as the Peninsular and Oriental Steam Navigation Company. This company is now simply known as "P & O," but as its full name suggests, its transnational business dates back to the heyday of British imperial expansion in the first half of the nineteenth century. Other inherently transnational companies including big commercial banks, insurance companies, and communications and information firms can all be added to this list, too. However, the forms of transnational corporate activity that are more immediately significant for scholars of global commodity chains are those relating to manufacturing and other businesses that, unlike oil, shipping, communication, and global finance companies, do not *have* to organize their activities on a transnational basis. The question of when manufacturing companies have expanded into foreign countries is in this sense much more interesting and important.

When a company like Ford moved into Britain in 1911 (and into France in 1913, and Germany in 1926), it was the leading edge of a phenomenon that other American companies were soon to follow (including GM which moved into Europe in 1925). These early foreign manufacturing initiatives were all about gaining **market access** to foreign consumers, and in this sense, they set the trend for much of the next half century. Not only were transport costs much more prohibitive back then, but so too were government regulations. Particularly after the Great Depression, nearly all the world's biggest economies became much more protectionist. Huge tariffs on imports and other legislative prohibitions prevented easy entry into foreign markets by non-national companies. In this regulatory context, the only way for firms to sell their products at a competitive price to foreign consumers was to actually make the products *in* the foreign country in which they were to be sold. By doing so, they avoided paying tariffs on imports, but by the same token, they had to go through elaborate adaptation processes as they set about establishing factories, transportation systems, marketing operations, and sales links in the foreign contexts. This approach was a response to more than just the regulatory restrictions and tariffs. At the time, it was much harder to coordinate production and source inputs on a global basis. However, during the 1970s, as the efforts America made to liberalize trade and open foreign markets began to lead to a steady decline in tariffs worldwide, the corporate rationales for becoming transnational started to change. In short, the key goal of selling products to new markets became complemented by another goal relating not to the last phase of the commodity chain but rather to the first, to the phase of production itself. As companies won more and more freedoms from national tariffs and regulations, as it became much easier and cheaper to source inputs from the cheapest and most reliable suppliers, this rationale for becoming transnational became about cutting costs, cheapening inputs, and, along way, whether deliberately or not, overcoming the legal protections established for workers in earlier eras. This other key rationale for transnationalization can be usefully understood in economic (albeit apolitical) terms as the quest for **sourcing efficiency**.

3.4.2 Why?

We have seen how the question of *when* TNCs transnationalize already tells us a great deal about *why* they transnationalize. If a TNC set up foreign activities before the twentieth century, it most likely did so as a trading company or as a producer of raw materials. If it established foreign activities in the middle of the twentieth century, it most likely did so to gain access to foreign markets that were closed off behind tariff walls or too costly to reach from abroad. And if a TNC set up or coordinated foreign activities more recently it is more likely to have done so for a *combined mixture* of market access and sourcing efficiency reasons. In order to understand this contemporary layering and inter-mixing of the rationales for transnationalization by TNCs, we first need to consider each rationale in more detail.

For companies seeking to improve profits for their shareholders, the prospect of finding foreign markets for their products is a persistent allure. Commentators from all ends of the political spectrum have always been in agreement on this. Back in 1848, for example, Karl Marx and Frederick Engels famously noted in *The Communist Manifesto* that it was precisely this need for new markets that made capitalism such a revolutionary force for change in the world. Their word for the business class of their time was "the bourgeoisie," and they sought to explain how the basic business desire of the bourgeoisie for market expansion was creating global economic interdependency.

> The need of a constantly expanding market for its products chases the bourgeoisie over the entire surface of the globe. It must nestle everywhere, settle everywhere, establish connections everywhere. The bourgeoisie has, through its exploitation of the world market, given a cosmopolitan character to production and consumption in every country. To the great chagrin of reactionaries, it has drawn from under the feet of industry the national ground on which it stood. All old-established national industries have been destroyed or are daily being destroyed. They are dislodged by new industries, whose introduction becomes a life and death question for all civilized nations, by industries that no longer work up indigenous raw material, but raw material drawn from the remotest zones; industries whose products are consumed, not only at home, but in every quarter of the globe. In place of the old wants, satisfied by the production of the country, we find new wants, requiring for their satisfaction the products of distant lands and climes. In place of the old local and national seclusion and self-sufficiency, we have intercourse in every direction, universal inter-dependence of nations.[12]

While their account betrayed a real excitement about the whirling changes wrought by capitalism, Marx and Engels simultaneously predicted that this vortex of capitalist interdependence would be transformed itself by "the specter haunting Europe": the specter being the Communist revolution that they hoped would follow and build upon the bourgeois revolution. Instead, over 150 years later, the same business imperatives about which Marx and Engels wrote so passionately remain largely unchanged. Communism has come and gone. Fordist national economic deve-lopment initiatives have come and gone. And we find ourselves confronted by a world where the basic business need for new markets continues to drive politics. Thus, to pick just one more recent example, on March 30, 2004 when President George W. Bush addressed entrepreneurs at the Fox Cities Chamber of Commerce in Appleton, Wisconsin he spoke directly to the same chronic business need. The White House press release noted that "he discussed his policies to strengthen the economy," and proceeded to list the president's primary proposal as: "Opening foreign markets to US products and services."[13]

Pro-market proposals from a pro-business president are hardly remarkable in themselves. However, the fact that President Bush made his Wisconsin comments in the midst of a fierce American debate over the job losses due to outsourcing by American companies makes the example more interesting. "Exports are vital to our Nation's economic strength," the president insisted.

> Especially because 95% of the potential customers for American products live outside the United States, America must reject the politics of economic isolationism.[14]

The clear aim of the speech was to suggest that Democrats calling for protectionist policies to keep jobs in America were wrong; that the benefits of transnational market access trumped concerns about TNCs transnationalizing their operations for the sake of sourcing efficiencies. In other words, job losses due to offshoring had to be understood as the price for wider market openness and thus ultimately more corporate growth for US TNCs. Whether or not one agrees that TNC growth leads to job creation in contemporary America, the link made by President Bush between the two main forms of contemporary business transnationalization remains an important one. Today, for most TNCs, the market access imperative has been joined by the sourcing efficiency imperative in the basic calculus of transnational strategic development. Both forms of transnationalization rely on regimes of market openness, and both can generate increased corporate profits. However, beyond these commonalities, both rationales still follow quite distinct patterns.

The pattern of transnationalization for market access is itself somewhat counter-intuitive. If world trade was really as open, unregulated, and tariff-free as neoliberals would like, then it would not be necessary for most TNCs to have to set up factories, affiliates, offices, and marketing, distribution, and retail systems abroad. They would only have to ship their products to various foreign destina-tions and let local firms take care of it. But such is the legacy of twentieth-century protectionism, and such is the power of still extant national and regional rules, that gaining access to foreign markets still often demands that TNCs employ local workers or at least make some part of their product in the area of the target market. This is one major reason why, for example, Japanese car manufacturers set up factories in the United States and Britain during the 1980s and early 1990s. They wanted to sell their cars to American and European customers without having to pay the tariffs that would still be imposed if the cars were made entirely in Japan. To be sure, there are other reasons why TNCs like Toyota and Nissan made these foreign investment decisions (including the appeal of tax breaks and cheaper labor costs in Ronald Reagan's America and Margaret Thatcher's Britain), but there is no doubting the importance of market access as a key explanatory factor. More recently, another example comes from China where the government has insisted that companies like Boeing should set up **joint ventures** with Chinese companies if they want to sell more planes in China. For other TNCs chasing larger markets, it is not so much the need to overcome tariffs and regulations that is the driving factor, but rather the more simple need to make products near the markets. Coke, for example, is not made in one giant factory in Atlanta (Coca Cola's headquarters) and shipped around the planet. Instead, it is mixed in bottling plants in different world regions close to target markets, and these regional bottling plants use local water and local supplies of sugar. In yet other cases, such as with retail and fast food companies, the rationale of market access is a still more immediate driver of TNC transnationalization. Home Depot sets up shops in Latin America, Starbucks opens stores in Europe, and Pizza Hut sets up restaurants in Southeast Asia precisely so they can sell to these foreign markets. Yet whether the transnational investments take place in order to get around trade regulations and tariffs, or whether they are designed simply to reach foreign customers directly, once they have been made they give TNCs a clear financial stake in staying in the foreign market area and continuing to operate transnationally. So, for this reason too, then, as a legacy of former investments made to access foreign markets, many TNCs find themselves today managing a complex web of foreign units. This complexity has only been further intensified by all the calculations surrounding the other major reason for transnationalizing: namely to source products and component parts more efficiently.

Sourcing efficiency is a cover term for many different business strategies ranging from reducing the costs of inputs to improving product quality to expediting production and transportation. Sometimes it is just a euphemism for extremely exploitative strategies of locating factories where labor costs are lower, where unions are banned or restricted, and where worker rights laws are poor or poorly enforced. But sourcing efficiency can also include strategies of finding a highly educated or linguistically talented workforce, or of locating a factory in an area where supply firms are already well established and where technical support is strong. More generally, TNCs seeking cost advantages in foreign operations are also frequently looking for an "efficient," which is to say business-friendly, political regime with low taxes and minimally intrusive corporate regulations, or, if there are taxes and regulations, at least an efficient supply of useful infrastructure (e.g. good roads) and legal protections (e.g. strong patent protection laws) to show for it. Normally it is a mix of all these different sorts of considerations that come into corporate transnationalization strategies. Depending on the type of commodity being made by the TNC, and depending in turn on whether the TNC adopts more vertically integrated or horizontally integrated commodity chain management approaches, different sorts of sourcing efficiencies will come into play. For mass-produced, labor intensive work in marketized, or relational commodity chains (such as the flexible chains used by apparel producers), sourcing efficiency often comes down to finding low-paid workers who are easy to exploit and easy to abandon when they organize. By contrast, for knowledge-intensive and specialized work in captive-supplier and in-house commodity chains (such as those in car and aircraft manufacturing), sourcing efficiency can involve locating abroad in sites where there are high levels of worker education and pre-established supply networks of key component parts. Recently, with TNC expansions into India and China, we have seen these strategies come together with business managers seeing both cost advantages and key skill assets in the foreign areas. The fact that China and India are also exciting for TNCs as potentially gigantic new markets reveals how all the key questions concerning *why* TNCs transnationalize help determine in turn *where* they transnationalize.

3.4.3   Where?

For most TNCs, the where question is posed and answered by all the factors we have examined thus far. The two big needs of market access and sourcing efficiency along with all their complex permutations, critically affect which foreign areas become the focus of transnational development strategy. Likewise, historical investments in particular foreign areas (including investments in the development of political relations and local knowledge, as well as into factories, buildings, and supply chains) shape decisions over where to make new rounds of transnational investments. In terms of reaching a large customer base, North America and Europe remain the key markets in the global economy. Thus, most European-based TNCs focus much of their energy on reaching North American consumers, and most North American TNCs are keenly concerned with selling their products to Europeans. Within these continental regions, they generally seek out as much sourcing efficiency as they can, often combining research and development investments in high-cost/high-education areas such as Silicon Valley and Southeast England with production investments in relatively low-cost areas such as Mexico and Poland. Whatever the more micro strategies developed in relation to sourcing efficiency, the big draw of market access remains a common denominator. By contrast, through most of the second half of the twentieth century, Asia has been a target for TNC activity mainly as a place to produce rather than to sell products. The low-cost factories of Taiwan, Hong Kong, Singapore, and South Korea have thus been followed by the low-cost factories of Indonesia, Malaysia, Thailand, the Philippines, and now China and India as the sourcing efficency workshops of the world. However, as a result of the development of sizable middle-class consumer populations in at least some of these countries, East Asia, Southeast Asia and South Asia are also now increasingly targeted as important growing markets for global TNCs. Here, for example, is how one North American consulting firm – Deloitte of Canada (a division of Deloitte and Touche, the global accounting firm) – characterized the twin advantages of China for its corporate clients.

> Once a low-tech, low cost producer, China is now graduating 450 000 engineers a year. Their capacity to compete is increasing in every way. China offers unprecedented opportunities in terms of operating efficiencies and access to a massive consumer market. Whether you make car parts or clothes, furniture or machinery, your organization's future will be affected by the China market.[15]

In other words, China is viewed not just as a place to produce products efficiently and cheaply but also as a "massive" consumer market in which to sell. This does not mean that the same young Chinese women workers who are laboring in the factories provide the core consumer base, but it does mean that China has become viewed as a key place to expand for *both* sourcing efficiency and market access reasons. For some TNCs, however, it is India that is more attractive as a combined production and sales base. For example, in 2004, Whirlpool, the US maker of kitchen and washing appliances, was reported to be moving much of its focus for Asian development from China to India because gaining access to the Indian market promised to be much easier. Whirlpool, like other foreign TNCs in China, faced tough competition from local Chinese firms who benefited from much cheaper borrowing and building costs as well as special promotion in government-owned department stores. By comparison, India was offering much better market access combined with a relative lack of local competition and a labor force that was meanwhile as cheap, well educated, and plentiful as China's.[16]

At a more local scale, the *where* question is also answered by the various efforts local governments make to attract TNC investment. Cities, counties, provinces, and nation-states right around the world have now been thrown into an extraordinarily intense and unprecedented global competition to attract the interest of TNCs. As we shall explore in greater detail in Chapter 8, the strategies used to win in this geographical competition are varied. They range from "bottom feeding" efforts to sell a region as a place where polluters go unpunished, and workers have no protections, to compromise strategies to promote regions with well-trained workers and a steady consumer base, to high-end advertising efforts aimed at attracting TNC management staff with boasts about "liveability," cultural amenities and recreational diversity. Across the range of these strategies, local and national governments strive to give TNCs what they demand in the hope that they will make the investments that generate local jobs and growth. Thus, in region after region, we have witnessed the rise of more corporate friendly government where a great emphasis is placed on the neoliberal norms of reducing taxes and regulations on business. In their efforts to win such concessions from governments, TNCs often present themselves as infinitely mobile. The idea that they can move anywhere in the world gives them considerable leverage against local politicians who fear their communities might lose out to other regions with lower corporate taxes or lax environmental laws. For the same reason, the idea of global mobility is one that TNCs greatly exaggerate (thereby both using and reinforcing the Globalization myths discussed in Chapter 1). This is not to deny that new free-trade agreements at both the regional and global level have increased TNC mobility. They have. An agreement like **NAFTA**, for example, gives companies the option to relocate to a low-cost country such as Mexico and still export tariff-free into the huge consumer market of the United States (see Chapter 6). This has led to real TNC shifts to northern Mexico as well as enabling other companies to extract huge concessions (such as tax breaks from American communities and pay and benefit cuts from American workers) by just threatening to leave. Nonetheless, TNCs are not exactly the placeless agents that they often suggest themselves to be. To understand why this is, we have to look more closely into *how* exactly TNCs transnationalize.

3.4.4　How?

There are basically just two main ways in which TNCs transnationalize their activities, and any single TNC can use one or both methods depending on the types of commodity chain they establish. The first method involves foreign direct investment, and the second involves various forms of **outsourcing**.

　1.　Foreign direct investment (**FDI**) is, just as it sounds, the direct investment by a TNC in a foreign country. The investment can be in the building of a new factory, the establishment of a chain of retail outlets, in the development of foreign offices, or even in the purchase of a foreign firm. The latter tactic which can involve mergers or outright acquisition of foreign companies is commonly called "*M & A investment*," whereas the other basic tactic of developing new foreign business operations from the ground up is referred to as "*Greenfield investment*." FDI of both the M & A and Greenfield types has historically been the main method through which TNCs have set about operating transnationally. For this reason, and because it also generates statistics that are tracked by national governments, FDI is often used alongside trade data as one of the main measures of growing global economic interdependency. As is shown in Figure 3.8, for example, the growth in the total global flows of FDI from 1970 to 2010 indicates a huge rise in global interdependency, especially when considered in relation to the much more moderate growth in total world GDP. Reaching a peak of almost US$2 trillion (2 thousand billion) in 2008 before a fall-off thanks to the global financial crisis, this historic rise outpaced the parallel rise in aggregate global GDP over the same period, indicating, like the growth in international trade, increasing functional integration across the global economy during the 1980s and 1990s. Just as with the trade data, it would be a mistake to assume that this increase in FDI indicates some sort of global leveling. Instead, the vast majority of FDI still *originates* in the world's wealthiest countries and, perhaps more surprisingly, still also tends to *go to* such countries, too. Nevertheless, in 2011, UN reports showed new records being set for FDI flows both

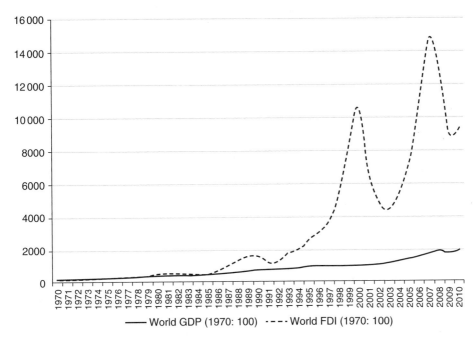

Figure 3.8 Total world FDI and total world GDP indexed from 1970 base forwards. *Source:* based on data from UNCTAD, http://unctad.org/en/Pages/Statistics.aspx.

into and out of Asia: with Asian investment in developed economies jumping from below 10% of global FDI before 2008 to over 17% in 2010, and with FDI going into East Asia leaping to $188 billion, mainly due to double-digit growth in inflows to China and Hong Kong.

2. Outsourcing, the second main method through which TNCs pursue transnational development, is a more recent phenomenon. It is true that the old global trading businesses technically "outsourced" as far back as the seventeenth century. The fur agents of the Hudson Bay Company, for example, outsourced in this sense when they contracted with native hunters to collect furs. But the large-scale use of foreign companies to produce components or to deliver services is a development that really only took off in the later years of the twentieth century: first with the subcontracting of manufacturing and assembly work, and second, more recently still with the outsourcing of service, back-office and even research and development work. Whereas FDI is more associated with in-house and captive supplier commodity chains, manufacturing outsourcing is clearly more a feature of marketized, relational, and modular commodity chains. It can take the simple form of subcontracted deliveries of parts from a single supplier, or of much more complex forms of multi-firm networking using intermediaries of all kinds (including shippers, logistics firms, marketing firms, vendors, and so on) to produce, distribute, and even organize the sales of commodities. Also, in contrast to FDI, outsourcing is much harder to track statistically or, for that matter, any way at all. It is this hard-to-track obscurity that has in turn created such a difficult challenge for the various corporate

accountability and anti-sweatshop groups that seek to reveal the conditions under which brand-name products are made. The big secret with Victoria's Secret lingerie, for instance, is not sex so much as the decidedly unsexy and untrackable subcontracting system through which the production process is outsourced. The same goes for Nike, Banana Republic, and other big brands, as well as for the outsourcing networks used by retailers such as Wal-Mart, Costco, Carrefour, and Target. Adding to the analytical challenge of tracking these commodity chains is the fact that the outsourcing networks are highly mobile and flexible. Precisely because they do not involve foreign direct investment, the lead companies have little to lose by abandoning one supply network and replacing it with another.

For all the above reasons, we cannot produce a world map of outsourcing along the lines of the world map of FDI. Nevertheless, by considering both FDI and outsourcing activities at the level of individual TNCs we can make some larger generalizations about the economic geography of global commodity production. It is this same geography that in turn helps put into question the "placeless TNC" myth. At its most extreme, the idea of the placeless TNC comes down to a vision of cosmopolitan capitalist business entirely unattached to any particular national context. Here, for example, is the vision as it was once articulated by the CEO of Dow Chemical Company.

> I have long dreamed of buying an island owned by no nation and of establishing the world headquarters of the Dow company on the truly neutral ground of such an island, beholden to no nation or society. If we were located on such truly neutral ground we could then really operate in the United States as US citizens, in Japan as Japanese citizens and in Brazil as Brazilians rather than being governed in prime by the laws of the United States . . . we could even pay any natives handsomely to move elsewhere.[17]

It is true that in recent years a few companies such as the global accounting firm Accenture have moved their headquarters to low-tax, business-friendly islands such as Bermuda. Likewise, CEOs such as IBM's Sam Palmisano like to talk about leading "a globally integrated company" rather than a multi-national with a home country."[18] However, by and large the fantasy of post-national corporate placelessness remains just that, a fantasy. FDI and outsourcing patterns of individual TNCs instead reveal at least three ways in which TNC activity reflects the *national places* in which TNCs are based and by which they remain shaped.

3.4.4.1   *The impact of national foreign policy on TNC development*
TNCs have always greatly benefited from the political support of particular national governments in the form of foreign interventions ranging from empire building to foreign policies of so-called "stabilization" and "securitization." British TNCs, for example, have generally had much more foreign involvement with parts of the world that used to be in the British empire, and the same goes for the French and the

Dutch, and, at least in Asia, for the Japanese, too. While the United States historically had a much smaller formal empire (the Philippines and various Pacific and Caribbean islands), there is also no doubting the close links that have long existed between US foreign policy and US TNCs. Indeed, the US experience in the twentieth century also shows that the ties between national foreign policy development and TNC development go both ways, with TNC needs often dictating foreign deployments of the nation's military forces. Here is how one of America's great military heroes, Major General Smedley Butler described the ties to TNCs in the early part of the century.

> I served in all commissioned ranks from Second Lieutenant to Major General . . . and during that period, I spent most of that time being a high-class muscle-man for Big Business, for Wall Street and for the Bankers. . . . I helped make Honduras "right" for American fruit companies in 1903. I helped make Mexico, especially Tampico, safe for American oil interests in 1914. I helped make Haiti and Cuba a decent place for the National City Bank boys to collect revenues in. I helped in the raping of half a dozen Central American republics for the benefit of Wall Street. . . . I helped purify Nicaragua for the international banking house of Brown Brothers in 1909–1912. I brought light to the Dominican Republic for American sugar interests in 1916. In China I helped to see to it that Standard Oil went its way unmolested.[19]

Writing in his retirement, Butler was obviously self-critical of his role, but others have followed in his footsteps, and whether one endorses or condemns what the US military has done on behalf of US TNCs, there can be no doubting the historic record of connection. These connections continue into the present (with US businesses such as Bechtel and Haliburton benefiting from, if not directing, the Iraq war) and are by no means unique to the United States. They indicate strong and ongoing ties between TNCs and the foreign policies of the nation-states in which they are based.

3.4.4.2   The impact of national economies and economic policy on TNC development
In his enormously useful book *Global Shift*, the economic geographer Peter Dicken presents a chart of the largest 100 TNCs in the world that ranks them on the basis of what he calls their "transnationality index."[20] This index is an average of three ratios: foreign assets to total assets; foreign sales to total sales; foreign employment to total employment. What the ranking shows is that the firms with the biggest transnationality indices are TNCs such as Nestlé, Electrolux, British American Tobacco, and Unilever from smaller nation-states such as Switzerland, Sweden, the United Kingdom, and the Netherlands. While the big US TNCs like ExxonMobil and McDonalds are still in the top 50, they are not as close to the top because their ratio of domestic to foreign activities is lower. Other American corporate giants such as General Electric and General Motors are yet further down the ranking at numbers 75 and 83, respectively. This place-shaped feature of TNC transnationality is perhaps not all that surprising. TNCs from small countries clearly are in no

position to rely solely on their national home markets. But it is not just the size of the domestic market and business base that shapes TNC's transnationality; it is also the effect of national economic and industrial development policies. Indeed, nothing contradicts the myth of the "placeless TNC" more than the financial support that is provided by national governments to domestic TNCs (most spectacularly during times of economic crisis, but frequently during normal years, too). Whether it is the French government providing grants and credit guarantees to a manufacturing giant like Alston (the maker of French TGV trains), the British government subsidizing British Aerospace, or the US government bailing out its national airlines (as happened after 9/11), this kind of financial intervention is a common practice around the world. Indeed, while it goes against the grain of all the neoliberal common-sense about the need for more free-market discipline, while it is at odds with TNC rhetoric about the need for less government, and while it is also often (as we shall see in Chapter 6) technically illegal under WTO, NAFTA, and EU trade laws, national governments continue to subsidize national TNCs in significant ways because of ongoing and close ties between government and business.

3.4.4.3   *The impact of national business norms*

TNCs are also shaped by their national contexts in less noticeable ways relating to actual business practices. National tax and accounting standards often stamp the internal workings of a TNC with a particular style of recording and reporting data. Indeed, as the American cases of Enron, Worldcom, and Xerox showed in 2001–2002, even a national tendency towards anti-tax and anti-government rhetoric can lead to a systematic style of doing business (a style which in the example of Enron took on the form of completely fraudulent accounting and reporting practices). Beyond accounting practices, TNCs are more broadly shaped by national cultural norms of doing business. Various Asian business cultures, for example, put a great emphasis on family and/or hometown networks. In South Korea, the now giant conglomerates like Hyundai called *chaebol* started out as networks of family firms. In Japan, the similar *zaibatsu* family firms of the pre-war era have now morphed into the vast *keiretsu* networks with names like Mitsubishi and Mitsui. These networks do not just make brand name products like Mitsubishi cars but also control hugely extensive corporate holdings across the whole spectrum of industrial, petrochemical, banking, and communications businesses. Overseas Chinese family business networks have led to yet other kinds of kin-based business practices where control of the firms and financing depends on personal relationships of reciprocity (*guanxi*). As these networks have spread out across the world wherever there is a Chinese migrant community, they have led to new names such as the "bamboo network" in the United States and *pibao gungsi* (suitcase companies) in Taiwan. Elsewhere in the world, German business practices remain heavily influenced by national traditions of rationalist long-term planning with control being mediated through banks. Meanwhile, in the United States and the United Kingdom, the role of shareholder and venture capitalist control of TNCs is just one symptom of a business culture more influenced by short-term casino-style calculations connected to stockmarket speculation and arbitrage.

Clearly, the stamp of national context continues to shape TNCs. Far from place-less, most of them have national homes, and these homes make an enormous difference to how TNCs go about the business of transnationalizing their activities. All this cuts against the grain of the neoliberal Globalization vision of hyper-mobile businesses on a global level playing field. However, contrary to a common *anti*-neoliberal myth, too, this is not to suggest that entrenched national TNCs are going to be the long-term winners of global free-market interdependency. While many in the global justice movement protest against TNCs taking over the world, it may well turn out in the end that established national TNCs (and especially their workers) will be among the long-term losers. This at least is the hypothesis of the pro-business *Financial Times* of London. In 2001, it conceded that "[f]ew components of globalisation are inevitable if there is a genuine popular will to stop them." However, it went on to argue that globalization will definitely have one big "business consequence."

> That consequence is the substitution of industrial structures based on competitive advantage for those based on historic market position. If that seems almost a truism, it is one that has not been obvious to either the business supporters or the protesting opponents of globalisation. They have shared a common belief that globalisation favours the established firm over the new entrant and the large business over the small firm. But globalisation has done harm, not good, to [established TNCs]. The principal victims of globalisation are companies, activities and individuals in rich countries with strong historic positions but no competitive advantages.[21]

Only time will tell whether the *Financial Times* hypothesis has lasting predictive power vis-à-vis the fate of big old TNCs. General Motors is suffering but still survives thanks to being supported by the US government after the crisis of 2008. Given all the complaints about this support from Tea Party supporters and other conservative critics of stimulus spending, what has changed more noticeably is the old consensus that: "What is good for General Motors is good for America." This was an axiom based on the idea that GM profits led to GM jobs and decent GM wages for American citizens who could then buy GM cars and all the other consumer durables defining a middle-class American lifestyle. In this respect, the *Financial Times* was surely right when it went on to list "US car workers" as its first example of the "victims" of global economic competition. These victims, the paper argued, were workers who were losing their strong historic position in rich countries because of the absolute competitive advantages (chiefly the low wages and poor legal protections) created by exploiting workers in poor countries. As we shall examine in more detail in Chapter 4, such changes are real, and they raise a whole set of new questions about the interconnected fate of workers everywhere in the context of globalization.

Student Exercises

Group:

1. Re-read the *Financial Times* argument about the fate of established TNCs. Form two debating teams, and have one team prepare to argue in favor of the hypothesis and one team against it. Both teams have to use at least two real-world examples to make their case either for or against the argument that established TNCs are going to lose out in the context of increasing global economic interdependency.

2. Decide as a group on a popular brand-name company and then compare the company's own representations of its commodity chains (including any obvious attempts at *non*-representation) with as many "corporate watch" and "anti-sweatshop" group analyses as possible.

Individual:

1. Try to write a new verse that brings John Masefield's *Cargoes* up to date. Here is an example:

> Mighty Container Ship from the Pearl River Delta,
> Steaming fast past Singapore, Batam, and Mallaka,
> With a cargo of TVs, tools,
> And intracorporate goods,
> Burning black gold from not so distant Nineveh.

2. Go to the website of a large shipping company such as Maersk, Sealand, or Evergreen and research how much it would cost to send 20 containers from the United States to China. Now try to find out the price for sending 20 containers from China to the United States. Write a short paragraph explaining the difference in pricing, and what it tells us about global trade flows.

Notes

1   WTO, *International Trade Statistics 2009*, 1–2, http://www.wto.org/english/res_e/statis_e/its2009_e/its09_toc_e.htm.

2   John Maynard Keynes, *The Economic Consequences of the Peace* (New York: Penguin, 1988) 10–12.

3   Data from WTO, *International Trade Statistics 2011*, 1, http://www.wto.org/english/res_e/statis_e/its2011_e/its11_toc_e.htm and Benjamin Mandel, "Why Is the U.S. Share of World Merchandise Exports Shrinking?" *Federal Reserve Bank of New York: Current Issues in Economics and Finance*, 18, no. 1 (2012)http://www.newyorkfed.org/research/current_issues/ci18-1.pdf.

4   WTO, *International Trade Statistics 2011*, 1, http://www.wto.org/english/res_e/statis_e/its2011_e/its11_toc_e.htm.

5   WTO, *International Trade Statistics 2009*, 1–2, http://www.wto.org/english/res_e/ statis_e/its2009_e/its09_toc_e.htm.

6   Another less dangerous strategy that has been employed by the BBC to great educational effect is to track a shipping container or "box" around the world and keep an inventory of the various contents it contains at different moments at different places on the world map. See http://news.bbc.co.uk/2/hi/in_depth/business/2008/the_box/default.stm.

7   It is also worth noting here that *outsourcing* does not necessarily involve *offshoring* either. It is quite possible and indeed quite common for companies to outsource within their own countries by subcontracting to external suppliers. The fact that so many commentators such as Thomas Friedman confuse these terms is indicative of the complex ways in which business practices have evolved hybrid mixes of the two strategies. This hybridity continues to grow in diverse ways, and with it we have also seen an evolution in the jargon, too. As a *Financial Times* article noted in 2006, this is why: "Offshoring and outsourcing have been joined by 'near-shoring' and 'on-shoring' under the umbrella of 'best-shoring' or 'smart-sourcing.'" Andrew Hill, "A Theory of evolution for outsourcers," *Financial Times* June 26 (2006): 15.

8   On the ascendancy of horizontal integration through market-mediated and buyer driven commodity chains, see Gary Hamilton and Robert Feenstra, *Emergent Economies, Divergent Path: Economic Organization and International Trade in South Korea and Taiwan* (New York: Cambridge University Press, 2006).

9   An especially useful set of studies outlining these five approaches has been developed by the American sociologist Gary Gereffi and his colleagues Tim Sturgeon and John Humphrey under the title of "The Global Value Chain Initiative": see http://www.ids. ac.uk/globalvaluechains/index.html. See especially Gereffi, Gary, John Humphrey, and Timothy Sturgeon, "The Governance of Global Value Chains." *Review of International Political Economy* 12, no. 1 (2005): 78–104. This textbook's account draws on many of the analyses and examples provided by these scholars, but retains the term "commodity chain" (instead of "value chain") because of its narrower and more precise meaning. As we shall see in Chapters 4 and 5, a comprehensive analysis of the value chains of production and circulation must also address how value is created by human labor and represented in its most abstract, socially generalized, and economically globalized form as money.

10 See Katharyne Mitchell, "Flexible Circulation in the Pacific Rim: Capitalisms in Cultural Context." *Economic Geography* 71, no. 4 (1995): 364–82.

11 See Hamilton and Feenstra, *Emergent Economies*, and for an excellent overview, including video footage detailing how Wal-Mart organizes its commodity chains see the materials presented by the American Public Broadcasting Service at http://www.pbs. org/wgbh/pages/frontline/shows/walmart/.

12 Karl Marx and Frederick Engels, *The Communist Manifesto* (London: Verso, 1998) originally published in 1848, 38.

13 http://www.whitehouse.gov/news/releases/2004/03/20040330-2.html.

14 http://www.whitehouse.gov/news/releases/2004/03/20040330-2.html.

15 On the webpage of Deloitte Canada, http://www.deloitte.com/dtt/brief/0,2298,sid%253 D3648%2526cid%253D29255,00.html.

16 Keith Bradsher, "India Gains on China Among Multinationals," *International Herald Tribune*, June 12–13 (2004): 13.

17 Quoted in Leslie Sklair, *The Transnational Capitalist Class* (Oxford: Blackwell, 2001): 12.

18   Quoted in Hill, *Theory of Evolution*.
19   Smedley Butler, "A Gangster for Capitalism," *Common Sense*, 1935.
20   Peter Dicken, *Global Shift: Reshaping the Global Economic Map in the 21st Century* (New York: The Guildford Press, 2004).
21   John Kay, "The Great Paradox of Globalisation: Rich-Country Multinationals Benefit from Wider Markets. but They Also Face More Competition," *The Financial Times* November 14 (2001): 18.

Keywords

commodification	NAFTA	sourcing efficiency
commodity chain	offshoring	TNCs
FDI	outsourcing	trade deficit
joint ventures	race to the bottom	
market access	sourcing efficiencies	

4

Labor

Chapter Contents

Chapter Concepts

1. The sourcing efficiencies created by cheap labor in poorer countries create downward harmonization pressures on wages and workplace protections in wealthier countries.
2. Downward harmonization pressures are creating new global divisions of labor.
3. The older Fordist divisions of labor that balanced national mass production with national mass consumption have been replaced.
4. Post-Fordist divisions of labor now link the fates of workers and consumers on a worldwide basis.
5. With the new global divisions of labor also come new social divisions of labor.
6. In response, organized labor has begun to develop transnational strategies of global organizing and solidarity-building, but these remain less extensive and influential than the global commodity chains of TNCs.

Introducing Globalization: Ties, Tensions, and Uneven Integration, First Edition. Matthew Sparke.
© 2013 Matthew Sparke. Published 2013 by Blackwell Publishing Ltd.

Key Concept

Businesses need labor both as workers who produce commodities and as consumers who then buy the commodities. In the mid twentieth century, the balance between this worker role and consumer role was generally achieved within particular national economies. The development of global commodity chains since the 1970s has transformed this previous balance. Businesses now seek out both workers and consumers globally, and the old need to pay national workers enough to buy nationally made goods no longer applies as a dominant business model.

4.1   Interdependence and the Far-from-Flat World of Workers

China is living through a gilded age of inequality, whose benefits are not trickling down to the 700 million or 800 million rural residents who live off the land or flock to the cities for factory or construction jobs. . . . This is partly a paradox of globalization. China has attracted more foreign investment by far than any other developing country, nearly $500 billion since it began internationalizing its economy. But it continues to draw capital essentially because it is willing to rent workers for falling returns.[1]

There is much hype about how India could become the global hub for outsourced businesses. But the reality is that the current boom is based on a single premise – cheap labor. But is cheap labor a virtue? Is it something to be proud of? The call center industry could move overnight to another country where the cost of labor would be lower.[2]

When we walk through a shopping mall or buy lunch or pay to play an online game such as *World of Warcraft*, we do not think about it very much. But behind every single commodity for sale in our world lies an act, or, more likely, many diverse and complexly integrated acts, of labor. Behind all the accounts of the global commodity chains we examined in Chapter 3, therefore, there are other stories to be told of what might, with poetic license, be called global commodity chain-gangs: in other words, the chains of interdependency connecting the fate of workers around the globe. Unfortunately, the image of imprisonment conjured up by the metaphor of "chain-gangs" is by no means inappropriate to describing the lives of numerous workers in today's world. Some Chinese prisoners, for example, even report being forced to work on old-fashioned manual labor chain gangs by day and new online gaming or "gold-farming" chain gangs by night. The latter involves doing tedious tasks on online games in order to win credits that prison guards can then sell for a profit. "As a prisoner at the Jixi labour camp, Liu Dali would slog through tough days breaking rocks and digging trenches in the open cast coalmines of north-east China. By night, he would slay demons, battle goblins and cast spells."[3] However, unlike Liu Dali and other prison laborers in the United States and the United Kingdom, most workers today, including those who play computer games for fun, and including even the Chinese and Indian workers cited in reports about "cheap labor" and globalization, willingly sell their labor. They obviously do not sell it under conditions of their own choosing: extreme poverty, family duty, and desperation often help explain their willingness. Likewise, intense and ongoing competition with other willing workers in other countries operates as a constant drag on the wages workers can expect to earn. Yet, in whatever way they come to enter the labor market, workers everywhere are daily selling their labor to employers, thereby turning it into a commodity. As such, labor plays a very special role in global capitalism. Four features distinguish this special role, and all of them need remembering before we begin to discuss the main features of labor and globalization examined subsequently.

First, in so far as employers use it to make other commodities that can then be sold for profit, labor is the basic source of the added value that lies at the heart of capitalist growth. It is true that individual businesses make profits in many different ways: beating competitors to the market with a hot new product; striking lucky in access to a rare raw material; successfully lobbying a government official for a subsidy; finding new customers in far-flung foreign markets; discovering a cheaper production technology; and so on. But the relative gains of some companies would always be balanced by the losses of others, were it not for the fact that there is one special commodity – labor – that can be bought systematically for less money than it enables its purchasers to produce. This in turn depends on workers being willing to sell their labor at a price that allows profits to be realized, and, while historic victories by unions have traditionally increased the price of labor, today the integration of countries such as India and China into the global economy means that there are hundreds of millions of new workers competing for work and pushing the cost of labor back down on a global scale. Thrown out of farm work by the entrance of new agriculture technologies and subsidized foodstuffs from North America and Europe; rendered redundant by the closing down of non-profitable state-run factories; or simply just desperate to make a living because of the destruction of forests, communal lands, and other traditional means of subsistence, over 2 billion new low-wage workers are trying to sell their labor worldwide, and the ongoing global competition keeps prices – wages, as well as the costs of the commodities that they make – down.[4]

Second, in so far as workers also buy commodities, they also represent a key consumer base whose purchases allow profits to be realized. During the mid twentieth century, national businesses in wealthy countries such as the United States and United Kingdom classically viewed their own national employees as a national consumer base. However, since the 1970s, this interest in the national worker as national consumer has been transcended by the turn TNCs have made towards transnational consumer markets. Of course, the very low-paid workers that have newly entered the world's labor pool can provide only a relatively small addition to effective demand globally, and, following the financial crises of 2008–2012, long-term trends suggest that finding effective demand in the future will be still more difficult as credit-dependent consumers in indebted countries such as the United States and United Kingdom increasingly find it hard to borrow in order to buy. Nevertheless, TNCs continue to search for new customers right around the world, and excited share-holder reports repeatedly reassure investors that the sheer size of countries such as China and India means that the small percentage of their populations who can afford to consume present significant new markets.

Third, since labor is human and therefore comprises thinking, feeling, social agents capable of all sorts of organizational activities, the way workers themselves negotiate their dual roles as laborers and consumers matters a great deal to the political organization of global capitalism.

And fourth, in addition to their dual role as both sellers of labor and purchasers of commodities, workers' lives are also profoundly shaped by all the non-paid work many of them do (most notably women) in reproducing new generations of workers.

These four core features of labor under capitalism have had significant implications for economic globalization. Recent rounds of economic integration, meanwhile, have reciprocally had significant implications for the ways in which these four core features of labor are connected with each other becoming interdependent on a global scale. Since the aim of this chapter is to explain the evolution of these two-way ties of labor globalization, we need to consider at the outset both how workers' fates are linked around the planet and how this interdependency relates to ongoing and often extreme inequalities between workers.

In June 2010, a *New York Times* front page featured two different stories that together told a story of global labor interdependencies in a particularly striking way. At the top of the page was a picture of Brenda and Kord Campbell sitting at their breakfast table in a typical American home hunched in private fascination over their separate iPads. The associated article entitled "Hooked on Gadgets, and Paying a Mental Price," proceeded to explain how the multiple electronic media occupying the Campbell's lives – iPads, phones, computers, email, text messaging, TV, social networking, and so on – illustrated the wider dominance of e-information over contemporary life in wealthy countries. The article highlighted in turn the addictive quality of such information for those seeking to multitask and get news fast. "You never know if something is going to be important," explained one e-addict in a related inside story. However, the main article on being "Hooked" online also explored the unfortunate irony that, far from creating efficiencies, such e-enabled multitasking was also becoming counter-productive and destructive: reducing task performance, eating into family time, undermining relationships, and allowing online practices such as social networking to become deeply anti-social. What was so striking about this story was that its conclusions about the destructive outcomes of e-enabled multitasking in America were directly connected to another story on the same front page of the newspaper about a very different kind of time-intensive multitasking focused on electronics but taking place in China: the work of laborers in the factories making iPads and other electronic gadgets for Apple, Dell, and Hewlett-Packard.[5]

No links were made by the different journalists writing the two stories, and the *New York Times* editorial staff did not address them in any obvious way. However, the connection was there for anyone interested in the interdependencies of global labor and the ways in which multi-tasking in one place is mentally, physically, and electronically tied to what might be called the over-tasking of workers in another place.

Evidently, the Chinese factory had intensified worker exploitation to such a high degree that over 10 young laborers had committed suicide because of the overwhelming workload and stress. Ma Xianquian, for example, whose body was found in front of his high-rise dormitory, had pay stubs showing that he had worked over 286 h in the month before he jumped to his death. These hours, including 112 in overtime, were mainly spent forging plastic and metal into electronic components in a dusty, fume-filled factory, but some were also spent cleaning toilets: an extra job with which the 19-year-old Xianquian had been tasked as a form of punishment after a run-in with his supervisor. In this case, the destructive consequences of multi-tasking and working on electronics were obviously much more severe and deadly than in the American setting where efforts to "unplug" were reported not as suicides but rather as work–life management problems overshadowed by e-addiction issues. Nevertheless, the human costs of speed-up, and the anti-social outcomes of being plugged into global economic integration dynamics (that in the form of business reports and opportunities simultaneously drive much of the news that news junkies try to keep up with online) are clearly shown in such stories to exist at both the production and consumption end of global commodity chains. For the same reasons, and despite all the ideas of wireless freedom that circulate around new e-gadgets like the iPad, being plugged in and hooked on looked a lot less liberating when considered from the point of view of workers.

Over-tasked Chinese factory workers and multitasking Americans preoccupied with email, blogs, and texting are just two of the many types of labor and many places of labor making up today's endlessly diverse world of work: a world evermore tightly bound by tensional ties to diverse worlds of social reproduction. Even if you only picked the products you have seen for sale in just the last 24 h, you could probably spend the rest of your entire time in college mapping the full variety of labor tasks, workplaces, and social settings involved in their production. Amidst this endless variety, however, there is a reason why scholars and reporters tend to focus on phenomena such as the recent outsourcing of factory and office work to China and India. It is because these developments represent the cutting edge of **downward harmonization** trends that tie together the fates of workers everywhere. This is not a downward harmonization of labor skills or labor quality; far from it: China and India are producing ever larger numbers of extremely well-trained BAs, MAs, and PhDs, and this reservoir of skilled workers in addition to the low average prices of Chinese and Indian labor helps explain why these countries have been attracting so much outsourced work. Downward harmonization instead refers to the relentless downward pressures on wages, worker benefits (such as pensions), and worker protections (such as workplace health and safety) at a global scale. When a business moves its assembly and research work to China, or when it moves its back-office data-entry, engineering, or call-center work to India, it not only creates **sourcing efficiencies**, but also creates systemic downward pressures on non-managerial wages and worker benefits globally. Even firms who do not move can extract new wage concessions and cuts in worker benefits by threatening to leave. And those that do move their facilities and reduce their costs can better compete against competitors who continue to employ more expensive and better-protected workers. When these less competitive companies start to lose money and go bankrupt, their workers lose their jobs, thereby increasing the numbers of those looking for work and further depressing non-managerial wages. At base, this is what the interdependency of workers comes down to (quite literally so): the downward harmonization of average wages and worker protections.

While downward harmonization dynamics are commonly criticized by labor activists as "whipsawing," neoliberal commentators respond by arguing that the resulting sourcing efficiencies increase economic growth and consumer choice while ultimately benefiting workers everywhere by providing jobs. Back in the 1980s, neoliberals also argued that the loss of labor-intensive manufacturing jobs from wealthy countries to places such as Mexico would be balanced by increases in better-paid **services** work. But as the Internet, email, and cheap long-distance phone calls have begun to make it possible for service-sector work to also become off-shored to offices in India and elsewhere, this argument has lost its allure. Thus, in 2003, the American business magazine *Business Week* published an article that instead worried out loud that downward harmonization might well leave US service workers worse off, despite the increased sourcing efficiencies created for American firms. "What happens if all those displaced white-collar workers can't find greener pastures?" the article asked.

> Sure, tech specialists, payroll administrators, and Wall Street analysts will land new jobs. But will they be able to make the same money as before? It's possible that lower salaries for skilled work will outweigh the gains in corporate efficiency.

Quoting a Harvard University economist, Robert Lawrence, the article acknowledged that the trends might therefore augur ill for Americans. "If foreign countries specialize in high-skilled areas where we have an advantage," Lawrence was quoted as saying, "we could be worse off. I still have faith that globalization will make us better off, but it's no more than faith."[6] The mixture of fear and faith in this comment is a telling reflection on how downward harmonization is testing the convictions of American neoliberals, but the bigger point that it illustrates is that no workers, not even American workers, are immune from the effects of global labor market interdependencies. Indeed, a notable aspect of Occupy Wall Street activism in the United States in 2011 was the large number of recently graduated but unemployed or under-employed students who took part: students who might have walked into six-figure salaried jobs on Wall Street in the preceding boom years, but who were exiting college from 2008 onwards into a precarious global workforce – a global *precariat*, as some call it – of desperate service workers with either low wage temping and part-time jobs or nothing at all.

Just as American workers are not unique, neither are Chinese and Indian workers. China and India are just the latest in a long line of countries where a mix of low wages, lax labor laws, poor worker benefits, and anti-union laws have given TNCs cost savings and other advantages over competitors (such as the flexibility to hire and fire without penalty). Mexico, Brazil, Jamaica, Malaysia, Indonesia, Thailand, the Philippines, and Poland, among others, have all also played this role during the 1980s and 1990s, and others – Bangladesh and Vietnam are both undermining China's attractiveness in this regard – will further leverage costs downwards in the future. As fresh workers from new countries such as China have come on line ("on chain" might be the more accurate metaphor), some of the other earlier venues of low-cost production such as Mexico and the Philippines have lost much of their former competitiveness. When workers in even these countries lose their jobs and income as a result of downward harmonization, the bleak underside of sourcing efficiency for labor becomes all too clear. There may be more choices of commodities in the stores, and business profitability may go up, but neither improvement is much consolation for workers whose low wages make the goods unobtainable and whose chronic risks of unemployment make life increasingly insecure.

As a representative from the Philippines told the UN's *World Commission on the Social Dimension of Globalization*: "There is no point to a globalization that reduces the price of a child's shoes, but costs the father his job."[7] Against such complaints, neoliberal promoters of free trade commonly remind us that a few countries, including the so-called "Asian Tigers" (Singapore, Taiwan, South Korea, and Hong Kong), have experienced considerable growth and the resulting expansion of a sizable consumption class as a result of early development as low wage production zones. But as consumerist as they are, these cases are by no means a clear vindication of market rule. There are a whole number of non-neoliberal reasons why they achieved such middle-class growth in consumption spending, including the significant government investments all these countries made in public education, public housing, and public health. More generally, export-led development has not turned poor workers into middle-class consumers. Most workers employed by TNCs in low-cost locations are not the chief market for the commodities they make. They remain too poor, and the commodities are too expensive. Workers in El Salvador, for example, earn about 24 cents a piece to make NBA jerseys that retail for $140.00 in the United States. Huge gaps therefore continue to exist between the low standards of living in low-wage production zones and the vastly higher levels of wealth in the main countries of consumption. It is these gaps that ensure in turn that inequality and contrasts just as much as interdependence and commonality define the fate of workers globally.

By reminding us of huge global inequalities between poor-country workers and rich-country consumers, the poverty of workers in places such as El Salvador and the more general differentials dividing worker experiences in different countries serve as potent correctives to the neoliberal myth of global leveling. Or, to put this more precisely, the fact that downward harmonization works by selling the products of ever-cheaper sources of labor to wealthier consumers highlights how the touted dynamics of leveling are based fundamentally on inequality. One tempting but difficult way of coming to terms with this inequality amidst interdependency is to try to convey to better-off consumers what working life is like in faraway production zones such as Guangdong province on China's Pearl River Delta. This, for instance, was how *The Irish Times* sought to jolt its readers into awareness about the ethical implications of economic interdependency during the 2002 Christmas shopping season. Under a headline referring to the "hidden downside of Santa's little helpers," it noted that:

> These days Santa's toys are all churned out in the crowded sweat shops of the Pearl River Delta, not by elves but by 1.5 million peasant girls sweating through a subtropical summer in 12- or even 14-hour shifts inhaling toxic fumes.[8]

Obviously, this is a provocative picture of extreme exploitation, and as such it builds on a long list of studies of sweatshop abuses going back centuries. From Frederick Engels' powerful account of what work was like in Britain's industrial revolution, to the muckraking American journalists who described the grim working conditions in the sweatshops of New York and Chicago at the turn of the twentieth century, to the recent ethnographies of worker exploitation and resistance in Asian **export processing zones**, empirical research that has gone back behind the shopwindow view of commodities has highlighted how hyper-exploitation has always been part of capitalism.[9] Yet despite the shock value of such accounts for educating workers and consumers in one place about work conditions in other places (i.e. about inequality amidst interdependency), we need to be very attentive to the ways in which examples of "cheap labor" can also be abused. The approach is problematic if it is not based on sustained study of work conditions and, most especially, if it does not attempt to give voice to the concerns of foreign workers themselves. Taken out of context, images of individual foreign workers alone are inadequate. They can also be quite easily appropriated by chauvinists, sexists, and racists in arguments that are essentially isolationist arguments that commonly stereotype the "cheap labor" of a foreign country along racial or cultural lines as "inferiors" who will take any job just to get ahead. A sentimental image like "Santa's little helpers," for example, could be turned in this way into an ethnicist insinuation about Chinese peasant girls working like thousands and thousands of oriental elves in order to steal white men's jobs. Such racist and sexist phobias are obviously a far cry from the ethic of consumer care that *The Irish Times* was attempting to encourage among its readers. But such reactions are no less real. They are often used by far-right demagogues in order to obscure the common fate created by downward harmonization dynamics while also turning the differences between workers into cultural and racial alibis for distrust and disengagement.

Instead of seeing the differences between workers in terms of ethnic stereotypes, we need to recognize how the diversity of workers globally is just as much the *product* of social and economic processes as is their interdependency. This means examining how workers experiences have been systematically divided up on a global basis at the very same time as they have been tied together. Individual accounts of workplace experiences and struggles are not adequate to this task, even if they can be relayed in a way that avoids ethnic stereotypes. Instead, the strategy adopted in what follows is to re-use an old concept from economics – the division of labor – employing it historically to interpret how the global ties of labor have led to different experiences for workers located in different places at different times. This also makes it possible to put earlier academic "theories" of the division of labor into their historical context. Adam Smith's account of the technical division of labor, David Ricardo's theory of an international division of labor (IDL), and the alternative theory of a so-called "new international division of labor" (NIDL) that developed in the early 1980s can all be understood in this way as academic reflections of their times. More than this, however, a historically grounded understanding of the division of labor makes it possible for us to do three things:

1. It allows us to explore the changing *geographical* division of labor, and, in particular, the transition from a largely national division of labor in the mid twentieth century to a transnational division of labor today (Section 4.2).
2. It allows us to examine the changing *social* division of labor, and, in particular, the role played by social power relations (such as class, sexism, and racism) in determining how work is allocated (Section 4.3).
3. It allows us to investigate the changing *political* division of labor and, most especially, the changing political positions and strategies of unions in the new transnational geographical division of labor (Section 4.4).

4.2 The Changing Geographical Division of Labor

The practice of creating "divisions of labor" is itself much older than capitalism. The Incas, the Egyptians, the Romans, and the ancient Indian and Chinese empires all developed elaborate divisions of labor using various combinations of slaves, soldiers, artisans, masons, and technicians to build monumental legacies that survive to this day. In its simplest technical sense, therefore, the idea is not about geographical, social, or political divisions of workers but rather refers simply to the splitting up of the work of production into a series of steps that can be carried out by different people with different specializations. Capitalist commodity production adopted this approach from the start and has since repeatedly revolutionized it with the aim of creating greater productivity (i.e. more production from fewer workers). In early forms of capitalism, the different steps of the division of labor were largely just different work roles in a single factory. Thus, in the first famous academic discussion of the division of labor by the Scottish economist, Adam Smith, the example of pin production served to illustrate simple divisions in the production process of a single "manufactory."

> One man draws out the wire, another straights it, a fourth points it, a fifth grinds it at the top for receiving the head; to make the head requires two or three distinct operations; to put it on, is a particular business, to whiten the pins is another; it is even a trade by itself to put them in the paper; and the important business of making a pin is, in this manner, divided into about eighteen distinct operations, which, in some manufactories, are all performed by distinct hands.[10]

In Smith's time, the mid 1700s, such technical divisions of labor were still quite rare. However, 100 years later at the height of the British industrial revolution, the process of dividing up commodity production into simplified tasks became the norm. Despite the deskilling and difficulty of much of this work, employers could easily find workers because the development of factory divisions of labor also coincided with huge social changes (most notably the enclosures of British farmland) that divided a vast class of laborers from their means of subsistence. Crowding into Britain's industrial towns and cities, such laborers created a workforce that could be hired to work for very low pay in the new factory production lines. By this time, too, significant communications developments – canals, roads, and the early railways – also began to make it possible for the *technical* division of labor by tasks and the *social* division of labor into an urbanized working class to be paralleled by an increasingly extensive, but still largely national, *geographical* division of labor, too. Another century and a half later, we have witnessed the widespread transnationalization of this geographical division of labor. It has led to the extension of the geographical division of labor across borders and ever-more expanded global networks of production. Today, more workers are therefore involved in more interconnected labor processes in more countries in the world than ever before. This widespread transnational extension of commodity and labor chains is really what is new about today's geographical division of labor, but to understand its significance for workers, we need to explore how it has also transformed the previous ways in which workers' work, workers' consumption, and workers' politics were tied together on a national basis in the twentieth century.

As the British industrial revolution was replicated in other countries in other parts of the world, the whole approach to managing production through ever more complex divisions of labor took off everywhere. Management gurus emerged who propounded advice on how to organize still more efficient technical divisions of labor. One such guru was the American, Frederick Winslow Taylor, who in 1911 published a popular treatise on the supposedly "scientific" principles of management. According to Taylor, managers had to strive to remake work tasks by developing rules of motion and standardized work stations. Workers were also meant to be carefully selected for each job, as well as being given adequate training and incentives in order to counter their resistance to the deskilling and alienation entailed by all the standardization. Notwithstanding Taylor's argument that this meant paying workers decent wages, the aim ultimately was to enable businesses to raise profits by increasing efficiency and reducing the amount of money paid out as wages to more highly skilled workers. This did not always happen in practice, because businesses had to employ a whole new class of managers in order to plan and implement all the standardization. Despite this, though, Taylor's basic approach (or Taylorism, as it came to be known) still began to dominate the organization of both factory and office work during the first part of the twentieth century. Most famously, it came to be enthusiastically embraced by big employers such as Henry Ford, and as such it became part of the approach to management that we now refer to as **Fordism.**

Alongside the giant factories with their Taylorized divisions of labor, the other main feature of Fordism as an overall approach to managing capitalism was its emphasis on turning factory workers into capable capitalist consumers. Not all managers pursued this goal with the zeal of Ford himself who, among other tactics, employed teams of social workers to ensure that his workers (many of whom were immigrants to Detroit) were adequately assimilated into a culture of orderly mass consumption. Nor, too, did all employers share Ford's commitment to paying workers at least $5 a day. The latter policy was probably what made Ford most famous. It was not a concession to organized labor. Ford was an ardent anti-unionist. Instead, it was based on the simple idea that if his workers were paid enough, they would be able to buy Ford motor cars thereby creating a bigger market and more profits. Unfortunately, for Ford's own workers he had to renege on his $5-a-day pledge in 1932 during the Great Depression. However, it was in the midst of this very same period of capitalist crisis that the governments of the world's wealthiest nation-states began to embrace the same basic "demand-side" economic idea that had inspired Ford. This was because the crisis of the Great Depression was fundamentally a crisis of oversupply or, as some political-economists call it, a crisis of overaccumulation. Businesses had seen the markets for their commodities disappear overnight. Workers in turn saw their jobs disappear, leading to yet further declines in demand. And thus, huge oversupplies of commodities, factories, and unemployed workers existed side by side without any obvious capitalist way of bringing them back together in a profitable combination. It was in this context that government demand management started to appeal. Thus, policies like the New Deal in the United States were based on the idea that government could and should intervene in order to remake and maintain economic demand. If workers could be supported financially through the worst of the economic downturn, if they could be gainfully employed in public works or at least kept fed, healthy, and educated, they could also serve once more as the mass consumers for all the mass-produced goods for which businesses lacked customers. Fears of workers turning to communism if conditions worsened also boosted the appeal of such policies, as did the academic credibility lent to them by the English economist, John Maynard Keynes, who urged governments to borrow in order to make demand-inducing macro-economic interventions. As a result, from the depression onwards and especially after World War II, most of the wealthy capitalist nation-states started to develop similar interventionist policies. Given that all these policies involved Ford's basic idea that mass production must be balanced with mass consumption, many scholars now use the term coined by the Italian political theorist, Antonio Gramsci, to describe the whole approach as Fordism.

Creating a notably *national* regime for managing capitalism, Fordist policies included national wage bargaining, government-enforced management–union arbitration, expanded public education, public housing, free and subsidized health care, and national systems of welfare. In short, Fordism comprised a whole approach to capitalist government which in the United States today is now commonly defined as "liberal" and which in Europe is seen as "social democratic." A rather more accurate but technical label for the sorts of national regime created by Fordist principles is "Keynesian Welfare-Statism," but, whatever the label one uses, it is worth remembering that the policies were pursued on a national basis, not transnationally. It also needs to be remembered that the struggles of national workers' movements strongly shaped the development of Fordist policies: sometimes speeding up their implementation, sometimes expanding their scope. For this reason, different nation-states implemented Fordism unevenly at different speeds and with different styles. In the United States, it had started early with President Roosevelt's New Deal, and in Britain it came late after the war, but whereas Britain very quickly built a universal National Health Service with free access to all, such a system never developed in the United States, and it was not until the Johnson and Nixon administrations of the 1960s that even a comprehensive social safety net for Americans was put in place. Whatever these national variations in Fordism in the wealthy countries, three key related features of the approach remained consistent:

- It was primarily organized as a *national* effort to bring the profit-making interests of national capitalists into harmony with the wage-making interests of national workers.
- It involved *Keynesian* macroeconomic fiscal measures involving government borrowing and public works schemes to rebalance production and consumption.
- It tended to produce *autarchic* patterns of economic development in which inter-national trade was managed so as to protect national industrial development.

Only the wealthiest and most developed economies could develop Fordism fully at a national scale and on an integrated national basis. Even some of these – Canada a nota-ble example – were highly dependent on foreign markets for the sorts of staple goods they were producing (such as oil, metals, fish, and wheat). For the same reason, the sorts of Fordism that developed in such staples-producing countries were intimately tied together with the ups and downs of mass consumption in the core market coun-tries such as the United States (not coincidentally, it was also in these countries – New Zealand and Australia, as well as Canada – that some of the earliest governmental experiments with neoliberalism were taken in the name of enhancing global competi-tiveness). For the rest of the non-communist world where dependency on the exports of staple raw materials was even more extreme, there were still more challenges to cre-ating a Fordist balance between mass production and mass consumption on a national basis. These countries in the periphery of the global economy – or what is now called "the **Global South**" – had developed principally as colonies of the wealthy capitalist countries and, for the same reason, had been treated economically as just sites from where raw materials could be extracted. This treatment continued long into the twen-tieth century, but it did not stop countries from the Global South from trying to develop forms of Fordism in the periphery. During the 1950s and 1960s, most sought in this way to develop **import substitution policies** that aimed to develop domestically man-ufactured production in place of the manufactured imports exported (often by force) by the wealthy Fordist economies of the north. These strategies met with uneven success, being continually undermined by difficulties in creating effective levels of domestic demand, as well as by all the vested interests involved in the ongoing extrac-

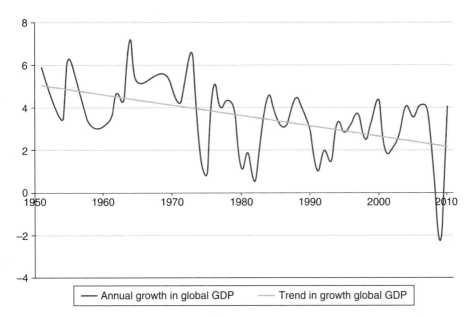

Figure 4.1 Global GDP growth rate (%) from 1950 to 2010. *Source*: based on data from UNCTAD, http://unctad.org/en/Pages/Statistics.aspx.

tion and export of raw materials. Nevertheless, in countries as diverse as Indonesia, Egypt, and Jamaica, Fordist patterns of domestic industrial production for domestic markets began to take shape. Thus, behind protectionist tariff walls, infant industries developed around much of the world, and alongside these initiatives considerable investments were made in national education, healthcare, and welfare programs as well as in the physical infrastructures (electricity supply, railways, roads, and ports) needed to sustain domestic manufacturing. Despite ongoing dependency on the export of raw materials (and the resulting turbulence created by the cyclical surges in global staples markets), the result was a remarkable, albeit episodic, period of global industrial development and growth. But it was not to last. Instead, we have seen a long-term trend towards slower annual growth rates for the global economy as a whole (see Figure 4.1).

By the end of the 1960s, global capitalism began to develop a new more global round of the oversupply problems that had created the crisis of the 1930s. Too many commodities were being produced for too few consumers, and now this was happening on an evermore global scale. The core causes of the problem lay in the post-war recoveries of Japan, Germany, and the rest of Europe whose economic output combined with ongoing American growth in production to create the bulk of the global oversupply. Initially, the problems were experienced nationally as country after country found itself unable to generate the national mass consumption to match national mass production. However, as producers everywhere began to increasingly look to foreign exports as the solution, the crises of oversupply were generalized globally through the world market. It was in this context that the whole emphasis on trade liberalization that we associate today with neoliberal Globalization began to gain in popularity as a political mantra for policy makers. American leaders had long been champions of global free trade, but now they were joined by other policy-making elites from across the western world. For all these leaders, protectionism and import substitution became dirty words. Controls on capital movements were loosened, and financial deregulation and free trade were trumpeted as the new norms of development (see Chapter 7). Gaining access to foreign markets for their countries' products became an ever-more important goal for governments, and thus high tariffs that kept out foreign exports were increasingly targeted as obstacles to continued economic growth in the core capitalist economies.

For a variety of reasons linked chiefly to global finance and the discipline of debt (see Chapter 5), the leaders of the world's wealthy countries were subsequently able to force free-trade policy on the countries of the Global South. The supposedly post-colonial countries were thus obliged to open their borders to foreign exports once again, to give up ideas about industrial development through import substitution, and to embrace a brave new world order of export-led development. Meanwhile, in the wealthy countries themselves, all the Fordist commitments to the Keynesian Welfare State came under attack, too. The many public services and worker rights won in large part through the struggles of organized labor in the mid twentieth century – pensions, welfare, family wages, public housing, free or at least affordable healthcare, workplace health and safety protections, rights to pregnancy- and parental leave, and the right to collective bargaining – all became subordinated to the single so-called "right to work." Instead of the national class compromise that lay at the heart of Fordism, therefore, instead of the attempts to balance the needs of employers with the needs of workers on a national basis, came the new transnational visions of **post-Fordism**, the transnational visions of a global level playing field and a high-stakes global competition for economic survival. Post-Fordist growth strategies thus gave up on the fundamental idea of achieving a balance between national production and national consumption. Businesses instead sought more and more to connect with consumers on a transnational basis. They were no longer so interested in maintaining a specifically national consumer base, and, by the same token, they were much less prepared to pay the taxes needed to maintain national public services. Thus was born the neoliberal era of global competitiveness and precariousness for workers worldwide, a decidedly post-Fordist era that nevertheless had its roots in the oversupply problems following all the global growth that occurred under Fordism after World War II.

According to the neoclassical economic theories that enjoyed a renaissance under neoliberalism, free trade and the removal of other impediments to the movement of commodities and money are meant to lead to increased economic growth. The basic idea is that under conditions of perfect competition, markets lead to prices that balance supply and demand in an efficient manner that minimizes costs, maximizes efficiency, and thereby leads to greater economic expansion. By letting the market operate in this way as an "invisible hand" guiding the organization of production and consumption, the belief is that capitalism will be freed up to create as much growth as possible. The nineteenth-century English economist, David Ricardo, had followed Adam Smith in this way by developing a theory of an ideal international division of labor based on the

neoliberalism

notion of **comparative advantage**. In Ricardo's abstract model, the goal of maximum growth is produced by making each country produce and export the commodities in which it has a *comparative advantage* in so-called "opportunity costs." Even if one country has an *absolute advantage* in making all the commodities under consideration (i.e. it can make them *all* more cheaply and efficiently), the model shows in an elegant mathematical way that greater global growth is attained if each country *specializes* in making the particular commodities that it makes *most* cheaply and efficiently. For example, India can make both underwear and software more cheaply than the United States, but since there are higher opportunity costs involved in the Americans giving up software to focus on underwear (because it is so expensive *relatively* to make underwear in the United States), the theory indicates that the international division of labor should involve the Indians mainly producing underwear and the Americans software. Few countries have ever been willing to accept for very long the ignominious and poor profit-making roles assigned by the theory to less wealthy countries. Moreover, academically as well as politically, the argument has always had it opponents. Most of these critics of Ricardo's theory have traditionally focused on its unrealistic assumptions (including the assumption that labor costs are constant between countries and the implicit underlying premise that greater global growth leads to greater global "welfare"). Yet a still more profound criticism is made possible by examining what has happened in the real world as a result of increasing free trade in the last quarter of the twentieth century. Has it led, as the theory of comparative advantage says it should, to increased global growth? As Figure 4.1 shows, the answer is a clear-cut no. In fact, the period since the mid 1970s in which neoliberalism has been ascendant and in which trade liberalization has proceeded most rapidly has actually seen increasingly *lower* growth rates each decade than under Fordism. Moreover, the poorer countries that were told that the export of key staple products like coffee, cotton, and cocoa would be their ticket to prosperity have seen just the reverse. Of the 10 poorest countries in the world, six are now *less* prosperous than they were 20 years ago. And this is to say nothing here of the increasing costs and human suffering caused by all the volatility created by liberalized financial markets, including most notably the steep reversal of world GDP growth following the crisis that started in 2008.

Despite its poor predictive performance, we should not underestimate the theory of the international division of labor based on comparative advantage. Indeed, its failure as a predictive model has been more than offset by its tremendous success as an academic argument in favor of what businesses in wealthy countries wanted to do anyway in response to the oversupply problems of the 1970s: namely, liberalize foreign markets. Irrespective of its inaccuracy, the theory has thus in practice become a fundamental axiom of neoliberal policy-making. This is hardly surprising given that Ricardo's original theory had been published and widely promoted at a time when British textile manufacturers wanted to legitimate free trade and the development of export markets for their cloth. Indeed, it was no accident that in Ricardo's own simplified model, the two countries compared were Britain and Portugal, that the two commodities in question were cloth and port, and that Ricardo concluded that the calculus of opportunity costs made it make sense for Britain to export cloth and Portugal to export port – exactly what the British manufacturers had wanted to hear. Since the 1940s, a revamped version of the same neoclassical theory referred to as the Heckscher–Ohlin–Samuelson model has done the same basic work of legitimation and is commonly taught in business schools and macroeconomics classes everywhere. Problems of oversupply continue to vex global capitalist development and stability, and while this would seem to diminish the value of a theory that assumes that "greater growth = greater welfare," the theory of the international division of labor based on comparative advantage nonetheless remains invaluable as an academic lever for prying open new markets.

Ironically, while problems of oversupply created the necessity of finding new markets, and while the breakdown of Fordism led businesses to seek out sourcing efficiencies abroad, the new free-trade orthodoxy has also led in practice to the massive post-1970s expansion in foreign direct investment and outsourcing discussed in Chapter 3. This is ironic because while these developments were legitimated by the neoclassical theory of the International Division of Labor, they led to changes in the global distribution of labor that, by the 1980s, many theorists were beginning to call a "*New* International Division of Labor" (**NIDL**).[11] With this term, scholars sought to describe the global ties between increasing unemployment in wealthy countries and increasing low-wage industrialization in poorer countries. Rather than allowing core capitalist countries to dominate manufacturing, as in Ricardo's day, trade liberalization was instead leading this time to widespread *deindustrialization* in the core. The resulting loss of blue collar jobs in places such as Ford's own Detroit was in this way interpreted as a symptom of a new globalized form of capitalism. Yet what exactly was "new" in all these arrangements needs to be examined very carefully. There was nothing particularly new about free trade itself. During the late nineteenth century and early twentieth century, global trade had been remarkably free. Likewise, going back still further, labor in the colonies and other peripheral parts of the global economy had been key to the supply of raw materials to the core since the beginning of capitalism in the sixteenth century. More generally, there was also nothing new in the capitalist need for sourcing efficiencies leading to new investments in some places and deindustrialization in others. What therefore was new in the late 1970s and early 1980s was instead the collapse of the national Fordist compromise between business and labor in the core capitalist countries. In this sense, the New International Division of labor was at once too sweeping and too limited a term: too sweeping because the capitalist imperatives involved were not really so new; and too limited because the idea of a new international division of labor did not really capture the historical significance of the collapse of Fordism.

In whatever way scholars choose to describe the subsequent period – and there are many other terms as well as post-Fordism and the New International Division of Labor, including "flexible accumulation," "disorganized capitalism" and "network capitalism" – the collapse of Fordism brought in its wake a profound reorganization of the geographical division of labor globally. With the breakdown of the commitment to balancing national production and national consumption in territorially defined units across planet came the newly transnational commodity chains in which the technical division of labor of any particular production process was increasingly extended over ever-longer distances involving ever-more disparate workers. Commentators often use terms like "the Global Assembly Line" and the "Global Office" to capture these innovations, and at one level the metaphors are very useful. There really is an intense assembly-line kind of integration that binds workers together functionally across the planet in the manufacture, assembly, distribution, marketing, and sales of something like a computer, or, as we saw with the two *New York Times* stories, an iPad. As you start work on your next term paper, and your fingers move across the keyboard, just think of all the other fingers that have been involved in creating this commodity for your use. There is a real interdependency there and, at one level, a certain sort of intimacy, too. However, as the overstressed lives and deaths linked by iPads illustrated, it is an intimacy fundamentally based on alienation. One would be hard pressed to make contact with even one of the workers involved in the production process – and this is to say nothing about problems reaching the people in the call center that is meant to answer queries about software compatability! Contrast this with a thought experiment about what it must have been like for a Ford worker to buy a Ford car and drive it around Detroit. It would have been easy to see the handiwork of a co-worker in the vehicle and feel connected to the labor process. More generally, and more importantly, workers under Fordism (at least in the wealthy countries) could see and feel part of a larger national project: a project in which their pay, their consumption, their taxes, their access to public services, and their overall standard of living were all intimately bound together on a national basis. It is that territorial consolidation of Fordism, that nationalized geographical division of labor, that has been so radically displaced by the global assembly lines and global offices of post-Fordism today. As a result, the chart of the changes from Fordism to post-Fordism can also be read as a listing of all the main tendencies in capitalism that contrast the era of *national welfare-state liberalism* with a now *globally ascendant neoliberalism* (Table 4.1).

Table 4.1   Changing capitalist approaches to labor management

Fordism	Post-Fordism
National mass production	Strategic global production
Factory assembly lines	Subcontracting and line teams
In-house commodity chains	Market network commodity chains
Just-in-case inventories	Just-in-time deliveries
Taylorism	Flexibility and benchmarking
Working-class solidarity and union growth	Workers divided and unions decline
National mass consumption	Uneven global consumption
Government demand support	Minimalist government
Government arbitration of labor and business disputes	Anti-union laws and pro-business facilitation
Development of welfare states	Development of workfare-states
Government provision of free or affordable public services	Government cutbacks in public services and universal access
Regulation of finance for long-term national interest	Deregulation of finance for short-term investor interest

4.3 The Changing Social Divisions of Labor

Spatial distance certainly plays a role in making it hard to track the connections of workers across today's commodity chains, but the newly transnational geographical division of labor is only one reason why workers know little about each other's conditions of work in the midst of increased global interdependency. Various other social divisions also serve to divide up workers from each other. Of these, three are particularly influential, and each will be discussed here in turn. The first is the class-based division of labor and, in particular, the widening class division between ordinary workers and an emerging transnational business class of managers. The second is the gender-based division of workers that, notwithstanding all the neoliberal hype about Globalization liberating women, continues to shape, and indeed often shapes in new and more powerful ways, how women are subordinated vis-à-vis men in the labor market. And third are the racialized and ethnically coded divisions of labor that operate globally in ways that frequently force people of color into more exploitative, more difficult, and often more dangerous work roles. With each of these social divisions of labor, we can see changes wrought by increased economic interdependency, but the changes have certainly not led to the leveling that is predicted by the celebrants of Globalization.

4.3.1 Changing pattern of class division

Under Fordism, the biggest class differences were effectively those in force between the rich countries and poor countries. The inequality between the working-class standard of living in a country such as the United Kingdom and even a middle-class standard of living in a country such as India was extreme, and much more significant than the differences between rich and poor within India, and the rich and the poor within the United Kingdom. With the demise of Fordism, however, these *transnational inequalities* have begun to be overtaken by *national inequalities* between classes of workers within individual countries. Thanks to new global business opportunities, extraordinarily wealthy elites have emerged in previously poor countries such as India and China. And meanwhile, in richer countries, pay and capital gains for the rich have increased at the same time as the flattening of taxes and cutbacks to social safety nets have impoverished the unemployed and non-unionized working class (including most especially part-time and temporary workers who lack benefits such as pensions and health insurance). From the early 1980s to today, the broad global trend has been towards increasing in-country inequality. It is scarcely surprising, therefore, that Occupy activism in 2011 and 2012 attracted widespread global interest and solidarity by highlighting the widening inequality between the so-called 99% and the 1% comprising the break-away global class elite.

According to the OECD or Organization for Economic Cooperation and Development (a generally pro-market think-tank and clearing house for economic data on its members – the world's wealthier economies), the trend towards increasing in-country inequality began first in countries such as the United States and United Kingdom.[12] These were the wealthy countries that experimented earliest with pro-market reforms and cutbacks to the redistributive Fordist welfare state, although as we shall see in Chapter 7, some middle-income countries in the Global South such as Chile were coerced to test such reforms very early, too. Yet more recently, the pattern has also been repeated in Germany, Denmark, and Sweden, countries that were traditionally low-inequality countries. Thus, despite a few enduring exceptions such as France and Japan, in nearly all the OECD economies the wages of the 10% best-paid workers have risen relative to the wages of the 10% lowest paid. Relatedly, the Gini coefficient (named after an Italian statistician, Corrado Gini), which measures income inequality on a scale from 0 (when all incomes are identical) to 1 (when all income goes to just one person), averaged 0.29 in OECD countries in the 1980s. By 2010, though, it had increased by almost 10% to 0.316. It rose in 17 out of 22 surveyed OECD countries, including significant increases in Finland, Germany, Israel, Luxembourg, New Zealand, Sweden, and the United States. It is true that in a few middle-income countries such as Turkey, income inequality decreased in the period from the 1980s to 2011. But such exceptions reflect only modest declines from what were initially very high levels of inequality at the start of the period.

Meanwhile, in the world's big, fast-developing economies such as Brazil, India, and China, high inequality has either persisted or increased in the context of rapid global integration. Despite the break-neck growth in GDP per capita in these countries, the share of GDP going to the richest versus the poor has only increased. Special factors that are less apparent in rich countries – factors such as huge rural–urban divisions and stratified citizenship rights – are involved in explaining these patterns. In China, for example, rural migrant workers who do not have an urban household registration (known as an urban *hukou*) are effectively reduced to the level of non-citizens in Chinese cities, and this in turn allows for extreme forms of hyper-exploitation and urban inequality. Elsewhere, in countries such as South Africa, the legacies of formalized forms of racialized and geographical inequality also contribute to high income inequalities, too. To be sure, yet other countries such as Brazil made new strides in the 2000s to address such legacies of dispossession. But, this was under a government that also sought to temper neoliberal reforms with new social protections too, and more generally the broader pattern of increasing inequality in the context of deepening global economic integration still holds (Figure 4.2).

Three key developments help explain the growing in-country inequalities. The first has been the reduction in the number of people living in absolute poverty in the world's poor countries. This number has declined more slowly during the era of free trade, but has nevertheless continued to go down from 1237 million in 1990 to 1100 million in 2000. Most of these changes, however, are explained by developments in India and China, which together represent 38% of the world's population. Indeed, in China, the reduction in the absolute poverty rate was phenomenal during the 1990s,

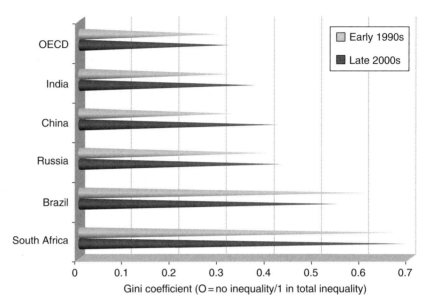

Figure 4.2   Increasing inequality measures from the early 1990s to late 2000s. *Source*: based on OECD data at http://dx.doi.org/10.1787/888932535432.

with a decline from 361 million to 204 million. Elsewhere in America, Canada, and Western Europe, as well as in Africa, Central Asia, Latin America, and the Caribbean, poverty has instead increased, in some cases quite significantly. This has happened at the same time as neoliberal reforms have removed social safety nets and pitted workers everywhere into an evermore desperate global competition for economic survival.

The second more profound and more general explanation for the increasing in-country inequalities shown in Figure 4.2 lies in the increase in the numbers of poor, unemployed, under-employed, and impoverished post-Fordist working classes around the world. Indeed, despite all the Globalization talk about providing jobs for the poor, global unemployment has actually increased over the last two decades to over 200 million in 2012. Unemployment of young people and recent school and university graduates has become an especially pressing global problem as a result of the financial crises that started to unfold in 2008. In 2011, 74.8 million people between the ages of 15 and 24 were unemployed, an increase of more than 4 million since 2007, creating a global youth unemployment rate of 12.7% (a full percentage point higher than the pre-crisis level). According to the UN's International Labor Organization, young people around the world are nearly three times as likely as adults to be unemployed.[13] To be sure, some of these developments clearly need to be explained in terms of particular historical global–local ties and feedback loops. The spread of HIV/AIDS in sub-Saharan Africa, for example, has further exacerbated the economic peripheralization and deprivation that enabled the original spread of the pandemic on the continent. In another way, in Southeast Asia and

Latin America, many of the problems for workers in the second half of the 1990s can be examined in terms of the knock-on effects of global **capital flight** and financial crisis. Elsewhere, in countries such as the United Kingdom and the United States, the increases in working class poverty in the 1980s and 1990s were related to deindustrialization and the roll-back of the welfare state. And elsewhere, most especially in Europe, the reverberations of financial crisis from 2008 onwards have led to economic depression, austerity, unemployment, and thus more economic depression.

There are clearly many complex and contextually contingent reasons for contemporary forms of working-class poverty. That said, a defining feature of post-Fordist development globally, and the third reason for the increasing in-country inequalities, is that the rising poverty has been accompanied by a parallel and equally dramatic rise in the wealth of managerial class elites, or, as Occupy and Indignado activists would have it, the global 1%. The ironic result of these tendencies is that, at the very same moment that the geographical division of labor has become transnationalized and at a time when the fate of workers in different countries is more and more closely tied together, class-based social division has increased *within particular nation-states*. National income inequalities have soared, and the classic class divide between ordinary workers on the one side and owners and managers on the other, the classic social division of labor under capitalism that Fordism had sought to subdue, has now returned with a vengeance.

The dramatic increases in managerial pay have been especially marked in countries such as the United States, the United Kingdom, Australia, New Zealand, and Canada, where the Fordist principles of class compromise were abandoned earliest. In these countries, income inequality has risen very significantly, with three-quarters of the workforce earning an ever-shrinking fraction of total income, while the take-home income of the top 5% of earners has increased by a staggering 1100%. In the United States, in 2011, the non-partisan Congressional Budget Office issued a report noting that between 1979 and 2007, the income of the top 1% of households rose by 275% while it rose by only 18% for the bottom 20% (see Figure 4.3).[14] By 2007, the top 1% received almost a quarter of all US income, the largest share of US national income going to the top 1% since the robber-baron days of the 1920s (Figure 4.4). However, in contrast to the pre-crash period of the 1920s, America's top 1% today is much more likely now to make its money through the activities of TNCs or investments in TNCs and, for the same reasons, is also much more likely to be globally mobile and concerned with managing capitalism globally. In this, it has led the way for other managerial elites in other countries, all of whom have increased their transnational mobility. The result is an emergent *transnational* business class whose members often have more in common with one another (whether it is MBA degrees, top-tier frequent-flier status, or favorite clubs in Hong Kong, Tokyo, and Frankfurt) than with their fellow national citizens. This is the class that has benefited most from neoliberal globalization. It largely consists of the executives, the majority shareholders, and the consultants of TNCs, the people with the biggest endowments of financial assets, the greatest access to information, and the most entrenched ties to the institutions of government, media, and elite education in the world's wealthiest

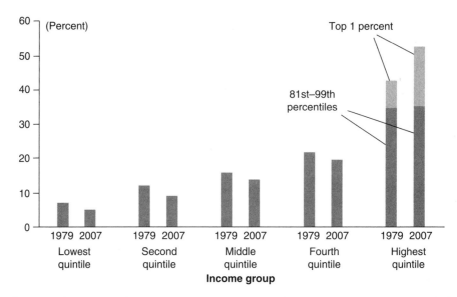

Figure 4.3   Shares of US income. *Source*: CBO, Trends in the Distribution of Household Income Between 1979 and 2007, http://www.cbo.gov/publication/42729.

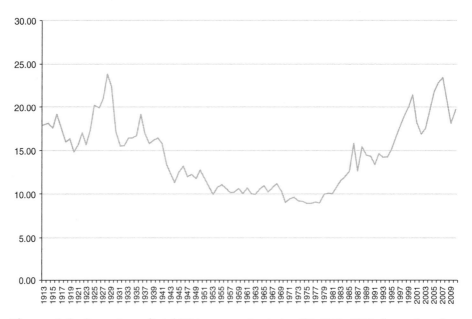

Figure 4.4   Percentage of total US income going to top 1%, 1913–2010. *Source*: based on data from Emmanuel Saez, http://elsa.berkeley.edu/~saez/TabFig2010.xls.

countries.) Often owning foreign bank accounts, foreign property, foreign investments, and foreign passports, and sometimes also making use of off-shore tax havens, it is a business class that has freed itself from many of the costs of national attachment.)

Clearly, though, the comfortable **cosmopolitanism** of today's transnational business class does not mean that it has altogether forsaken national symbols and refused national assistance. For example, the same American business elites who insistently demand cuts in national welfare and social security also pinned national flags to their business suits after 9/11 and did not hesitate to lobby for special support from the US government. Yet, despite such flag-waving, these American elites remain a key component of the transnational business class in so far as they share an overarching worldview with business elites from other countries. They see the world as a flat playing field, and as a class, the transnational business class has the jet-set perspective and mobility that makes this planar, friction-free "borderless world" seem real. Indeed, working together across borders to expand and entrench neoliberal reforms, it is a class that is also expanding the free-market economic constitution of the level playing field all over the world. And it this economic constitution, a constitution that replaces the old Fordist preoccupations with balancing national production and national consumption with a new focus on the rights and liberties of property owners and corporations, that the transnational business class is progressively entrenching globally through the new patchwork quilt of free-trade agreements (see Chapter 6). Neoliberals argue that this process of free-market entrenchment serves the interests of consumers, but this downplays the question of who exactly is able to play the role of a consumer on the global stage. While it is true that the transnational business class is constantly seeking to tear down trade barriers and widen access to consumers, it is also just as true that the consumers that most interest TNCs comprise wealthy elites and upwardly mobile middle classes. Other consumers, including the increasingly sidelined working classes of the wealthy countries, are faced by contrast with ever-diminishing choices as the welfare state becomes a so-called "workfare state," and access to privatized public services becomes more and more mediated by the market.

Compared with the hyper-mobile world that the transnational business class enjoys, working classes around the world have faced ever-bigger obstacles to mobility. Extreme poverty and low pay are the biggest obstacle for most, and over 900 million people worldwide are still earning *less than* $2 a day. Meanwhile, for those living in the wealthy nation-states, declining pay and declining public services have led to declining educational opportunities for the children of working class families, and all these problems have led to not only less intergenerational class mobility, but also less geographical mobility. Living in rustbelt cities like Sheffield in the United Kingdom, and Flint in the United States, they survive as impoverished and increasingly isolated populations. Their despair is hard to capture with statistics, but it is a form of economic isolation that has been powerfully documented in films like *The Full Monty* and *Roger and Me*. Meanwhile, for the unemployed and underemployed of poorer nation-states such as Mexico and Hungary, still more extreme levels of impoverishment have driven workers, including even child workers, to seek out work abroad. Many of these migrant laborers come from rural farming families who have been displaced from their traditional work by cheap foreign agricultural imports (often consisting of highly subsidized exports from the United States, Canada, and the EU). For such workers, moving is vital, but this does not mean that they enjoy the same comfortable mobility of transnational business elites. Indeed, even compared to the prior free trade era of the early twentieth century when poorer Europeans freely crossed borders and oceans looking for work, today's poor migrant workers face many more obstacles and dangers when they travel. Among the most vulnerable of all are the young women workers who, whether as seamstresses, machinists, maids, nannies, or prostitutes, frequently fill some of the most precarious and exploitative jobs in today's global economy. While the plight of these workers certainly represents a form of class subordination, it also clearly needs to be understood simultaneously in terms of gendered divisions of labor.

4.3.2   Changing pattern of gender division

Reports show that women globally still earn on average only about 60% of what men earn. The gender pay gap may vary widely from one country to another, but the fact that there is a gap by which men earn more than women remains stubbornly consistent (Figure 4.5). Women also receive less than 10% of financial credit and own less than 2% of the planet's land. Meanwhile, they are estimated to do over 75% of unpaid labor in the world while constituting about 70% of the

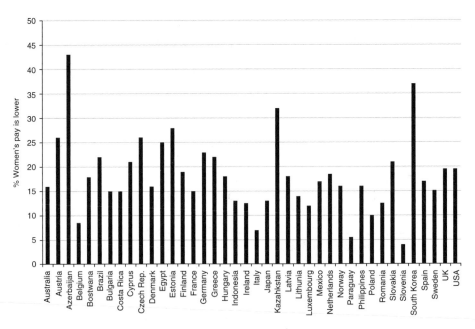

Figure 4.5   Gender pay gap in 40 countries. *Source*: data from 2012 ITUC report, Frozen in time: Gender pay gap unchanged for 10 years, available at http://www.ituc-csi.org/IMG/pdf/pay_gap_en_final.pdf.

global population living on less than $1 a day.[15] All these statistics point to a wide-spread form of sexism in most societies around the planet, a socially systemic rather than just interpersonal form of sexism that persistently and powerfully creates a gendered social division of labor. Globalization when promoted as a leveler by neoliberals is often said to promise the end of such systemic social bias against women. But has it? It is certainly true that millions of women workers around the world have found waged employment for the first time because of outsourcing and the rapid development of global assembly lines and global offices. Moreover, in wealthy countries such as the United States and the United Kingdom, women now make up about 45% of the paid labor force. Such paid work has provided real money and, for some women at least, a chance to raise their social status and escape either the domestic servitude of patriarchal families or the inse-curity of informal labor in work such as rag-picking and street vending. However, the same sexist social norms from which women have sought escape have never-theless continued to structure much of what they experience working in the new global economy. Women's paid jobs have therefore tended to be more insecure, more temporary, and, most significantly, less well paid than those that men have traditionally occupied in wealthy countries under Fordism. At the same time, though, because of global downward harmonization pressures, many men have increasingly begun to experience similar types of insecurity, unpredictability, and low pay to those experienced by women. Critics sometimes describe these dual trends as the "feminization of labor," but, rather than use this abstract term which confuses two meanings of feminization – the first meaning more women entering the labor force, and the second meaning more female *and* male workers becoming poorly paid and insecure – we will here instead focus simply on how the changing gendered division of labor is affecting women.

To begin with, it is not as if the unpaid work that women have traditionally done has suddenly disappeared. Looking after children, cooking food, cleaning houses, washing clothes, and caring for the elderly all continue to be treated in most societies around the world as women's work. Unless it is turned into paid work, it is work that is seen as secondary and trivial compared to waged labor. It nevertheless remains vital to everyone's daily life everywhere and, as such, a crucial but often unnoticed underpinning of economic globalization. Moreover, even though women have entered the ranks of the waged workforce in huge numbers over the last two decades, they continue to be expected to accept this unpaid work as their particular social responsibility. Unpaid domestic labor has thus effectively become a *second shift* for the world's working women: a second shift that contributes an estimated $11 trillion annually to the global economy but a second shift that is systematically devalued because it is assumed to be women's natural duty.

Assumptions about a naturally gendered social division of labor run deep despite the fact that they are socially reproduced. They are inculcated in both girls and boys from a young age, and reinforced by social institutions ranging from families to schools to organized religions. They are also commonly understood by individu-als and governments alike as a practical matter of economic common sense. As a result, sexist social divisions of labor remain remarkably resistant to change. Indeed, even wealthy women in professional positions in wealthy countries, even women who might be said to be members of the new transnational business class, still have to deal with dominant assumptions (including sometimes their own) that enforce the second shift and other gendered work roles. If such women find freedom through hiring nannies and cleaners, it is still quite likely that their personal escape rests on the assignment of the low-status work to other women from less privileged backgrounds. Globalization has certainly increased the availability of such women – not least of all by transforming rural economies and displacing subsistence farmers in poor countries. However, increased world trade and economic interdependency have not fundamentally altered the traditional gendering of the social division of labor. Thus, despite the occasional announcement of the arrival of the so-called "New Man" (normally by marketing executives launching new product lines such as recipe books for men), we have not seen millions of men rushing into the unpaid menial work roles traditionally assigned to women. Meanwhile, neoliberal reforms that have cut back state spending on professional childcare, nursing, and welfare have only increased the amount of unpaid work that needs doing. This means that the social costs of neoliberal globalization have also tended to fall disproportionately on women.

When women do actually enter waged work, it is by no means an escape into a gender-neutral oasis. Instead, paid labor is itself very often assigned on the basis of highly gendered assumptions about what work is appropriate for women and men. The so-called "glass ceilings" at the top of most TNCs mean that the majority of the best-paying jobs opened up by increasing global economic interdependency – the top jobs in management, finance, and high-technology – tend to remain closed off to women. Meanwhile, business managers recruiting workers for assembly work in the electronics, toy, and textiles sectors have tended to seek out female recruits on the basis of completely unscientific and socially constructed ideas about women being more nimble and more flexible. Researchers studying how gendered divisions of labor work in practice have also shown that it is not just the division of work assignments and pay rates that are gendered, but also the whole approach to disciplining workers. Managers commonly assume in this regard that women workers will be more pliant and docile. Whether it is temp agencies that boast about how their female counselors help train and maintain more "flexible" female temps, or whether it is an export processing zone advertising the adaptability and discipline of its women workers, the recurring idea is that women workers are much more likely to accommodate the changing demands of TNCs without resistance.

While such sexist assumptions about political docility have often been proved wrong in practice (Thai women, for example, have in fact tended to be more militant workplace organizers than Thai men), the practices of disciplining workers on the basis of traditional gendered stereotypes persist. One reason why is that female workers are frequently coded as dutiful daughters. In her research in Dongguan, China, for example, the feminist geographer, Melissa Wright, found that the male managers related to their female workforce through distinctly patriarchal attitudes:

viewing the young women as daughters and themselves as grown-up fathers. "We have naive girls," explained one manager to Wright. "Here we are like their parents. They have to obey us. We will do what is right for them and right for us."[16] In Wright's study, the managers were putting themselves in the place of the real fathers that the women workers had left behind when they traveled from faraway parts of rural China to find work. In other contexts, the real fathers are closer by, and patriarchal assumptions work to structure women's work lives still more powerfully. Another feminist geographer, Rachel Silvey, for example, found that in an Indonesian community on Java, assumptions about family duty helped in this way to discipline women workers and strongly curtail their activism. A 22-year-old called Sri who was living with her parents reported to Silvey that: "My parents wouldn't like it if I joined in strikes. We have to stick together and keep Sunda orderly."[17] In this case, just as in Wright's study, we therefore see a woman worker being disciplined by social conventions defining what it means to be a dutiful daughter.

Both Silvey and Wright emphasize that while patriarchal assumptions about women's roles are commonly repeated in different countries, the way in which gendered divisions of labor actually develop remains strongly shaped by local contexts. While young, single women appear to be the preferred factory labor force for low-wage assembly work in China, for example, factory employers in export processing zones in the Philippines have been found to express a greater interest in recruiting older, married women. Such findings highlight how we must be careful to avoid making the same stereotyping assumptions as managers themselves typically make. What counts as "femininity" is socially constructed, just as what counts as "flexible" is socially constructed. It is also social conventions that link ideals about "femininity" and "flexibility" in particular ways in particular places. Whether they are old or young, women workers are not destined by nature to be flexible. They can be disciplined by social conventions to be more pliant, but, just like men, given the right context they can obviously be agents of workplace activism and resistance. That said, it also needs to be remembered that women's agency worldwide is repeatedly undermined by the systemic ties between sexist assumptions and physical practices of sexual subordination directed at women's bodies. Whether it is the Mexican assembly plant workers who are forced to take birth-control pills and are fired if they become pregnant, or whether it is the 120 000 women who are trafficked each year to work in the global sex industry, women's bodies repeatedly become the focus of domineering and demeaning social forces that most men simply do not experience.

The example of the transnational movement of women in the sex industry introduces another way in which globalization has mobilized gendered divisions of labor. In addition to drawing women into factories and offices in their own countries, increasing global integration has also led to a phenomenal rise in the number of women going abroad to find work. About half of the world's 120 million migrants are now believed to be women, and whether they work as prostitutes, or as nannies, nurses, and cleaners, the gendering of the division of labor has affected their global experiences in profound ways. One very significant result has been the creation of global "care chains" that need to be considered as another global labor market interdependency alongside all the competitive cost-cutting dynamics associated with downward harmonization.[18] Two important global care chains – the work of foreign nannies and the work of foreign nurses – make this interdependency and its unequal impacts on donor and recipient countries especially clear.

Studies show that when parents in wealthy countries employ nannies from poorer countries, it creates a whole cascade of effects down the gendered chain of care.[19] The nannies who come from countries such as the Philippines have usually chosen to become transnational care-workers because they need to make money for their own families. They nevertheless have to leave behind these families (including, quite often, their young children) in order to begin earning the US dollars, Canadian dollars, Hong Kong dollars, Singapore dollars, and British pounds that they will send back to the Philippines. This means in turn that nannies either have to ask elderly relatives to care for their own children or pay for a local nanny using their foreign earnings. That local nanny might in turn rely on one of her older children – normally the eldest girl – to look after her other children. In such ways, the hiring decisions made by relatively wealthy families in recipient countries – decisions that themselves reflect a new gendered division of labor with women entering the paid workforce – create worldwide ties that have implications for the gendering of labor all the way back in the families of the local nannies used to replace long-distance nannies in the donor countries. Such care chains not only create far-reaching transnational interdependencies but also clearly involve huge inequalities, and it is the nannies at the center of the chains that feel this inequality most painfully. The following testimonial from a Filipino nanny working in Italy underlines how the transnational care chain can also in this way involve a personal chain of pain.

> When the girl that I take care of calls her mother "Mama," my heart jumps all the time because my children also call me "Mama." . . . The work that I do here is done for my family, but the problem is they are not close to me but are far away in the Philippines. If I had wings, I would fly home to my children. Just for a moment, to see my children and take care of their needs, help them, then fly back over here to continue my work.[20]

With this poignant quotation, we hear close-up the voice of someone in the heart – in some senses, the broken heart – of the global care chain. The quotation comes from the research of Rhacel Parreñas, who has followed up her work on nannies with further studies of the knock-on impacts on their families.[21] Such families, Parreñas shows, face other big challenges, too: including the risks of overburdening extended kin networks and the great strains on marriages. But most of all, there remains the disturbing separation of nannies from their own children, a separation made all the more difficult to deal with emotionally because of the ways in which nannies are constantly having to give loving care to the children of their employers. Thus, while there is much academic and journalistic attention paid to landscapes where nannies congregate in London, Hong Kong, and Singapore, and while there is much parental guidance literature on how to pick, control, and monitor nannies most effectively, wealthy western consumers of nannies' labor too often overlook what is happening at the other end of the care chain and how this other end – cut off by a complex transnational gendered division of labor – remains physically distant from nannies themselves.

Remembering the ways in which inequality shapes interdependency also provides a useful analytical approach for exploring the care chains in which foreign nurses work. Their labor outside the home is generally better paid and more secure than that of nannies, but it remains gendered by assumptions that care-work is women's work. These assumptions have in fact played a large role in creating widespread nursing shortages in wealthy countries as more and more women have sought better-paid, higher-status work in other sectors. It is these shortages that have in turn driven nursing recruitment agencies to look more and more to foreign nurses to fill their needs, and the result has been a phenomenal rise in the transnational flows of female nursing labor into wealthy countries. Australia, for example, received 11 757 foreign nurses between 1995 and 2000. Over the same period, the US Immigration and Naturalization Service reported more than 10 000 foreign nurses were admitted to the United States on H-1A visas. And still more stunningly, in the 4-year period between 1998 and 2002, the United Kingdom admitted 26 286 foreign nurses.[22] The United Kingdom, the United States, and Australia have some of the highest nurse-per-capita ratios in the world. By contrast, the so-called "donor" countries from which they are pulling in many of the foreign nurses – including the Philippines, India, South Africa, and Zimbabwe – are countries that have very low nurse-per-capita ratios. Thus, while the United States, for example, has about 1000 nurses per 100 000 people, India has only 45 per 100 000. Herein lies the inequality amidst the interdependency of nursing care.

It should be noted that some healthcare workers are also recruited to move between the rich countries. Australian and British nurses, for instance, are often attracted by the higher pay offered to technically sophisticated nursing staff in private US hospitals and care homes. However, these movements have only further increased the need in the United Kingdom and Australia for well-trained nurses from the Philippines, India, and South Africa. Already faced with overwhelming healthcare crises caused by the spread of HIV/AIDS and diverse political and economic upheavals, these are countries that can ill afford to lose their best-trained nurses. Not only do they lose the technical skills that they have invested sparse public funds in developing, but also they often lose tremendous amounts of local knowledge and experience when the nurses leave. Sometimes the results are devastating, and healthcare managers in both the Philippines and South Africa have spoken about the looming collapse of their domestic hospital systems as a result of what they criticize as the "poaching" of their nurses.[23] It is true that foreign nurses learn new skills in their transnational jobs, and it is also true that they sometimes send back significant remittances (monies sent back to relatives in their home countries). However, because their foreign jobs are insecure, because they tend to be at the bottom of the pay scales and professional development ladders in the rich countries, and because the nurses frequently end up staying in the recipient countries, the reverse flow of benefits to the donor countries remains limited and unreliable (see Chapter 9). Meanwhile, the racist insults foreign nurses sometimes face on the job, and the testing for HIV and tuberculosis imposed by recipient country governments, can create high personal costs that run counter to the individualized economic benefits of transnational nursing.

4.3.3   Changing patterns of racial division

Just as Filipino nannies and South African nurses sometimes fall prey to racist treatment in recipient countries, so too do many male migrant workers. Racism, just like sexism, remains in this way a persistent and pervasive force structuring the global division of labor. Under slavery and European imperialism, of course, racist arguments were used to legitimate much starker and more brutal divisions of labor globally. The key commodities of early rounds of economic globalization in the sixteenth, seventeenth, eighteenth, and nineteenth centuries – gold, sugar, cotton, and rubber – were thus all produced by workers who were captured and controlled by white men of property who deployed ideologies about racial inferiority to justify their use of African slaves, and Indian and Chinese coolie laborers. Today it is still largely white men of property who are in the positions of authority. They represent over 95% of the managers of the world's largest 500 TNCs. However, the way in which racial and ethnic ideas are mobilized to organize and position other workers has become much more complex. It is mediated by the ethnically organized creation of particular economic sectors and by the effects of affirmative action policies, as well as by the racist exclusions enforced by labor market gatekeepers. The results vary greatly from country to country, and indeed from city to city, depending on particular histories of migration, marginalization, ethnic organization, and resistance. Nevertheless, there can be no doubt that race and ethnicity still deeply structure today's divisions of labor. Californian farmworkers, New York city cab drivers, London newsagents, and maids in the middle east, all have predictable ethnic characteristics, and research into how their labor is mobilized requires a sensitivity to the ethnic ties as well as the ethnic exclusions that lead Mexicans to Californian fields, Sikhs to New York taxis, Bangladeshis to British city corner stores, and Indonesians, Indians, and Pakistanis to private Saudi Arabian homes.

More generally, racism continues to structure labor politics in many different countries. During the debates over **NAFTA** in the United States in the early 1990s, for example, the conservative commentator Patrick Buchanan was able to drum up considerable working-class support for his campaign against the free-trade agreement by implying that Mexicans were stealing the jobs of white Americans. "Heh José!" he shouted to cheering crowds of white men, "go away!" Another demagogic contributor to this "debate"-turned-shouting-match, Ross Perot, refrained from directly racist remarks but nevertheless also tended to dehumanize Mexican workers when he waxed lyrical about the "giant sucking sound" of American jobs heading south. Using ethnic stereotypes about Mexican untrustworthiness, he also suggested that the US government may well have been swindled by Mexican negotiators. As free trade and processes of outsourcing and deindustrialization continue to transform the economies of North America and Western Europe, and as white workers in these countries continue to lose blue-collar jobs, the possibilities for this sort of racialized posturing about foreign and migrant workers remain all too apparent. Many unions that represent ordinary workers and which developed most successfully under Fordism initially did little to deal with this type of international inter-worker rivalry. However, after over two decades of transformation and struggle, these same unions have now begun to develop more successfully the only obvious alternative to national chauvinism and its allied, albeit often implicit, forms of racism. This alternative strategy is transnational union solidarity: the sort of internationalist strategy that has always been an official part of union rhetoric, but a strategy, too, which in many ways was suppressed under regimes of nationally organized Fordism. It is to the re-emergence of this strategy and its various formations that we now turn.

4.4 Transnational Responses of Organized Labor

"Workers of all countries, unite!"[24] Ever since the famous call for global worker solidarity at the end of *The Communist Manifesto*, left-wing unions have appealed for transnational collaboration among workers as a way of negotiating more effectively in and with the transnational networks of global capitalism. While the rhetoric has always continued, the actual organizational practices of workers in unions have nonetheless varied greatly from extremely open transnational outlooks to much more closed nationalist and localist orientations. Notably, the mid-twentieth century years of Fordism tended to make single-country union negotiation strategies such as national wage-bargaining much more significant. These were years when unions won other important victories for workers on a national basis: establishing national pensions, national unemployment benefits, national public holidays, and national health and safety rights in the workplace. However, now that the commodity chains of globalization have brought transnational worker interdependencies to the fore again, transnational worker solidarity has also returned as an important practical objective of organized labor.

We can chart the slow collapse of the national-based union organizing model by looking at the American example. During the Fordist period, the main umbrella organization for US unions, the **AFL-CIO**, was notably nationalist, its foreign engagements mainly shaped by the anti-communist American priorities of the Cold War. At the turn of the new millennium, however, its incoming leader, John Sweeney, made an internationalist case for a change in strategy: "the global economy that corporations have forged," he said "can only be tamed by the international solidarity of working families everywhere."[25] Thus, while Marx and Engels had said that workers of the world had "nothing to lose but their chains," it is today the chains of downward harmonization that are raising consciousness among unions that nationally focused strategies alone will not win them the world. Once they see how their fate is linked to the fate of workers elsewhere, unions also see quite clearly the practical need for transnational solidarity. Within the broader context of downward harmonization, two particular sorts of challenges have come to the forefront. The first has been the way in which national governments have adopted neoliberalism and abandoned the national protections that were won by workers in the Fordist period; and the second has been the way in which individual firms have used transnational mobility (or just the threat of such mobility) to extract new concessions from workers including lower pay, longer work hours, and fewer benefits. Faced with these challenges, unions have begun to develop a wide range of transnational responses: some involving the formation and revitalization of international union organizations, others involving more grassroots union-to-union solidarity efforts by individual activists in different countries, and yet others including new forms of collaboration with non-union organizers in global social justice movements such as the World Social Forum.[26]

At the global scale, there are three main institutions that serve to mediate transnational worker interests and union organizing. First, there is the ILO, the International Labor Organization, which is a Geneva-based agency of the United Nations. While it is not a union organization itself, it works to formulate global conventions about labor rights (including conventions against child labor, and conventions protecting the right of workers to unionize) and operates as a mediator between business, governments, and unions in debates over global governance. Second is ICFTU, the International Confederation of Free Trade Unions, which is a Brussels-based body that seeks to facilitate the collaboration of national union confederations on a global scale. And third are the **Global Union Federations** that until quite recently were known as "International Trade Secretariats." These were the original pioneers of international cooperation among individual unions in particular economic sectors, and, while they started as trade guilds in the late nineteenth century, they have been redeveloped today as global unions concerned with worker rights in particular economic sectors. ICEM, for example, the International Federation of Chemical, Energy, Mine and General Workers' Union, is concerned with workers in the energy, chemical, and mining industries; PSI (Public Services International) with government and other workers in the public sector around the world; UNI (Union Network International) with workers in private service sector industries; and so on.

One way in which the Global Union Federations, ICFTU, and the ILO effectively come together at a global scale is through campaigns targeted against obvious breaches of ILO labor rights conventions. Whether it is the ban on worker-organized unions in China, the use of child labor in Pakistan, or the use of forced labor in Burma, these campaigns raise public awareness and can lead towards international political efforts at forcing change. It should be noted, however, that the ILO has very little enforcement capacity, and it is in this context that ICFTU and the Global Union Federations have turned to other more powerful institutions of global governance such as the **World Bank**, the **IMF**, and the **WTO** as vehicles through which worker rights can be advanced. ICFTU, for example, has an ongoing campaign to make the ILO's Declaration on Rights at Work a part of new trade agreements negotiated through the WTO. The insertion of a workers' rights charter based on the ILO Declaration would ideally make it possible for workers to form unions in all the countries that sign on to the trade agreements. This in turn would provide the bite of potential trade sanctions to the Declaration, enabling it to become more than just a fine-sounding statement of principles. In a similar way, the global union federation of Building and Wood Workers (IFBWW) has sought to make the World Bank promote and protect workers' rights through its contract-bidding process. The goal is to incorporate the protections of the eight ILO fundamental conventions (No.s 87 and 98 on freedom of association and the right to bargain collectively, No.s 29 and 105 on the abolition of forced labor, No.s 100 and 111 on the prevention of discrimination in employment and equal pay for work of equal value, and No.s 138 and 182 on child labor) in loan agreements created by the World Bank. This would make it possible to disqualify anti-union and anti-worker bidders from the bidding process while expanding the protections of basic worker rights to all contractors and subcontractors receiving World Bank project funding. More generally, the aim of these sorts of global campaigns is to develop what ICFTU and the Global Union Federations see as the best antidote to downward harmonization, namely, the upward harmonization of labor rights, pay, and protection on a global scale.[27]

One of the attractions of upward harmonization is that it offers an alternative inclusive approach to the more exclusive nationalist approaches that many unions developed during the Fordist era. Instead of viewing low-wage workers in foreign countries as competitors, the goal is therefore to see them more as co-workers in global assembly lines and global offices. Based on this more collaborative view, global union federations have also sought to create transnational unions alliances and so-called "framework agreements" relating to *all* the transnational operations and workers of particular TNCs. The Union Network International (UNI), for example, has developed a number of union alliances for the global employees of TNCs such as SBC/Ameritech, Cable & Wireless, Telefónica, Barclays Bank and the Quebecor Group. The alliances run websites and share information about company developments around the world, collaborate in joint actions, participate in the annual stockholders meetings, and work to create framework agreements with the TNCs so that workers in any part of the global alliance are guaranteed the same rights and resources. UNI aims in this way to show companies like Ameritech that wherever they move operations in the world, the union will be there to help local workers stand up for their rights. Sometimes, these sorts of coordinated union actions can take the more traditional form of the strike, but with the difference that strikes now often have to be planned and implemented on a global scale in order to be successful.

One particularly impressive example of such a coordinated joint strike action by global workers was the late 1990s campaign by the ITF, the global union federation of transportation workers in support of Australian dockworkers. The local

Australian stevedore company, in collaboration with the neoliberal Australian government, had wanted to break the union by dismissing all employees who were union members and employing cheaper and unprotected non-union laborers. They had even planned to send some serving Australian soldiers to the United Arab Emirates (where unions are banned) to train to become replacement dock-workers in the case of a strike. Successfully fighting a legal action in London against its involvement, the ITF sent funds to support the dismissed workers, and also successfully lobbied the United Arab Emirates government to revoke the visas of the Australian soldiers. Most impressively, it coordinated with affiliated unions in ports around the world to refuse unloading services to ships loaded with non-union labor in Australia. Thus, when the *Columbus Canada* arrived in the port of Los Angeles, workers from the International Longshore workers Union (ILWU) refused to unload it, forcing the ship to return with its cargo (including approximately 60 containers of meat and dairy products) to Australia. Similarly, the *CGM Gaugin* was diverted from Bombay after an ITF action by workers there, and the *Endeavor* met with hundreds of protesting dockworkers in Japan. Faced with this coordinated global resistance, the Australian employers ultimately had to back down. They reinstated dismissed workers and ended up renewing union contracts for all their Australian employees. It was a significant victory for the ITF and a symbol of what global workers can achieve through coordinated collaborative action.

In addition to the influence and actions of the ILO, ICFTU, and the global union federations, there are many other factors that shape the direction and type of transnational union activities. Traditions of union leadership, for instance, play a key role. Some union leaders, like those at the helm of the ILWU in America, have longstanding traditions of internationalism that go back decades. Others have only become reluctantly involved in transnational actions for the purpose of protecting their own domestic interests.[28] However, even localist actions by nationalist unions can have transnational impacts because of yet another important factor, namely, the ways in which the global networks of TNCs can make them more rather than less vulnerable to union action. In other words, it is not always necessary to organize globally the way the ITF did because the interdependency of the global network of a TNC gives particular unions in particular places extraordinary leverage. For example, in 1998, a strike by United Auto Workers at just two plants in Flint Michigan over local work issues brought GM's global "just in time" sourcing system to a spectacular halt. The giant car company was forced to close or severely cut back work at 27 of its 29 North American assembly plants and at 117 components plants in the United States, Canada, Mexico, and Singapore. As a result, the company lost production of half a million vehicles and ended with a loss of $2.3 billion. One lesson for labor from the Flint strike is therefore that the globalization of commodity chains may actually lead to increased union strength. With equal success, other unions have also exploited the links in global commodity chains by politicizing consumption sites as well as production sites. For example, the American Union of Needletrades, Industrial and Textiles Employees (UNITE) has developed a "Stop Sweatshops Campaign" designed to get consumers to put pressure on the big shops who set prices within the industry. This kind of consumer activism provides not only a way of leveraging union strength over long distances but also a strategy through which unions can collaborate with non-union activists from non-governmental organizations (NGOs) that are concerned about social justice for workers. Such collaboration is not always simple, and unions tend to have serious concerns about initiatives such as "social labeling" and "social auditing" when they do not have worker and union involvement. Nevertheless, some labeling strategies such as that developed in the United States by the student-initiated Workers Rights Consortium do insist on just such involvement and therefore provide another opportunity for transnationalizing union struggles for worker justice.

If the extensive economic geographies of transnational commodity chains are an important influence on union transnationalism, so, too, are the political geographies of transnational governance (see Chapter 7). Most notably, different regional free-trade regimes tend to lead to different kinds of union strategies. In the European Union (**EU**), for instance, the development of pan-European legislation has enabled labor parties and union groups to push for the establishment of new worker rights at a continental level. Most significant in this context has been the pan-European law known as the European Works Council Directive that, since 1994, has required any company with more than 1000 workers in the EU and with over 150 in at least two member countries to establish a European Work Council. Such councils allow employees of the same TNC from different countries to come together with each other as well as with the management of the company on a regular basis. Language difficulties and different traditions of industrial relations can create obstacles, and the Works Councils are also often used by TNCs as a way of diffusing worker agitation, but for many union activists the Works Councils also offer a novel chance to develop real relations of transnational solidarity with co-workers from other countries.[29] In the context of North American free trade, by contrast, **NAFTA** provides for no such firm level collaboration opportunities between workers. Instead, the North American Agreement on Labor Cooperation (NAALC) – negotiated by the Clinton administration as a side-agreement in its last minute bid to win Democratic support for NAFTA in the US Congress – has provided only a procedural complaints mechanism that workers and unions can use to publicize infractions of nationally defined worker rights.[30] Thus, while American unions such as the United Electrical Radio and Machine Workers (UE) appealed through the NAALC mechanisms to contest labor rights infractions in Mexico, they only met with obstacles and inaction because of the toothless nature of the side agreement. For example, in the UE case brought against a Honeywell plant in Chihuahua, the US authorities concluded that, while the timing of dismissals at the plant coincided with an independent union's organizing drive, it could not recommend any remedies. A subsequent UE appeal about the violation of the organizing rights of another independent Mexican union led to an even more serious disappointment. The union in question, called "October 6," had attempted to organize workers at the Han Young plant in Tijuana. The US government found the claims about rights violations to be justified but only saw fit to respond by coordinating with the Mexican authorities to arrange a seminar near the plant to educate workers about their rights under Mexican law. Even this feeble response turned to failure when, after protesting their rights at this seminar, members of the October 6 union were physically brutalized in front of the Mexican social welfare secretary and the US government representative by men from the Mexican government's own union. The UE letter to US labor secretary, Alexis Herman, complained about this disastrous outcome in the following terms:

> It is the height of irony, shame and tragedy that workers were permitted to be physically beaten at a seminar which purported to educate them about their rights as workers. The fact that nothing was done to protect these workers highlights both the inadequacy of NAFTA and the NAALC and indicates a lack of political will to protect workers' rights.[31]

It is worth noting examples of the ongoing challenges facing transnational union organizing because all too often, scholarship on labor and globalization ends with upbeat accounts of conditions steadily improving. In reality, the challenges for workers remain enormous, and, as in the Han Young case, they include the obstacles created by nationalist unions fighting transnational activism. More generally, the changing divisions of labor we have explored in this chapter – the development of global assembly lines and global offices, and the transnationalization of new gendered and racialized divisions of labor – mean that it continues to be easier to talk about the workers of the world uniting as opposed to making the rhetoric into reality. Nevertheless, because they are at the cutting edge of economic globalization, workers and their unions also continue to be at the leading edge of resistance to neoliberalism.[32] Whether or not one actually supports union organization efforts, it is therefore possible to learn from them in at least three ways. First, transnational union solidarity underlines again that neoliberalism is not uncontested and that other forms of globalization are imaginable and possible. Second, and more practically, the actual educational efforts of unions to teach workers about their interdependencies with other "co-workers" on other sides of the planet also provide everyone else who is interested in globalization with valuable insider information on the emerging forms of economic interdependency. And third, union struggles for worker rights also remind us that behind all the economic flows in our world, and behind all the abstract talk of new investments leading to new profits, remains the labor of individual human beings. As we move forward in the next chapter to examine the global flows of money, it will remain critical to keep this vital human role in mind.

Student Exercises

Group:

Research where your university's sportswear is made, by who, and for what pay. This may sound impossibly daunting, but for American students there is a useful Internet research resource provided by the Workers Rights Consortium at http://www.workersrights.org/search/. This site enables searches on the companies, countries, and factories that source sportswear to colleges and universities who are members of the consortium. It provides you with information about the particular types of commodities made in particular factories as well as giving the name, phone number, and even sometimes email address of someone you can contact to find out about the conditions of work in a particular factory. As a result, this project can be done in five easy steps:

1. Working as a group, allocate five factories for each group member to contact. Use the linguistic skills of your group as best as possible by allocating Chinese speakers to research Chinese factories, Spanish speakers to research Latin American factories, and so on.
2. Each group member should try to discover pay rates in the factory, the health and safety conditions, and the average length of time workers normally stay at the factory on both a daily and yearly basis.
3. When the group comes back together, you should be able to create a map of the world showing where most of the sportswear comes from and what conditions are like in the factories in question.
4. If any of the factories that supply your university or college have been made subject to a WRC complaints investigation, summarize the factual findings, recommendations, and results of the investigation.
5. If your university or college is not part of the consortium, the group's research project should instead be focused on asking the university administration why they have not done so.

Individual:

In its 1995 *Workers in an Integrating World* development report, the World Bank offered a portrait of three workers' lives. At first glance, the three anecdotes triangulate a compelling portrait of how the global economy affects labor. However, the underlying narrative of the three examples also presents an exceedingly optimistic argument about global development trends. Read the anecdotes and reflect on what the personal stories might be leaving out.

> "Joe lives in a small town in southern Texas. His old job as an accounts clerk in a textile firm . . . was not very secure. He earned $50 a day, but promises of a promotion never came through, and the firm eventually went out of business as cheap imports from Mexico forced textile prices down. Joe went back to college to study business administration and was recently hired by one of the new banks in the area. He enjoys

a comfortable living even after making the monthly payments on his government subsidized student loan.

Maria recently moved from her central Mexican village and now works in a US owned firm in Mexico's maquiladora sector. Her husband Juan runs a small car uphol-stery business and sometimes crosses the border during the harvest season to work illegally on farms in California. Maria, Juan, and their son have improved their stand-ard of living since moving out of subsistence agriculture, but Maria's wage has not increased in years: she still earns about $10 a day. . . .

Xiao Zhi is an industrial worker in Shenzhen, a Special Economic Zone in China. After three difficult years on the road as part of China's floating population, fleeing the poverty of nearby Sizhuan province, he has finally settled with a new firm from Hong Kong that produces garments for the US market. He can now afford more than a bowl of rice for his daily meal. He makes $2 a day and is hopeful for the future."[33]

Having reflected on what is missing from these anecdotes, go to the Global Union Federations website (http://www.global-unions.org/) and use whatever material you can find about real workers and their struggles to write three other anecdotes about other possible worker experiences in today's global economy.

Notes

1   Joseph Kahn, "Workers Face Uphill Battle on Road to Globalization," *International Herald Tribune* January 27 (2004).

2   Nidhi Kumar and Nidhi Verghese, "Money for Nothing and Calls for Free," from *Corporate Watch* February 17 (2004), http://www.globalpolicy.org/globaliz/special/2004/0217 callcenters.htm.

3   Danny Vincent, "China Used Prisoners in Lucrative Internet Gaming Work," *The Guardian* 25 May (2011), http://www.guardian.co.uk/world/2011/may/25/china-prisoners-internet-gaming-scam.

4   For a fascinating discussion of the entrance of Chinese workers into the global labor market, see Giovanni Arrighi, *Adam Smith in Beijing: Lineages of the Twenty-First Century* (New York: Verso, 2007).

5   Matt Richtel, "Hooked on Gadgets, and Paying a Mental Price," *New York Times*, June 7 (2010) A1; and, David Barboza, "After Suicides, Scrutiny of China's Grim Factories," *New York Times* (2010): A1. Later on in 2010, Foxconn, the Chinese company under most criticism for the suicides, responded to the related worker unrest with a mix of higher wages for workers in coastal cities, and a new push to relocate its operations to cities with cheaper labor in the interior of China. Kathrin Hille, "Factory of the World Does Rethink As Workers Use the Strike Weapon," *Financial Times*, Oct 27 (2010), *China supplement* 3. The same article noted in closing that the higher wages being paid to Foxconn workers such as Ms Liu in Shenzhen would not have much impact on the prices paid at the other end of the commodity chain. "For consumers of the products she helps make–electronics gadgets including iPhones, game consoles, and personal computers – the impact is limited, as Chinese labour continues to account for a fraction of the final retail price. Last year, wage costs amounted to just 3.5 per cent of company revenues in the electronics industry, according to Credit Suisse."

6   *Business Week*, "At the New Global Job Shift: the Next Round of Globalization Is Sending Upscale Jobs Offshore," *Business Week*, February 3 (2003): 50.

7   Quoted in The International Labor Organization's report, *The World Commission on the Social Dimension of Globalization* (ILO: Geneva, 2004), 13.

8   Jasper Becker, "The Hidden Downside of Santa's Little Helpers," *The Irish Times*, December 21 (2002).

9   Friedrich Engels, *The Condition of the Working Class in England* (New York: Macmillan, 1958);Upton Sinclair, *The Jungle* (New York: Infobase Pub, 2010); Carla Freeman, *High Tech and High Heels in the Global Economy: Women, Work and Pink-Collar Identities in the Caribbean* (Durham, NC: Duke University Press, 2000); Aihwa Ong, *Spirits of Resistance and Capitalist Discipline: Factory Women in Malaysia* (Albany: State University of New York Press, 1987); and Melissa W. Wright, *Disposable Women and Other Myths of Global Capitalism* (New York: Routledge, 2006).

10 Adam Smith, *An Inquiry into the Nature and Causes of the Wealth of Nations* (Oxford: Clarendon Press, 1976), 5.

11 The initial use of the phrase was in Folker Fröbel, Jürgen Heinrichs, and Otto Kreye, *The New International Division of Labour: Structural Unemployment in Industrialized Countries and Industrialization in Developing Countries* (Cambridge: Cambridge University Press, 1980).

12 These data and the subsequent facts about global inequality trends are all taken from the 2011 OECD report, *Divided We Stand: Why Inequality Keeps Rising*, OECD 2011 http://www.oecd.org/document/51/0,3746,en_2649_33933_49147827_1_1_1_1,00.html.

13 ILO, *Global Employment Trends 2012: Preventing a Deeper Jobs Crisis*, http://www.ilo.org/global/publications/books/global-employment-trends/WCMS_171571/lang--nl/index.htm See also Michael Denning, "Wageless life," *New Left Review* 66 (2010): 79–97.

14 CBO, *Trends in the Distribution of Household Income Between 1979 and 2007*, http://www.cbo.gov/publication/42729.

15 See ILO, *Global Employment Trends for Women*, Geneva: ILO, 2004, http://www.ilo.org/public/english/employment/strat/global.htm; and, UNDP, *Human Development Report* (New York: United Nations, 1995).

16 Melissa W. Wright, "Factory Daughters and Chinese Modernity: a Case from Dongguan," *Geoforum* 34 (2003): 291–301, 296.

17 Rachel Silvey, "Spaces of Protest: Gendered Migration, Social Networks, and Labor Activism in West Java, Indonesia," *Political Geography* 22 (2003): 129–55, 147.

18 A useful set of studies of the "global women" involved in this global care chain are included in *Global Woman: Nannies, Maids, and Sex Workers in the New Economy*, eds Barbara Ehrenreich and Arlie Russell Hochschild (New York: Metropolitan Books, 2003).

19 Arlie Russell Hochschild, "The Nanny Chain," *The American Prospect January 3*, 11, no. 4 (2000): 32–39.

20 Quoted in Rhacel Salazar Parrenas, "Mothering from a distance: emotions, gender, and intergenerational relations in Filipino transnational families," *Feminist Studies* 27, no. 2 (2001): 361–91.

21 Rhacel Parrenàs, *Servants of Globalization: Women, Migration and Domestic Work* (Stanford, CA: Stanford University Press, 2001).

22 Donna Kline, "Push and Pull Factors in International Nurse Migration," *Journal of Nursing Scholarship* 35, no. 2 (2003): 107–12.

23   Mark Rice-Oxley, "Britain Looks Abroad for Nurses," *Christian Science Monitor* July 29, 2003.
24   Karl Marx and Frederick Engels, "The Manifesto of the Communist Party," *Marx/Engels Selected Works*, Volume 1 (Moscow: Progress Publishers, 1969), 98–137, at page 137.
25   Quoted in Andrew Herod, "Geographies of Labor Internationalism," *Social Science History* 27, no. 4 (2003): 501–23.
26   On the importance of this latter development, see Peter Waterman, "The Forward March of Labour (and Unions?) Recommenced: Reflections on an Emancipatory Labour Internationalism and International Labor Studies, *Antipode* 37, no. 2 (2005): 208–18.
27   ICFTU, *A Trade Union Guide to Globalization* (ICTFU: Geneva, 2001).
28   Rebecca Johns, "Bridging the Gap between Class and Space: US Worker Solidarity with Guatemala," *Economic Geography* 74, no. 3 (1998): 252–71.
29   Jane Wills, "Uneven Geographies of Capital and Labour: The Lessons of European Works Councils," *Antipode* 33, no. 3 (2001): 484–509.
30   That said, the NAFTA regime created by the NAALC has set the stage for a whole set of new union activist networks. See Joel Stillerman, "Transnational Activist Networks and the Emergence of Labor Internationalism in the NAFTA Countries," *Social Science History* 27, no. 4 (2003): 577–601.
31   Letter from John H. Hovis, President of the UE, to Alexis Herman, dated August 17, 2000. A copy of this letter and others relating to the incident were kindly sent to the author by Robin Alexander of the UE. For an extensive review of the lessons about the limits of transnational solidarity presented by Han Young case, see Heather Williams, "Of Labor Tragedy and Legal Farce: The Han Young Factory Struggle in Tijuana, Mexico," *Social Science History* 27, no. 4 (2003): 525–50.
32   For more information, see Kim Moody, *Workers in a Lean World: Unions in the International Economy* (London: Verso, 1997).
33   World Bank, *World Development Report 1995: Workers in an Integrating World* (New York: Oxford University Press, 1995), 50.

Keywords

AFL-CIO	Fordism	NIDL
capital flight	Global South	post-Fordism
comparative advantage	Global Union Federations	services
cosmopolitanism	ICFTU	sourcing efficiencies
downward harmonization	IMF	World Bank
EU	import substitution policies	WTO
export processing zones	NAFTA	

5

Money

Chapter Contents

Chapter Concepts

1. Money market movements reflect global financial interdependencies.
2. The 1944 Bretton Woods conference created a global regime of financial regulation.
3. Bretton Woods also formalized the US dollar's function as a global reserve currency.
4. Up until 1971, dollar dominance was based on the strength of the US economy, its trade surpluses, and the dollar–gold peg arranged at Bretton Woods.
5. After 1971, when the United States abandoned the dollar–gold peg, dollar dominance continued but based increasingly on the expansion of dollar-denominated debt.
6. The financial volatility created by debt-based dollar dominance prompted the expansion of 24/7 currency and derivatives trading and the rise of debt crises globally.
7. The debt crises have led to new systems of global regulation based not on controlling finance but on managing societies through "financialization" and the discipline of debt.
8. Three forms of debt-based global societal management are: (a) structural adjustment; (b) debt risk management; and (c) microfinance.

Introducing Globalization: Ties, Tensions, and Uneven Integration, First Edition. Matthew Sparke.
© 2013 Matthew Sparke. Published 2013 by Blackwell Publishing Ltd.

Key Concept

Bretton Woods represented the high point of governmental control over global finance. The dollar reserve system that was established in 1944 survived the delinking of gold and the dollar in 1971, but dollar volatility, the increasing debt of the United States, and the related development of debt crises globally all reflect the ways in which both dollar dominance and governmental control over finance have declined. The 2008–2009 "subprime crisis" and subsequent global recession are indicators of the end of the ability of even the United States to control global money movements. In the place of a global system of government regulation over finance, we have seen increasing regulation of societies through finance, most notably through the rise of new global systems of poverty management made possible by the disciplinary force of debt globally.

5.1   The Meanings of Money

> Concerns about sovereign risk [drove] market action this week as any relief that eurozone leaders had finally agreed a rescue package for Greece was tempered by growing fears about the US government's burgeoning debt level. Indeed, worries about the US drove the yield on the 10-year Treasury bond to its highest level for nine months. Equities had a broadly positive week in spite of renewed concerns about the fragile nature of the US housing market. But the Vix volatility index – closely watched as a gauge of investors' risk aversion – rose nearly 5 per cent over the week.
>
> *Financial Times*, March 27, 2010

Welcome to the casino of global finance! Everyday about 2 or so trillion dollars ricochet around the planet, and everyday these rapid-fire movements are traced in financial reports like that quoted here, or at least registered in the figures at the bottom of TV screens, or reduced to something like a weather report in news about the "strengthening" or "weakening" of a particular market or a synopsis on whether stock indices such as the "S&P 500" (an index created by averaging the stock price movements of 500 different equities) or the "Dow" or "Nikkei" or "FTSE" (pronounced "FOOT-SY") has gone up or down in "heavy" or "light" trading. We are so accustomed to the sounds and sights of these financial newsbites that we frequently take them for granted. We rarely stop to think about how so much money can move so far and so fast. Nor really do we often contemplate the meaning of the sums involve (did you know there are 12 zeros in a trillion?), nor stop to think about how all this economic value has been produced in the first place. In Chapter 4, we saw that it is ordinary workers that produce the value in the commodities that are traded for money. But while it is easy to grasp how money is produced by putting human labor to work and selling the resulting products for a profit, it is much more difficult to understand how the resulting value also *circulates* as money and thereby facilitates trade, investment, and all kinds of commerce and speculation on a global scale. Money is a store of value, but it is also a means of exchange and financial arbitrage, and it is this market-mediated circulation of money that in turn represents the interdependencies of economic globalization at their most consequential, fast, and electrifyingly intense. In this chapter we turn our attention to precisely this: to what happens when value's representation as money enters into circulation in global financial markets.

One of the core goals here is to make it easier to understand what all the jargon surrounding global finance actually means. By the end of this chapter you should be able to understand why worries about so-called "sovereign risk" might generate "the key drivers for market action." However, to begin with, we need to examine the more straightforward currency trading details also noted in the *Financial Times* weekly wrap-up report cited above: "In currencies, the euro rallied back above $1.34 after reaching a succession of 10-month lows below the $1.33 level earlier in the week. The dollar enjoyed a week of broad strength as worries about turbulence elsewhere drove investors towards the perceived safety of the US currency."

We can at least make a first cut into the meanings of money by considering how the prices of currencies such as these go up and down in the market simply on the basis of supply and demand (most obviously, for example, a currency that is in high demand will tend to fetch a higher price). As will become clear, though, even a brief review of these simple supply-and-demand relationships quickly raises all sorts of complex questions about the asymmetries that characterize today's unbalanced global money flows, including the asymmetries in the distribution of sovereign debt and risk in global markets.

The historical evolution and structuring of the asymmetries in global money movements are the focus of Section 5.2 on the twentieth-century organization of international finance. To understand this organizational structure we have to trace how it developed historically out of the famous **Bretton Woods Conference** that was orchestrated by the United States as World War II drew to a close in 1944. The resulting Bretton Woods system (BWS) with its use of the US dollar as the world's reserve currency still has an important influence even now, despite growing concerns about US debt (including US corporate and consumer debt as well as the sovereign debt owed by the US government). But we also have to come to terms with how the breakdown of the Bretton Woods system in the early 1970s has had huge consequences for economic life in today's world. These consequences include the volatile casino-like developments in global financial trading. But they also include disturbing trade-offs between financial profits and debt, and it is into this uneven and strangely warped world of global indebtedness that we go in Section 5.3. A close examination of the development of the **debt** crises in which many of the world's poor have been trapped reveals the deep links between global indebtedness and the development of global credit markets. However, looking into these links also helps us come to terms with how the breakdown of Bretton Woods regulations over global finance has also created two distinct worlds of money, with unregulated global finance on one side and deeply regulating forms of global poverty management on the other.

To begin with, we need to come back to the basic meaning of money. Pick up a dollar, a euro, a rupee, a pound coin, or a piece of loose change. They are all forms of money, and they are all so vital to our lives that we always have at least one form of money close at hand, even if it's just a plastic debit card. So, touch some money. Stare at it. And think about the lives it links together as a representation of the value produced by human labor, the ways in which it enables everyone's work everywhere on the planet to be measured, compared, and thus ultimately valued (or devalued) in monetary terms. As a widely accepted but abstract representation of value, money connects all the ties and tensions of globalization in some of their most mobile, volatile, and powerful forms. Indeed, a little like globalization itself, it both embodies diverse global relations and operates as a symbolic force in its own right, an abstraction with enormous, almost occult, power over social and political life. As such, money is both a medium and manifestation of the ways in which globalization creates ties that bind (think, for example, of the ties between the need to pay back debts to international banks and the restrictions placed on investments in education and health care in many impoverished countries). For these sorts of reasons, money has been charged with multiple meanings. "Filthy lucre," "awful offal," and "cold hard cash" are all terms that have been used to capture the dehumanizing and radically alienating side of money: its symbolization of greed, its role in the **commodification** of social relations, and its connection to debt, dependence, and political disorder.[1] But at the same time, money always somehow retains its golden promise, its associations with choice, freedom, independence, and investment in the future. And whether they are defensive and cautious market "bears" or aggressive hardcharging market "bulls," financial experts everywhere always tend to see global money movements as a world of opportunity.

Of course, after the collapse of Lehman Brothers and all the other defaults associated with the crashing value of US mortgage-backed securities in 2008, even many financial experts worried about the rising likelihood of an apocalyptic global financial meltdown brought on by speculation in complex financial products that everyone finds hard to understand (mortgage-backed securities or "MBS" in market jargon being structured financial products backed by thousands and thousands of individual mortgages that were then sliced into "tranches" according to what turned out to be completely unreliable risk ratings of default). When American homeowners started defaulting, and the crashing MBS market brought most other bank-to-bank lending to a halt in 2009, the US government was effectively forced to provide free money to both American banks and foreign banks in order to avert disaster, and this raised anxieties everywhere about the long-term value of the dollar. The global economy's over-reliance on American indebtedness and American consumption came to seem increasingly unsustainable in this light. Meanwhile, the ways in which money-market interdependencies relayed problems in one part of the world to everywhere else (the so-called contagion effects represented by the worldwide stock market falls that followed the 1997 Asian financial crisis and 2008–2009 US subprime meltdown) further suggested that finding a secure place to store value amidst financial globalization was next to impossible.

Despite all the turmoil of 2009, and despite all the continuing concerns about debt defaults in Greece and other poorer Euro-zone countries in 2010 and 2011, most financial professionals still have faith in global money markets as the best and most flexible tools capitalism can create for managing risk, enabling development, and mediating all the complex political and economic relations of global society. Of course, critics in the Occupy Wall Street movement strongly disagree. In 2011, this anti-neoliberal movement clearly hit a nerve all around the world as protestors camped out in the nerve-centers of financial globalization, condemning the violence, volatility, and inequality unleashed by Wall Street speculators and associated champions of casino capitalism in other global cities. However, these champions of financial neoliberalization still retain close control over the policy-making process, not to mention the media. Moreover, whether one approves or disapproves of their actions, the post-Bretton Woods "system" of deregulated global finance that they have created remains undeniably powerful and consequential as a truly planetary system of interdependency. It is the resulting importance and significance of financial markets that accounts in turn for the omnipresence of reports like that from the *FT* quoted above – this being the inhouse name for the *Financial Times* among global financial dealers themselves. Examining this typical report more closely now and translating some of its jargon also allows us to consider what sorts of global interdependencies are implicated in the simple sound bites we take for granted in news items about global finance.

So, let's look again at the comments on currency trading in the *FT* summary. "The dollar enjoyed a week of broad strength as worries about turbulence elsewhere drove investors towards the perceived safety of the US currency." On the surface of things, this announcement seems very simple to understand. Ever since Bretton Woods, the US dollar has been seen as a safe haven currency, a good store of value when other currencies and other assets have looked risky. Foreign governments and foreign investors have therefore had a long history of buying the US dollar because of its "perceived safety," a pattern that has intensified since the 1997 Asian financial crisis because of the ways countries in Asia and elsewhere have increasingly bought dollars and dollar-denominated bonds as a store of value that they can liquidate to prop up their own currencies in times of crisis. And now that they own so much dollar-denominated debt, they also have a vested interest in seeing the dollar retain its value. The result is heightened global demand for the US currency and hence its heightened value against the other currencies that are sold off to purchase dollars, a reciprocal relationship that is also of course deliberately used by countries such as Japan and China to depress their own currencies and make their exports cheaper and more competitive.

Ironically – given the dollar appreciation involved – the same 24/7 foreign exchange markets (Forex markets) that allow currencies to be bought and sold like this have developed since the 1970s as a direct result of the breakdown of the deal reached at Bretton Woods pegging the value of the dollar to gold and making the US currency "as good as gold." As we shall explore in detail in the next section, this development of floating currencies in foreign exchange markets did depress the value of the dollar for a time but did not destroy its credibility. Instead, it led to the ongoing use of the US currency as a de facto global reserve currency while meanwhile spurring the development of complex derivatives trading designed to hedge against (or speculate upon) greater dollar volatility in global markets. **Derivatives** such as the interest-rate swaps noted in the *FT* article are a collective name for a diverse set of financial products that *derive* their value – hence the name – from the price movements of another underlying set of assets. They are important to understand, and we will have reason to come back to them more than once in what follows. Here, the important point to make in terms of understanding the *FT* report is that what looks like an initially simple assessment of dollar appreciation based on perceived safety turns out to be complicated by a more systemic point about market movements signaling longer-term concerns about a floating dollar beginning to sink in value, concerns especially intensified in the context of increasing sovereign debt crises around the world and the parallel post-housing-bubble weakness of the American economy itself.

Why, then, was sovereign debt seen as such an important market mover in the *FT* report? Three points are key here. First, the early part of 2010 saw financial markets coming to terms with the increasing likelihood of Greece defaulting on its national debt, a default that in turn imperiled the value of the Euro – the currency in which Greek debt along with the debt of all the other "Eurozone" countries (including equally vulnerable Portugal, Spain, and Ireland) is denominated. Second, concerns about America's own sovereign debt were also intensifying at this time, the bond markets indicating that the US government was having to offer higher interest rates (called "yields") on its Treasury Bonds to attract buyers in auctions of government debt. And third, in a way that underlines how the movements of particular currencies together tell a story of global market interdependency, both the Yen and the Euro moved down against the dollar, indicating that the dollar was appreciating not only because of the search for safety in dollar-denominated assets, but also because of short-term speculative bets based on the rising interest-rate differentials. What is so interesting and paradoxical about this is that these same interest-rate differentials were in turn indexing growing anxiety about the US currency as a store of value.

That third and especially ironic point certainly seems counter-intuitive, but think of it this way. Short-term speculators are not so worried about finding a long-term store of value for their money. Precisely because of financial globalization, they can keep on moving their assets around the world in and out of different countries and currency denominations, always selling faster than ordinary savers when new risks appear to threaten the value of a particular currency. As a result, such speculators are apt to see the threats to the long-term value of the dollar as a good reason to buy dollars! Why? Because these same threats, including anxieties about the long-term inflationary impact of all the "free money" measures the Fed took to avert disaster in 2009 (ultra low interest rates plus so-called quantitative easing in which the Fed purchases bonds), were translating into rising US interest rates on longer maturity bonds. The raised rates on US bonds in turn represented an opportunity for short-term gains by providing a speculative opportunity to borrow cheaply elsewhere in another currency (say in Japanese Yen) and to then "carry" over and use this money to buy US Treasury bonds and benefit from their higher yields. Finally, in addition to such global carry trades, we should note that the particular derivatives cited in the *FT* report – interest-rate swaps – provided a further way of speculating on such interest-rate differentials in 2010: the historically unprecedented negative swap rate – the "10-year US swap rate [that] fell below the 10-year Treasury yield rate" – indicating that market players were betting that more could be made by swapping the returns on riskier government debt for what markets deemed less risky private banking debt.

The previous paragraph only begins to point to the complexities of contemporary globalized finance, but it has already taken us into some challenging market jargon. The initial cuts into the tangled relations may seem simple, but they soon begin to reveal an extraordinarily messy mix of ties and tensions bundled in arcane market terminology that takes much patience and practice to decode. Nevertheless, two analytical principles can help make global finance more comprehensible so long as they are held in tension with one another. On the more technical and micro side, most market movements can be reduced to a set of supply-and-demand relations that dictate market pricing: low supply and high demand creating high prices and vice versa. For example, much of the mind-twisting ties between bond prices and bond yields can be easily understood this way. When a bond is in short supply, and demand for it is high, it fetches a higher price, and its seller does not have to offer such a high interest rate to attract investors. Reciprocally when bonds are being oversupplied, and demand is diminished, as in the case of US Treasuries in March 2010, bond prices fall, and their interest rates rise. This may seem simple enough, but as we have already begun to see with the *FT* report, these micro-market mediations do not happen in a vacuum. Thus, on the other more macro and political side, all the supply and demand pricing mechanisms for financial assets must also be understood as operating within a global political–economic system that works with and reproduces complex asymmetries and complications. Governments, for instance, and particularly the US government, are able to intervene in the markets in a variety of ways: buying or selling their own currencies and their own government bonds, and sometimes, as in the US case, creating more of their own currency to do so (i.e. "printing money," although it is now just done digitally and referred to as "quantitative easing" or "monetization"). As we shall examine in the next section, one of the great global advantages enjoyed by the US from Bretton Woods onwards was an easy ability to borrow in its own currency because of foreigners' desire to preserve their savings in the global reserve currency. Yet it was exactly this privileged American leverage over finance that was being tested in March 2010 as the Treasury struggled to find buyers in its auctions of newly issued debt. Understanding global speculation on dollars, bond prices, and yields, therefore, cannot be done without putting the day-to-day supply-and-demand forces into a global political–economic context.

Holding on to both micro- and macro-analytical approaches is not always easy. Most financial players tend to put their faith in the technical modeling of the micro relations as they hone their skills at speculating on particular market differentials. Meanwhile, the big macro picture demands a historical understanding of global political economy, which takes patience and eludes easy summary. However, both analytical approaches are vital if you really want to be able to decode global market reports. Some of the best commentators in the financial press – Gillian Tett and Martin Wolf of the *Financial Times*, for example, or Floyd Norris and Gretchen Morgenson, who write for the *New York Times* business pages – manage to do both the micro- and macro analysis effectively, albeit with a view to helping investors maximize their financial returns. Here, with a view to helping readers maximize their understanding of global money, the two-pronged analytical approach is the same. Thus, to show how the micro-market movements we started with are related to the macro legacy of Bretton Woods explored in the next section, we will end this section by reviewing the main factors shaping global foreign exchange market movements. The next time you hear about a currency going up or down in value, try using the following points to understand why.

Starting with discrete supply-and-demand relations themselves, we can generate 10 simple rules to follow in interpreting everyday currency movements (see Table 5.1). Alongside higher national interest rates, therefore, rises in the value of national currencies can be generally explained as a result of export surpluses, increasing security for investors, national bank currency purchases, and national price stability. Reciprocally, putting any of these key drivers into reverse can lead currency speculators to sell the national currency and drive down its value.

All of these supply-and-demand explanations of why currencies rise and fall can work together, but they can also sometimes operate in countervailing ways, too, because of the different time horizons of different actors in the market. For instance, governments can take actions such as investments in education and infrastructure that might generate long-term security for investment but which, in the short term, might look like inflation-inducing deficit spending. Also complicating the picture, direct government interventions in currency markets may invert the impact of particular factors, thereby causing exactly the reverse effect to that normally expected. For example, China's trade surpluses would normally make its national currency the renminbi appreciate, but, because China fears that this would choke off demand for its exports, it keeps on intervening, buying dollars, sterling, euros, and now gold in order to keep the renminbi artificially low against the currencies of its trading partners. These sorts of interventions in foreign exchange markets highlight in turn the need to introduce the macro global context in which all the national currency movements are happening.

China is by no means the first country to manipulate exchange rates. The practice has a long history, and, as we shall see, the United States itself has engaged in it from time to time, too. However, the US experience also highlights how the ability of countries to intervene in money markets changes over time as a result of changing degrees of economic autonomy and influence. When the United States was the industrial power-house and workshop of the world in the mid twentieth century, it enjoyed immense influence over global money movements, and the dollar was

Table 5.1   Ten tips for understanding everyday money-market movements

1. Other things being equal, a national currency tends to *rise* in value when its national interest rates rise – because foreign investors tend to *buy* more of the currency in order to buy bonds and other assets that will provide increased returns due to the rising interest rates.
2. Other things being equal, a national currency tends to *rise* in value against other currencies when the country in question exports more than it imports – because foreigners tend to have to *buy* more of the country's currency in order to purchase its exports.
3. Other things being equal, a national currency tends to *rise* in value when foreign investors believe that the country is a safe and profitable place for investment – because they tend in such cases to make more investments in the country, and to do this they need to *buy* more of the country's currency.
4. Other things being equal, a national currency tends to *rise* in value when the country's central bank and/or other central banks *buy* the currency – because such central bank interventions deliberately increase demand for the currency and hence its value in global currency markets.
5. Other things being equal, a national currency tends to *rise* in value when the national rate of inflation is reduced – because reducing inflation equates with stabilized purchasing power for the currency and thus its reliability as a holder of value.
6. Other things being equal, a national currency tends to *fall* in value when its national interest rates go down – because foreign investors tend to *sell* more of the currency in order to abandon investments that will have reduced returns because of the falling interest rate.
7. Other things being equal, a national currency tends to *fall* in value against other currencies when the country in question imports more than it exports – because importers have to *sell* their own currency and buy foreigners' currencies in order to buy foreign exports.
8. Other things being equal, a national currency tends to *fall* in value when foreign investors believe that investments in the country are risky and/or when the government of the country becomes highly indebted – because in under such conditions there are more pressures to *sell* more of the country's currency.
9. Other things being equal, a national currency tends to *fall* in value when the country's central bank and/or other central banks *sell* the currency – because such actions are deliberately designed to lower the value of the currency in global currency markets.
10. Other things being equal, a national currency tends to *fall* in value when the national rate of inflation increases – because inflation equates with decreasing purchasing power for the currency and thus its eroding reliability as a holder of value.

supremely dominant. But now, having become the world's largest debtor nation with giant trade and budget deficits, American autonomy and influence are on the wane. Even the US Federal Reserve, the most powerful institutional guardian of the value of money anywhere in the world, finds itself hemmed in by global forces. Thus, while it was able to bail out banks and provide liquidity to the markets in ways that prevented a complete financial crash in 2009, it nevertheless found itself a year later trapped between the need to deal with ongoing US unemployment and foreclosures on the one side and the threat of inflation on the other. This threat of inflation (price rises) was in turn further magnified by the long-term downward trajectory of the dollar, the diminishing value of the national currency effectively making all the foreign goods imported by Americans more expensive. And imported inflation aside, even the Fed's traditional ability to manipulate interest rates on supposedly risk-free short-term government bonds (by either buying back the bonds to reduce rates or selling them to raise rates) look set in 2010 and 2011 to become increasingly straitjacketed by global market speculation over the heightened risk attached to US sovereign debt.

In short, the United States, which once benefited so much from dollar dominance, has begun to experience global money movements in the same way as other countries have experienced them for much longer: namely, as constraining and controlling rather than enabling. The ability of the US government and US Federal Reserve to intervene in the markets remains significant, but their room for maneuver is gradually getting smaller as the markets themselves begin to treat US debt as something less creditworthy than the "risk-free" benchmark it represented for over half a century. It was no surprise therefore to see the Vix market volatility index rising in early 2010 despite the US stock-market recovery that marked the start of the year. The surface may have looked calm, and the *FT* report may only have registered the cause of some of the volatility in its esoteric acknowledgment of an unusual interest rate inversion in the swaps market. However, underneath these derivative signs on the surface, oceanic pulls in global money were creating all sorts of deeper disturbances in the structure of dollar dominance first established at Bretton Woods. In 2011, other signs of trouble emerged when the credit ratings firm Standard and Poor's downgraded the sovereign credit rating of the United States, thereby suggesting increasing risks associated with US Treasury bonds that had always been seen since Bretton Woods as a basic benchmark of "risk-free" investment. To understand the epochal significance of these global disturbances, we now need to travel back to the time and town in New Hampshire where global dollar dominance was first put in place.

5.2   From Bretton Woods to the Rise of Global Finance

The accelerated movement of money around our world and the 24/7 casino of financial speculation it enables have not always existed in the current form of instantaneous currency trading. Money has never moved before with the electronic speed or the geographic scope with which it moves today. Indeed, if there is an example of a global development in which the three big myths about Globalization would seem to make some sense, it is the rise of global finance. The novelty of today's electronic financial marketplace, the immense power of its movements over government policy, and the flat revisioning of the world by financial investors looking only at the bottom line, would all seem to illustrate global forces that are in some notable respects new, inevitable, and leveling. However, even with global finance, the connection of the

Globalization myths to reality remains tenuous. While the immense power of today's global financial system should never be doubted, the story of its rise indicates a much more complex reality: a reality rooted partly in a historic attempt by policy-makers to address the crises associated with the speculative financial flows of an earlier era, and thus also a reality shaped as much by a governmental attempt to control earlier rounds of financial volatility as by some radically new financial influence over government. The name of this historic attempt at governmental control was the Bretton Woods agreement, and because it was an effort at global financial governance that was chiefly organized by the United States, it also created an institutional legacy designed to protect specifically American interests, a legacy that was and remains therefore far from "leveling" in its implications for global financial flows.

Officially known as the *United Nations Monetary and Financial Conference*, the Bretton Woods meeting took place in July 1944 while British and American troops were still battling their way against the Nazis through France and while the Soviet Army was still losing large numbers of its soldiers fighting its way towards Germany from the east. Far from all the death and destruction, ministers of the US, Britain, and France met with representatives of 41 other Allied countries, including the Soviet Union, in the small New Hampshire town of Bretton Woods to develop a plan for world economic development after the expected defeat of the Japanese and German regimes. While distant from the violence of the war itself, the meeting was nonetheless overshadowed by a deep concern with how the global financial crises of the 1930s had created the opportunity for fascism to develop in the first place. Henry Morgenthau, the US Treasury Secretary at the time, captured this concern concisely in his own address to the conference.

> All of us have seen the great economic tragedy of our time. We saw the world-wide depression of the 1930s. We saw currency disorders develop and spread from land to land, destroying the basis for international trade and international investment and even international faith. In their wake we saw unemployment and wretchedness – idle tools, wasted wealth. We saw their victims fall prey, in places to demagogues and dictators. We saw bewilderment and bitterness become breeders of fascism and, finally, of war.[2]

Thus it was with a view to preventing more global depression, unemployment, fascism, and war that the organizers and attendees came together at the Mount Washington Hotel in Bretton Woods to plan for what was hoped would be a more stable post-war financial order (Figure 5.1).

The agreement that the US representatives secured at the conference had four major outcomes, three of them institutional, and one of them more organizational in nature. The first institutional outcome was the creation of the International Monetary Fund (**IMF**), which was planned with a view to providing a solution to the short-term **balance of payments** crises that, along with all sorts of related competitive currency devaluations, had been such a disruptive feature of economic depression during the 1930s. The second institutional outcome was the creation of the **World Bank** whose original name at Bretton Woods was the International Bank for Reconstruction and Development (IBRD). The purpose of this bank was conceived

Figure 5.1   Meeting of 44 countries at Bretton Woods in 1944. *Source*: US National Archives (NARA): 208-N-29536.

primarily in terms of redeveloping the economies ravaged by the war. Only later did it take on the much more global development mandate that it has now as the World Bank. Still more limited at the time, the third institutional outcome of Bretton Woods was a plan to create an international trade organization that would work towards expanding and enforcing free trade at a global level. It was this plan that led through the many decades of talks over a General Agreement on Tariffs and Trade (GATT) to the eventual establishment of the World Trade Organization (**WTO**) in 1995. Much more immediate in its impact, but just as long-lasting in its influence as the three Bretton Woods institutions, the fourth major outcome of the conference was to formalize a dollar-based organizational structure for the global monetary system. By 1944, the United States owned three-quarters of the existing monetary gold in the world. This, combined with the underlying fact that the US economy was emerging from the war in much better shape than the European and Asian economies, meant that the US dollar looked set to remain "as good as gold" as a stable store of value. After the Wall Street crash of 1929, the dollar had been "pegged" to gold at the rate of $35 per ounce. It was therefore with an assumption that this dollar/gold peg would remain stable into the future that the participants at Bretton Woods proceeded to envision a global system of currency controls in which foreign currencies would only be allowed to fluctuate within a narrow band around agreed "par values" vis-à-vis the dollar/gold standard. In turn, the purpose of the three Bretton Woods institutions and, most particularly, the primary purpose of the IMF, was envisioned at the conference as one of facilitating and stabilizing this dollar-standardized monetary regime. Overall, therefore, the framework for the global economic system that was constructed at Bretton Woods was characterized by three regulative

Figure 5.2   John Maynard Keynes of the UK (center) with Mikhail Stepanovich Stepanov of the USSR and Vladimir Rybar of Yugoslavia at the Bretton Woods conference in July 1944. *Source*: US National Archives (NARA): 208-N-29538.

commitments: (1) to privileging free trade over free finance; (2) to managing global money movements through global institutions; and (3) to basing this whole system of control on the strength of the dollar.

By creating the dollar-standard system of managed flexibility – a sort of half-way house between free and totally fixed exchange rates – the hope was to provide enough governmental control and coordination to prevent the competitive devaluations that had so destabilized global finance in the 1930s. Countries would no longer be able to deliberately reduce the value of their currencies in order to boost their exports and reduce their imports. However, the resulting approach to managing global financial markets remained nonetheless very much a "made-in-America" compromise. At a philosophical level, therefore, the desire to manage global markets and prevent financial crisis was balanced by a parallel American desire for free-market solutions. Even though Harry Dexter White, the main US representative at the conference, had to work alongside the influential British economist, John Maynard Keynes, and even though White's thinking, like that of many other New Deal policy-makers in the United States, had been influenced by Keynesianism (an economic philosophy emphasizing the need for macroeconomic management by governments), the Bretton Woods agreement rested on a still-unyielding American commitment to free-market principles (Figure 5.2). The fact that Keynes himself did not get many of the things he came to Bretton Woods demanding (e.g. ongoing protection for trade within the system of British imperial preference or the establishment of an international currency based neither on the dollar nor on gold), reflected how as the main British representative he was the voice of a weakened world power that would now be dependent after the war on American aid. More than just indicating the new American command over economic thinking, at a practical level the plans made at Bretton Woods also secured the basis for extending America's actual economic dominance into the future. The commitments to free trade clearly benefited the United States as the world's dominant exporter of the time. The plan for the IMF voting system using subscription-based quotas effectively gave the United States a veto over all IMF decisions. And the establishment of a dollar-based global monetary system not only gave the United States the power to print as many dollars as would be required to rebuild Europe and Japan (the redevelopment work for which the IBRD/World Bank was primarily established), but also provided the United States with all sorts of other advantages over other national economies. This asymmetric outcome of Bretton Woods in turn had huge repercussions for the development and organization of global finance in the latter half of the twentieth century. We shall explore how America's uneven influence in the three Bretton Woods institutions has changed over the years both in Chapter 6, which examines the legal ramifications of the WTO, and in Chapter 7, when we turn to consider the role the IMF and World Bank play in enforcing neoliberal global governance. Here, in the next three subsections, it is the impact that the Bretton Woods regime had on global financial interdependencies that is the focus.

5.2.1   From Bretton Woods to the breakdown of the dollar–gold peg

In the 1950s and early 1960s, the global financial order based on managed exchange rates remained fairly stable – although it took some time for the post-war economies of Europe to accumulate the reserves officially demanded by the par values system. During this time, the United States continued to function as the workshop of the world, exporting much more than it imported from the rest of the world. The resulting trade surplus helped in turn to keep the dollar in high demand and its value stable. Meanwhile, as US development aid distributed through the Marshall Plan, and the IBRD helped redevelop the economies of Europe and Asia, the initial result was to produce still more demand for US exports. However, by the 1960s, this had begun to change. All the investments in redeveloping Japanese, German, and other European industry had led to a massive increase in global productive capacity, including the increasing capacity generated by the overseas investments by American TNCs, too. The commodities produced in these factories outside of America became internationally competitive in global markets. As a result, there was increasing price competition as yet more industrial capacity came on stream globally. More and more commodities were chasing a limited number of consumers. In this increasingly competitive late 1960s context, profits were squeezed, and US exporters lost market share to the newer and cheaper international competitors. As US consumers started to buy larger numbers of foreign made products – German cars and Japanese electronics, for example – the US trade surplus became the deficit we noted in Chapter 3 (Figure 5.3). The resulting downward drag on the value of the dollar created by this balance of payments deficit was then further exacerbated by an

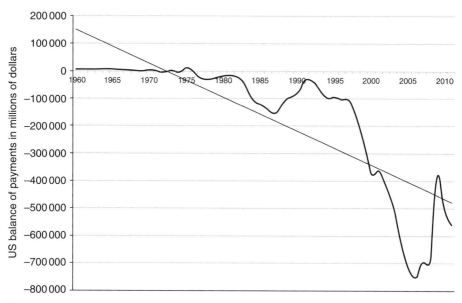

Figure 5.3   US balance of payments deficits (US$ million). *Source:* based on data from the US Census, http://www.census.gov/foreign-trade/statistics/historical/.

increasing fiscal deficit (national budget deficit) as American government spending only continued to increase.

To understand why the fiscal deficit developed in the late 1960s, we have to remember that the Cold War had led the United States to expand its development spending overseas as part of an effort to stop the spread of communism. Then, the direct military confrontation in Vietnam also became a heavy drain on government reserves in the late 1960s. And, back on the home front, the costs of trying to manage domestic discontent about inequality through the expansion of welfare, health care, and educational access also sent the government's budget into the red. To pay for this fiscal deficit, the US government began printing ever larger numbers of dollars. In effect, this meant that the United States was issuing paper IOUs which it no longer had enough gold reserves to cover but which as dollars were at the same time still being treated by foreign governments as a gold convertible currency. Already in 1965, French leaders complained that this dollar "seigneurage" – the American government's ability to control and print what remained a global reserve currency – conferred an "exorbitant privilege" on the United States. Notwithstanding the complaints, though, the privilege continued, and from 1967 onwards the result of this increasing supply of dollars was increasing inflation in America (i.e. a decreasing value in the purchasing power of American money), and, as we shall explore further below, a parallel increase in offshore dollar-denominated loans (so-called Eurodollars) put into circulation by banks based in London. By 1970, the real global value of the dollar had declined so significantly that the government could no longer pretend that it was convertible to gold at $35 an ounce. Indeed, in 1970, Eurodollar deposits alone amounted to about $10 billion, a figure equal itself to what was left of all US gold reserves. By this point, foreign governments who demanded gold in exchange for their increasingly devalued dollar reserves were told to suspend such demands altogether (an American request that was impossible to refuse when so many of these foreign governments were dependent on the United States for military support). Thus, in 1971, President Richard Nixon came to formalize officially what was already a practical reality. He closed the "Gold Window" by ending any convertibility between the dollar and gold. The US currency's value was no longer pegged to gold at all and would now be set in global foreign exchange markets. By this point, too, financial pressures throughout the rest of the industrialized world had also led other governments to abandon their own efforts at maintaining the currency stabilization arrangements agreed to in 1944. The Bretton Woods system was dead! Or was it?

Many accounts of Nixon's abandonment of the dollar–gold peg do indeed describe it as the break-up of Bretton Woods. His personal opposition to Roosevelt's New Deal and Bretton Woods was well known. Previously, as a first-term congressman from California, it was Nixon who had charged Harry Dexter White before the House un-American Activities Committee in 1948. The accusations did not stick, but White suffered a fatal heart attack on his way home from the hearings, and thus the notion of Nixon as the breaker of Bretton Woods had a personal pre-history. In any event, 1971 certainly marked an important watershed moment in the global history of finance. Managed currency controls based on a dollar standard thereby came to be replaced in the subsequent years by an entirely market-based currency-trading system, and it is this system that has produced the global casino of non-stop worldwide money market movement that we have today. However, in another sense, Bretton Woods did not die at all, and nor did 1971 represent the collapse of American economic dominance either. As we shall see later, the institutions born at Bretton Woods actually enjoyed increasing influence in the subsequent period with the IMF, World Bank, and later even the WTO all becoming much more important command centers for global capitalism. More than this, the dominance of the dollar that Bretton Woods had formalized still continued, albeit in informal and increasingly unstable ways. Coming to terms with this precarious dollar dominance after 1971 involves examining both the implications of the floating of the dollar for financial markets and all the knock-on effects for economic development patterns more generally.

5.2.2   Floating exchange rates and the development of the global casino

In financial terms, the floating of the dollar turned the US currency into a purely paper representation of value with no fixed connection to gold (this is sometimes called "fiat money," although a floating currency does not really fit the old Roman reference to money given value by governmental decree – today it is global forex markets that do the decrees). The value of the currency – along with all the other currencies over which Bretton Woods had established a regulated regime of price bands – was now primarily set by the ups and downs of supply and demand for dollars and dollar-denominated securities in the market. It was in turn the uncertainty surrounding the resulting floating exchange rates that precipitated the subsequent development of increasingly complex financial derivatives designed to allow investors to either hedge their exposure to volatile currency market movements or speculate on the associated risks. Simply put, derivatives derive their value from global market expectations about the changing values of other assets. They generally allow one party to hedge against volatility in the future value of this underlying asset, and another party to speculate on this volatility by selling the hedge. Their history goes back a long way, but with the emergence of floating currencies and with the evermore consequential development of foreign exchange markets in the 1970s, the three main kinds – futures, options, and swaps – took off.

Futures, which had long existed for commodities like pork bellies, were now created to allow investors to hedge or speculate on the risk associated with the future values of currencies and bonds. Options trading also increased parallel to this, allowing investors to put a price on an option to buy or sell particular assets at particular prices at particular dates in the future. And still more complexly, swaps also took off after this period, providing for further risk trading based on differentials in currencies and bonds in different parts of the world economy with different rates of interest. For example, interest-rate swaps between fixed interest and floating interest rate loans were developed in order to allow the sellers to speculate that future floating interest rates would generate higher payments while also allowing the buyers of the fixed rate payments to reduce their exposure to the risks associated with interest-rate volatility. After the 1970s, many more complex swaps developed with exotic names like "accreting swaps," "amortizing swaps," "seasonal swaps," "roller coaster swaps," "off-market swaps," "yield curve swaps," "flavored currency swaps," and "CIRCUS swaps." And, fast-forwarding through to the 1990s and new millennium, the evermore complex development of financial derivatives was highlighted by the extraordinary growth of hedge funds and diverse sorts of banking innovations associated with securitizing and then speculating on debt: including most infamously mortgage-backed securities and collateralized debt obligations (CDOs) using credit default swaps (CDSs) as insurance against default. These innovations became infamous because the casino of debt trading and speculation they made possible abruptly collapsed in 2008, causing a massive global financial crisis. The reasons why this happened need to be picked apart carefully. Here, we begin with US financial industry innovations and then work back historically and outwards geographically to put the crisis into a more long-term global perspective.

US hedge funds were originally advertised as offering extra returns for wealthy investors willing to make extra risks by betting on short-term market movements in derivatives and other more risky assets (such as the high-yield, high-risk corporate loans sometime referred to as "junk bonds"). Meanwhile, big investment banks from around the world were able to capitalize on the eagerness of such investors to overlook traditional banking reserve requirements and the accumulation of risky assets in special investment vehicles (SIVs) and other sorts of off-the-books "conduits." All this so-called shadow banking was seen by many market players and regulators as just an extension of the free-market in finance that had opened with the closing of the dollar–gold window in 1971: a continuation, in other words, of the financial deregulation that had taken off in the 1980s and 1990s as Presidents Reagan, Bush, and Clinton all gave up on the mid-twentieth century effort to assert governmental authority over finance. Leading authorities now believed that financial markets were better suited to measuring and managing financial risk themselves in the context of global money movements. Alan Greenspan, the US Federal Reserve Chairman and cheerleader of further financial deregulation, argued thus that Wall Street innovations in securitization and collateralization helped disperse and thereby reduce risk. Instead, the 2008 financial crisis showed that big banks, hedge funds, and the whole shadow-banking system had in fact concentrated and heightened risk. More than this, the crisis also showed that the most sophisticated risk-management and hedging tools were actually the most dangerous risk aggregators, too, creating accumulations of risk that were so huge they also became systemic for the whole global financial system.

One notable example of risk aggregation that created a systemic shock wave was and remains the global market in credit default swaps. These derivatives, which the esteemed US investor Warren Buffett had once called "financial weapons of mass destruction," exploded with especially destructive consequences in 2008. Initially, they had seemed relatively benign, allowing purchasers of securitized loans to hedge against the risk of loan defaults by buying insurance against the danger of borrowers failing to pay. In reality, though, CDS contracts were not like ordinary insurance at all. A bit like the "horcruxes" in Harry Potter novels, they promised to preserve the immortality or at least the financial futures of their creators, and yet by creating them, the wizards of global finance ended up both concentrating and concealing risk in instruments scattered right across world markets. All sorts of international speculators could trade in the swaps, whether they owned a security that might be undermined by default or not: a form of so-called "naked trading" analogous to being able to take out fire insurance on your neighbor's house. This in turn created perverse incentives to mis-measure risk or even exacerbate it directly (imagine taking out fire insurance on your neighbor's house and then starting a fire or cutting off the water supply). Meanwhile, issuers of credit default swaps were gambling, too: taking the money and offering the insurance while hoping against hope that there would never be a default. So, when overextended US borrowers started to miss their mortgage payments in 2007 and 2008, and when the mortgage-backed securities based on their payments therefore crashed in value, the issuers of credit default swaps such as AIG had no way of paying off the swaps and honoring the pledge of insurance. The result was an extraordinarily systemic global market crash. The risk had become so widespread globally that pension funds and local government investors in places as remote as northern Norway discovered that their investments had collapsed in value. In response, to rescue the global financial system and get credit moving again, the US government had to go global, too: paying out billions of US dollars to foreign banks such as United Bank of Switzerland (UBS), Hong Kong Shanghai Banking Corporation (HSBC), and Deutsche Bank (DB) as part of honoring the credit default swap contracts that AIG had originally issued (and, while this may stretch the metaphor too far, maybe we can see the related extraordinary expansion of its balance sheet by the Federal Reserve – effectively printing dollars to pay for all the bailouts – as similar to Harry Potter chasing down horcruxes to the point of ultimate existential crisis).

For many who work at the heart of the financial industry, the global nature of the risks on which they gamble and trade was obvious long before the 2008 crisis. The financial deregulation that ensued after 1971 involved evermore global trades in currencies, bonds, and equities, as well as derivatives like credit default swaps. Borders were crossed by ever-larger investments at the push of the button, the huge distances across the Atlantic and Pacific completely compressed by electronic transfers. As a result, for jet-setting financial elites, the myth of the flat world was made into something of a daily reality. Meanwhile, as geography became history for investors, history itself was speeded up with financial professionals living lives totally focused on the aspatial abstractions of minute-by-minute market movements. Describing this almost artistic sensibility well, a retired trader has reflected that the abstractions of risk trading at the end of the twentieth century meant that in his experience:

> many traded by feel rather than by fundamentals, forgetting about things like leading economic indicators, government policies, and even supplies of commodities. They simply tried to catch the market on the way up and ditch it on the way down. In the trading pits they could do it faster and better than any outside speculators because they were squarely in the heart of the action.[3]

Since the start of the twenty-first century, most financial trading has moved online, becoming yet more accelerated, abstract, and aspatial. Outside of the pits, speculators have sought to beat the market with complex "quant" models of derivatives, but these strategies, too, have proved just as disconnected from global economic fundamentals. There were already signs of these increasing dangers of abstracted and concentrated risk in the 1990s when the infamous hedge fund Long Term Capital Management collapsed in 1998 after losing $4.6 billion in under 4 months. This collapse was contained by the emergency injection of Fed funding into the markets. And so far, all of the financial crises since have also been contained by similar interventions, mainly by using the governmental capacity to buy up failing assets, lower interest rates, and create liquidity through providing banks with access to virtually free loans. The costs of all these interventions, though, have also been increasing exponentially since 2008. And each time governments have made borrowing cheaper in order to get credit moving again, they have also allowed bigger and yet more unstable credit bubbles to balloon and explode in the future.

The losers in the Long Term Capital Management fiasco were bailed out to the tune of $3.6 billion by an intervention organized by the Federal Reserve Bank of New York. But the US costs of propping up AIG and all the other bank failures in 2008–2009 exceeded $300 billion, with over $700 billion set aside by Congress for the so-called Toxic Asset Relief Program or TARP. Subsequently, in 2011, European governments had to plan even bigger bailout funds because of the debt-default dangers posed by Greece, Spain, Portugal, and Italy. And yet as they did so, the limits of such financialized crisis management also became clear, too, with the coordination challenges facing the European central bank and the vulnerability of the EU as the world's biggest economy becoming especially obvious when it became clear that China was not willing to contribute significant new reserves to the European bailout facility. A key question going forward therefore concerns how much longer such governmental interventions can be sustained as the amounts involved and the imbalances hedged by derivatives trading continue to expand. This expansion of risk and imbalance is undoubtedly ongoing, and attempts to re-regulate derivative trading continue to face stiff opposition both from Wall Street speculators and from the big corporations that rely on derivatives to hedge against their exposure to commodity price and currency volatility. Moreover, the vast volumes of money involved are increasingly dwarfing the power of even the American central bank to intervene, forcing the government to do the equivalent of printing money (monetization through "quantitative easing"), and thereby undermining also the ability of the dollar to function as a stable reserve currency. In this sense, the American attempt to regulate global finance that was established at Bretton Woods and the dollar hegemony it established now appear to have entered a terminal state of decline. To really understand why, though, we need to consider some of the other financial challenges to regulation that resulted from what happened to global trading relations and the dollar after Nixon's formal abandonment of the dollar/gold peg in 1971.

5.2.3   Floating exchange rates and global recession

The immediate economic aftermath of the switch to floating currency rates in the early 1970s was a worldwide recession that was felt more strongly outside the United States than domestically. Even though it was the weakening of the US economy and the dollar that had forced the change, the sudden drop in the value of the US currency served to displace much of the economic damage abroad. Foreign exporters could no longer compete so effectively in the US market, and Europeans who had built up their dollar reserves by exporting to America found themselves now holding devalued assets. Meanwhile, US exporters regained a competitive foothold in global markets because they were now paying their own workers in lower-valued dollars. At the same time, though, producers of staple commodities such as oil, coffee, and iron ore that were traded in dollars saw their real profits plummet because of the lower-valued dollar. In the face of the complaints from foreign holders of dollar reserves, the United States was quite cavalier. For example, John Connally, the Treasury Secretary at the time, famously replied to European concerns about the falling dollar by saying that it was "our currency" and "your problem." However, the impact of dollar devaluation on staples producers was to create problems that ultimately became an American problem, too. Confronted with falling profits, many of these staples producers formed cartels in order to control supply and thereby push up prices. Most famously, in 1973, Middle Eastern oil producers cartelized the Organization of Petroleum Exporting Countries (OPEC), which restricted the flow of oil globally and pushed up oil prices drastically. The consolidation of OPEC was undoubtedly underpinned by the anger many Arab leaders felt about America's support for Israel's war with its neighbors. Nevertheless, it was the economic imperative of the falling dollar that created the underlying need to increase oil prices, and the higher prices when they came created in turn another blow to developing and developed economies all around the world. Already suffering from global overcapacity and falling profits, the higher prices of staple commodities simultaneously created sharp inflationary pressures, lowering the value of savings, increasing the cost of borrowing, and reducing investment. The grim result was what economists at the time called stagflation, an unusual and unpleasant mix of economic recession and inflation.

5.2.4   The rise of debt-based dollar dominance

Out of the stagflation of the 1970s, two key developments emerged that further heightened global financial interdependencies. One was the creation of the global debt crisis, which we will examine in the next section. But another result, and an important precursor of the debt crisis, was the restoration of the US dollar as a global reserve currency based not on gold but rather on America's ability to sell its own debt globally (i.e. its ability to borrow in its own currency from the rest of the world). This restoration of dollar dominance via dollar debt occurred for a number of reasons. Large volumes of global savings were already denominated in dollars because of the legacy of Bretton Woods, and dollar-based staples trading in commodities such as oil continued to create dollar-denominated profits which were recycled as dollar-denominated loans. But in addition, it was the way in which US monetary policy developed at the end of 1970s that set the stage for the revival of the dollar as a floating but nevertheless still widely used reserve currency.

Faced with ongoing stagflation and the falling value of domestic dollar savings, the US Fed finally intervened by drastically increasing US interest rates and, because this increased the yields on dollar-denominated loans, the value of the dollar. Led by Paul Volcker, a new Fed chairman appointed by President Jimmy Carter in 1979, the Fed's switch to a high-interest-rate policy represented a shift away from a Keynesian philosophy – that emphasized maintaining high employment by using government borrowing to stimulate economic activity – to a now ascendant monetarist philosophy – which was based on the neoliberal nostrums of Milton Friedman and the Chicago School. Advocating against government borrowing and deficit-spending, Friedman had famously argued that "inflation is always and everywhere a monetary phenomenon" (an argument focused on the importance of central bank monetary policy that has now been eclipsed by the same transnational money movements that Friedman's emphasis on deregulated finance ironically helped advance). Monetarists following Friedman thought in turn that the job of the Fed should be reduced to simply fighting inflation while meanwhile allowing unemployment to rise to levels that depressed wages. Volcker was not a purist in this respect, but he did bring a strong anti-inflationary emphasis to his work as Fed chairman, and his hiking of interest rates reflected that. The result was that inflation in America was reduced from 9% in 1980 to only 3.2% by 1983. It was a great result for bankers and others who owned significant savings, but the radical reduction in money supply created by the increased interest rates also reduced investment in commodity production, thereby precipitating a recession and a sharp increase in unemployment. Inflation was nevertheless beaten, and as prices stabilized and the value of savings and the dollar increased, the monetarists declared victory.

Through the rest of the 1980s, the reverberations of high US interest rates and the high dollar continued to be felt. While it was a boom time for lenders, and while it increased the buying power of US consumers who retained their jobs and income (not to mention the investment power of US TNCs who were also thereby enabled to make more foreign direct investment in overseas production), the strong dollar was nevertheless crippling for domestic US producers, especially auto-makers. By the mid 1980s, the increasingly desperate plight of American manufacturers there-fore led the Reagan administration to orchestrate a shift in currency policy. With the 1985 Plaza Accords, they succeeded in persuading the leaders of foreign central banks to sell dollar assets in a globally coordinated fashion and thereby push down the value of the dollar in global currency markets. While this hurt foreign businesses that were dependent on exporting into America, their governments nevertheless went along with the American requests in order to secure ongoing access to the US market. When subsequent speculation in financial markets against the dollar continued to push it too low, however, another so-called Louvre accord was made in 1987, this time to stop the dollar's fall. Then again in 1995, President Clinton's treasury secretary Robert Rubin engineered a further set of accords – sometimes called the Reverse Plaza Accords – to revalue the dollar once more. By this point, there was much less resistance from within US manufacturing. Many American TNCs had adjusted to global competition by outsourcing or otherwise moving more produc-tion overseas while also developing strategies for profit generation in the United States that relied more on finance and real estate (and thus a strong dollar). This so-called financialization of US corporate strategy also came together with the nota-bly financial worldview that Rubin himself brought with him from a background in derivatives trading at the investment bank Goldman Sachs. Indeed, it marked a new era in which the old industrialist idea that "What is good for General Motors is good for America" became replaced by a new worldview that "What is good for Goldman Sachs is good for America." It was not a worldview that jived very well with the American public and so was never articulated as such. However, shaped by con-cerns about contagion effects in global financial markets and by a desire to secure the value of dollar based savings, it became dominant among American leaders. Not surprisingly, it therefore led to a policy emphasizing US price stability as a protec-tion against global volatility. Yet beyond just the banking biases of Rubin and the financialization of US corporate strategy, the dollar hike that resulted from the 1995 Reverse Plaza Accords also indicated a victory of financial interests over the basic concept of governmental control over finance. It was in this sense a neoliberal intervention to end interventions, an intervention that simultaneously represented the final vanquishing of the Bretton Woods idea that governments should regulate global financial interdependency.

Since 1995, the maintenance of dollar dominance has become so dependent on the casino of global financial trading that any coordinated global governmental intervention appears evermore implausible. The immediate result of the 1995 return to strong dollar policy was a huge influx of foreign funds into dollar-denominated assets. This helped make possible the late-1990s run-up in US stocks (the so-called technology or dot.com boom) on Wall Street, but, in another case of "our currency, your problem," it also set the scene for the 1997 Asian financial crisis. In order to bring stability to their export trade with the United States, many of these countries had pegged their currencies to the dollar. When the US currency suddenly increased in value, their central banks did not have enough dollar reserves to maintain the pegs (i.e. they needed more reserves to buy back their own currencies and maintain the pegged values of these currencies vis-à-vis the newly expensive dollar). Global currency speculators who saw this weakness then profited grandly from "short-selling" the Southeast Asian currencies – borrowing them, selling them, and then buying them back after they crashed in order to pay back the original loans. This casino-like gambling on the Asian currencies drove them into an even speedier decline all the while the speculators retained their gains in dollars. After suffering capital flight and disinvestment, most of the affected economies eventually recovered. Ironically, however, one of the main outcomes of their experience has been a subsequent tendency by countries such as South Korea and Thailand to buy up more dollar securities as emergency reserves, and this has in turn increased the global demand for the dollar, further increasing its value.

Other bigger factors also account for the continuing debt-based strength (and thus underlying precariousness) of the dollar since 2000. Most notably, the dollar's value has come to depend on vast purchases of US Treasury bonds by the central banks of China and Japan. Their main reason for making these purchases of US debt has been to push down the value of their own currencies and thereby increase the competitiveness of their exports in America – the very sort of competitive devaluation that Bretton Woods had hoped to end. In devaluing their currencies this way, the Asian central banks have created a risky relationship of trans-Pacific codependency (Figure 5.4). Recycling the profits they make from selling to American consumers, China and Japan in particular have continued to buy yet more dollar-denominated debt securities, and by thereby inflating US bond prices and simultaneously pushing down bond yields, they have effectively reduced US interest rates and ensured that the cost of borrowing in America remains low. This in turn has ensured that Americans can keep consuming because the cheap credit has reduced the cost of financing everything from corporate loans to mortgages to personal credit card debt. All the while US borrowers keep spending this cheap credit

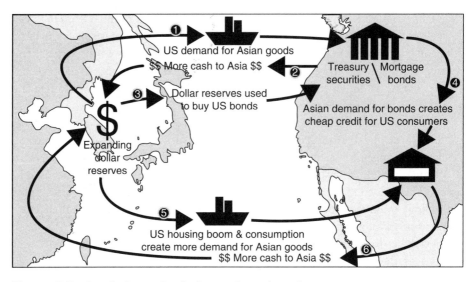

US demand for Asian goods
$$ More cash to Asia $$
Treasury \ Mortgage
securities \ bonds
Dollar reserves used
to buy US bonds
Asian demand for bonds creates
cheap credit for US consumers
Expanding
dollar
reserves
US housing boom & consumption
create more demand for Asian goods
$$ More cash to Asia $$

Figure 5.4   Spiral of trans-Pacific financial interdependency.

on Asian exports, this trans-Pacific codependency keeps on growing. But it clearly rests on extremely speculative foundations, and the 2008–2009 collapse in credit markets in the United States significantly destabilized the situation further: reducing the access to cheap credit for poor and middle-class American borrowers, and thereby undermining their ability to contribute to global consumer demand.

Eventually, the American economy will have to generate enough income to pay back all the debt, and all the while the United States puts off the day of reckoning, it borrows yet more money to cover its deficits. In 2004, America was importing a dollar in loans for every dollar of goods it sold abroad, a sign for many observers that, far from being able to generate income from exports, the United States was just digging itself deeper into debt. A record of more than $90 billion flowed into US bonds from abroad in September alone in 2005 – well over $2 billion a day. Thus, by late 2005, foreigners owned $8 trillion of US debt instruments, including 40% of the US government's tradable debt (mainly Treasury bonds), 26% of US corporate bonds, and 13% of US equities. And by 2011, foreign investors held 53.8% of tradable US government debt. The resulting dependency on foreign creditors has in turn significantly eroded America's ability to influence foreign central banks the way it did with the Plaza accords and their successors. It is true, as Keynes himself once noted, that big borrowers still have a certain leverage over lenders who cannot afford to see the borrower default. As the world's biggest borrower – sucking in about 75% of the world's savings in the first decade of the new millennium – the United States has in this sense locked its lenders into long-term commitments to a strong dollar. Anyone anywhere who has invested in dollar-denominated bonds has a great deal to lose from a dollar devaluation. But when borrowers need to keep on borrowing – as the United States clearly is – it is still lenders, *not* borrowers, who ultimately set the terms of financial interdependency. Thus, when President Obama was visiting

China in November 2009, Liu Mingkang, the chief Chinese banking regulator, saw fit to complain that America's ultra-loose monetary policies were creating real and insurmountable risks to the global economy. No longer, then, can the United States so easily say "our currency, your problem." It is now more a case of "our debt, your loans, and the whole world's problem."

The basic economic facts on which the problem of US indebtedness is based are clear. Having never recovered the trade surpluses it enjoyed before the mid 1960s, the country continues to import increasingly more than it exports, thereby creating an ever-larger current account deficit (the trade deficit in goods plus what is also now an increasing deficit in services). Meanwhile, the US government has behaved just like American consumers and American companies in building up its own fiscal deficit. As exemplified by Greece, Spain, and Italy from 2010 onwards, any other country in the world with this combination of current account and fiscal deficits would be in deep financial trouble, its sovereign debt being bet against in the credit default swap market, its government pressured by lenders to make drastic austerity measures and cuts in government spending, its businesses and consumers facing runaway inflation and high interest rates, and its good standing among global investors undermined by worries about capital flight. But not America; at least up till now. Despite a few financiers making bets on a dollar decline and becoming famous as "dollar bears," and despite the associated interest in assets such as Gold and Treasury Inflation Protected Securities that provide a hedge against a dollar crash and hyperinflation, the United States has continued to benefit from the dollar dominance established at Bretton Woods. As a result, Americans and their government just continue to consume and pile up the debt. Nevertheless, the worries have been piling up, too, worries that have been increasingly articulated inside as well as outside of America about the downsides of debt-based dollar dominance. Paul Volcker – the former Fed chairman who engineered the strong dollar policy of the 1980s by pushing up interest rates – expressed fears thus in 2005 about the ways in which dollar debt was creating dangerous disequilibria in the global economy. "Under the placid surface," he said, "there are disturbing trends: huge imbalances, disequilibria, risks – call them what you will. Altogether the circumstances seem to me as dangerous and intractable as any I can remember, and I can remember quite a lot."[4] Likewise, Lawrence Summers, Rubin's successor as US Treasury secretary, argued that

America's spending addiction now threatens to undermine that virtuous global economic cycle. The country that is more economically central than it has been in decades is borrowing more than any other country in the world. In many respects, the world economy is dependent on an American engine that is running on fumes. Unless it is brought under control, the US savings crisis will soon be the world's problem.[5]

Subsequently, in the period following the 2008–2009 financial crisis, the basic reality of this prediction has come to pass. Moreover, with Summers himself serving as the chief of President Obama's council of economic advisors and with Volcker chairing the US Economic Recovery Advisory Board, and yet with still nothing being done to change the fundamental imbalances and problems, the inability of the US government to control the global movement of money has become obvious for all to see. And because ultra-low US interest rates (designed to expand the monetary base and restart the US economy) are inflating new speculative bubbles in equity and commodity prices around the world, the fumes that Summers spoke of are looking increasingly explosive.

The worries of finance chiefs are worth noting because they also usefully underline the degree to which financial interdependencies have political as well as economic implications. Remember that Milton Friedman inaugurated the Chicago School arguments against fiscal debt and deficit-spending as responses to recession by claiming that "inflation is always and everywhere a monetary phenomenon." Today, however, those who continue in his tradition of being spokesmen for the bond markets know that Friedman's monetarist axiom is simply not plausible anymore. They know that inflationary threats now loom in the form of a run on the dollar in foreign exchange markets, in other words, from external threats that go far beyond Friedman's focus on an autonomous national economy. They therefore understand instead that the danger of inflation in the United States is also all about a global situation in which Americans have become completely dependent on the willingness of foreigners to keep on buying dollar denominated debt. In addition, and far from just a monetary phenomenon relating to the supply and demand for US dollar debt, inflation in America and many other wealthy countries is also now increasingly determined by price levels in other poorer countries such as China. Thus, in a telling online *Wall Street Journal* report of 2011 entitled "Chinese Inflation Goes Global," a *Market Watch* reporter explained that the rising cost of labor and raw materials in China was creating a new, and significantly higher, "China Price" that was in turn being passed on to consumers of Chinese-made commodities right around the world.[6] Through the 1990s and into the new millennium, he reported, China had been a source of global deflation to the extent that its poorly paid workers also effectively worked to reduce the global prices charged for a vast range of consumer goods. But by 2011, this pattern was put into reverse, thereby also exporting price inflation along with all the Chinese-made goods on which the world had come to depend. And to the degree that this was coinciding with increasing Chinese government concerns about putting its sovereign savings into Treasuries and other US dollar denominated assets, the inflationary impact looks set to be further exacerbated by a possible sell-off of dollars in foreign exchange markets, too. So much, then, for inflation only being a matter of national monetary policy.

The dollar-depreciating danger of China selling off its US assets (or even of just reducing its regular purchases of Treasuries), and the reciprocal and often protectionist angst in America about China's rising economic clout, indicate in turn the salience of a metaphor used by many to describe the precarious global financial ties as a form of "mutually assured destruction." Having emerged from the threat of mutually assured nuclear destruction in the Cold War, the United States in the new millennium is positioned in another mutually destructive scenario vis-à-vis its codependency on foreign producers-cum-creditors. It is this new balance of financial terror in which the world lives today. America's creditors have the nuclear option of withholding their loans, sending the dollar into free-fall and crashing the US economy, but in doing so, they would destroy the value of their dollar assets and also their main export market. This means that the nuclear option would also destroy their own economies. There is, as many have commented, something extremely odd and unnerving about the world's greatest power being the world's greatest debtor. However, as this section has shown, the United States is no ordinary debtor. It has historically borrowed easily from world financial markets in its own currency, and while this exorbitant privilege is no longer linked to controlling the world's supply of gold or being the workshop of the world, and while it is now based on the much more shaky arrangement of mutually assured financial destruction across the Pacific, it remains a privilege that can be traced back to the glory days of US power at Bretton Woods. In the next section, we examine what has happened to other debtor nation-states who have never enjoyed such power and privilege, nation-states that had little or no say at Bretton Woods but whose fate nonetheless has been deeply entangled with the ups and downs of the dollar reserve system that was established in 1944.

5.3   Debt, Inequality, and Global Poverty Management

Debt and economic crisis have long been linked in the global development of capitalism. Historians have shown that intense periods of growth in production have always been followed by periods of growth in finance and indebtedness, and that these have always in turn led into bouts of devaluation and economic depression.[7] This was the story of the 1929 Wall Street crash and the great depression that followed, and, before this, it was also the story with the Latin American and Middle Eastern crises of the 1870s. However, the debt crises that developed in developing countries in the aftermath of 1971 were different in so far as they were tied together globally. Thanks both to the increased integration of the world economy and the increased integration of the global finance industry itself, the end of the dollar–gold peg set the conditions for a perfect storm of debt and depression in the developing world.

5.3.1   The development of the debt crises

In terms of the world economy, let us recall what happened during the 1970s when the dollar was allowed to float in the market and thus fall in value. First, there was the global recession that depressed demand for exports right around the world. Second, there were the rapid price rises for basic staple commodities priced in dollars, notably oil. While the United States and other wealthier countries suffered stagflation as a result, the double hit of the decline in global demand for exports and the rise in the price of oil was much more debilitating for developing countries. For them, the basic economic decline was compounded by a significant drop in the amount of official development assistance that the United States and other developed countries were willing to provide. As a result, they suddenly found themselves without any money to pay for the national development initiatives that they had begun in the post-colonial period of the 1950s and 1960s. Moreover, in many places, these economic troubles came together with the Cold War militarization of the developing world to create political instabilities that in turn allowed a number of brutal military dictatorships to come to power. Often, these military dictatorships borrowed huge sums from foreign creditors in order to build up their armies and personal fortunes. Yet even when dictators were not involved, the underlying economic problems of falling export profits and rising oil prices combined to create a widespread "push" towards borrowing.

Added to all the "push" factors, there was also a "pull" factor. The dollar profits generated by OPEC and the other commodity cartels in the mid 1970s had to go somewhere. Not wanting to invest their petrodollars (profits from selling oil in dollars) in the United States itself, oil producers followed the Soviet Union's more long-standing practice of placing dollar savings in dollar accounts in banks in London. Known as Eurodollars, these dollar accounts were outside of direct US government control. For the same reason, they operated under extremely liberalized free-market rules. Although often managed by American-owned banks, Eurodollar deposits could therefore be loaned out without the traditional demands for minimal cash reserves that applied in the United States itself. Replacing such reserve requirements, the investment banks making Eurodollar loans did so merely on the basis of their own assessment of the creditworthiness of their borrowers. In addition, instead of applying interest rates based on the Federal Reserve's target overnight rate, Eurodollar accounts were subject to interest rates based on the London Inter-Bank Offered Rate or LIBOR. These distinctions might seem small, but they were to have extremely significant implications when developing countries began to default on the loans, and the spread between LIBOR and the Fed funds target rate increased. Moreover, they also helped create the "pull" into debt in the first place because the distinctly deregulated quality of the Eurodollar markets enabled reckless lending practices. While initially based on the recycling of petrodollars, this lending really took off in the late 1970s when the United States itself added to the global oversupply of dollars by printing yet more money to balance the federal budget. Awash in cash that they needed to turn into loans and free to make loans even when they did not have cash reserves, the Eurodollar lenders became increasingly aggressive in lending to the increasingly desperate developing-country borrowers. Moreover – and this is extremely important – they made the loans in dollars at *low* but *adjustable* LIBOR-based interest rates. Most of the bankers did not think the big developing countries would go bankrupt. They also tended to be paid on commission. Thus, they aggressively competed with one another to lend billions of dollars, and it was this aggressive lending that led in turn to the pull into indebtedness for so many developing countries.

The aggressive lending by the commercial banks reached its height between 1978 and 1982 when a number of smaller African and Eastern European economies had already begun to default because of rising interest rates and a falling export market. But in 1982, the risk associated with the much bigger loans to Latin American counties also started to become clear. The 1982 war between Argentina and Britain over the Malvinas/Falkland islands so unnerved the big banks that they stopped all new loans to Argentina. This led to Argentina's effective default on its existing loan payments, and this then created the catalyst for the much bigger default of Mexico in August 1982, then Brazil in November 1982, and then Venezuela in February 1983. By 1984, virtually the whole of Latin America and the Caribbean was engulfed by debt crises. The actual financial mechanics of the loan defaults varied from one country to the next. Likewise, the problems were exacerbated in some countries by bad leadership, militarization, and corruption, in others by bad planning and waste, and in yet other cases by plain bad luck. However, the underlying reason for why all these developing countries went into crisis at the same time in the early 1980s lies in the structure of global finance and the asymmetric influence therein of the dollar. Remember what was happening to the dollar in America during the same period. President Carter had appointed Volcker as an inflation-fighting Fed chairman, and he had rapidly raised interest rates. This had two extremely significant results vis-à-vis developing-country debt. First, by increasing the global supply of dollar denominated bonds available to investors (and thereby forcing the commercial issuers of bonds to increase interest rates to attract new investors), the Fed move also increased the LIBOR interest-rate – from 9.2% in 1978 to about 16.6% in 1981. Second, it simultaneously increased the value of the dollar in which most of the loans to the developing world had been denominated. So, developing countries suddenly saw their interest-rate payments rise while also seeing the overall value of their dollar denominated debts become much larger vis-à-vis the payment power of their own domestic currencies. Added to these financial challenges, many of them also meanwhile had to confront the fact that the value of their own exports was declining because of the global economic downturn in export markets brought on by the recession caused by the high interest rates in North America and Europe. The perfect storm of debt had hit, and much destruction was to follow in its wake.

5.3.2 Debt and dispossession

The damaging impacts of the debt crises in the developing countries have been many. They have included widespread increases in poverty, unemployment, ill-health, famine, disease, child mortality, political instability, and civil war. Yet these social, medical, and political problems – which continue and which we examine more closely in later chapters – are by no means the whole story. They have been worsened over time by a terrible spiral of decreasing economic productivity, decreasing autonomy, and decreasing investment in infrastructure, education, and health care. The more the crises have continued, the more the decline and disinvestment have taken developing countries down this destructive spiral towards deeper and more desperate forms of dependency. Many accounts of the 1980s debt crises focus solely on these problems of dependency and tend either to blame the victims or to decry their victimization. Some critics talk endlessly about the corruption of debt-dependent governments, while others point to the ways in which the United States and other wealthy countries initially encouraged developing countries to go into debt to fund projects designed to bolster capitalism in the context of the Cold War. Relatedly, there are also the many extremely tragic cases of odious debt. This is the sort of debt burden created by the borrowing of military dictators such as General Suharto in Indonesia or the Duvalier regimes in Haiti: borrowing that paid for weapons that were used to persecute national populations who then, in a horrendous twist of fate, also ended up later having to pay back the dictators' debts. Yet, while the history of the debt crises is filled with these examples of corruption, victimization, and odious debt, it is important to remember that the financial dependency of these countries was also from the very start a form of *interdependency* involving the exposure and vulnerability of the big banks who had made so many of the loans. For example, the debts of Brazil, Argentina, and Mexico alone exceeded the assets owned by the American banks that had leant to them by 32% in 1984. In other words, the developing-world debt crises were also simultaneously developed-world banking crises. Considered from the point of view of global financial ties, the two sets of problems were one, and it was this money-mediated global interdependency, much more than any concern for the tragedy of the developing world, that led leaders of global finance to talk about the need for a coordinated global response. As Paul Volcker himself said in 1983: "Our concern for maintaining a well functioning financial system is rooted in self-interest, not in altruism."[8]

Understanding that the response by developed countries was rooted in self-interest is crucial because it helps explain both the character and the limits of the three main strategies that have subsequently developed to address the debt crises. The first and by far the most enduring and influential of these strategies has been *structural adjustment*; the second has been *debt relief*; and the third and most recent development has been *microfinance*. We shall deal with each of these three strategies in turn, but it is worth noting at the start that, despite their difference from one another, all three strategies are based on models of managing global patterns of poverty rather than directly regulating global finance itself. As such, they can all also be described as neoliberal strategies in so far as they are based upon the idea that free-market practices provide the best way of organizing behavior.

5.3.3   Structural adjustment

Initially, structural adjustment was the most obvious approach for developed-country financial leaders to take in order to protect their banks and bank investors from the debt crises. It took the form of the IMF and World Bank providing new loans on the condition that the structures of political and economic regulation in the indebted countries be changed. The whole emphasis of this re-regulation was in turn focused on creating economies that would be able to make prompt and reliable loan repayments for the remaining period of the rescheduled loans. It was not meant to stop the downward spiral of dependency by restoring development initiatives based on social and educational investment. In other words, the narrow goal was simply to ensure that the developing countries would eventually pay back the loans and thereby prevent a collapse of commercial banking in the developed world. Based on neoliberal assumptions that the best way to do this was through the introduction of free-market reforms, the resulting structural adjustment plans (SAPs) always took the same form in whatever country they were imposed. Their rules, also known as "conditionalities," generally took the form of the neoliberal norms discussed in Chapter 2, including most importantly for the IMF and World Bank:

1. cutting public spending
2. reducing inflation
3. expanding free trade
4. encouraging foreign investment
5. business flexibility and deregulation.

As we shall see in Chapter 7, these five key conditionalities of structural adjustment created a form of disciplinary neoliberalism, replacing diverse national-state policies with a one-size-fits-all recipe for pro-market governance. While the expansion and entrenchment of this regime of policy-making were and continue to be contested by citizens complaining about the loss of national sovereignty, it is important to note here though that among economists at the IMF and World Bank in DC there was (through the 1980s and early 1990s at least) a great deal of agreement on the benefits of these policies. For the same reason, they are commonly referred to collectively as the **Washington Consensus**.

Given that the IMF and World Bank are based in Washington DC, and given that these two Bretton Woods institutions came to take an increasingly important role in imposing and monitoring structural adjustment in the years that followed, the term Washington Consensus made sense. It was also a useful term in so far as it underlined the centrality of the US government – in particular the US Treasury and Federal Reserve – in guiding the imposition of structural adjustment on developing countries. But in other ways, the notion of a Washington Consensus was always a bit misleading. Presented as expert advice from the father figures of the global economy to their errant children in the developing world, the focus on structurally re-regulating developing world economies simultaneously let developed world banks and their investors off the hook. Their lending practices did not have to be structurally readjusted, and nor did they have to accept any kind of austerity. The whole focus on implementing neoliberal norms in the developing world therefore meant that the banks and their investors did not have to share either the blame or the pain of the debt crises. By putting Washington at the center, the city centers of world banking could be ignored. London with its Eurodollar lenders in "the City," New York with its investment banks on "Wall Street," and Paris with its "Paris Club" consortium of creditors could all continue with business as usual while the talk was about structural adjustment being imposed by institutions based in Washington DC. Of course, developing countries complained about this, and in this respect, the notion of a Washington Consensus was also off the mark because there never really was a consensus, certainly not a global one. It is true that increasing numbers of developing-country leaders – many of them trained in US economics programs – bought into the idea that structural adjustment was a necessary response to the debt crises. But there were always cogent complaints, too, including, for example, the Jamaican leader Michael Manley's articulate criticisms of the IMF and World Bank recalled in the film *Life and Debt*. Similarly, it should be noted that there were also active efforts by developing countries (notably Brazil, Mexico, Venezuela, and Argentina) to forge a cartel of debtors and thereby threaten a collaborative refusal to pay back the debt. When these efforts collapsed, it had less to do with agreement on the Washington Consensus, and much more with the raw power of the creditors to break up the consensus of the debtors by offering special deals to particular countries such as Mexico.

5.3.4   From debt rescheduling to debt relief

Over time, however, even the consensus among economic leaders in Washington has broken down because of the global trail of disaster that followed in the wake of structural adjustment. The countries that have come back from the debt crisis years most successfully – countries such as South Korea, Malaysia, and Singapore – have done so by implementing all sorts of non-neoliberal controls over finance and business, as well as making big investments in public services such as housing, education, and transportation. Meanwhile, the countries that implemented structural adjustment experienced "lost decades" in which the problems of debt continued to fester and build. By sending all of their domestic savings abroad to service their debt, they lost any capacity to make investments in the sorts of development policies that would turn the situation around. Moreover, the conditionalities of structural adjustment, including the insistence on public-sector cuts, privatization, and reduced taxation, all further eroded their economic control over development thereby making the countries more vulnerable to the kinds of external financial shocks that created the debt crises in the first place. The result was a debt trap, a vicious cycle of increasing indebtedness and decreasing developmental opportunity. Despite delivering millions of dollars in debt service payments to the banks, countries from Asia to Latin America to Africa found themselves owing yet more money in the 1990s than when the crises began. In 1980, the total publicly guaranteed debt owed by developing countries was about $324 billion, which represented 20% of the GNP of these countries. By 1992, after all the structural adjustments, austerity, and debt-service payments, this total debt had ballooned to the figure $865 billion, which by this point represented 31% of their collective GNP. As a result, the self-reinforcing problems of indebtedness only increased.

The problems of the debt trap and the related need for debt relief were only acknowledged very slowly by global financial leaders. They preferred to talk about the "moral hazard" of debt cancellation (i.e. the idea that if you cancel a country's debts, it simply rewards bad governments and bad lenders – a view that was often also shared by borrowers like South Korea that *did* pay back their loans). Only in the late 1990s, as the unfairness, rigidity, and outright failures of structural adjustment became painfully clear, did world economic experts talk about the need for a "post-Washington Consensus." Joseph Stiglitz, for example, a former chief economist at the World Bank, discussed his discontent with the IMF's ongoing insistence on financial liberalization; and even the IMF itself came to acknowledge, albeit rather begrudgingly, that structural adjustment conditionalities were not always and every-where appropriate.[9] There was therefore no longer any consensus that structural adjustment was the right thing to do. It had worked in the short term as a solution to the developed world's banking crisis. Likewise, as we shall see in Chapter 7, it enabled the development of a whole new global system of neoliberal governance mediated by financial markets and risk-ratings agencies. However, the strategy of making the developing countries carry all the burden of the debt merely extended the underlying problems by creating dependency and thus more instability, crisis, and debt. In the face of these failures, the initial responses of financial leaders simply represented more elaborate mechanisms for implementing structural adjustment. Even when debt relief was discussed in the late 1980s and early 1990s, it was used to refer to various sorts of debt for equity swaps, not outright debt cancellation. But over time, the various plans developed to deal with the debt crises have led slowly from the banking model of debt restructuring towards a new global governance model incorporating debt cancellation. In so far as this post-Washington consensus on debt relief is in some senses a response to the increasing global criticism of the IMF and World Bank, we therefore need to trace its development by going back to events in Washington in the 1980s when US leaders shifted debt management away from the commercial banks by expanding the roles of the two DC-based Bretton Woods institutions.

The 1985 plan of US Treasury Secretary, James Baker, sought to diffuse some of the pressures on the investment banks by increasing the role of the IMF and empha-sizing that structural adjustment needed to come with growth. When this growth failed to materialize, and when the debt-related problems of disease, famine, and civil war in sub-Saharan Africa started to become more obvious at the end of the 1980s, US Secretary of State Nicholas Brady articulated another plan in 1989 that focused further on the need for the World Bank to join with the IMF in providing new loans that would pay off the older debts to the banks. By this point, the exposure of the banks had been reduced considerably. Official debt owed to governments, the IMF, and the World Bank now represented a much larger share of overall develop-ing-country debt. But still there was little sign of growth and development in the indebted countries. Indeed, for many of them, the ongoing attempts at structural adjustment had led only to more misery and, despite paying back billions in loan payments, still increasing debt burdens. World Bank data for the 33 most severely

indebted countries indicate thus that from 1982 to 1992, their debts had almost tri-
pled in relation to their ability to pay (their debt-to-export ratios rising over the 10
years from 266% to 620%). It was this deepening crisis – including the related disaster of the AIDS pandemic in sub-Saharan Africa (see Chapter 9) – that provoked
increasing global criticism. The supposed moral hazard of providing debt relief
came thus to be surpassed by the moral failure to halt the increasing suffering and
death due to debt all around the world. It was in this context that the World Bank
and IMF jointly launched a new debt-management program in 1996, called the
Heavily Indebted Poor Country initiative (or HIPC).

Promoted as a form of debt relief, HIPC still remained a hybrid form of structural
adjustment designed on the basis of a poverty-management model. The aim was not
to cancel debt altogether, but simply reduce it to levels of so-called debt sustainability. Moreover, the 38 countries identified as eligible for the relief based on their
chronic poverty problems had to sign on to a new hybrid regime of conditionalities.
They had to show a strong commitment to privatization and other neoliberal policies that were part of the old structural adjustment package, but, at the same time,
they also had to target what little new public spending they could muster on poverty
reduction, health, and education. In order to do this targeting, the World Bank and
IMF obliged the HIPC countries to develop Poverty Reduction Strategy Papers
(PRSPs) through extensive public dialogue. The aim of this process was to reduce
the danger that funds provided for debt relief might go to corrupt officials rather
than the poor. There was in this respect a genuine concern for the poor. But the
process of developing Poverty Reduction Strategies that satisfied World Bank and
IMF managers also meant that the whole HIPC approach has continued to enforce
neoliberal policy norms based on assumptions – still consistently assumed at the
IMF if not always at the World Bank – that export-led growth, privatization, and the
liberalization of trade and finance are the only way out of poverty. Even the World
Bank web page that heralds the HIPC initiative notes in this respect that: "A stable
macro-economic environment underpins the growth-friendly reforms undertaken
in such areas as legal system reforms, the establishment of a reliable and accountable
financial system, and the fostering of a self-sustaining private sector development."[10]
The same page points in turn to the "Payoffs for Poor People" delivered by the initiative, arguing that "HIPC Initiative participants have already shown how funds
freed up by lower debt levels can be channeled into deserving poverty-reducing programs." But despite small examples of success, the results of HIPC programs have
remained overshadowed by the vast scale of ongoing poverty in the indebted countries. Against the backcloth of this ongoing poverty and the neoliberal conditionalities (which continue to make countries vulnerable to external shocks), debt
sustainability has sounded more and more like a contradiction in terms.

In 2000, the ongoing desperate poverty of the developing world led the UN to
articulate eight Millennium Development Goals (MDGs) to be achieved by 2015
(see Table 5.2).

With its eighth goal calling explicitly for debt relief as part of new development
partnerships, the UN underlined the need to replace debt service payments with

Table 5.2[11]   Millennium development goals to be achieved by 2015

1. Halve extreme poverty and hunger
2. Achieve universal primary education
3. Empower women and promote equality between women and men
4. Reduce under-five mortality
5. Reduce maternal mortality
6. Reverse the spread of diseases, especially HIV/AIDS and malaria
7. Ensure environmental sustainability
8. Create a global partnership for development

social service payments and other forms of anti-poverty investment. NGO groups such as Oxfam and Jubilee have insisted still more strongly that the realization of *all* the UN development goals will not be possible without real debt relief. All eight goals will be impossible to achieve by 2015, they point out, unless the debt trap is eliminated through complete debt cancellation. With many other voices making similar arguments – voices ranging from the Pope, Madonna, and Bono to street protesters in Seattle, Porto Alegre, and Mumbai – world finance leaders finally made their first meaningful move towards real debt relief with the announcement in 2005 of a new Gleneagles consensus: a new deal for the world's most impoverished countries announced by the leaders of the G8 at a luxury golf course – Gleneagles – in Scotland. At first blush, the announcement appeared radically new because it introduced the principle of 100% debt cancellation. Even Oxfam declared the initiative "a serious step forward." But on closer inspection, the step remained limited in relation to the full scale of the problems. To put the deal in perspective, Oxfam therefore also noted that: "at present a child dies every three seconds as a result of poverty; on the basis of the G8 deal, by 2010 a child will die every three and a half seconds as a result of poverty."[12]

Under the Gleneagles deal, 18 countries will cease making any payments on debts owed to the World Bank, the African Development Bank, and the IMF, and over time, their overall debt will be reduced to zero. In the medium term, the same deal could also be extended to another 20 countries, thereby including all of the countries currently covered under the HIPC poverty management system. However, another large set of countries (including Angola, Burundi, Côte d'Ivoire, Kenya, Nigeria, Sudan, Somalia, and Zimbabwe) that do not currently qualify for HIPC treatment will be excluded because they have the wrong kind of government (e.g. a dictatorship or ongoing civil war) or the wrong kind of economy (e.g. an oil industry that can turn a profit even if, as in Nigeria, these dividends reach very few in a vast population). In sub-Saharan Africa, these excluded countries collectively account for a third of the population, and numbering more than 260 million, they represent a populace almost the size of the United States living with chronic debt and associated disease and poverty problems that will not be addressed under the Gleneagles plans. Moreover, even those countries who do qualify face two big challenges with the Gleneagles deal. First, since most of the $17 billion of debt being cancelled is owed to the World Bank, and since the World Bank will finance this write-off by simultaneously cutting aid budgets to the countries in question, the net benefit to these countries will be much reduced. Second, since the whole deal comes under World Bank control, it will not be a radical departure from the HIPC poverty-management model. In this sense, the small print produced by the World Bank in its own upbeat assessment of Gleneagles also exposes the limits of the deal – its cuts to aid, its hybrid HIPC conditionalities, and thus its underlying emphasis on neoliberal austerity. Under the title of "Potential Benefits," the World Bank notes thus that:

> Moral hazard and equity concerns associated with previous debt relief would be avoided since "gross assistance flows" from [the World Bank] to eligible countries would be reduced by the volume of debt relief. Re-allocating "replacement" donor contributions using [the World Bank's] performance based allocation system would help strengthen the link between resource transfers and country performance.[13]

5.3.5   Microcredit and microfinance

The World Bank's neoliberal "performance based allocation system" is not unrelated to the third and newest global response to debt and poverty problems: microfinance. As well as being the year of Gleneagles, 2005 was also declared by the UN as the year of microcredit, and, just as the Gleneagles deal was conditioned by the World Bank's emphasis on fiscal prudence at a national level, so microcredit in turn is conditioned by a neoliberal emphasis on fiscal prudence at a personal level. A related note about vocabulary is needed here: namely that the transition from the original term "microcredit" to the now common designation of "microfinance" serves to flag the degree to which for-profit interests have taken over this micro approach to poverty management. To put this in more technical terms, the micro-neoliberalism of encouraging personal entrepreneurship has now with micro-finance been effectively twinned with the macro-neoliberalism of for-profit global banking. An ironic but telling result in the age of the new millennium development goals is that microfinance is commonly described as a new profit-making frontier by big private banks. However, it did not start this way.

The original concept of microcredit was to give small loans to individual poor people in developing countries to overcome historical, geographical, and social exclusions from financing and develop entrepreneurial initiatives in their communities. It was not a direct response to the chronic problems of developing country debt, but rather a strategy for addressing the related problems of personal poverty and the usury of loan sharks to which poor people in developing countries are commonly vulnerable. To be sure, the fact that microfinance now uses the mechanism of debt to manage poverty means that – like structural adjustment and debt relief – it retains a post-Bretton Woods emphasis on regulating the poor rather than global finance. However, unlike the Washington consensus and unlike the Gleneagles consensus on debt cancellation, microcredit was for three reasons rather different (at least when it began). First, it originated not as a global plan of rich country financial experts, but rather as a local initiative of a poor country economist, Muhammad Yunus, for addressing chronic poverty problems in his own nation-state, Bangladesh. Second, right from these Bangladeshi beginnings, microcredit has been associated with the targeting of loans at women. Since Yunus founded the non-profit Grameen Bank in 1976, it has issued more than $3 billion in loans to approximately 2.4 million borrowers, and 94% of these borrowers have been women. And third, as it spread to other countries, it adapted to the particular political, social, and cultural contexts of implementation in a wide variety of ways: sometimes addressing the infrastructure needs and non-financial services (such as health care) necessary for ensuring a successful business environment for borrowers; and other times ignoring these wider development needs and focusing solely on transforming and scaling up microcredit as high-profit microfinance.

With its Bangladeshi beginnings and its distinctive focus on loans to individual women, microcredit initially marked a novel "Bangladesh consensus" on development policy. Successful development according to this consensus was assumed to come from the work of rational economic women becoming entrepreneurs in their villages rather than from the expertise of rational economic men at the IMF and World Bank dispensing advice in Washington. But as the IMF and World Bank have begun to embrace and remake microcredit as microfinance, the results of merging the Bangladesh and Washington visions have led to widespread profiteering and thus interest rates and fees that make microfinance just as bad as the loan shark business it was originally meant to replace. It is always important therefore to ask about the interest rates charged by for-profit microfinance organizations. They may treat you as if you had just farted at a fancy conference, and, indeed, if you are at a conference that is full of boasts about helping vulnerable women to become smiling entrepreneurs, such a question may appear very unseemly. But it is no less important to ask, because it cuts to the heart of the economics involved in turning non-profit microcredit into for-profit microfinance. This, then, is not to deny the many successes of non-profit microcredit. Women previously excluded from economic activities were often given the chance to join both informal and formal work-worlds. They were also thereby enabled to provide much needed financial support to their families, and this in turn has often improved opportunities for their children as well as for the women borrowers themselves. For example, a study in Bangladesh found that almost 100% of girls in Grameen Bank client households went to school, whereas the rate of school attendance by girls in non-client households was only 60%. Moreover, since the average rate of default on their loans is very low, and, because many microcredit banks like Grameen are not run primarily for profit, most of the monies that are paid back are recycled as new loans at low interest rates to new borrowers. However, as microcredit has turned to microfinance and spread to other countries through the huge global expansion of Microfinance Institutions (MFIs), there has been widespread criticism from NGOs, governments, and borrowers themselves that it is becoming just another form of credit-baiting targeted at some of the most vulnerable people in the world.

In Nicaragua in 2009, for instance, protestors took to the streets to launch non-payment protests against MFIs in much the same way as developing countries saw anti-IMF street protests against structural adjustment in the 1980s. And in 2010, Indian policy-makers in the state of Andhra Pradesh adopted a tough new ordinance on MFIs after a spate of 35 suicides associated with harassment by micro-loan debt collectors.[14] Meanwhile, critics also argue that women in the programs often exploit their own children in the entrepreneurial activities they set up; that they are also often driven to compete with one another in ways that destroy successful and enduring forms of social collaboration; and that the "solidarity groups" used by microcredit banks to instill good entrepreneurial practice have meanwhile effectively financialized everyday life among poor women, reducing their autonomy and increasing their stress and vulnerability to external market-based shocks.[15]

For the critics, the broader problem with global transformation of microcredit into microfinance is precisely the way it has become taken over by profit-making imperatives in the course of being incorporated into a broader panoply of post-Washington consensus anti-poverty programs.[16] When commentators talk about microfinance instead of microcredit, it is a signal that the non-profit aspect of the Grameen Bank's original approach (which relied on grants for start-up money) has been overtaken by the *for*-profit approaches of the financial-service industry. Big commercial banks such as HSCB, Deutsche Bank, and Citibank increasingly view microfinance as a profit-making basis for their own financial good health, and, recovering from the mass defaults of US sub-prime borrowers, the bankers are especially excited it seems by the extremely high loan-repayment rates recorded on microloans in Bangladesh. In another indication of the increasing business interest in turning non-profit microcredit into for-profit microfinance, there is also a website called The Mix Market. While it began as a UN development project, The Mix Market aspires to be a NASDAQ for microfinance and looks like any other financial services website offering investors the opportunity to investigate the risk ratings and benchmarks for returns on investment through "heat-maps" of microfinance projects around the globe. The remaking of microcredit as microfinance has also been marked by the World Bank's own embrace of the concept, an embrace that acknowledges the south Asia roots of the ideas (and the importance of women within them), but then very quickly returns to conventional banking jargon about financial services and infrastructure. Thus, the Bank's own webpage *Celebrating the year of microcredit*, uses the following revealing language:

> The World Bank Group's portfolio in microfinance initiatives has risen to over $1 billion in recent years. The key challenge for microfinance today is not money, but scale – providing high quality financial services and offering financial products to the broadest group possible, and those with the greatest need.[17]

It should be emphasized that the World Bank's own stated goal is not the for-profit expansion of microfinance. It clearly views microloans as another way of pursuing the UN's anti-poverty Millennium Development Goals. But, all the while it is also simultaneously encouraging the expansion of a new for-profit frontier for commercial banks, the chances of reaching these goals through microfinance seem remote.

The concerns about co-optation and the credit-baiting of women noted, it also needs to be remembered in conclusion that microcredit remains an extremely diverse global phenomenon. All kinds of NGOs and philanthropic organizations remain committed to developing non-profit microcredit opportunities that are community-based and locally managed (e.g. FINCA). Others, such as the Gates Foundation, are now focusing instead on supporting micro-savings rather than pushing loans. Moreover, through other still more informal forms of family-based credit pooling in Asian migrant communities and transnational charity networks among Islamic communities there are also a vast range of other kinds of global financial networks being developed today that seek to tackle the problems of poverty created by the ongoing global debt crises. The complexities of these networks are the subject of extensive study and elaboration elsewhere.[18] However, this chapter has set the scene for understanding the significance of such globally networked responses by explaining how the global debt crises emerged after the unraveling of Bretton Woods in the 1970s. By charting the financial history of the rise and fall of the Bretton Woods regime, the chapter has also explained how the dollar has come to be such an important but precarious global reserve currency, and how the twentieth century was marked by the rise and fall of attempts to regulate global finance. Now that we live in a world of unregulated finance and regulated poverty, much attention has been placed on whether and how developing countries can export their way out of poverty through free trade. However, as we shall now turn to examine in Chapter 6, free trade also has all sorts of legal and quasi-constitutional implications that in turn make it just as regulatory for developing countries and poor communities as the other aspects of structural adjustment and poverty management explored in this chapter.

Student Exercises

Group:
The following is a suggestion for a group debate on the implications of global financial flows on the longterm value of the dollar.

In July 2006, the *Financial Times* "Currencies" section puzzled through the implications of new data on global portfolio investment coming into the United States. It noted that: "Cross-border portfolio flows data compiled by the US Treasury showed the United States attracted net inflows of $69.6 bn in May up from $51.1 bn in April and enough to cover May's trade deficit." It also highlighted that "foreign official institutions (such as central banks) were small net sellers of long-term securities, and the inflows were driven by private demand." Summing up the views of market players, the report suggested that opinion was divided on whether this was good or bad sign about the long-term prospects for the dollar. On the one side, Monica Fan from RBC Capital Markets said that "The composition and size of US securities inflows, especially the reduced reliance on central bank appetite for US Treasuries, is neutral to broadly positive for the dollar." On the other side, Simon Hayley from Capital Economics disagreed: "arguing that while Asian central banks were no longer propping up the dollar, a sharp upturn in buying from the United Kingdom merely pointed to the recycling of Middle Eastern petrodollars." (*FinancialTimes*, July 19, 2006: 20).

Divide into two subgroups. Let one side argue the case of Fan that the reduced reliance on Asian central bank purchases and the increased private demand was positive news for the dollar. Let the other side argue the case of Hayley that the increased private demand merely indicated a switch in dependency onto the investments by oil-rich individuals from the Middle East.

Based on the discussion of debt-based dollar dominance in this chapter, each side must explain why the dollar is likely to go up (following Fan) or down (following Hayley) in the longer term as a result of these changing global buying patterns. After the debate, discuss the degree to which the financial crises starting in 2008 have changed (or not) these underlying trends.

Individual:

Write a list of all the ways in which your own personal everyday life is governed by financial market processes and practices. Be sure to include both macro market forces (such as the way in which the government austerity forced by bond-market concerns leads to things like tuition increases) and micro market imperatives (such as the way a concern with your FICO score or other credit scores leads you to make certain sorts of consumption choices). When you look at the list as a whole, to what degree do you see your whole life being structured and managed as a kind of investment fund?

Notes

1   For a brilliant discussion of the monstrous side of money and its ties to the "black gold" of oil, see Michael Watts, "Oil as Money: The Devil's Excrement and the Spectacle of Black Gold," in *Reading Economic Geography*, eds, Trevor J. Barnes, Jamie Peck, Eric Sheppard, and Adam Tickell (Oxford: Blackwell, 2004), 204–19.
2   Quoted in United States Department of State, Proceedings and Documents of the United Nations Monetary and Financial Conference – Bretton Woods, New Hampshire July 1–22, 1944, vol. 1 (Washington, DC: US Government Printing Office, 1948), 81.
3   Bob Tamarkin quoted in Robert Kolb, *Futures, Options and Swaps*, 3rd edition (Oxford: Blackwell, 2000, 89.)
4   Paul A. Volcker, "An Economy On Thin Ice," *Washington Post* Sunday, April 10 (2005): B07.
5   Lawrence Summers, "America Overdrawn," *Foreign Policy* July–August 1, 43 (2004): 46–50.
6   Craig Stephen, "Chinese Inflation Goes Global: New China Price, As We All Pay for Wage Hikes," *MarketWatch*, March 27, 2011, http://www.marketwatch.com/story/chinese-inflation-goes-global-2011-03-27.

7   See Giovanni Arrighi, *Adam Smith in Beijing: Lineages of the Twenty-First Century* (New York: Verso, 2007).

8   Paul Volker, "Remarks before the Subcomittee on International Finance and Monetary Policy of the Committee on Banking, Housing and Urban Affairs, US Senate, February 17th," *Federal Reserve Bulletin* 69 (1982): 175–77.

9   Joseph Stiglitz, *Globalization and Its Discontents* (New York: Norton and Company, 2002); IMF, *Distilling the Lessons from the ESAF Reviews* (Washington, DC: IMF, 1998), http://www.imf.org/external/pubs/ft/distill/index.HTM.

10 World Bank, "Debt Relief," http://web.worldbank.org/WBSITE/EXTERNAL/NEWS/0,contentMDK:20040942~menuPK:34480~pagePK:34370~theSitePK:4607,00.html.

11 Listed on the UN MDG website at http://www.un.org/millenniumgoals/.

12 Oxfam, "Justice for the World's Poor: Did the G8 Deliver?" Oxfam (2005), http://www.oxfam.org.uk/what_you_can_do/campaign/mph/g8/downloads/g8_report.pdf.

13 World Bank, "Note on the G8 Debt Relief Proposal," *World Bank* (2005), http://siteresources.worldbank.org/DEVCOMMINT/Documentation/20656508/DC2005-0023(E)-DebtRelief.pdf.

14 Elyssa Pachico, "'No Pago' Confronts Microfinance in Nicaragua," *NACLA*, Oct 28 (2009), https://nacla.org/node/6180.

15 For sophisticated evaluations of these criticisms, see Ananya Roy, *Poverty Capital: Microfinance and the Frontiers of Millennial Development* (New York: Routledge, 2010); Katherin Rankin and Yogendra Shakya, 2007, "Neoliberalising the Grassroots: Microfinance and the Politics of Development in Nepal," in Kim England and Kevin Ward, eds., *Neo-liberalization: Networks, States, Peoples:* (Oxford Blackwell, 2009), 48–76; and Milford Bateman, *Why Doesn't Microfinance Work? The Destructive Rise of Local Neoliberalism* (New York: Zed Press, 2010).

16 Mark Engler, "The Godfather of Microcredit: Is Muhammad Yunus Selling "Free Market" Neoliberalism in the Guise of Liberal Do-Gooderism?," *Dissent*, Fall (2009) http://www.dissentmagazine.org/article/?article=1976.

17 World Bank, "Celebrating the Year of Microcredit," (2005), http://web.worldbank.org/WBSITE/EXTERNAL/NEWS/0,contentMDK:20643650~menuPK:34459~pagePK:34370~piPK:34424~theSitePK:4607,00.html.

18 See, for example, Marieke de Goode, *Virtue, Fortune and Faith: A Genealogy of Finance* (Minneapolis, University of Minnesota Press, 2005); and Bill Maurer, *Mutual Life, Limited: Islamic Banking, Alternative Currencies, Lateral Reason* (Princeton, NJ: Princeton University Press, 2005).

Keywords

balance of payments	derivatives	Washington Consensus
Bretton Woods Conference	fall	World Bank
commodification	IMF	WTO
debt	rise	

6

Law

Chapter Contents

Chapter Concepts

1.   Commercial law has always been at the cutting edge of transnational law.
2.   Both regional trade agreements and the WTO have globalized commercial law.
3.   Compared to trade tribunals, the power of other international courts remains limited.
4.   While judicial globalization through international courts has been uneven, it is still changing both national and international law, especially human-rights law.
5.   Human-rights law has also been globally transformed and extended through the legal struggles of transnational advocacy networks and other social movements.
6.   The transnational fields of global law constitute a kaleidoscope of hard laws and soft laws that themselves unevenly reflect both hard and soft forms of national law-making.

Key Concept

The globalization of law has plural dimensions that are unevenly developed. While commercial law has globalized rapidly through an overlapping and globe-spanning system of trade agreements, other forms of international law relating to non-market

Introducing Globalization: Ties, Tensions, and Uneven Integration, First Edition. Matthew Sparke.
© 2013 Matthew Sparke. Published 2013 by Blackwell Publishing Ltd.

norms – such as human rights – have developed much more slowly and inconsistently, restrained, and repeatedly redefined by dominant national norms and legal frameworks. Nevertheless, these diverse fields of law do often interconnect and affect one another, creating new challenges and new opportunities for all those struggling for justice.

6.1   Trade Agreements and the Globalization of Commercial Law

It may seem surprising to see a chapter on law in a book on globalization. What could seem less globalized than tradition-bound national legal systems with their distinctive national courts, national laws, and national histories of legal precedent? And this is to say nothing of more quirky local legal traditions that range globally from judges wearing wigs to witnesses making oaths on everything from the Bible, Koran, and the Torah to animal-skins and broken plates. But, despite the wigs and all the other appearances, legal processes are integral to contemporary globalization. One reason for this is the growing significance of international courts and human-rights laws globally. Another is the offshoring of legal service work, including the outsourcing of legal research, copying, inputting, filing, and other forms of archiving to low-cost locations such as India. And yet another is the transnational spread of American legal norms thanks to Hollywood. So-called Miranda rights, for example, are commonly assumed to apply in many English-speaking countries where they do not exist because TV audiences repeatedly see American police saying: "You have a right to remain silent." Mainly, though, globalization and law are so closely entwined because of the ways in which new laws and regulations created by trade agreements have underwritten the recent growth in global economic integration. They have done so by creating transnational spaces of market competition and legally locking in pro-business market reforms. It is for these reasons, too, that law lies at the heart of some of the most contentious political debates over the regulative force of market-led globalization. Such claims may seem counter-intuitive when so much of the popular Globalization discourse that we reviewed in Chapter 2 is based on ideas about deregulation. But, by focusing directly on how law is itself changing and trans-nationalizing today, we can instead come to see how pro-business deregulation depends fundamentally on re-regulation through the creation of new transnational legal regimes. Moreover, addressing the globalization of law more generally highlights once again the inaccuracies in the myths about the newness, inevitability, and leveling of globalization.

The development of space-spanning transnational legal regimes is not new. It goes back at least to the *lex mercatoria* or merchant law of the middle ages in Europe and, before this, the sweeping imposition of Roman law, including punishments such as crucifixion, under ancient Roman imperialism. This is not to minimize the much more global and economically consequential expansion of transnational trade and investment law in the last two decades. However, these recent developments in turn indicate that the touted inevitability of Globalization has actually depended on the much-disputed and often difficult development of numerous new laws. Far from an inevitable deregulatory juggernaut, the extension of free-market systems has had to rely on a complex global patchwork of new regulations sown together with much effort and at great cost by trade lawyers writing and invoking the codes of trade agreements. These legal codes, complicated and difficult to negotiate as they have been, now effectively comprise the rulebook of market-based globalization or, as some critics have called it, the new "transnational constitution of disciplinary neoliberalism."[1]

Whether we call it a global market rulebook or a transnational neoliberal constitution, we need to understand its laws. This is not especially easy because most media discussion of legal globalization is served up as an unpalatable alphabet soup of acronyms ranging from the GATT, EU, CUFTA, NAFTA, CAFTA, FTAA, ASEAN, and MERCOSUR to the World Trade Organization's AGP, MFN, SPS, GATS, TBT, TRIMS, and TRIPS. By decoding some of the more important of these acronyms in what follows, the first goal is to make the trade agreements and their legal jargon comprehensible (if not necessarily digestible).[2] In addition, the second goal is to highlight how, contrary to flat-world visions, the so-called level playing field of so-called free trade actually relies upon a complex patchwork of bilateral, regional, and global agreements that re-regulate rather than deregulate trade. Further complicating the simple myth of leveling, the global patchwork of free-trade regimes is not only geographically varied and uneven itself, but also quite distinct from the much more frail and fraying legal initiatives that have been advanced globally to protect human rights and social justice around the world. We shall come back to these latter topics in Sections 6.2 and 6.3, where there will be occasion to discuss some of the national forces that continue to complicate the globalization of human-rights law. To begin with, though, we start here by considering the more consequential global expansion of commercial law that has been advanced through the last two decades by trade agreements and the associated development of global arbitration, global conventions, and the global business practices of law firms.

The history of medieval merchant law gives us some clues as to why and how commercial law lies on the cutting edge of today's transnational law-making. As merchants traveled far and wide through Europe to different trade fairs in the late middle ages, they needed to find ways to settle their disputes and have their business practices and contracts protected. They did so in part by agreeing to let merchant courts intervene in cases of conflict over breaches of contractual agreement. Established in trade centers on important trade routes where merchants came together, these courts were also administered by merchants as well as serving their needs. They therefore operated a system of customary law outside the traditional feudal systems of medieval government by lords, princes, and the church. This externality of merchant courts from feudal government meant that they were deprived of formal state powers of enforcement. However, they were nevertheless able to use the commercial force of exclusion – that is, refusing market access to traders who had been found guilty – to make merchant law meaningful for the trading parties brought together in the merchant courts. Meanwhile, feudal lords and princes themselves tolerated the merchant courts as separate sites of legal authority because of the increased trade and tax-collection possibilities they brought to local areas of rule.

The parallels between the medieval law merchant and today's transnational commercial laws are many. Contemporary trade and investment law has also developed to facilitate the long-distance trading of goods and capital. It, too, operates through market agencies, market professionals and semi-private tribunals operated at a remove from the national courts and the formal jurisdiction of sovereign governments. Similarly, it also leverages the penalty of trade sanctions and other forms of market exclusion to impose punishment and facilitate enforcement. However, and this is a big "however," the intervening centuries between the medieval era and the contemporary global era have involved two big transformations in the relationship between commercial law and the laws of governments, transformations that in turn have important implications for the ways in which today's transnational legal regimes are being expanded and entrenched.

The first big transformation that occurred from the development of capitalism in the sixteenth century to the nineteenth century involved the integration of the previously private merchant laws into the formal public laws of national governments. The second big transformation happened as economic exchange took off anew between nation-states in the nineteenth and twentieth centuries, leading to the redevelopment of new forms of international business law developed to handle all the commercial transactions between nation-states. While this second internationalizing transformation may seem on the surface to have reversed the nationalizing changes of the earlier period, and while it certainly created new legal regimes that transcended the borders of national-state sovereignty, it nevertheless operated in a context now completely dominated by the public law-making of national-state governments. This is important because it means that nearly all of today's transnational legal regimes remain deeply dependent on forms of national legal authority established under modern state rule. As a result, contemporary commercial law only has its transnational regulative reach because nation-states endorse and enforce it. The structural contrast with medieval merchant law is in this sense just as significant as the vast increase in the scale of global economic interactions governed by contemporary commercial laws.[3]

By far the most important feature of today's commercial legal landscape is transnational trade law. It is true that international lawyering connected to mergers and acquisitions, arbitration, asset securitization, and insurance is significant, too. Moreover, this global legal work (along with the not-always-legal lawyering that makes it possible for wealthy elites to offshore assets in tax havens such as the British Virgin Islands) has generated increasing business for a growing group of global law firms that specialize in transnational corporate legal services. The biggest and most globalized of these firms (most of them American and British) routinely have a large percentage of their lawyers working outside their home country (see Table 6.1). And even after the financial crises that started in 2008 caused

Table 6.1   Top 10 global law firms based on data from *The American Lawyer* October, 2007

Firm (home country)	Number of lawyers	Countries in which firms have offices	Percentage of lawyers operating outside of home country
Baker and Mackenzie (United States)	3335	38	81
Clifford Chance (United Kingdom)	2654	20	61
Piper International (United Kingdom)	2219	25	52
Linklaters (United Kingdom)	2197	23	63
Jones Day (United States)	2195	14	27
Freshfields Bruckhaus Deringer (United Kingdom)	2009	15	68
Allan and Overy (United Kingdom)	1895	19	56
White and Case (United States)	1826	24	63
Latham and Watkins (United States)	1810	10	23
Garrigues (Spain)	1800	8	8

widespread cutbacks amidst law firms more generally, a *Law 360* survey of the top 20 global law firms found that: "they continued to expand into nearly every corner of the world, opening offices in Asia, Africa, South America, Europe, and the Middle East, as well as at home."[4]

Indeed, this same report noted that "the top three firms have at least 70% of their attorneys stationed outside of the firm's home country, and together boast 120 international offices in more than 40 countries." At the same time, most of the world's largest TNCs also have their own internal legal teams who are constantly traveling the world negotiating contracts and litigating cases on the basis of both national laws and emerging transnational legal rules and conventions. Nevertheless, it is the core business of establishing such rules and conventions through legally binding trade agreements that dominates the debate over commercial law and globalization.

By removing barriers to trade, harmonizing national laws relating to business, and providing corporations with quasi-constitutional rights to protect their property and profits across transnational spaces, trade agreements have underwritten the huge increases in global trade and investment flows that we explored in Chapters 3 and 5. They have also thereby advanced the collective class interests of a new global *mercatocracy*: the global business class of trade lawyers, trade officials, financiers, economic experts and pro-business politicians who have put the global patchwork of trade treaties in place. As well as advancing the interests of the global business class (or the 1% as the Occupy activists refer to it), the re-regulation of global law through trade treaties has also impacted everyone else (i.e. the so-called 99%) on the planet because it has effectively re-written an enormous number of national laws in all the countries involved. These include laws affecting our health, our consumer rights, our rights as workers, our environmental protections, our mobility rights, and even our democratic rights to vote and be represented by legislators who can write new laws. Most of these areas of law may not initially appear to be directly tied to trade. To understand why they are in fact tied very tightly to trade law, we therefore have to explore the economic history and internal mechanics of trade agreements. In particular, we have to come to terms with the three main ways through which they have had their re-regulative effects, namely (1) competition, (2) harmonization, and (3) monopolization.

6.1.1　Competition

The traditional mechanism through which trade agreements operate and through which they also have many re-regulative effects is by removing barriers to cross-border trade and unleashing transnational competition. The main barriers targeted for removal in this way are **tariffs**. These are principally the fees or taxes charged by government customs agencies on imports coming into a country. Sometimes, countries also charge tariffs on exports, too, when they want to increase in-country supply and reduce costs of key commodities for domestic consumers. The imposition of export tariffs on staples such as rice and cooking oil, for instance, has happened with increasing frequency in recent times as prices have soared in many developing countries. The use of import tariffs, though, is much more widespread and has a much longer history. As we saw in Chapter 3, both during and after the Great Depression of the 1930s, many countries imposed tariffs on imports as a way of protecting domestic industries and domestic jobs from foreign competition. A scaled-back kind of tariff protectionism also continued on after World War II, even though one of the main American government goals at Bretton Woods in 1944 was to open up markets for American exports by fostering free trade. It was these free-trade goals of removing tariff barriers that subsequently became the basis of international talks over the **GATT**, the General Agreement on Tariffs and Trade. Such were the obstacles of ongoing protectionism, though, that the running joke about the GATT was that it really stood for the "General Agreement to Talk and Talk." After an initial failed attempt to create an International Trade Organization (ITO), the GATT only seemed to lead to round after round of inter-governmental talks. While agreements on tariff reductions were made in each round, they were slow to be implemented, occasionally dodged with deliberate distortions of trade such as the Multi Fiber Arrangement (MFA) in textile trade, and, in some areas such as agricultural trade, hardly advanced at all. Nevertheless, half a century later, the conclusion of the so-called Uruguay Round of GATT talks culminated in January 1995 with the creation of the World Trade Organization (**WTO**).

Governments now agree to considerable tariff reductions and "tariff-binding" (commitments to reduce tariffs to a narrow range) as part of becoming WTO members (of which there were 157 in 2012). However, tariffs have still by no means been eliminated on all trade globally. Partly because it is much harder to move farms to low-wage countries than factories, agricultural production continues to be highly protected by wealthy European countries, the United States, and Japan. It is for this reason (and because of the reciprocal calls for free trade from agricultural exporters such as Brazil who want to export into the protected markets) that further trade liberalization continues to be one of the main ongoing goals of WTO negotiations. However, the slow pace of the GATT and WTO trade liberalization process has also led over time to a long list of regional free-trade agreements that have also sought to open up cross-border competition by removing or lowering tariff barriers. The European Union (EU), the North American Free Trade Agreement (**NAFTA**), and Latin America's Southern Common Market (**MERCOSUR**) are all good examples in this respect, and they have all operated at a regional level to facilitate further tariff reductions for trade among their signatory countries. We shall come back to their differences below, but for the moment the key point to note is that all these trade agreements, both global and regional, have enabled commodities and investments to move much more cheaply across borders, and by doing this, they have in turn significantly increased cross-border competition, including both competition *between businesses* and, much more significantly from a legal perspective, competition *between places* competing for business activity and the jobs and wealth generation it promises to bring.

The competition happens because free-trade agreements allow TNCs to chose where to locate operations, or where to source components from, free from the constraint of having to make commodities in the same countries as they are sold. High tariffs in the middle of the twentieth century imposed these market-access constraints, and this is partly why big multi-national companies such as Ford set up foreign operations in the first place. It was not always cheaper to make cars in European countries, but it allowed a US company such as Ford to access the markets of European countries tariff-free. Reciprocally, by removing the tariff barriers, trade agreements have also removed this "market access" rationale for foreign production. In its place, they have introduced instead a new "market efficiency" rationale, making it possible for TNCs to locate different parts of their commodity chains in different places chosen on the basis of their cost-savings and profitability. Sometimes, this means locating certain sorts of capital-intensive or research-intensive activities in rich countries that have the necessary high-tech infrastructure and universities. But more commonly, it means relocating to lower-cost countries, some of which, like China and India, also increasingly have the infrastructure and universities, too. Consequently, TNCs can take advantage of cheaper costs of production in poorer countries without having to worry about paying tariffs when they move goods from these low-cost locations into countries with wealthier consumers (or, at least, as happened with the expansion of the consumer class in America from 1990 to 2008, to consumers who have access to cheaper credit). It is for this reason that they move production to places where labor is cheaper or less unionized, or where taxes are lower, or where environmental laws are less demanding or more weakly enforced. Just as significantly, they can also *threaten* to move to such low-cost locations as a way of forcing local governments in places where they are already located to adopt more business-friendly laws. This in turn provides pro-business politicians with the basis for their arguments that new laws are necessary to reduce taxes, to disempower unions, or to curtail environmental regulations in order to create the "flexibility" needed for competition in a cross-border economy. For these reasons, "flexibility" has become a favorite euphemism for pro-business re-regulation in the context of heightened transnational competition.

Business leaders and market fundamentalist economists tend to praise the competition unleashed by tariff reductions by pointing to the economic efficiencies generated by exploiting the so-called **comparative advantage** of different locations. Recalling in this way the "gains from trade" arguments of the nineteenth-century English economist, David Ricardo, this is how the WTO itself explains the benefits on its webpage:

> All countries, including the poorest, have assets – human, industrial, natural, financial – which they can employ to produce goods and services for their domestic markets or to compete overseas. Economics tells us that we can benefit when these goods and services are traded. Simply put, the principle of "comparative advantage" says that countries prosper first by taking advantage of their assets in order to concentrate on what they can produce best, and then by trading these products for products that other countries produce best. In other words, liberal trade policies – policies that allow the unrestricted flow of goods and services – sharpen competition, motivate innovation and breed success. They multiply the rewards that result from producing the best products, with the best design, at the best price.[5]

Such utilitarian arguments enable free-trade proponents to assert that the invisible hand of market competition will allocate the different parts of the production process to the most economically rational sites available and in this way generate the greatest growth and thus, it is assumed, greatest good for the greatest number of people. By contrast, citizen groups, unions, and environmentalists frequently contest this competitive rationalization, arguing that the market competition simultaneously creates a **"race to the bottom"** in which the "whipsawing" involved in playing one location off against another becomes an end-run on democracy itself. They point out in this way that concerns about losing local businesses and jobs to cheaper foreign production sites frequently force elected politicians to abandon their commitments to local citizens and give business whatever neoliberal legislative reform it wants. In formal legal theory, this phenomenon is referred to as a "democracy deficit." As such, it leads to complex questions about the blending of public and private authority and the related rise of bargaining-based and marketized models of administrative law.

In more informal public commentary, the terms are less polite – witness "whipsawing" and "race to the bottom" – and the questions are more urgent. What is the use of having elections for political representatives, critics ask, if those representatives end up being forced by market competition to change laws and re-write regulations designed to give business more flexibility and citizens less representation? This concern with the destruction of democracy is why, for example, both union members and environmentalists, held up signs in the anti-WTO protests in Seattle saying: "No Globalization Without Representation!"

Against the criticisms that trade agreements are anti-democratic, proponents commonly offer two standard answers. First, that it has been democratically elected national governments that have signed on to the agreements in the first place (exceptions such as the Chinese Communist Party admitted); and second, that the agreements are really just about trade law and should not therefore be mixed up with concerns about the demise of democracy. In turn, the critics retort that both counter-arguments are misleading: that, while national governments willingly sign on because they want the access to foreign markets for their country's exports, there remains no democratically elected *transnational* government that can represent the interests of non-business stakeholders across the whole space covered by a particular trade agreement (one notable counter-example to this, though, is the EU parliament discussed below). Moreover, the critics contend, at the same time as the economic integration is occurring without any sort of integrated and democratic political oversight, the trade agreements' legal effects really do reach beyond trade to affect a vast range of social, health, environmental, and cultural rights previously protected by national laws. In making the latter case, critics point to concessions made by local law-makers in order to compete with each other to keep or attract business in the tariff-free spaces of cross-border competition. In addition, though, critics also high-light the second main mechanism through which the agreements actually operate: namely, legal harmonization.

6.1.2   Harmonization

Whether they are critics or proponents of contemporary commercial law, no one denies that the binding contracts agreed to in trade agreements have direct legal effects in addition to the indirect legislative reforms and pro-business laws spurred by transnational competition. These direct legal effects are referred to in more tech-nical publications under the title of "harmonization." They result from the ways in which the agreements are generally designed to remove *non-tariff barriers* to trade in addition to removing or lowering tariffs. Non-tariff barriers, or "**NTBs**" as they are often called by trade lawyers, come in many different forms. The most common types one hears about are anti-dumping laws (passed by governments to allow for retaliatory trade sanctions), national procurement laws (to mandate government purchases from national companies), labeling and rules of origin requirements (that can be used to block imports from certain places), buy-national laws (designed to spur national job growth), and various sorts of import license, export subsidy and certification deliberately designed to allow governments to manipulate trade. In addition, though, a whole set of laws that are less obviously related to trade are now commonly treated as NTBs, too. A national law designed to protect consumers from dangerous pesticides can be an NTB. A law designed to protect national cultural industries, including magazine, film and TV industries, can be an NTB. And any sort of law aimed at providing health and social services or insurance or even educa-tion through governmental programs can also be coded as an NTB. Faced with this enormous reach of the NTB designation and all the revisions of national law it therefore makes possible, the most obvious question to ask is *why*?

Why are so many areas of national and local law subject to revision as non-tariff-barriers to trade? One way of answering this question is to consider the double-meaning of the word "protection." From the perspective of law-makers and the citizens they represent, protection often means something quite literal like protecting the food chain or water supply, protecting national cultural traditions, or protecting the sick and vulnerable. However, from the perspective of trade liberalization, the diverse laws used to provide such protection are also often considered protect*ionist* in the economic sense because they close off markets to foreign competition. The pro-competition response is therefore to remove the NTB by writing new transnational laws (what critics call a "corporate bill of rights") that effectively make the protections illegal. This is what legal harmonization through trade agreements is all about, and while the word is simple and innocuous, the actual processes of harmonization set in motion by trade agreements have proved deeply challenging for those keeping track. This is because the generalized business interest in expanding markets for goods and services has led through the complicated process of writing and implementing trade agreements to a steady *downward* harmonization of the standards governments are legally able to set for everything from food and environmental protection to public health and educational services. Let us consider a few key examples.

At the global level of the WTO, the harmonization process is linked to two core GATT agreements on Most Favored Nation (MFN) and National Treatment. The MFN agreement means that all members of the WTO are legally obligated to treat all trading parties equally. They cannot discriminate between countries, and they cannot grant a special privilege to one "most favored" country without having to do the same for all other WTO members. The National Treatment agreement in turn means that all WTO members are contractually obligated to treat imported goods and locally made goods in the same way once they are inside the market. It should be noted that while these core WTO agreements use the words "Nation" and "National," they ultimately underpin a process of *trans*national legal harmonization by controlling the shape of national legislation. They make it very hard for WTO members to introduce new national laws designed to exert governmental control over particular kinds of trade from particular countries, and they make it virtually impossible to repeal national laws allowing foreign goods and services into a country.

In addition, there are a whole set of WTO agreements that further expand the organization's legal scope in, through, and over the domestic laws of its members. These legally binding WTO contracts include:

1. Article XVI-4 of the agreement establishing the WTO that specifically requires each signatory country to ensure that its laws, regulations, and administrative procedures conform to all WTO terms.
2. The Dispute Settlement Understanding (DSU) that transfers final legal authority over any trade-related dispute to closed tribunals (closed, that is, to the press

and public, but not to TNCs and their lawyers). Staffed only by trade professionals (somewhat like medieval merchant courts), these tribunals are empowered to endorse binding trade sanctions as punishment on a member state for failing to re-write any laws found to constitute an illegal trade barrier. It was one of these tribunals that in 1998 overruled the US Endangered Species Act ban on shrimp caught in nets that kill sea turtles. The WTO tribunal found in favor of the complaint brought by India, Malaysia, Pakistan, and Thailand that the US ban was an illegal trade barrier, and concluded thus that the United States should re-write its national law to make it WTO-compliant.

3.   The Sanitary and Phyto-Sanitary (SPS) agreement that constrains precautionary public health and food policies by setting low and therefore limiting global standards for what can be treated as a health risk from contaminants, toxins, pesticides, veterinary drugs, and other disease-causing additives in foods and drinks. To harmonize food standards, the SPS agreement names the Codex Alimentarius Commission based in Rome as the ultimate arbiter of how much pesticide residue and what levels of irradiation, artificial hormones, toxic chemicals, and carcinogens are permissible in food. If member countries impose higher standards of food safety than the Codex allows, the higher standards are treated as illegal NTBs. This, for example, is what has happened to the EU's ban on artificial hormone treated beef, even though the EU was able to show that the hormone 17 beta oestradiol was carcinogenic.

4.   The Technical Barriers to Trade (TBT) agreement that sets constraints on national and local policies regarding labeling products and product standards, including warning labels on tobacco and alcohol products, and limits on lead, asbestos, PVCs, and toxic waste. If member countries impose higher public health and consumer safety requirements than the TBT allows, they are treated as illegal NTBs. It is in this way that the United States has claimed that European rules requiring producers to safely dispose of computers, cell phones, and other chemically toxic products are more onerous than they should be for American TNCs.

5.   The General Agreement on Trade in Services (**GATS**) that constrains national and local law-makers abilities to expand or create public services (such as education, health-care services or universal government insurance programs) by treating such services as traded goods and thereby allowing TNCs to claim they must be compensated for lost market share when the goods are newly provided by the government. While the GATS does not explicitly require privatization of public services and while it has some limited exceptions, it works systematically to lock in privatization where it has happened, and meanwhile creates huge disincentives against maintaining public services once private-sector services are allowed into a particular field. The break-up of Canadian Medicare, for example, seems set to continue thanks in part to the way GATS locks in the privatization of particular medical services by particular Canadian provinces. Meanwhile, post-Enron US legislation designed to make accounting practices more transparent and open (the 2002 Sarbanes-Oxley law) has been challenged by EU officials as an illegal NTB under GATS.

6. The Trade Related Investment Measures (TRIMs) agreement that limits the ability of national law-makers to shape the development of domestic businesses by setting rules for how foreign investors in such businesses should import and export goods and capital.
7. The Agreement on Government Procurement (AGP) which constrains the ability of national law-makers to set rules (such as environmental impact standards) on how goods purchased by governments are made. This preempts attempts by member governments to pass legislation insisting that products paid for with tax-payer money should meet certain environmental or labor-rights requirements.

This list of seven sanctionable agreements encoded into global trade law provides a good indication of the sweeping legal force of the WTO over law-making activities in its member countries. In this respect, it is important to remember that the WTO's force over national laws exists only because it leverages the economic force of international trade itself. Based in Geneva, the offices of the WTO secretariat are not big, and with a staff of only 625 (much smaller than the average university or municipal government), it represents a tiny bureaucracy with no independent powers of its own, let alone the traditional recourse states have to using police and military forces. The power of the organization instead lies in the way its extensive legal rules are enforced by member nation-states under the threat of trade sanctions and monetary penalties from other nation-states. When national and local law-makers are writing new legislation, they do not ask whether it is WTO-compliant because they fear an air-strike from Geneva, but rather because they have to contemplate the likelihood of trade penalties (such as countervailing duties) from other members if they are found to be creating NTBs by a WTO dispute resolution tribunal. For these reasons, nationalistic representations of the WTO as an evil foreign force miss the point, and miss the underlying basis of the authority invoked at WTO ministerial meetings. They fail to register how the organization's downward harmonization of standards to a low global common denominator works through the market-mediated contractual force of agreements signed by government ministers from every single member country.

While it is true that, during most of the GATT talks that led up to the WTO's creation, US government officials drove the process forward with their insistent calls for trade liberalization, it is nowadays inaccurate to represent the WTO as an agent of American dominion. WTO negotiations still tend to be dominated by issues of most interest to the world's wealthiest countries (such as the Intellectual Property rules we will examine in Section 6.1.3). But, because all WTO member countries have just one vote each (unlike in the IMF and World Bank), no one country can set the terms of the NTB harmonization process. It is instead systemic market forces themselves that tend to drive forward the process of downward harmonization by constantly working to expand the cross-border trade of as many goods and services as possible.

Partly as a result of frustrations with the multilateralism of WTO negotiations, and partly because of historical and geopolitical factors, many countries with large trading relationships with their neighbors have turned to bilateral agreements instead. Indeed, as the United States has increasingly lost control of the WTO agenda since the Seattle protests of 1999, it has been especially eager to pursue bilateral forms of harmonization that expand markets for US services, financial products, and intellectual property (IP) without having to reciprocate in opening up the American agricultural sector to foreign competition. The United States–Singapore Free Trade Agreement, and the United States–Chile Free Trade Agreement, are both examples of this new asymmetric bilateralism in trade negotiations in the new millennium. However, both these agreements are themselves modeled on an older form of regional trade agreement that the United States developed in concert with its Canadian and Mexican neighbors. First, in 1989, came the Canada–United States Free Trade Agreement (CUFTA), and next, with the inclusion of Mexico too, came the trilateral North American Free Trade Agreement (NAFTA) in 1994. Both agreements involved considerable commitments to cut tariffs on cross-border trade, but both too also involved all sorts of NTB reduction agreements that expanded and entrenched at a regional level the same sorts of market-mediated downward harmonization tendencies associated with WTO rules at a global level.

Most notoriously from the point of view of critics, NAFTA's **Chapter 11** gave TNCs new rights to sue national and local governments for any laws or policies that are "tantamount to nationalization or expropriation." This has led to the downward harmonization of all sorts of public health and environmental standards because it has made legislatures vulnerable to lawsuits from foreign businesses who can sue and win damages in a NAFTA tribunal by arguing that something such as a government ban on a toxic fuel additive, or a toxic waste dump, to cite two of the more infamous cases, constitutes an expropriative regulatory infringement on their rights as foreign investors. In the case of the Canadian ban on the fuel additive MMT, the company that brought the lawsuit was the Ethyl Corporation. It successfully used NAFTA's Chapter 11 to force the Canadians to repeal their ban, and also won $13 million in compensation for profits that it argued it lost while the ban was in place. In the case of the Mexican municipality of Guadalacazar refusing to give the Metalclad Corporation the right to expand a hazardous waste dump, the corporation also won in a NAFTA trade tribunal with Chapter 11, arguing that the municipality's refusal of expansion permission amounted to a form of expropriation without compensation. The NAFTA tribunal ruled against the Mexicans and awarded Metalclad compensation of $16 685 000. In addition, there have been all sorts of other Chapter 11 cases brought by Canadian and, though to a much lesser extent, Mexican TNCs against US governments. As a result, disquiet about the huge legal implications of NAFTA has also spread to the United States itself. John Echeverria, a noted legal scholar at Georgetown University, has stated thus that "this is the biggest threat to US judicial independence that no one has heard of and even fewer people understand." Similarly, Chief Justice Ronald George of the California Supreme Court has complained that: "it's rather shocking that the highest courts of the state and federal governments could have their judgments circumvented by these tribunals." And, still more revealing about the retroactive concerns raised by

Chapter 11, Abner Mikva, a former Chief Justice on the US Court of Appeals for the District of Columbia, a former congressman, and, most amazingly, one of the three NAFTA judges on a tribunal, concluded: "If Congress had known that there was anything like this in NAFTA," he said, "they would never have voted for it."

The legal outcomes may seem troubling enough to judges, but from the perspective of critics, they represent only the tip of the iceberg of pro-business re-regulation. This is because the threat of being sued under Chapter 11 constantly undermines legislative efforts to pass new public health and environmental laws. "We can't do that," say business lobbyists and the politicians they influence, "it's not NAFTA-compliant!" Moreover, pressured by such lobbyists, American leaders continue to seek to *expand* NAFTA's pro-business framework to the whole continent. They have therefore used it as a model for a new series of regional and bilateral trade agreements including the Central American Free Trade Agreement (CAFTA), United States–Chile Trade Agreement, United States–Peru Trade Promotion Agreement, United States–Columbia Trade Agreement, and United States–Andean Trade Agreement. These agreements are in turn seen as stepping stones to including the whole hemisphere from Alaska to Chile in one giant Free Trade Area of the Americas (FTAA).

Ironically, although it would be included in the envisioned FTAA, the Latin American MERCOSUR community has actually come to serve at times as a counterweight to the US-led efforts to expand the NAFTA model southwards. Originally founded in 1991, MERCOSUR's main members are Argentina, Brazil, Paraguay, and Uruguay. In addition, Bolivia, Chile, Colombia, Ecuador, and Peru currently have associate member status, and Venezuela's membership is awaiting ratification by Brazil and Paraguay's parliaments. MERCOSUR has primarily focused on reducing tariff barriers within the region. However, as centrist and leftist political reformers have recently won elections across Latin America, and as many of them look for alternatives to the downward harmonization of neoliberalism, expectations are high that MERCOSUR members can now work to harmonize standards of social security and economic welfare *upwards*. Certainly, this is the stated hope of President Hugo Chavez of Venezuela, who has meanwhile promoted the Bolivarian Alternative for the People of Our America as a regional grouping named in Spanish as *Alternativa Bolivariana para los Pueblos de Nuestra América* or ALBA (which also means "dawn" in Spanish). The main five members of ALBA are Cuba, Venezuela, Nicaragua, Bolivia, and the Dominican Republic, and, while the main agreement of the group to date is only a commitment to exchange Cuban medical experts and Venezuelan oil, the new dawn vision of ALBA still represents a radical alternative to the US-led FTAA.

Much less radical, but much more economically consequential, is the other global alternative represented by the EU. Here, harmonization takes yet another form, shaped by the long and complex evolution of the European Union out of the 1951 European Coal and Steel Community and the 1957 Treaty of Rome. Today, with 27 member countries, a vast population (over 500 million) and a giant economy (over $17 trillion), the EU is no longer just a customs association coordinated to liberalize trade – which is primarily how it functioned for over 20 years as the European Economic Community (**EEC**). It certainly has expanded transnational trade in Europe, eliminating tariffs on practically all cross-border trade in goods and services, and it has also introduced a long list of common laws and regulations that harmonize standards within the union. However, unlike the WTO and unlike NAFTA, the EU has also evolved into a cross-border form of government whose law-making power is much more democratically accessible and accountable. There is now, therefore, both an elected European Parliament and a European Court, and many groups, including environmentalists, unions, and human-rights organizations, are able to take part in and shape the deliberations over law in these institutions. For these reasons, legal harmonization in Europe has also included diverse forms of environmental protection, public-health improvement, and pro-union regulation. For example, EU laws surrounding European Works Councils actually mandate TNCs to pay for worker representatives from factories across the EU to come together to coordinate their efforts to improve working conditions.

Advancing labor rights through European Works Councils clearly represents a very different kind of harmonization of rights to that advanced by the WTO rules that even make it hard for governments to regulate something like worker rights in companies making products for government procurement. Yet, all this said, over the long term the EU has still tended to privilege business interests over those of other stakeholders in the regional economy, especially as it has grown to incorporate many poor countries (and thus many low-wage workers) from the former eastern bloc. Moreover, any national attempt by an individual EU member state to block low standard imports from *outside* the EU is close to impossible because of the ease with which buyers can import goods through other member states and then move them freely across the EU's internal borders. This same pro-business bias is also reflected in some of the most conspicuous and consequential developments of EU sovereignty over member states' national sovereignty. These include: the continent-wide constitutionalization of property rights; the singularity of the European central bank's focus on fighting inflation (with no parallel commitment to support full employment); and the steady development of the European single currency, the Euro. Meanwhile, attempts to write a non-economic constitution for the EU that would harmonize commitments to social security, advance the EU's ability to defend human rights, and enable the EU to act as a single unified agent in foreign policy have faltered repeatedly in the face of populist nationalism in member countries. A 1989 Social Charter was never fully adopted by all members, and two subsequent proposals for an EU constitution, the Treaty of Nice (2001) and the Treaty of Lisbon (2007), have both suffered embarrassing setbacks as a result of public "no" votes on ratification. Ironically, in both these cases, nationalist opposition to a formal EU constitution was augmented by anti-neoliberal opposition to the economic rights for business written into the Treaties. Nevertheless, such anti-neoliberal activism has not been able to halt the broader global advance of market-based harmonization, and so even in the EU with its parliament and court, it has been business interests that have benefited most from the process of cross-border re-regulation.

6.1.3   Monopolization

One other important area where EU economic harmonization has advanced legally is in "competition policy." This is policy designed to prevent cartels and monopolies from forming, and to punish and dismantle them when they do. It is of note here because it is a kind of broad pro-market policy that has also ended up pitting the EU against some major market players in the global economy, most notably the Microsoft Corporation, which was recently fined €777 million by the EU Competition Commission after a nine-year legal case found that the US company was guilty of monopolistic practices. What is so significant about this in terms of globalization and law is that such a finding at the EU regional scale has meanwhile been countered at a global scale by the success that companies such as Microsoft have had in having their IP defined and protected under WTO rules.

IP is any creation of the mind that is turned into a tradable commodity. Key to this process of commodifying intellectual creations is the legal demarcation and monopolization of the intellectual creation as something that can be privately owned and rented or otherwise sold on for use. Music, books, and movies can all be legally enclosed in this way with copyrights. Likewise, by using patents and trademarks, IP rights can also be claimed over everything from pharmaceuticals to genetically modified organisms to computer operating systems. The WTO has in turn authorized and enforced such monopolistic claims on IP globally through the agreement known as TRIPS, Trade Related Aspects of Intellectual Property. While some of this agreement's provisions on copyright were imported from the Berne Convention for the Protection of Literary and Artistic Works, and, while some of its patent and trademark provisions were imported from the Paris Convention for the Protection of Industrial Property, the TRIPS agreement nevertheless represents the first legally enforceable introduction of IP law into the global trading system.

The eight agreed laws of the TRIPS agreement are as follows:

1. Copyright terms must extend to 50 years after the death of the author.
2. Copyright must be granted automatically, and not based upon any "formality," such as registrations or systems of renewal.
3. Computer programs must be regarded as "literary works" under copyright law and receive the same terms of protection.
4. Patents must be granted in all "fields of technology," and must be enforceable for at least 20 years.
5. Exceptions to the exclusive rights must be limited, provided that a normal exploitation of the work and normal exploitation of the patent is not in conflict.
6. No unreasonably prejudice to the legitimate interests of the right holders of computer programs and patents is allowed.
7. Legitimate interests of third parties have to be taken into account by patent rights.
8. In each WTO member state, IP laws may not offer any benefits to local citizens which are not available to citizens of other TRIPs signatories by the principles of National Treatment.[6]

This list of WTO law says nothing directly about granting owners of IP monopolistic rights to extract rents from copyrighted, trademarked, and patented material. Nevertheless, this is exactly what TRIPS does in practice, working like the rules of the board game *Monopoly* to allow owners of IP to charge rents to anyone who uses their WTO-protected private property. To some extent, the metaphor of the *Monopoly* board game is geographically misleading because in contrast to claiming city streets, the TRIPS rules effectively place everywhere in every member country under the control of private IP ownership. The reach of this WTO IP law is in this way staggeringly global. However, just like the board game *Monopoly* (which was itself patented by an American, Charles Brace Darrow), TRIPS has American origins. And until recently at least, it has also tended to serve the private corporate interests of American TNCs, particularly those holding market monopolies in the pharmaceutical and high-tech sectors.

While TRIPS transforms intellectual knowledge and innovation into monopolizable commodities, it should be noted that the preamble of the agreement begins by asserting that its broad goals are to "take into account the need to promote effective and adequate protection of intellectual property rights" while *also* "ensur[ing] that measures and procedures to enforce IP rights do not themselves become barriers to legitimate trade."[7] There is in this legal language, then, some acknowledgment of the monopoly-building dangers inherent in granting extensive property rights over IP to private corporations. So far, though, the implementation of TRIPS has functioned only to protect corporate monopolies over intellectual innovation. Software and media companies like Microsoft along with big pharmaceutical companies such as Pfizer, Eli Lilly, and Novartis have in this way become the principal beneficiaries of the new global legal protections. For these companies, the argument in favor of TRIPS is simple. Unless they can protect IP globally, they say, there would be no profit in intellectual innovation, and without the profit motive, there would be no innovation. They claim thus that it is principally private profit through private monopolies on intellectual creation that offers the best hope of new scientific breakthroughs and cures. "For the foreseeable future," asserts the head of corporate research for Novartis in a characteristic claim, "the discovery and development of new medicines will be driven almost exclusively by commercial pharmaceutical companies." For the same reason, he insists, TRIPS is vital: "The only way that these firms can remain viable is through a robust intellectual-property protection system." And he defends this whole market-based approach by arguing it is the best way to produce "new drugs for any disease, regardless of whether it afflicts the rich or the poor."[8]

Many poor people, many poor countries, and many organizations working to improve global health for the poor, disagree with the corporate claims about TRIPS. For them the acronym points instead towards the problems the agreement produces as it systematically *trips up* efforts to develop cheap and universally available medicines for all those who cannot afford the high costs of patented drug discoveries. Not only do IP rules put life-saving discoveries out of reach for those who most need them, but also they create a system of profit-driven innovation that draws research away from diseases such as malaria and tuberculosis that tend to afflict only the poor. While supporters of open-source computer software are also frustrated by the monopolistic privileges granted to companies such as Microsoft under TRIPS, it is a much wider set of activists and organizations – including even the Gates foundation of former Microsoft CEO Bill Gates – that has argued that the TRIPS-protected corporate approach to global health has been marked by market failure. This, for instance, was how Joe Cerrell, the Director of Global Health Policy and Advocacy for the Gates Foundation, put it in a speech that – in a sign of how broad-based the criticisms have become – ended up being published on the website of the IMF.

> Some of the greatest inequities in global health result from markets that are not structured to serve the poor. Every year, millions of people in developing countries die from diseases, including malaria and tuberculosis, that have been all but forgotten in rich countries. For these diseases, the economics of the marketplace are not sufficient to commercially justify the large-scale investment needed to develop and deliver vaccines and drugs. Through global advocacy, the Bill & Melinda Gates Foundation is working to address this market failure by promoting innovative health financing mechanisms that provide better incentives to the private sector to create global public goods. The guiding principle is to bring together public agencies and private industry to deal with grossly inadequate health care for the poor resulting from failures of the marketplace.[9]

Plausibly some defenders of TRIPS might claim that here at least we are seeing the profits generated by an IP monopoly over patented computer operating systems being reinvested in a philanthropic strategy to correct the damage of IP monopolies in patented drug therapies. Critics, however, contend that it is the very monopolization process itself that is the problem, that life-saving knowledge should not be privatized but rather shared as widely and as freely as possible. Moreover, they argue in the case of TRIPS that the problems it poses for human and planetary health are made all the more grave by the ways in which its enforcement of monopoly rights over life-forms also enables new forms of corporate bio-piracy and bio-engineering.

The bio-piracy criticism concerns the ways in which TRIPS rules allow TNCs to patent and extract profits from pre-existing genetic material. Traditional plant-based medicines, traditional seed stocks and naturally developed forms of immunity to disease, have all become targets of opportunity for corporations in this respect. The plants, seeds, and genomic immunities involved already exist, but, by patenting their biological features and genetic codes, corporations can create monopolistic rights over any market-mediated distribution of such biological information. This in turn means that something such as a special seed or plant that has been shared freely for centuries by farming communities – the Indian Neem tree and the Mexican Enola Bean are famously contested cases – can suddenly become monopolized as private property on which rents are charged by a corporation. In many developing countries, the sense of being dispossessed through these dynamics is strong. In Thailand, for example, the Plao Noi, a plant traditionally used to treat ulcers, was patented by a Japanese company, and the Thais lost all rights to market it. For the corporation, the process of registering such a patent and collecting the rents hardly seems unethical at all, especially as it often involves recoding the biological information in a neutral-sounding scientific language. However, for communities that have experienced the process first hand, it is no less unethical and immoral. This, for instance, is how many Indian activists saw the problem of legalized biopiracy under TRIPS when they wrote to the Director General of the WTO in 1999:

> India is a country which has centuries' old indigenous knowledge systems based on its rich biodiversity which the Indian people have conserved through their traditional lifestyles and local economies. Two-thirds of our population even today is directly dependent on the biological resources and the indigenous knowledge. These resources and knowledge are used in an ethic of sharing so that the livelihoods and needs of the poorest are met. This is in direct contradiction with the ethics (or the lack of it) perpetrated by the World Trade Organization through the Agreement on Trade-Related Aspects of Intellectual Property Rights (TRIPs). TRIPs has globalised and legalised a perverse and unethical intellectual property rights system which encourages the piracy of our indigenous knowledge and subverts our decentralised democratic system.[10]

The WTO Director General's response to these criticisms of biopiracy was that TRIPS only protects property claims over biological materials that have involved some sort of inventive step of innovation on the part of the patent holder. He argued thus that the "TRIPS Agreement does not provide for the patentability of biological material in its natural state or for indigenous knowledge in the public domain." Critics such as the American consumer rights group *Public Citizen* respond in turn that the monopolization process still dispossesses traditional users in so far as they are forced to go to extraordinarily expensive lengths to document how their knowledge was in the public domain in the first place. Moreover, argue the *Public Citizen* activists, the TRIPS agreement definition of "innovation" is so weak as to allow even the most minor forms of recoding and recalibration to qualify. "The TRIPS notion of innovation," they argue,

> allows a distant company to modify an existing process or "product" and then patent it as new. Given the fact that the generations-old innovations of subsistence farmers and forest dwellers are not patented, a foreign bio-prospecting firm can seize ownership over such knowledge by slightly modifying it and patenting it.[11]

The *Public Citizen* criticisms about bio-prospecting reveal in turn how the legal battles over bio-piracy connect to the broader issue of bio-engineering in which genetic innovations, even only small ones, are precisely what is at stake. Here, while the central question of monopolization remains the key concern of critics, the economic impacts involved are far bigger with still more far-ranging implications for global health and well-being. Some of the health impacts in developing countries surround basic nutrition because one of the main areas in which TRIPS comes together with bio-engineering is in the patenting of genetically modified seeds and plants. TNCs such as Monsanto that develop and market genetically modified seeds have invoked the threat of TRIPS to stop farmers saving seed from one year to the next. Led by savvy scholar-activists such as Vandana Shiva, Indian farmers and politicians have resisted in various ways, including twice refusing to amend India's 1970 patent act that had previously excluded plants and agricultural methods from patentability. But, over time, India's parliament has been forced to pass new TRIPS-compliant legislation. Meanwhile, Monsanto has patented new "Terminator" seeds that are genetically modified to grow into plants with infertile seeds that destroy the whole point of seed saving. As a result, more and more of the food supply around the world has become monopolized by corporate actors whose property rights over seeds are more and more protected by TRIPS-compliant national legislation.

An even wider set of health impacts can be charted in relation to the extension of TRIPS protection to patents on genomic code and pharmaceuticals more generally. In this respect, we see TRIPS coming together with what geneticists call "Snips" or SNPS, the shorthand term for the Single Nucleotide Polymorphisms that are the DNA markers that enable geneticists to sequence the human genome and locate genes linked to particular biological traits. The result is an explosion of patent registration applications for patents on the human genome, and this has in turn ignited much controversy over whether the rapid growth of IP monopoly rights will either impede or enable research aimed at developing genetic therapies for disease such as AIDS, cystic fibrosis, malaria, muscular dystrophy and diabetes. Some global health professionals argue that strong international IP laws are the only practical way of ensuring that genetic therapies will be developed. Other researchers argue in response that relying on the profit motive to guide genetic research will only lead to a focus on developing therapies for diseases afflicting those who can pay for high-cost treatments (which is to say nothing of diverting research to cosmetic concerns such as male-pattern baldness). Thus, even in relation to a single disease such as AIDS, much more research effort has been spent on developing a vaccine for the form of AIDS affecting Americans and Europeans (known as Clade B) and much less on the slightly different form (Clade C) that predominates in Africa (even though Sub-Saharan Africa has over 60% of the total global cases of HIV/AIDS).[12] It is just such inequalities in market-led research that lie at the heart of the market failure mentioned by the Gates Foundation director.

More generally, the commodification of pharmaceutical and medical knowledge as corporate-owned and privately managed IP looks set to limit access to health globally for some time to come. Nevertheless, because the WTO negotiation process allows each member state to have one vote and at least a limited voice in deliberations, some of the discontent around TRIPS has led to changes. Thus, at the WTO meetings of 2001 in Doha, the criticisms of many poor-country governments about the limitations on producing low-cost drugs imposed by TRIPS led to the development of some legal loopholes that allow a little latitude in providing cheap copies of patented medicines in cases of national public-health crises. This 2001 agreement is known as the Doha Declaration. It states categorically that:

> The TRIPS Agreement does not and should not prevent Members from taking measures to protect public health. Accordingly, while reiterating our commitment to

the TRIPS Agreement, we affirm that the Agreement can and should be interpreted and implemented in a manner supportive of WTO Members' right to protect public health and, in particular, to promote access to medicines for all.[13]

The main legal mechanism defined in the Doha Declaration for providing medicines is through compulsory licenses. These are government-mandated exceptions to patent law in particular places for a particular time period, exceptions that force the patent holders to grant rights for the use of the property to the government or a government-defined producer of, in this medical case, cheap medicines.[14] As such, the legal loophole around TRIPS-mandated monopolies on drug patents has been useful for countries such as Brazil and India that have had the industrial and technological capacity to reverse-engineer cheap domestic copies of patented drugs. Despite further lobbying of the WTO by South Africa and Nigeria, though, the Doha declaration has done little to help most African governments who do not have such capacity to mass-produce generic medicines domestically. Medical NGOs working in Africa such as Médecins Sans Frontières (MSF) have therefore been obliged to import cheap generic drugs, and, according to MSF's comprehensive online information source, this transnational trade in cheap medicines has been increasingly imperiled by lawsuits by companies such as Novartis (lawsuits that have sought to further revise patent law in supplier countries such as India). Notwithstanding these uneven outcomes, the Doha Declaration did nevertheless signal a significant victory on the part of health activists over the interests of the big pharmaceutical companies, and, as such, it is an example of grassroots legal globalization to which we return in Section 6.3.

For exactly the same reason that global health advocates were buoyed by the Doha departure from TRIPS legal norms, American trade negotiators who had originally fought for strong global IP laws behalf of the US pharmaceutical industry have been deeply frustrated by developments at WTO meetings since 1999 (one of the reasons for the move to bilateralism and hemispheric trade agreements noted above). They had originally hoped that the Doha meetings in 2001 would put the WTO back on track after the US failures to win concessions from developing countries in Seattle. It was also hoped that Qatar's authoritarian approach to policing would prevent another show of unrest in the streets. However, while the protests were limited in Doha, the Doha Declaration still presented another kind of debacle to all the trade negotiators trained to think legally only in terms of corporate rights. Subsequently, at the next set of WTO meetings in Cancun in 2003, they had to fight another rearguard action to block attempts to make it easier for countries without their own pharmaceutical manufacturing sectors to import generic drugs. But at least on this health-related side of TRIPS, they have continued to lose ground to the many governments and agencies demanding wider access to patented therapies. Most recently, for example, the United Nations international drug purchase agency (UNITAID) has developed a "patent pool" system also supported by the World Health Organization (WHO) to make it easier for generic producers to acquire permission to use patented components in new formulas. As these sorts of global health-based derogations from TRIPS norms continue to be developed, it is notable that global health activists simultaneously employ another sort of global legal language that is quite distinct from the corporate language of planetary patent rights. This other language is the language of universal *human* rights, and while such rights have not had the concerted institutional enforcement that the WTO has given to IP rights, they remain another important part of the law and globalization story. It is to the various declarations and courts involved in telling this human-rights part of the story that we now turn.

6.2   Courts, Human Rights, and Judicial Globalization

The kind of transnational law-making that is expanded and entrenched through trade agreements is a formal and, as we have seen, powerfully enforceable form of legal globalization. Transnational human-rights law which is not backed up by the threat of trade sanctions is instead referred to as customary law and is not so easily enforced. Indeed, portrayed as "international law," it is often ignored or trivialized. "I'd better call my lawyer," said President Bush when asked a question about it. "I don't know what you're talking about by international law."[15] Such insouciance is possible because, unlike a trade treaty in which the laws are ratified by member states who agree to subject themselves to binding disputes arbitration by trade tribunals, international customary laws are instead formed and upheld only by consistent state practices undertaken with a sense of legal obligation (known in legal jargon as *opinio juris*). It is only when state practice and *opinio juris* become integrated and generalized by a large number of states that the globalization of customary law starts to become legally binding, and even then it is vulnerable to disputation and disavowal by powerful governments.

The most important example of globalized customary law is the *Universal Declaration of Human Rights* (online at http://www.un.org/en/documents/udhr/). Impelled by the horrors of the Holocaust and World War II, the humanitarian rights enshrined in the *Universal Declaration* became increasingly influential through the second half of the twentieth century as governments around the world committed themselves to repudiating the abuses that marked the war years by signing on to human-rights protections encoded in treaties such as the Geneva Conventions (the latter being revised and ratified in 1949 to encode the rights of non-combatants, the wounded, and prisoners of war). American officials in key venues such as the Nuremberg and Tokyo war crimes trials were often in the lead in articulating these human-rights protections, and it was Eleanor Roosevelt who led the international committee that first drafted the *Universal Declaration*. More recently, however, in the context of its new declaration of a Global War on Terror (GWOT), the US government has been leading a new global movement away from human-rights conventions, with Alberto Gonzales – the White House legal adviser who went on to become Attorney General under President Bush – even going so far as to issue a memo stating that the war on terror "renders obsolete Geneva's strict limitations on questioning of enemy prisoners and renders quaint some of its provisions."[16] We will start this section by reviewing the *Universal Declaration* and the global law-making it has inspired. We will then turn to examine how the expansion of global human rights protections have been undermined by exceptions, including, as in the recent American exceptionalism, exceptions justified in terms of fighting for freedom.

When it was originally introduced as a resolution of the United Nations General Assembly in 1948, the *Universal Declaration* was widely seen as an aspirational document that set high global standards without offering any way of making them legally enforceable. Over half a century later, however, a combination of consistent state practices and an emergent consensus around the obligatory implications of the *Universal Declaration* have led many to view it as a customary global legal code with real judicial force. Certainly, its rising global stature has enabled many claims against injustice globally. Yet, remedies for wrongs identified as breaches of the *Universal Declaration* have been enacted only unevenly, if at all. In this respect, it is worth reminding ourselves that some of the key articles such as Article 25 on the rights to health, still remain all too aspirational at a time when so many people continue to die everyday from diseases for which there are perfectly well-known treatments and solutions (see Chapter 9).

One major reason for why it has been hard to develop remedies for wrongs defined under the customary law of the *Universal Declaration* is that there is nothing like the WTO's dispute settlement mechanism to facilitate enforcement. Instead, there are two global courts based in The Hague in the Netherlands. These are the International Criminal Court (**ICC**) and the World Court, the latter being referred to formally as the International Court of Justice (ICJ). While both of these courts represent important institutional enactors of global human-rights norms, and while they have made The Hague the global center of international human-rights law, neither court can boast the case load or the consequential global enforcement capacity of the WTO's dispute tribunals. In what follows, therefore, we have to explore what the courts reveal about the globalization of human-rights laws without assuming that their judicial activation of the ideals in the *Universal Declaration* has been universally endorsed and enforced. Close attention must be paid to exceptions to the jurisdiction of the ICC and ICJ made in the name of "national sovereignty," and, in particular, we must address the ways in which US national leaders have argued that America's global interests necessitate military strategies and interrogation techniques that violate global human rights norms.

The ICJ is the main judicial arm of the UN having been established by the UN Charter in 1945. Its main functions are to settle legal disputes and to deliberate on questions submitted to it by member states and the UN General Assembly. However, in its half-century-plus history, the ICJ has settled relatively few cases, and only about a third of the countries in the world accept the compulsory jurisdiction of the court. Moreover, while it is called the World Court, and while its founding Articles demand respect for the "general principles of law recognized by civilized nations," its approach to legal reasoning and convention is not entirely universal. It is shaped primarily by the "Civil Law" tradition of continental Europe, a tradition that emerged out of ancient Roman law and subsequent European legal systems of *ius civile* such as the Napoleonic Code, the Italian civil code, and the German civil code. This legal tradition was globalized to some extent by European imperialism, but the two other great global legal traditions – the "Common Law" tradition that the Normans brought to England and the British brought to their empire, and the "Islamic Law" tradition that moved across Asia and Africa along with the spread of Islam – use important legal doctrines that are not directly recognized in the ICJ. For example, the common law doctrine of *stare decisis* that involves the use of evolving precedents to make judgments is not a feature of the World Court where no one judgment is viewed as having binding implications for others later on. Likewise, the formal importance attached in Islamic law to honoring contracts or *pacta sunt servanda* is effectively subordinated in the ICJ to the civil law doctrine of *bona fides* or good faith in keeping promises. Scholars studying these discrepancies suggest in turn that they account in part for why countries that have civil law traditions are much more likely to recognize the jurisdiction of the ICJ than countries with common law and Islamic law traditions.

Notwithstanding regionalized reservations surrounding its legal doctrines, the ICJ has been used with increasing frequency since the 1980s, especially for resolving a number of contentious border disputes. It has been during this more recent period of activity that the United States has withdrawn from compulsory ICJ jurisdiction. The withdrawal happened in 1986 after the ICJ demanded that the United States pay $2 billion in war reparations to Nicaragua. This came in a 14-to-1 ruling by the court's judges – an American judge being the one dissenter – that the US attacks on Nicaragua and the CIA's support for the counter-revolutionary paramilitary movement known as the "Contras" were illegal. In response to this decision, the United States now accepts the ICJ's judicial authority only on a case-by-case basis. Chapter XIV of the United Nations Charter authorizes the UN Security Council to enforce ICJ rulings, but this is subject to the veto of the permanent five members of the Council, including the United States along with the United Kingdom, China, Russia, and France. It is this same veto power held by the United States in the UN Security Council that has allowed it to repeatedly block enforcement of UN resolutions that call on Israel to withdraw its forces and settlers from the occupied Palestinian territories of the West Bank and Gaza. And it is this same occupation that brought an ICJ decision against Israel on July 9, 2004. The court's judges again came to a 14-to-1 decision – again with the American judge being the lone dissenter – ruling that the Israeli government's building of a separation wall through the occupied Palestinian West Bank was illegal. The court called on Israel to stop building the wall, to dismantle what had been built, and to compensate the Palestinians who had suffered as a result of its construction. The reasoning for this was based in part on the fourth Geneva Convention under which it is unlawful for an occupying power to transfer any parts of its civilian population into an area seized by military force. This is precisely what the separation wall has done because it is not built along Israel's internationally recognized border, as was originally proposed by the Israeli moderates who planned a "separation fence." Instead, the vast concrete wall erected by the government of Ariel Sharon winds its way through the occupied Palestinian lands, snaking back and forth to incorporate illegal Israeli settlements all the while isolating Palestinian communities and cutting many off from their farm lands and olive groves. The court acknowledged Israel's right to self defense against terror attacks, but insisted that to be legal, any separation wall should be built along the legal border of the state of Israel, the 1949 armistice line.

In Israel, no less a figure than the chief justice of the Supreme Court has written that: "Only a separation fence built on the basis of law will grant security to the state and its citizens. Only a separation route based on the path of law will lead to the security so yearned for."[17] In the United States, by contrast, both Democrats and Republicans alike have instead attacked the ICJ, arguing that its judgment was biased against Israel and wrong. These attacks on the ICJ have generally been interpreted in the US media as simply being "pro-Israel." However, such interpretations downplay the degree to which the US antagonism towards the World Court is part of a wider exceptionalism in America's own approach to global humanitarian law. The war on terror, which is presented as a "global" war for universal human freedom, has thereby become increasingly associated with arguments that US forces should be exempted from the rule of global human-rights conventions. This means that the same legal exceptionalism underpinning American attacks on the ICJ has also led the United States to oppose the global jurisdiction of the other main international court based in the Hague, the International Criminal Court.

The ICC was established in 2002 as a permanent tribunal to prosecute perpetrators of genocide, war crimes, and other crimes against humanity such as torture. Based on the idea that universal humanitarian norms protect and bind all humans together no matter what their national identity, the Rome Statute on which the ICC is based was signed by 139 countries by early 2003. To date, it has addressed war crimes in four separate conflicts: in Darfur, Sudan, in the Democratic Republic of the Congo, in the Central African Republic, and in Uganda. In each case, it has issued arrest warrants for leaders it seeks to prosecute for war crimes and human-rights abuses. Thus, for example, on July 14, 2008, the ICC Prosecutor issued an arrest warrant for Sudanese President Omar al-Bashir, accusing him of genocide, crimes against humanity, and war crimes. Whether or not the court will ever be able to prosecute someone such as al-Bashir depends of course on whether world powers will allow his arrest and extradition to the Hague. In this respect, it should be noted that the successful extradition of Slobodan Milošević to the Hague (where he died before the end of his trial) was not to the ICC, but rather for prosecution in an ad hoc court set up by the UN called the International Criminal Tribunal for the former Yugoslavia or ICTY. It is to this court that Radovan Karadžić, the former Bosnian Serb leader, was also sent to be prosecuted after his capture in the summer of 2008. This distinction noted, the ICC shares with the ICTY a focus on individual perpetrators of human-rights violations. Thus, unlike the ICJ, which addresses state practices, the ICC is instead concerned with individuals who have perpetrated major crimes against humanity. Like the ICJ, though, the ICC's jurisdiction can be exercised only when the individuals are citizens of states who have signed on to its founding charter and when the crimes in question take place in the territory of such signed-on states. Herein lies the rub with the refusal of some of the world's largest and most powerful states to submit to the court's jurisdiction.

The United States is by no means alone in refusing to accept the jurisdiction of the ICC. It has been joined in its refusal by China, Russia, India, and Israel. All these countries argue that the ICC infringes on their national sovereignty. Even though the court can only intervene and exercise its jurisdiction when national courts have been unwilling or unable to take on the cases, the concern is that the ICC will prosecute national citizens for crimes that are not recognized as crimes in their home countries. In the US case, this concern is further compounded by an awareness that American military interventions around the world involve American military personnel in acts of violence that are seen by many other world citizens to be breaches of international law. It was for this reason that the US Congress passed the American Service Members' Protection Act (ASPA) in December 2001, a law banning the United States from cooperating with the ICC and establishing a presidential prerogative to use "all means necessary" in preventing the prosecution of US citizens by the ICC. Subsequently, the administration of President Bush Jr worked systematically to ensure immunity from the court, sometimes using the carrot of trade and aid agreements to put in place deals with other countries expressly forbidding ICC extradition of US nationals. That so much effort might be made to work against a global humanitarian legal institution might seem odd given prior American efforts to establish and support international human-rights laws such as the 1984 Convention against Torture. That the anti-ICC efforts were led by a US president who has himself questioned the actual existence of international law might also appear strange. But while President Bush might have publicly jested about needing to call his lawyers about the meaning of international law, it is clear that his administration was repeatedly consulting lawyers as US violations of global humanitarian law mounted in the Global War on Terror.

The torture and abuse at the American-run prison of Abu Ghraib in Iraq are one example of the sorts of US violations vulnerable to ICC prosecution. While the lower-level perpetrators of these atrocities have been prosecuted as isolated "bad apples" in US military courts (a process that removes them from ICC jurisdiction), many critics of American policy argue that there is a global "poison orchard" of exceptionalism that has allowed US forces to violate human rights right around the world.[18] Joining the critics are many Americans, too, including such prominent journalists as Jane Meyer who have documented in detail the "dark side" of American dominance stretching from the torturing of prisoners at the US military base "Gitmo" on Guantánamo Bay, Cuba to the outsourcing of torture to other countries through the CIA's extraordinary rendition programs.[19] Tracing the global ties between these sites of human rights abuse, the critical geographer Derek Gregory argues that they have become "spaces of exception" in the new world order, a global gulag of human-rights exceptionalism that represents the vanishing points of global humanitarian law.[20] We will come back to the global geography of such spaces of exception in Chapter 8 where we will examine how they relate to other emerging forms of enclaved space that range from gated communities and malls to export processing zones and privatized prisons. Here, just three key concluding points should be made about the implications of American human-rights exceptionalism as regards the globalization of law more generally.

The first is a historical point and reminds us again once more why the newness myth about Globalization can be so misleading. In short, the double standards surrounding human rights today are nothing new in the annals of global integration. Human-rights conventions during the times of traditional imperialism were also notably marked by double standards. For example, French revolutionaries who proposed *liberté, egalité*, and *fraternité* in France in 1789 were simultaneously involved in attempts to suppress the freedoms of revolutionary slaves in Haiti, even as Toussaint L'Ouverture, the leader of the slave revolution in the former French colony, drafted a constitution for a free Haiti based on the basic human-rights ideals of the revolution in France. Likewise, nineteenth-century British liberal thinkers such as John Stuart Mill advocated expanding human rights and freedoms in Britain at the very same time as defending the British East India company and supporting the brutal suppression of Indian advocates of independence and freedom in the British colony.[21]

Mill's defense of a Victorian trading empire is also worth remembering because the way he combined arguments about Britain's "civilizing mission" with others about the advantages of trade is similar to the way the Bush administration itself made its own case for pre-emptive global war. This is a second point we should note about American legal exceptionalism: namely, that officials have obscured the inconsistency between global human rights and the global war on terror by consistently combining their calls for freedom with calls for free trade. "[T]he United States will use this moment of opportunity," declared the *National Security Strategy* of 2002, "to extend the benefits of freedom across the globe. We will actively work to bring the hope of democracy, development, free markets and free trade to every corner of the world."[22]

Finally, a third concluding point about exceptionalism and global humanitarian law follows in turn from what we can now observe about the limits of the militarized approach taken by the Bush administration to spreading its own brand of freedom. While American war-making has certainly advanced the US Middle East Free Trade Area (MEFTA) initiative, and while it has been successful in freeing up Iraqi oil contracts for legal possession by foreign oil companies, the attempt to impose "democracy, development, and free markets" militarily has also clearly run into enormous and often brutally inhuman challenges on the ground. One pessimistic conclusion that is increasingly drawn from the ongoing insurgencies in the Middle East is that some parts of the world and some cultures are just not inclined towards freedom, whether it be of the human-rights kind or the sort associated with trade liberalization. However, other observers who study law comparatively from the ground up are more optimistic. They suggest that if we stop thinking about law simply in terms of something that is imposed abstractly from above by states, and if we consider instead the way it is made and remade through processes of social struggle in and between societies, it is possible to see a whole new world of law-making taking shape that is more about freeing people from injustice and dispossession than making abstract equations of freedom with free trade.[23] The so-called Arab Spring of 2011 in which multiple Middle Eastern despots were deposed by popular uprisings also illustrated just such social law-making in action. It is to other non-governmental examples of this "legal globalization from below" that we now turn.

6.3   Social Justice and the Grassroots Globalization of Law

Legal struggles for social justice are a common feature of many societies around the world. They involve diverse efforts to show how the human rights enshrined in national constitutions and global human rights conventions have not been honored and enforced on the ground, and they range from mass social mobilizations and campaigns to the focused litigation efforts of lawyers working on behalf of disempowered and dispossessed groups. Civil rights for racially disempowered groups, labor rights for workers, health and safety rights for consumers, indigenous rights, women's rights, gay, lesbian, and bisexual rights, disabled people's rights, and (although not always in the same way) community and environmental rights have all been the subject of this sort of social justice lawyering. While many of these legal mobilizations have been successful in expanding the reach and meaningfulness of rights on a national level, however, they have only more recently been expanded into transnational struggles. It would be wrong therefore to suggest that some sort of informal global legal revolution from below has developed that matches the scope, scale, and long-term development trajectory of the transnational legal regimes of commercial law examined in Section 6.1. Nevertheless, by both building on and responding to some of the same cross-border ties that have been expanded by trade agreements, and drawing on such customary consensus as exists globally about humanitarian law, social justice legal mobilization is still becoming globalized. In this section, we will examine just three key developments that are enabling this process of legal globalization from below:

1.   the cross-border movement of judicial reform and rights-based harmonization;
2.   the use of existing courts to fight transnational social justice cases;
3.   the development of transnational advocacy networks (TANs).

6.3.1   Cross-border judicial reform and harmonization

While the global jurisdiction of the ICC and ICJ has been limited by exceptionalist opposition, jurists around the world have been busy globalizing judicial norms and conventions from the ground up. In these cases, the harmonization has not been downwards towards the kinds of minimal global standards we examined in relation to the lowered ceilings for environmental, health, and nutrition protections set by the WTO. Instead, the legal harmonization around social justice has involved judges and lawyers sharing ideas transnationally about judicial norms and reforms. "In the area of human rights," stated US Supreme Court Justice Ruth Ginsburg, "experience in one nation or region may inspire or inform other nations or regions."[24] Of course, this viewpoint has also been challenged by conservative constitutionalists who argue precisely the opposite. Thus, in the US case, Justice Ginsburg's colleague Justice Clarence Thomas has criticized her and other judicial globalists on the Supreme Court, saying that their resort to foreign precedents and norms reveals just how weak and unconstitutional their arguments actually are. "Were there any support in our own jurisprudence," he argued, "it would be unnecessary for proponents of the claim to rely on the European Court of Human Rights, the Supreme Court of Zimbabwe, the Supreme Court of India, or the Privy Council."[25] Notwithstanding such opposition and the attendant effort to belittle foreign courts, the importance of foreign legal findings has still started to gain traction in the US Supreme Court. For example, in a 2003 ruling that found a Texan anti-sodomy law to be unconstitutional, Justice Anthony Kennedy cited as support for the ruling a 1981 decision by the European Court of Human Rights that struck down an anti-sodomy law in Northern Ireland. In such a case, we see how what is already a transnationalization of law in the EU becoming transnationalized again, crossing the Atlantic to support an argument in the US supreme court that global society is increasingly acknowledging and judicially upholding gay rights. Border-crossing global precedent was thus invoked to support a judicial overruling of a prior national norm in US courts of condemning and prosecuting homosexuality.

Transnational judicial reform is by no means always towards the progressive expansion of rights for formerly disempowered and marginalized groups. The reality is much more complex when we consider contexts shaped by hybrid histories of colonial, post-colonial, and neo-colonial law-making. It needs remembering in this respect that the sorts of double standards we examined in relation to global human-rights exceptionalism have complicated the colonial transfer of legal norms from 1492 onwards. As a result, the legal dispossession of colonized peoples by European powers and settler societies can well be argued to constitute both the primary principle and the principle paradox of international law. The refinement of colonial legal doctrines such as *discovery* (which denied legal possession of land to those inhabiting it prior to colonialism), *terra nullius* (which formalized the colonists' conceit that colonies were legally empty) and *colonial state sovereignty* (which relied on denying colonized peoples the legal right to nationhood) created a fundamentally asymmetric system of international rights in which colonial subjects were considered uncivilized children in need of training and trusteeship before ever being able to claim rights as legal actors on their own behalf. As we shall see in the next chapter on governance, this same global asymmetry and its attendant assumptions about the need to train the uncivilized have continued from the age of empire into today's talk of the need for "good governance" in the developing world. However, over all this time, another kind of cross-border legal movement occurred that traveled in the opposite direction as a result of resistance from colonized societies to the very asymmetries inaugurated by western law. Anti-colonial resistance in the twentieth century led in this way to the achievement of independent statehood for former colonies and, with it, their international recognition as legally sovereign nation-states. Such legal recognition in turn enabled post-colonial nation-states to exercise new forms of legal agency in international forums ranging from the non-aligned Cold War position staked out by newly independent states under the name of the Third World to more recent organizing by countries of the Global South in the UN. These forms of international agency have not only overturned the colonial legal doctrines that denied colonies sovereignty but also substantially informed important innovations in global customary law – such as the 1973 UN Convention against Apartheid (which overruled an obdurate aspect of white colonial rule in South Africa) and the 1993 Convention on Biological Diversity (which aimed in part at protecting developing country ecologies from TRIPS-based bioprospecting). Yet another aspect of this post-colonial legal agency has been a series of global declarations ranging from UN Resolution 1514, the Declaration on the Granting of Independence to Colonial Countries and Peoples, to the 2001 UNESCO Universal Declaration on Cultural Diversity, to the recent 2007 UN Declaration on the Rights of Indigenous Peoples.

Notwithstanding all the articulations of legal sovereignty by colonized peoples around the world, gaining recognition for such sovereignty and making it meaningful continues to be a challenging form of judicial reform globally. Disconcertingly, one of the challenges can even be the rule of law itself. For example, much of the late twentieth-century importation of US ideas about the rule of law in Latin America is by no means simply a *liberal* response to the authoritarianism of the 1970s and 1980s when military dictatorships replaced civilian government across much of the continent. Instead, research shows that this Latin American importation of the rule of law has been caught up in extending and entrenching *neo*liberal pro-business policies that the authoritarian generals and juntas had themselves implemented with so much *illiberal* violence. Property rights have therefore tended to be privileged over most other social rights, all the while legal processes such as land titling (turning commonly shared land into lots of privately owned property) have taken pride of place over prosecuting the former authoritarian elites for their human-rights violations. It is true that elsewhere in the Americas, in Canada the importation of American legal conventions has sometimes contributed to new national norms that expand human rights, including notably the Canadian Supreme Court's ruling that Canadian citizens should actually have the same Miranda rights they see on American TV. However, even in Canada, many critics charge that the importation of American constitutionalism with its emphasis on individual rights diminishes important group rights and communal rights, including most notably the collective rights of French-speaking citizens in Québèc and the First Nations sovereignty rights of numerous native communities.[26] It is these same tensions that in turn drive and shape one of the main strategies taken by native communities in Canada and elsewhere as they continue to seek recognition of their land rights: namely, using existing colonial-turned-national courts to make the case for their group rights.

6.3.2   Use of existing courts to fight transnational social justice cases

It may not appear transnational in the same way as a lawsuit in the European Court
of Human Rights or a prosecution at the ICC, but for many native communities
around the world, the strategy of going into a national court to fight for recognition
of their communal legal claims remains very much a process of transnational
translation and contestation. In Canada, where most native communities are organized explicitly as First Nations, the legal process of suing in Canadian courts for
recognition of their sovereignty and for compensation for losses due to colonization
has become an important element in the struggle to decolonize native nations. In
such cases, the First Nations well know that the legal strategy puts them at a
disadvantage in so far as the courts operate on the basis of western norms of sovereignty and property, which have been linked from the beginnings of empire to the
simultaneous denial of rights to native peoples. Even something so simple as legally
demarcating native land on a map thereby becomes complicated by radically
different norms of native mapping for communal stewardship versus settler mapping for private property.[27] And each time there is such a complication, the courts
tend to side with the authority accorded to legal norms derived from colonial concepts of ruling and administering land as a new found possession. But it has also
become clear that our own era's expanded recognition of native rights globally –
including the 2007 UN declaration on indigenous rights – has made local legal
struggles for recognition of native sovereignty much more viable. Moreover, in
today's world of instant information sharing around the planet, the so-called global
village of mass communication has made it increasingly easy for particular native
villages in particular places to tell the world about the injustices inflicted on them in
the name of development and civilization. Thus, even if indigenous groups lose in
national courts of law, many still win enough support and solidarity in the courts of
world opinion that national governments are forced to concede some of the local
rights claims made global in the big public trials.

Another set of actors involved in transnational struggles within national legal systems are immigrants. We will address the ways in which migrants' trajectories transcend traditional territorial norms of citizenship in Chapter 8 on space and the
geography of globalization. Here, though, we should still note the ways in which the
relations between law and migration are being changed in the context of the other
transnational legal developments described in the prior sections of this chapter. First
of all, the development of continental legal regimes based on trade agreements has
had the effect of legalizing certain sorts of migration while simultaneously expanding flows of unauthorized migrants, too. Second, the already uneven expansion of
humanitarian law has often been bifurcated and further compromised by the divisions between legal and illegal migration, with illegal entry to a country often being
used as an excuse to deny migrants basic human rights.

The double dynamic of creating both legal and illegal flows at the same time is
especially clear in the NAFTA context. On the one hand, Chapter 16 of NAFTA

legalized the transnational movement of professional workers such as business executives, doctors, and academics, providing such business persons and their employers with a more flexible set of legal options for expedited travel and temporary residency across a tri-national space. On the other hand, NAFTA's tariff reductions allowed subsidized American and Canadian grain exports to flood Mexican markets. While this has not provided a sustainable source of cheap food for ordinary Mexicans (the retail prices being held high by monopolistic food processing and retailing within Mexico), it has nonetheless had a devastating effect on small and medium-sized Mexican grain producers. When they could no longer make a profit, they went out of business, and their former workers were forced to find new jobs, first in Mexico's own cities and border towns, and then, second, in the booming US economy across the border. Entering the United States without legal authorization, these migrants were vulnerable from the start to workplace abuses, being systematically deprived of legal leverage against their employers. More recently, as the US economy has turned recessionary, and the need for extra workers has declined, increasing legal measures are being taken to deport Mexican laborers. New US laws, including the *PATRIOT Act* and the *Enhanced Border Security Act* (along with the aggressive implementation of the 1996 *Immigrant Responsibility and Illegal Immigration Reform Act*), mandate US border patrol and immigration agents to expedite the removal of so-called "illegal aliens." Tellingly, this language of expediting the removal of working-class migrants parallels but reverses the language of expediting the travel of border-crossing business-class migrants. And while the latter enjoy all sorts of new transnational citizenship rights to travel freely across borders, it is clear that there is no parallel expansion of civil rights for working-class migrants whose status as "illegal aliens" tends instead to be used as a justification for removing their human rights even more speedily than removing them from the country.[28]

Notwithstanding the rise of anti-immigrant laws and law enforcement in countries such as the United States, migrants still continue to pursue strategies of legal-rights defense. For Mexicans in the United States, such strategies have ranged from fighting removal in the courts, to regularizing local rights of residency, to organizing mass protests aimed at making manifest the integral part played by immigrants as workers and taxpayers in American communities. Seeking to aid such efforts at regularizing immigrants as rights-bearing human beings, the Mexican government (along with other Latin American governments) has itself sought to provide workers and their families with a form of substitute passport documentation – a *Matrícula Consular* – so that they can set up bank accounts, businesses, and residential arrangements with at least some sort of legally binding means of identification.[29] Elsewhere in the world, other attempts to regularize migrant rights from below have proceeded still further. Most notably, in Europe, longstanding migrant communities, including many with links to the former Eastern Bloc countries of Europe, have slowly seen their home countries become part of the EU and their own status shift to that of rights-bearing citizens with most of the same sorts of health rights, workplace rights, and education rights wherever they move across the continent (with the notable exception of Romanians, who are increasingly being treated as outcasts in countries such as Italy). All the new EU citizens also have recourse to the European Court of Human Rights and European Court of Justice in cases where such rights have been withheld or suspended by host societies. However, even in the European context, the regularization of many migrants' citizenship rights has been paralleled by a growing anti-immigrant approach to managing the movement of poor and vulnerable migrants from outside of the EU's Schengen Zone (the transnational zone in which EU member states have abolished immigration and border controls for their citizens). Consequently, in Europe, as in the United States and elsewhere, the rights of such vulnerable migrants continue to the be subject of legal-aid efforts by organizations that range from Amnesty International (when cases can be made that the migrants in question are refugees from war zones or otherwise violent contexts of abuse, torture, and ill-treatment) to Human Rights Watch (which works on a broader set of human-rights concerns for migrants) to a diversity of special-focus legal-aid groups (which may work with immigrants, for example, on labor rights, women's rights, or community rights). Sometimes supported by law school clinics, and sometimes criticized as limited by a legalistic approach to politics, such immigrant rights lawyering continues to negotiate within national legal systems, even as it runs into all the transnational power relations that make so many migrants disempowered in the first place.

In addition to working for migrant rights, public-interest activists and lawyers also use existing courts to expand human rights for other disempowered groups, too. In the EU, activists ranging from unions to women's rights groups to environmentalist organizations are able to take such cases to the European Court of Justice and European Court of Human Rights based on transnational laws and conventions such as the European social charter. In the Americas and Asia, by contrast, no formal transnational courts and transnational laws exist to protect work rights and other broadly interpreted human rights. Nonetheless, in the United States, there remains one notable legal tool known as the Alien Tort Claims Act or ATCA that has seen increasing use from 1980 onwards as a way of prosecuting TNCs for violating human-rights law. What is remarkable about this little-known American law dating back to 1789 is that it can be applied even if the alleged violation occurs outside of the United States. Sometimes also referred to as the Alien Tort Statute (ATS) or the "pirate law," it has allowed a considerable number of corporations to face prosecution in American courts for overseas abuses of non-American workers. Unocal has been sued in this way for human-rights violations, including allegations of forced labor and torture, in building a gas pipeline through Burma. Coca-Cola has been sued for violations that allegedly involved terrorizing and murdering union organizers at a bottling plant in Columbia. Texaco has been sued for alleged violations in Ecuador. And, having been sued under ATCA for complicity in the Nigerian government's execution of Ken Saro-Wiwa and other leaders of the Movement for the Survival of the Ogoni People, Royal Dutch Shell paid $15.5 million in June 2009 to settle.

All the ATCA suits have moved forward because the US law provides that: "the district courts shall have original jurisdiction of any civil action by an alien for a tort only, committed in violation of the law of nations or a treaty of the United States."[30] While the accused parties must be in the United States to be served court papers, neither they nor the aggrieved parties need be US citizens. This means that the scope of ATCA is just as global as the global networks of TNCs themselves, and while no corporations have been forced to pay court-mandated penalties yet, settlements are increasing. Moreover, because of growing global consensus around the ways environmental damage constitutes a violation of the human right to health, legal scholars indicate that ATCA may well be used in the future for environmentalist legal action and, as such, may even provide a critical counter-mechanism to NAFTA's chapter 11 erosion of environmental-health laws.[31]

The rising risk of liability under ATCA has not surprisingly also led to corporate concern. Thus, after Unocal settled in the Burma case in 2005, the rising number of ATCA suits has led some significant voices of corporate America to sound the alarm. Elliot Schrag of the Council on Foreign Relations (but formerly a vice president of The Gap) spoke of 2005 as a turning point. "The Unocal settlement legitimates the idea that [ATCA] is a real business risk," he said. In response, TNCs have grouped together to file briefs seeking to undermine ATCA cases, and the National Foreign Trade Council has been circulating a study warning that ATCA suits could "seriously damage the world economy."[32] Despite the lobbying, in June 2008 in a complicated cross-border case known as *Sosa v. Alvarez-Machain*, the US Supreme Court ruled that ATCA remained a viable judicial tool for prosecuting human-rights abuses occurring outside of the United States. However, as ATCA is used to prosecute abuse by private military contractors in Iraq, and as this abuse also implicates American government officials, it is unclear going forward whether the US courts and law-makers will continue to allow ATCA to exist in its current form.

A big reason for the corporate concern about ATCA is that while the suits have not led to immediate financial penalties, they still cost TNCs their reputation in the court of consumer opinion. For example, in November 2007, Yahoo settled an ATCA case for an undisclosed amount of money just as it was coming under public pressure in the United States for being too accommodating with the Chinese communist government. The suit against the TNC had been brought by the mother of a Chinese dissident, Wang Xiaoning. Using a Yahoo e-mail account, he had been posting anonymous writings to an Internet mailing list that were critical of human-rights abuses in China. The suit alleged that Yahoo, under pressure from the Chinese government, first blocked his account and then gave officials information that allowed them to identify, arrest, and prosecute Wang. In its settlement, Yahoo agreed to provide "financial, humanitarian and legal support to these families" and create a separate "humanitarian relief fund" for other dissidents and their families. Such concessions by global corporations seeking to balance the conflicting demands of different business contexts look set to increase more and more as courts continue to be used by activists to raise public awareness about corporate crimes. In this respect, ATCA suits in the United States are just one example out of a burgeoning set of legal strategies used by activists in national courts around the world.

Sometimes, in some places, the court cases may even be initiated by TNCs themselves only to backfire because of adverse publicity generated by the trials. Most famously, this is what happened in the "McLibel case" in the United Kingdom when activists who had circulated a pamphlet critical of McDonalds were sued by the corporation for libel. In UK courts, libel laws are particularly stringent (because the burden of proving the full truth of every disparaging statement is on the defendant), and so McDonalds was initially successful in the courtroom in arguing that the offending pamphlet had made untrue claims about the company's practices. However, the court case that is officially known as *McDonald's Restaurants v Morris & Steel* eventually became a giant public-relations fiasco for the corporation, leading to years and years of repeated reevaluations of the claims originally made in the pamphlet, a 20-year legal struggle that ended up with the UK government being judged guilty by the European Court of Human Rights for not giving the activists a fair trial and, finally, a critical 2005 documentary film called *McLibel*.[33] The original 1986 pamphlet entitled *What's wrong with McDonald's: Everything they don't want you to know* had not originally enjoyed anything like the same wide circulation, being just a small specialist publication in London. To be sure, its claims against McDonalds were big, including allegations that the company:

- sells unhealthy, addictive junk food;
- alters its food with artificial chemistry;
- practices economic imperialism;
- is complicit in Third World starvation;
- buys from greedy rulers and elites;
- wastes vast quantities of grain and water;
- destroys rain forests with lethal poisons and colonial invasions;
- deliberately exploits children with its advertising;
- is responsible for torture and murder of animals;
- poisons customers with contaminated meat; and
- exploits its workers and bans unions[34]

But all these big claims about the "Big Mac" brand would never have reached such a big audience had McDonalds not sued the activists. Subsequently, all of the company's actions – including both spending several million pounds litigating the case and then offering to settle with the defendants – could not make the bad PR go away. And as the case got appealed, first in the high courts in the United Kingdom and then at the European Court of Human Rights, all the original allegations were repeatedly revisited, some of them being authoritatively corroborated by scientists and judges in ways that were much more damaging to McDonald's reputation than the original pamphlet had ever been.

The risk of bad PR may make some TNCs hesitate to turn to the courts, but meanwhile equally real risks of legal liability continue to force them into courts to defend themselves.[35] National human-rights laws are increasingly being used in this way to target corporate malfeasance, and meanwhile with ICC membership enlargement combined with increasing attention by the UN to the need for global corporate accountability, the prospect of liability in transnational courts is growing, too.[36] A major force behind this progressive transnational expansion of legal rights for those negatively affected by corporations is the work of transnational advocacy networks (TANs). Expanding the net of corporate liability and continually working to show how human-rights protections necessarily entail rights for workers, women, and indigenous people, such networks are the grassroots rooters of legal globalization from below. It is to their organization and development that we now turn.

6.3.3   Transnational advocacy networks (TANs)

As should be clear by this point, the uneven global expansion of different sorts of legal regimes has created a complex, stratified, and highly pluralized system of global law. Networking across these plural legal regimes, and finding new ways to advocate for the disempowered within them, TANs have taken the national model of social movement legalization global. The legal advocacy involved can range from organizing for workers' rights to women's rights to environmental rights to health rights, but in every case we see efforts by the transnational activists to draw out transnational links and liabilities that are more normally ignored. Starting with some examples of TANs working on labor issues, a review of such transnational networking reveals that there is therefore an important legal side to the economic ties of the commodity chains examined in Chapter 3.

For TNCs offshore outsourcing is not only a cost saving, but also often a way of offloading legal liability, too. Companies such as Nike that outsource all production work to foreign vendors thereby seek to avoid the sorts of litigation normally faced by corporations in home-country courts for factory violations of home-country laws. It is precisely such side-stepping of the law through the use of subcontractors that labor-rights TANs seek to address by harmonizing legal protections for workers upwards. They do so through anti-sweatshop mobilization and the establishment of codes of corporate conduct which, by making producer–consumer connections more transparent, also make TNC activities more accountable. One good illustration of such transnational advocacy is the Kukdong case that resulted in the successful improvement of worker rights at a Mexican factory run by a Korean TNC supplying, among others, Nike. An engineering unit for Kukdong is famous for its role in building the skybridge linking the twin Patronas towers in Malaysia, one of the world's tallest buildings. However, in Mexico, Kukdong's business was all about building a supply-chain bridge to Nike's customers without those customers ever being able to hold Nike accountable for the treatment of the workers in the Kukdong factory. Engineering economic linkage without legal liability is clearly very common in a world of global commodity chains, but with transnational advocacy the economic ties can be retrofitted with legal ties, too, and this is what happened with the Kukdong factory in Puebla, Mexico.[37]

In 2001, workers went on strike and occupied part of the Kukdong factory in an effort to win recognition of their independent union and to improve working conditions. The factory management fired the strike's leaders, sued them for property damage, and had the local police evict the strikers by force. In response a US–Mexican anti-sweatshop TAN organized a publicity campaign to pressure Nike and other companies supplied by Kukdong to improve conditions in the factory by making the management implement a new code of conduct and follow local labor laws giving workers organizing rights. This transnational campaign – involving US students picketing Nike stores, unions coming together across borders, and transnational code of conduct organizations – quickly accomplished its goals. The striking workers were reinstated, the independent union was recognized, and the management signed a contract with this union that included a 40% wage increase and improved working conditions. Critically, one of the keys to this success was the anti-sweatshop campaign's ability to leverage the power of Nike as a big-buyer backwards down the commodity chain to a local legal context where court action was being used by the management and local politicians to block the development of the independent union. In this way, the long-distance and offshore requests of a TNC concerned for its global reputation came to reverse and literally replace the long-distance offloading of the foreign factory as an accountability-free area for labor exploitation. Instead of corrupt politicians and legal elites enforcing exceptions from Mexico's formal labor laws, an informal code of conduct forced on Nike by transnational advocacy came to provide Mexican workers with workplace rights more commonly honored in the breach.

Alongside *Global Exchange*, the **AFL-CIO**, the *International Labor Rights Fund*, and the *Korean House of Solidarity*, another vitally important organization involved in the Kukdong campaign was the *Workers Rights Consortium* (WRC). The WRC is a labor-rights watchdog that was founded by United Students Against Sweatshops (USAS). Working together, the WRC and USAS have had remarkable success in making global commodity chains visible to consumers. For example, the WRC website provides American college students with a terrific tool for determining where exactly apparel, shoes, and other products bearing college logos are made (see http://www.workersrights.org/). In addition to making the ties between students and factory workers clear, the WRC and USAS have also had notable victories in improving labor conditions at suppliers' factories. In a 2009 case concerning the rights of factory workers in Honduras, for instance, Russell Athletic was forced through USAS/WRC activism to put workers that it had fired for their efforts to unionize back to work. The company was also forced to provide compensation for lost wages to the workers it had fired, and to recognize their union for purposes of collective bargaining both at the factory where the struggle began and at all other Russell apparel plants in Honduras. "This is the first time we know of where a factory that was shut down to eliminate a union was later re-opened after a worker-activist campaign," said Rod Palmquist, USAS International Campaign Coordinator and former student organizer from the University of Washington in Seattle.

> This is also the first company-wide neutrality agreement in the history of the Central America apparel export industry – and it has been entered into by the largest private

employer in Honduras, the largest exporter of t-shirts to the US market in the world. This is a breakthrough of enormous significance for the right to organize – and worker rights in general – in one of the harshest labor rights environments in the world.[38]

Despite such successes, however, the WRC and USAS have nevertheless been frustrated by the ability of TNCs to move work from one factory to another or otherwise escape consistent compliance with the anti-sweatshop code of conduct. As a result, the WRC has now developed what it calls a Designated Supplier Program, designed to foster long-term commitments between university customers and specific supplier factories in which the price for a stable student market is a clear-cut commitment by producers to abide by a strict labor-rights code of conduct.[39]

The tie of responsibility articulated by the WRC's Designated Supplier Program takes transnational labor-rights advocacy in a direction that has already been popularized by Fair Trade advocacy. With products such as Fair Trade coffee and Fair Trade chocolate, the core legal commitment of the vendor to the consumer is that the farming communities and workers have been paid good prices and a living wage. Such commitments are enforced by Fair Trade certification programs that work like code of conduct-monitoring programs as third-party guarantors that the supply chain is working on the basis of Fair Trade commitments. As the website of TransFair USA explains:

> The Fair Trade Certified™ label guarantees consumers that strict economic, social and environmental criteria were met in the production and trade of an agricultural product. Fair Trade Certification is currently available in the US for coffee, tea and herbs, cocoa and chocolate, fresh fruit, flowers, sugar, rice, and vanilla. TransFair USA licenses companies to display the Fair Trade Certified label on products that meet strict international Fair Trade standards (http://www.transfairusa.org/).

TransFair's description of Fair Trade also highlights how TAN advocacy has increasingly come to include environmental protections alongside assuring labor and community development rights and benefits. These are all called soft law assurances, and they do not have the hard law enforcement implications of free trade treaties or even the semi-hard implications of customary human-rights law. However, by connecting the world of trade with the worlds of workers and the environments in which they live, soft law codes of conduct are increasingly establishing consequential conventions for sustainable ecological development in many parts of the Global South.

Of course, in much of the **Global South**, especially in areas affected by mining, oil drilling and other economic activities that are less susceptible to consumer campaigns, sustainable development remains far out of reach. Meanwhile, even in the home countries of wealthy consumers, we are witnessing a reactive co-optation of the language of sustainable development. In the EU case, for example, legal scholars argue that European lawyering on environmental issues has now become so closely intertwined with the business of setting up markets for carbon credits and pollution credits that the environmentalist idea of legally mandating sustainable development has been taken over by the legal logistics of simply sustaining business. The landscape of environmental lawyering thus becomes just a fertile field for the sorts of corporate greenery made infamous by BP: the oil company officially listed as British Petroleum but which branded itself as green as "Beyond Petroleum" before the 2010 disaster in the Gulf of Mexico created one of the biggest environmental catastrophes in American history and thereby exposed the ugly and unsustainable underside of green PR more generally.[40]

Beyond BP and beyond all the legal debates over sustainable development, we must remember that all of the soft law strategies developed by TANs remain vulnerable to co-optation. Fair Trade food can simply become a niche-market brand that big vendors use to burnish their reputations while changing none of their other supply chains. And codes of conduct can be controlled by corporations in ways that actually end up reducing liability and public relations pressures without improving worker rights on the factory floor. Indeed, the language and practices of Corporate Social Responsibility (CSR) have become so dominant that they are more often viewed today as an important tool of professional development and crisis management than as radical reforms to business as usual. Nevertheless, such softening of soft law can itself become a target of transnational advocacy. In this respect, global organizing around the human right to health is especially telling and a good way to illustrate in closing how all the different developments in global law examined in this chapter shape one another in a continual process of convergence, conflict, and kaleidoscopic recombination.

The revolving kaleidoscope of global law is in fact key to understanding some of the most urgent debates today about global health. Developments such as the WTO's TRIPS protections for patent monopolies that we examined in Section 6.1 limit access to life-saving pharmaceuticals for the world's poor. Meanwhile, the protection of the right to health remains an important aspect of the universal human rights that we reviewed in Section 6.2. In turn, illustrating the social movement legal mobilization discussed in this section, grassroots advocates of health as a human right have highlighted the clear contradictions between the global property rights regime of TRIPS and the human right to health. It was precisely in this way that they won the notable victory of the Doha Declaration (see page 200), the TRIPS modifying declaration that acknowledged "WTO Members' right to protect public health and, in particular, to promote access to medicines for all." The legal language of the Doha Declaration sounds muted and mild, but here we should remember that as a new aspect of global commercial law, it represents a legal outcome of enormously contentious life-and-death struggles among health activists, policy-makers, and drug companies that continue all around the world. Stretching from the clinics of community health workers to street protests to national courts to the transnational networks of advocacy groups to global trade missions and trade negotiations, these struggles have been especially urgent and contradictory in African countries dealing with deadly pandemics such as HIV/AIDS. In South Africa, for example, the sorts of struggle that led to the Doha Declaration were particularly hard fought, and, for the same reason, the contradictions between property rights and human rights particularly clear. It is with this case that we shall conclude because it shows how interlinked the global kaleidoscope of national and transnational law-making is in practice.

In 1994, South Africans finally won freedom from the white-supremacist apartheid regime. It was an extraordinary historical moment of human-rights expansion where the legal implications and expectations of freedom were huge. In the words of Archbishop Desmond Tutu, the chair of the country's *Truth and Reconciliation Commission*:

> Reconciliation means that those who have been on the underside of history must see that there is a qualitative difference between repression and freedom. And for them freedom translates into having a supply of clean water, having electricity on tap; being able to live in a decent home and have a good job; to be able to send your children to school and to have accessible health care.[41]

These were all deeply humanitarian ideals of freedom, but they fast became eclipsed by a different market-based understanding of freedom that severely curtailed their realization. This was because in 1994, the African National Congress (ANC), the party that had come to lead the freedom struggle, also agreed to sign South Africa up as a founding member of the WTO. The ANC's leaders had hoped the new South Africa could capitalize on the end of apartheid-era international trade sanctions. They were also driven by an acute awareness of the need to rebuild the country's post-apartheid economy. However, while they saw a direct link between the free-trade commitments of WTO membership and the new freedom of all those who had suffered under apartheid, the contradictions between TRIPS private property rights and South Africans' human rights soon became brutally clear, too.

Among other developments, the 1996 post-apartheid constitution for the country included a clause stating that access to health care services was a right of all South Africans, and this led advocates working on behalf of the increasing numbers of people suffering and dying from HIV/AIDS to turn to the courts as part of their wider political struggle for treatment. Ultimately, this hybrid political–legal struggle resulted in a new law, the 1997 Medicines Act, that mandated measures to ensure the supply of affordable medicines to all South Africans and opened the door to trade management practices such as parallel importation (of cheap generics) and compulsory licensing. Immediately, the pharmaceutical companies saw the danger in the new law and the more general victory it represented for all those arguing that access to essential medicines is a basic human right. They pressured the office of the United States Trade Representative to challenge South Africa for its likely violation of TRIPS, and they organized to appeal the law directly in South Africa's own courts. These transnational and national pressures to revoke the new South African law continued to heighten through 1999, but against them there also developed new national and transnational advocacy networks organized to fight for universal access to essential medicines. The networks included South African organizations such as the Treatment Action Campaign, but also US organizations and activists such as ACT-UP and the Congressional Black Caucus. It was in turn this transnational advocacy networking that eventually turned the tide at Doha (although the US government's own 2001 issuance of a compulsory license to override Bayer's Cipro patent during the anthrax scare also undermined the USTR's previous hardline against compulsory licensing). As a result, a new form of legal exceptionalism from global law was inaugurated in the name of health as a human right.

Of course, the pharmaceutical TNCs have by no means given up their legal struggles to limit global access to low-profit medicine through generic drugs and compulsory licensing. They continue to press for "TRIPSplus" protections for their patents, even as they present elaborate social responsibility codes of conduct in their websites and advertisements. But, by the same token, transnational advocacy organizations also continue to network at events such as the World Social Forum (see Chapters 2 and 10) to press for wider reforms in global medical governance that might eventually make the universal rights to health recognized in constitutions such as South Africa's a reality for everyone on the planet. In the next chapter, we will turn to investigate what such reform plans represent in terms of wider global struggles over free-market governance and the political advocacy of alternatives. Here we can simply conclude by noting again that the connections between South African health advocacy and the Doha Declaration reflect the complex kaleidoscope of today's global legal regimes. From TRIPS to transnational human-rights lawyering, this kaleidoscope continues to turn. But hopefully now, its complexity and convolutions are more comprehensible than they were at the start of the chapter.

Student Exercises

Individual:
1. One of the notable contradictions of the global commercial law that was highlighted in Section 6.1 concerned the ways in which recent trade agreements have simultaneously expanded transnational market competition at the same time as creating private property monopoly rights for a privileged set of marketplayers. A useful exercise in this respect is to examine how the contradiction is dealt with by the World Trade Organization itself. Go to the WTO teaching module website – http://www.wto.org/english/res_e/webcas_e/webcas_e.htm – and review the training provided on: first "Why is it important to liberalize?" by Patrick Low, and second, "The Trade-Related Intellectual Property Rights Agreement (TRIPS)" by Adrian Otten. Try to track how the presenters reconcile liberalization with monopoly rights, and make up your own mind as to whether they present a convincing case.

Group:
2. Read aloud the following quotation from John Steinbeck's *The Grapes of Wrath*, and then work together as a group to create a list of similar situations where we

have recently seen groups of dispossessed people coming together to establish codes of conduct that recognize and call for basic human rights in the context of globalization.

In the evening a strange thing happened: the twenty families became one family, the children were children of all. The loss of home became one loss . . . Every night a world created, complete with furniture – friends made and enemies established; a world complete with braggarts and cowards, with quiet men, with humble men, with kindly men . . . At first the families were timid in the building and tumbling worlds, but gradually the technique of building worlds became their technique. Then leaders emerged, then laws were made, then codes came into being . . . And the families learned what rights must be observed – the right of privacy in the tent; the right to keep the past black hidden in the heart; the right to talk and to listen; the right to refuse help or accept, to offer help or decline it . . . the right of the hungry to be fed; the right of the pregnant and sick to transcend all other rights.

Notes

1   Stephen Gill, a Canadian theorist of political-economy who early on saw the disciplinary effects of the Canada–United States Free Trade Agreement (CUFTA), has been especially clear about the resulting market constitutionalism. Stephen Gill, "Globalisation, Market Civilisation and Disciplinary Neoliberalism," *Millennium* 24 (1995): 399–423; Stephen Gill, "New Constitutionalism, Democratisation and Global Political Economy," *Pacifica Review* 10 (1998): 23–38; Stephen Gill, "The Constitution of Global Capitalism," Mimeo, http://www.theglobalsite.ac.uk/press/010gill.htm. See also David Schneiderman, Investment Rules and the Rule of Law, *Constellations*, 8, no. 4 (2001): 521–37.
2   For further critical decoding of many of these terms, see Lori Wallach, *Public Citizen's Pocket Trade Lawyer: The Alphabet Soup of Globalization* http://www.citizen.org/documents/Pocket_Trade_Lawyer_January_2006_Final.pdf.
3   For further discussion of the similarities and contrasts between medieval merchant law and contemporary global commercial law, see Saskia Sassen, *Territory, Authority, Rights: From Medieval to Global Assemblages* (Princeton, NJ: Princeton University Press, 2006).
4   Law360, "Global 20 Firms Blaze Trails Abroad," http://www.law360.com/topnews/articles/245194/law360-global-20-firms-blaze-trails-abroad.
5   See WTO, *The Case for Open Trade*, http://www.wto.org/english/thewto_e/whatis_e/tif_e/fact3_e.htm. In 2008, this website also provided a short instructional video on the basic "reduced opportunity costs" theory of comparative advantage for anyone who did not know it. If this video is no longer there when you read this footnote, you will not have to go far. The need to train new generations of students in neoclassical economic orthodoxy means that lessons on the gains of "comparative advantage" are almost as omnipresent as advertisements on the benefits of new cell phones. Elsewhere, though, many criticisms are available, too: see, Walden Bello, *Deglobalization: Ideas for a New World Economy* (New York: Zed Books, 2002), and websites such as http://openconcept.ca/wtoaction_wtocaravan. Most such critiques come from an alter-globalization perspective that is interested in advancing and protecting global social and environmental justice. However, for another nationally protectionist, but still critical take on

comparative advantage from a partisan of American business interests, see William R. Hawkins, Comparative Advantage and Competition, http://www.americaneconomi-calert.org/view_art.asp?Prod_ID=1070.

6 Summarized from the texts of the WTO agreement and posted by the WTO, http://www.wto.org/english/docs_e/legal_e/27-trips.pdf.

7 WTO, 2008: Preamble to TRIPS, Trade-Related Aspects of Intellectual Property Rights, http://www.wto.org/english/docs_e/legal_e/27-trips_02_e.htm.

8 Paul Herrling, "Patent Sense." *Nature* 449 (2007): 174–75.

9 Joe Cerrell, "Making Markets Work," http://www.imf.org/external/pubs/ft/fandd/2007/12/view.htm.

10 http://www.ratical.org/co-globalize/BPandWTO.html.

11 Lori Wallach and Peter Woodall, *Whose Trade Organization? a Comprehensive Guide to the WTO* (New York: The New Press, 2004) 202.

12 Susan Craddock, "Market Incentives, Human Lives, and AIDS Vaccines," *Social Science & Medicine* 64, no. 5 (2007): 1042–57.

13 http://www.wto.org/english/thewto_e/minist_e/min01_e/mindecl_trips_e.htm.

14 For an excellent online guide to the many legal complexities surrounding compulsory licenses for specific drugs in specific countries, see http://www.cptech.org/ip/health/.

15 George W. Bush, "President Discusses Year-End Accomplishments in Cabinet Meeting," http://www.whitehouse.gov/news/releases, 11 December 2003.

16 Quoted in the David Sanger and Eric Lichtblau, "Bush Nominates his Top Counsel for Justice Post," *New York Times* November 11 (2004) A1.

17 This quotation and the summary of the debate are taken from Stephen Zunes, "Implications of US Reaction to the World Court Ruling Against Israel's 'Separation Barrier,'" *Middle East Policy* XI, 4 (2004): 72–85. While many Israeli liberals concur with the chief justice, it would be wrong to suggest that all legal professionals, let alone all Israelis politicians and citizens, agree. For a valuable enquiry into legal liberalism in Israel, including its limits, silences, and often space-spanning construction through global ties to US law schools, see the study of the American-Israeli legal scholar, Gad Barzilai, "The Ambivalent Language of Lawyers in Israel: Liberal Politics, Economic Liberalism, Silence and Dissent," in *Fighting for Political Freedom*, eds Terence Halliday, Lucien Karpik, Malcolm Feeley (Portland, OR: Hart Publishing, 2007): 247–79.

18 Philippe Sands, *Lawless World: America and the Making and Breaking of Global Rules* (London: Allen Lane, 2005).

19 Jane Meyer, *The Dark Side: The Inside Story of How The War on Terror Turned into a War on American Ideals* (New York: Doubleday, 2008).

20 See Derek Gregory, "Vanishing Points: Law, Violence and Exception in the Global War Prison," in Derek Gregory and Allan Pred, eds., *Violent Geographies: Fear, Terror, and Political Violence* (New York: Routledge, 2007).

21 For some excellent studies of these double standards in the history of human-rights law, see: Uday Singh Metha, *Liberalism and Empire: a Study in Nineteenth Century British Liberal Thought* (Chicago: University of Chicago Press, 1999); Louis Sala-Molins, *Dark Side of the Light: Slavery and the French Enlightenment translated and with an introduction by John Conteh-Morgan* (Minneapolis: University of Minnesota Press, 2006); and Tayyab Mahmud, "Geography and International Law: Towards a Postcolonial Mapping," *Santa Clara Journal of International Law* 2 (2007): 525–61.

22 The White House, *The National Security Strategy of the United States of America* (Washington, DC: The White House, 2002), preface, 1.

23   Boaventura de Sousa Santos and César Rodríguez-Garavito, eds., *Law and Globalization from Below: Toward a Cosmopolitan Legality* (Cambridge: Cambridge University Press, 2005).

24   This quotation and the two that follow are taken from an excellent article by Anne Marie Slaughter, "Courting the World," *Foreign Policy* March/April (2004): 78–79.

25   A still more critical position was made of the Supreme Court's appeal to global humanitarian norms by John Yoo, the Bush administration legal adviser who also notoriously authored the White House memoranda legitimating torture as executive privilege. "When the court starts taking things like that into account," Yoo wrote of the Supreme Court's appeal to global convention, "it reveals itself as more interested in making policy than interpreting the fixed texts of the Constitution or statutes," quoted in Charles Lane, "Thinking Outside the US," *Washington Post*, August 4 (2003).

26   Michael Mandel, *The Charter of Rights & the Legalization of Politics in Canada* (Toronto: Thompson Educational Pub, 1994).

27   See Chapter 1 of Matthew Sparke, *In the Space of Theory: Postfoundational Geographies of the Nation-State* (Minneapolis: University of Minnesota Press, 2005).

28   Matthew Sparke, "A Neoliberal Nexus: Citizenship, Security and the Future of the Border," *Political Geography* 25, no. 2 (2006): 151–80.

29   Monica W. Varsanyi, Documenting Undocumented Migrants: The Matrículas Consulares as Neoliberal Local Membership. *Geopolitics* 12, no. 2 (2007): 299–319.

30   28 U.S.C. § 1350.

31   Kevin Scott Prussia, "NAFTA and the Alien Tort Claims Act: Making a Case for Actionable Offenses Based on Environmental Harms and Injuries to the Public Health," *American Journal of Law and Medicine* 32 (2006): 381–404; and Natalie L. Bridgeman, "Human Rights Litigation under the ATCA As a Proxy for Environmental Claims," *Yale Human Rights and Development Law Journal* (2003): 1–43.

32   Quoted in Joshua Kurlantzick, "Pirates of the Corporation," http://www.rutherford.org/oldspeak/articles/law/oldspeak-pirates.htm.

33   For more information on the film, see http://www.spannerfilms.net/?lid=161.

34   See the activists' own webpage at http://www.mcspotlight.org/case/factsheet.html.

35   For a detailed survey of 16 countries, see Anita Ramasastry and Robert C. Thompson, Commerce, Crime and Conflict: Legal Remedies for Private Sector Liability for Grave Breaches of International Law – Executive Summary (2006), http://www.fafo.no/liabilities.

36   Special Representative of the UN Secretary-General, "Business and Human Rights: Mapping International Standards of Responsibility and Accountability for Corporate Acts," New York: UN. http://www.business-humanrights.org/Documents/SRSG-report-Human-Rights-Council-19-Feb-2007.pdf.

37   For a much more detailed and nuanced analysis of the case on which this summary is based, see César Rodríguez-Garavito, "Nike's Law: The Anti-Sweatshop Movements, Transnational Corporations, and the Struggle over International Labor Rights in the Americas," in Boaventura de Sousa Santos and César Rodríguez-Garavito, eds., *Law and Globalization from Below: Toward a Cosmopolitan Legality* (Cambridge: Cambridge University Press, 2005): 64–91.

38   See http://www.globalexchange.org/countries/americas/honduras/6423.html.

39   See http://www.workersrights.org/dsp/#DSP.

40   Yves Dezelay, "From a Symbolic Boom to a Marketing Bust: Genesis and Reconstruction of a Field of Legal and Political Expertise at the Crossroads of a Europe Opening to the

Atlantic," *Law & Social Inquiry* 32, no. 1 (2007): 161–81. For another more metaphorical but brilliant reading of the changing relationship between the fields of landscape and law in the context of cross-border European networking, see Eve Darian-Smith, *Bridging Divides: The Channel Tunnel and English Legal Identity in the New Europe* (Berkeley: University of California Press, 1999).

41 Quoted in Naomi Klein, *The Shock Doctrine: The Rise of Disaster Capitalism* (New York: Metropolitan Books, 2007), 194.

Keywords

AFL-CIO	Global South	race to the bottom
Chapter 11	ICC	tariffs
comparative advantage	MERCOSUR	WTO
GATS	NAFTA	
GATT	NTB	

7

Governance

Chapter Contents

Chapter Concepts

1. Claims about the "end of the nation-state" obscure a more complex reality in which national governments enforce global market discipline through neoliberal policies.
2. The United States has exceptional global influence as a nation-state amidst globalization yet uses it most often to force other governments to conform with market discipline.
3. Enforcement of pro-market governance globally has been further expanded by inter-governmental institutions, including the IMF and World Bank.
4. Non-governmental organizations (NGOs) are developing governmental capacity amidst the roll-back of the state, and the entrenchment of neoliberalism.
5. NGO networks are part of a patchwork of global governance also structured by the non-governmental but organizing effects of market forces on personal behavior.

Key Concept

The main transformation in governance associated with globalization today is the emergence, expansion, and entrenchment of a pro-market, neoliberal approach to

Introducing Globalization: Ties, Tensions, and Uneven Integration, First Edition. Matthew Sparke.
© 2013 Matthew Sparke. Published 2013 by Blackwell Publishing Ltd.

government. This neoliberalization of governance is widely enforced by agencies ranging from national-state governments, to global financial institutions, to NGOs and individuals operating on the basis of free market ideals and incentives. Even the global financial market crises of 2008–2012 did not shake the broadly held neoliberal orthodoxy that markets should be liberalized, respected, and used by governing agencies. Thus, while it does so unevenly, incompletely, and with the visible helping hands of diverse state sponsors and NGOs, the invisible hand of "the market" increasingly rules.

7.1   The End of the Nation-State?

When policy-makers receive advice on how to govern from global business consultants – and many have done so from the 1980s onwards – they hear repeatedly about how globalization is bringing the era of national-state government to an end. According to Kenichi Ohmae, a widely cited management guru and one of the earliest and boldest announcers of this kind of obituary, policy-makers should therefore come to terms with the fact that globalization means "the end of the nation-state."[1] Though they lived in different times, American writer Mark Twain, Swedish inventor Alfred Nobel, and Jamaican hero Marcus Garvey might all have recognized this sort of message. They, too, received premature obituaries, and in at least three ways the parallels with announcements of "the end of the nation-state" are telling. First, there is the issue of exaggeration – as in Twain's famous retort "The report of my death is an exaggeration." In the case of the nation-state, this parallel forces us to remember that, along with their national passports, national borders, and national armies, nation-states still retain their role as the basic building blocks of governance globally. They are certainly not dead and gone! Second, there is the question of influence. Nobel apparently was so influenced by a premature obituary condemning his wealth made from weapons manufacturing that he went on to use some of his fortune to establish the Nobel peace prizes. National-state governance can in this sense also be analyzed in terms of how premature obituaries actually end up influencing governmental policy: not creating global peace prize legacies, but nevertheless transforming multiple aspects of government, including even the ways in which nation-states approach war and peace. And third there is the shock impact illustrated by Garvey's death, which was supposedly precipitated by his reading a premature and negative obituary of himself in a Chicago newspaper. The way such shock works with national-state governance is obviously not so direct or psychological. However, as we shall see in what follows, shocks to national governments created by some of the global economic upheavals examined in Chapter 5 have frequently combined with the shock impact of experts invoking "the end of the nation-state" to make neoliberal policies the end, which is to say, the goal, vision, and destiny of governments all around the world (to remind yourself of the main policies of **neoliberalism**, see Table 7.1).[2]

Table 7.1   Top 10 neoliberal policy norms

1. Free trade
2. Privatization
3. Deregulation
4. Austerity
5. Tax cuts
6. Encourage foreign investment
7. Reduce union power
8. Export led development
9. Reduce inflation
10. Enforce property rights

Another way of summing up the argument here about premature "end of the nation-state" announcements is that they represent a recurring sub-plot of the larger, capital "G" Globalization story we explored in Chapter 2. As such, they clearly draw on the same basic Globalization myths: that it is new, that it is inevitable, and that it is leveling. Indeed, Ohmae's work is a good example in this respect because one of his other books prior to publishing *The End of the Nation-State* was entitled *The Borderless World*. In it, Ohmae makes the case that the new and inevitable juggernaut of Globalization is such a profound leveler that it is ushering in a world without borders. Here, the exaggeration is obvious, and no doubt Ohmae, just like any other frequent flyer, is regularly reminded of his hyperbole every time he steps off a plane and presents his passport to a border guard. What is more important to note about his arguments, though, is that they illustrate the way premature obituaries to national government seek to influence governmental policy-making, and how they employ the shock value of big "G" Globalization myths to do so. Ohmae explains thus in *The Borderless World* that he wants his readers to be roused enough by his account of the new interlinked global economy that they will "throw the bureaucrats out," the bureaucrats being any policy-makers in national government who refuse to acknowledge Globalization's inevitability and who therefore also refuse to cede influence to global companies and their global customers. "Traditional governments," he says, "will have to establish a new single framework of global governance."

Not surprisingly, the single framework advocated by Ohmae and so many other business leaders is governance *for* and, as much as possible, *through* the liberalized capitalist market. Indeed, their use of the word "governance" – particularly in ongoing demands for what business magazines and commentators call "good governance" – tends to index the ways in which the ideals of market discipline are elevated as an alternative to so-called "big government." By constantly complaining about how clunky national government rules no longer work well in the era of Globalization, pro-market experts therefore use "end of the nation-state" appeals to persuade national governments to adopt neoliberal governance instead. Of course, from the point of view of anti-neoliberal critics, such an approach to governing for and through the market is better understood as a kind of cage that imprisons governments and forces them to wear a singular one-size-fits-all "market fundamentalist" straitjacket. Despite their differences, though, advocates and critics alike agree that, amidst all the connections and crises of economic globalization over the last four decades, national governments have repeatedly been shocked into governing in new ways that better serve the transnational market interests and enable the transnational market movements of global business. The nation-state is not therefore dead. But the old "Fordist-Keynesian" or "welfare-statist" systems of national-state governance in the rich countries; the post-colonial nation-building development plans of former colonies; and the state-managed economies of former socialist countries have all now been eclipsed by a decidedly post-Fordist, post-development, and post-socialist model of market-driven and market-disciplined policy-making. Even in China, where the Communist party retains its authoritarian command, cadres have turned their far-from-dead state powers to a single-minded focus on capitalist growth as measured by market metrics. Thus, in 2009, while Western governments agonized over whether the financial market crises pointed to broader failings in pro-market models of governance, Chinese leaders pressed ahead with their command capitalism, aggressively promoting market lending, creating more market stimulus, and generating more economic growth than any other country in the world.

Governance, as we will go on to explore in greater detail in Sections 7.2 and 7.3, is about more than just national governments and their policies. There is intellectual reason for using the word here instead of just "government." As an umbrella term for diverse forms of both formal *and* informal systems of control, governance helps us name some of the important ways that government has been augmented, extended, and transformed amidst contemporary globalization. It thus includes the controlling effects on policy-making of the main international financial institutions (IFIs) – the World Bank and IMF, the regulative effects of sub-national governments such as cities and counties, the coordinating effects of Inter-Governmental Organizations (IGOs that themselves range widely from the UN, to the EU to the **G8** and OPEC), and, despite their name, the governmental effects of diverse Non-Governmental Organizations (NGOs). More than just these institutions, governance also comprises a whole series of *practices*, too. These are practices that create social systems of political control – what some theorists of modern power call governmentality – that in turn have their regulative effects on how we conduct our lives by shaping behaviors commonly seen as personal choices. Routine decisions over everything from childcare, to health care, to shopping, religion, and even dating, can all in this sense be understood as being both the outcomes and enablers of governmental effects. Theorists of governmentality suggest that neoliberalism has been expanded at this very behavioral level, too. They therefore argue that alongside the macro management of neoliberalism exemplified by World Bank Structural Adjustment Programs (**SAPs**), we should also examine the neoliberal micro management of personal practices such as learning from self-help gurus to think of one's life as an investment opportunity. Even enrolling in college and taking a course on globalization can be considered thus as another aspect of governance!

The latter point may sound suspiciously like conspiratorial conjecture about one world government. But for precisely the same reason that social practices enlist people all around the world into systems of governance, the complete consolidation of a singular post-national framework for global governance of the sort advocated by Ohmae is ultimately impossible. Too many people, places, and possibilities exist for such singularized simplicity. One kind of college course – say in Microeconomics – may tend to make you see free-market neoliberalism as rational and right, but another kind of course – say in Cultural Anthropology or International Development or Human Geography – may lead you to think and act in favor of fair trade and new protections for worker rights and the environment. So, while global business leaders demand a single system of global government to serve a single global market, and while critics decry the straitjacketing of governments by a single one-size-fits-all neoliberal uniform code of conduct, we must remember that governance is contested and continues to be remade in different ways in different places. It can always therefore be remade again, and, given that it includes all sorts of non-governmental organizations and informal social practices, the possible participants in such movements for remaking governance include everyone on the planet.

The possibilities for contestation noted, the trend towards more pro-market patterns of governance globally is real. Moreover, and this is especially ironic given all the obituaries to the nation-state announced in support of such a trend, neoliberal governance has been vitally enabled in practice by some of the same structures of national-state government that are said to be finished. In other words, the very same nation-states that the big "G" Globalization storytellers say have reached their "end" remain key to understanding how little "g" globalization is being governed in more neoliberal ways. In the rest of this section, we will examine why, by reversing the terms of this ironic contradiction. In short, we will use the problems with the myths of newness, inevitability, and leveling as prompts for investigating how national government has endured as a building block of global governance. As it turns out, the fact that globalization has a long history, the fact that it has had to depend on all sorts of non-inevitable regulatory shifts, and the fact that it is extremely uneven are all facts that centrally involve the role played by nation-states in governing global relations. Thus, the following three sub-sections examine in further detail how nation-states at once complement and complicate our understanding of globalization. In doing so, they also outline how, far from being at an end, nation-states today endure as managed mediators of market discipline.

7.1.1   New-ness and national-state sovereignty

The new-ness myth recurs repeatedly in the retelling of the "end of the nation-state" sub-plot. New globalization trends have made national governments "history," so the story goes. States have been rendered redundant by the new economic interdependencies, and they are therefore little more than crumbling ruins of a bygone era when national exchange rates, national interest rates, national trade policy, national investment policy, national labor policy and a vast sweep of national legislation could be developed with little regard for global relations and global rules. At least this is the big "G" Globalization story-line. As with all the myths about Globalization, there is a grain of truth involved. Global market pressures are undoubtedly disciplinary for national governments, dimming hopes for national independence of even the most visionary national leaders. Having finally won freedom from apartheid in South Africa, for example, Nelson Mandela told the ANC's 1997 national conference that freedom from global market forces was another issue altogether. "The very mobility of capital and the globalization of the capital and other markets," he said, "make it impossible for countries . . . to decide national economic policy without regard to the likely response of these markets."[3] However, Mandela was by no means ready to draw the conclusion that national government was as a result now suddenly history. Like many other leaders in the post-colonial countries of the **Global South**, his leadership of South Africa was instead informed by an acute sense of how national governance has always been both enabled and constrained amidst global political–economic entanglements. For anyone knowledgeable of such history, the idea that national governments once enjoyed great freedom to set policy would be ridiculed as a fairy tale. Citizens of former colonies – which, it bares remembering, make up the majority of the world's nation-states – instead know well that national-state policy-making has always been tied in key and consequential ways to global relations. Likewise, while their leaders are less ready to acknowledge such historical interdependencies, former imperial powers such as Britain and France cannot be understood as nation-states themselves without full consideration of how they industrialized, grew, and transformed their systems of government in tandem with establishing global networks of economic and political dominance overseas.[4] One problem with the notion of new-ness, then, is that in relation to national-state governments, it obscures their foundational formation amidst earlier rounds of globalization.

More than just hiding history, though, another bigger problem with the new-ness myth is that it obscures *how* this history of globally shaped national state-making has in turn shaped the ways nation-states are tied into the ordering and regulation of contemporary global interdependencies. In particular, one enduring aspect of national state government that resulted from transnational ties and tensions in the past remains – notwithstanding "end of the nation-state" obituaries – absolutely central to explaining the global expansion and entrenchment of neoliberal governance today: namely, sovereignty.[5]

The norms and practices of sovereignty reach back beyond the beginning of modern national state-making to an era in European history – from the late Middle Ages through the sixteenth century – when sovereigns in the form of kings, queens, and emperors established systems of absolute rule over increasingly consolidated territories. These territories only slowly developed as meaningfully "national" communities later, and even then, very unevenly such that the hyphenated formula of "the nation-state" covered over all sorts of resistance by city, regional, ethnic, and linguistic communities to being governed by a single sovereign. Sovereign state-making over a single national territory has since developed as a precarious and processual achievement rather than a fixed and finalized result, and the space-spanning hyphen in between the two words "nation" and "state" has remained a reminder of all sorts of space-grabbing, space-contesting, and space-defending struggles ever since. Nevertheless, over time, and as a result of ongoing international ties and tensions, five features of sovereignty became normalized from the seventeenth century onwards. Today, each of these features has also come to play a role in expanding or entrenching neoliberal governance.

Sovereignty i: The first feature is what is commonly called "Westphalian sovereignty." This is named after the 1648 treaties of Westphalia that ended both the Thirty Years War in the Holy Roman Empire and the Eighty Years War between Spain and the Republic of the Seven United Netherlands. The treaties were themselves complex diplomatic compromises between diverse religious and monarchical players, and they recognized all sorts of territories, principalities, and political regimes. However, what they are now remembered for and what Westphalian sovereignty basically means is the principle that *one state should not interfere within the territory of another state*. Today, even as their fates become ever more interwoven, nation-states and their populations hold this principle high. Countries as diverse as the United States, China, and the Sudan all insist thus on respect for their territorial sovereignty.

Yet, while Westphalian sovereignty clearly persists, it has nevertheless been complicated today by the need for sovereign nation-states to manage transnational interdependencies. This is where pro-market policies enter the picture. Since so many of today's global interdependencies – trade ties, financial ties, and labor market ties, for example – are mediated by the capitalist market, their management often involves market-based rule as a default mode of global governance. Moreover, even when the global interdependencies in question are only indirectly interconnected with economic globalization (e.g. environmental ties), Westphalian sovereignty works to advance pro-market rule by blocking the development of transnational governmental institutions that might regulate globalization in non-neoliberal ways. Why? Because when national governments assert sovereignty, they object to more visible transnational governmental agencies and rules all the while they accept and adapt to the invisible regulatory effects of the market.

To illustrate how Westphalian sovereignty tends to lead to more pro-market responses to global governance challenges, let us consider a call for international cooperation put forward by the Chinese premier at the UN in 2008. "In the long history of mankind," he concluded,

> the destinies of countries have never been so closely linked as they are today. Given the global nature of issues threatening the survival and development of mankind such as climate change, environmental degradation, resource constraints, frequent outbreaks of diseases and natural disasters and the spread of terrorism, and in the face of the intertwining challenges of finance, energy and food, no country can expect to stay away from the difficulties or handle the problems all by itself.

All these key global concerns – the global environment, global diseases, global terrorism, and global financial crisis – are clearly problems for global governance, and they all invite many different solutions. However, because world leaders tend to approach them with an insistence on ongoing Westphalian sovereignty, they also tend to privilege as "solutions" the invisible regulative hand of market forces over the visible hands of global government, global regulations, and global enforcement. Thus, carbon trading, corporate pharmaceutical innovation, the freezing of terrorists' assets, and an enhanced crisis management role for the IMF and World Bank are the sorts of "working together" that are repeatedly privileged as more viable. Creating a global environmental agency with real regulatory and enforcement powers, by contrast, an agency that could go into a country such as China and close down big polluters, is – as we saw with the failed 2009 Copenhagen climate summit – considered unrealistic. After all, in the same speech, the Chinese premier insisted that China "will never tolerate any external interference." And nor for that matter will the United States or India, or even a small nation-state such as Singapore. At the same time, though, all these countries are willing to tolerate the rules that come with WTO membership, even when, as we saw in Chapter 6, these market rules clearly have huge implications for domestic development and law. Thus, we see Westphalian sovereignty and market-based regulation coming together in a kind of global governance marriage – state power + market power – of capitalist convenience.

It would be wrong to suggest that Westphalian sovereignty and neoliberalism always come together so synergistically. In the European Union (**EU**), the story is a little more complex. For this reason, one of the best places to test the limits of Westphalian sovereignty today is in the historical site of Westphalia itself. Now known as *Westfalen* and located in northern Germany on the border with the Netherlands, the region lies at the heart of the EU. Here, some of the principles of Westphalian sovereignty have clearly been supplanted by something new. All 27 EU members, including Germany and the Netherlands, have pooled important aspects of their national sovereignty, agreeing to create and enforce a vast set of common laws and policies. The resulting system of EU government comprises a transnational regime of formal and institutionalized cooperative governance that is based on transnational democratic principles and the transnational rule of law. It has an elected supra-national parliament and a supra-national court, along with the supra-national executive – the European Commission – that controls the budget and bureaucracy for a diverse set of supra-national agencies. Yet while all these elements of EU governance supercede territorially bounded Westphalian sovereignty, and while EU agencies play a direct role in all sorts of planning and development initiatives inside the territories of member nation-states, other aspects of Westphalian sovereignty endure – not least of all in peaceful Westfalen itself. German citizens here would no more accept direct political rule from Paris (as once happened when Napoleon turned Westphalia into a vassal state of France) than the French would accept political rule from Berlin (as happened in World War II under the Nazis). Instead, precisely because prior rounds of international conflict have led to respect for the principles of Westphalian sovereignty, it has been possible for these neighboring nation-states to come together and negotiate all the new agreements that lie at the heart of shared EU governance. Moreover, as EU leaders continue to make the case for EU governance to skeptical nationalists in their home countries, they also frequently end up appealing to the Westphalian ideal of post-war peace as a way of advancing neoliberal policies. They claim thus that it is the peace of commercial exchange between respectful sovereign nation-states that operates as the most enabling alternative to the wars that once devastated and divided the continent in the past.

The emphasis on making profits rather than war is one of the reasons why neoliberal norms have tended – as we saw in Chapter 6 – to be privileged in many of the EU's laws. It also accounts for why neoliberal norms also tend to predominate in EU regional development initiatives, including the cross-border region linking the German state of Nordrhein-Westfalen with the Dutch provinces of Gelderland, North-Brabant, and Limburg. Known as Euregio Rhine-Waal, this region, which incorporates historic Westphalia, now serves as a model for other EU cross-border regions because it has transformed an area once defined by deadly nationalistic war-making into a zone of peaceful growth and profit-making. Key initiatives of the Euregio Rhine-Waal that are funded by the EU therefore emphasize helping businesses connect with each other and collaborate across the German–Dutch border, as well as promoting the region as a site for foreign direct investment.[6] As such, the Euregio illustrates at a regional level the ways in which the most widely enforced elements in EU governance have tended to emphasize a pro-market model of development. It is true that there have also been some other initiatives in the region, too, for example, in pooling cross-border health services and educational innovation. Like the health, labor, and environmental protections put in place at the pan-EU scale, these have been enabled by an element of transnational democratic accountability in the Euregio. However, both in the cross-border region and across the EU as a whole, the non-neoliberal application of many of these sorts of health, labor, and environmental protections is constantly frustrated by other aspects of sovereignty that persist in Europe as elsewhere. It is these that we must now consider in more detail.

Sovereignty ii: The second enduring feature of sovereignty is "recognition sovereignty." This also emerged out of the same sorts of post-war diplomatic developments represented by the peace of Westphalia. However, it has since gained a more social significance of its own in a world where national governments are understood to serve as representational agents of national societies. It refers to the principle that *nation-states recognize one another as representatives of populations in international negotiations and activities*. A number of notable examples including Taiwan and Palestine do not enjoy universal recognition of their sovereignty in this way. But these are the exceptions that show how intact the general rule is, even in the EU where Westphalian sovereignty has been supra-nationally supplemented. Whether it is at the UN, or in national legal representations at the International Court of Justice, or in symbolic flag-waving and anthem-playing at events such as the Olympic games, recognition sovereignty remains a commonplace of global events. Moreover, while its emergence was historically based in the prosecution and resolution of international wars, its contemporary relevance stretches into more peaceful events – as the Olympic games exemplifies – associated with the rule-based management of international competition. As a transnational regime enabled by agreements on the cooperative, rule-based management of competition, the EU illustrates this very well. EU rules still have to acknowledge the recognition sovereignty held dear by member governments. Sometimes these same national governments are obliged to recognize in turn the ways in which they are recognized by anxious citizens as national protectors from the problems of economic integration.

Yet while such paradoxes point to tensions between globalization and national sovereignty, the more general outcome of the recognition sovereignty revived by integration angst – angst about foreign workers, angst about foreign bureaucrats, angst about foreign laws, and so on – is a systematic bias towards privileging neoliberal policy across transnational space. This is what some theorists call "negative integration": the process of EU integration which limits non-neoliberal innovations by repeatedly restricting the ability of non-governmental organizations such as feminist groups and unions to make the case that they better represent the interests of particular populations ignored or marginalized by national governments. Finally, it should be noted that, even when they do successfully make their cases, such transnational activists have to deal with a third feature of sovereignty, the crossing of which tends to be much easier for national diplomats, goods, and money than for grassroots political organizations.

Sovereignty iii: The third feature of national-state sovereignty is "border sovereignty." It rests on the principle that *nation-states control their territorial borders, including the flow of commodities, capital, and people into and out of their territories*. Though clearly related to the international diplomacy and territorial maps associated with Westphalian and recognition sovereignty, border sovereignty also has historical roots in the international negotiations and management practices associated with marking and enforcing the borders of nation-states on the ground. As Ohmae's work illustrates, borders feature prominently as obstacles to be overcome in "end of the nation-state" story-telling. However, their historical establishment as sites where national-state sovereignty is negotiated and performed means in fact that border-management processes constitute one of the main places where conformity with emerging pro-market governance is enforced. Borders are key to neoliberal management practices ranging from the implementation of free-trade tariff reductions to expedited passport processing of business travelers to the ongoing balancing of migration management with labor market needs. Border regions around the world are therefore marked by new norms of neoliberal citizenship and exclusion (see Chapter 8). They are sites where the transformation of sovereignty into a tool for managing globalization in more neoliberal ways becomes especially clear – even as they continue to make clear that we do not live in Ohmae's borderless world.

Sovereignty iv: A fourth feature of national-state sovereignty is "administrative sovereignty." It rests on the principle that *a nation-state is the chief administrative authority enforcing laws for and on its national population.* Although the transnational legal harmonization processes associated with trade agreements often end-up overruling pre-existing national laws, they still crucially depend on the regulatory authority of national administrative sovereignty to do so. It is this sovereignty – itself an outcome of both the prior globalization of national administrative practices under imperialism and ongoing international efforts to expand so-called good governance today – that is invoked repeatedly in **WTO, World Bank**, and **IMF** agreements as the constitutional basis of new global rules. Member nation-states and client governments of these institutions are thereby recognized as having the administrative authority to sign binding contracts that in turn lock in the market rules. When later governments, sub-national governments, or non-governmental groups subsequently seek to overturn such rules, they see them as being enforced by the global economic institutions themselves. However, this enforcement would not even be possible were it not for the national-state administrative sovereignty invoked to establish the rules in the first place.

Sovereignty v: Finally, a fifth feature of sovereignty, a feature that is commonly ignored in less global analyses, is "resistance sovereignty." While all of the other four features tend to obscure the class interests and religious, racial, or regional biases of state leaders making sovereignty claims for a wider population, *resistance sovereignty represents the interests of dispossessed populations with new appeals to sovereignty.* An early example was Haiti, declared a free sovereign nation-state by former slaves after their successful revolution against French rulers in 1791. Subsequently, in the twentieth century, formerly colonized countries all around the world have fought for independence in the same name of national sovereignty. And even today, autonomist "sub-national" nations such as that represented by Québec in Canada demand recognition and respect for their resistant sovereignty as part of their broader efforts to set their own laws and policies. All these examples also illustrate the ways in which resistance sovereignty has itself been informed by global ties, tensions, and inspirations. The Haitian leader, Toussaint L'Ouverture, deliberately adapted and expanded the *liberté, egalité*, and *fraternité* of the French revolution to write the revolutionary constitution of the newly sovereign Haiti, making the ideal of equality much more of a reality there than it could become in a France still committed post-revolution to the racist double standards of slavery.[7] Likewise, anti-colonial national independence struggles of the twentieth century – in, for example, India, Indonesia, and Mozambique – generally used the geographical outlines and administrative structures established by imperial powers as the basis for their resistant claims for sovereignty. And much more recently, among First Nations in Canada, the Gitxsan and Wet'suwet'en have used modern maps of their territories and invoked UN recognition of native rights to make the case for recognition of their sovereignty before Canadian courts.[8]

While anti-colonial resistance sovereignty clearly illustrates how national sovereignty claims emerge out of international ties, tensions, and inspirations, recent developments in post-colonial countries show in turn how sovereignty remains a two-edged sword: at times an instrument for expanding independence while at others an instrument for disciplining national governments. As we shall examine in more detail in Section 7.3, the national treatment once demanded by newly inde-pendent colonies has now become a disciplining device which, in the context of contemporary globalization and in the hands of all sorts of accountants of global business, is being used to penalize resistance to pro-market governance. Used as the basis for diverse national rankings, ratings, and risk assessments aimed at measuring and ultimately ensuring compliance with neoliberal rule, resistance sovereignty has thus been turned into a form of what critics call "market sovereignty." One other important illustration of this disciplinary neoliberalism was already introduced in Chapter 6: the so-called "national treatment" rule of the WTO according to which all signatory members have to treat goods made in other countries the same as goods made domestically (see page 190). The larger point here, again, is that we are not seeing the end of the nation-state so much as the re-working of national sovereignty: its retention, but also its re-use for purposes of expanding and entrenching norms of pro-market governance.

The example of national treatment being used to implement a piece of transnational neoliberal legislation takes us in turn from problems with the new-ness myth to problems with the inevitability myth. Global changes that require legal changes that require recourse to the historically established sovereignty of the nation-state can hardly be inevitable. They have to be authorized, legislated into place, and enforced by governments. To understand why and how this happens, we have to explore another enduring feature of nation-states that is also obscured by "end of the nation-state" story tellers: the capacity of national governments to authorize new policies.

7.1.2   Inevitability and national-state authority

If the new-ness myth conceals the ongoing importance of sovereignty, the enduring feature of nation-states obscured by inevitability arguments is national authority: including the legislative authority, judicial authority, policing authority, and military authority of nation-states to shape and enforce their sovereignty. Saying that the "end of the nation-state" is inevitable thereby ignores the important ways in which national authority is used to legislate and enforce neoliberal reforms. Though they prefer to present neoliberalism as natural, pro-market policy advocates know that this national-state authorization matters. This is why they fund authors, educators, think-tanks, lobbyists, and politicians the world over to promote the neoliberal policies as normal, rational, and good. It is worth remembering in this respect the older eighteenth- and nineteenth-century politics of the term *laissez-faire* to which today's neoliberalism harkens back. On the one hand, *laissez-faire* meant "letting the economy do what it wants" and not having government interfere. Yet, on the other hand, the very fact that it had to be named and framed as a policy meant that "letting do" was not enough; that the supposedly inevitable market-based organization of capitalism instead had to be actively authorized and enforced as a matter (and thus a slogan) of policy. As the Hungarian political-economist Karl Polanyi famously reflected in 1944: "There was nothing natural about *laissez-faire*; free markets could never have come into being merely by allowing things to take their course.... *Laissez-faire* was itself enforced by the state . . . *Laissez-faire* was planned."

While his book *The Great Transformation* is now enjoying an academic renaissance, Polanyi remains far less famous than a fellow native of Austria–Hungary, Friedrich August von Hayek. Polanyi was Jewish and had to flea from Austria in 1933 as the fascists rose to power. Von Hayek, by contrast, was descended from Bohemian nobility and had already left for London in 1931 for a post at the London School of Economics. Nevertheless, his transnational travels across the Atlantic after the 1940s were also haunted by Nazi authoritarianism and, as such, offered a radically different interpretation of capitalist crisis. While Polanyi saw the crises caused by unfettered market capitalism as the basic explanation for the social breakdown that brought the Nazis to power, Hayek believed the exact opposite. For him, the lesson of National Socialism was simply that all government planning had authoritarian tendencies: that it was, in the terms of the title of his widely acclaimed book, *The Road to Serfdom*. Hayek's opposition to government regulation of the market subsequently put him at odds with the Keynesian policies of the post-war Labour government in Britain (even though Keynes himself professed to find himself in agreement with virtually all of Hayek's arguments). However, over the years, as Hayek moved to the United States and the University of Chicago and then back to Germany (where he died in Freiburg in 1992), his arguments against interventionist government attracted more and more followers, leading him to become one of the most important intellectual authorities invoked by advocates of neoliberal governance. Margaret Thatcher, for instance, famously slammed a copy of Hayek's *The Constitution of Freedom* down on the table in front of Conservative party planners, saying authoritatively: "This is what we believe."

The irony involved in being authoritarian about a critique of authoritarianism provides a clue in turn to the fact that invoking Hayek as an authority for neoliberal reforms was also never going to be enough on its own. Even when combined with the work of other early advocates of pro-market governance such as Milton Friedman (a professor of economics who, guided by Hayek, made the University of Chicago economics department the national and global leader in promoting pro-market "shock therapy"), and even as Hayek's and Friedman's fundamentalist formulation of free-market freedom started to gain traction in former bastions of Keynesian orthodoxy, the academic Chicago School ideas about the market knowing best could not force through the needed changes in policy without national government action. Pro-market leaders such as Thatcher therefore had to use all the authoritative powers of the nation-state itself to put the neoliberal notions into practice. To paraphrase Polanyi, *laissez-faire* had to be planned and enforced all over again, and the authority of the same national governments so demonized by Hayek and Friedman had to be used to put their planning philosophy into place as a new regime of pro-market governance.

In some parts of the world, the use of governmental authority to expand and entrench neoliberal policies involved especially authoritarian transformations of government, too. For example, the rise of Singapore, Hong Kong, Taiwan, and South Korea as the free-market "Asian Tigers" could not have been accomplished without far-from-free governmental controls over political, economic, and social life.[9] In still more shocking illustrations of authoritarian enforcement, Latin American countries such as Chile saw military coups bring dictators into power in the 1970s who then violently strong-armed their countries into implementing the shock therapy of Chicago School economists overnight. Elsewhere, though, as Thatcher herself explained to Hayek after he had recommended the Chilean example to her in 1981, such rapid revolutions in governmental policy were not feasible. She wrote back to him:

> I am sure you will agree that in Britain with our democratic institutions and the need for a high degree of consent, some of the measures adopted in Chile are quite unacceptable. Our reform must be in line with our traditions and our Constitution. At times the process may seem painfully slow.[10]

For these very same reasons, "the process" in many countries took all the more governmental planning and enforcement to make the supposedly inevitable neoliberal reforms really inevitable. Starting with the British case, let us consider some of the more notable examples.

From electoral victory in 1979 and all through the 1980s, Thatcher's governments continued to work hard to authorize neoliberal reform. They privatized state-owned industries, utilities, and public housing. They deregulated banking and the City of London's financial-services industry. They reduced redistributive income taxes. And, far from letting the economy do its own thing, they shifted away from the view that inflation would go away naturally and towards monetarist policies of reducing the money supply, pushing up interest rates, and imposing fiscal austerity in order to restore price stability. The resulting cutbacks in education, health, and welfare spending may have sometimes been depicted as attacks on what Thatcher disparaged as "the nanny state." But in her hands, these actions were by no means associated with a shrinking of state power and authority. Notwithstanding her hesitations about "some of the measures adopted in Chile," her governments were unhesitatingly authoritarian in their punitive treatment of striking unions, most notably of the National Union of Mineworkers who Thatcher depicted as an "enemy" of the nation. Such use of traditional national war-talk was also famously amplified by the foreign war Thatcher led Britain into against Argentina in 1982. In turn, she used the shock of this campaign alongside the shock of Globalization myths to destabilize a tradition-bound society and force the British to accept neoliberal reform. This political–economic achievement enabled her to press ahead with more privatizations. British Airways, British Airport Authority, British Gas, British Steel, and British Telecom all went the same way into private ownership: British in name, but privatized under the authority of national government, and no longer owned and managed by the nation-state.

Thatcher's success lay in part in articulating her neoliberal revolution with nationalism. She could thereby use the authority of the national government to make the changes legitimate enough to be lasting. While she said "There Is No Alternative" to pro-market reform and while she is therefore credited with being the original TINA-tout, it is important to underline therefore that her enthusiasm for inevitability arguments never led her to give up national governmental authority. Thatcher's position on the EU was to become especially telling in this respect. On the one hand she adamantly opposed the deepening of the EU and any associated developments of democratic supranational governance. "We have not successfully rolled back the frontiers of the state in Britain," she said in her famous 1988 Bruges speech, "only to see them reimposed at a European level, with a European super state exercising a new dominance from Brussels."[11] Yet on the other hand, she was a big fan of widening the EU's liberalized market to as many new trading partners as possible. This second position was her ultimate undoing as the leader of the Conservative party whose xenophobic base remained nationalistically anti-EU in every way imaginable. Nevertheless, in the years that have followed, it is also these pro-market aspects of EU governance – including pan-European free trade and financial liberalization – that have been most successfully expanded and entrenched, and the opposition to EU institutional deepening led by politicians such as Thatcher goes a long way to explaining this result.

Thatcher's use of national state authority to roll back the Fordist state was paralleled elsewhere by leaders in New Zealand, Canada, Australia, and also, though more slowly, in many other parts of Europe, too. However, it was back in Henry Ford's own country where the roll-back of the Fordist arrangements and the roll-out of neoliberal governance had the greatest global significance. Here, Thatcher's friend President Ronald Reagan led the United States through a sweeping set of pro-market policy reforms (sometimes referred to as Reaganomics) right through the 1980s. Like Thatcher, Reagan saw no contradiction in using state authority to entrench neoliberalism. As nationalistic as he might have been about the US constitution making America a shining "beacon of freedom," Reagan was also keen to recommend CUFTA (the Canada–United States Free Trade Agreement) as "a new economic constitution for North America."[12] Like Thatcher, too, Reagan waged war-like struggles domestically against unions, most notably against PATCO (the Professional Air Traffic Controllers Organization) whose 1981 strike he declared a "peril to national safety." And Reagan was adept in using the authority of the White House to deregulate business and cut taxes for the wealthy, despite the ways these policies actually did more to imperil consumer safety and undermine welfare safety nets for America's middle class and poor.

For American students, criticisms of Reagan-era reforms may sound like the purely partisan points of "liberal" critics. For the same reason, it is important to emphasize two further facts about neoliberalism in America. First, while Reagan undoubtedly used state authority to authorize pro-market reforms, he was by no means the first or last president to do so. Indeed, Democratic President Jimmy Carter who preceded him initiated a number of neoliberal reforms himself, including appointing the monetarist Paul Volcker as Chairman of the US Federal Reserve. Subsequently, in the 1990s, it was another Democrat, President Bill Clinton, who enthusiastically expanded CUFTA to Mexico under NAFTA and who signed a 1996 welfare reform act in order, as he boasted himself, "to end welfare as we know it." Still more recently, coming to the Oval office after the biggest cataclysm in global financial markets since the Great Depression, Democratic President Barack Obama still appointed a set of pro-market neoliberals to be his main economic advisers. Alongside such notables as Lawrence Summers and Timothy Geithner, Obama also re-enlisted Paul Volcker, pulling him out of retirement and into a group whose pro-market predilections have made his own monetarism seem mild. Obama's memoir of organizing community groups to fight racial injustice in the Southside of Chicago indicates he may not be a Chicago Boy of the classic Milton Friedman mould. But his actions as president suggest he is following the same free-market rule book as his predecessors. Thus, while the styles and social concerns of presidencies have changed, the underlying advancement of neoliberal norms persists as a mainstay of US government. Moreover, the second more complex truth about neoliberalism in America is that this domestic advancement of pro-market policy-making also *reflected* as well as *reinforced* the wider uptake and enforcement of pro-market governance globally.

The way Democratic administrations have continued to enforce and expand the pro-market reforms of Reagan reflects specifically the wider rise of what is best described as an executive class "group think" on the virtues of neoliberal policies all around the world. Sometimes referred to as a "Third Way" or "Middle Way" between Right and Left, the pattern has been remarkably global. In Britain, Thatcher was followed by neoliberal advocates Tony Blair and Gordon Brown, who, as leaders of the old socialist Labour Party, turned it into a neoliberal party branded "New Labour." Similar neoliberal rebrandings have also been made to the Social Democratic Party of Germany, the French Socialist Party, and others across Western Europe. Elsewhere, in Australia the Labor Party governments of Bob Hawke and Paul Keating early on adopted pro-market policies such as floating the Australian Dollar in 1983, reducing trade tariffs, making taxes less redistributive, switching government wage-fixing for "enterprise bargaining," deregulating the banking system, and privatizing Qantas airlines. Similarly, in New Zealand the early 1980s saw the uptake of so-called Rogernomics – a name for the Reaganomic pro-market policies introduced by the Finance Minister of the New Zealand Labor Party, Roger Douglas. Meanwhile, in Canada, following neoliberal reforms initiated in the 1980s by the awkwardly named Progressive Conservatives, the Liberal Party of Jean Chretien and Paul Martin abandoned its social liberalism and remembered for the new millennium that it had started in the nineteenth century as the party of business and liberal capitalism.

More widely, in Eastern Europe, Southeast Asia, Latin America, South Africa, and the so-called BRIC countries of Brazil, Russia, India, and China, similar transformations have taken hold, too. The leaders of governing parties may once have been socialists, communists, Peronists, Maoists, ANC activists, "non-aligned" modernisers, or supporters of landless peasants, but now, even if they have not abandoned all the party uniforms of the past, they have all, in one way or another, donned the business suits of neoliberalism. Coming out of the Cold War, it has been an impressive realignment in global governance. But just as it was never inevitable, it has hardly been a story of leveling either (except in the sense that leaders of re-branded pro-market parties have been obsessed the world over with the leveling idea of "wiping the slate clean"). As Reagan well knew when he referred to America as a shining city on the hill, the global uptake and enforcement of pro-market rule has instead also involved the uniquely powerful national influence of the United States.

7.1.3   Leveling and national-state hegemony

While the new-ness and inevitability myths obscure the enduring importance of nation-states in authorizing neoliberal governance, the leveling myth hides hierarchies of national-state power globally, including the very special power the United States has as a global pro-market enforcer. Sometimes called leadership and praised for bringing "Pax Americana" to the world, and at other times criticized as imperialism and a "Pox Americana," there is no doubting that this enforcement role has been important in pushing through neoliberal reforms globally. It is not new, though, and the American emphasis on opening up markets abroad and using military power to secure access for US business interests has a long history that predates Fordism as well as neoliberalism. To understand it, we therefore have to turn from the topics of sovereignty and authority to a third enduring feature of national-state power that is equally obscured by ahistorical "end of the nation-state" obituaries: namely, hegemony.

Hegemony refers here to two interrelated sorts of power. First, as it is used by international relations and world systems theorists, hegemony means global dominance, most often through military means. Second, as it is used by social and cultural theorists, hegemony refers rather differently to the ways in which dominant social classes secure consent from subordinated classes, including consent to their own subordination, by shaping popular representations of what policies and social norms make good sense. In historical empires, the two forms of hegemony sometimes operated in distinct spatial zones with military hegemony abroad and sociocultural hegemony at home. For example, during the original *Pax Romana* of the ancient Romans, brutal hegemonic dominance of the empire's enemies in the periphery combined with the hegemony of free "Bread and Circuses" to ensure support from the plebs in Rome. With a famous mix of architecture, infrastructure, and pubic displays of beneficence, the Romans also tried to supplement their military hegemony with efforts to enlist peaceful consent in the colonies. But as with many empires that followed, the efforts at sociocultural hegemony still worked much better at home. Victorian imperialists, to use an English example (itself a place that the Romans never fully pacified), may have deeply believed in their empire's "civilizing mission," but their overseas dominance depended much more on weapons and military violence than on successful Christian conversions.[13] A nineteenth-century parody of a popular hymn captured the resulting contradictions all too well:

> Onward Christian soldiers, on to heathen lands,
> Prayer-books in your pockets, rifles in your hands,
> Take the glorious tidings where trade can be done,
> Spread the peaceful gospel – with the Maxim gun.

However, when we fast forward to contemporary globalization, we see that the two kinds of hegemony have blurred the inside/outside division and come to shape one another. Beginning from the Jeffersonian ideal of America being an "empire of liberty," US leaders have generally seen themselves as advancing American interests abroad consensually in the name of freedom and over time rather than coercively in the name of the nation-state and over space. Henry Luce, the founder of *Time, Life, and Fortune* magazines, spoke of the twentieth century thus as an American Century. He did not talk about an American Empire, and, like other US leaders before and especially after, he pointed instead to the popularity of American ideas and innovations abroad. Hollywood movies, "**McDonaldization**," and what is sometimes called "Coca-Colonization" are all illustrations in this way of the sorts of consensual hegemony-building orchestrated by American corporate interests outside America. Along with the less noticed but deeply influential spread of American business education norms (e.g. MBAs), American accounting norms (e.g. Generally Accepted Auditing Standards), and American shopping and investment norms (e.g. big box malls and 24/7 market reporting), they illustrate the ways in which the United States has modeled a form of market society for world societies.[14] And, of course, in another sign of economic hegemony that is ignored by leveling myths, since 1945 the US national currency has in turn provided a de facto global reserve currency for multiple foreign markets and commodities.

As popular as many American business products have been abroad, and as much as the dollar has been used to buy and sell them, the label of Coca-Colonization reminds us that there has been more than modeling and money involved. There has also been the US military and its establishment of bases and garrisons around the world as quasi-colonial outposts. It was American military superiority from World War II through the Cold War that gave the United States its "exorbitant privilege" to print the world's reserve currency. The French could complain all they liked about the unfair advantage this gave the United States to export inflation, but, while they depended on the American nuclear umbrella, there was very little that they and other Europeans could do about US unwillingness to exchange European dollar savings for gold. Likewise, while Keynes and the British may have had other plans at Bretton Woods, the way the United States emerged from World War II as a superpower allowed US leaders to set up the IMF and World Bank in ways that locked US influence into place. The form of pro-market governance these institutions have enforced globally has therefore been bound up from the beginning with US business interests. This is also why the term **Washington Consensus** has been picked up and used as a synonym for neoliberalism in studies of global governance. It captures the American economic interests relayed through Washington DC, as well as the neoliberal consensus of economists working in the IMF, World Bank, and US Treasury. We will examine the creation of this consensus and its enforcement by the two Bretton Woods financial institutions in the next section, but here it should be noted that, notwithstanding the consensus among DC-based economists, there has not always been consensus on neoliberalism outside of America. As the self-styled "neoconservatives" behind the "Project for a New American Century" advised President Bush (the younger), the empire of liberty has also had to rely at times on using the brute force of the US military to coerce unwilling nation-states into global economic integration.

One of the main sites for hegemonic maintenance cited by the neoconservatives during President Bush's two terms in office was Iraq. In terms of governance, it is worth remembering that while support for the Iraq war was rallied with dystopian depictions of Saddam Hussein as a nuclear-armed terrorist, the longer-term vision of the neoconservatives was more utopian, being centered on the "benevolent" idea of expanding and entrenching neoliberalism in Iraq as a way of incorporating the wider region into market-led globalization.[15] The goal was to use military force to remove a corrupt dictator, free-up Iraqi oil supply for privatization, and integrate the middle of the Middle East into the global economy with a new Middle East Free Trade Agreement (MEFTA). The ties of market bonds, it was thought, would soon therefore follow the skies full of bombs. It was hoped thus that, having been born of neoconservative war-making, Iraq would in turn come to be a bastion of neoliberal profit-making – a Tiger on the Tigris, it was imagined – serving as an example for the rest of the region of the benefits of pro-market governance. Of course, on the ground, the war and occupation fast became much less "benevolent," its vast costs in both blood and dollars also threatening the active maintenance of US hegemony in other parts of the world, too. As a result, Americans turned against the neoconservatives. President Bush himself ousted some of the movement's more confrontational characters from his administration (notably Paul Wolfowitz who was moved from the Pentagon to the presidency of the World Bank), and, subsequently, with the victory of President Obama, Washington saw the return of a global governance emphasis on international cooperation and alliances.

The political defeat of the neoconservatives notwithstanding, their lasting intellectual success has been to remind a new generation of students and scholars that, beneath all the talk of cooperation and alliances, global governance throughout the twentieth century has been deeply shaped by American force. In short, American military hegemony has been used repeatedly to open markets and expand a pro-market form of socio-economic hegemony to other parts of the world. Back in 1907, when he was still president of Princeton University, Woodrow Wilson explained this hegemonic project very directly:

> Since trade ignores national boundaries and the manufacturer insists on having the world as a market, the flag of his nation must follow him, and the doors of the nations which are closed must be battered down. . . . Concessions obtained by financiers must be safeguarded by ministers of state, even if the sovereignty of unwilling nations be outraged in the process.[16]

Figure 7.1 Worldmapper cartogram showing country share of world military spending. *Source:* http://www.worldmapper.org/display.php?selected=279. © Copyright SASI Group (University of Sheffield) and Mark Newman (University of Michigan) (CC BY-NC-ND 3.0).

More recently, with American economic influence declining and dependency on foreign finance growing, US presidents (and university presidents) speak more carefully about respecting the sovereignty of other countries. But, as we saw in Chapter 2, US commentators such as Thomas Friedman still talk of McDonalds needing McDonnell Douglas. And meanwhile, with over 700 bases spread across the entire planet, and with US military spending still accounting in 2011 for almost 50% of total world spending on "defense," American military hegemony remains as imposing as it is enduring (Figure 7.1).

Throughout the Cold War, the United States continued to follow the Wilsonian approach, intervening militarily to open or protect markets in Latin America, the Caribbean, and Asia, while also expanding into new regions and continents, including the Middle East and Africa in a competition with the Soviet Union for influence. Yet during the Cold War, when there was a real possibility that other nation-states might have moved in more communist directions, the United States was sometimes willing to tolerate and even actively support social-democratic systems of government that put tight regulatory controls on market capitalism. Indeed, in West Germany, where the Pentagon permanently stationed bases to protect the country from Soviet tanks, and where the US government delivered massive amounts of economic aid in the form of the Marshall Plan, American leaders let German governments impose import bans on American goods and develop command economy controls that were the very opposite of openness and market liberalization.

As time went by, though, the United States was much less tolerant of democracies that turned from liberal market capitalism towards more socialized systems of economic organization. Most significant in signaling the rise of neoliberalism in the 1970s, the Nixon administration supported the violent 1973 overthrow of President Salvador Allende's democratically elected socialist government in Chile by General Augusto Pinochet. Not only did the American Central Intelligence Agency play an important role in training and enabling the leaders of this military coup, but American influence prevailed at the level of policy and socio-economic hegemony, too. It was in this way that Pinochet's dictatorship turned Chile into a grand experiment in top-down neoliberal reform based on the pro-market ideas of the Chicago School. Almost immediately after seizing power, and before the mass murders of socialist leaders were over, the General invited Chicago School trained economists – the "Chicago Boys" – to draft a new economic plan for Chile based on neoliberal ideals. Government spending for health, education, and human services (though not for the military) was drastically cut. Foreign banks and corporations were given free access to the country. And companies that had been nationalized by Allende's government were privatized anew. This whole experiment in forced neoliberalization occurred, it should be remembered, at a time when Nixon's administration continued to fund the Great Society programs within America, programs such as Medicaid, Medicare, Head Start, and Food Stamps that are now traditionally seen as "liberal" in the "Big Government" sense. In other words, American hegemony was such in the 1970s that it led to neoliberalism abroad with ongoing welfare-state liberalism at home. It was not until the Reagan era when ongoing American support for anti-socialist violence in Latin America (e.g. for the Contras campaign in Nicaragua) finally came together with a domestic version of the Chilean experiment inside the United States itself.

Reagan's attacks on "Big Government" were also informed by enduring American anxieties about the Soviet Union. But in 1989, the year he left the presidency, what he had once called the "Evil Empire" itself began to crumble with the fall of the Berlin Wall. With the collapse of the Soviet system shortly thereafter in 1991, the idea that there was no alternative to free market capitalism took on a new geopolitical meaning. The absence of a Soviet military threat to backup alternative approaches to governance – what foreign-policy pundits described as a new "unipolar" moment in global governance – meant that US influence abroad was less dependent on the military and evermore mediated by market institutions and ideas. Illustrations of this were especially obvious in the countries of the former Soviet Union, many of which were suffering severe economic crises. Newly elected leaders in Poland and Russia turned to the United States for support, but instead of the sorts of direct financial aid once enjoyed by West Germany during the Cold War, America only sent economists as assistance this time. These experts – including the then Harvard-based Jeffrey Sachs – in turn advised the "Shock Therapy" of overnight neoliberalization that had been pioneered in Chile in 1973. And, because of the already shocked state of many of these countries, the process did not have to be "painfully slow" – as Thatcher had put it with regret to Hayek. Instead, across much of the former Communist bloc, and thus across a vast region that America had once sought to contain geopolitically, a reverse process of incorporation into global capitalism was painfully fast. Moreover, while other Western models of social-democratic govern-ance in capitalist countries such as Sweden may have previously seemed appealing alternatives to their neighbors behind the Iron Curtain, now the only model for incorporation available – or so advised the American Shock Therapy experts – was that of radical pro-market neoliberalism.

In the years that have followed the market incorporation of the former Soviet Union, other crises – some unplanned and economically induced and some delib-erately planned and militarily introduced – have gone on providing opportunities for US-led pro-market reforms in other parts of the world. In 1997, for example, the Asian financial crises opened the door for US corporations to gain significant new footholds in Thailand, South Korea, and Indonesia at the same time as the credit problems facing these countries made it possible for American economic advisers to recommend more of the Chicago School teachings about the virtues of trade liberalization, financial deregulation, and privatization. In a different and strikingly militaristic way, the "shock and awe" approach to crisis creation presented by the Iraq war also allowed its neoconservative planners – including the defense-secretary and die-hard Milton Friedman fan Donald Rumsfeld – to try an especially extreme experiment in overnight neoliberalization. Thus it was that the first acts of Paul Bremer, the head of the American occupation govern-ment in Iraq, included implementing a flat tax, closing down most of the Iraqi governmental bureaucracy, removing food and fuel subsidies, and opening Iraq's market to foreign imports. However, what the Iraq war also made clear was that the US military as an instrument of coercive hegemony was also being radically remodeled along the lines of neoliberal hegemony. Privatization and outsourcing were common, with the war effort becoming dependent on diverse private mili-tary contractors. It was also a war managed at long distance using many of the tools developed for managing long-distance commodity chains, and a war mar-keted to an increasingly skeptical US public with all the branding, imagery, and 24/7 TV promotion one would normally associate with a coordinated corpo-rate PR blitz. And all this is to say nothing about how the $3 trillion bill for the hostilities was and continues to be paid, like much of the deregulated and over-mortgaged US economy itself, by borrowing and building up dollar debts for the future.[17]

As we conclude this section on the far-from-level features of American-led neoliberal hegemony, it is worth remembering that borrowing and credit-based development are not necessarily neoliberal. Traditional Keynesianism rested on the idea that government borrowing in a recession can fund new production and consumption, and thereby kick-start a depressed economy. That said, as we shall examine in the next sections, debt is now linked with distinctly post-Keynesian norms of neoliberal governance globally because of the way it makes countries and individuals subject to global market discipline. How much longer the US govern-ment itself can escape such discipline while it goes on borrowing to pay for its mili-tary by selling Treasury bonds to China, Japan, and Middle Eastern governments remains very much in doubt. It may not be much longer now before American leaders find themselves in a similar situation to the very same Asian countries they instructed on adopting pro-market reforms after the financial crisis of 1997. When this happens, the United States will also have to come to renegotiate its relationship with the same international financial institutions – the IMF and World Bank – that have historically helped it use such crises to implement Washington Consensus policy. These, of course, are the very institutions that American hegemony helped establish in the first place at Bretton Woods. In order to understand how their role developed subsequently, how they operate today, and how they might therefore deal with a defaulting US government, we now turn to examine the IMF and World Bank directly.

7.2   Inter-Governmental Institutions of Global Governance

In Chapter 5, we saw how the 1944 *United Nations Monetary and Financial Conference* at Bretton Woods laid the foundations for the global financial system and the dollar dominance that defined the decades that followed. We also considered the ways in which the specific concern of US leaders with preventing another Great Depression underpinned an emphasis on economic internationalism at the conference. What we did not look at so closely was how this emphasis on the part of President Roosevelt and the internationalist New Dealers at the US Treasury remained in tension at the time with the more conservative and nationalistic leanings of the US Congress. This tension crucially shaped the mandates of the World Bank and International Monetary Fund, and their subsequent development as two of the most important institutions – commonly referred to simply as "the Bank" and "the Fund" – of pro-market global governance. We start here by tracing how the initial shaping process led to the Bank and Fund becoming such important agencies of global market discipline, and we then proceed to examine how this disciplinary process has actually worked in practice. The ultimate lesson of examining the two international financial institutions (IFIs) in this way is that their power to govern globally derives from the way in which they mediate global financial ties. This is important to understand because, as we shall explore further in Section 7.3, other global market intermediaries – such as bond and risk ratings agencies – are also now increasingly capturing some of the global governance capacities once assigned to the Bank and the Fund. To begin with, though, we need to review: (1) how American influence was originally encoded in the governance structures of the two Bretton Woods IFIs; and (2) how that influence in turn led the Bank and Fund to become the two most important inter-governmental agencies involved in enforcing Washington Consensus norms of "good governance" – that is, neoliberal governance – on the rest of the world.

Finally, before proceeding it should be noted that the focus here on the two big IFIs means that this section does not address other less influential institutions of global governance in any depth. These other intergovernmental organizations

(IGOs) – for example, the United Nations (UN) and its agencies such as the Food and Agriculture Organization (FAO) and the World Health Organization (WHO) – still remain significant centers for debate, data-gathering, and policy coordination. They also can influence deep shifts in government too, especially when they work in tandem with the IFIs to encourage or enforce pro-market governance such as the privatization of public services, export-oriented agriculture, and the protection of pharmaceutical patents. However, with the exception of the UN Security Council (which remains dominated by its permanent members – the United States, United Kingdom, France, China, and Russia) the internal governance mechanisms of most UN agencies and associated IGOs allow for much more democratic deliberation. This means that while they might sometimes take up neoliberal initiatives in common with the World Bank and IMF, they also generally allow the "good" of good governance to be more actively contested. In Chapter 9 on Heath and in Chapter 10 on Responses, we return to consider such moments of contestation. Here, by contrast, we focus instead on the two institutions that have defined good governance in terms of neoliberal norms most persistently and powerfully. To understand how they have done so, we now need to consider how the Fund and the Bank were originally set up both to articulate and to administrate global market forces.

7.2.1   The IMF, World Bank, and the Institutionalization of American Interest

At Bretton Woods, the chief US conference negotiator, Harry Dexter White, imagined the Fund and the Bank as agencies of New Deal type Keynesian market management at a supranational level. Similarly, Keynes himself led the British delegation to the conference with a vision of setting up a global clearing union in which no currency was special and all transfers were automatic. But set against both these visions, the concerns of a domestically minded and budget-conscious US Congress created a rather more precarious foundational footing for the international institution-building undertaken at the conference. White himself was well aware that the new institutions had to be as international as possible in order to have any chance of success in creating consensus and a lasting post-war peace. But while he therefore saw the need to fashion international agreement at the conference, the American negotiator could not go along with the supranational power-sharing and administrative automaticity imagined by Keynes. He knew that a skeptical US Congress was asking questions about both the costs and the threats to US economic dominance. Robert Taft had argued thus on the US Senate floor that providing funds to the Bank and the Fund would be tantamount to "pouring money down a rat hole."[18] In consequence, both IFIs were designed in such a way that they maximized US influence while minimizing the US budgetary burden. The Bank and the Fund were not therefore set up as international aid organizations, as is often thought. Instead, from the start, they were tied – bonded, in fact, is a better verb – to the world of private finance and Wall Street bond markets.

For the Bank, the bonding meant turning directly to the markets for funds. As John McCloy, the second Bank president, put it in 1947: "The Bank is, I believe, a rather unique institution in that although it is an intergovernmental organization, it relies primarily on the private investment community and not upon its member governments for the major part of its loanable resources."[19] For the Fund, which depended instead on the member country reserves it held, private banking nevertheless provided the model for its lending: the country reserves being more like shareholder equity than an aid budget. Thus, while both IFIs are now seen by client countries as the last places to go when all other banks have shut their doors, and while the IFIs see themselves in this light as "global lenders of last resort," they still impose on their borrowers the same sorts of conditions normally attached by American investment banks and other private lenders to market-issued loans. IFI internationalism, then, is at root the internationalism of banking, not an internationalism of aid; it is an internationalism of Wall Street institutions and financialized governance, not an internationalism of international deliberation and democratic governance.

To be sure, both IFIs had the word "International" in their titles at the start: the formal name for the Bank at Bretton Woods being the *International Bank of Reconstruction and Development* (IBRD). More profoundly, this titular tilt towards internationalism reflected the fact that both IFIs were also designed with clear international mandates: the Fund to deal with short-term balance of payments and currency crises; the Bank to address the longer-range challenges of development. While their initial focus was on rebuilding the war-ravaged economies of Western Europe and not on the development of the "developing world" or Global South as we understand it today, American negotiators wanted the IFIs to address more global development initiatives in the end, and White announced that the Bank "must not be a rich man's club."[20] Yet, the international aims acknowledged, the underlying interest of the United States remained on building a post-war global governance system centered on and supportive of American hegemony. The choice of Washington DC as the location for the headquarters of both the Fund and Bank symbolized this hegemony, and it was not surprising therefore that when Keynes heard about the locational choice, he complained that: "[the Americans] plainly intend to force their own conceptions through regardless of the rest of us. The result is that the institutions look like becoming American concerns, run by gigantic American staffs, with the rest of us very much on the side-lines."[21]

Keynes's complaints were no doubt inspired in part by resentment about Britain's own imperial decline. At any rate, the concerns with staffing and office location have, over time, come to look like pomp and circumstance when compared to the ongoing US influence on the actual governance of the two IFIs. Thanks to the weighted quota and subscription systems set up at Bretton Woods, America secured effective vetoes and dominant voting power in both the Bank and the Fund going forward.[22] While conference delegates were told that their country quotas and votes were based on a scientific formula, and while the weightings mainly just meant that member countries were allocated votes in proportion to their economic size and significance within the global economy, the US Treasury official charged with

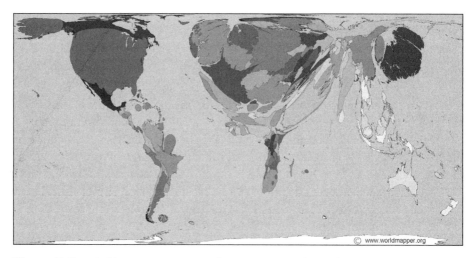

Figure 7.2 Worldmapper cartogram showing country share of votes at the IMF in 2006. *Source:* http://www.worldmapper.org/display.php?selected=365. © Copyright SASI Group (University of Sheffield) and Mark Newman (University of Michigan) (CC BY-NC-ND 3.0).

defining the quotas for the Fund, later revealed that the weighting strongly favored American alliances, being driven by war-time geopolitics as much as economics. And this US influence through the weighted voting structure of the IMF continues to this day, notwithstanding increasing complaints from China and other US creditors that they should now have more votes (Figure 7.2).

American influence at the Bank also took the form of a disproportionate voting share: the original US "subscription" constituting about a third of 10-plus-billion-dollar capitalization of the institution during its first 10 years. This, combined with the need to raise the other 85% of the Bank's loanable funds on Wall Street, entailed in turn the wholesale dollarization of Bank lending, further buttressing the dollar hegemony established by the Fund and the dollar–gold peg. Thus, in contrast to the UN's constitutional order of "one country, one vote" (formalized a year after Bretton Woods in 1945 in San Francisco), the internal governance structure of the Bretton Woods institutions was instead effectively "one dollar, one vote."

Also, in contrast to the UN, the Bank designated English as its official language, and later in the early 1960s when the UN attempted to set up a more internationalized development bank – the Special United Nations Fund for Economic Development (SUNFED) – the American interest again became explicit in the establishment of the Bank's International Development Association (IDA) arm. This is an important chapter in Bank history to know about because it also reveals much about how dependency on private funding led the Bank to enforce Wall Street lending standards and goals. Prior to the 1960s, US leadership at the Bank had focused on making sure its bonds (bonds sold on Wall Street to raise money for its loans) achieved **AAA** ratings from the private investment community. It therefore avoided making so-called "soft" loans for health, education, and housing, and instead depicted desirable "Development" purely in terms of "hard" profit-making projects: dams, roads, railways, and other infrastructure projects that promised relatively quick economic returns. But when newly decolonized developing countries in the Global South sought to set up SUNFED as an alternative that would fund longer-term social development needs, American leaders argued it was time to establish a new arm of the Bank – the IDA – that could "assist" and "guide" new development initiatives in the former colonies of the West. In short, when control from DC was threatened, the Bank was adapted in order to preserve US governmental influence – even at the cost of introducing development ideals and investment strategies that did not appeal so much to Wall Street.

American influence in both the Bank and the Fund has continued ever since. This is hardly surprising given the considerable returns – both economic and geopolitical – that the United States has enjoyed on its highly leveraged investments. Always keen to allay congressional concerns that these investments are wasteful, IFI leaders have often been quite candid on the US benefits outweighing the costs. Back in 1947, for example, when the United States was still the world's greatest exporter of manufactured commodities, the director of the Bank's loan department explained explicitly that its dollar-denominated loans were in America's best interest. A borrowing country, he highlighted, "is given the immediate means of buying turbines or agricultural machinery or electrical equipment or some other goods and services which the United States is able to produce." Another Bank official subsequently said that: "Most of our money doesn't go to the South, it goes straight from Washington to Pennsylvania, where they manufacture turbines, or Frankfurt, where they produce dredging equipment." And by the 1990s, one study of the Bank's lending indicated that that the US influence had returned more than just dollar-denominated interest payments: the cumulative $1.94 billion of US funds invested in the IBRD generating more than 10 times its value in profits for US business.[23] More recently still, ongoing research into IMF lending in the new millennium also reveals an ongoing return on American investment in the Fund – in the shape of benefits for US commercial banks and in securing ongoing geopolitical allegiances, too.[24]

In order to hold on to its advantages, the United States has also held on to its weighted voting and veto powers over the internal decision-making of the Bank and the Fund. Minor modifications have been made to the "one dollar one vote" system over time, and as the BRIC countries – that is, Brazil, Russia, India, and China – have started to become bigger components of the global economy, their leaders have made increasing calls for a bigger say in the running of the IFIs. But despite this, and despite the fact that both the Bank and Fund have now developed new sources of loans that further diminish the importance of US funding, the basic allocation of votes based on the weighted quotas and subscriptions established at Bretton Woods remains largely unchanged.[25] Of course, given their international mandates, both IFIs are at pains to explain on their websites that they are globally representative and not US-owned and operated agencies. However, if you continue to explore both websites further, you soon begin to see the ways in which a dominant US influence endures. For the Fund, the distribution of the quotas and the proportional voting power for each member country are listed in an online chart that in 2009 showed the United States controlling 16.77% of the vote, far higher than any other country and significantly more than the 4.6% controlled by all the countries of sub-Saharan Africa put together.[26] Likewise, in the IDA arm of the Bank the United States controls 12.06% of the vote, and within the IBRD arm of the Bank (the arm that deals with "middle income and more creditworthy poor countries"), the United States still has 16.36% of the vote, while all 47 countries of Africa control just 6%.[27] These weighted voting formulae are now being questioned more intensely than ever before, especially in global governance gatherings such as the G20 meetings where American influence is diluted. But despite the misrepresentation concerns being raised by rising economic powers, progress towards a new allocation of IFI votes reflecting America's increasing indebtedness seems set to be very slow indeed. Thus, although there was much talk in 2010 of the Bank raising $86 billion in new capital to expand the IBRD votes of emerging economy countries – the largest expansion of new money and votes in 20 years – this only meant that the rich countries were giving up 3.1% of their voting shares.

The larger point here is that the American influence at Bretton Woods was effectively institutionalized in the internal workings of both the Bank and the Fund all the while the two IFIs retained an inter-governmental architecture with an enough organizational internationalism to build long-term global buy-in. Defenders of this compromise suggest it was the best outcome possible given opposition to deeper and more democratic internationalism from the US Congress. They also argue that US support for the IFIs has helped over time stave off multiple financial crises. Critics, by contrast, argue that this very same crisis-management by the Bank and Fund has merely served to expand the American model of market capitalism globally, allowing the United States to secure extraordinary political bang for its buck while institutionalizing the significance of that same buck – the dollar – as the international reserve currency. Whether you agree with the critics or the defenders, it remains vital to understand the economic ties through which the Fund and Bank have come to be such important agencies of global governance. It is to these ties that we now turn.

7.2.2   Structural adjustment and the global entrenchment of "good governance"

The history of Bretton Woods is just as important for understanding the global market-based governance exercised by the Fund and the Bank as it is in explaining US influence in their internal governance. It is worth comparing the IFIs in this respect with the third institution to emerge out of Bretton Woods – the WTO – which also derives its governance capacity from global market forces. As we saw in Chapter 6, the WTO operates as an agency of global governance because of how it turns the trade dependency of member countries into the legal enforceability of its trade rules. Noting this here helps introduce in turn how the global governance capabilities of the IMF and World Bank also emerge out of economic intermediation.

In short, their power derives from their institutional capacity to turn the credit dependency of applicant countries into the conditionality of stabilization plans, Structural Adjustment Programs (**SAPs**) and other "conditionalized" poverty management schemes.

At Bretton Woods, the Fund was seen as the more important institution, and subsequently it has always remained the senior partner in its relations with the Bank, its supervisory and surveillance capacities setting the standard for their combined management of client countries. The IMF's two main purposes as originally designed were: (1) to regulate the rates at which currencies were exchanged among member countries; and (2) to ensure international monetary stability by making short-term loans to countries suffering balance of payments crises (i.e. not taking in enough money from exports and foreign investments to pay for imports and debt payments). Referred to initially as the International Stabilization Fund, it was designed to have supervisory and surveillance capabilities in order to defend the post-war international financial regime from non-conformist national actions (such as the deliberate currency depreciations that had led into World War II). As well as addressing these sorts beggar-thy-neighbor problems, Roosevelt's team at Bretton Woods saw the Fund's stabilization mission in directly geopolitical terms, too: the key goal being to stabilize Britain in particular in the post-war years. "The real nub of the situation," explained the president, "is to keep Britain from going into complete bankruptcy at the end of the war."[28] But as the post-war peace persisted, and the stabilization mission turned to other countries, the principles and priorities of economic stability took over from wartime worries about geopolitical instability. As a result, the supervisory role of the Fund also came to be increasingly about enforcing pro-market policies. In expanding and entrenching this system of neoliberal governance, these surveillance capacities were also effectively augmented by the Bank's developmentalist interventions. They operated as a one–two neoliberal development tag team: the Bank offering all sorts of advice and loans to promote market-led development, and the Fund serving to monitor compliance with the loan **conditionalities**. Initially, in the 1940s and 1950s, these conditions had simply consisted of requests for "an effective program for establishing or keeping the stability of the currency of the member country at a realistic exchange rate."[29] However, since the 1970s, the conditions have grown to become the familiar regime of pro-market "conditionality" that has made the IFIs such powerful enforcers of neoliberalism.

The enforcement power of the Bank and the Fund, it needs re-emphasizing, lies in being market-sensitive mediators of market discipline. It is not as if they can threaten non-compliant nation-states with military violence. Nor were they "given" the power of global governance in some sort of ceremonial handover of governmental authority. Instead, the way in which they have developed the capacity to discipline through debt has emerged historically amidst the convolutions of decolonization, development, and increasingly denationalized financial flows. As the movie *Life and Debt* shows in all its geographical complexity and human tragedy, typical applicants to the Fund in the 1980s and 1990s were decolonized countries such as Jamaica: countries that, having won independence and sovereignty only after much twentieth-century struggle, experienced IFI conditionality at the end of the century as a sort of recolonizing return to foreign control. Ironically, though, given this neocolonial aspect of IMF-enforced neoliberalism, the original targets for Fund stabilization efforts in the immediate post-war years were countries such as Britain: the former colonial powers whose own economic collapse and subjection to IMF surveillance were closely linked to the end of empire. Like all member countries – with the exception of the United States – they had to surrender considerable economic sovereignty in joining the Fund, agreeing to fix and maintain their currency exchange rates on the basis of a set of "par values" anchored on the dollar–gold rate of $35 per ounce (and this also entailed an ongoing commitment to intervene in currency markets to restore the par value of their currencies if they went up or down or to work with the Fund to re-set the original par value). Also, former colonizers just like former colonies had to reserve their quota of reserves at the Fund. In return, they received the assurance of being able to borrow back the same reserves, including the ability to draw immediately on the first 25% of the quota known as the "low tranche," which was originally deposited with the Fund in the form of hard currency or gold. Such borrowing came with low conditionality, and it was largely on this basis that Britain became the Fund's biggest borrower in its first 25 years of operation – just as Roosevelt had envisioned. However, events in the late 1960s and early 1970s were to change all this, leading to an extremely high conditionality loan to the UK Labor government in 1976, and ushering in the new era of IMF neoliberal enforcement that was to sweep over countries such as Jamaica later in the 1980s.

After the debacle for Labour in Britain (which ended up bringing Thatcher to power), other wealthier nation-states generally tried to avoid the IFIs (oftentimes appeasing investors and markets by capitulating pre-emptively to neoliberal norms). Instead, because of ongoing debt crises through the 1980s and 1990s, it was the formerly colonized countries of the Global South who found themselves turning to the Fund and Bank for loans and loan rescheduling because of their debt crises. The basic economic history of these debt crises was reviewed in Chapter 5, where it was also noted that many of the interventions of the Fund and Bank were driven more by the short-term financial needs of private banks (whose profitability was jeopardized by outstanding and unpaid loans to developing countries). Here, the key point that needs noting is that the conditionalities delivered in the form of the Fund's stabilization programs and the Bank's structural adjustment plans effectively turned the financial pressures into governmental pressures. In short, they transformed the economic force of debt into the political enforcement of neoliberal governance, and the result has been a remarkably consistent top-down global application of one-size-fits-all pro-market policy reforms.

The countries that have turned to the Bank and Fund for loans may have been plunged into financial crisis for very different reasons – a run on the currency by foreign speculators, a sudden spike in the costs of debt servicing, a natural disaster, a war, a borrowing binge by a corrupt dictator buying weapons to terrorize his own people – but whatever the reasons, the stabilization and structural adjustment policies are generally the same and always involve the same sorts of conditions: cut government spending, cut subsidies on food, cut tariffs on imports, cut regulations on foreign investments and business, and meanwhile impose higher interest rates to control inflation and adopt pro-growth over pro-welfare economic policies. These then are the typical conditionalities that countries are obliged to abide by in order to receive loans and loan rescheduling. For economists in DC, the rationale for these policies is mainly economic. It is about restoring a country's short-term ability to pay its external creditors and balance its books. But for national governments, by contrast, it represents the complete loss of policy-making autonomy. Disciplined by conditionalities, they have to submit to surveillance and control by international agencies that set neoliberal policies as national policies while undoing and undermining all governmental alternatives. Despite the destruction of government services, austerity is enforced. Despite starvation and food riots, subsidies for food are eliminated. Despite the loss of local jobs, trade is liberalized. And despite increasing inequalities and instability, Gross Domestic Product (GDP) and price stability become the only economic metrics of importance. Citizens in these countries who lose their livelihoods, or their access to public hospitals and schools, or their ability to feed themselves, can and do contest the rights of an unelected group of DC-based banking bureaucrats to override the policies of their national governments. And allies in the global justice movement make ongoing arguments about SAPs sapping the long-term capacity of national governments to provide healthy, fair, and sustainable development for their people. But after the worker strikes, student sit-ins, street protests, and parliamentary polemics are over, Fund and Bank managers know the indebted governments will usually come back to DC seeking support and promising obedience. Such is the disciplinary power of debt.

No word better summarizes the disciplinary powers of the Fund and Bank than "conditionality." It is obviously on the one hand a banking term, and yet it also aptly describes a market-conditioned regime of governance on the other. The IFIs themselves tend to describe obedience with this regime as "good governance," associating it also with governmental norms of transparency and accountability that make their work of financial surveillance and international accounting more straightforward. But conditionality is simultaneously understood by its critics as disempowering. Far from promoting accountable and inclusive democratic decision-making in client countries, conditionalities are seen instead as externally imposed neocolonial control and thus, for many in the Global South, as bad governance. Yet, whether one sees conditionality thus as bad governance or as good governance, there can be no doubting the fact that in practice it means market-conditioned neoliberalization. It means being obliged under the discipline of debt, under the surveillance of the IMF and under the expert supervision of the Bank to implement Washington Consensus policies of privatization, trade liberalization, financial deregulation, fiscal austerity, and export-led development.

The key point to underline again here is that the Fund and Bank gain their power to govern by serving as global financial intermediaries that articulate and administrate market forces. They do not have global governance powers because of some sort of one-world-government agreement or constitutional arrangement.

Moreover, the power of conditionality has itself depended on the intersection of two sets of conditions that are far from constitutionally stable and fixed. These are, on the one side, the existence of a policy-making consensus in DC and, on the other side, the global economic context. These conditions for conditionality are worth considering in more detail now because in recent years, both have begun to break down. Today, therefore, there is talk of *dissensus* in DC over the practices of market discipline. And meanwhile, global economic developments – including most importantly the phenomenal rise of Asian capitalism and the resulting availability of new non-Western lending – have undermined the US-centric system of debt-based discipline managed by the Bank and Fund. We will conclude this section of the chapter by reviewing both of these developments in turn.

The apparent breakdown of the Washington Consensus occurred most obviously after the Asian financial crisis of 1997. World Bank economist Joseph Stiglitz, along with some other influential development economists such as Jeffrey Sachs, attacked the IMF for continuing to emphasize neoliberal conditionalities such as removing capital controls even as it became clear that financial deregulation had caused many of the economic problems at the heart of the crisis.[30] Meanwhile, from the 1999 Seattle protests onwards, both the Bank and the Fund experienced increasingly vociferous criticisms from the global justice movement, including the large "Spank the Bank" protests that took place in DC in April 2000. As a result of all these diverse criticisms coming from both inside and outside of the IFIs, talk of a Washington Consensus was increasingly replaced by talk of dissensus. Yet, despite what you might think after reading this, the relations between the Bank and the Fund have not radically broken down in the subsequent years. There is still an underground tunnel linking their respective buildings beneath 19th Street in DC and it might well be interpreted as a physical sign of their ongoing cooperation on enforcing neoliberal governance, too. Where they have parted ways is instead in tone, emphasis, and methods. Thus, while the IMF has tended to stick with its traditional surveillance and policy-making enforcement at the macro-scale of countries and the global economy, and while it also retains its crisis-management focus on the short-term gyrations of financial markets, the World Bank has increasingly embraced more micro projects of poverty management such as microfinance, combining them with initiatives aimed at addressing global health and global climate change over a longer-term time horizon than traditional IMF actions.

The reason why we hear of dissensus despite the ongoing cooperation of the IFIs has mainly to do with public statements by World Bank leaders themselves. Whether it has been in attempts to change the conversation within the Bank or to respond to external critics, they have tended to exaggerate the story of institutional change. In 2000, for example, as the "Spank the Bank" critics descended on DC, World Bank president James Wolfensohn declared that: "We are way ahead of the protestors." What he meant, it seems, was that by launching new micro projects and health initiatives, the Bank was already addressing the problems of one-size-fits-all structural adjustment planning. No longer an old-fashioned top-down "Development Bank," the World Bank in this new millennium view was born again as a "Knowledge Bank," a center for expertise aimed at ending poverty. Supporting their story of transformation, Wolfensohn and his staff could (with the help of a public-relations machine led by a former writer from *The Economist*) further point to stylistic contrasts with previous leadership at the Bank, including most notably the contrast with Robert McNamara, the legendary Bank president of the 1970s who had previously worked as US Secretary of Defense as the principal planner of the Vietnam war. Many commentators interpreted McNamara's leadership of the Bank as serving as some sort of extended expiation for Vietnam, and thus also as an effort to restore faith in American global leadership with big commitments to large-scale development projects. The contrast with new millennium micro initiatives seems clear in this regard, but it is misleading if it is interpreted as a symbol of radical change and a turn away from neoliberal norms. Such accounts of change downplay the degree to which significant continuities connect the McNamara years (1968–1981) with the Wolfensohn years (1995–2005), including, not least of all, ongoing dependence on Wall Street's support for World Bank bond issuance. Moreover, many of the new Knowledge Bank initiatives actually had their start in the Development Bank of the 1970s: Wolfensohn's interest in global health challenges such as AIDS, for instance, clearly having had a precedent in McNamara's pioneering concern with river blindness. Even the attempt to present the Bank as a poverty-fighting Knowledge Bank can itself be traced back to McNamara's calls for the Bank to reduce poverty by remaking itself as a development agency. For these reasons, critics argue that the new language of "poverty reduction" and "good governance" associated with the so-called Wolfensohn reforms came with plans that simply continued with structural adjustment and the other "discredited" neoliberal policies of earlier periods.[31]

A more nuanced account of recent changes must instead address two more minor but novel innovations in the Bank's approach to global governance in the new millennium. First, there is the turn to micro initiatives, including most notably the support for microfinance led by the Consultative Group to Assist the Poor (CGAP) that is housed at the Bank.[32] Second, there is the parallel emphasis on having client countries themselves write the conditionalities for their loans: namely, Poverty Reduction Strategy Papers (PRSPs). Both developments can be seen as responses to the accusations of top-down SAPs, and both thereby stress bottom-up inclusion and accountability. CGAP coordinates the largest pool of money allocated for microfinance in the world, and, while using this leverage to push for a market-responsive approach to the sector that accommodates large financial firms, it still emphasizes the need to advance financial access for the poor. In doing so, as was noted in Chapter 5, microfinance simultaneously extends the discipline of debt to individual borrowers, enlisting them in all sorts of microenterprise projects that are managed through the relations of personalized responsibility set up between individual borrowers and the microfinance institutions (MFIs) that make the microloans. It is this same pattern of market-responsive "responsibilization" that has also come to define PRSPs, too. Under these, individual countries are enlisted into drafting their own conditionalities for new loans and debt relief. Even this practice has a precedent in previous protocols requiring client countries to submit their own "statements of intent" about structural adjustment. However, with PRSPs the emphasis on countries taking responsibility for restructuring themselves is definitely heightened. And just as with microfinance, the associated policy language is all about reducing poverty by reaching out more effectively to the poor, thereby expanding inclusivity and accountability at the same time.

While the bottom-up approach to crafting PRSPs reflects some of the same sort of responsibilization found in microfinance, the way in which the resulting strategies end up reproducing a very normative and disciplinary neoliberalism is not always paralleled by the more eclectic innovation of microfinance itself. Recent work on the innovations in microfinance pursued by the Grameen Bank and BRAC in Bangladesh, for example, indicates that they sometimes run afoul of World Bank neoliberal norms as articulated by CGAP, particularly the goal of making microfinance profitable for the financial industry.[33] Indeed, Ananya Roy's research of what she calls the Bangladesh Consensus shows thus that the Bank has increasingly been involved in trying to discipline the very institutions – Grameen in particular – World Bank leaders once upheld as models for its wider new millennium turn towards micro-managing poverty. The problems have occurred, it seems, when the founders of microcredit have focused more on the access of the poor to credit rather than on the access of financial firms to the "bankable poor." By helping impoverished families simply survive through times of extreme hardship, or stressing women's empowerment over and above the market imperative to make bigger profits, the Bangladesh Consensus organizations therefore sometimes depart from both Washington Consensus and post-Washington Consensus norms alike.

The lesson of recent research on microfinance is that while the micro approach provided a model for the World Bank in its new millennium moves towards expanding neoliberalism from below, the actual methods of expanding credit through micro loans may sometimes not sit so well with what remains a DC-based IFI: an institution, after all, that remains answerable to the same influences – the US Treasury and Wall Street – that structured it in the first place. This brings us back to the fact of the ongoing partnership between the Bank and IMF, a partnership which itself endures in part because of the way both institutions serve to relay and reflect the interests of investment banks and bond holders. To the extent that Bank leaders depart from articulating policies in line with these Wall Street interests – the previously noted criticisms of Stiglitz, for example – they themselves start to become criticized and taken less seriously. This is why the notion of a Washington Dissensus became a focus of concern in the first place. The criticisms were in effect destabilizing one of the main conditions for market fundamentalist conditionalities. However, if we turn now to address some of the recent developments at the IMF – the very institution that Stiglitz was criticizing – they bring in to focus how the second main condition determining neoliberal conditionality – the global economy – is itself beginning to shake the foundations of IFI global governance still more.

The IMF today continues its original work of global and national economic surveillance with which it was charged at Bretton Woods. In doing so, it also partners with the Bank in monitoring country compliance with PRSPs and all the related conditionalities. At the same time, however, the Fund is now having to respond to the aftershocks of what was widely seen as the worst global financial crisis since 1929. In this new context, the Fund continues to function as an authoritative voice on and of global financial markets. But in so far as these same markets have been blamed for the economic damage inflicted in 2008 and 2009, and in so far as it has been the "markets-know-best" ideas routinely repeated by the Fund that have been singled out for criticism, it has also had to deal with accusations that it is part of the problem. Moreover, given that it is simultaneously having to respond to the concerns of emerging economies such as China, and given that these concerns are deeply troubling to a debt-ridden United States, the IMF with its French managing director has found itself buffeted on all sides.

Two challenges in 2010 usefully illustrated the changing global conditions shaping the world's ultimate arbiter of conditionality. On the one side, the IMF was brought in by EU leaders to deal with the likelihood of Greece defaulting on its sovereign debt. German and French leaders were particularly worried about such a default: both because much of the debt was owed to German and French banks, and because a Greek default would radically undermine the Euro as a stable store of value and create contagion effects in the EU's other vulnerable economies (disparagingly referred to along with Greece as the PIGS – Portugal, Italy, Greece, and Spain – an acronym which in a further sign of contagion concerns among financial commentators grew to include Ireland and Great Britain, too, with PIIGGS, and further still to register the debt-binging United States itself in PIG IS US). In relation to Greece, Germany and France did not want to further destabilize the Euro and the overall EU project of shared governance by issuing their own edicts about the vital necessity of Greek austerity measures. And so, like a *deus ex machina* in an ancient Greek tragedy, the IMF was invited in as the stern disciplinarian ready to dispense the usual market adjustment medicine of shock neoliberalization. This was all IMF business as usual, and, also as usual, it prompted all sorts of anti-austerity anti-IMF street protests in Athens, too. However, this was not the only direction from which IMF authority was challenged.

On the other side of the Atlantic in the United States, the ability of the IMF to present itself as the rational and god-like voice of financial markets was also being questioned. And it was being questioned precisely because the rationality of those same markets was itself in question after the sub-prime debacle of 2008–2009. To the degree that the IMF had previously aligned itself with market sentiment about there not being any credit bubble, it too was coming in for criticism. It had said, for example, that the Irish economy had strong fundamentals in 2007, only to realize in 2009 that this same Irish economy had been completely overleveraged and imperiled because of credit bubbles in both its own housing market and the market that Irish banks had invested in of US mortgage-backed securities. Moreover, in the aftermath of the US subprime crisis, the IMF could no longer argue – as it had done in the Asian crisis in 1997 – that national controls on capital movements were bad policy or that some sort of "Tobin tax" on global financial movements was bad economics. Instead, it began to make moves towards recommending both capital controls and a financial activities tax as good global governance, and it even floated the additional idea – an especially unusual one in terms of neoliberal monetarist orthodoxy – of possibly revising its recommended inflation targets upwards. These IMF policy innovations came hesitantly alongside equally inconsistent notes of concern about America's own financial institutions and increasing indebtedness. Yet it was in these very vacillations and hesitations that it was possible to start to see the break-up of the Bretton Woods US-centric system. As a telling result, the IMF no longer looked likely to enjoy unwavering Wall Street support: its new ideas about regulating and taxing finance making it increasingly unpopular with its traditional backers in investment banking.[34]

Meanwhile, on the other side of the Pacific and Caribbean, the break-up of Bretton Woods legacies was also influenced by the growing economic clout of countries that were not on the guest list for the New Hampshire meeting back in 1944. With their new-found wealth, India, Brazil, and especially China were effectively crashing the party, demanding respect for their own interests at the IMF and, in China's case, also becoming a significant source of non-IMF-controlled lending in other parts of the developing world. Even if they still had fewer IMF voting shares than Luxembourg, the Netherlands, and Belgium in 2010, these emerging economies were using their influence to raise concerns about the long-term credit worthiness of the United States, and demanding national rights to regulate capital flows. With China also eyeing the advantages of the IMF's accounting unit – the SDR – as a currency in which to put savings and thereby hedge against future dollar depreciations, these emerging economy interests were increasingly influencing IMF policy statements, too, even if the effort to acquire IMF executive voting quotas continued to meet resistance from the European countries that would lose them.[35] The Fund had never so clearly voiced concern in the past about the dangers of US debt issuance or deregulated capital markets. But struggling to regain its own credibility, and thereby morphing into an institution increasingly answerable to emerging economies, the IMF in 2010 was beginning to articulate a more internationally inclusive account of financial risk. Entering into this new IMF accounting as a particularly large aggregator of risk and debt, the United States was also no longer the unquestioned global economic leader and lender that had first established the Fund as a tool of global risk management at Bretton Woods. Thus, to come back to where we first began our analysis of the IFIs, global governance by institutions set up to be super-sensitive to market forces is changing because of disruptions to the global ordering of the very same markets they were originally designed to manage.

7.3   Non-Governmental Organizations of Global Governance

One of the net results of the government cutbacks, privatization, and market-led development plans enforced around the world by the IMF and World Bank over the last three decades has been the rising importance of Non-Governmental

Organizations or NGOs. Their collective name and acronym reflect the traditional separation of these civil society organizations from formal governments. However, the emergence of NGOs and their phenomenal growth in number and variety are also fundamentally tied to the perceived need for government-like intervention on issues that neoliberal governments tend to retreat from, privatize, deregulate, or ignore. This does not mean that all NGOs are anti-neoliberal organizations. Far from it, as we shall see in what follows, NGOs can still be organized in profoundly pro-market ways and can pursue all sorts of pro-market policy goals, even if they count as "non-profits" under national tax codes. Indeed, two acronyms commonly used to designate particular kinds of corporate-sponsored NGO make this especially clear: thus BINGO is short for Business-friendly International NGOs, and MANGO is short for market advocacy NGOs. Beyond these more obviously market-oriented sub-categories, even NGOs that are famous for directly challenging corporate power – Greenpeace, Oxfam, and Médecins Sans Frontières, for example – still have to work in contexts and in ways that remain deeply shaped by market forces. For the same reason, as they go about managing their projects, their budgets, their staff, and their public relations, many NGOs reproduce some of the same market-expanding and government-contracting practices that created the need for their involvement in the first place. Indeed, "government-contracting" has a double-meaning as a result – with governments increasingly contracting out work to NGOs at the same time as they have rolled back and contracted the scale and scope of their own operations. To understand these tendencies, we have to look in turn at the ways in which civil society more generally – the whole world of social and political life outside of governments and businesses – has itself become increasingly governed through competitive market forces, including diverse forms of marketing, ranking, risk-rating, and individualized risk-management. Even historic forms of non-governmental organization that you would not normally think of as NGOs – religious organizations and universities, for example – can be seen thus as caught up in some of the same sorts of market-mediated regulatory practices. To begin with, though, let us look more closely at how the governance roles of formal NGOs have developed over time, before turning to exam such market-mediated non-governmental governmentality more generally.

The historical emergence of NGOs was itself tied to prior rounds of globalization. Improvements in communications technologies from the mid 1800s onwards – including the telegraph and print media that developed with imperialism – enabled transnational civil society organizations such as anti-slavery groups, labor groups, women's suffrage groups, and peace groups to work long distance as well as to articulate international consciousness about shared problems. Later on, the legalistic designation of "Non-Governmental" for such organizations itself emerged thanks to the 1945 United Nations Charter, a charter in which Article 71 of Chapter 10 permitted a consultative role for organizations that were designated neither governments nor member states. Subsequently, decolonization in the Global South, followed by the Cold War, followed by the debt and structural adjustment crises of the 1980s and 1990s, created numerous new development and humanitarian challenges

264   *Governance*

to which more and more NGOs sought to respond. The collapse of the geopolitical divisions of the Cold War (marked by the collapse of the Berlin Wall in 1989), further opened up the possibility of expanding NGO work internationally in areas that had previously been shaped more by the state-sponsored machinations of militaries and government-controlled aid organizations. And, as the twentieth century came to an end, increasing economic instability, increasing emphasis by the World Bank and UN on civil society participation, and increasing demands for democratization led to a global "NGO revolution."[36]

By the new millennium, there were over 40 000 International NGOs (INGOs). And within nation-states, NGO numbers have multiplied still more, creating what are sometimes called "shadow-states" within states as more and more organizations seek to provide services and policy advocacy in issue areas ranging from the environment, health, and emergency relief to transportation, housing, education, women's rights, minority rights, and children's rights as well as human rights and social justice more generally. In India alone, for example, there are estimated to be over 1 million NGOs.[37] Meanwhile, still poorer countries such as Haiti have effectively become NGO republics. Even before the terrible earthquake of 2010, over 80% of "public services" in Haiti were being provided privately by non-public NGOs, giving the country the highest NGO per capita ratio in the world.[38] While many commentators reported that the earthquake had effectively "decapitated" the Haitian government by killing numerous politicians and officials, looked at as an NGO republic Haiti had already lost its sovereign government long before.

Not surprisingly, the loss of governmental authority seen in countries such as Haiti often stirs criticism of NGOs. Unelected and under suspicion for making money out of other people's misery, they are sometimes condemned as offering professionalized profiteering opportunities for their project managers along with "indulgences" (i.e. ethics for purchase) for their donors. For example, in 2004 when the BBC ran a live debate on NGOs in Africa, a critical respondent from Ghana expressed the common concern with NGO profiteering as follows:

> the majority of them are in it to make money. There are instances where some will just go to the villages, take photographs, and present them to the donors, pretending they are going to put proper structures for developments in the villages. It's a pity that the people who claim they are helping the deprived are fattening themselves and their families whilst the helpless are suffering.[39]

Another similar critique of NGOs is that their workers' privileged lifestyles reveal elitist attitudes and an underlying business-class affiliation even when they are really trying to help. Beyond the obvious economic inequalities, the differences in mobility in and across space, and the ties between NGOs, neoliberalization, and disaster profiteering are all often involved, too. Before turning to these concerns, however, it is important first to note that criticisms of NGO privilege are strikingly different to the images of NGO work we normally see. The normal picture, by contrast, is of NGOs making heroic efforts without personal profit or gain, and NGOs remain remarkably popular in public opinion polling around the world. In 2006, when the BBC commissioned a global opinion survey, it found that 60% of respondents thought that NGOs had a mainly positive influence, winning far more acclaim in this respect than the IMF, World Bank, global companies, or the news media.[40] The support was stronger in richer countries – 80% in France, 70% in the United Kingdom, and 64% in the United States – but even in poorer Mexico where there was a 23% negative, still 39% of the population held a positive perspective on NGOs. Given the wide discrepancies between these positive perspectives and the criticisms of NGO privilege, it is key to avoid simple generalizations about "all" NGOs. The aim here is to provide a more analytical and less judgmental approach guided by two questions that are specifically about NGOs and governance. Following the way in which we examined IFI governance both internally and externally, these questions can be posed as: (1) How are NGOs and their practices governed? (2) How does NGO governance relate to global governance?

7.3.1   How are NGOs and their practices governed?

As the Ghanaian commentator suggested, NGOs vary a great deal in the way they are run on the ground. The diversity of NGO organizational structures and purposes shows up in turn in the alphabet soup of acronyms used to distinguish different types of NGO. Thus, alongside the BINGOs and MANGOs mentioned already, all sorts of weird and wonderful NGO sub-types have blossomed in recent years. DONGO is short for Donor Organized NGO; ENGO for Environmental NGO; FBO for Faith Based Organization; NNGO for Northern NGOs funded by wealthy governments to deliver aid in the Global South; SNGO for Southern NGOs that are based and run in the Global South yet often enabled by World Bank PRSP protocols; INGO for International NGO, some of which increasingly aspire to cross the North–South divide in their own internal governance; TANGO for Technical Assistance NGOs; TANs for the Transnational Advocacy Networks through which NGOs often collaborate in international forums; and, most exotically of all, GONGO stands for a Government Operated NGO such as, but not limited to, QUANGOs or Quasi Autonomous NGOs! One obvious lesson of this acronymic explosion is that as well as crossing North–South divides globally, NGOs also tend to blur the boundaries of civil society on both the business side and the state side. Thus, while some introductions locate NGO activity in a "Third Sector" existing in a neatly compartmentalized zone of social organization beyond the "private sector" and "state sector," the reality is much more messy and mixed. There are, for example, "astroturf" or synthetic grassroots NGOs that represent efforts on the part of corporations to promote initiatives that normal business advertising and lobbying cannot accomplish (e.g. the US National Smokers' Alliance). There are the aforementioned GONGOs and QUANGOs that represent efforts by government to enlist civil society in their projects and thereby avoid accusations of big bad government (e.g. the London Docklands Development Association). And then there are the less well-funded and more radical NGOs that persist in offering services at the same time as agonizing about how their receipt of government or donor funding makes them complicit with government or business agendas.

Amidst all the diversity, however, some common themes and common ways in which NGOs govern themselves and their projects still stand out. Thus, the common, albeit contested, categories of NGO governance are indexed by the keywords "participation," "accountability," and "empowerment." Undoubtedly, much of the popularity of NGOs in opinion polls is due to how they are perceived to facilitate fuller and more meaningful public participation while at the same time offering an accountable and empowering alternative for citizens struggling against (or at least with) big government and big business. Sometimes seeing themselves as the organized executive arm of new social movements, NGOs also on occasion aspire thus to be the leaders of social resistance or social change. Yet, as they have participated more and more in the provision of services traditionally provided by governments, as they have come to rely on government funding or support from private philanthropy or a mix of IFI, IGO, and EU funding, and as they have also offered more business-like accounting of how they spend donor money, the claims NGOs make about empowering citizens have also been questioned by critics who point out that – to use the title of a book-length critique – "The Revolution will Not be Funded."[41] Instead of providing transformative participatory democracy, critics argue thus that NGOs too often become technocratic elites that disempower ordinary people and reinforce the status quo. Instead of providing transparency and new knowledge networks for grassroots communities, the charge is that NGOs create clubby and nebulous associations that actually block access and obscure information. And instead of really offering a civil society counterweight to deregulated market forces, critics therefore argue that NGOs offer a market-dependent and market-expanding model of accountability that further undermines democratic state authority over market transactions.

Even if NGOs seek in their advocacy work to contest neoliberal policies and priorities, the argument is that by effectively substituting NGO services for state services and by going along with a contracting-out approach to government, they are helping to consolidate the roll-back of macro state control and the end of efforts to discipline and "embed" market forces through governmental regulation. Defenders of such a deregulatory roll-back might point out that much of the state control seen around the world in the twentieth century rarely involved participatory democracy, and that replacing it with new micro initiatives led by NGOs offers much more grassroots accountability. However, the concern of the critics is that relying on new NGO networks to "deliver" participation only substitutes another democratically unaccountable and disempowering approach to governance all the while it rolls out innumerable new market metrics of efficiency and cost-effectiveness as the ultimate benchmarks of the promised accountability.[42] The rhetoric of "delivering" participation and empowerment along with services would seem in this sense to speak to the market-mediated model of citizenship and governance that is entailed: the ability of political citizens to hold representatives in a parliament or congress accountable for their use of public resources being replaced by the idea of economic citizens consuming services provided by NGOs who are in turn monitored by accountants for their use of private and public funds.[43] This disempowering outcome of empowerment-speak has been most distressing in the developing world where the interest in public participation has been especially heightened (due to the legacies of colonialism as well as the sorts of World Bank PRSP participation policy noted above). Here, though, anthropologists have found that the NGO-boom in Africa and Asia has instead created a kind of "anti-politics machine," a machine that systematically obscures the ruling regimes, power politics, and structural inequalities that continue to disempower people on the ground.[44] Meanwhile, research on NGOs in Europe that are actually funded by the EU to promote public debate finds that their work on democratic mobilization is also frequently thwarted by the daily struggle to manage grants and find further funding. "Grant writing, pursuing project cooperation, and managing human resources are cited by all networks as central to survival, and occupy up to 60% of work time," concludes a recent study of European women's rights NGOs.[45] And even when the struggle for funding does not present an obstacle, the same study found that real democratic engagement tended to be subordinated by the proclivity of NGOs towards working with intergovernmental institutions and other NGOs rather than broader publics.

Reflecting on what they sometimes refer to disparagingly as the "NGO-ization of politics," NGO workers (if not their managers) are often their own most vociferous critics. They voice worries about the transformation of social justice struggles into professionalized nine to five jobs; about being part of wider neoliberal shifts in governance; about the tokenistic use of images of smiling aid recipients in various brochures and online efforts to raise money; about the reproduction of social hierarchies within NGO chains of command; about the short-termism and narrow foci of NGO projects dictated by funding cycles and the issue-oriented nature of donor grants; and about the privileges of NGO mobility and living situations that so often stand in stark contrast to the immobility and vulnerability of those they seek to help.[46] Nevertheless, rather than give up in the face of these concerns, many NGO workers and leaders are struggling to find solutions that counteract some of the problems associated with practicing forms of governance so deeply shaped by neoliberal norms. For example, a progressive global health NGO based in Seattle called Health Alliance International (HAI) is involved in efforts to provide vital medical services in Africa while simultaneously working to mitigate the problem of undermining public health systems in the countries where it works. This problem involves the brain-drain phenomenon of NGOs hiring high-skilled health professionals away from government health ministries with higher pay. In response, HAI has worked with Partners in Health, Oxfam, and other health NGOs to develop an "NGO code of conduct" designed to help NGO project managers reduce such brain-draining developments by working more collaboratively with local and national governments.[47] This, it seems, is a new development in relations between NGOs and nation states. It has the long-term goal of building up rather than replacing public government in poor countries, and yet it is a goal pursued while still retaining the NGO approach to winning and distributing grant support from wealthy governments and foundations. Such hybrid developments are obviously at odds with the neoliberal nostrum that NGOs are simply an alternative to big bad government corruption. Nevertheless, this nostrum remains influential globally and therefore shapes how the contested common denominators of NGO governance – participation, empowerment, and accountability – relate in turn to global governance more generally.

7.3.2   How does NGO governance relate to global governance?

The most obvious way in which NGOs relate to global governance is that they are associated with the wider subordination of national-state governance to neoliberal norms. Neoliberal reformers tend to see NGOs as accountable, efficient, and appropriate alternatives to corrupt, inefficient, and anachronistic governments precisely because they are "non-governmental." However, not all NGOs are Trojan horses for global neoliberalism. There is clearly a world of difference between a BINGO such as the American Smokers' Alliance and a progressive health NGO such as HAI, and there is a still wider range of divergent positions staked out by different NGOs about the degrees to which they oppose or support anti-neoliberal ideas about disciplining corporations and making markets accountable. Despite these differences, trends can still be identified. It is increasingly clear, therefore, that, just like nation-states themselves, NGOs tend to be given more authority and incentives to shape, implement, and monitor programs if they provide services that complement or at least compensate for the rise of pro-market governance. Whether they are enlisted by the World Bank in the implementation of a PRSP, or supported by giant global philanthropies such as the Ford Foundation, or are funded by national governments themselves, the constellation of forces at work tends to elevate and expand NGO activities that are consistent with privatization, cutbacks in state services, financial deregulation, and international free-trade agreements.

By crossing national borders, international NGOs or INGOs also transcend traditional national-state governance in another way, too. They create and expand networks that cross the boundaries of national territorial sovereignty, and for many hopeful commentators they therefore also offer an antidote to the forms of territorialized anger and xenophobia that shape so many political reactions to globalization.[48] Working on global humanitarian crises, global health, global human-rights issues, or global climate-change challenges, INGO activities often also identify governmental challenges that are global or at least transnational in nature. And for the same reason, they often collaborate with or within global institutions. These include United Nations agencies (e.g. the UNDP – UN Development Program, the FAO, and the WHO), the World Bank, and global scientific organizations such as the IPCC – International Panel on Climate Change, as well as associated transgovernmental networks such as the Global Alliance for Vaccines and Immunization (GAVI), the Global Water Partnership, and the World Commission on Dams Forum. With all this international networking, it is clear that INGOs have been considerably enabled by the global communications revolution created by the Internet, jet travel, and global news organizations. Not only are they responding to problems and challenges about which people are informed and concerned because of global media, but also INGOs have much of their own transnational influence and government-like effects because of the ways in which they can communicate and shape opinion across borders with a mix of technical, moral, and policy ideas that travel. Of course, many INGOs, especially in the development, health, and human-rights fields, remain deeply dependent on the national governments of wealthy countries for their funding. This means that, contrary to the "end of the nation-state" myth-making, they have not superceded national governance altogether. But it remains true all the same that the transnational networking of INGOs really does represent a distinctly transnational influence on global governance.

The networked nature of INGO operations, the ways they work with all sorts of agencies and governments across international borders, and the processes through which these ties construct effective forms of global governance prompt further questions about how transnationally networked governance is being governed itself. Who or what coordinates global governance in the absence of a global sovereign? Who or what is in charge? Unlike at the World Bank and IMF, there is no one sitting in a "Global Governance" executive office ready to pick up a red phone and respond to a call from the American president. Indeed, there is no unitary regime of global governance, let alone a unitary executive. Notwithstanding the paranoid fears of militia groups in the United States, the UN does not have squadrons of black helicopters ready to dominate the world. It is much more of a talking shop than a powerful governing body, and its agencies are deeply dependent on networks of member governments and NGOs to pursue policy targets such as the Millennium Development Goals. Even the UN Security Council is itself highly dependent on coalitions of national governments to pass resolutions, although its five permanent members (the United States, China, Russia, France, and the United Kingdom) have enduring veto powers as a result of the geopolitical circumstances surrounding the creation of the UN at the end of World War II. And, outside of the UN, other intergovernmental talking shops such as the G8 and G20 have only very limited norm-setting power on economic issues, itself shaped by business-affiliated think tanks and forums such as the Organization of Economic Cooperation and Development (OECD) and the World Economic Forum. NGOs themselves network within and between meetings of all these institutions: sometimes just monitoring, sometimes lobbying, and sometimes actually being involved in making and implementing policy. Thus, the result in terms of global governance is a system that is profoundly pluralistic, multidimensional, and, as the overlapping networks of NGO involvement underline, also complexly connected to the regimes of expertise surrounding issue-specific subsystems of governance.

Even to use the language of systems is somewhat misleading here because there is little that is systematic about global governance. However, there are at least two tendencies that can be said to be *systemic*. First, as was highlighted in Section 7.1, there is the hegemonic role that the United States plays in steering the direction of policy and norm-setting in most of these intergovernmental and INGO networks. Whether it is the US military, the office of the US trade representative (USTR), or the US Agency for International Development (USAID), there is the direct steering undertaken by the formal agencies of US government. And especially salient in NGO networks, there is also the more informal steering through which American media, norms, and standards further shape the ideals and practices of global institutions. Whether it is an American emphasis on supporting faith-based organizations or on emphasizing the empowerment of women and girls, these US influences have gone global as they have been taken up and extended through NGO networks. Second, and not unrelated to the global dominance of American norm-setting which has increasingly included an emphasis on using bond ratings to assess risk in development planning, there has been the still more systemic influence of market models and metrics in the organization of global governance. As we already noted, routine NGO practices of accounting are shaped by this influence, and this in turn shapes how NGOs of all kinds interact within global networks and communications. For example, the ways in which health and development NGOs report back to donors on the numbers of lives saved is increasingly structured by competitive dynamics that can even make metrics such as the Millennium Development Goals come to seem more like the bottom-line numbers of a stock-market score card (with all the dangers therein of the speculative and innovative book-keeping we have come to expect from TNCs in earnings reporting season).

In addition to the influence on NGOs themselves, there is also a much broader way in which market systems of ranking, rating, and risk management shape global governance, and, by doing so, considerably expand and redefine what "non-governmental organization" might actually be considered to include. At the heart of this non-governmental but yet profoundly regulative mode of market organization is the underlying capitalist mechanism of competition. As most famously evoked in Adam Smith's invisible hand metaphor, this is a mechanism of governance that rules systemically through unseen market relations rather than through the more visible actions and edicts of a sovereign. The market still creates enormous regulative and state-like effects, but it does so without being seen as a formal government or regulatory authority. It organizes in extensive and influential ways; it disciplines, distributes, enables, and controls, but yet not in the traditional top-down manner of a national government. We will conclude the section, therefore, by addressing how this enlarged market mechanism of non-governmental organization relates to global governance more generally.

There have been various concepts developed by scholars to describe the global influence of market-based governance on other institutions and organizations. They include: "governance beyond the state," "governance without government," "network governance," "market civilization," and, most evocatively, "the new nebuleuse of neoliberal hegemony."[49] Running through these concepts – sometimes as an explicit object of criticism, other times more as a tacit assumption – is an understanding that market forces are not simply unleashed by macroeconomic neoliberal policy reforms, but also enabled in micro social networks and institutions that predispose individuals and organizations to act in enterprising or other market-calculating ways (as we saw earlier in this chapter, for example, with the governance of NGOs through their dependence on grant funding). This is where the complementary concept of "governmentality" comes into play, giving us a term with which to describe the ways in which modern government involves micro practices of regulation that operate at the level of individuals. Historically, these regulatory practices of discipline and training have not always intensified market rule at an individual level. Instead, traditional nineteenth- and twentieth-century governmentality in modern institutions such as public schools, barracks, clinics, and factories, tended to lead people to think of their identities and regulate their behavior through appeals to more collective concepts of national territory, national population, and national security.[50] Today, by contrast, governmentality in the age of post-national and trans-territorial markets instead entails much more individualized identity formations in which training increasingly involves being taught to be an enterprising or prudential individual who manages risk and security on a personal level. Of course, we have not witnessed the end of training in national identity or the destruction of national territory and security operations. Yet, in the context of neoliberalization, conceptions of collective responsibility and collective care for national populations have been increasingly subordinated to personalized forms of "responsibilization" that stress personal accountability and enterprising approaches to risk management by individuals.

The neoliberal shifts in governmentality are occurring in culturally distinct ways in different countries and at varying speeds based in part on the degree to which national governments have themselves embraced or resisted macroeconomic neoliberal reforms. But the market-molded developments of neoliberal governmentality have nevertheless had a profound global impact because they have enabled governance to be reworked and reformed from the bottom up in line with the operational principles and practices of capitalist competition. One of the most obvious examples of neoliberal governmentality today is the omnipresence of competitive rankings in our lives – think, for example, of how important your own personal credit score is. And beyond the ways we are trained to regulate our behavior so as to have a "good credit" score, other sorts of risk or competitive ratings that are based on market metrics now shape regulative and organizational practices (i.e. governance) across a wide range of scales from the global to the local. Whether it is rankings of best nation-states in which to do business, safest emerging markets in which to invest, or most livable cities in which to buy real estate, or whether it takes the more banal form of ranking top restaurants, top sports teams, top celebrities, and top electronic gadgets, or yet, at a still more basic level, of best local electricians, car mechanics, and hair dressers, there is simply no avoiding the omnipresent organizational influences of competitive rankings in everyday life today. And the rankings clearly have an impact: not only shaping consumption choices, but also profoundly shaping the ways in which people ranging from national and urban leaders to mechanics and hair dressers go about setting policy, developing growth plans, and providing or cutting back new services.

Perhaps most remarkable is the rise of ranking systems in parts of the world and parts of social life that were historically governed by forces considered older or somehow more transcendent than modern market metrics of demand, consumption, and risk. In the Global South, microfinance market rankings now map and rank some of the remotest parts of the world based on the expected returns for microfinance investors. At the same time, in wealthy countries parts of the "public sector" long viewed as autonomous from market forces have been taken over by the organizational imperatives of ranking. Thus, public services that were once seen as national rights and collective entitlements are now seen as privately consumed goods provided to calculating individuals and their families by rankable institutions. Schools and colleges are ranked on the basis of student demand or "value added education"; doctors and dentists are ranked on the basis of patient satisfaction; and parks and playgrounds are ranked for recreational opportunity and safety. Most strikingly of all, we are seeing much older pre-modern institutions such as Christian churches, Muslim mosques, and Jewish synagogues ranked on online city guides of "best places of worship." This does not mean that all churches, mosques, and synagogues have themselves become institutional enablers of neoliberalism in the same way as the German sociologist Max Weber once argued that Protestantism prepared its adherents to become especially spirited and well-suited pioneers of capitalism.[51] Just because they make decisions on where to pray based on a ranked list does not necessarily mean that Muslim, Jewish, and Christian fundamentalists are all becoming market fundamentalists in the neoliberal sense! But the use of competitive rankings certainly indicates the extraordinary extent to which market metrics have come to organize some of the oldest and most obviously pre-capitalist aspects of social life.

Moving from religious practices back to the main institutions of governance we have explored in this chapter, what might be the parallel conclusions about the increasing intrusion of market mechanisms? Clearly the nation-state with which we began remains an influential form of governmental authority notwithstanding the ways in which this same authority is increasingly used to enforce neoliberal policy norms. As they are enlisted into these processes of government-enabled neoliberalization, it is also not hard to see the ways in which politicians and state bureaucrats are themselves also involved in recognizing and reinforcing all sorts of micro practices of competitive ranking, benchmarking, and risk calculation, too. For example, national leaders, along with city and regional leaders around the world, now find themselves evermore preoccupied with how to make sure that their particular polity gains a high ranking from the three big credit and risk ratings firms – Moody's, Standard and Poor's, and Fitch's. The main reason why is that without high ratings, the cost of borrowing money goes up as lenders charge an additional premium or spread over the so-called risk free rate in any particular bond market. Traditionally, the risk-free rate in national bond markets was a national government's prime rate on its own debt, but, as the sovereign debt crises of late have shown with the repeated downgradings of Greek, Spanish, and even French debt, national governments now have to work hard themselves to retain the esteemed AAA ratings.

Reciprocally, it should be noted that even though the **credit-ratings agencies** had themselves attracted widespread criticism in the aftermath of the sub-prime market melt down of 2008 – having given out strong ratings for what turned out to be the highly risky structured debt "products" created by banks – the sovereign debt crises of 2010–2012 indicated that they still enjoyed much more credibility and thus more power in the markets than the European governments that were trying to re-regulate them but which they "downgraded" into economic collapse.

Aided and abetted by political leaders who have internalized the competitive logic of ratings, these same ranking systems have now been extended into other aspects of global governance, too.[52] Thus, beyond the spectacle of national governments bowing down before the assessments of the credit-ratings firms, it is also possible to point to the more generalized uptake of government-through-ratings across a wide swathe of global governance. Not surprisingly, the IMF and World Bank have long been concerned with the ways in which their administration of austerity through structural adjustment and PRSPs is interconnected with securing better ratings for borrowing countries. Again and again, therefore, we have witnessed IFI policies explained and justified in terms of improving market risk assessments for indebted countries, and thus as a way of putting them on the path to cheaper borrowing and economic growth. Further afield, when development NGOs or their donors make the case for tackling a particular development challenge in order to put a country on the so-called ladder of growth, one can also see the ways in which their efforts contribute to a league-table regime in global governance in which basic market benchmarks of growth and risk predominate. However, it is also true that as ratings regimes have developed further away from the corporate sector in which they first originated – Moody's and Standard and Poor's, it should be noted, began life in the nineteenth century by publishing evaluations of US railroad companies – the actual basis of competitive comparisons has shifted. For the same reason, as neoliberal norms of governance have become increasingly questioned around the world, all sorts of new league tables have been proposed. There is the Human Development Index, for example, which takes into account life expectancy and literacy as well as average standards of living within a country or community. Moving further away from simple economic metrics, there are also Gender Parity, Child Development, and Democracy index rankings, too. And as the most obvious, anti-neoliberal antidote to using GDP as a way of ranking nation-states with an economic growth index, alternatives now include the Gross National Happiness, Genuine Progress Indicator (GPI), and Happy Planet indexes that seek to re-evaluate and re-rank countries on the basis of all round human and environmental well-being.

The possibility that a basic device of neoliberal governmentality – the competitively ranked list – might become a mechanism for prioritizing non-neoliberal development goals and alternative market-controlling approaches to governance is another example of why we need to question the myth of inevitability so often attached to the big G Globalization story about the death of the nation-state. Nothing is inevitable when governance remains such a contested focus of struggle over human and environmental priorities on the planet. In subsequent chapters, we will move on to consider how these struggles in areas such as health and sustainability may well move global governance in new directions in the future. For the moment, though, we should conclude this chapter by acknowledging the fact that despite the existence of alternatives, it is the sorts of ranking that retain the economic metrics of traditional credit ratings that remain most dominant in our world. From the IMF and World Bank, down to nation-states and cities, down to all of us as individuals applying for credit cards, car loans, student loans, and mortgages, the rulings that come with credit ratings and rankings also come with enormously consequential implications for how we live our lives. Ultimately, this is because the power of credit ratings is deeply material. Compliance is ensured because without good credit ratings, credit goes away. It is not just a matter of representation, rhetoric, or the reality-framing quality of a competitive ranking based on financial risk, although superficial market "opinion" measures can certainly trigger herd-like behavior from investors. It is because market rankings also make a material difference by regulating access to resources, and enabling or eroding the capacity of both institutions and individuals to control their destinies. In this respect, while the nation-state is not dead, and while NGOs complicate the patchwork pattern of neoliberal global governance, the invisible force of the market rules like no other non-governmental organization ever seen.

Student Exercises

Individual:
Compare and contrast how neoliberal policy norms were brought into Chile with how they were introduced in New Zealand. What do the differences tell us about the importance of local context in understanding the global expansion of pro-market rules?

Group:
Ask everyone in your group to develop and define their own ranking system for nation-states designed to encode their own personal values in calculable and competitive metrics. Then work as a group to examine what sorts of challenges and consequences would arise from attempting to implement each system given the current state of global governance.

Notes

1   Kenichi Ohmae, *The End of the Nation-State: The Rise of Regional Economies* (New York: Free Press, 1995).
2   Naomi Klein, *The Shock Doctrine: The Rise of Disaster Capitalism* (New York: Metropolitan Books, 2007).
3   Quoted in Klein, *Shock Doctrine*, 207.

4   Lauren Benton, *A Search for Sovereignty: Law and Geography in European Empires, 1400–1900* (Cambridge: Cambridge University Press, 2010).

5   See John Agnew, *Globalization and Sovereignty* (Lantham: Rowman and Littlefield, 2009).

6   http://www.euregio.org/index.cfm?action=ShowPage&PageID=DD57853A-5F10-43A2-B443-D5FE25FE15CC.

7   Laurent Dubois, *Avengers of the New World: The Story of the Haitian Revolution* (Cambridge,MA: Harvard University Press, 2004).

8   Matthew Sparke, "A Map that Roared and an Original Atlas: Canada, Cartography and the Narration of Nation," *Annals of the Association of American Geographers*, 88, no. 3 (1998): 464–95.

9   Eun Mee Kim, ed., *The Four Asian Tigers Economic Development and the Global Political Economy* (New York: Elsevier, 1998).

10 Quoted in Klein, *Shock Doctrine*, 6.

11 See Margaret Thatcher, "Speech to the College of Europe ("The Bruges Speech")" at http://www.margaretthatcher.org/speeches/displaydocument.asp?docid=107332.

12 See Stephen Clarkson, "Constitutionalising the Canadian–American Relationship," in Duncan Cameron and Mel Watkins, eds., *Canada Under Free Trade* (Toronto: James Lorimer and Co, 1993): 3–20.

13 See Piers Brendon, *The Decline and Fall of the British Empire, 1776–1997* (New York: Knopf, 2007).

14 For an excellent account of this form of market-based and market-developing hegemony, see John Agnew, *Hegemony: The New Shape of Global Power* (Philadelphia: Temple University Press, 2005).

15 See Matthew Sparke, "Geopolitical Fear, Geoeconomic Hope and the Responsibilities of Geography," *Annals of the Association of American Geographers* 97, no. 2 (2007): 338–49.

16 Quoted in William Appleman Williams, *The Tragedy of American Diplomacy* (New York: Norton, 1988), 72.

17 For a full economic costing of the war, see Joseph E. Stiglitz and Linda J. Bilmes, *The Three Trillion Dollar War: The True Cost of the Iraq Conflict* (New York: W.W. Norton, 2008).

18 Quoted in Bret Benjamin, *Invested Interests: Capital, Culture and the World Bank* (Minneapolis: University of Minnesota Press, 2007), 21.

19 Quoted in Benjamin, *Invested Interests*, 27.

20 Quoted in Benjamin, *Invested Interests*, 16–17.

21 Quoted in Ngaire Woods, *The Globalisers: The IMF, World Bank and their Borrowers* (Ithaca, NY: Cornell University Press, 2006), 17.

22 Stephen Cohen, *The Making of United States International Economic Policy* (New York: Praeger, 2000).

23 These data and the two prior quotes are all from Benjamin, *Invested Interests*, 29.

24 Thomas Oatley and Jason Yackee, "American Interests and IMF Lending," *International Politics* 41, no. 3 (2004): 415–29.

25 John Glenn, "Global Governance and the Democratic Deficit: stifling the voice of the South," *Third World Quarterly* 29, no. 2 (2008): 217–38.

26 http://www.imf.org/external/np/sec/memdir/members.htm.

27 http://siteresources.worldbank.org/BODINT/Resources/278027-1215524804501/IBRDCountryVotingTable.pdf.

28   Quoted in Richard Peet, *Unholy Trinity: The IMF World Bank and WTO* (London: Zed Books, 2003), 41.

29   IMF, *International Reserves and Liquidity* (Washington, DC: IMF, 1958).

30   See Joseph Stiglitz, *Making Globalization Work* (New York: Norton, 2006).

31   Walden Bellow and Shalmail Guttal, "The Limits of Reform: the Wolfensohn era at the World Banks," *Race and Class* 47, no. 3 (2006): 68–91.

32   See http://www.cgap.org/p/site/c/aboutus/.

33   Ananya Roy, *Poverty Capital: Microfinance and the Making of Development* (New York: Routledge, 2010).

34   Chris Giles, "IMF Needs No Sympathy When It Comes to New Levies on Banks," *Financial Times*, April 22 (2010): 2.

35   Peter Lee, "China discovers value in the IMF, *Asia Times*, June 10 (2009) at http://www.atimes.com/atimes/China_Business/KF10Cb01.html; and on the struggle over quotas in 2010, Alan Beattie and Christian Oliver, "Accord on IMF Board Masks Lack of Progress," *Financial Times* October 25, (2010): 6.

36   http://www.ngohandbook.org/index.php?title=Main_Page.

37   See http://www.indianngos.com/ for latest figures and examples of internal national NGO diversity.

38   Peter Hallward, *Damming the Flood: Haiti, Aristide, and the Politics of Containment* (New York: Verso, 2007).

39   See http://news.bbc.co.uk/2/hi/africa/3502733.stm.

40   Quoted in Jeffrey Unerman and Brendan O'Dwyer, "On James Bond and the Importance of NGO Accountability," *Accounting, Auditing & Accountability Journal*, 19, no. 3 (2006): 305–18.

41   Incite! Women of Color Against Violence, *The Revolution Will Not Be Funded: Beyond the Non-Profit Industrial Complex* (Cambridge, MA: South End Press, 2007).

42   Erik Swyngedouw, "Governance Innovation and the Citizen: The Janus Face of Governance-beyond-the-State," *Urban Studies* 42, 11 (2005): 1991–2006.

43   Jeffrey Unerman and Brendan O'Dwyer, On James Bond.

44   James Ferguson, *Global Shadows: Africa in the Neoliberal World Order* (Durham, NC: Duke University Press, 2006); and Tania Murray Li, *The Will to Improve: Governmentality, Development, and the Practice of Politics* (Durham, NC: Duke University Press, 2007).

45   Sabine Lang, "Assessing Advocacy: European Transnational Women's Networks. and Gender Mainstreaming," *Social Politics: International Studies in Gender, State and Society* 16, no. 3 (2009): 327–57, at 350.

46   Sangtin Writers and Richa Nagar, *Playing with Fire: Feminist Thought and Activism through Seven Lives in India, foreword by Chandra Talpade Mohanty* (Minneapolis: University of Minnesota Press, 2006).

47   See http://ngocodeofconduct.org/.

48   See, for example, the discussion of international slum dweller NGOs in Arjun Appadurai, *Fear of Small Numbers: An Essay on the Geography of Anger* (Durham, NC: Duke University Press, 2006): 131–37.

49   David Roberts, *Global Governance and Biopolitics: Regulating Human Security* (New York: Zed Press, 2010).

50   Michel Foucault, "Governmentality," trans. Rosi Braidotti and revised by Colin Gordon, in Graham Burchell, Colin Gordon, and Peter Miller, eds., *The Foucault Effect: Studies in Governmentality* (Chicago, IL: University of Chicago Press, 1991): 87–104.

51 Max Weber, *The Protestant Ethic and the Spirit of Capitalism*. Translated by Talcott Parsons (New York: Scribner, 1958).

52 For a great introduction to the rising influence of ratings firms see Timothy Sinclair, *The New Masters of Capital: American Bond Rating Agencies and the Politics of Credit-worthiness* (Ithaca, NY: Cornell University Press, 2005).

Keywords

AAA	Global South	SAP
conditionalities	IMF	Washington Consensus
credit ratings agencies	McDonaldization	World Bank
G8	neoliberalism	WTO

8

Space

Chapter Contents

Chapter Concepts

1. Globalization has shrunk distances but led to uneven geographical development.
2. Global unevenness leads to new entanglements of geopolitics with geoeconomics.
3. Speculative urbanism in global cities reflects and reinforces uneven development.
4. Global city competition creates both spatial spectacle and splintering.
5. Spectacular city developments create a spatial fix for global investment.
6. Splintered development involves enclaving alongside slums.
7. Enclaves and slums make manifest the neoliberalization of citizenship.

Key Concept

Globalization and the shrinking of distance have not led to the end of geography. Instead, they have led to uneven development and diverse forms of reterritorialization. Examples of such reterritorialization range in scale and type from the redefinition of geopolitical conflict zones to the promotion of global cities as sites for inward investment, to the creation of local landscapes of stark inequality where enclaves of privilege and possessive individualism exist right beside slums and communal spaces of dispossession.

Introducing Globalization: Ties, Tensions, and Uneven Integration, First Edition. Matthew Sparke.
© 2013 Matthew Sparke. Published 2013 by Blackwell Publishing Ltd.

8.1   Uneven Development, Geopolitics, and Geoeconomics

Space, the title of this chapter, may well make you think first about "Outer-Space" and the "Final Frontier" made memorable by the opening of *Star Trek*. But this is not the main sort of space we will be examining here. Instead, it is terrestrial space, the space of geographical relationships on and around the planet Earth that provides our focus. This space has a complex and fast-changing human geography, including a patchwork of continental trade regimes, nation-states, cities, and enclaves that has been significantly reworked by the transnational networks of contemporary globalization. Continents have been connected by commerce and capital, distances shrunk by the speed-up of transportation and communication, borders crossed by tourists and transnational workers, public lands privatized, and landscapes and territories of all kinds radically revisioned through world-framing representational technologies ranging from Google Earth to online games like *World of Warcraft* to the sorts of competitive ranking regimes we examined in the previous chapter on governance. Some commentators, as we have already seen, describe these changes as the "destruction" or "leveling" or "smoothing" of space. Focusing only on so-called deterritorialization or the moments in which territory is transcended, myth-makers argue that Globalization is so revolutionary that it has completely overcome the friction of distance, flattened the Earth, and thereby brought about an end of geography altogether. A conclusion that might well be drawn from these sorts of "endist" arguments is that *Star Trek*'s final frontier in outer-space is really the only space left worth exploring. Such a conclusion, though, is wrong because it ignores all the ways in which today's deterritorializing developments – *global commodity chains, integrated financial markets, inter-continental jet travel, the Internet, the sale of public land*, and so on – simultaneously create patterns of reterritorialization – *digital divides, resource wars, trade blocs, global cities, cross-border regions, export processing zones, gated communities, shopping malls, privatized prisons*, and so on. Globalization clearly has the capacity to destroy old spatial patterns and barriers, but it simultaneously creates new geographies that are just as powerful when it comes to territorializing and, in some cases, terrorizing human lives. As a result, uneven geographical distributions of growth and decline, wealth and poverty, and hope and despair all remain enduring landmarks of global capitalism.

Just think, for example, of the European Union, which we examined in relation to governance in the last chapter. It was once a region violently divided by national borders: a continent carved up by geopolitical divisions ranging from the trenches of World War I to Check Point Charlie and the Berlin Wall. Today, by contrast, the EU has been reterritorialized as a supranational free-trade area with shared governance, shared spatial planning, and a shared external border. For many tourists and business people traveling across this new geoeconomic space, the old internal national borders within the EU seem to have been rendered obsolete. National landscapes are reduced thus to niche vacation markets lined up in travel shop advertisements; the names of historic national capitals added to lists of destinations on airport and station monitors with no sign of their significance as centers of sovereignty; and old customs houses on Europe's road borders transformed into bars and restaurants that commercialize frontier landscapes as quaint reminders of a bygone geopolitical age. But for external "applicant" countries such as Turkey who want EU membership and free-trade access to European markets, and for all sorts of immigrants and refugees traveling from Africa, the Middle East, and the Balkans, the external borders of today's new Europe represent a geopolitically fraught and deeply consequential territorial divide. Internal deterritorialization has been matched in this sense by a reterritorialization of the external border, along with all sorts of draconian detention and deportation efforts to impose the legal meaning of this new EU territory on the bodies of individual migrants. Thus, far from ending geography, we see a double dynamic of deterritorialization and reterritorialization that creates new patterns of uneven geographical development that are also unevenly experienced depending on where you come from and who you are. These uneven geographical patterns are, as we shall explore here, often in turn represented and discussed in terms of a global tension between "geoeconomic" spaces of cooperation, inclusion and integration, and "geopolitical" zones of conflict, isolation, and military intervention. Yet as commonplace as these sorts of mappings of uneven development may be, noticing the geographical dynamics that underpin and connect them is not so easy. And it is made all the more difficult if we begin with a simple-minded mythic view of the globalized earth as a flat earth. By contrast, a couple of observations about the *Star Trek* view of space ironically provide useful correctives as well as insight into why the flat earth vision has, so to speak, taken off in the context of globalization.

First, the voyages of the *Starship Enterprise*, like so many other space fantasy movies and books, actually reflect very earthly preoccupations with exploring, pacifying, and making use of foreign lands. By recalling imperial enterprises on Earth itself, they remind us of the geographically uneven development of earlier empire-building rounds of globalization on the planet. After all, 15 ships of the British Royal Navy have had the name HMS Enterprise, including the oldest, a 24-gun jackass frigate which began service as *L'Enterprise* in the French navy before being captured in 1705 in the inter-imperial Anglo-French wars. Reusing this same name, and often addressing issues of inter-imperial conflict, the sci-fi *Starship Enterprise*'s explorations of outer space effectively allegorize age-old conflicts over terrestial space. In doing so, they also point to uneven geographical development, not a level playing field. While the adventures of the *Enterprise* also certainly reflect excitement, interest, and angst about how to live with interdependency, as stories recalling earthly spatial exploration they emphasize asymmetries and uneven incorporation under centralized control, not leveling. Indeed, Gene Roddenberry, who first developed the *Star Trek* TV series in 1966, marketed it as a Western in outer space – "a wagon train to the stars," he called it – hoping to use the similarities with America's Wild West expansion to address, among other things, the Vietnam war and enduring concerns about what Thomas Jefferson once called America's "empire of liberty."

Figure 8.1   Earth from Apollo 17. *Source:* astronaut photograph AS17-148-22727, courtesy NASA Johnson Space Center Gateway to Astronaut Photography of Earth (http://eol.jsc.nasa.gov).

Efforts to use outer-space fantasy to reflect on the geopolitical space of the planet indicate in turn a second *Star Trek* corrective to flat-earth fantasies: namely, insight into the technological and historical developments that make them possible. The *Star Trek* view of earth – the Earth seen from outer space, the Earth as single, spinning globe – is telling in this regard because it reflects the rise of a "space-travel" view of the planet in the 1960s. Obviously many different developments made this distant and abstract perspective possible, including all the investments in the Cold War space race as well as the rise of jet travel into the 1970s and beyond. Out of these there came new visions of the globe, including most famously the first outer-space picture of earth (image 22727) photographed by an Apollo 17 astronaut in 1972 (Figure 8.1). About the same time but often in opposition to the militarism of the space race, there were the efforts by the peace and environmentalist movements to recycle whole earth imagery (including image 22727) to – in John Lennon's famous 1971 lyrics – "Imagine all the people, living life in peace." And then, in the years after Lennon's invitation to "Imagine there's no countries," his other more anti-capitalist call to "Imagine no possessions" was left far behind as the postnational pursuit of peace was overtaken by a postnational pursuit of profit by post-Fordist TNCs. As we saw in Chapter 3, one of the distinguishing features of TNCs in the period after **Fordism** was that they started to see the whole planet strategically, moving on from the Fordist balancing of national mass production with national mass consumption to seek out new sites around the world for both sourcing and selling their goods with reduced concern for national workers, national consumers, and national borders. The rising prevalence of a postnational "globalist" perspective on the planet owes a great deal to these basic economic imperatives, and thus today's omnipresent representations of the world as a globe seen from outer space share what are in fact very earthly and, what might well be called, enterprising origins.

It is also primarily because of the association with the globalizing TNC world view that most books on globalization (and every other advert for a global MBA program anywhere) repeatedly use *Star Trek* style imagery of abstract globes seen from outer space to illustrate the idea of an increasingly globalized planet. By contrast, this book does not, and the reasons why should by now be clear. First, abstract globe imagery tends to reinforce the myth of global leveling. To be sure, it reminds us that the world is round, not flat. But globes and even low-orbit satellite images still tend to abstract away from all the Earthly unevenness, helping us ignore inequalities and asymmetries on the ground. Barbed-wire borders, inequalities in access to communications and mobility, enclaves within countries and cities, and extraordinarily uneven geographical concentrations of wealth and poverty all disappear from view. Second, a further problem with using globe images is that they also abstract away from enduring struggles over the political implications and consequences of the spatial representations themselves. By downplaying the political stakes of spatial representation, the relentless repetition of abstract global imagery thereby also tends to obscure its own ties to the practices of managing or at least moving across the world as if geography was, as travel, and telecommunications adverts so often aver, history.

Another way of stating the argument here is that we need to pay attention to how representations of the geography of globalization are tied to real world interdependencies and practices. The distant space-travel view of the world as an abstract globe looks the way it does and appears as often as it does because it is associated with strategic and privileged modes of traveling across the spaces of the real world. Sometimes, these practices are tied to ecologically or ethically integrative calls to global community such as those made by environmental, human rights, and global health NGOs. More commonly, however, the globalist imagery is associated with the logistically integrated world of business management.

In the business world, the representational ties go at least three ways. First, images of globes reflect the ways in which business management and movement have gone global in the search for sourcing efficiencies and new markets. And, second, because global managers are surrounded by such images everywhere they study, work, and move, they are in turn tempted to see and represent the world as an evermore level playing field. However, this self-reinforcing relay of practices and representations is in turn complicated in the real world of global business development by a third and disruptive relationship: namely the need for business leaders to track how different parts of the world offer different assets and advantages amidst all the global competition. This third point means that most business decisions and actions are not "placeless" at all. They depend instead on very detailed knowledge of local specificities.

Thus, beneath all the globalist imagery, and often tied to all sorts of global mapping technologies, there is an underlying economic interest in the particularities of place. Indeed, precisely because business today can move goods and capital around the world so easily, the differences distinguishing different production locations and different markets are all the more important. Business managers greatly value local knowledge and expertise, and for the same reason, news agencies and research firms compete aggressively to supply it. "Think you know global markets?" challenged one such supplier in a 2010 advertisement before inviting online readers into a so-called SmartDart game designed to test place-specific knowledge.[1] The point here is that in order to advertise itself as a useful window onto global markets, the company in question – Dow Jones – sought to use a game to present itself as an authority on place-based knowledge and news.

Given the clear economic importance attached to local knowledge about the particularities of place, one might well ask: why is the abstract globalist imagery of world space still so common? The Dow Jones SmartDart game provides something of an answer. Despite its effort to create a global competition about local knowledge, the game's interactive online global map still has a flattening and abstracting aspect to it because of the way it invites participants to treat the whole planet as a giant dartboard over which they can claim mastery (while also functioning as a commercial for a global news corporation and its 90-plus news bureaus). This reflects the broader way in which space-visualization technologies produce a "God's Eye View" that tends to hide the actual processes and embodied experience of uneven geographical development on the ground even when designed to draw attention to local details and territorial distinctions. Thus, despite the clear business interest in local knowledge, despite all the news coverage of business-relevant developments in particular places, and notwithstanding the many ways in which business education aims at teaching future managers about how to tailor their products for distinct local markets ("localization"), most globalist imagery tends to cover up the processes that produce geographic differences and uneven experience on the ground. This chapter responds to this problem by exploring the historical–geographical dynamics of uneven development that the abstract space-travel imagery obscures. We have to boldy go, as it were, and study the shifting human geographies of development and destruction that have been hidden by the outer-space view.

In the rest of this section, we will proceed by exploring further the economic imperatives underlying uneven development. While these imperatives have clearly led to the transcendence of diverse spatial barriers, and while they have created technologies such as jet planes and the Internet that have radically reduced the influence of spatial distance over our lives, they have simultaneously generated new forms of uneven geographical development marked by extreme inequalities. After all, only a small fraction of the world's population can actually afford to travel by jet, and a vast digital divide exists between Internet users in wealthier settings and the desperately poor communities in Africa where old computers are stripped for precious metals by bare hands that have never typed letters on a keyboard. One of the broadest scales at which this sort of unevenness and inequality becomes evident is in the world of international relations: the world of military and diplomatic struggle over territory and security that is commonly conceptualized today in terms of **geopolitics** and **geoeconomics**. Thus, after reviewing the global mechanics of uneven geographical development, we will examine how the spatial ideas and visions of international relations strategists and military planners have mapped and made sense of unevenness at a global scale by distinguishing zones of danger, disconnection, and conflict from areas of market integration. Then, in Section 8.2, we will turn to consider how cities and regions at the sub-national scale also exhibit new (as well as old) forms of uneven geographical development, including the expansion of giant global cities whose economic, political, and cultural significance around the world stands apart from and often, like their ever-higher sky-scrapers, taller in global standing than the countries in which they are located. Finally, in Section 8.3, we link these macro developments in international relations and global cities to some of the more micro geographical outcomes of uneven development occurring locally inside the spaces of globally networked city regions: geographical outcomes that including enclaves of privilege bounded off from the slums and impoverishment that surround them. To begin with, though, we need to come to terms with the basic economic forces that continue to drive the processes of reterritorialization at and across all these different spatial scales.

8.1.1 Between territorial fixing and geographical expansion

At the heart of the process of uneven geographical development lies the dynamism and growth-oriented nature of capitalism. Rather than some sort of steady-state regime based on stationary equilibrium, our world's economic system is instead based on the ongoing expansion of profit-making production and consumption. It is this need to expand capital that in turn leads capitalists to go beyond fixed geographic constraints. To find cheaper inputs, to locate new markets, and to speed up the turnover time between producing goods and selling them, businesses are constantly working to overcome spatial barriers and reduce the frictions of distance. At the very same time, though, they are always also having to make investments in particular places – including in farms, factories, offices, and retail outlets. These sorts of investments in place-based production, management, and marketing also in turn have to be augmented with further investments in the wider political–economic contexts that ensure ongoing profit-making. Whether these investments are designed to secure direct government subsidies and tax concessions for business, or the more indirect support represented by educational, health, and social services for workers, there is always a complex political–economic cost–benefit calculus at work that leads corporations to make investments in particular polities. And whether these are cities, counties, states, nation-states or even continents (as in the EU context), there can be no doubting that at a certain scale, the ties between a particular business and a particular political–economic space go very deep indeed (think, for instance, of the ties in the United States between the auto-industry and the region around

Detroit, or between high-tech electronics and Silicon Valley, or, in the United Kingdom, between financial services and the City of London). The big challenge for business, therefore, is to balance the benefits that accrue from these place-bound investments with an ability to pursue opportunities in new external places. Clearly, some businesses tend to be more place-bound than others (farming conglomerates and ship builders in contrast to shoe and toy makers, for instance). But, averaged out across an entire economy, the basic balancing act remains in force. On the one hand, there is the need to commit to place-bound investments, and, on the other hand, there is the constant competitive pressure to pursue new opportunities beyond the borders of the places in which business has invested already. It is this essential tension between the *territorial fix* of place-investment and the *geographical expansion* of place-transcendence that drives uneven geographical development.

In the context of the recent, market-liberalizing rounds of globalization, the tension between the place-investing and place-transcending imperatives at the heart of uneven development has become especially acute at the same time as it has become evermore global. Competitive pressures unleashed at a global scale push TNCs to search out new opportunities right around the world. Yet because of the long time periods needed to make a return on prior place-bound investments, particularly large or institutionally mediated ones (e.g. an airplane factory, or a training institute at a university), and because of all sorts of social and familial networks that also tend to generate strong business ties to particular places, the challenges of moving out and transcending place are much more significant than talk of "footloose firms" and "placeless corporations" generally implies. Of course, businesses often present themselves as hyper-mobile because this allows them to win greater concessions from place-bound politicians and communities. Indeed, this is another reason why the myth of a global level playing field is so common. It helps improve the hand of business in negotiations with governments and communities by painting a picture of easy exits to other places (normally other places with lower taxes, fewer unions, and less environmental and worker protections). But in reality, the expense of abandoning investments that have already been made in place is far from negligible.

The costs of movement obviously include the failure to realize a full return on money sunk into buildings and equipment. In addition to such fixed capital investments, though, businesses are also bound into local economies through networks of interdependency with local suppliers, service firms, educational institutions, social clubs, and so on. On top of this, there are the monopolistic advantages many firms enjoy as prime investors in particular places (e.g. ownership of expensive real estate, or special access to infrastructure, or cozy relationships with local government). And, meanwhile, the uncertainties of global financial volatility mean that corporate leaders increasingly depend on the security provided by place-bound ties too, especially in places where national governments and treasuries can help mitigate the risks of economic crisis with guarantees and stimuli that sustain credit markets, labor markets, and consumption markets through tough times.

The way in which recent financial crises have highlighted business dependency on place-based security also highlights how the tensional relationship between territorial fixity and geographical transcendence shifts over time. Some historical periods see more fixity and place-bound consolidation, while other periods witness more spatial transcendence and geographical expansion. At the most macro global level, these tendencies have waxed and waned over decades-long periods. For example, from the late 1980s, through the 1990s, and into the new millennium, global capitalism as a whole saw spectacular space-transcending expansion. The phenomenal growth of production and consumption in Asia, especially China and India, was clearly accompanied in this period by multiple space-transcending developments in global networking, transportation, and communications. It has in turn been these distance-shrinking developments that have led to so much of the hype about Globalization as a leveling juggernaut of global integration and change. Yet, just as this hype misses the unevenness of the resulting growth patterns, it also ignores the history of prior periods of expansion in which the tension between fixity and transcendence has been similarly tilted towards expansionary movements into new places of production and consumption. For instance, in the mid nineteenth century, as the countries of western Europe industrialized and sought foreign markets for their new manufacturing output, a similar burst of expansionary activity was widely noted. At the time, even capitalism's critics were impressed, and it was in this way that Karl Marx and Frederick Engels came to write about the border-crossing feats of the business class (who they referred to as the "bourgeoisie") in the famously lyrical terms of *The Communist Manifesto*.

> The need of a constantly expanding market for its products chases the bourgeoisie over the entire surface of the globe. It must nestle everywhere, settle everywhere, establish connections everywhere. The bourgeoisie has, through its exploitation of the world market, given a cosmopolitan character to production and consumption in every country. To the great chagrin of reactionaries, it has drawn from under the feet of industry the national ground on which it stood. All old-established national industries have been destroyed or are daily being destroyed. They are dislodged by new industries, whose introduction becomes a life and death question for all civilized nations, by industries that no longer work up indigenous raw material, but raw material drawn from the remotest zones; industries whose products are consumed, not only at home, but in every quarter of the globe. In place of the old wants, satisfied by the production of the country, we find new wants, requiring for their satisfaction the products of distant lands and climes. In place of the old local and national seclusion and self-sufficiency, we have intercourse in every direction, universal inter-dependence of nations.[2]

One great historical irony surrounding this depiction of global capitalism in the mid-nineteenth century is that both it and the global communism that Marx and Engels hoped would follow in its tracks fell victim in the twentieth century to authoritarian brands of nationalistic territoriality. Hitler's Germany and Stalin's Soviet Union brought back the seclusion of national industries on national ground with land-grabbing militaristic vengeance (although, as an Austrian in Germany and as a Georgian in Russia, Hitler and Stalin also brought personal anxieties about being "outsiders" to their totalitarian projects of territorial aggrandizement). Beyond the especially violent and reactionary returns to "fatherland" and "motherland" fixation by demagogic nationalists, it is clear that other responses to the economic crises of the early twentieth century also led elsewhere to more nationally self-contained models of economic development, including Roosevelt's New Deal nationalism in America. It was in this way that the economic depression and retrenchment in the 1930s was followed by the Fordist forms of national economic management that we examined in Chapter 3. As we saw, these generally involved balancing national mass production with national mass consumption. Not surprisingly, therefore, this mid-twentieth-century Fordist period also tended to be characterized (at least at a global scale) by a tendency towards national spatial fixity and investments in place. Nevertheless, it was also in this period that the seeds were sown for a new round of global expansion. Thus, foreign competition and foreign opportunities made more and more TNCs go global from the 1960s forwards.

After the fiscal and monetary crises of national Fordism in the 1970s, the solution to uneven national surpluses of capital and labor was increasingly sought in yet more transnational expansion. As we saw in Chapter 7, this new moment of territory-transcending globalization also coincided with a widespread neoliberalization of governance, too. This in turn created a second sort of historical irony in so far as former Fordist and socialist countries were forced one after another to adopt the sorts of pro-market reforms advocated by the disciples of Von Hayek and Friedman. Landscapes previously associated with state control and territories previously managed in the interests of national publics were thus rapidly deterritorialized and reterritorialized for the purposes of capitalist integration and exploitation. As Naomi Klein explains with a cartographic metaphor in her gripping account of neoliberal shock therapy, this also represented a certain sort of spatial remapping by the planners of anti-planning.

> Under Chicago School economics, the state acts as the colonial frontier which corporate conquistadors pillage with the same ruthless determination and energy as their predecessors showed when they hauled home the gold and silver of the Andes. Where [Adam] Smith saw fertile green fields turned into profitable farmlands on the pampas and the prairies, Wall Street saw "green field opportunities" in Chile's phone system, Argentina's airline, Russia's oil fields, Bolivia's water system, the United States' public airwaves, Poland's factories – all built with public wealth, then sold for a trifle. . . . By relentlessly searching for new profit frontiers in the public domain, Chicago School economists are like the mapmakers of the colonial era, identifying new waterways through the Amazon, making off the location of a hidden cache of gold inside an Inca temple.[3]

Klein's cartographic metaphor for neoliberal globalization does more than draw the historical parallel with the early periods of mercantilist expansion. In addition, with her attention to the diverse landscapes targeted for exploration and exploitation, she also usefully underlines how reterritorialization occurred across a wide range of spatial scales (from airwaves and oil fields to genes). This same range in spatial scale also therefore has to be taken into account in any attempt to chart the historical waxing and waning of uneven development. Most notably, throughout the long periods in which fixity and transcendence came and went as predominant imperatives for nation-states on the global stage, all sorts of reterritorializing and sometimes countervailing processes of uneven development operated at smaller scales within nation-states. We shall therefore go on to explore sub-national urban and regional dynamics in the next section when we consider new forms of territorial fixity in today's global city-regions. And in the final section of the chapter, we will turn to sub-national processes unfolding within cities and more personal spaces as we turn to consider the creation of enclaves and slums. Here, however, we need to look first at how the patterns of global uneven development already introduced have in turn been reframed by the grand foreign policy visions of geopolitics and geoeconomics. The important point to remember in this respect is that these geographical representations of international relations reflect the tensions of uneven development but in ways that tend to abstract particular territorial problems or ideals out of the processes of historical-geographical transformation that produce them. An "arc of instability" or "disputed border" might thereby be blamed for causing geopolitical unrest; while a "free trade region" or "free zone" may be idealized as bringing geoeconomic peace and prosperity.

For many of the diplomats and geostrategic visionaries involved in statecraft and geopolitical planning, space goes from being something that needs to be explained to something that is used to explain, and, as a result, the historical-geographical processes through which unevenness evolves tend to be obscured. Here, by contrast, uneven development remains the focus, and this approach in turn provides a useful way of creating some analytical distance from the high stakes, nationalistic feelings and often deadly struggles associated with the spatial visions and war-making associated with geopolitics and geoeconomics. Analytically this also means coming to terms with how geopolitics and geoeconomics are actually *entangled* with one another today in the form of a "double vision": a double vision that maps the divergent economic imperatives towards territorial fixing and geographical expansion in a distortive way that repeatedly divides the world into distinct zones – zones of geopolitical conflict on the one side and spaces of geoeconomic peace on the other – rather than coming to terms with the global ties between the two. By tracing how territorial struggles reflect historical–geographical processes of uneven development, we can instead correct for the distortion and better understand the connections.

For example, the development of anti-immigration sentiment among unemployed working-class communities in the United States today is often explained in terms of the geopolitical failure of US border defenses (by anti-immigration groups themselves) or in terms of nationalistic geopolitics (by immigrants' rights groups) rather than as a result of a shift in class alliances generated by American business expanding abroad, rising unemployment and the intensified global competition for jobs. If we consider the changing patterns of uneven development, therefore, we are better able to put simplistic geopolitical and ethnicist interpretations into context. Another good example of where this critical approach is useful relates to the debate in American foreign policy between Samuel Huntington's geopolitical vision of a looming "Clash of Civilizations" and his student Francis Fukuyama's countervailing geoeconomic vision of the "End of History."[4] Whereas these two positions are often introduced and explained as polar opposites – with Huntington interpreted as having said that a struggle between "Western civilization" and "muslim civilization" was inevitable, and Fukuyama interpreted as saying that such cultural and ideological struggles will ultimately be superceded by processes of economic globalization – they are in fact better understood as two inter-related sides of the same capitalist coin. By introducing an awareness of capitalism's uneven global development to this debate, it is therefore possible to develop a much more complex and nuanced understanding. In short, much of the struggle that is associated with cultural conflict by Huntington and other geopolitical interpreters is actually caused by the exploitative ways in which Middle Eastern countries have, contrary to Fukuyama and the would-be geo-economic peace makers, *already* been economically integrated into the global system. The entanglement of geopolitics and geoeconomics in this major area of foreign policy debate therefore conceals the connections of economic integration processes (such as oil extraction) that repeatedly create conditions for international conflict.

Of course, the economic influences of capitalism do not explain everything. Geopolitical visions and feelings are also influential in their own right, and often have roots in other cultural imperatives associated with religion and racism. Take, for example, the geopolitics of evangelical "dispensationalists" who call fellow Christians to support of Israel ahead of so-called end-times in which they believe Jesus Christ will return to rule the world from Jerusalem. And consider the commonalities as well as the obvious contrasts between this ultimately anti-Semitic worldview and what was the widely reported geopolitical ambition of Osama Bin Laden to build a New Caliphate from the Middle East right across Mediterranean Europe. As geopolitically antagonistic and iconoclastic as these visions may be, if we only consider the cultural politics in such geopolitics, we miss the ways in which geopolitical plans more generally refract and reframe underlying patterns of uneven development. Even extreme cases such as the New Caliphate and new Christian dispensation vision cannot therefore simply be understood in their own fantastical-turned-fanatical terms. They have emerged in uneasy tension with other more enduring political and economic realities in the region, including everything from the geography of oil exploitation in the Persian Gulf and the expansion of US military bases to investment in the state of Israel.

The need to contextualize and complicate simple visions applies equally to moments when ahistorical geoeconomic maps are offered as antidotes to simplified geopolitical visions. For example, we often hear in this way from US business leaders that geopolitically antagonistic and xenophobic depictions of China are precisely the wrong way of looking at the country into which they are investing. They argue thus that geopolitical anxieties about China becoming a geopolitical competitor to the United States ignore the dividend of peace and prosperity that will result from the PRC's geoeconomic integration into the global economy. It is these sorts of claims and counter-claims that need to be understood in terms of uneven development. Doing so, we also need to be mindful of the ways in which the depictions and divisions of geopolitics and geoeconomics still have consequences. And to do this, we must first trace the way in which they have been developed as expert discourses in international relations.

Geopolitics has a much longer history as a term associated with statecraft and the formal geostrategic mapping of international relations. It developed at the end of the nineteenth century and in the early twentieth century as a way of both representing and reterritorializing the world in terms, literally, of inter-*national* conflict. As such, it mediated a historical moment in which empires were struggling to control territories around the world while the nation-state was becoming consolidated as a successor territorial system based on states enforcing national borders and advancing national security with citizen soldiers. Viewed by academic innovators such as Friedrich Ratzel in Germany and Halford Mackinder in Britain as a serious academic field, geopolitical theories emerged in this context to formalize and legitimize notions of asserting territorial control for national societies. They drew at times, as the Nazis did in developing Ratzel's notion of *Lebensraum* (living space), on racist social-Darwinian ideas about an "organic" fit between an ethnically defined national population and a so-called national homeland. But whether they used such ideas or not, most geopolitical theories tended to naturalize the nation-state as the sovereign space of a national population, putting much emphasis on defining and defending national borders. War was conceptualized thus as occurring beyond the borders of national territory, while economists, demographers, planners, and health officials used the same borders to define the internal national population as a focus for non-militarized policing and regulation. In this way, geopolitics represented an extension turned externalization of politics by military means, and the role of the military came to be viewed in terms of pursuing national security with external "foreign policy" operations. In countries with more expansionary business interests abroad, this in turn led to increasing geopolitical arguments about the need to use national militaries to advance national interests globally. And then came World War II.

After the Nazis brought shame on the geopolitical justification of aggressive territorial land grabs, geoeconomic ideas stressing global market-based integration became increasingly articulated as an alternative. Such ideas had already been promoted in the early decades of the century, especially in the United States where the Open Door policy before World War I was followed by President Woodrow Wilson's "Fourteen Points" vision of liberal internationalism based on open trade and respect for international borders. Appeals to America's "Mission" in these times often emphasized the economic opportunities of an internationally integrative commercial geography. And, even back in 1909, US companies heralded the prospects of productive and profitable opportunities across the globe as harbingers of peace. However, these ideals and commercial campaigns remained in tension at the time with all sorts of nationalistic and territorial ambitions (both in America and elsewhere), and it was not until after World War II that the United States was finally able to advance its integrative internationalism via the Bretton Woods plans: institutionally entrenching and globally expanding a liberalized yet dollar-based market capitalism. During the same period, former colonies were winning independence around the world, and in this context geopolitical ideas about expanding territorial claims in the name of empire fell further into disgrace (France's and Britain's brutal efforts to hold onto empire in Africa notwithstanding). It was no wonder therefore that American leaders preferred to talk about an "American century" rather than an "American empire," and, for the same reason, appeals to the geopolitics of the "organic state" were no longer used to legitimize national borders and territorial transcendence by major world powers. Where such geopolitical appeals were made in the Cold War was instead to criticize and contain the territorial ambitions of the Soviet Union and Third World countries, being augmented at times by accusations of "oriental" despotism that ironically turned European ideas about the "organic state" into criticisms of post-colonial nation-building.

In the 1960s, the actual word geoeconomics was still not widely used, and the work of the French economic geographer (Jacques Boudeville) who first developed it as an alternative to geopolitics remained largely unknown. He never did become famous, yet as the Bretton Woods regime evolved through the 1970s, 1980s, and 1990s into today's more deeply interdependent system of market-based integration, geoeconomic arguments and visions have become increasingly popular. Associated most obviously with the ideas, ideals, and perspectives on the planet of the transnationally mobile business class, geoeconomic visions have also moved transnationally, too, repeatedly replacing militaristic concerns with territorial dominance with networked notions of partnerships for peace. Thus, in place of orthodox geopolitics and its concerns for soldiers and citizens, this geoeconomic outlook tends to elevate the entrepreneurial interests of investors and customers; in contrast to a geopolitical focus on national borders and place, it privileges networks and pace; and instead of concentrating international politics on building alliances for "security" against supposed "evil empires," geoeconomics is primarily concerned with building international partnerships that advance "growth," "integration," "harmonization," and "efficiency," against the threats of "traditionalism," "isolationism," "anachronism," and "anarchy."

Not all advocates of these geoeconomic business perspectives actually use the term geoeconomics, and the would-be Ratzels and Mackinders of geoeconomics are still struggling to formalize its meaning. Most prominently, for example, the American strategist Edward Luttwak advocated geoeconomics in the 1990s as a new vocabulary for international relations better suited to a world system defined by border-crossing market competition. For him, this involved national leaders and security specialists changing their overall "grammar": conducting international relations with a view to protecting "vital economic interests by geo-economic defenses, geo-economic offensives, geo-economic diplomacy, and geo-economic intelligence."[5] More generally, other visionaries tend to work more with geoeconomic ideas rather than the term itself, using the grammar, as it were, while developing their own jargon to describe a deterritorialized world order in which economic integration is argued to overcome traditional geopolitical borders and battles. Thomas Friedman's "flat world" and Kenichi Ohmae's "borderless world" are in this sense just two of the more popular geoeconomic concepts among a much larger lexicon of "level-playing field," "fast world," and "wired world" cover-terms characteristic of a post-geopolitical perspective on the planet.

Commentators such as Friedman and consultants such as Ohmae are by no means the only purveyors of the emerging geoeconomic common-sense about globalization and the eclipse of geopolitical borders. Even military strategists in the most state-centric centers of geopolitical calculation have come to use related geoeconomic mappings of borderless global networks to conceptualize how militaries can themselves use market management models in an era of market-based globalization. Admiral Cebrowski, a former marine aviator who was appointed by defense secretary Donald Rumsfeld in 2001 to serve as director of Force Transformation at the Pentagon, took precisely this approach when he recommended that the US military should pursue "Network Centric Warfare" as a way of managing its geographically dispersed global forces through high-speed networks. "The organizing principle of network-centric warfare," he explained, "has its antecedent in the dynamics of growth and competition that have emerged in the modern economy."[6] Cebrowski argued thus that the US military could and should learn from corporations such as Wal-Mart in order to coordinate strategy, tactics, and operations across a borderless global "ecosystem." Moreover, in a complete reversal of Cold War containment geopolitics, Cebrowski also suggested that the geostrategic point of US foreign policy should also now be about connecting the disconnected. In this sense, Network Centric Warfare was not just about using connectivity for force transformation, but also for defining allies and enemies anew. "If you reject connectivity," he said in words aimed at defining threats to US security in the post-Cold War era, "you are probably going to be of interest to the United States Department of Defense."[7]

Perhaps most remarkable of all in terms of actually mapping the new geoeconomic world view has been the work of Thomas Barnett, a Pentagon planner who worked under Cebrowski in the office of Force Transformation. Coming to the Pentagon as a researcher from the US Naval War college, Barnett developed a powerpoint brief that he subsequently went on to publish as a magazine article and book under the title *The Pentagon's New Map*.[8] Given that this map exemplifies geoeconomics in an especially graphic way, given that Barnett also often highlights his experience taking part in a workshop on geoeconomic themes with a Wall Street brokerage company, and given that his blog *Globlogization* continues to offer geoeconomic perspectives on foreign affairs, Barnett's map-making efforts make a useful example through which to highlight the links between geoeconomic perspectives and globalization more generally.

In its bold cartographic outline, Barnett's map is simple and binary (see Figure 8.2). It divides the planet into two clear zones: "The Functioning Core" and "The Non-Integrating Gap." The Core is thereby conceptualized as the heartland of successf[ul] and peaceful integration into economic globalization, whereas the Gap is dep[icted] as the drop-put zone of countries and communities who have failed to in[tegrate]. Barnett explains in his writing that his map of the Gap was based on a re[view of] the places where the US military has been deployed in recent years[. Mapping] these places as the Non-Integrating Gap, he argues in the same wa[y]

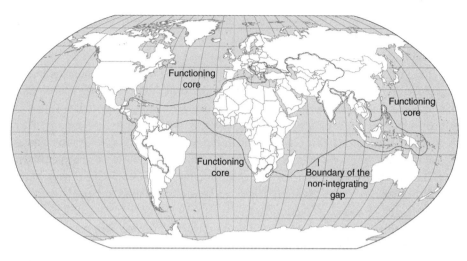

Figure 8.2   Barnett's mapping of Core and Non-Integrating Gap. *Source:* map drawn by Dick Gilbreath.

that the basic underlying purpose of US military interventions has been to reconnect the disconnected parts of the world by bringing them forcibly into the Functioning Core of globalization. This is obviously a different map to the bipolar cartographies of the Cold War. It is not premised on a geopolitics of containing communism or stopping the dominoes of Sino-Soviet influence spreading through Southeast Asia. Instead, it is a geoeconomic map that appeals to ideals of economic integration over containment and which explains terrorism and other security threats in terms of the alienation, isolation, anger, and envy of those that the map maps as globalization's outsiders. In Barnett's bullet points, "Disconnection Defines Danger," and international security become all about reconnecting the disconnected. Near the end of his book, he argues:

> In sum, shrinking the Gap gets us the final piece to the puzzle that is global peace. . . .
> What stands between us and the goal of making globalization truly global is the threat
> ~~forces~~ of disconnectedness – the bad individual actors that plague the
> n the Gap as their own, and the Core wins this war

sort of geoeconomic argument is just a new rhetoy the world's only remaining super-power. Yet such ies between the geoeconomic ideas expressed by shared, indeed globally shared, business views on he earnest investment in hopes about the benefits of policy-makers themselves. This institutionalized nternational appeal of the geoeconomic perspective in turn why American leaders have used it to justify recent wars in Iraq and Afghanistan. The 2002 *National Security Strategy* of President Bush, for example, explained the rationale for the Iraq War in the following terms:

> [T]he United States will use this moment of opportunity to extend the benefits of freedom across the globe. We will actively work to bring the hope of democracy, development, free markets and free trade to every corner of the world.

Similarly, President Obama's 2010 *National Security Strategy* continued with the theme of expanding freedom into the gap by asserting that: "In Afghanistan, we must deny al-Qa'ida a safe haven," while arguing that the "we" involved in such efforts should consist of all countries who can and do live at peace within the context of globalization.[10] And, even though they note that global economic integration will likely cause resource conflicts, disruptive migration, and other geopolitical tensions in the future, recent assessments by the US National Intelligence Council also continue to argue that the "benefits of globalization" outweigh the costs, that it is ultimately a benign development that will increase democratic opportunity, reduce poverty, and increase long-term social harmony by expanding a global middle class.[11] They therefore suggest repeatedly that the United States should collaborate globally to address problems like the 2008 financial crisis and keep the processes of global economic integration on track.

As popular as the geoeconomic arguments have been, however, at least two big contradictions reveal that their globalist vision remains deeply entangled with nationalist geopolitics at the same time. The first and most obvious contradiction is that while the geoeconomic outlook on expanding the Core and closing the Gap may be widely shared internationally in venues ranging from the World Economic Forum to G20 meetings to the UN general assembly, its implementation has involved all sorts of unilateral actions by the United States that have in turn been explained in the old-fashioned geopolitical terms of defending the "homeland" and maintaining national security. US National Security Strategy documents remain "National" in precisely this way, and whether they refer to "Our Nation" with a capital "N" or speak in elaborate terms about "Advancing Our Interests," they continue to articulate a strong geopolitical interest in national defense alongside their investment in more geoeconomic hopes about global peace through economic integration. Another second contradiction with the whole geoeconomic idea of reconnecting the disconnected is that it ignores the many ways in which geopolitical action by the United States and its allies in places like the Middle East and Central Asia repeatedly sets the scene for further instabilities. In reality, and in direct contradiction with Barnett's neatly partitioned world map, much of the anger, alienation, and terroristic organizing witnessed in the so-called Gap can be tied back thus to *the ways in which it has already been connected*, not to disconnection at all. And whether it's the long-term geopolitics of oil extraction from the Middle East, or the Cold War geopolitics of defeating the Soviets and funding the insurgency that became the Taliban in Afghanistan, or the contemporary geopolitics of attacks on insurgents across south Asia, the connections created by US national interests and interventions have much to do with longer-term patterns of global uneven development.

To summarize, we cannot look at contemporary geoeconomic maps of the world without noticing their entanglement with geopolitical ideas and engagements. We cannot pretend that we have entered some sort of post-geopolitical era. Instead, geoeconomic perspectives ranging from Luttwak's new grammar to the Pentagon discourse of disconnection defining danger all exist in uneasy tension with ongoing geopolitical assertions about national interests, national homelands, and national security. Indeed, just as the early efforts to articulate geoeconomic outlooks at the start of the twentieth century were attended by some of the starkest geopolitical expressions of nationalism the world has ever seen, today's proponents of geoeconomics also frequently betray their own geopolitical interest. After all, Luttwak conceptualized his own grammar primarily for the purposes of national state-craft, and it is geopolitical leaders that he therefore calls upon to protect "vital economic interests by geo-economic defenses, geo-economic offensives, geo-economic diplomacy, and geo-economic intelligence." Similarly, as we saw in Chapter 2, Friedman's flat-world geoeconomics assumes nationalistically the vital role of the US military in bulldozing the level-playing field and making the world safe for free markets. And notwithstanding all the ways in which the wars in Iraq and Afghanistan have been fought by the United States using network models and private-sector methods (including all sorts of outsourcing to private military contractors), the repeated recourse to patriotic public relations by the US government in the so-called "homeland" and the simultaneous assertion of American interests in oil and the geopolitical fate of allies abroad has remained a reminder that the geoeconomics of expanding the Core globally continues to be closely associated with the geopolitics of protecting fixed investments in national territories, too.

Meanwhile, notwithstanding all the geoeconomic visions of Pacific cooperation between the United States and East Asia, and despite even the paradigmatic post-Cold War economic threat of mutually assured financial destruction discussed in Chapter 5, China continues to make geopolitical plans and invest in weapon systems such as anti-ship ballistic missiles (including the much-mentioned Dong Feng "carrier killers") that threaten to undermine US military dominance in the Western Pacific and South China Sea. More generally geopolitical contentions are widespread across the whole of Asia. Thus, even as US National Intelligence Council reports wax lyrical about the rising wealth and benefits flowing from the global economic integration of China, India, and other parts of Asia, the region remains rife with enormous and enduring geopolitical disputes over national territories. Alongside the old Cold War legacy conflicts over the Korean peninsula, then, are all sorts of evolving disputes between newly powerful, or at least, increasingly well-armed neighbors: China versus India over Arunchal Pradesh; India versus Pakistan over Kashmir; China versus Taiwan over the autonomy of Taiwan and control of the Taiwan Straits; Japan versus Russia over the "Southern Kuriles"/"Northern Territories"; and China, Vietnam, Taiwan, Malaysia, Brunei, and the Philippines all in contention over the Spratly Islands. In so far as these very basic sorts of geopolitical dispute continue over national territories, it is a mistake to think that globalization has led magically to a post-geopolitical age. Uneven development persists, and with it ongoing entanglements of geopolitical and geoeconomic plans that in turn shape policies and practices, including military practices, in consequential ways that create unequal outcomes on the ground.

8.2 Global Cities and Speculative Urbanism

The tension between territorial fixity and geographical expansion at the heart of uneven development also operates at sub-national spatial scales to create other unstable entanglements of growth and decline. Geoeconomic plans for global integration here take the form of more localized efforts by the governments of cities, regions, and economic development zones to reach beyond national territory and fix global financial flows in local space. Most notably, the phenomenal growth of global cities or globally integrated mega-urban areas in the last three decades is a significant form of such post-national reterritorialization. Driving the growth of these cities across the planet are a series of processes that we will introduce and examine here under the title of "speculative urbanism." The processes of global city formation are speculative in part because they are organized directly by the financial speculation of investors seeking to secure and build their investments through urban development. But they are also speculative in the broader sense that they involve bets by wider communities of planners, governments, and privileged transnational consumers and real-estate buyers about the future shape of city regions, too. As we will see in Section 8.3, these spectacular bets and visions also involve significant revisions to the traditionally universal social and political rights of national citizenship. Even as the growth of global cities revitalizes ancient ideas about cities being the basis of citizenship and sovereignty, then, their uneven development and attendant forms of exclusion and marginalization create new kinds of social splintering and political division. To begin with, though, we must first review the big picture of urban development across the planet: a picture that makes the territorial scope of citizenship and sovereignty in the cities of the ancient Greece, Egypt, and Babylonia seem tiny.

Over half of humanity now inhabits cities, and in the Global South, densely populated urban areas are gaining an average of 5 million residents every month.[12] Not all such urban areas are always addressed in traditional accounts of global cities, and even some of the most graphic illustrations of global urbanization can sometimes obscure such city growth. Take, for example, a NASA image of the Earth's city lights that is frequently used to illustrate patterns of urban development across the world (Figure 8.3). The first things you notice about this image are the amazing clusters of bright lights across North America, Europe, and East Asia, and perhaps most revealingly of all, across the rapidly urbanizing areas of the Gulf States and coastal Arabia. Next, you see the lattice lights of transportation corridors linking urban nodes around the world, including the Nile river in north Africa and the Japanese bullet train network, as well as the US interstate system, the glittering maze of European networks, and the rather fainter trace of the Trans-Siberian railroad. All of these bright spots, however, contrast with the relative darkness depicted in much of Africa as well as in several areas of India and

Figure 8.3 NASA image of the earth's city lights. *Source:* http://eoimages.gsfc.nasa.gov/
images/imagerecords/55000/55167/land_ocean_ice_lights_8192.tif (accessed 31/05/2012).

Southeast Asia: areas that are highly populated and increasingly urbanized but not yet
burning energy through the night to light their cities.

Given the history of imperial racism that represented Africa as a "Heart of
Darkness" – a phrase used by Joseph Conrad as a title for a book about European
fears and fantasies about "Darkest Africa" – we need to be careful not to assume that
the lack of big city lights implies a lack of urban life or an absence of globally networked civilization. For the same reason, we need to approach the challenge of
understanding global cities with an awareness of their global variety as well as their
growing similarities. Some of the fastest-growing cities in Africa such as Nairobi,
Lagos, and Kinshasa may not be mentioned in traditional accounts of global cities.
But with their mobile and often globally traveled populations, their innovations in
hybrid world music, their recycling of western electronics and second-hand clothing, their consumption of foreign food and medicines, and their expatriate NGO
communities, they are every bit as "global" as London, New York, and Tokyo. Lighted
or not, then, global cities represent diverse kinds of urban cosmopolitanism as well
as linked patterns of capitalist integration, and our approach to understanding their
uneven development therefore needs to be attentive to both the varieties and similarities at the same time.

In terms of the similarities, global cities of all kinds teach us useful lessons about
the impact of global economic integration on territory, space, and place. Of course,
there have been many historical examples of cities defined in earlier periods by their
long-distance ties to other peoples and places. Imperial Rome, Caliphate Baghdad,
and Ch'ing Peking illustrated the pattern in ancient times, and London, Lisbon, and
Paris all grew rapidly as capital cities at the controlling centers of modern empires in
the eighteenth and nineteenth centuries. But today's global cities are distinct in their
scale, global proliferation, and trans-territorial ties. In 1950, there were 83 cities on

1	Tokyo	34.2
[flag]	Canada	34.0
2	Guangzhou	24.5
3	Seoul	24.5
[flag]	Ghana	24.2
4	Delhi	23.9
5	Mumbai	23.3
[flag]	Taiwan	23.0
6	Mexico City	22.8
7	New York	22.2
[flag]	Australia	21.2
8	Sao Paulo	20.8
9	Manila	20.1
[flag]	Cameroon	19.7
10	Shanghai	18.8
11	Jakarta	18.7
12	Los Angeles	17.9
13	Osaka	16.8
[flag]	Chile	16.8
14	Karachi	16.7
15	Kolkata	16.6
16	Cairo	15.3
[flag]	Ecuador	15.0
17	Buenos Aires	14.9
18	Moscow	14.8
[flag]	Cambodia	14.7
19	Dhaka	14.0
20	Beijing	13.9
[flag]	Zambia	13.8
21	Tehran	13.1
22	Istanbul	13.0
[flag]	Senegal	12.9
23	London	12.6
24	Rio de Janeiro	12.5
25	Lagos	12.1
[flag]	Portugal	10.8
26	Paris	10.5
[flag]	Israel	7.4

Figure 8.4   Ranked list of world's biggest cities with comparative examples of selected national populations. *Source:* data from 2011 CIA factbook at https://www.cia.gov/library/ publications/the-world-factbook/fields/2119.html?countryName=World&countryCode=x x&regionCode=oc&#xx, and from Peter Taylor, 2011, Mega-Cities in Theoretical Perspective, at http://www.lboro.ac.uk/gawc/rb/rb373.html.

the planet with a population of over one million; by 2007, this number had risen to 468, including 26 "mega-cities" with populations over 10 million. The UN estimates that the world's current urban population of 3.2 billion will rise to 5 billion by 2030, and global cities lead this urbanization trend. They are historically unprecedented concentrations of population that produce remarkable juxtapositions of wealth and poverty in landscapes that rise above – both literally and figuratively – the nation-states, regions, and provinces in which they are located. Ranked lists of the world's biggest urban populations further indicate their remarkable significance vis-à-vis the comparative size of significant national populations (Figure 8.4). But as well as having populations on a par with whole countries, it is the global networking of global cities and their internal extremes of wealth and poverty that stand out. Better linked to other global cities than to the rural hinterlands that supply them with land, utilities, food, and migrant workers, and often important as command and control nodes of global-spanning networks, global cities are also places that increasingly evidence parallel patterns of urban inequality with slums and zones of abandonment located right next to gentrified neighborhoods, private malls, gated communities, and some of the richest real estate on the planet.

The underlying processes of uneven development that produce global cities are themselves revealed by the tell-tale juxtapositions of affluence and extreme poverty. It is as if *A Tale of Two Cities* told by Charles Dickens about wealthy excess and hellish squalor in eighteenth-century London and Paris suddenly had new relevance, giving us a way of reading both the landscapes of global cities for the stories they tell about world-changing political–economic developments. "It was the best of times, it was the worst of times," began Dickens.

> It was the age of wisdom, it was the age of foolishness, it was the epoch of belief, it was the epoch of incredulity, it was the season of Light, it was the season of Darkness, it was the spring of hope, it was the winter of despair, we had everything before us, we had nothing before us, we were all going direct to Heaven, we were all going direct the other way – in short, the period was so far like the present period, that some of its noisiest authorities insisted on its being received, for good or for evil, in the superlative degree of comparison only.[13]

The noisiest authorities today must surely be the endless eye-catching online rankings of best and worst cities. Google "Best Cities" and you will quickly enter this ranked world of place-names and place-promoting lists that are themselves competing with one another to grab your attention at the same time as perpetuating a competitive way of looking at how cities relate to one another globally. We are invited thus to click lists of the most livable cities, or most miserable cities, best fine-dining cities, or most dangerous cities, most green cities, or most polluted cities, most sexy cities or most haunted cities, or, in a remarkable ranked list of US cities promoted in 2010 by a prominent pesticide manufacturer, most bedbug-infested cities! International rankings are run all the time too, of course, and whether it is best cities for tourists or best cities for business, or worst cities for corruption or pollution or health or violence, it is always the extremes that are used by the list-makers to attract interest. *Foreign Policy* magazine's famous annual indexing of the world's most global cities (as measured by the magazine's own metrics of trans-territorial influence) is just one of many examples.[14]

Rather than take all the rankings at face value, it is useful now to consider the ways in which they reflect wider global tendencies towards a new kind of *speculative urbanism*. Based on widely replicated entrepreneurial schemes of place promotion, tourism marketing, and investment incentivization, speculative urbanism has led to a familiar kind of global city boosterism right around the world. The most obvious and superficial signs of this boosterism are all the city rankings that have been driven by marketeers promoting particular cities or particular sorts of products. But beyond the promotion schemes, there is clearly a wider and deeper link between such ranking regimes and the individualistic forms of neoliberal governmentality we reviewed in Chapter 7. It is this disciplinary linkage that in turn explains the wider popularity and everyday acceptance of speculative urbanism. If we choose to visit or move to a city based on where it falls on one of these ranked lists, our decisions are linked in part to the ways in which we are individually enlisted and guided by the competitive logic of the list. Likewise, if urban leaders make policy in order to move their city up one of these lists, there is a direct governmental effect created by the ranking. Thus, if we examine the extremes and superlatives more closely, we can begin to investigate how speculative urbanism spawns neoliberal urban government and, with it, a suite of competition-induced commonalities.

On the one side, the wealth represented by all the expensive commercial and private properties in global cities monumentalizes the results of the relentless global competition for investment under neoliberal forms of globalization. Speculative urbanism in this sense introduces what is often called "spectacular urbanism." The palatial clubs and compounds, the luxury penthouse condominiums, and the massive sky-scrapers that provide an almost orbital world-view all serve thus as stunning illustrations of the material consequences that follow from competing for investment. Based on borrowed money it may have been, and empty though many of its offices remained after the global financial crisis in 2008–2009, the world's tallest building – the 828-meter-high Burj Dubai – stands as an especially spectacular testament to what the global competition for investment can achieve. And looking down from the Burj at Dubai's sinking attempt to create "The World" (a failed luxury resort made of artificial islands in the shape of the world map) one can also see how precarious and fleeting the attempts to fix global capital in local space can be (Figure 8.5). Nevertheless, it is the global competition to do precisely this – to reterritorialize deterritorialized financial flows – that has driven the endless promotion, branding, and ranking of global cities everywhere as great places to invest and visit. More than this, the global competition for capital has also been the big background influence shaping global city governance and networking, along with the ways global cities have thereby come to stand apart from the nation-states in which they are located (except, as happened in Dubai, when the property developers needed to turn to fellow UAE nationals to bail them out of the bankrupting effects of global financial failure). And as the governance of global cities has become increasingly disciplined by global market forces, so to in turn have their landscapes come to share similar landmarks. Neoliberal global cities therefore all tend to exhibit at least three out of the following four features of spectacular urbanism: (1) high-end mega-malls; (2) "gentrified" and "beautified" downtown cores; (3) big-budget mega-projects such as museums, concert halls, and sports stadiums; and (4) luxury apartment towers, gated communities, and other securitized domestic spaces.

On the other side, the devastating poverty of global city slums, shacks, and decayed public housing makes manifest processes of dispossession. Speculative urbanism in this way leads to another sort of spectacle altogether: shattered and shuttered landscapes of loss, division, and violent crime that have sometimes been called "splintered

Figure 8.5   World in Dubai from NASA. *Source:* http://eoimages.gsfc.nasa.gov/images/ imagerecords/42000/42477/ISS022-E-024940_lrg.jpg.

urbanism." Four main features of such splintering are: (1) informal squatter settle-ments and slums; (2) neighborhood gang violence; (3) police violence; and (4), in response, urban struggles by the marginalized for rights to the city. From rural land confiscations in countries such as India and Indonesia, to the chronic unemployment and welfare roll-backs that have helped foster inner-city drug dependency in countries such as the United States and United Kingdom, the processes producing splintered urbanism create fractured spaces that are often viewed as dead (or just deadly) when compared to the high-end residences, gated enclaves, and offices of global city afflu-ence. For the same reasons, the landscapes of the dispossessed are generally seen as a world apart or as totally different kinds of "world cities" from the global cities that regularly make it to the top of all the ranked lists. Yet such tales of two types of cities – glittering global cities that have apparently won the global competition for invest-ment on the one side, and poor world cities that are left behind like losers on the other – are deeply misleading. They hide the ways in which these divergent spaces of accumulation and dispossession are connected: that the wealth of one is tied to the poverty of the other. So instead, we need to trace the linkages. Following the way Dickens depicted the ties between London and Paris, and told a single tale linking the two cities, it is equally possible to trace ties between the vast variety of today's global cities, and to do this, we need to examine how they have evolved historically.

When global cities first began to be discussed in the 1980s and 1990s, their novelty as world cities was seen in terms of how they served as entrepreneurial command and control hubs for global capitalism in a period of post-Fordist economic restructuring. Their post-national or "denationalized" development was explained thus as the outcome of both, on the one side, national government cutbacks and, on the other, transnational networking by financial businesses (banking, insurance, and investment services) and other high-profit service industries (real estate, marketing, and media). As a result of the mega-profits and rents available at these pinnacles of global economic influence, global cities also experienced growth in low-pay service work catering to the consumption needs of the high-income earners (work in restaurants, hotels, cleaning, and chauffeur services, for example). And whether it was is in the high-paying jobs in finance or, as was more common, in the low-paying menial jobs, immigrant labor played a key role in making these cities more multi-lingual and cosmopolitan as well as more connected. London, New York, and Tokyo were the "big three" archetypal examples of this global city growth through services, and their dual track mix of concentrated development in financial and managerial services combined with low-income service work remains a common denominator (albeit with immigrant labor playing a much bigger role in London and New York than in Tokyo).

As primary or "primate" cities in their respective national contexts, and as places with long histories of international importance, the global networking of London, New York, and Tokyo is by no means new. Indeed, their growth as global cities is another reminder that the networks and nodes of contemporary globalization frequently build on historical forms of global interconnection, including the networks going out from older centers of colonial calculation. Yet, the ability of the big three to capture command and control roles in an increasingly liberalized global economy, and their rising stature in relation to older industrial centers such as Birmingham, Manchester, Detroit, Cleveland, and Nagoya, meant that they also enjoyed a newly global form of urban primacy. Like a number of other wealthy financial, media, and business service hubs – most notably, Brussels, Chicago, Frankfurt, Hong Kong, Los Angeles, Montreal, Paris, San Francisco, Singapore, Sydney, and Toronto – they also saw increasing social inequalities among their inhabitants as the differences in pay between high-income and low-income service work expanded. And it was precisely this primacy-plus-inequality that the term global city came to capture.

More recently, other global cities have emerged out of the shadow of the wealthy-world financial, business services, and media hubs. Bangalore, Beijing, Buenos Aires, Cairo, Cape Town, Dubai, Istanbul, Jakarta, Johannesburg, Karachi, Kuala Lumpur, Lagos, Mexico City, Manila, Mumbai, Nairobi, Shanghai, Seoul, and São Paolo have to varying degrees also become global hubs in their own right (although Beijing, Shanghai, and Mumbai obviously have much more influence as important new centers of global finance and global media control than cities such as Jakarta, Karachi, and Lagos). More than just places of population growth with their own home-grown patterns of inequality, they have become cities shaped by similar patterns. This does not mean that they are all witnessing the same sorts of post-Fordist service-sector-led restructuring seen in London, New York, and Tokyo. Nor have they become command and control hubs of transnational corporations. Indeed, recent attempts to map the interlocking directorates of the world's biggest firms show that London and western European cities remain dominant, with only New York and Montreal showing up as major hubs in North America, while Tokyo has become less linked as a result of Japan's decade of economic decline.[15] Rather than becoming hubs of corporate control, the commonalities shared by the new global cities have more to do with the competitive inter-referencing and internationally familiar forms of inequality that the global competition for investment now entails. The disciplinary neoliberal influence on urban governance of global competition and competitive rankings is an especially consequential common denominator in this respect, as too are associated increases in privatization and the role played in city government by public–private partnerships. These tendencies have in turn created the global convergence around newly entrepreneurial and investment-oriented approaches to managing cities. Urban boosterism is therefore no longer just about one-off attempts to attract investors or tourists or sports teams or big global events like the Olympics and World Cup. It is about doing all of this all the time in a newly intensified non-stop 24/7 global competition of speculative urbanism: a sustained, if not sustainable, multi-sectoral speculative exploration, speculative visioning, and speculative development of city spaces as if they were stock-market listings.

If speculative urbanism is what all the ranked lists of cities are representing and reproducing at the same time, how exactly does the process of speculation come to create common effects in global cities despite all the differentiation and comparison highlighted by the competitive lists themselves? Key to understanding these commonalities in global cities are three main mediating influences that shape speculative urbanism and make it so powerful: (1) the controlling role of global investors and associated investor ratings; (2) the steering role of consultants, meetings, and institutes offering expert advice on how to remake cities to attract global interest and investment; and (3) the governmental role of city leaders and new para-state agencies seeking to remake urban governance to attract speculative capital. Let us now consider each of these three influences in turn.

1. Look at the property news and advertisements in a business newspaper like the *Financial Times*, or go to the website of an online urban investment company, and you will quickly see how urban speculation and spectacle are linked. For the wealthy, global cities are not just places in which to store, secure, and show off wealth. They are also places that promise to make investors more money. This, for example, is how Citiesinvest.com explains the underlying opportunity to individual investors on a fairly typical, albeit verbose, website.

> We believe that to make the very most from a property investment, a would-be buyer should look to the world's urban centres. . . . Cities are expanding at a faster rate than ever before . . . [I]f it's profit you're after . . . the flourishing and rapidly expanding cities of the world are the logical choice for the modern investor.[16]

The underlying investment interest in global cities, then, lies in the way that they offer the prospect of making profits through property speculation, and this applies just as much in the brutal land grabs going on in Global South cities such as Bangalore as it does in the discrete sales of offices and apartments in historically rich cities such as Paris. Indeed, the beautiful boulevards and vistas of Paris were themselves once produced by brutal forms of dispossession in the mid-nineteenth century, and the way French financiers and the state conspired thus to takeover and make-over the streets of Paris has provided the model ever since. It showed that remaking city space can remove obstacles to city management and the policing of protest while also offering elites a way of soaking up surplus profits and putting them to profitable use. Particularly in periods of overproduction and overcapacity, this "urban spatial fix" strategy has gone on to be reproduced the world over. When there have been too many goods chasing too few consumers, the geographical displacement of the associated surpluses of capital and labor from commodity production into property development has thereby provided a provisional fix, allowing for the reinvestment of the money and redirection of the labor to develop new spaces. Global cities have simply taken this enduring capitalist need for spatial fixing to a new and gigantic global scale. Thus, the particular forms of architectural gigantism exemplified today by Burj Dubai and the mega-buildings of East Asia's fast-growing mega-cities can be explained in part as spatial fixes for the especially enormous financial surpluses being created by oil exporters and low-wage commodity producers.

Organized by diverse developers and property-management firms, the actual global speculation on city space serves the interests of a huge global investment industry that is constantly chasing better returns by moving money between different areas of the global economy. It should not be surprising therefore that the resulting processes of spatial selectivity mirror stock market selectivity, too. Just as stock pickers are constantly measuring risk versus return for particular stocks and funds, so, too, does the property investment industry look at the world map of global cities as a kind of stock market listing of opportunity and danger. In some cases, there are even formal financial market metrics and assessment mechanisms involved, too. In the United States, for example, investors consult the risk ratings for particular cities produced by the big three bond ratings firms: Moody's, Standard and Poor's, and Fitch. Ranging from the top **AAA** "investment grade" scores down to the Bbs and Ccs of so-called "speculative" and "junk bond" categories, the primary purpose of these ratings is to provide investors with a tool for pricing the risks associated with the bonds sold by cities. Just as with the similar credit scores issued by the ratings firms for corporate debt and national debt, municipal bonds that receive higher ratings are considered less risky and therefore benefit from higher investor demand, which in turn means higher bond prices and lower interest rates. By contrast, cities issuing bonds that receive only low ratings attract less investor demand (in part because some pension funds are forbidden from investing in any bonds below "investment grade"), and therefore have to offer higher interest rates to attract buyers. This, then, is the primary reason why so many cities strive to win high ratings. The closer they are to AAA, the lower the interest rate they have to pay on their debt.

In narrow accounting terms, what cities have to do to win high ratings is demonstrate a good financial history free from defaults, a reliable administrative structure, predictable cash flow and a promising fiscal outlook. Yet, as the impacts and implications of ratings have increased, city governments have gone to increasingly strenuous and sometimes desperate efforts to make the case for high scores. Such desperation reflects in turn the way a high rating effects more than just the costs of financing municipal debt. In addition, it also communicates greater security and promise to investors who are buying land and other assets in a city. Thus, receiving a high rating can also boost all sorts of private equity and venture capital inflows as well as reduce financing costs on municipal bonds. This, combined with the fact that US cities have continued to lose Federal government financial support from the 1980s onwards, explains why the ratings firms have so much leverage over American city government. Even though they are private companies focused principally on rating very specific financial instruments, they serve at the same time as gatekeepers of investment inflows more generally. And even after the 2008 subprime mortgage fiasco in which Moody's, Standard and Poor's, and Fitch were widely castigated for their misleadingly high ratings for "troubled" and "toxic" mortgage-backed securities, US cities have still had to knuckle down and do whatever it takes to win their high ratings.

The discipline of debt dependency and ratings forces cities to focus more and more on creating a so-called favorable investment climate. Promoting themselves with ritzy downtown development schemes, high-end shopping malls, and subsidies for attention-grabbing buildings and entertainment facilities, the constant mantra is that city government must do everything possible to win approval from potential investors. To be sure, the need to finance municipal debt does not always translate directly into crass Donald Trump-style urban boosterism. Parks and urban beautification projects can sometimes benefit from the efforts, as can plans for public transportation, or even efforts to introduce non-punitive "harm-reduction" drug policies in which addicts are given clean needles and safe places to inject in ways that are meant to reduce street violence and deaths. But even if the effects sometimes improve public health, the general direction in urban governance enforced by a preoccupation with investor confidence tends ultimately to be focused more on market well-being than on the well-being of all urban citizens. A plan for more social housing advanced by one city leader, for example, may be vetoed by others who argue that the short-term drain on the budget will lower the city's bond rating and reduce the attractiveness of the city to investors more generally. Speculative urbanism in this way represents another version of the disciplinary neoliberalism we examined in Chapter 7. It enables the invisible hands of the market to rule city governments in much the same way as they rule indebted national governments.

While urban bond markets are growing elsewhere in the world, including in emerging economies such as South Africa, Brazil, and Indonesia, the main corollary of American municipal bond market ratings in other countries are the sovereign ratings of national debt that, as we have already seen, enforce neoliberal norms at a national scale. Parallel private-sector risk assessments carried out by management consultants and accounting firms also generate powerful pressures over where speculative capital is invested at the scale of urban real-estate markets. Moreover, thanks to national neoliberal reforms that have deregulated capital mobility, the world's real-estate markets have effectively been globalized, which in turn increases the influence of these urban assessments. As city leaders around the world feel and see the resulting pressure from transnational investors, they also respond with more intense efforts at self-promotion and market-friendly self-regulation. Land clearances for big eye-catching infrastructure projects often get a go-ahead from officials this way, as do all sorts of mall-building, hotel-building, and luxury-apartment-building property developments, too. The resulting speculative landscapes do not always succeed in winning investor confidence, of course. Anxieties about speculative bubbles or overly ambitious and unsustainable development plans can even sometimes dampen confidence. Equally investors might be put off by other worries about the political stability of the country or region in which a city is located, or the long-term prospects for the national currency. But, despite these many complicating factors, speculative urbanism does have consequences globally as well as in the United States. It is not just an "American" or "western" way of looking at cities in terms of competitive rankings, promotional hype, and fancy real-estate advertisements. And it is more than a discourse or mindset. It is also a very practical way of organizing cities that creates real urban transformations wherever it goes, including the widespread tendency towards the privatization of public space, the building of malls and gated communities, and the more generalized depoliticization of civic life through the market-mediated management of development. To explore how and why this pattern is repeated the world over, it is necessary now to explore in more detail the role of expert urban consultants.

2. The urban expertise industry that has developed to advise city leaders on how best to attract and retain investment is now something of a profit-making business in its own right. Aided by multilateral agencies such as the World Bank Cities Alliance and UN HABITAT, co-sponsored by big banks and TNCs such as HSBC and Siemens, and co-organized by global management consultants such as McKinsey and PricewaterhouseCoopers, there are now multitudinous meetings, forums, and summits on the subject of how best to promote and manage globally "successful cities." Events such as the World Cities Summit, the Global City Forum, the Global Cities Dialogue, and the C40 Cities Mayors Summit thereby provide a steady stream of work for a wide range of expert institutions, consultants, and urban gurus. It is important to note, though, that not all these experts speak with one voice or hold to a single political orientation. Let us consider, therefore, some examples of the variety.

One of the most well-organized and omnipresent of the institutions offering advice on urban governance is the World Bank. The bank's pro-market vision of the economic geography of global cities has led it to offer predictably neoliberal nostrums on how best to work with market forces in order to expand the reach of speculative urbanism. "Many policy makers perceive cities as constructs of the state – to be managed and manipulated to serve some social objective," warned an influential 2009 world development report from the bank. Against such social objectives, the report's authors instead advised that cities should be serving market objectives.

In reality, cities and towns, just like firms and farms, are creatures of the market. Just as firms and farms deliver final and intermediate goods and services, towns and cities deliver agglomeration economies to producers and workers. So city administrators are better advised to learn what their city does, and to help it do this well, rather than try to abruptly change the course of their city's destiny. Planners and policy makers should see their role as prudent managers of a portfolio of places, to get the most from agglomeration economies.[17]

This is speculative urbanism in its purest form. City government is reduced to prudently managing a portfolio of places as if they comprise a stock fund, and the idea of having social objectives for cities is seen simply as an error.

Other expert discourses diverge, however, frequently making very clear social recommendations for global cities. Neoconservative neoliberals, for example, Giuliani Partners and The Bratton Group L.L.C., advocate for an aggressive law enforcement approach to city government. Their argument, based in part on Rudi Giuliani's record as mayor of New York City, is that "zero-tolerance" for crime and the punitive policing of the poor and homeless is vital for "securing" the city, making it feel safe for investors, and thereby ensuring the successful financial "securitization" of urban investment. The "[k]ey to attracting capital, tourists, and residents with disposable income," argues Giulani, "is the promotion of the city as a safe place to live, work, travel, and shop."[18] And thanks to the consulting work of Giuliani and others, his "broken windows policing" approach has been taken up elsewhere in urban areas as different as Mexico City and US-occupied Baghdad.

Yet another approach to securing investment in cities is offered by the Stanford economist Paul Romer. Proposed as a solution to governmental corruption and inefficiency rather than as a way for city governments to take over the streets, Romer recommends creating wholly new global cities as enclaves of technocratic rationality located on uninhabited sites with their own city charters. "Charter Cities," argues Romer, would be therefore run like charter schools, providing new freedoms for innovations in urban governance.[19] Instead of needing foreign aid, Romer thinks charter cities will develop like Hong Kong did historically, attracting private capital because of their freedoms and market-friendly rules. And having started out with radical plans to turn Guantanamo Bay into a Hong Kong for Cuba – an enclave in which to nurture free-market capitalism with clear-cut trading rules – he has more recently promoted efforts by the Honduran government to create a model charter city for Latin America in Honduras.

Instead of thinking in terms of building model global cities on uninhabited land, there are yet others who maintain that it is the quality of the inhabitants in already-existing cities that matters. Richard Florida, an American planner now based in Toronto, argues thus that the best way for cities to build investor confidence is by attracting the "creative class." He advises that cities should do all they can to make themselves into pleasant places for well-educated upper-middle-class residents to live, work, and play.[20] They should be clean, green, culturally diverse, and as open to gay and immigrant communities as they are to business. Florida presents himself thus as a fiscally conservative social liberal: annoying right-wing homophobes and anti-immigration activists, on the one side, and left-wing supporters of social welfare, on the other.[21] Advocating for gentrification in the name of creativity, he says cities should deliberately foster funky and hip downtown neighborhoods using their tax dollars to build bike lanes and other amenities for the affluent. Replacing the traditional business inducements of tax abatements and transport infrastructure, he argues the new "Ts" of global city government should instead be: tolerance, technology, and talent. And, as testament to his own talent for spreading these "Ts" transnationally, Florida's faith in the creative class has recently been heralded by the British prime minister, David Cameron, as a guide for redeveloping what was once the working-class east end of London.

From "creativity" to "sustainability," yet another set of urban experts talk about the need to fashion global cities as "eco-cities." There are traces of these ideas in Florida's enthusiasm for recreational amenities, and in Romer's suggestions that cities are the most efficient way of accommodating the world's burgeoning population, but other advocates for sustainable cities take the arguments much further. From the Australian "ecocity" architect, Paul Downton, to the American biophilic planner, Timothy Beatley, to Canadian bioregionalist, William Rees, who argues directly for measuring and reducing urban carbon footprints, these experts offer more criticism of unsustainable urbanism than city elites usually want to hear.[22] But this has not stopped "sustainable city" ideas and other related appeals to "green cities" and "healthy cities" from attracting the interest of both urban governments and corporate investors. Thus, coordinated by multilateral agencies such as the United Nations Global Compact Cities program, we are now seeing global cities attempting to attract new rounds of interest and investment with high-profile efforts at eco-city planning. And ranging from relatively radical proposals such as the City of Melbourne's "zero net emissions" plan to more entrepreneurial initiatives such as San Francisco's Business Council on Climate Change, these efforts are in turn attracting buy-in (to use the appropriate business metaphor) from corporations themselves.

There are many more schools of thought about how best to attract and retain investor confidence in urban areas. For the same reason, it would be mistaken to ignore the differences distinguishing all the experts advising global cities on how to be more "successful." Indeed, amidst the cacophony, more nuanced studies have even discerned the voices of critics asking the all important question: success for whom?[23] However, it is just as important to acknowledge the degree to which the whole urban expertise industry still buys into an underlying competitive idea that success is possible and that there are therefore necessarily market winners and losers. This explains in turn why so much of the global discourse over global cities resonates with marketing assumptions about branding, rebranding, and place promotion. Take, for example, a "global city blog" posting from the 2011 Abu Dhabi Global City Forum. In it, "global advisor" Greg Clark offers tips on "The Seven habits of highly successful cities," suggesting that cities should hire experts like himself to create a unifying promotional story that speaks to multiple competitive markets simultaneously.

> It is not enough for a city to have a brand that attracts tourists, cities must have an identity
> that reaches across different markets and customers and tell a unifying story about the
> value the city can add to the activity that is looking for a home. We cannot tell one story
> to the students and another to the business people, for example, because the students
> may become business people, and the business people sometimes also study. We need an
> organising story across many markets, not just a sales campaign within one of them.[24]

Ultimately it seems that what global city leaders are being told by experts such as
Clark is that they need to be able to fashion authentic and coherent stories about
their cities. Not surprisingly, the experts are ready in turn to provide many hours of
high-paid contract work to craft just such stories. What is surprising, though, is that
investors or anyone else can be persuaded by such globally outsourced and globally
circulated storytelling. Still more surprising is that city leaders themselves buy in to
the stories themselves. And yet, as we shall now see, this is what is happening with
significant effects on urban governance.

3. Picking up ideas from all the global city meetings and consultation sessions,
urban leaders start to look at their own cities in new ways. "Thanks to these types of
meetings and experiences and conversations," explained a city commissioner from
Jaipur in the Northwest of India, "I have begun to see my home city differently."[25]
Following the lead of ethnographers of speculative urbanism, such comments are
worth exploring further for what they reveal about the reinvention of the city
through global city story-telling. The reinvention, it seems, occurs through a two-
step re-vision process. First comes the moment when the old city is reappraised as
traditional, inefficient, unchanging and, thus, unproductive.

> When I look out from Jaipur's main railway station, I can see makeshift huts with women
> cleaning dishes and children playing and grazing their animals, the dhobis washing
> clothing, the small food carts setting up for the day, people meeting the call of nature. I
> have always seen this as a typical city scene in India, the way it has been and will always be.

Then comes the second moment when this deadened landscape is reimagined anew
as exciting, productive and, thus, potentially profitable, too.

> But why couldn't we build right along the station a line of nice hotels, corporate centers,
> and shopping malls? Now, I can imagine that Jaipur, too, can become a world city that can
> generate jobs and money and bring in tourists and make the city and its people much
> more productive. From this view, our cities are full of untapped value and potential,
> making them a very exciting place to be.

Such processes of urban reimagination are being repeated the world over. As this
happens, they also repeatedly reference one another, with the globally mobile city
experts and leaders picking up "success stories" from one meeting and taking them
to the next. This inter-referencing is in turn further encouraged and enabled by the
circulation of reports about particular pilot programs and demonstration projects
by global governance institutions that celebrate the successful make-over of one city
or neighborhood in order to demonstrate the salience of a particular approach to

others. The World Bank, for example, is especially keen to push aspiring global cities to develop land reforms that involve the privatization and titling of land. To do this, they not only promote titling programs directly through the World Bank Cities Alliance but have made use of a supposed success story of titling in Lima, Peru.[26] Here, in a few chosen neighborhoods, a pilot project designed to secure property title for the poor was strongly correlated with increased employment outside the home by adults and decreased employment outside the home by children (i.e. decreased child labor). The World Bank concluded that this showed how creating property rights for the urban poor generated positive social outcomes. Even though the study was biased by the fact that the neighborhoods that showed the positive correlation had easier access to employment opportunities, and even though the project failed to deliver on its original promise, which was to enable the poor to borrow more easily by using their newly titled property as collateral (instead they had to work longer hours), the story was taken out of context and circulated by World Bank-affiliated economists to justify titling elsewhere. The flaws in the Lima study have subsequently been highlighted by Columbia University political scientist, Timothy Mitchell.[27] But what Mitchell has also shown is that it is precisely the process of taking the demonstration project out of context that actually makes it more compelling. A one-off place-specific correlation thereby becomes a project-proven rule, and by becoming a rule, it is then used to help make rules for other places, too.

Whether or not the World Bank is involved in the reporting and associated neoliberal rule-making, global city inter-referencing conducted by city mayors and other leaders tends to work in exactly the same way. The resulting form of governance through demonstration projects is therefore very common in global cities everywhere. It is for this reason that we constantly hear such familiar refrains as the following: "Singapore benefited from recruiting creative capitalists from elsewhere, so can we"; "Bangalore benefited from becoming an IT and outsourcing center, so can we"; "Dubai benefited from making itself into a major global airline hub, so can we"; "Macao benefited from becoming a giant gambling center, so can we"; "Sydney benefited from hosting an Olympics, so can we"; and, perhaps most commonly, "Boston, Baltimore, and San Francisco all benefited from the gentrification of waterfront markets and neighborhoods, so can we." Reciting such "success" stories, urban leaders try to re-site them too, and, however speculative the attempts at replication might be, the resulting general trend is towards more speculative urbanism. To be sure, not all of this inter-referencing leads inevitably towards the neoliberal common denominators of spectacular urbanism. For example, many left-leaning city governments have sought to turn the success story of Porto Alegre's collective budget-making process in southern Brazil into a model for participatory budget-making in their own cities. Likewise, living-wage campaigns by workers, unions, and religious groups in big global cities reference one another for support, too.[28] But the more general trend is towards much less inclusive initiatives that are aimed first and foremost at winning investor approval. These market-friendly outcomes are explained by more than just the direct influence of market imperatives such as bond ratings, and the steering role of experts from institutions such as the World Bank.

In addition, a further transformation in the political organization and political geography of urban governance has also helped to expand and entrench the neoliberal norms. This is the development of public–private parastatal agencies of urban governance which are either unelected or otherwise disconnected from traditional institutions of city government.

Just as New York City emerged early on as paradigmatic example of a global city, so, too, has it illustrated how public–private parastatal agencies can takeover authority from city hall. In 1975, after New York endured its worst ever fiscal crisis and began to default on its bond payments, the big Wall Street banks that underwrote the city's debts grew frustrated with the unwillingness of the city government to lay off workers and enforce massive spending cuts. In response, they orchestrated the creation of a new parastatal agency sponsored by the state of New York called the Municipal Assistance Corporation or MAC. MAC simultaneously took over the city's outstanding debts and implemented the austerity the banks had been demanding. The resulting layoffs and fee increases, including big tuition increases at CUNY, led to a summer of labor unrest. Nevertheless, the transition in governing authority over the city's finance remained in force. As a result, MAC was subsequently able to promote a new investor-friendly set of development initiatives in the city, encouraging more gentrification in SoHo and Greenwich Village, but also broader and more ambitious mega-projects that included the redevelopment of Battery Park City, Times Square, South Street Seaport, and the Upper West Side. Over three decades later, having sold almost $10 billion in bonds, MAC settled its accounts in 2008 and shut down. Its work was done, and New York City was completely remade as a neoliberal city famous for its gentrified neighborhoods and spectacular city-scape.

During this same time, and particularly in the last 10 years, many other aspiring global cities have meanwhile seen similar methods used to sideline traditional government agencies. Sometimes supported by neoliberal national governments, at other times introduced by the World Bank, new urban governance principles founded on treating citizens of cities as consumers have simultaneously led to the creation of new public–private partnerships and agencies to serve the customers who can pay. As a result, parastatals have developed across the cities of the Global South to manage everything from garbage collection and telephone services to electricity and water supply. And just as in New York, this neoliberalization of city government has in turn enabled investor-friendly development initiatives and spectacular mega-projects. In Bangalore, for example, a whole suite of parastatals have basically taken over urban governance, flying over the old rules and offices of city officials in much the same way as a new monorail to the airport has been designed to provide for swift passage of the city's creative classes over the resentful populations, public health dangers, pollution, and slow-moving traffic jams on the ground.

Speculative urbanism in this sense is not just creating the spectacular urbanism of the monorail and other associated office parks and mega-projects. It is also very clearly related to splintered urbanism in which the rich and the poor of the global city live apart and move in radically different ways through space. It is to this process of spatial splintering, including all the ways enclaving emerges as a reterritorializing response to the inequalities and instabilities of speculative uneven development, that we now turn in more detail.

8.3   Enclaves, Slums, and Citizenship

As soon as you start to notice the spatial enclaves that are emerging in the context of contemporary globalization, they seem to be everywhere. Along with the private malls, gentrified neighborhoods, enclosed entertainment complexes, and high-security high-rises of spectacular urbanism, enclaving is also happening in a wide variety of other venues, too. The projects and landscapes involved range in spatial scale from large transnational regions and special economic zones, to sub-national resource-extraction enclaves, to business improvement districts within cities and towns, to self-contained tourism resorts such as Disneyland and cruise ships, to personal strategies of self-securitization that range from buying weapons and fortified deadbolts to investment in such mobile enclaves as SUVs, yachts, and, for the most mobile yet enclaved of all, private executive jets. Some of the original US enclaves – the suburbs of southern California, for example – are now so splintered by foreclosures and inequality that internal enclaving is also all the rage: elaborate security camera systems can be bought at Costco and Wal-Mart, the old-fashioned American mailbox can be replaced by a Secure Mail Vault ("the perfect curb side solution to mail box theft and vandalism"), and, for the extra-anxious there are always "antibiological invasion technologies." You can even tour the resulting landscape of division, defense, and decay in an SUV that has been branded and sold by General Motors as the *Buick Enclave*! Meanwhile, urban scholars such as Mike Davis (who is famous for his work on the enclaving of LA) report that the southern California pattern has now gone global, with elites around the world seeking to disembed their lives from surrounding cities and slums.[29] Davis sees a fundamental reorganization of global space going on in this way with elites creating a transnational archipelago of guarded spaces that are joined together through fortified global networks while also simultaneously delinking from the local poor.

Enclaving, then, is another way in which the deterritorializing ties and upheavals of globalization have simultaneously led to reterritorialization, too. Global networking, whether in the global city, in global commodity chains or in global movements of people, is coupled thus with local space-making. Even if it's the space-shrinking space-making of an expedited airport security line or EZ-PASS toll lane on a highway, it still involves the creation of a special purpose territorial control system in order to speed up the movements of elites and other customers who can afford to pay for acceleration. To explain these reciprocal ties between deterritorialization and reterritorialization, we need to recognize from the start the ways in which they reflect the broader neoliberalization of *citizenship*. In this broader process, transnational capitalist imperatives are increasingly undermining forms of national citizenship that used to provide – after much struggle in the nineteenth and twentieth centuries – social, political, and economic rights for large majorities of national populations living in the same national territory. Social rights to education, health, and housing were the last to be won in most countries and, for the same reason, have been the first to be undercut. Despite a deeper history in many democracies, political rights to run for office and to be represented democratically have also been undermined by the increasing corruption of politics by money and transnational media monopolies. And even in countries such as China where the historic lack of political rights was supposedly counterbalanced by social rights for citizens, neoliberal reforms are now creating staggering social inequalities. Meanwhile, across the world, something still more complex and bifurcated is happening to the old economic rights of national citizenship: on the one side, workers are losing national legal protections over the conditions in which they sell their labor; and on the other side, businesses increasingly enjoy the ability to protect property, make contracts, and move transnationally. Although the exact circumstances vary widely, what we are seeing emerge thus as a general global pattern is a neoliberal reworking of citizenship that tends to expand the economic rights, including transnational mobility rights, of the business class and the wealthy at the same time as it curtails the social and political rights of the working class and the poor. How then, we need to ask, is this neoliberalization of citizenship connected back to the deterritorialization and reterritorialization of space?

By exploring the emerging landscapes of global enclaving here, we can begin to offer answers by tracing the ways in which the reciprocal dynamics of deterritorialization and reterritorialization both reflect the wider reworking of citizenship. Key in this respect is another reciprocal relationship that is operative in enclaving itself. On the one side, enclaves generally involve forms of *economic opportunism* by the business class. On the other side, they also involve regimes of *political exceptionalism*: regimes in which traditional forms of national sovereignty, political rule, and collective rights are suspended so as to allow for the pursuit of space-specific and class-specific economic opportunities. The opportunism and exceptionalism are therefore linked, albeit in unstable and uneven ways, and the hybrid formation of enclaves reproduces the resulting contradictions on the ground through the boundary-redrawing processes of reterritorialization. Here, we will proceed by examining some select examples of enclaving from around the world.

We will focus most closely on: (1) a sub-set of special economic zones and cross-border regions; and (2) a sub-set of urban enclaving examples. As we do so, we need to trace how the reciprocal relationship between economic opportunism and political exceptionalism creates new boundaries affecting who can move where and with what sorts of citizenship rights. The lessons here highlight again the problem with the myth of the "borderless world": namely, that it obscures uneven development and the many ways in which deterritorializing ties also create reterritorializing responses. But more than this, what the enclaved examples of reterritorialization also reveal are processes of marginalization in which the expanded economic opportunities of some are predicated on efforts to exclude and/or suspend the rights of others. The exclusionary underside of economic opportunism thereby comes into view and, along with it, all the ways in which enclaving involves controlling and banishing those who the wealthy and privileged fear. In the last part of the section, we therefore end by examining the actual spaces of this global specter: the diverse slums of the world. Despite all the fears that inspire enclaving, these spaces of suffering and simmering resentment are hardly hotbeds of revolutionary radicalism. Nor exactly are they the inspiring examples of urban entrepreneurialism and self-improvement sometimes pictured by romantics. Instead, they are places where opportunism and exceptionalism return in informal and innovative, if also uneven and extremely unstable, combinations of personal resilience and shared vulnerability.

1. Special Economic Zones (also known as SEZs, Special Administrative Zones, Free Trade Zones, and Free Zones) represent especially opportunistic economic efforts to fix global capital in local space through political exceptionalism. The exceptions involved generally include: freedom from (or big reductions in) customs duties, business taxes, sales taxes, employment taxes, and real-estate taxes; exemptions from full compliance with national labor protection rules; exemption from full compliance with national environmental protection rules; and a whole suite of special privileges such as subsidized infrastructure and "one stop shopping" planning approval designed to expedite new building and development. Normal national laws and procedures, and routine practices of governmental oversight and management are thereby suspended or at least minimized in the zones in order to attract inward investment. Meanwhile, the young, often university-aged workers in SEZs see their rights to unionize, organize, or even just socialize with each other suspended, too. Housed in enclave-operated dormitories, often brought in from faraway communities on short-term contracts, and selected in countries such as China on the basis of *not* holding household registration rights to live locally outside of the enclave, workers are also effectively denied basic citizenship rights to move about and build personal lives beyond the boundary of the SEZ. As soon as work in the enclave dries up, as happened in southern China during the country's brief 2008 recession, they are sent back home to the rural areas and their families. Moreover, when there is work in the SEZ, workers tend to be disciplined with draconian in-house rules that use familial codes to discipline. "Good girls should behave like dutiful daughters," is a particularly common discourse in this respect, reflecting the sexist as well as exploitative ways in which male factory managers use the in-house enclaving of SEZs to exert the disciplinary authority of family patriarchs.[30]

In order to combine economic opportunism and exceptionalism, SEZs are highly territorialized, too: marked off on planning maps as distinct spaces, managed and policed by their own parastatal agencies, promoted in marketing materials as if they were sovereign entities, and bounded on the ground frequently by high-security fences, check-points and elaborate surveillance systems. It is a much-noted irony that all these so-called free zones therefore have landscapes that look more like concentration camps, military bases, and fortified national frontiers. But such ironies should be no surprise. As a number of scholars have noted, they are completely predictable outcomes of the neoliberal transformations in sovereignty and citizenship within enclaves.[31] Moreover, while freedom for contract workers and unions remains in deliberately short supply in such zones, the freedom for business is real. From the point of view of TNCs, the market-friendly neoliberal strategies of political–geographical reorganization are truly freeing, and, as advocates of such free zones also often point out, a common reason for all the barbed-wire fences and security measures is to keep people out as much as in. In other words, the desperation of workers in many parts of the world leads them to want to work inside such zones. Even if the working and living conditions inside are grim, the options on the outside are still worse. And thus, appealing to peasant farmers who have lost their farmlands as much as to economists who have lost faith in traditional governments, SEZs are an increasingly popular development strategy.

The popularity of SEZs is obvious in many parts of the world, not least of all in Asia where there has been a contagious outbreak of "zone fever" over the last two decades. Following the impressive growth of the first Chinese SEZs established by Deng Xiaoping in the early 1980s in Shantou, Shenzhen, Zhuhai, and Xiamen, many others have followed in Indonesia, India, Pakistan, Korea, and the Philippines. Yet more have been developed subsequently in China, too: on the Liaodong Peninsula, Shandong Peninsula, and Yangtze River Delta, and in the Xiamen–Zhangzhou–Quanzhou Triangle as well as across other parts of the Pearl River Delta. Competing with one another, and inter-referencing one another like global cities competing and conversing over success stories, SEZs have also increasingly experimented with a variety of economic zoning themes. We therefore see high-technology zones, bio-technology zones, and tourism-designated zones, as well as the old-fashioned, standard-issue "bonded" free-trade export processing zones (EPZs). There is also a growing "enclaves within the enclave" approach represented by Subic Bay Freeport Zone in the Philippines, the Aqaba SEZ in Jordan, and the Mundra SEZ in India. In these cases, sub-zones for particular industries and specialized economic activities are specified within the broader SEZ. Taking this approach to its most opportunistic and exceptionalist extreme, the emirate of Dubai now in turn boasts having multiple internal enclaves – media city, health care city, high-tech city, humanitarian aid city, and so on – even at the same time as it fashions itself as the Middle East's premier global city enclave, too.

Just as Dubai's differentiated sub-enclaves strive to fill distinct economic niches, the economic approaches of specialized SEZ enclaves vary quite dramatically. Some of the high-tech zones involve so-called top-feeding, high-paying strategies aimed at achieving "global excellence." A notable example in this respect is Singapore's *Biopolis*: a biotech business park which is appealing to investment from global pharmaceutical companies with a mix of financial inducements for world-renowned researchers, support for human subjects testing, and legal freedom from laws imposed elsewhere against embryonic stem-cell research (Figure 8.6). By contrast, other SEZs can be seen as following the model of bottom-feeding, low-paying "hyper-exploitation plus pollution" pioneered on the United States–Mexico border by one of the first forms of global EPZ development, the *maquiladoras* (Figure 8.7). Also known as *maquilas* (a Spanish reference to the "miller's portion" taken as a fee for processing other people's grain) these were originally set up back in the 1960s as sweatshops using low-paid women workers to assemble consumer goods headed for

Figure 8.6 Entrance to Biopolis in Singapore. Photo by Matthew Sparke.

Figure 8.7 Inside a maquiladora EPZ in Mexico. Photo by Guldhammer. http://en.
wikipedia.org/wiki/File:Maquiladora.JPG.

the United States. Following the implementation of NAFTA in 1994, there was a big expansion in *maquiladoras*, in border cities such as Tijuana and Juarez as well as deeper within Mexico. By 2001, over 3700 had been created, and as their numbers expanded, they also increasingly sought to win higher-skilled and better-paid work. However, since then, competition from Asia's cheaper and better-positioned SEZs has seen considerable trade diversion away from the *maquiladoras*, leaving a bleak lesson about the precariousness of EPZ development, as well as a bitter local legacies of high unemployment, gang violence, and murderous attacks on women.

While the Singaporean and Mexican examples provide striking contrasts, they are also worth highlighting for what they share, too. Like most other SEZs around the world, they have been developed within the wider context of increasing cross-border economic integration and liberalized (if not fully free) trade. This is important to note because this same context has also led to a further territorially distinct innovation in the standard SEZ: namely, the cross-border economic region. Seen as another exceptional way of spatially fixing the economic opportunities unleashed by transnational free-trade agreements, cross-border economic regions have been imagined and promoted in the NAFTA area and the EU as well as across Asia. The basic idea is that by spanning an international frontier, they can internalize the gains from liberalized transnational trade – including all the opportunities for economic complementarity, specialization, and thus efficiency – while simultaneously being promoted as "gateway regions" or "global city regions" that are open to international investment. Tellingly, it was this very same idea about reterritorializing at a regional scale in the context of globalization that originally inspired Kenichi Ohmae's announcement of the end of the nation-state. The full title of his book was *The End of the Nation State: The Rise of Regional Economies*, and many of Ohmae's leading examples were cross-border regions. One of these, the so-called Singapore Growth Triangle, has since become something of an exemplary case, used by other aspiring cross-border regions in other parts of Asia, North America, and Europe as an illustration of the benefits of the strategy. However, while this model of reterritorialization has gone global, the particular patterns it has created have varied as a result of contrasting continental trade regimes. We will conclude this survey of special economic regions, therefore, by reflecting on how cross-border regionalism illustrates both the similarities and variations that ensue (including variations in the place-specific forms of political exceptionalism) from pursuing a singular idea about regionalizing economic opportunity in different global contexts.

The Growth Triangle cross-border region links Singapore with the province of Johor in southern Malaysia and the Riau Islands of Indonesia. For this reason, it has also been called SIJORI (using the first two letters of each sub-regional part). However, since both this name and the Singapore Growth Triangle name have raised concerns in Indonesia and Malaysia about Singaporean primacy, its promoters have gone on to refer to the region as the Indonesia–Malaysia–Singapore or IMS Growth Triangle (Figure 8.8). Despite the name changes, Singapore remains the primary player in the design and organization of the region. From the initial planning by the

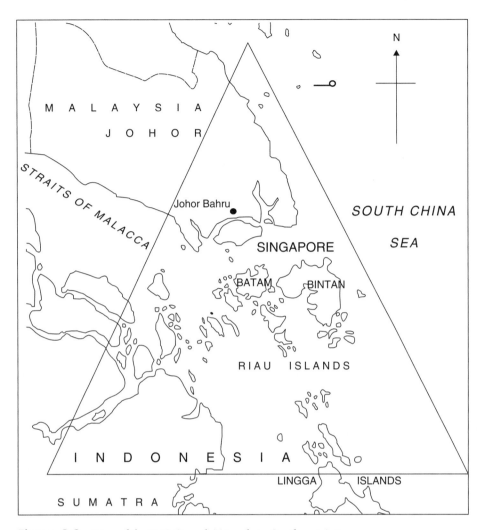

Figure 8.8 Map of the IMS Growth Triangle in Southeast Asia.

city-state's Economic Development Board, to its inaugural announcement by Deputy Prime Minister, Goh Chok Tong, in 1989, the Growth Triangle was envisioned as a way to enable Singapore's onward climb up the global development rankings by accessing cheaper labor, land, and associated resources such as water and food in neighboring parts of Indonesia and Malaysia. In this way, smaller EPZs on the Indonesian islands of Batam and Bintam have been incorporated into the larger triangular arrangement and, on this basis, are now also included as if they were part of Singapore for the trade preference purposes of the bilateral United States–Singapore free-trade agreement. But while the goods produced on Batam and Bintam qualify for free-trade treatment and easy cross-border movement, the contract workers brought in from Java and other parts of Indonesia to assemble them are doubly enclaved away: working and living inside fenced EPZs like Batamindo on

Batam, and standing no chance at all of ever crossing the straits of Singapore, the busiest shipping lane in the world, to see the head offices and big banks where much of their work is coordinated. Meanwhile, Singaporeans can enjoy visits to holiday resorts across Batam, Bintam, and Johor, finding increased mobility rather than restriction as a result of the cross-border enclaved development efforts. The Growth Triangle is thus in no way an equilateral triangle, being skewed not only by the dominance of Singapore's booming economy, but also by highly stratified and unequal mobility rights for the region's different inhabitants.

The NAFTA region also has its asymmetrical cross-border regions too, most notably that linking wealthy and militarized San Diego in the United States with the gang-controlled Mexican border city of Tijuana. Elsewhere, on the border between the United States and Canada, the more symmetrical wealth and development levels on either side of the 49th parallel have led to more co-equal kinds of cross-border cooperation. The Cascadia region, for example, spanning the 49th parallel and linking the US states of Washington and Oregon with the Canadian province of British Columbia, has been witness to almost two decades of two-way talk about "bi-national business opportunity," "two-nation vacations," as well as constant calls to "collaborate regionally in order to compete globally" (Figure 8.9). The idealized post-national "citizens" of Cascadia are thereby imagined most often as business people and transnational tourists: not national citizens with rights, but rather transnationals with money and access to the cooperative cross-border networks of twenty-first century technology. It was with this vision in mind that two high-profile promoters put their case for the region back in the 1990s.

> Cascadia is organizing itself around what will be the new realities of the next century – open borders, free trade, regional cooperation, and the instant transfer of information, money and technology. The nineteenth- and twentieth century realities of the nation-state, with guarded borders and nationalistic traditions are giving way.[32]

However, despite such post-national hype about Cascadia's economic opportunities in the age of NAFTA, the only significant achievement in terms of realizing the promoters' goals on the ground has been the development of an expedited-border crossing lane for frequent travelers. Now named NEXUS, even this project has been mired in funding challenges and concerns about US border security. Nevertheless, the underlying reterritorializing idea – of creating an enclave of post-national mobility for a subset of trusted transnationals and their trading relations – remains very much part of the local entrepreneurial imagination. And so, despite numerous setbacks, local Chambers of Commerce and business think-tanks on both sides of the border continue to pursue the Cascadian vision of fashioning a real cross-border region with its own maps, high speed rail connections and branded identity.

In the EU context, there are both symmetrical and asymmetrical cross-border regions, the latter being a notable feature of the regions linking new members such as Hungary, Slovakia, and Poland with wealthier western European countries such as Germany and Austria. However, cross-border regionalism within the EU is globally

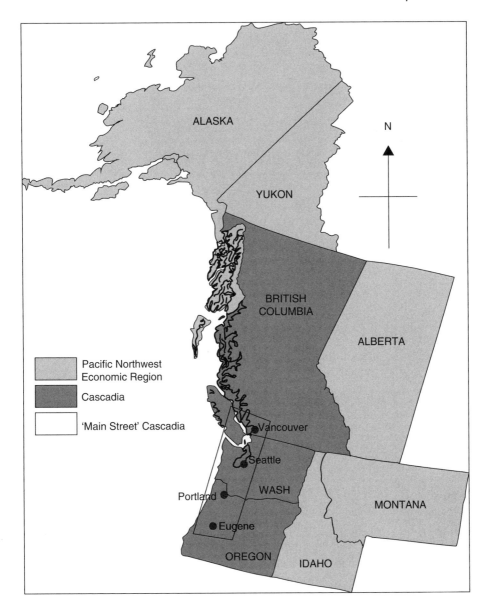

Figure 8.9 Map of the Cascadia region in North America.

distinct in so far as it has also been directly supported by government funding coming out of the EU *Interreg* program in Brussels. This EU governmental involvement has meant that local governments have been invited to take the lead in developing cross-border regional connections. Moreover, the EU has also provided additional support for certain sorts of social and environmental services that are not commonly supported in the cross-border regions of North America and Asia. Job training, health-service improvements, and local environmental protection efforts have all benefited in this way. Nevertheless, it is still the entrepreneurial visions of

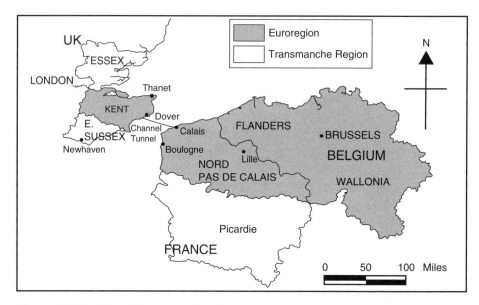

Figure 8.10   Map of Transmanche within the Euroregion.

competitive regionalism that tend to prevail. As was discussed in Chapter 7, this is the case in the Dutch–German cross-border region of Euregio Rhine-Waal. And there are many other illustrations, too. One especially unlikely example is Transmanche, a cross-border region between south-east England and north-east France that is joined by the underground and underwater Channel Tunnel. Beyond the obvious challenge of crossing the sea, history, too, also makes this an especially unlikely cross-border regional alliance. After all, from the Roman and Norman invasions of England to the Battle of Britain and D-Day, this has been a border defined by aggression, not cross-border collaboration. Moreover, since World War II, Nord-Pas de Calais has traditionally been a strongly socialist-voting area of France, and Kent is famous in the United Kingdom for being a county where the conservative majority is so big that it is "weighed, not counted"! So, it is especially striking that, despite these historic differences, the main collaborative efforts organized under the banner of Transmanche have been about promoting the region around the world (including in Asia) as a great place to locate business and benefit from speedy rail access to London, Paris, and Brussels. In turn, this is why Transmanche plans for cooperating locally to compete globally have also been tied to various other place-promotional cross-border initiatives, including a wider regional project that encompasses Belgium and which is advertised thus as another one of the EU's Euroregions (Figure 8.10).

From the Singapore Growth Triangle, to Cascadia, to Transmanche, these examples of cross-border regionalism illustrate how economic enclaving can be projected across international borders: the opportunity of promoting transnational gateway regions inspiring exceptions from national territorial norms. But clearly, this does not represent the end of the nation-state. Far from ushering in a borderless world and a complete eclipse of national-state territoriality, these cross-border reterritori-alizations create new regimes of social-sorting that advance the mobility rights of class-specific and nationality-specific sub-populations. Other people, by contrast, effectively become sub-citizens without rights amidst all the cross-border mobility. In Southeast Asia, unwanted migrants frequently find themselves held immobile for months on special island camps. In the NAFTA region, the NEXUS expedited cross-ing system is paralleled by the US government's "expedited removal" program for "illegal aliens," as well as by ongoing innovations in gatekeeping and fence-building on the United States–Mexico border. And, while the annual death tolls of the Sonoran desert and of southern California's freeways are globally infamous exam-ples of what happens when migrants are treated as sub-human sub-citizens, in Transmanche, too, the inequalities between trusted transnationals and their others are equally sobering. For paying passengers with the right passports, fast train trips on the Eurostar through the channel tunnel reduce the time taken to enter the United Kingdom from France to a mere 15 min. Yet, while creating cross-border connections for some, the Eurostar and the region it connects are not equally open to all. At Sangatte near Calais in France, one testament to this for a time was a camp for migrants (many of them refugees from Iraq, Kurdistan, and Kosovo) attempting to find their way into the United Kingdom. Referred to by supporters as "Sans-Gate" ("Without-Gate") and by critics as "The Jungle," the camp and its inhabitants became a symbol of the enclaved underside of the "Europe without borders" celebrated by advocates of cross-border regionalism. It was eventually closed down by the French government in 2009, but not before a number of its more desperate inhabitants had tried to jump on to moving Eurostar trains, some of them being killed or seriously injured in the process. In such tragic cases as these, the imagination of cross-border transnationalism is turned on its head, the hopes for attracting cosmopolitan capital with the promise of a networked cross-border future being replaced by scenes of cosmopolitan refugees losing the future and everything else as they attempt to join the network and cross the border.

2. Urban enclaving has also been marked by similarly stark divisions between the privileged spaces of class-advantaged citizenship and the dangerous and dispos-sessed margins of sub-citizenship. Homeless people regularly die on the streets of the world's "most livable" cities. Informal housing is regularly bulldozed to make way for new malls and mega-projects. And beggars, street vendors, drug addicts, and sex-workers are regularly banished from downtown neighborhoods in the inter-ests of encouraging gentrification and suburban shoppers. Meanwhile, as cities defund public services for the poor, the wealthy frequently attempt to delink altogether from public urban space by moving in to segregated and securitized pri-vate communities. One notable sub-type of this privatizing spatial response to urban malaise are suburban gated communities. While set apart from the other worlds of urban poverty that their residents flee, gated communities nevertheless remain worldly in their own way, frequently referencing one another in attempts to normal-ize the landscapes of neoliberal privilege. They are thus "often imagineered as replica Southern Californias," argues Mike Davis, and as such have subsequently globalized

an idealized vision of American suburban escape around the rest of the world. "'Beverly Hills' does not exist only in the 90210 zip code," he reports:

> it is also with Utopia and Dreamland, a suburb of Cairo, an affluent private city whose inhabitants can keep their distances from the sight and severity of poverty and the violence and political Islam which is seemingly permeating the localities. Likewise "Orange County" is a gated estate of sprawling million California-style dollar homes, designed by a Newport Beach architect and with Martha Stewart décor, on the northern outskirts of Beijing. . . . Long Beach – which the New York Times designated as "the epicenter of faux L.A. in China" is also north of Beijing, astride a new six-lane highway. Palm Springs, meanwhile, is a heavily guarded enclave in Hong Kong where affluent residents can "play tennis and stroll through the theme park, where Disney comic strip characters are surrounded by mock Greek columns and neoclassical pavilions."[33]

The globalization of the gated community model clearly involves architectural and symbolic inter-referencing as well as reflecting the wider neoliberalization of citizenship. Just as with the inter-referencing of global cities, there is a profoundly speculative logic at work in this respect. Much hope and much money are invested in the idea that building gated communities will attract capital and capitalists, and sometimes the speculation does not lead to the anticipated growth. The architectural and place-name references alone by no means guarantee that a gated enclave will attract privileged neoliberal elites. Uneven development may instead leave a gated community project looking like a failure even in its own terms. For example, on Batam Island, not so far from some of the EPZs that have been linked across the border through the trade ties of the Singapore Growth Triangle, there is another gated community development project named Beverly. Its location boasts views in the distance of Singapore (undoubtedly itself an influential enclave model and reference for many Indonesian developers), and the signs advertising the project evoke Southern California once more, albeit with a tropical twist (Figure 8.11). But when I visited the site myself, Batam's Beverly seemed a very risky bet indeed: the building was rickety, the construction was moving slowly, and the surrounding landscape looked more like a peri-urban slum (Figure 8.12).

When speculative plans to develop suburban gated communities fail (and even when they succeed), uneven development still tends to lead to other sorts of urban enclaving, too. Downtown gentrification, for example, is now a common feature of older cities all around the world. It involves wealthier social classes (hence the reference to the English word "gentry") recolonizing run-down low-rent areas of the urban core, buying up cheaper properties, and fixing them up in ways that signal the class transformation of a neighborhood. The metaphor of "recolonizing" is exact because the process really is about claiming and marking territory, frequently reclaiming it from renters and other populations who are considered in class terms as unworthy. In US cities, this class colonial aspect of gentrification is also often associated with the recycling of racist codes that depict gentrifiers as "white pioneers" moving into the "new frontier" of "the black inner city." But, whether colored by racism or not, gentrified enclaves everywhere tend to be marked by an aesthetic

Figure 8.11   Advertisement in Batam, Indonesia for a gated community. Photo by Matthew Sparke.

Figure 8.12   Building the gate in a speculative landscape. Photo by Matthew Sparke.

code of class control. Glossy paint, cast iron railings, and things like *Restoration Hardware* door handles frequently do signature service in this way as markers of the elite enclave. And in addition to the aesthetics, in certain cases the fortification of the gentrified area may go far beyond railings, reflecting the defensive concerns of pioneer settlement with conspicuous alarm systems, gated entryways, and security cameras (concealed though they might be in places like London in antique street utilities). In these defensive ways, the urban frontier of gentrification therefore often merges with another related enclaving trend: the fortified in-city enclave.

Particularly within inner cities where gang violence, drug wars, and militaristic policing have followed neoliberal reforms and cutbacks, elites are giving up on the traditional public sphere altogether, securing themselves in the equivalent of urban fortresses. Fortified urban enclaving has therefore gone global. Concrete walls, barbed wire fences, electronic surveillance, militarized private patrols, and a new focus on security concerns in urban design and architecture can therefore be found around the world. Of course, such enclaving does not simply unfold in the same way everywhere. Local histories and geographies are always more complex than this, with the processes of neoliberalization and enclosure often inspiring counter-movements to reclaim and revalue public space by cross-class social alliances. Another complicating factor in many cities in the Middle East and South Asia is the direct state-led militarization of space, too. As a result, private forms of fortification are being built right next to military compounds and enclaves, the most obvious being Baghdad's Green Zone. These are imposed forms of hyper-fortified enclaving that obviously owe more to state security needs than to the social class concerns of defensive neoliberal elites (even if they inspire such elites to buy Humvees and create similar spaces themselves, and even if they have been justified back in America in the neoliberal name of spreading freedom and free enterprise). Meanwhile, if we consider peace-making instead of war-making, Katharyne Mitchell's work comparing Paris and Marseille suggests that the ways in which cities are networked with other peoples and places plays an important role in determining whether fortified enclaving or peaceful coexistence develop in the context of neoliberal restructuring and austerity.[34] Marseille, she argues, with its interethnic networks and links across the Mediterranean, models another, less violent way of being a global city, distinct from Paris with its speculative investments (old and new) in a more enclaved urban landscape. In other words, all the while global cities and their elites repeatedly refer to similar models, fortified urban enclaving is by no means inevitable, or always created in the same way by local-global ties.

Other patterns of neoliberal urban enclaving that are more consistent around the world relate directly to the business activities and organizing influences of TNCs. Private shopping malls, for example, with their familiar clusters of brand-name stores, fast-food outlets, and coffee shops illustrate this most obviously. Striving to recreate the feel of traditional public spaces with architectural cues and vernacular street signage, malls nevertheless remain definitively and legally private spaces, where behaviors that diverge from shopping and consumption are strictly curtailed. Many young kids escape to malls with their friends, often seeing them as a safe zone of freedom and experimentation away from family surveillance. But when they try taking photographs or organizing a consumer protest of some kind, the freedom quickly ends, mall security intervenes, and everyone is reminded that the mall is not the same as the city street. Indeed, like the EPZs and SEZs where most of the commodities sold in malls are assembled, shopping malls clearly mix economic opportunism with political exceptionalism. Your rights as a citizen to speak freely are suspended, at the same time as your right to spend freely is enlisted as part of the mall's economic opportunity structure. And should you actually want to encourage fellow consumers to consider a political concern such as the rights of workers in the zones that supplied the commodities, you would find that this is not allowed within the urban enclave of shopping. As Naomi Klein puts it with great passion and verve in *No Logo*, the shopping mall and the EPZ thereby parallel one another as enclaves of unfreedom at opposite ends of global commodity chains.[35] They are obviously tied together as spaces, but most of the shoppers and most of the workers do not know or think about this because they are so profoundly enclaved apart.

One final example of urban enclaving that is also business-related is closely associated with the forms of speculative urbanism discussed in Section 8.2. Known appropriately by the speculative-sounding acronym "BID," the "Business Improvement District" is another fast-spreading form of spatial privatization in cities both large and small. BIDs are particularly common in global cities and towns where neoliberal cutbacks in services have come to undermine business confidence. In response, local businesses band together to create a kind of corporate gated community within urban space: a zone in which the BID raises fees from members to pay for services that may no longer be provided by the public city government. Almost 1000 BIDs now exist in the United States, including 64 in New York City alone, and many more have been developed in the United Kingdom, Ireland, Germany, New Zealand, South Africa, Jamaica, Serbia, and Canada (which actually experimented with the world's first BID in Toronto in 1970). Sometimes also referred to as business revitalization zones (BRZs), community improvement district (CIDs), special services area (SSAs), or special improvement district (SIDs), the basic idea is to compensate within a select sub-area of the city for declining or non-existent city-wide services. Within the BID, businesses therefore agree to tax themselves to fund special services (such as private security) and urban development (such as streetscape beautification). This in turn allows members to fund the shared services they want and need without being obliged to support similar services through the whole city. Not only does this protect them from service cutbacks and other forms of citywide austerity and decline. It also allows BID members to further delink from and defund the project of shared city governance. They can join anti-tax revolts with impunity, and they can support politicians who campaign for "smaller government" and other neoliberal reforms without worrying that this will diminish their own special services. BIDs therefore also represent a political and economic bid to entrench neoliberal norms of citizenship in urban space.

Running through all the examples of urban enclaves we have reviewed here is a common concern with security. Unsurprisingly, therefore, it is widely assumed that enclaving involves attempts to make exceptions not only for reasons of economic opportunity, but also for reasons of defense. Enclaves are interpreted in this way by both their defenders and critics as spatial efforts by wealthier classes to protect themselves and their assets from others deemed to be a threat. And this is how we come to the slum, a term long associated with concerns among elites about the threats posed to social and economic order by the geographical concentration of an urban underclass. The term goes back to the 1800s and early references by Dickens and other Victorians to the co-development of "back slums" behind the expansion of London, Manchester, and other big cities at the center of global imperial networks. As the link to Dickens might suggest, there was always also a *Tale of Two Cities* aspect to slums in so far as they were seen to threaten or at least overshadow the very processes of city development that they supported. Today it seems these same ties and tensions persist in global cities everywhere. Enclaves of privilege that have benefited from neoliberal reforms are thereby juxtaposed to their urbanized inverse: the spatial concentrations of poverty, poor housing, unemployment, hunger, sickness, and rising crime that are the widespread global legacy of structural adjustment and other neoliberal policy reforms. It is almost as if some sort of "global slum space" haunts the globally networked spaces of neoliberal enclaving like a ghost or shadow. But while such ghost stories may well reveal the fears that inspire enclaving, they repeatedly fail to describe the reality of slum life and what slum dwellers – many of whom reject the word "slum" as derogatory – find fearful and threatening themselves. We therefore need to go beyond the slurs about slums and learn from research that has actually compared their complex reality with the fearful view from the enclave.

We know from the reporting work of *UN-Habitat* – the UN Agency dedicated to addressing city and settlement problems around the world – that the global slum population is growing fast. In 2007, it was close to a billion people worldwide, and the agency estimates that by 2020 the total worldwide slum population will be about 1.4 billion – meaning that at least one out of every three city dwellers on the planet will be living in slum conditions.[36] Given these enormous numbers and their global prevalence, it should hardly be surprising that slums are also very varied. They have diverse local histories of development, and the importance of local context in defining the character of slums is indexed by the long list of alternative names used to describe slum-like developments globally. Vernacular terms include: *shanty towns* (Jamaica and Trinidad), *townships* (South Africa), *new villages* (Malaysia), *favelas* (Brazil), *colonias* (Mexico), *desakotas* (Indonesia), *chawls* (India), *gecekondus* (Turkey), *pueblos jóvenes* (Peru), *bidonvilles* (France, Tunisia, Haiti), *asentamientos* (Guatemala), *campamentos* (Chile), and *barrios* or *Villas Miseria* (Argentina). Other names also come and go. In the United States, for example, we no longer talk about *Hoovervilles*, but today there is much discussion of *Tent Cities*, the homeless encampments that have proliferated across the United States in the aftermath of the recent foreclosure crises (and which as such have inspired in turn the protest tent cities of the Occupy movement). Part of the purpose of calling these encampments Tent Cities is to reject negative stereotypes about street people as social "outcasts" and "bums." By instead creating spaces, albeit temporary ones, that are premised on the idea that the homeless are also citizens with enduring social relations, organizational skills, and rights to the city, Tent Cities force urban elites to confront the problems producing homelessness rather than pretend they do not exist. This is of wider relevance because similar organizational strategies underpin other related alternatives to the word slum, too. Thus, *squatter settlements* and *shack settlements* are also both frequently used as more affirmative names: names that point towards the agency and constructive capabilities of slum dwellers (actively squatting and shack-building) in opposition to ideas about their delinquency and capacity for disorder.

Beyond the global variation and organization of slums, there is another bigger problem with attempts to present them as a singular source of danger from which elites need to enclave themselves away. In short, these enclaving impulses obscure how it is the dangers facing slum dwellers themselves rather than the dangers they pose to enclaves that ultimately define slums. Four main sets of dangers stand out in this respect as the most common threats facing slum dwellers around the world. (1) Slums are first and foremost places of extreme poverty, poor employment options, and hyper-exploitation. (2) They are also places where the inhabitants face constant dangers because of the lack of durable and sufficiently sized living quarters. (3) The inadequacy of slum housing is in turn closely connected to threats to slum dwellers' health and well-being that stem from unreliable utilities, including bad water, sanitation, and electricity supply in slums. And (4) slum dwellers are also threatened by their lack of tenure and associated urban citizenship rights, a form of legal and political insecurity that makes them especially vulnerable to evictions, land grabs, and gang violence. These dangers come together to define slums, but they by no means make all the landscapes of slum-living look the same. Slums may be situated in the middle of cities or on the outskirts; they may involve precarious forms of land title or, as is more common, complex renting and sub-renting relationships; and they may be located anywhere from public housing towers to flophouses to pirate subdivisions, city streets, graveyards, flood plains and landslide-prone hillsides. Nevertheless, despite all of these and other variations, the extreme poverty, the crowded fragility, the unhealthy unreliability of utilities, and the insecure tenure and citizenship protections, all remain constant.

Summing up its own assessment of slum dweller vulnerabilities around the world, UN Habitat suggests that they reveal huge inequalities in the state of the world's cities: "a tale of two cities within one city, where non-slum populations enjoy good health and education, while slum communities suffer from both poor health and lack of opportunities." Slums, the agency concludes, "are not only a manifestation of poor housing standards, lack of basic services and denial of human rights, they are also a symptom of dysfunctional urban societies where inequalities are not only tolerated, but allowed to fester." To be sure, the word "fester" here might be claimed to play on the fearful image of slums as pathological breeding grounds of social disorder. Critics charge that when government officials replicate this sort of rhetoric and repeat slogans like "Cities Without Slums," they tend to focus on slum clearance strategies rather than addressing the underlying processes creating inequality and slum development in the first place. Relatedly, a critical concern with the UN's pursuit of Millennium Development Goal 7, target 11 – "to improve the lives of at least 100 million slum dwellers by 2020" – is that it encourages forced slum evictions as a simple way to meet the target. But on this threat to slum-dwellers, UN Habitat sees the danger coming from a different direction entirely: namely the rise of intolerant attitudes among urban elites associated with the global competition for investment (and the various forms of speculative urbanism we examined in Section 8.2). Rejecting this neoliberal splintering of urban citizenship, UN Habitat instead argues that slums can be improved by reducing the threats facing slum-dwellers themselves. By focusing on the improvement of slum lives rather than on the clean up of slum-space, slum transformation becomes part of creating more just and sustainable cities, and these efforts can in turn, it is argued, contribute towards achieving the UN's wider Millennium Development Goals.

One of the main strategies repeatedly recommended as a way of reducing the vulnerabilities of slum dwellers is that of securing tenure. Secure tenure means protection against eviction, and this generally means having some sort of documentation or other widely recognized public understanding that indicates that slum dwellers have legitimate tenure and rights to live in a particular part of city space. Many global experts and agencies, including (as we saw in Section 8.2) the World Bank, believe that secure tenure simply means holding private property or "title." They argue that "slum upgrading" – with the provision of more durable buildings and more reliable utilities – should also therefore be legally founded on the titling of slum property. However, slum-dweller organizations themselves indicate that the challenges are more complex. Thus, the website of *Slum Dwellers International* concurs about secure tenure being vital, but also explains the associated problems when the titling of private property is used as the method amidst the wider pressures of speculative urbanism.

> Securing tenure is not without its complexities and often leads to the softest form of eviction yet. In many cases, simply giving out title deeds has created an increase in poverty by placing slumdwellers at the mercy of a voracious property market. Slightly richer people, with an eye toward entrepreneurial development, scoop up newly secured property to resell or rent. And what family isn't going to trade in a shack for more money than they could get in 5 years?[37]

Despite all the evidence of its problems, the strategy of upgrading through titling slum property still has its fans, and to explain why, we need to return to the ways in which slums have been repeatedly reinterpreted amidst the wider patterns of uneven development we have been exploring throughout the whole chapter. Slums have been regularly viewed through history as recuperable sites of salvation through innovations in "self-help" entrepreneurialism. They thus become proving grounds for various experiments in pushing forward the global frontiers of capitalism and integrating its perceived outside and other. Contemporary efforts to promote titling and private property as a form of slum upgrading need in this way to be seen as part of an integrative inversion of enclave fears: an inversion that reconnects slums directly to the territorial tensions at the heart of uneven development. In short, titling extends the "private property to the rescue" solution of the enclave itself, offering planning proposals focused on the heroism and future fortunes to be found "at the bottom of the pyramid."

Many romantic impulses come together to make praise for the entrepreneurialism of the poor popular, leading to what Ananya Roy describes as "Slumdog City" storytelling.[38] Taking off from the basic humanitarian urge to repudiate dehumanizing depictions of slums as danger zones filled with sub-human sub-citizens, these stories reinterpret the slum anew as a space of hope. Thus, the typical romantic story has two parts. First comes an account of the horrible reality of slum life; and second comes the invitation to see the squalor afresh as a site of entrepreneurial opportunity. "Across a filthy, rubbish-filled creek we enter the slum's heaving residential area," reads a typical example of the genre.

> Live wires hang from wobbly walls; we crouch through corridor-like passages between houses made from reclaimed rubble as the sky disappears above our heads. Behind flimsy doorway curtains we spy babies sleeping on dirty mattresses in tiny single room homes, mothers busy washing, cooking and cleaning. The few hours I spend touring Mumbai's teeming Dharavi slum are uncomfortable and upsetting, teetering on voyeuristic. They are also among the most uplifting of my life. Instead of a neighbourhood characterised by misery, I find a bustling and enterprising place, packed with smallscale industries defying their circumstances to flourish amidst the squalor. Rather than pity, I am inspired by man's alchemic ability to thrive when the chips are down.[39]

Thus, while discomfort and suffering may be all around, romantic responses such as this offer revisionist accounts of slums providing training grounds and resources for building better lives. It is a compelling kind of storyline because instead of demeaning slum dwellers, it presents them as heroic figures of human perseverance. For the same reason, it should be no surprise that successful movies such as *Slumdog Millionaire* take us on the same romantic ride. From the initial depiction of slum horrors in India, we are transported thus to a satisfying story-book conclusion in which a single successful individual climbs the class ladder out of the slum. The big problem with all the story-telling, of course, is that in reality we are not seeing so many happy endings. Roy suggests thus that the romantic vision of the "Slumdog City" instead obscures what is in fact a much more complicated and less satisfying reality of "subaltern urbanism."

Subaltern urbanism for Roy is a name for all the different ways in which the informal urban lives of the poor and marginal complicate simple stories of the slum as a dangerous dystopia turned enterprising utopia. Instead of these simple stories with their "poverty pornography" and "entrepreneurial escapes," Roy suggests we need to keep track of the multiple ways slum-dwellers innovate urban space in diverse informal peripheries, gray spaces, and zones of exception. Like Mike Davis, she suggests that a politics of opportunistic occupancy is more important to this informality for slum-dwellers than the entrepreneurialism so prized by neoliberal policy makers. And, by highlighting these complexities of subaltern urbanism, she, Davis, and other scholars of slum-dweller agency make it possible to notice the ways in which slums ultimately capsize the economic opportunism and political exceptionalism of enclaves. For example, *Slum Dwellers International* argue that better opportunities for secure tenure can be found in taking exception to the global titling trends and developing collective regimes instead.

> For SDI, the goal then is to create tenure situations that work for communities without subjecting them to increased market forces. Poor people in South Africa, India, Brazil and Kenya have been instrumental in designing communal tenure arrangements that ensure the current residents actually benefit from increased security, and can set about building their dream houses little by little.

In efforts such as these, the economic opportunitism involved is clearly quite different to the more possessive and individualistic opportunism of the enclave. Slum dwellers *have* to be opportunistic in this way to survive all the while they are treated as political exceptions by governments and landlords that try to evict them. Political exceptionalism is not something that they choose, unemployment and underemployment are their normal experience, and any economic opportunities they can secure are therefore both limited and precarious. Moreover, as we shall examine in Chapter 9 on global health, the life-shortening consequences of slum poverty and vulnerability create very different health outcomes to those enjoyed in enclaves of privilege. But, in so far as slums capsize the enclaving imperatives of opportunism and exceptionalism, they also obviously reterritorialize the landscape, too. They serve thus as another especially sobering reminder that the deterritorializing impacts of neoliberal globalization have not created a borderless or flattened world with mobility rights for all.

To end by returning to the reterritorializing tensions between geopolitics and geoeconomics examined in the first section of this chapter, we should conclude here by noting that slums are also now a major territorial preoccupation of Pentagon planners, too. In a globalized world where a so-called "youth bulge" is massed in giant slums like Baghdad's Sadr City, the specter of global slum space returns to haunt US global military strategy (and the over 200 foreign bases and compounds that create the fortified global network of America's military dominance). As a result, "Military Operations in Urban Terrain" now has its own strategic specialists as well as an acronym (MOUT). For these specialists, the opportunistic urbanism of the slum presents a target of opportunity, too. Sometimes, this opportunity is conceptualized in geoeconomic terms as a target for economic integration and the kinds of social and cultural outreach that General David Petraeus has promoted in Iraq and Afghanistan. At other times, it is seen instead in geopolitical terms as a danger zone better approached through the targeting protocols of bombers and Predator drones. So, here again, then, we find uneven development at work. And as this chapter has shown throughout, and as the enclaves and slum developments discussed in this last section make especially clear, the resulting connections *across* space simultaneously create deep divides *in* space at the very same time.

Student Exercises

Individual:

1. A common complaint around mobile communications and networking technology today is that it is ironically leading to more alienated individual lives cut off from embodied social relations. Read the following comments on the pros and cons of constant contact social networking, and explain, based on your reading of this chapter, whether you think the space-transcending technologies are simultaneously turning their users into spatially disconnected enclaves.

> *I Will Check My Phone At Dinner And You Will Deal With It.*
> Love it or hate it, this is becoming the norm. And when it fully becomes the norm, there will no longer be the same stigma attached to checking your phone at a restaurant. Naturally, my mother refuses to believe this will happen, but it's happening already. Go out to dinner with people in their 20s or 30s. Or worse, go out to dinner with teenagers. When I go out to dinner with my peers these days, it's not considered weird at all to pull out your phone. In fact, the situation has sort of reversed itself: you feel awkward if everyone else is using their phones and you're not. It happens. A lot. And it has made going to dinner so much better.[40]

> Then there is also a specific kind of narcissism that the social Web engenders. By grooming and updating your various avatars, you are making sure you remain at the popular kid's table. One of the more seductive data points in real-time media is what people think of you. The metrics of followers and retweets beget a kind of always-on day trading in the unstable currency of the self.[41]

Group:

2. In a 2011 *Financial Times* essay reflecting on the limits of "most livable cities" lists, Edwin Heathcote complained that they miss much that he prefers about the cities he loves. He also quotes the US urbanist Joel Garreau as saying: "These lists are journalistic catnip. Fun to read and look at the pictures, but I find the liveable cities lists intellectually on a par with People magazine's 'sexiest people' lists." However, Heathcote still could not resist offering his own list of most "lovable" cities. New York makes the top. "The only city that gives me a thrill every single time I walk through it." And meanwhile, Jerusalem hits the bottom. "I know, I know beautiful, holy, history lingers in its every shady corner. Yet the treatment of Arabs as second class citizens, the ghastly security wall smashing through its edges and the omnipresent guns have spoilt it."[42]

Have everyone in your group come up with their own ranked list of best cities, then compare and contrast each other's listings and pull out what sorts of city landscapes are being variously privileged and subordinated as a result. To what extent can you create lists that avoid the competitive pressures and disciplinary implications of the sorts of liveable city rankings that bother Heathcote and Garreau?

Notes

1   See http://www.dowjones.com/algo/smartdarts/.
2   Karl Marx and Frederick Engels, *The Communist Manifesto* (London: Verso, 1998), 38.
3   Naomi Klein, *The Shock Doctrine: The Rise of Disaster Capitalism* (New York: Metropolitan Books, 2007), 262.
4   Samuel P. Huntington, *The Clash of Civilizations and the Remaking of World Order* (New York: Simon & Schuster, 1996); Francis Fukuyama, *The End of History and the Last Man* (New York: Free Press, 1992).
5   Edward Luttwak, "The Coming Global War for Economic Power: There Are No Nice Guys on the Battlefield of Geo-Economics," *The International Economy* 75 (1993): 18–67, 19. See also Edward Luttwak, "From Geopolitics to Geo-Economics: Logic of Conflict, Grammar of Commerce," *The National Interest* 20 (1990): 17–23.
6   Arthur Cebrowski and John Garstka, "Network-Centric Warfare: Its Origin and Future," *Naval Institute Proceedings* (1998), http://all.net/books/iw/iwarstuff/www.usni.org/Proceedings/Articles98/PROcebrowski.htm.
7   Cebrowski and John Garstka, Network-Centric Warfare, 7.
8   Thomas Barnett, *The Pentagon's New Map: War and Peace in the Twenty-First Century* (New York: G.P. Putnam's Sons, 2004).
9   Barnett, *New Map*, 304.
10 http://www.whitehouse.gov/sites/default/files/rss_viewer/national_security_strategy.pdf.
11 See especially NIC, *Global Trends 2025: A Transformed World* and *Mapping the Global Future*, http://www.dni.gov/nic/NIC_2025_project.html.
12 UN-HABITAT, *State of the World's Cities* (New York: UN, 2008), http://www.unhabitat.org/pmss/listItemDetails.aspx?publicationID=2562.
13 Charles Dickens, *A Tale of Two Cities* (London: Dent, 1906).
14 http://www.foreignpolicy.com/articles/2010/08/11/the_global_cities_index_2010.
15 William Carroll, *The Making of a Transnational Capitalist Class: Corporate Power in the 21st Century* (New York: Zed Press, 2010).
16 http://www.citiesinvest.com/whyinvest.php.
17 World Bank, *World Development Report 2009: Reshaping Economic Geography*, Washington, DC: World Bank, http://econ.worldbank.org/external/default/main?pagePK=64165259&theSitePK=469372&piPK=64165421&menuPK=64166093&entityID=000333038_20081203234958.
18 Quoted in Katharyne Mitchell and Katherine Beckett, "Securing the Global City: Crime, Consulting, Risk, and Ratings in the Production of Urban Space," *Indiana Journal of Global Legal Studies* 15, no. 1 (2008): 75–99.
19 http://www.chartercities.org/.
20 http://www.creativeclass.com/richard_florida/.
21 Jamie Peck, "Struggling with the Creative Class," *International Journal of Urban and Regional Research* 29, no. 4 (2005): 740–70.
22 Paul Downton, *Ecopolis: Architecture and Cities for a Changing Climate* (Dordrecht: Springer Science, 2009); Timothy Beatley, *Biophilic Cities: Integrating Nature Into Urban Design and Planning* (Washington, DC: Island Press, 2010); and William Rees, "Building More Sustainable Cities," *Scientific American*, March 12 (2009), http://www.scientificamerican.com/article.cfm?id=building-more-sustainable-cities.

23   For a valuable collection of critical essays asking exactly this, see Helga Leitner, Jamie Peck, and Eric Sheppard, eds, *Contesting Neoliberalism: Urban Frontiers* (New York: The Guilford Press, 2007).

24   http://www.globalcityforum.com/en/global-city-blog.aspx.

25   Quoted in Michael Goldman, "Speculative Urbanism and the Making of the Next World City," *International Journal of Urban and Regional Research* 35, no. 3 (2011): 555–81.

26   World Bank, *Implementation Completion Report (SCL-43840): On a Loan in the Amount of US $36.12 Million to the Republic Of Peru for an Urban Property Rights Project* (Washington, DC: World Bank, 2004); and Erica Field, "Entitled to Work: Urban Property Rights and Labor Supply in Peru" (2003), http://rwj.harvard.edu/scholarsbio/field/field.htm.

27   Timothy Mitchell, "How Neoliberalism Makes Its World: The Urban Property Rights Project in Peru," in Philip Mirowski and Dieter Plehwe, eds., *The Road from Mont Pèlerin: the Making of the Neoliberal Thought Collective* (Cambridge, MA: Harvard University Press, 2009): 386–90.

28   Deborah Figart, *Living Wage Movements: A Global Perspective* (New York: Routledge, 2004); and Kavita Datta, Yara Evans, Joanna Herbert, Jon May, Cathy McIlwaine, and Jane Wills, *Global Cities at Work: New Migrant Divisions of Labour* (Pluto: London, 2010).

29   An awareness of enclaving is a recurring concern in the extensive work of Davis. See Mike Davis, *Planet of slums* (New York: Verso, 2006); Mike Davis, *City of Quartz: Excavating the Future in Los Angeles* (New York: Verso, 1990); Mike Davis and Daniel Monk, eds., *Evil Paradises: Dreamworlds of Neoliberalism* (New York: W.W. Norton & 2007).

30   The documentary movie, *Mardi Gras Made in China* (directed by David Redmon) makes the exploitative effects of this discourse horribly clear, as too does important ethnographic research by feminist geographers: Rachel Silvey, "Spaces of Protest: Gendered Migration, Social Networks, and Labor Activism in West Java, Indonesia," *Political Geography* 22 (2003): 129–55; and Melissa Wright, "Factory Daughters and Chinese Modernity: A Case from Dongguan," *Geoforum* 34 (2003): 291–301.

31   Naomi Klein, *Fences and Windows: Dispatches from the Front Lines of the Globalization Debate* (New York: Picador USA, 2002); and Aihwa Ong, *Neoliberalism As Exception: Mutations In Citizenship And Sovereignty* (Durham, NC: Duke University Press, 2006).

32   Paul Schell and John Hamer, "Cascadia: The New Binationalism of Western Canada and the U.S. Pacific Northwest," in Robert Earle and John Wirth, eds., *Identities in North America: The Search for Community* (Palo Alto, CA: Stanford University Press, 1995): 140–56, 141.

33   Davis, *Planet of Slums*, 115.

34   Katharyne Mitchell, "Marseille's Not for Burning," *Annals of the Association of American Geographers* 101, no. 2 (2011): 404–23.

35   Naomi Klein, *No Space, No Choice, No Jobs No Logo*, (New York: Picador USA, 2002); see also her movie: *No Logo: Brands, Globalization, Resistance*, Media Education Foundation (2003).

36   UN Habitat, *State of the World's Cities, 2006–2007*, http://www.unhabitat.org/.

37   http://www.sdinet.org/ritual/land-tenure/.

38   Ananya Roy, "Slumdog Cities: Rethinking Subaltern Urbanism," *International Journal of Urban and Regional Research*, 35, no. 2 (2011): 223–38.

39   Stephan Crerar, "Mumbai Slum Tour: Why You Should See Dharavi" *The Times* 13 May (2010), http://www.timesonline.co.uk/tol/travel/destinations/india/article7124205.ece.

40   http://techcrunch.com/2011/02/21/phones-at-dinner/.

41 http://www.nytimes.com/2011/04/17/fashion/17TEXT.html?pagewanted=2&_r=1&sq=David%20Carr&st=cse&scp=4. For further discussion of this enclaving of the self, see Arlie Russell Hochschild, *The Outsourced Self: Intimate Life in Market Times* (New York: Metropolitan Books, 2012).

42 Edwin Healthcote, "Liveable v Lovable," *Financial Times*, May 7, 2011, House and Home Section, 1.

Keywords

AAA
Fordism
geoeconomics
geopolitics

9

Health

Chapter Contents

Chapter Concepts

1. Ecological globalization has taken a new form with global climate change.
2. Today's environmental interdependencies are deeply shaped by inequalities.
3. Genomics and biomedicine open unequal access to biological citizenship.
4. Inequalities shape the ties of disease, drugs, organ trading, and health workers.
5. Globalization influences non-biological social determinants of health.
6. Debate over the impact of market capitalism shapes global health policy.
7. Both market fundamentalism and critiques of market failure have increasingly lost ground to ideas about global health as market foster care.

Key Concept

Global health is the ultimate way in which the interdependencies of globalization come together to shape destinies. While the global ties involved are inescapable, they are embodied in radically different and unequal experiences of interdependency. The improved health and biological citizenship of some are often dependent on the sub-citizenship and exploitation of others, and while many global health initiatives have been launched to reach out to those whose health has been undermined by global

Introducing Globalization: Ties, Tensions, and Uneven Integration, First Edition. Matthew Sparke.
© 2013 Matthew Sparke. Published 2013 by Blackwell Publishing Ltd.

market ties, the resulting development of disease-specific donor-driven vertical programs and grant competitions remains profoundly shaped by market forces.

9.1 Interdependent Ecologies of Global Change

In an important ecological sense, life on earth has always been globalized. Our evolution and health as human beings have been dependent from the start on our interactions with a planetary ecosystem. Other life forms and environmental systems ranging from microbes, plants, and animals to forests, oceans, and the global climate have all played a vital role in creating the global ecology necessary for human development and health. Nevertheless, the anthropocentric forms of globalization we have been examining in this book up till now have fundamentally changed these ecological interdependencies, making us the dominant global species and creating today what some scientists refer to as a new ecological-turned-geological era: the *anthropocene*.[1] In addition, anthropogenic globalization has been centrally involved in increasing and ordering our knowledge of human–environment interdependencies, including most recently the push to analyze eco-system services in the name of market-friendly conservation.[2] Based on at least 500 years of global exploration, discovery, and development, this knowledge has in turned considerably increased our ability to change the conditions that originally nurtured human life.

As we shall see in what follows, some of the anthropogenic changes, including global climate change, do not bode well for sustaining a healthy planet. However, other human capacities connected to science, medicine, and health systems governance have made it possible for us to at least protect and increase human health, making the knowledge underpinning these capacities one of the more widely valued aspects of contemporary globalization. Even where there have been conflicts with religious interpretations of nature and biology, and even where the contemporary convergence of science with business raises concerns about the commodification of nature, patenting, and unequal access to life-saving innovations, societies have generally come to respect the benefits of global knowledge that improves health (and therefore to complain about religious and business barriers to accessing such knowledge). As a result, most humans now live much longer than they did in 1500, and the same knowledge that helps make this longevity possible also means that most people grow up learning that the world is neither flat nor the center of the cosmos, that it is instead a single planet spinning in the solar system, a planet on which humans, along with all other living beings, share a precarious planetary fate with the ecology of the global environment.

The processes of exploration and integration that have made modern science and medicine globally dominant have also brought much death and destruction along the way. European conquest of the Americas, for example, both exposed and expanded human–disease relations globally by setting off the most devastating health disaster the world has ever seen. Though they did not understand most of the interconnections themselves, the explorers and conquistadors were accompanied from the start by deadly diseases. Columbus is thought to have brought swine flu to Hispaniola in 1493; Cortés came with smallpox to Aztec Mexico; and measles, typhus, and other forms of influenza served as shock troops of European colonialism right across the Americas.[3] After 25 years of the resulting devastation, there were hardly any native people left to exploit as workers in the gold and silver mines. In response, Europeans turned to the enslavement of Africans, devastating societies on yet one more continent while also spreading other deadly epidemics among native Americans, thanks to the yellow fever and malaria that traveled with the slaves from Africa. Meanwhile, explorers returned to Europe with syphilis, and even though they had scoffed at the limits of native American healing practices, the main European treatment for the new venereal disease came to be a Caribbean folk remedy using guaiac wood. One might have thought that these globe-traveling diseases would have also nurtured a globalized appreciation of a shared human vulnerability. Instead, alongside the international spread of syphilis, an international blame game broke out, setting an early precedent for how modern societies have repeatedly turned their common vulnerability into the basis of division and discord. The medical historian Roy Porter captures the resulting ironies and idiocies surrounding syphilis all too well:

> Initially it was called the "disease of Naples," but rapidly became the "French Pox" and other terms accusing this or that nation: the Spanish disease in Holland, the Polish disease in Russia, the Russian disease in Siberia, the Christian disease in Turkey and the Portuguese disease in India and Japan. For their part the Portugese called it the Castilian disease, and a couple of centuries later Captain Cook (1728–79), exploring the Pacific, rued that the Tahitians "call the veneral disease Apa no Britannia – the British disease" (he thought they'd caught it from the French).[4]

Clearly no one in Europe or the Americas in the 1500s understood that syphilis is caused by the *Treponema* group of corkscrew-shaped bacteria that we now call *spirochaetes*. It was only 350 years later – after Louis Pasteur made his pioneering advances in bacteriology and microscopy in late nineteenth-century France – that modern biomedical science could start to see and interpret biological–ecological interconnections at this microscopic scale. Thus, while the voyages of colonial discovery certainly helped expand geographical knowledge, and while they eventually enabled advances in botany, biology, and the natural sciences more generally, the more consequential Columbian "code-sharing" occurred unseen at a microbial level in ways that none of the humans involved understood. Today, by contrast, a simple search on *Wikipedia* by anyone anywhere with an Internet connection reveals how shared science about *spirochaetes* points to a co-evolutionary global history with humans and other mammals going back long before Columbus:

> The recent sequencing of the genomes of several spirochaetes permits a thorough analysis of the similarities and differences within this bacterial phylum. Treponema pallidum has one of the smallest bacterial genomes at 1.14 million base pairs (Mb) and has limited metabolic capabilities, reflecting its adaptation through genome reduction to the rich environment of mammalian tissue.[5]

At least two important observations can be made about these historical snapshots of how globalization, knowledge about health, and changing human–environment relations are linked. First is that while anthropogenic globalization has often exposed and extended particular forms of human–environment interdependency, our knowledge about such interdependencies has rarely developed synchronously. However, a second important observation is that when such knowledge has been developed in subsequent periods, anthropogenic globalization has often been centrally involved. Pasteur's explorations on the microscopic frontiers of science, for example, were directly tied to the macro frontiers of French colonialism: the budget for what became the *Institut Pasteur* coming to be justified in terms of protecting French colonies from "their most fearsome, because invisible, enemies."[6] And these sorts of ties with political and economic forms of globalization have continued into the present, too: the recent revolutions in genetics that make it possible to map the genome of something like *Treponema pallidum* being linked to the capitalist incentives and intellectual property laws of our own global era's global market. Innovations in genetics were accelerated in the late 1990s by corporate pressure to patent human DNA: the publically funded Human Genome Project being pitched into competition with the private for-profit efforts of Craig Venter's Celera Corporation.[7] From Columbus to Celera, then, knowledge about the underlying bio-ecologies of global health has been linked with political and economic forms of global interdependency. While the ties and time lags have been many and complex, they underline that our ability to understand global ecological change as well as our capacity to create it are at once outcomes and enablers of ongoing globalization.

As the example of North American colonization also illustrates, the global interdependency of life on earth has gone through a number of dramatic moments of transformation in which human-induced global change alters the underlying conditions for life and death in different parts of the world. Here, in Section 9.1, we will address another similarly traumatic period of life-changing global integration and transformation: namely, global environmental change at a planetary scale. Subsequently, in Section 9.2, we turn to the equally transformative but micro-scaled implications of recent revolutions in microbiology and genomics. Despite their vast differences in scale, both of these developments are often presented as all-encompassing stories of global transformation affecting health. Likewise, while environmental change has been unintended and the biomedical innovation deliberately planned, both can also be seen as clear indications of a shared planetary fate: the first because it introduces new threats to human health, and the second because it offers hopes of successful scientific health management. On closer examination, however, both developments also reveal ways in which increasing global interdependencies are structured by global asymmetries that in turn generate huge global inequalities. Both the fears about environmental apocalypse and the hopes about biomedical risk management appear a great deal less universal when considered in this way, and both therefore also have much to teach us about wider patterns of inequality amidst global interdependency.

While global environmental change and molecular biomedicine are uneven in their impacts and implications, they have both still spurred an increasingly global understanding of human health as global health. For the same reason, the third and final section of this chapter takes up the topic of global health and globalization directly. We examine the ways in which different understandings of globalization – from the most pro-market to the most pro-justice – thereby come to shape the ways in which the global determinants of global health outcomes are understood. Here we will review how older policies about developing national primary health and other "horizontal" health systems have become increasingly replaced today by space-selective, and often disease-specific, strategies that turn macro global targets (such as the health-related Millennium Development Goals) into micro targets for "vertical" intervention by NGOs and global public–private partnerships (PPPs). To begin with, though, we need first to consider the broader context of global changes to the environment and to biomedicine that set the parameters for so much of this work.

9.1.1   Global environmental change and health

Humans have been changing the global ecosystem that supports human life ever since the first forest clearings and simple irrigation systems. This process of trans-formation nevertheless accelerated after Europeans introduced horses to the Americas and returned with potatoes, tomatoes, turkeys, and tobacco. The agricultural impacts of the trans-Atlantic Columbian exchange came to be surpassed in due course by the rise of industrial capitalism and the burning of fossil fuels, albeit with the ongoing trans-Atlantic trade in slaves playing an integral role in sustaining an industrial workforce in Europe with a sugar-rich diet.[8] The subsequent twentieth century globalization of capitalism has been attended in turn by the most rapid transformations in our worldwide environment that humanity has ever created. The resulting global impacts and landmarks are as enormous as they are innumerable, including the building of over 43 000 airports, 1 371 000 km of railroads and 68 936 000 km of roadways.[9] Even just these statistics indicate the vast amounts of energy humanity uses in deliberate projects of global networking. But the resulting non-deliberate global transformations are still more environmentally significant. By unleashing the Earth-sequestered energy of the Sun through the intensive use of coal, oil, and gas, we have begun to change the overall climate of the planet, warming the atmosphere and oceans, melting vast amounts of ice, shifting the jet streams and ocean currents, and increasing the energy available for tropical storms, hurricanes, and tornadoes. By also introducing new technologies such as nuclear power, chemical fertilizers, and synthetic pesticides, we have simultaneously created unwanted changes in the basic ecological support system for life. And by urbanizing we have also created another kind of environment altogether, a new built environment of global urbanization that has huge implications for human health. Indeed, alongside the global climate change impact of cities (which account for more than 70% of global carbon-dioxide emissions), urban areas are also associated around the world

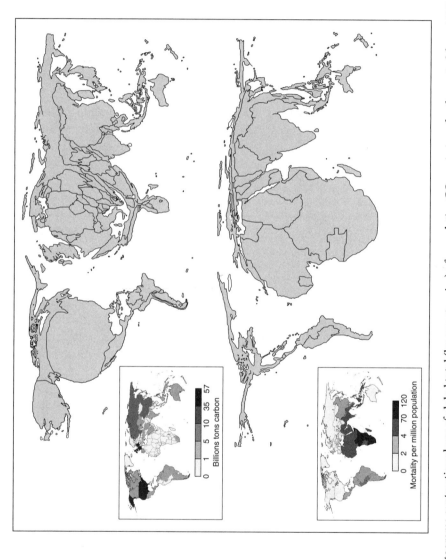

Figure 9.1 Cartograms contrasting share of global total (by country size) of cumulative CO_2 emissions for the period from 1950 to 2000 versus share of global total of excess mortality based on WHO estimates across four health outcomes: malaria, malnutrition, diarrhea, and inland flooding fatalities.

Source: Jonathan A. Patz, Holly K. Gibbs, Jonathan A. Foley, Jamesine Rogers, and Kirk R. Smith, 2007, "Climate Change and Global Health: Quantifying a Growing Ethical Crisis," *EcoHealth* 4, 397–405.

with increased local rates of diabetes, heart disease, obesity, mental-health problems, drug misuse, and road-traffic injuries. So, while there is nothing quite like a tour of a big global city to highlight how humanity can rise above nature, urban areas also keep reminding us that human life still remains profoundly dependent on its environment.

As energy-efficient "sustainable city" and "healthy city" initiatives are further showing with successful mass transit, cycling, and tree-planting projects, some outcomes of anthropogenic environmental change can be life-improving, too. The twentieth century, we must remember, saw the doubling of average human life expectancy, the quadrupling of earth's human population, and a more than sixfold increase in global food production. But these benefits have not been shared equally across the planet, and meanwhile the more damaging and destructive downsides of the global growth in human population and health are not being shared equally either: neither in terms of generational nor in terms of geographical justice. The sixfold increase in water consumption, the 12-fold increase in carbon dioxide emissions, and the 20-fold increase in economic activity globally during the twentieth century mean that humanity as a whole is operating now at an unsustainable ecological deficit that is imposing enormous costs on future generations.[10] And in addition to these obvious intergenerational inequalities, the uneven geographic experience of our global ecological deficit is felt most powerfully and damagingly in places where the growth and improvements in health have been most limited. For instance, conservative estimates suggest that by the year 2000, global climate change had already led to about 150 000 deaths worldwide, most of them among the world's poorest 1 billion.[11] These same populations, meanwhile, have accounted for only around 3% of the world's total carbon emissions (Figure 9.1). To understand this picture of inequality alongside interdependency, we need to examine in more detail some of the most obvious health-threatening implications of global environmental change.

The Intergovernmental Panel on Climate Change (IPCC), the global group of scientists and policy-makers studying climate change and its environmental consequences, issued a conclusive report in 2007 stating that the warming of the global climate system is real, and that it far exceeds natural ranges recorded in evidence such as ice cores (the 10 warmest years on record, for example, have all occurred since 1990).[12] The major driver of this overall warming trend, according to the global scientific consensus, is the atmospheric accumulation of greenhouse gases (chiefly carbon dioxide, methane, and nitrous oxide). These are the gases that trap Earth-reflected solar energy and thereby alter the global climate's radiative balance. Of the gases, CO_2 emissions from the use of fossil fuels account for over 56% of the atmospheric accumulation, with CO_2 emissions from deforestation and biomass decay accounting for 17%, and methane, mainly from livestock and other agricultural emissions, accounting for another 14.3%. The IPCC and other analysts make clear that various feedback dynamics complicate the warming effects forced by these greenhouse-gas accumulations. In some cases, this leads to a further acceleration of warming. For example, the melting of arctic ice and other glaciers accelerates warming by reducing the amount of solar energy reflected from the Earth's ice fields. Similarly, the melting of permafrost in northern latitudes accelerates emissions of greenhouse gases that were previously frozen underground. In other cases, the complex ties between ocean temperatures, conveyor currents, jet streams, and sea levels can lead to counter-intuitive outcomes such as colder winters in certain regions (e.g. in northern Europe) and increases in the storm-flooding of drought-stricken farmlands (e.g. the southern Mississippi basin in the United States). Nevertheless, the overall global warming trend is undeniable, and the IPCC concludes thus by stating as its most robust global finding that the "warming of the climate system is unequivocal."[13]

The obvious inequalities within the global picture of climate change are also many. First and most obviously, they relate to responsibility for greenhouse-gas emissions (Figure 9.1). The world's wealthiest countries in Europe and North America are home to only 12% of the global population, and yet they account today for over 60% of global private energy consumption. As a result of developing fossil-fuel use first, they also owe the rest of the world a huge historical "climate debt" in emissions.[14] And the ongoing inequalities in the present remain staggering. The United States alone with about 4% of the world's total population accounts for 25% of the planet's greenhouse-gas emissions. India, by contrast, is home to 16% of the world's population but accounts for only about 4% of global carbon emissions. China, meanwhile, has recently overtaken the United States to become the world's biggest polluter, yet its per capita emissions are still less than a third of America's, and much of China's emissions anyway include the long-distance carbon footprints made by North American and European consumers when they buy goods made by burning fossil fuels in China (Figure 9.2).[15] More complex still are the climate change paradoxes presented by countries such as Norway and Australia: countries that are leaders in efforts to reduce their domestic carbon emissions, but countries, too, that can afford to invest in green technologies in large part due to the profits derived from exporting oil, coal, and other carbon-emitting resources to countries such as China.

A second set of inequalities relate to the direct impacts of global climate change, and while many of these are mediated by interdependent ties to other global environmental and food systems, the results remain unequally distributed as a result. Changing weather patterns and rising sea levels have the most obviously uneven effects. While some parts of the world are especially threatened by droughts, desertification, and heatwaves, other regions are coming to experience severe flooding, devastating tidal surges, and more frequent extreme weather events such as hurricanes, cyclones, tornadoes, and blizzards. Disrupted agricultural activity through desertification and flooding, and the displacement of rural communities and living conditions present some of the biggest systemic dangers of these developments. Climate change is also thereby creating huge global problems of food insecurity and food-price inflation (problems that are not being counteracted, as was once thought they might be, by any fertilizer effects created by increased atmospheric carbon dioxide).[16] Moreover, as the British-based NGO Oxfam argued in 2011, the food insecurity problems are unequally concentrated in places in the developing world where the production of staple foods is threatened most. There will be "adverse

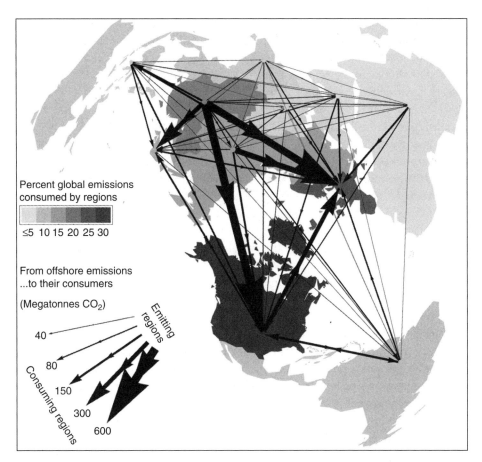

Figure 9.2 Global linkages between locations of carbon emissions and regions where consumption of resulting goods occurs, 2004. *Source:* analysis and map provided by Dr. Luke Bergmann, University of Washington.

effects on aggregate production volumes, as well as agricultural productivity, across all developing regions," notes the Oxfam report.

> Projections raise particularly worrying concerns for maize production in sub-Saharan Africa. Moreover, . . . analysis points to a marked climate change effect in reducing yields of sweet potatoes and yams, cassava, and wheat by 2050 (respectively, 13, 8, and 22 per cent lower than under a scenario without climate change).[17]

Elsewhere in the world, poor coastal communities that are threatened directly by rising sea levels and extreme storm events also face food insecurity effects, too. For example, the degradation of the world's great coral reef systems due to the increasing acidification of the oceans (due to the increasing amounts of carbon dioxide mixing with the water) is an especially worrying concern because reefs contain about 25% of the ocean's biodiversity and supply over 500 million people with a crucial source of protein. As a result of these sorts of changes, increasing malnutrition in the world's poorest populations is a widely anticipated outcome of global climate change, including as well all the problems of obesity and diabetes that develop when poor populations replace lost calories from fish, grains, and vegetables with the cheap calories provided by corn-based sugars and other energy-rich but nutrient-poor processed foods. In addition, the IPCC and other global health researchers predict increasing diarrhoeal diseases, and increasing threats from the extended border-crossing range of diseases such as malaria and dengue as likely outcomes of warming trends, as well as the direct mortality increases among vulnerable populations due to droughts, fires, and extreme weather. *Global Health Watch* estimates thus that 12 million people are at risk from hunger due to failing crops; 220 million from malaria; and 2240 million from water shortages.[18] And none of these vulnerabilities are spread evenly across the face of the planet.

A third set of inequalities shape the overall experience of global climate change in so far as some societies are far better able to protect themselves and mitigate the worst of the damage. Poor communities, coastal villages, urban slums, and already unhealthy populations such as the elderly are much more vulnerable. For example, increasing droughts and heatwaves hit subsistence farmers especially hard. While wealthy farmers are better able to adapt with new crops, pesticides, and irrigation, peasant farmers can lose everything, leaving behind ruined landscapes as "water refugees" while also leaving their communities and countries with worsening problems of food insecurity and malnutrition. Meanwhile, other sorts of water refugees are being created among poor coastal communities threatened by rising sea levels and deadly storm surges. These populations cannot turn to the expensive engineering adaptations available in wealthy countries. The UN Development Program notes thus that while the United Kingdom is spending $1.2 billion on new flood defenses, and the Dutch are investing in homes that float on water, the poor in less wealthy countries literally sink or swim based on their own precarious efforts at "adaptation."

> In the Horn of Africa, "adaptation" means that women and young girls walk further to collect water. In the Ganges Delta, people are erecting bamboo flood shelters on stilts. And in the Mekong Delta people are planting mangroves to protect themselves against storm surges, and women and children are being taught to swim.[19]

As Hurricane Katrina made clear in New Orleans in 2005, wealthier and healthier residents are generally able to escape extreme storm events, but impoverished communities, especially the elderly, infirm, and those abandoned because of racism, remain terribly vulnerable. In the same way, high-tech fixes for the ill effects of urban heatwaves and drought are also available only to the world's wealthiest cities. For example, both Perth in Australia and New Delhi in India are forecast to suffer from dwindling freshwater supplies and increasing numbers of super-hot days with temperatures over 35 °C (95 °F). But whereas Perth can invest in desalination and air conditioning, and take public-health steps to protect manual workers, poor communities and workers in Delhi look set to suffer significant increases in heat-related deaths. More generally, it seems that inequalities like these threaten to split the world's population between the "climate exposed" and the "climate insulated," a split that also maps directly onto the division between slums and enclaves of protection we examined in Chapter 8. As South Africa's veteran anti-apartheid campaigner, Bishop Desmond Tutu, has therefore warned, the world looks set to see a new apartheid in adaptational capacity emerge between those who are ecologically at risk and those who can manage and mitigate their vulnerability more effectively.[20]

Fourth, we should note that the main risk-management response being developed and debated as a collective global solution to climate change is also itself organized through global market interdependencies and the inequalities that structure them. This is *carbon trading*, a market-based fix that aims to put a price on carbon emissions by allowing big polluters to purchase carbon credit "off-sets" from smaller polluters, non-polluters, and providers of additional carbon-sinks such as newly replanted forests. The approach has led to the creation of multiple carbon exchanges around the world – in London (www.ecx.eu), Chicago (www.chicagoclimatex.com), Montreal (www.mcex.ca), and China (www.chinatcx.com.cn) – and it allows for traders to create an extraordinary extension of offset options that capitalize on the concept of ecosystem services (including most shockingly "PopOffsets" or population offsets in which the lives of supposedly "unwanted" African babies are priced vis-à-vis the reductions in estimated carbon emissions saved by their not being born).[21] Initially promoted by the United States as a way for high-polluting countries to meet the carbon-reduction targets of the 1997 Kyoto Protocol, carbon trading has so far failed to deliver on the promise that market incentives will reduce emissions and solve the problem of increasing greenhouse-gas accumulations. "Cap and trade" legislation has gone nowhere in the United States itself, and Kyoto's modest goal of an average 5.2% *reduction* by 2012 now looks totally unrealistic next to the actual *increases* in emissions by New Zealand (+62.4%), Spain (+43.7%), Canada (+33%), Australia (+33.1%), the United States (+15.3%), and other big polluters.[22]

Instead of lowering global emissions, the carbon-trading system has created a global currency in "Certified Emissions Reductions" (CERs) and other associated derivatives which, because they are freely printed by global governmental agencies, keep losing value. As a result, the price of offsets for emissions has fallen below the price that would represent anything like the real costs of greenhouse-gas pollution. It would take a global carbon price of over $50 a ton to make renewable energy a truly competitive global alternative, but instead the carbon market keeps crashing with prices falling to lower than $10 a ton by 2011. Key market watchers conclude therefore that the ultimate floor for carbon credits is going to be zero (in other words, the same free and fully uncosted right to pollute that existed before the carbon market was invented). Moreover, since the "survival emissions" of the Global South are given the same global price as the "luxury emissions" of the wealthy world, carbon trading allows polluting populations to get away with much more than their fair share of the Earth's carbon-cycling capacity.[23] Most problematically, the future oriented nature of the global markets in carbon also obviously fails to address the *historically* unequal shares in pollution that are the legacy costs of the wealthy world's early adoption of fossil fuels. Meanwhile, other global markets in catastrophe bonds and weather derivatives have simultaneously allowed wealthy institutions, insurance companies, and investors to hedge against and bet on climate-change risks, redistributing them through global finance in ways that are totally impossible for the world's poor.[24]

None of the inequalities and problems surrounding global carbon trading take away from the urgent importance of measuring the costs of pollution or of assessing the price of environmental change more generally. Our global incapacity in this regard is remarkable given how practiced we are at affixing and interpreting prices on everything else. From food prices to fuel prices to all the endless discount prices announced in advertisements, price numbers completely dominate our everyday lives. After all, the invisible hand of global capitalist coordination is fundamentally based on the frenetic 24/7 pricing of all the goods moving through global commodity chains. By contrast, the environmental "bads" created by the global system for producing, distributing, and consuming all these goods are rarely priced effectively at all (hence also the reason for using this play on words "goods vs. bads" to highlight the unacknowledged environmental costs). The toxic metals in computers, cell phones, and TVs, the persistent organic pollutants (POPs) in coolants and electrical equipment, the cadmium and lead in batteries, and the benzene in all sorts of plastics, fuels, dyes, and detergents are just a few examples of such hidden and unpriced "bads" in the goods we consume. More complexly, and yet also more pervasively, the foods that we eat frequently come with their own environmental ill effects as well. These may include pesticide traces in both the food itself and the ecologies of the farmland used in production; they may be the deforestation and species destruction necessitated to create farmland in the first place; or they may consist in the less traceable, but no less damaging, implications of the multiple petroleum-based inputs – fuel, chemical fertilizers, and fertilizer-fed corn, cattle, and corn syrup – that are such a striking feature of the farming used to create fast food.

Given the ways poorer populations are becoming dependent on nutrient-poor food in the context of global environmental change, and given, too, that this is better than dying from hunger (which the World Food Program tells us is the fate of about 25 000 people every single day), there is a distinct danger of sounding elitist in criticizing the carbon costs of fast food.[25] There are also dangers of sounding moralistic and apocalyptic when introducing the idea that the goods in global commodity chains have environmental "bads" associated with them. The point here, however, is to underline the uncosted environmental impacts of so many of the commodities for which finding ordinary market prices otherwise remains easy. More than this, another advantage of the term "bad" is that it also points towards the bad health outcomes associated with producing, distributing, and consuming so many of these goods. In other words, what the above examples also illustrate is that there is in fact a place where all the invisible costs do start to become felt and recorded over the long term: namely, the human body.

Pesticide poisoning can cause tremors and other nervous-system disorders. Toxic metals are associated with increased cancer rates, as well as skin and blood-vessel damage. POPs cause damage to the kidneys and liver, and are associated with reproductive disorders. Cadmium and lead cause kidney, brain, and liver damage. Benzene in high doses can lead to anemia and leukemia. And as we have already seen, the climate changes that ensue from burning fossil fuels are going to create a wide range of negative health outcomes that are spread, albeit unevenly, across the whole world. The obesity epidemic that is associated with the global adoption of high-energy low-nutrition diets is in this sense just one of the more obvious aspects of the wider problems. All these dangers mean that our health as human beings literally embodies both the goods and "bads" of global capitalism at the same time.[26] As we will see in Section 9.3, global health statistics reveal in turn how the ways in which we organize capitalism and address its inequalities have significant implications for global health. Before this, though, let us examine more closely another important global development that is often thought to offer a way of managing many of the dangers of the changing global environment as they relate to our health.

9.2 Molecular Biomedicine and Global Health

While global environmental change puts our shared fate as human beings into collective question, recent innovations in microbiology and genetics have underlined how being human also depends upon something else equally profound, equally changeable, and equally global in its implications: a shared inheritance of the same basic genetic code. Our DNA itself encodes a global journey, indicating in the words of *National Geographic*'s transnational "Genographic Project" "that all humans today descend from a group of African ancestors who – about 60 000 years ago – began a remarkable journey."[27] More than this, advances in genomics, pharmacogenomics, and genetically targeted therapies now promise a new global era in medicine in which many biological risks facing humans as a species can be more effectively managed at a personal level. These include the biological risks presented by global environmental change itself. Thus, emerging sub-fields such as *epigenetics* are heralded as offering new insight into how a changing environment can trigger the bad genetic transcriptions that cause cancer and other chronic diseases.[28] Molecular research into new seed hybrids and genetically modified foods is offered as an adaptation strategy to the droughts and flooding set off by climate change. And meanwhile, microbiological entrepreneurs are winning grants and investing venture capital to study how synthetic organisms can be created to transform the overaccumulation of atmospheric carbon back into usable energy.[29]

The anthropocene would in these ways seem to offer a microbiological response mechanism to some of the macro-ecological perturbations of anthropogenic change. However, even as these innovations make manifest the basic biological interdependencies of being human, they also, as we shall now examine, illustrate how the underlying interdependency remains structured today by inequality.

Not surprisingly, the species-wide implications of the new biotechnologies are often announced in epochal statements about their global significance, and descriptions of genomic mapping in particular tend to borrow metaphors of global exploration that emphasize the planetary scope of both the new knowledge and the scientific collaborations that have made it possible. One particularly telling example of the macro claims being made about microbiology came on June 26, 2000. President Bill Clinton walked into the East Room of the White House with Celera's Craig Venter and Francis Collins, the director of the Human Genome Project, to announce that the sequencing of the human genome was nearing completion. Joined via satellite by the United Kingdom's Tony Blair (in what was a further communicational display of international collaboration), the president proceeded to explain the significance of the science using a mapping metaphor and a historical comparison:

> Nearly two centuries ago, in this room, on this floor, Thomas Jefferson and a trusted aide spread out a magnificent map – a map Jefferson had long prayed he would see in his lifetime. The aide was Meriwether Lewis and the map was the product of a courageous expedition across the American frontier, all the way to the Pacific. It was a map that defined the contours and forever expanded the frontiers of our continent and our imagination. Today, the world is joining us here in the East Room to behold a map of even greater significance. We are here to celebrate the completion of the first survey of the entire human genome. Without a doubt, this is the most important, most wondrous map ever produced by humankind.[30]

This was not just effusive presidential rhetoric. The map metaphor and all the associated ideas about global exploration yielding new insight into humanity's shared biological inheritance also became a commonplace characterization of the new knowledge by scientists, too. Thus declares the National Institutes of Health website that:

> The Human Genome Project was one of the great feats of exploration in history – an inward voyage of discovery rather than an outward exploration of the planet or the cosmos; an international research effort to sequence and map all of the genes – together known as the genome – of members of our species, Homo sapiens. Completed in April 2003, the HGP gave us the ability, for the first time, to read nature's complete genetic blueprint for building a human being.[31]

This description also obviously illustrates other influential metaphors used to describe the power of genomics: notably the genesis idea that the human genome constitutes a book of life or "genetic blueprint" that can be "read." However, the same basic mapping metaphor used by Clinton in his veneration of "the most wondrous map ever produced by humankind" is used here, too, and again it makes a direct link between biological exploration and global exploration.

The linkage between the "inward voyage" of genomics and the "outward exploration" of the world associated with historic rounds of globalization raises in turn two obvious and interconnected questions about microbiology and globalization. The first is about the ways in which genetic research might itself be haunted by the sorts of colonial power relations that have been traditionally associated with mapping and colonizing "new worlds"; and the second concerns how such moments of "discovery" relate to access and ownership rights over new microbiological knowledge.[32] By considering each of these questions in turn, we begin to examine how the metaphors of genomic mapping help highlight the ways in which molecular biomedicine is also marked by the asymmetries and inequalities associated with other aspects of globalization.

In terms of the parallels with colonial mapping, it should come as no surprise that native peoples have raised concerns about the biocolonialism and bioprospecting involved in certain forms of genetic research. The Human Genome Diversity Project started at Stanford University, for example, has been condemned by the World Council of Indigenous Peoples as a "vampire project" that represents an "unconscionable attempt by genetic researchers to pirate indigenous DNA for their own means."[33] Likewise, despite deliberate efforts to collaborate and support indigenous conservation and revitalization, *National Geographic*'s Genographic project has also been criticized by the Indigenous People's Council as another example of biocolonialism, too. Given that the Lewis and Clark map mentioned by Clinton opened the American west to colonization, these concerns with dispossession are not hard to understand. Nevertheless, its advocates argue that genomics can serve the interests of repossession and restoration, too. For example, a 2009 article in *Nature* on "The genome of the American West" has made the case that another use for genomics is the biological restoration of the pre-colonial buffalo, a species that almost went extinct in the late 1800s after being hunted down by settlers (partly as a way of depriving native people of food).[34] Genomic science is presented in this sort of way as a basis for post-colonial conservation strategies. However, the degree to which such efforts might also empower the native communities who once depended on the buffalo, and the degree to which genomics more generally might help all the people worldwide that it "maps," crucially depends in turn on the second big question raised by the parallels between genomic mapping and colonial mapping: namely, access rights to the new knowledge. This was something that Francis Collins and his colleagues stressed very strongly themselves.

> To ensure that genomics research benefits all, it will be critical to examine how genomics-based health care is accessed and used. What are the barriers to equitable access, and how can they be removed? This is relevant not only in resource-poor nations, but also in wealthier countries where segments of society, such as indigenous populations, the uninsured, or rural and inner city communities, have traditionally not received adequate health care.[35]

Access was especially important to Collins and his colleagues in the Human Genome Project because of the competition with Celera's private sector genomic mapping. For the same reason, Clinton himself emphasized that despite the public–private competition, the results would be open to all: "Public and private research teams are committed to publishing their genomic data simultaneously later this year, for the benefit of researchers in every corner of the globe."[36] That this would be truly global access was a point that Blair was keen to insist on, too, not least of all because it had been one of the main priorities of the British-based Wellcome Trust, which had funded the United Kingdom's involvement in the project. And that the access should continue to be free and unfettered by patents and proprietary business interests was subsequently an ongoing emphasis of Collins, too. "The availability of the highly accurate human genome sequence in free public databases," he argued, "enables researchers around the world to conduct even more precise studies of our genetic instruction book and how it influences health and disease."[37]

On one level, these arguments about making the new knowledge freely available in the interests of protecting human health across the planet proved very successful in terms of guaranteeing access to the actual data. As a result, the finished human genome sequence can now be accessed online through at least five different "genome browser" websites: GenBank (http://www.ncbi.nih.gov/Genbank); the UCSC Genome Browser (www.genome.ucsc.edu); the Wellcome Trust Sanger Institute browser (www.ensembl.org); the DNA Data Bank of Japan (www.ddbj.nih.ac.jp); and EMBL-Bank (http://www.ebi.ac.uk/embl/index.html) at the European Molecular Biology Laboratory's Nucleotide Sequence Database. However, at another level, access to the health benefits of the new genomic knowledge remains far more limited, and these limitations in turn point towards wider inequalities across the global landscape of molecular biomedicine.

Key to understanding the inequalities in access to the benefits of molecular biomedicine is the global mismatch between the focus on individualized risk management and the ability of individuals to pay and participate. The new genomics-based technologies open up the possibility of personal genome sequencing as a diagnostic tool for individuals concerned with inherited risk factors, and molecular biomedicine more generally makes it possible to develop targeted therapies and personalized risk management at an individual level. This represents an unprecedented turn towards individualistic approaches to protecting and increasing human health at the very same time as we are seeing rising levels of economic inequality around the world. As a result, traditional forms of health citizenship look set to change, with conventional population-level access and exclusion being both undermined and overtaken by the molecularization of life and medicine.[38] What we are witnessing as a result looks like a rather Janus-faced or double-sided development in access in which old barriers of bureaucracy, nationality, and ethnicity are falling at the very same time as new barriers associated with socio-economic class are rising.

On the one side, the new molecular map of human being opens up the prospect of genetic understanding to individuals everywhere no matter what country they live in. What came to be defined in the nineteenth and twentieth centuries as national health citizenship is thereby redefined as a newly transnational form of "biological citizenship."[39] If health used to depend more on your position within a national population with population-specific vulnerabilities and protections, now it is said to depend more on your personal inheritance and the ways in which you individually manage your personal risks. And according to the proponents of this individualized approach to health, the molecular technologies that enable us to predict and prevent certain sorts of genetic trigger mechanisms therefore also promise to open up a much more participatory as well as personalized form of medicine. Indeed, in the promotional language of a leading advocate of genomics-enhanced health management, they will usher in a new era of "P4 medicine" that is at once "predictive, preventive, personalized, and participatory."[40]

On the other side of this open and engaging world of biological citizenship, there remain many other worlds of sub-citizenship and non-citizenship comprising all the people globally who cannot afford to use the technologies of molecular biomedicine. They may no longer be excluded for reasons of nationality and ethnicity, and in this sense the coverage of the wondrous map evoked by Clinton might well be universal and global in scope. Wealthy people around the world will be able to participate with all sorts of new body-counting metrics and precautionary investments in diet, exercise, and biomedicine that parallel the actuarial approach they take to managing their finances, their education, and so much else in the context of wider neoliberal social norms. But to the extent that billions of people around the world are not covered by health programs and heath insurance that can pay for innovations in molecular medicine, the barriers to inclusion are huge. For the world's poor, then, the possibility of participation as engaged biological citizens is completely out of reach. Biological citizenship is therefore nothing like as universal as our shared human DNA. Instead, two very different and economically distinct worlds of body-counting and health management are emerging. On the one side, we have the privileged world of prudential risk management in which individuals invest in and take responsibility for their own body counts – whether just counting cholesterol or sequencing DNA and counting their chances of falling victim to cancers, mental disorders, and other diseases that have genetic pre-conditions.[41] And on the other side, there is the much more populous impoverished world where body counts are still conducted simply in terms of lives lost per day and per hour to treatable diseases. People living in this underworld of poverty are vulnerable to such a wide array of political, economic, and social determinants of ill health that inheritable factors simply do not count as important, and the same dearth of resources that makes personalized risk management impossible meanwhile makes malnutrition, infant mortality, and the big infectious diseases (HIV/AIDS, TB, and malaria) especially devastating.[42]

We will return in Section 9.3 to examine how global determinants of health relate to economic globalization. In the rest of this section, though, we will examine a further set of lessons about globalization that relate directly to the global links between the two worlds of "body counting" associated with the molecularization of medicine. In short, these two worlds – the world of biological citizenship and the world of its impoverished others – are tied tightly together, even as they create radically different health outcomes. They present us therefore with yet another picture of interdependency *with* asymmetry, creating connected but unequal fates at the very same time. While molecular biomedicine promises to provide personalized therapy for the privileged, those who cannot afford the "P4" possibilities are not so much globally disconnected as disempowered. They lack enduring access to the health benefits of biological citizenship, but they are still connected to the processes that produce them for others. Indeed, in this respect, they share an analogous fate with the African American woman Henrietta Lacks whose immortalized "HeLa" cancer cells have been widely used after her death for microbiological research into everything from the polio vaccine to *in vitro* fertilization to genetic cloning.[43] Today these sorts of connections stretch further still. They include the living as well as the dead, and involve many more complex and contemporaneous global interdependencies than just those of genomic mapping itself. At least four sorts of interconnected global ties and sub-citizenship need to be considered: the ties of drug development, the ties of pandemic disease, the ties of organ trading, and the ties of traveling health workers.

1. First, there are the pharmaceutical research interdependencies that involve the recruitment of "experimental subjects" in poor communities for the testing of drugs needed to treat biological citizens in more privileged contexts. A series of biological, economic, and bioethical considerations come together to make this globalization of testing especially important for drug development. The biological advantage, indeed microbiological advantage, of recruiting experimental subjects in poor country settings is that their bodies allow researchers to test new drugs in living laboratories that are free from the pharmacological interference of other drugs. In the language of drug-testing science, the bodies of fully enfranchised biological citizens make for far less optimal clinical trials because they are "treatment saturated" – which is to say, full of pills. Poor people's bodies, by contrast, are usually much better for research because they are said to be "treatment naïve" (itself a term with imperial implications going back to the scoffing conquistadors). This means that new drugs can be tested on poor people without the risk of the drug-to-drug interactions that make it hard to show the specific effects of a single drug and which therefore undermine the statistical significance of drug trials conducted on "treatment saturated" bodies.[44]

A global industry of contract research organizations (CROs) now caters to the need to find suitable experimental subjects all over the world. It does so in turn with cost-effectiveness as another key consideration. Economically it is much cheaper to recruit drug trial subjects in resource-poor contexts, and it is also more cost-effective to conduct trials in countries where there are well-trained but less well-paid medical staff. This accounts for the rapid recent increases in CRO-administered trials in countries such as India, Russia, and Hungary. Researchers writing in the *New England Journal of Medicine* report a pharmaceutical executive as saying that "a first-rate academic medical center in India charges approximately $1,500 to $2,000 per case report, less than one tenth the cost at a second-tier center in the United States."[45] Such huge cost savings mean that poor people in countries such as India are far more likely to encounter the world of biological citizenship through drug trials than through affordable access to medicines. One of the most thorough empirical studies yet conducted on the interconnections between economic influences and pharmacogenomic drug development explains that as a result, "the more likely subject position for Indian populations with respect to genomics is not that of a *consumer* as much as that of *experimental subject*."[46] Meanwhile, in many parts of sub-Saharan Africa, volunteering for clinical trials and experimental treatment programs is often the only way to secure access to any medical attention whatsoever.[47] In such contexts of extreme poverty, therefore, CROs do not have to pay much or explain much in order to find ready and willing human subjects. The economics of poverty and the economics of pharmacological research therefore come to match supply and demand globally to create ties between the poor and the biological citizens who benefit from all the ongoing experimentation.

Worse still, as movies and books such as *The Constant Gardener* dramatize, recruiting experimental subjects in poor country settings also offers researchers a way of avoiding the bioethical regulations that apply to clinical trials in wealthy countries.[48] Even if the resulting abuses do not lead to the murder and conspiracy depicted in fiction, the inequalities in political–economic power and protection are all too real, and the resulting loss of rights for experimental subjects all too common. Here again we come back to the basic question of access to benefits. The World Medical Association's *Helsinki Declaration* on the treatment of human subjects states that at the end of a clinical trial, participating subjects should have access to the best therapy identified by the study.[49] However, very few of the drugs being tested in offshored trials are ever affordable to local communities, and so they effectively have no access. Relatedly, there is also a common disconnect between the wealthy-country diseases (such as allergies) for which new drugs are being tested and the more acute and deadly diseases (such as malaria) that create the biggest burden in poor countries. As a result, poor research subjects who may never benefit from the new therapies and who may not even understand their purpose are systematically exposed to pharmacological testing risks precisely so that risk-managing biological citizens elsewhere can avoid them.

2. A second set of ties between the two worlds of body counting exist because of the ways in which global responses to pandemic threats and the microbiology of treatment are organized in the context of economic globalization. Advocates of global health repeatedly remind us that infectious diseases know no boundaries; that in the age of jet travel, global food chains, global tourism, and widespread mass migration, the whole planet shares a common vulnerability to microscopic and molecular pathogens. At the same time, however, recent responses to global pandemics indicate that our ability to turn shared vulnerability into division persists, with the ties and tensions between today's unequal worlds of body-counting being centrally involved in reproducing different experiences of the same disease. For example, no disease more than HIV (the virus that causes AIDS) has highlighted how humanity shares a common global vulnerability, in this case a shared strength-turned-weakness in our inherited immune system. Yet the global response to the HIV/AIDS pandemic has evolved in ways that underline how inequality persistently structures the experience of this biological interconnection, highlighting along the way that the counting of T-cells by people living with AIDS in the world of participatory biological citizenship is intimately bound up with the counting of the dead in poorer populations.

The most obvious impacts of inequality on the experience of HIV/AIDS have involved ties between vulnerability and blame. Poor people already suffering from diseases that tend to afflict the poor (such as malnutrition and TB) are especially vulnerable when AIDS attacks their immune systems. The resulting death counts due to the disease in poor communities have in turn tended to lead them to be treated as pathological places that can be blamed for the spread or origination of AIDS. In the early years of the pandemic, health experts in wealthier spaces of per-sonalized risk management tended thus to create what the physician and anthro-pologist Paul Farmer criticized as "geographies of blame" that literally *placed* blame for the global HIV/AIDS risks on poor countries such as Haiti.[50] Offering what has become an especially influential rebuttal to this tendency to locate and externalize blame, Farmer countered with a rigorous analysis of the transnational ties linking infection and inequality between biological citizens and their impoverished others. "The ties that bind Haiti to urban North America have a historical basis," he argued.

> These connections are economic and affective; they are political and personal. The AIDS pandemic is a striking reminder that even a [remote] village in [central Haiti] is linked to a network that includes Port-au-Prince and Brooklyn, voodoo and chemo-therapy, divination and serology, poverty and plenty.[51]

Subsequently, in the 1990s, the development of anti-retroviral (ARV) therapy created new ways in which inequality structured the ties between the worlds of biomedical risk management and impoverished spaces of what epidemiologists call "excess morbidity." The new medicines started to make AIDS a treatable "life sentence" for those with access to ARVs, even as the disease remained a lethal "death sentence" for those without access.[52] We now know that this ARV treatment and associated public-health education efforts also considerably reduced the risks of HIV transmission. Maps of global HIV prevalence indicate in turn how a lack of treatment and public health education has led to the disproportionate spread of the disease in sub-Saharan Africa and, to a lesser extent, South Asia (Figure 9.3). Meanwhile, microbiological research into a vaccine for HIV further encoded these sorts of inequalities at a molecular level, with drug companies and researchers focus-ing far less of their effort on the viral varieties or "clades" of HIV found in the Global South despite the fact that these clades account for many more untreated cases and thus deaths.[53]

More recently, however, new and more complex microbiological ties have emerged between biological citizens living with AIDS and the excluded others of the Global South. Pushed by treatment action campaigns around the world, a huge global effort to bring ARV therapy to poor people has now led to a significant improvement in access for those needing treatment. Swaziland, for example, which had the world's worst HIV prevalence rate in 2004 (about a quarter of all adults), now has 89% of its adults needing treatment receiving ARVs.[54] At the same time, though, the historical achievement of rolling out treatment globally continues to be complicated by the dif-ferences between the divided worlds of body-counting that it links. The sorts of public testimonials about infection pioneered by biological citizens fighting disease stigma in wealthy settings have led to a strange and strained triage system for selecting who

Figure 9.3 Worldmapper cartogram showing country share of global HIV cases. *Source:* http://www.worldmapper.org/display.php?selected=227. © Copyright SASI Group (University of Sheffield) and Mark Newman (University of Michigan) (CC BY-NC-ND 3.0).

receives ARVs in poor countries based in part on how well patients tell their personal stories of molecular seropositivity.[55] The poor who do gain access to treatment find in turn that the hunger pangs set off in their bodies by the ARV-enabled recovery process are often not adequately met by a personal diet of food that can match the personal prescription of ARVs (a radical contrast, therefore, with the comprehensive body-counting of more enfranchised biological citizens who can match up exercise, diet, and drugs using a wide array of personal health metrics).[56] Furthermore, such uneven and partial experiences of inclusion into the world of biological citizenship also mean that ARV recipients in poor countries rarely have access to the sophisticated diagnostic tools needed to track drug resistance with regular point-of-care CD4 counting.[57] As a result, their experience of body-counting still tends to be impersonal and alienating, their involvement in ARV treatment being part of a global calculus of population metrics that has less to do with personalized body-counting than with the estimations, indicators, and competitive grant-driven counting of programs claiming the mantle of global action on AIDS.

In the cases of other global pandemic challenges, the ways in which the divided worlds of body-counting are linked can be still more compromising for the poor. In the case of the 2008–2009 H1N1 or "swine flu" scare, for example, it soon became clear that poor countries would be unable to access vaccines and anti-viral medicines even as they were asked by the World Health Organization to expend precious public-health resources gathering and forwarding surveillance data on the case fatality rates and spread of the disease. The stockpiling of anti-virals by rich countries along with their advance purchase agreements with vaccine makers left poor countries looking very vulnerable.[58] Fortunately, H1N1 turned out to be much less lethal than was originally feared, but, as the epidemiological data were gathered to show this, it also became clear that the fate of poor countries deprived of vaccines and anti-virals was little better than that of canaries in coalmines.[59] Their epidemio-logical data and viral specimens were used to support the risk-management strate-gies of biological citizens in wealthier parts of the world (including such individualistic innovations as the iPhone "Outbreaks Near Me" app) at the same time as they were left with only a tiny fraction of the global vaccine and anti-viral stockpiles. Unlike canaries, moreover, some poor countries were also singled out for blame for the outbreak, with many anti-immigrant commentators in the United States continuing to blame Mexico, calling H1N1 the "Mexican Flu" long after it became clear that the North American trajectory of the disease in 2008 started in the US states of Wisconsin, Ohio, and Texas *before* going to Mexico.

As Paul Farmer has shown, the best antidote to the international blame game around any pandemic involves tracing how multiple global ties intersect, transport viruses, and create new vulnerabilities. In the case of H1N1, this means exploring its interconnections with the global factory farming that feeds the global factory work-ers that supply global commodity chains, and some of the best research that makes these global connections points in turn to the viral ties in the factory zones of Asia between swine flu and its avian flu relation, H5N1.[60] These ties are also important to note here because H5N1 has itself generated a huge global debate over the compro-mised sub-citizenship position of poorer populations in relation to the world's risk-managing biological citizens. Asian countries such as Indonesia with high prevalence and relatively high human case fatalities due to H5N1 are expected to follow global health regulations that demand the prompt sharing of tissue from victims with WHO reference laboratories. However, in 2007, Indonesia's health minister informed the WHO that the country would no longer provide samples of tissue from Indonesians killed by H5N1. Her objections were based on the fact that after being handed over, the Indonesian tissue was being turned into patented intellectual prop-erty and used to develop vaccines which, because of the patenting and associated profit-making, would be unaffordable and therefore inaccessible to ordinary Indonesians.[61] While these concerns were often mocked by western commentators, and while the health minister engaged in some geopolitical grandstanding, the issue at base was still about the way that freely donated specimens would be used to develop unaffordable medicines because of the profit-making interests of the pharmaceutical companies controlling global vaccine development. These same concerns have gone on to shape continuing struggles at the WHO over specimen-and-benefit sharing more generally, and despite being reactivated by the inequalities in vaccine access evidenced by the H1N1 scare, drug companies and wealthy coun-tries continue to resist changes to the asymmetric system of sharing microbiological samples without sharing microbiological benefits.[62]

3. Alongside the inequalities in biological citizenship highlighted by sample-and-benefit sharing controversies, there are still more stark asymmetries involved in organ exchanges between the world's poor and rich. In the global trade in "fresh" organs, we also therefore see the risk-managing strategies of today's biological citizens being supported by the risk-increasing experiences of others (as well as by key advances in the molecular suppression of the immune system needed to prevent

the rejection of transplants). The kidneys, corneas, intestines, tendons, livers, and even lungs that are globally traded are not all sourced in the same way, with some "donations" remaining genuine gifts, while others involve the legalized sale of tissues-turned-commodities by so-called Commercial Living Donors (CLDs), and yet others involve illegal transactions and trafficking of the sort depicted in movies such as *Dirty Pretty Things*.[63] By adding commodified organs and tissue to global biomedical supply chains, and by also enabling a growing global business in medical transplant tourism in countries such as Pakistan, India, and the Philippines, today's transplant trading systems eclipse older ethical boundaries between gift economies and commercial economies at the same time as they transcend the old territorial boundaries of national organ donation systems, national waiting lists and associated national regulations.[64]

The boundary between legal and illegal transplant trading is itself constantly moving, with both new laws and new biomedical technologies – such as those that support the transnational outsourcing of pregnancy and childbirth to surrogate mothers – frequently forcing or enabling the global trading to go in new directions. Some countries such as India and the Philippines have imposed bans on what were once highly liberalized transplant markets, while notably illiberal governments such as China's allow for the procurement of prisoner organs after they are executed. In 2006, 11 000 transplants involved the organs of executed Chinese prisoners: including 8000 kidneys, 3000 livers, and 200 hearts.[65] Since 2007, when China passed a human-transplantation act banning commercial organ trading, it is estimated that the number of transplants going to foreigners was cut in half, but many other places can provide for the lost supply. Indeed, a large global network of supply chains exists, and the key nodes in this network – Bombay, Chisenau, Johannesburg, Lima, Lvov, Manila, and Tel Aviv –have become the "global cities" of the transplant business.[66]

According to the anthropologist and anti-trafficking activist, Nancy Scheper-Hughes, the global circulation of organs through the transplant cities network follows the pattern of financial globalization with value moving from the Global South to the North: "from poorer to more affluent bodies, from black and brown bodies to white ones, and from females to males."[67] Despite these underlying inequalities, though, privileged consumers of traded organs often justify their purchases with appeals to the "win–win" advantages of free-market exchange, deterritorialized appeals that simultaneously disparage the territorialized problems of waiting on a national non-commercial list for a donated organ. "Why should I have to wait for years for a kidney from somebody who was in a traffic accident," asked one such consumer.

> After all that trauma . . . that organ isn't going to be any good! Or worse, I could get the organ of an old person, or an alcoholic, or someone who died of a stroke. That kidney has already done its work! No, obviously it's much better to get a kidney from a healthy person who can benefit from the money I can afford to pay. Believe me, where I went the people were so poor they didn't even have bread to eat. Do you have any idea of what one, let alone five thousand dollars, means to a peasant? The money I paid him was a "gift of life" equal to what I received.[68]

Here we come face to face with a biological citizen doing personalized risk management. He brings an actuarial approach to assessing his own personal odds of securing a low-risk transplantation and then applies an equally economic logic to justifying his commercial kinship with the impoverished seller of "his" new kidney.

By contrast, the sellers of organs report another set of calculations altogether. For them, coming of age in places such as the Bangon Lupa slum of Manila means becoming legally old enough to sell a kidney. These desperate kinds of personal calculations may also often lead to lies about their ages, their names, and their medical histories of exposure to diseases such as TB, AIDS, and dengue fever. Such is the desperation involved in fact that some scholars disagree with the arguments made by Scheper-Hughes and others for legislative bans on commercialized transplants. They counter that the economic forces driving people to sell parts of their bodies will continue, and so the best alternative to forcing organ trafficking further underground is to regulate it and thereby extend a very basic form of medical citizenship with monitoring and post-operative health care to the biological progenitors of the "gift of life."[69]

Many other economic imperatives can be found structuring the global ties of transplants. While not all consumers of commercially traded organs and tissues may justify their actions with frank appeals to market-based logic, they all nevertheless have to engage in a wide suite of personalized calculations concerning the costs and benefits of a transplant operation. Moreover, many of these same calculations apply equally to biological citizens navigating the hybrid public–private systems shaping access to tissue and transplants within national programs such as the United Network for Organ Sharing (http://www.unos.org/) in the United States (which notably allows non-national citizens to become biological citizens of the program so long as they can pay). Actuarial approaches predominate in these systems, too, turning the health of the self into a complex numbers game mixing up molecular and market data in the calculation of individualized risk and reward. Ranging from strictly microbiological body counts relating to antibody levels and blood types, to medical–situational numbers relating to things like time left to organ failure, to the socio-economic counts associated with insurance coverage, income, and financial net worth, these individualized body-counting practices become the basis of each individual's biological citizenship. Not surprisingly, given the wider market metrics and influences, socio-economic class thereby also tends to become a key determinant of who is most advantaged and who stands a poorer chance of being approved for a transplant. Biological citizenship is in this sense internally stratified by economics, too, and not just a matter of insiders versus outsiders.

Bereft of rights within transplant systems for which they serve as the ultimate external short cut, commercial living donors remain global outsiders when it comes to personal risk management. They have no health citizenship rights or protections against risk, and instead are integrated into the global trading of organs and tissue through the biology of the genetic-matching designed to reduce risk for others. Indeed, inverting the actuarial approach of transplant beneficiaries, an individual decision to sell an organ at a particular moment of economic crisis is generally followed by *increasing* forms of risk thereafter. Post-operative complications and chronic pain are common, and CLDs also often have to deal with forms of social stigma and exclusion, too, including being seen as weak, disabled, or unviable for marriage. They therefore endure underclass experiences of extreme vulnerability and significant personal danger all the while they provide the vital biological material that helps other people in more privileged global positions to manage their own risks more effectively. In the end, however, some of the same vulnerabilities and dangers that drive CLDs to sell their organs can still eventually come back to haunt recipients of their organs and the biomedical infrastructure of biological citizenship, too. "Even physicians who would have no part in the organ trade," note two contributors to the *American Journal of Transplantation*, "now bear a responsibility for the medical care of those recipients who return … with unknown risks of donor transmitted infection (such as hepatitis or tuberculosis) or a donor-transmitted malignancy."[70]

4. While some doctors do global work when they confront diseases that are transmitted transnationally, many other health workers, including large numbers of nurses as well as physicians, work globally because they move themselves. Traditionally, this involved younger nurses and doctors moving between the world's richer countries, but over the last two decades, global health-worker migration from poor countries to rich countries has also increased significantly, representing an especially important interdependency between the divided worlds of body-counting we have been considering here. Poor countries that spend already-limited health budgets training doctors and nurses for domestic work are losing these workers to higher-paying jobs with better benefits and working conditions overseas. It is estimated that about $500 million is lost this way each year on the training of health workers who leave for richer countries.[71] Sometimes leaving within two years of finishing their training, these departing health workers represent an especially tragic loss for the 57 poor countries that the WHO lists as already suffering from critical shortages of fewer than 23 doctors, nurses, and midwives per 10 000 population.[72]

At the same time, rich countries have seen their share of foreign-trained doctors and nurses climb, adding to what are already especially high ratios of health workers per capita (physician density in the United States and United Kingdom, for example is about 27 doctors per 10 000 population).[73] In 2008, the percentage of foreign-trained doctors was 23% in Australia, 26% in the United States, 32% in the United Kingdom, and an enormous 36% and 39% in Ireland and New Zealand, respectively. Similarly, the percentages for nurses show a significant dependence on foreign-trained workers with Ireland at 47%, New Zealand at 22%, Australia at 16%, and the United Kingdom and the United States at 8% and 4%, respectively.[74] As a result of these sorts of data, scholars now regularly write about the problem of health worker "brain drain" from poor countries, with one 2003 article in the *British Medical Journal* asking whether we should call it "the great brain robbery" and another in the *New England Journal of Medicine* in 2005 answering that: "the exodus constitutes a silent theft from the poorest countries through the loss of public subsidies for medical education.”[75] More recently and more urgently, an article in *The Lancet* has even described the active recruitment of health workers from sub-Saharan Africa as an international crime against humanity.[76]

The damaging impact of the loss of health workers in poor countries is especially heightened because of the big burdens of disease these countries face. Unmet needs for health workers to counter the devastating death counts due to AIDS, TB, malaria, malnutrition, and maternal and infant mortality are only exacerbated by the exodus, and so discussion of the "fatal flows" from this perspective is couched in terms of body-counting at its most macro and non-personal. "With just 600 000 doctors, nurses, and midwives for 600 million people," note the *New England Journal* authors,

> African countries need the equivalent of at least 1 million additional workers in order to offer basic services consistent with the United Nations Millennium Development Goals. Instead, these countries are moving backward, with the hemorrhaging of clini-cal and professional leaders crippling the already fragile health care systems.

Juxtaposed to such critical commentaries, the websites used to recruit health work-ers into rich-country labor markets focus not surprisingly on personal development opportunities, the chance to learn about new biomedical technologies, and the promise of better pay and benefits. Thus, as well as advertising immigration-support services, recruitment agencies such as O'Grady Peyton International (www.ogradypeyton.com/) and Allied Health (www.alliedhealth.com/) highlight how travel is exciting for individual medical professionals, how it allows for new experi-ences and how these in turn translate into the acquisition of new career-enhancing skills. As agencies providing passage into the world of biological citizenship, the recruiters notably also offer medical, dental, and life insurance along with moving expenses. Here, then, the distinctions between the two worlds of body-counting loom large: one being defined by the big body counts generated by unmet care needs in poor countries, and the other by the personal counting of the pay, insurance ben-efits and human capital acquired in providing biomedical services to the rich world's biological citizens.

Connecting the two worlds of body-counting with their own bodies and care work, migrant health-workers experience the divisions very personally. Just as with the global care chains involving nannies that we examined in Chapter 4, they can be torn quite painfully between their own personal needs for reasonable pay and the costs to the countries and communities they leave behind. These costs are certainly very real. For example, a 2004 report indicated that with Ghana losing so many health workers to the United Kingdom, the country had lost around £35 million of the investment it put into medical and nursing training (representing simultaneously a saving of £65 million in training costs for the United Kingdom).[77] However, as policy makers have struggled to respond to these and other injustices produced by global health worker migration, they have had to remain mindful of the personal needs and rights of individual health workers, too. As a result, the

WHO's Global Health Workforce Alliance mostly focuses on attempting to strengthen retention and remuneration in poor countries, rather than banning health-worker migration itself. Similarly, the *Global Code of Practice on the International Recruitment of Health Personnel* developed and announced by the WHO in 2010 counterpoints observations about global needs and principles with an ongoing emphasis on health-worker migration rights.[78] It does say that member states should "strive to meet their health personnel needs with their own human resources for health." And it calls on recruiters and employers to "consider the outstanding legal responsibility of health personnel to the health system of their own country . . . and not seek to recruit them." But it also insists that nothing in the Code "should be interpreted as limiting the freedom of health personnel, in accordance with applicable laws, to migrate to countries that wish to admit and employ them."

One other kind of compromise written into the WHO's 2010 *Global Code of Practice* concerns another criticism commonly made about the recruitment of health-worker migrants by rich countries: namely, that it leads to forms of training in poor countries that are not well suited to local needs.[79] Whereas the complicated diagnostics of biological citizenship in rich countries require health workers with a working knowledge of diverse microbiological metrics and tools, these skills are of little use in low-income settings that lack expensive diagnostic technology. In response, the WHO calls specifically for member states to "educate, retain and sustain a health workforce *that is appropriate for the specific conditions of each country, including areas of greatest need.*" However, there is also an awareness built into the Code that mutual educational benefits come out of health-worker migration if it is sufficiently well managed with bilateral and multilateral measures. "Such measures," declares the Code,

> may include the provision of effective and appropriate technical assistance, support for health personnel retention, social and professional recognition of health personnel, support for training in source countries that is appropriate for the disease profile of such countries, twinning of health facilities, support for capacity building in the development of appropriate regulatory frameworks, access to specialized training, technology and skills transfers, and the support of return migration.[80]

Whether or not member states will honor these principles remains to be seen, but they are important to note here because they highlight how the global ecology of global health can ultimately lead to interdependency overcoming inequality (rather than the other way round). For related reasons, other recent calls for transnational training with reciprocal benefits for all have now begun to shape plans for global health education more generally.[81] Moving beyond technical biomedical training, these plans call for future health workers to be educated about the unequal contexts of care globally and the political, economic, and social determinants of unequal global health outcomes. It is these non-biological determinants of global health and their links to globalization that are the focus of Section 9.3.

9.3 Globalization and Global Determinants of Health

The paradox of global health interdependency coming together with global health inequalities raises an obvious and important question: namely, how do the divergent global health outcomes relate to the political, economic, and social integration effects of contemporary globalization? Ironically, in earlier periods of global integration, when our scientific understanding of human biology and the environment was more limited, worldwide variations in human health tended to be explained in terms of what were conceptualized as "natural causes." Erroneous assumptions about race and nature thus led many eighteenth- and nineteenth-century writers to think that certain human types tended to live longer or shorter lives based on how well suited they were to particular climatological or environmental conditions.[82] Imperialists not only justified the shortened lives of their colonized subjects in terms of race but also had racial preoccupations about ensuring the health of colonial administrators under tropical conditions that they considered especially dangerous for white bodies. Today, by contrast, our understanding of shared DNA has invalidated these sorts of racist assumptions while also showing that our common vulnerability to disease as human beings actually makes unnatural causes – including all the social changes associated with globalization – much more important in explaining global variations in mortality and morbidity. To be sure, genetic research has also highlighted the role of inheritable risk factors for particular diseases such as cancers, cystic fibrosis, and hemophilia, but these do not in any sense line up with imperial understandings of race and nature. Instead, insights into shared DNA created by the microbiological voyage "inwards" have made it all the more important to pursue other social-science voyages "outwards" to understand how non-biological influences determine divergences in personal health outcomes. These studies of the so-called "social determinants of health" have shown that individual experiences of sickness and health are determined by a wide range of mediating and distal factors stretching from the local to the national to the global.

Re-tracing the influence of distal "non-biological" factors from the top down highlights in turn how many changes associated with economic globalization – including growth, trade agreements, market discipline, and uneven development – deeply influence our health (Figure 9.4). But while there is widespread agreement on the importance of these social determinants in shaping health outcomes around the world, there also remains widespread debate about exactly how the inequalities in such outcomes relate to contemporary forms of globalization. Not surprisingly, given all the contention we have already examined around Globalization and neoliberalization, much of the disagreement surrounds the pros and cons of market integration and capitalist growth, including the ways in which the mediating role of local and national policy is explained as either good or bad for health based on the degree to which it is aligned with the norms of neoliberal governance. Contrary to what one might initially think, though, there are more than simply

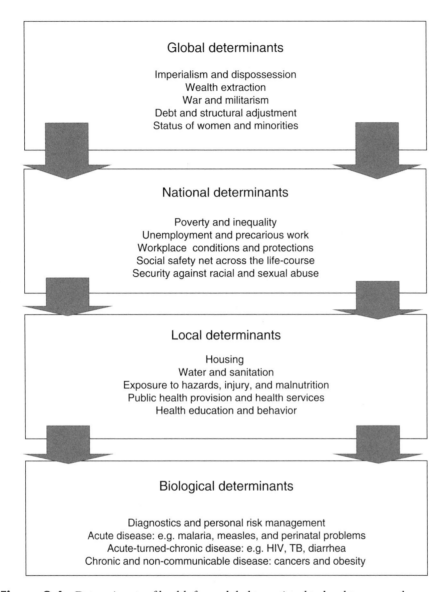

Figure 9.4   Determinants of health from global to national to local to personal.

two argumentative positions on how global market integration and neoliberal reforms thereby come to shape global health outcomes.

There are certainly market fundamentalists who argue that market liberalization and capitalist growth create strong links between wealth and health. And there are also many market critics who argue that it is the inequalities and instabilities of neoliberal capitalism that end up being embodied in illness. But there are also a third and increasingly dominant group of global health advocates who reverse the terms of this debate and argue that bad health outcomes represent one of the biggest problems facing and thwarting global market integration. For them, health needs to be

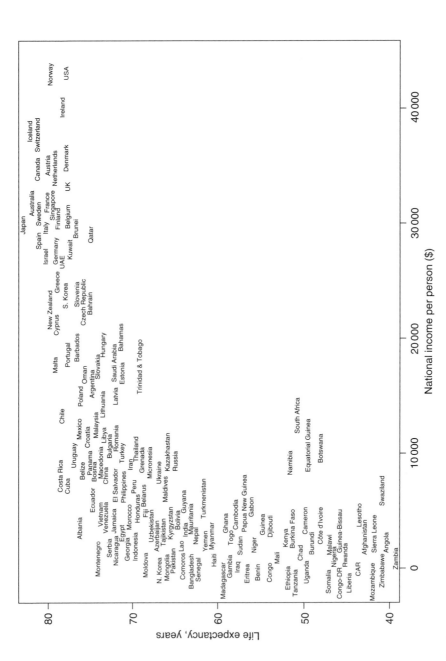

Figure 9.5 "Preston curve" showing the association of national income per capita and life expectancy. *Source:* reprinted from Richard Wilkinson and Kate Pickett, *The Spirit Level: Why Greater Equality Makes Societies Stronger* (New York: Bloomsbury, 2010), with the kind permission of the Equality Trust.

fostered as a *prerequisite* for economic integration and growth. In what follows, we will examine each of these three main argumentative positions about globalization and global health in turn: (1) the market fundamentalists who believe market integration and wealth lead to health; (2) the critics of market failure who explain ill health in terms of economic inequalities and the global impacts of neoliberalization; and (3) the advocates of what is best described as market foster care, advocates, in other words, who argue that particular sites of poor health need good health as a way of fostering global economic integration, growth, and the eventual realization of human value.

1. The claim that good growth leads to good health is most commonly supported by macro-historical data that link long-term increases in population life expectancy (average per capita life span) with increases in per capita gross domestic product (GDP/population). Most famously, this link is illustrated graphically by the "Preston curve," named after an American demographer, Samuel Preston, who first depicted the empirical association between life expectancy and per capita income in 1975. As we shall examine further below, this is a curve that also levels off after a certain level of income per capita is achieved, and after this point, further increases in income do not correlate with increases in average life expectancy at birth (compare the United States and Costa Rica in Figure 9.5). Nevertheless, the initial upward trajectory in the association of health and wealth remains an influential starting-point for a global health story about the benefits of growth. More recently, demographers have begun to use online tools that allow them to "animate" this story by charting the changing distribution of countries across Preston-like curves over time. Thus, if you go to a global health data visualization website such as www.gapminder.org, and watch the animated graph of average income and life expectancy rising from 1800 till today, it offers a graphic (and quite gripping) account of how income growth is associated over time with improved population health.

Of course, wars and associated public-health crises (for example, the so-called Spanish Flu that followed troops home after World War I) create big drops in average life-expectancy along the way. Likewise, other key covariates such as decolonization and education complicate the story in so far as they produce the conditions for economic growth but also directly improve life expectancy (also creating a relationship between multiple variables statisticians call "multicolinearity"). For this reason, it remains crucial to remember that the link between rising life expectancy and rising GDP is a statistical correlation, not a causal explanation. But the strong correlation is still undeniable, with the second half of the twentieth century being notably marked around the world by both income growth and rising average global life expectancy (from 48 in 1955 to 66 in 2000). In the words of *Gapminder*'s creator, the statistician turned Internet professor, Hans Rosling, the 200-year global history of rising wealth and health has led thus to a new global convergence around higher incomes and longer lives. "I see a clear trend into the future," he says, pointing at the end of his 4 min BBC video to an on-screen arrow that points to rising wealth and health, "with aid, trade, green technology and peace, it's fully possible that everyone can make it to the healthy wealthy corner."[83]

In the bolder terms of economists arguing for pro-growth economic policies, the take-home message comes with fewer caveats and is simpler: "wealthier nations are healthier nations."[84] Conversely, they conclude that policies that reduce economic growth rates "substantially slow the improvement of child (and adult) health." Given the market fundamentalist orthodoxy that growth-reducing policies involve more taxes, worker protections, and public-welfare services; and given, too, that market fundamentalists believe that good growth is attained by liberalizing markets, joining free trade agreements, and pursuing export led development, it should not be surprising that they conclude from the "wealthier is healthier" story that a distinctly neoliberal form of globalization is the best route to take to assuring improved health for a population. Poor health, by contrast, is explained in terms of a lack of growth, a lack of pro-market reforms, and a lack of global market integration.

While wealth and health make for a nicely poetic couplet, and while poverty and premature death are undoubtedly (and unpoetically) related, other data complicate the story of association between population health, income growth, and global integration. Preston himself estimated that only 20% of life-expectancy improvements in developing countries could be attributed to increases in income, indicating that deliberate social policies addressing nutrition, education, and sanitation were much more important.[85] More recent research confirms these findings, indicating that the main reason why wealthier countries enjoy better health relates to increases in social welfare spending (with rises in such spending being associated with about *seven* times more of a population health improvement than comparable rises in GDP).[86] Complicating the story further, there are different causal dynamics unfolding at different places along the curve. Initial increases in income growth appear to pay much bigger health dividends because they are associated with basic improvements in health systems. Then, after the so-called "epidemiological transition" to lower infant mortality and longer life expectancy, we come to the point when the curve "flattens out" as the longer-term challenges of chronic and non-communicable diseases (such as cancer and heart disease) replace the earlier and more urgent problems of acute disease (such as cholera). After this inflection point, increasing growth per capita can even be associated (as in the United States) with *lower* average life expectancy than that found in relatively poorer countries. A major reason for this is a lack of wealth redistribution and a transformation of health services into commodities that only wealthier classes can afford. Historical studies of countries experiencing rapid rises in income – including mid-nineteenth-century Britain, late-twentieth-century America, and twenty-first-century China – indicate thus that mortality rates stagnate or even deteriorate in the context of wealth increases that come without wealth redistribution.[87] Going forward, moreover, global developments such as increasing carbon emissions and obesity that are associated with rising wealth indicate still more downsides ahead for the "wealthier is healthier" argument.

Despite all the complications, though, the individuals and institutions that support neoliberalization have still been able to act on the argument that pro-growth wealth-generating policies will inevitably lead to better health, too. For example, respectively as a senior World Bank economist and a rising star in the US Treasury,

Lant Pritchett and Lawrence Summers (the two economists cited above) were able to promote their view that "wealthier is healthier" at two of the most influential institutions of the Washington Consensus. Summers himself also went on to become President of Harvard University and then returned as US Treasury Secretary under President Obama, providing pro-market advocacy at a time when both US health-care reform and banking reform could have instead gone in more market-replacing and market-regulating directions.

Beyond the powerful personalities involved, it is has been the ongoing institutional support for the market fundamentalist arguments that has been most influential globally. Joined by the IMF, the WTO, and more neoliberal agencies within the UN (including elements within the WHO), the Washington Consensus commitment to the "wealthier is healthier" worldview has had huge consequences. It provided legitimation as the World Bank moved away from its older policy statements (of 1975 and 1980) that actually warned against the "market failures" associated with relying on the private sector to provide health services. It made it justifiable for the IMF to make new loans conditional on cutbacks in spending for health, education, and nutrition. And it led both the Bank and IMF to pursue policies from the mid-1980s onwards that systematically undermined investment in social welfare more generally, replacing it with an emphasis on "user fees" that amplified class inequalities by limiting access on the basis of ability to pay.[88] We will examine the impacts of these neoliberal policies and related increases in inequality in relation to critiques of market failure below. Here, to conclude these reflections on the influence of market fundamentalism, one other indirect but important effect needs noting: namely, the impact of this global neoliberalization on the policy-making space in which governments and other health-promoting agencies are obliged to operate.

In sum, the impact of market fundamentalism on health policy-making space has been enclosure. As documented by the WHO's Commission on the Social Determinants of Health, the global entrenchment of pro-market neoliberal norms has boxed in national policy-making thereby "shrinking national policy space."[89] As we saw in Chapter 7, structural adjustment plans, trade agreements, and the ongoing market demands for a "good investment climate" have all taken regulative authority away from national and local governments. Advanced as pro-growth policies, they are all neoliberal policies that can be justified in the terms of the "wealthier is healthier" maxim. And yet they have all restricted the ability of governments to pursue non-neoliberal policies that have much larger health benefits than growth alone. SAPs are a particularly obvious example in this respect. Government investments in public-health services, food subsidies, sanitation systems, and education have repeatedly been cut as a condition of IMF and World Bank lending. As a result, poor countries have been confronted by rising levels of malnutrition and infant mortality as well as by the increased vulnerability of their populations to diseases such AIDS, TB, and malaria.[90] Moreover, as wealthy country governments have sought to provide assistance in the Global South to tackle these diseases, IMF influence has even at times blocked or diverted the assistance with budget managers saying that the additional expenditures risk increasing inflation and threatening growth.[91]

Another example of neoliberalization shrinking the health-related policy space of governments is provided by trade agreements. As we saw in Chapter 6, these allow pharmaceutical companies to create intellectual property right monopolies that then restrict the ability of governments to produce and distribute free medicines and cheap generic drugs. Beyond the TRIPS patent provisions, there are many other WTO rules relating to services (GATS) and sanitary and phytosanitary standards (SPS) through which other important public-health measures are also controlled, conditionalized, and curtailed, too. From direct government provision of health care, to national procurement programs, to subsidized pharmaceutical research, to the regulation of toxic pesticides and carcinogenic additives, to the application of precautionary principles to risky foods, to the enforcement of environmental clean-up laws, the forms of health governance that thereby become re-regulated by trade law are many.[92] Moreover, considering the case of NAFTA's Chapter 11 with its rules allowing private companies to sue national governments for actions "tantamount to expropriation," we also can note that, as well as making it difficult for governments to ban toxic chemicals and waste, the trade agreement also features a lock-in mechanism that makes it impossible for more progressive politicians to reverse neoliberal reforms such as the privatization of health services.[93] And yet defenders of NAFTA continue to argue that free trade increases the choices of health-care consumers, even when it means restricting access to new drugs and other medical advance on the basis of ability to pay.[94]

2. While market fundamentalists have undoubtedly succeeded in shaping health governance globally, and while this has also enabled innovations in biological citizenship for the world's wealthy, critics contend that the outcomes have been a failure in terms of delivering health for all. Instead, health problems associated with the structural reforms and the shocks of market-led globalization have combined with increasing in-country inequalities to create a remarkable record of heightened vulnerability, lost opportunity, and shortened lives. A long list of global health books with titles such as *Dying for Growth*, *Pathologies of Power*, and *Sickness and Wealth* document these failures in detail, and an extensive range of public health articles and reports show that increasing economic inequality is tied to decreasing population health.[95] Amidst these multiple critiques, two distinct sets of integration effects stand out: health problems and vulnerabilities directly produced by market-led globalization; and health problems and vulnerabilities resulting from the ways neoliberalization has undermined existing health systems and economic redistribution mechanisms. Epidemiological and anthropological studies suggest that in reality, these different effects come together in an embodied and material form, affecting personal experiences of sickness and health across the life-course in ways that are also influenced by context-contingent patterns of racial, sexual, and geopolitical domination.[96] Here, we will distinguish between the two sorts of economic effect for the sake of analytical clarity.

The health problems and vulnerabilities directly created by global market integration range from the impact of inequality on everyday life to the creation and spread of new infectious diseases. On the inequality effects, epidemiological

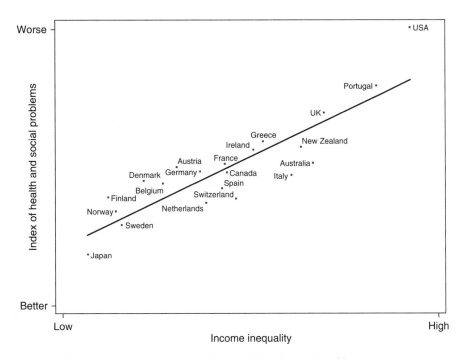

Figure 9.6   Regression line showing that health and social problems are worse in more unequal societies. *Source:* reprinted from Richard Wilkinson and Kate Pickett, *The Spirit Level: Why Greater Equality Makes Societies Stronger*, New York: Bloomsbury, 2010, with the kind permission of the Equality Trust.

studies are especially extensive: including regression analyses of personal and social health that contradict the claim of market fundamentalists that wealthier is healthier (Figure 9.6). Instead, some of the world's richest countries including the United States and the United Kingdom fall behind less wealthy but more egalitarian societies such as Belgium and Sweden. Moreover, according to UN and CIA factbook data, the average life expectancy of about 78.3 in the United States (per capita income $47 284) is by some counts worse than Jordan (per capita income $5644) and Costa Rica (per capita income $11 216), and about the same as Cuba (per capita income $9900), a country which, thanks to both American and Cuban politics, represents a form of ongoing experiment in what isolation from the global market economy does to a country's health.[97] Beyond these crude sorts of global league tables, nuanced analysis of variations among the world's wealthiest countries tends to show the same patterns repeatedly.[98] The more unequal and less redistributive societies such as the United States tend to have worse health outcomes, including higher infant mortality, higher rates of murder, depression, obesity, and stress-related disease, and thus on average lower average life expectancy at birth. By contrast, populations that benefit from higher social-welfare redistribution in the form of better education, housing, and public safety live healthier, longer lives.[99]

Here again, we confront the problem of a correlation (between in-country income inequality and ill health) not being a causal explanation. Scholars still disagree on the actual causal pathways through which economic inequality relates to health. Some suggest a directly bio-physical effect of illness induced by the stress created by living in a highly hierarchical society.[100] Others emphasize the intervening effects of weakened social solidarity in unequal societies.[101] And yet others argue that the association has developed in more unequal countries from the 1980s onwards because these countries have tended to push pro-market reforms more quickly and have therefore also had more radical neoliberal cutbacks in social welfare and public-health systems.[102] Putting all these explanations together in a more global synthesis, the 2008 WHO report of the Commission on the Social Determinants of Health summarizes that: "social injustice is killing people on a grand scale."[103] Backed up by hundreds of pages of data and contributions from multiple experts, the report argues thus that globally the "unequal distribution of health-damaging experiences is not in any sense a 'natural' phenomenon but is the result of a toxic combination of poor social policies and programmes, unfair economic arrangements and bad politics."

Many physicians and other scholars concerned with the embodiment of global inequality take the materialist critique of "toxic" injustice one step further by noting that the social determinants of health end up manifesting themselves in what look and feel like natural experiences of pathology, disease, and death. Books like *Infections and Inequalities* by Paul Farmer and *Late Victorian Holocausts* by Mike Davis thereby remind us that deadly epidemics, famines, and other events that appear as terrible natural disasters are as physically devastating as they are because of political–economic forces that come together with particular forms of racial, sexual, and geopolitical domination.[104] Farmer thereby describes the suffering of his patients in places such as rural Haiti and urban Peru as the result of "structural violence."[105] The effects on the body look and feel like the natural result of violent assaults by disease, malnutrition, and ecological disaster, and yet the mediating mechanisms involve complex chains of structural ties that bind and curtail life-sustaining opportunities through social, political, and economic relations. The examples used by Farmer – case histories that highlight the connections between the sickness of the Haitian poor and, for instance, the dealings of French banks handling claims on Haitian debt – also highlight in turn that many of the structural ties that produce experiences of illness operate transnationally, too. They are therefore not just about in-country inequalities effecting ill health. In this way, Farmer's critical awareness of transnational capitalist ties recalls an early insight of one of the pioneers of social medicine in the nineteenth century, the German physician, Rudolph Virchow, who argued that disease had to be understood in relation to long-distance economic interdependencies. "May the rich remember during the winter," he once said, "when they sit in front of their hot stoves and give Christmas apples to their little ones, that the ship hands who brought the coal and the apples died from cholera."[106]

As was noted in relation to swine flu H1N1 and avian flu H1N5, the global economic inequalities that enable and organize today's transnational commodity chains are also implicated in the actual biological development of disease, too. It is not just that workers working in low-income settings are especially vulnerable to falling ill because of the stresses of slum-dwelling, dangerous work conditions, and hyper-exploitation. Nor is it simply an issue of today's high-speed global trading links spreading epidemics such as SARS further and faster than ever before. In addition, these features of today's globalized world have also combined to create new processes of disease development at a molecular level. As a result, the inequalities of the global economy are effectively being encoded microbiologically in newly pathogenic viral reassortments. "Factory practices provide what seems to be an amenable environment for the evolution of a variety of virulent influenzas," explains political virologist, Robert Wallace.

> Swine flu H1N1, the most recent example arising early 2009 appears by definition industrial in origin. The closest ancestor for each of this H1N1's eight genomic segments is of swine origin. The segments have been identified as originating from different parts of the world: neuraminidase and the matrix protein from strains circulating in Eurasia, the other six from North America. No small farmer has the industrial capacity necessary to export livestock of any consequence across such long distances, nor the market entree livestock influenzas need to spread through international commodity chains.[107]

Thus, a disease that Columbus first brought to North America in the fifteenth century has been re-exported and remade globally in the twenty-first century, and the transnational movements of animal stock, migrant workers, and the innumerable commodities made by migrant workers in the sweatshops of Asia have all been involved and encoded in the newly virulent virus.

Alongside new assortments of acute infectious diseases, we can further note that there is a now a growing scholarly consensus that today's global trading ties are also increasingly implicated in the spread of chronic diseases such as obesity, diabetes, and heart disease, too. In this sense, they have converted what epidemiologists have traditionally referred to as non-communicable diseases (NCDs) into communicable health problems that spread across borders like infections.[108] The promotion of cigarettes and smoking in the Global South is the most egregious and deadly example, but more generally it is global shifts in food supply and eating habits that create the widest systemic risks. Transnational food corporations and retailers ranging from Cargill and ADM to Coca Cola and Pepsi-Co to Wal-Mart and Carrefour are all involved in this respect, as are the transnational trade agreements that allow highly subsidized and often highly processed European and American food products to penetrate foreign markets. High in energy but low in nutrition, these foods are simultaneously accelerating the spread of obesity and undermining long-term food security. Defenders of transnational food corporations argue that they are helping to lower food costs and tackle global hunger problems. And it is true that consumers often buy the new processed foods at lower prices, or at least at prices that seem worth paying, given the dangers of food preparation in unhealthy environments. However, when local farmers are forced to shut down because they cannot compete with the cheap foreign imports, it undermines the long-term food security of poor countries as well as often reducing the nutritional quality of the available food. Meanwhile, the trade agreements that allow for all the new imports also at the same time restrict the ability of governments to regulate food safety and public health, making it harder to reduce pesticides in food or to control the availability of cigarettes.

Returning us to the problem of shrinking governmental policy space, the example of trade agreements also illustrates the way market-led integration and neoliberalization can undermine existing health services. Financial globalization is especially influential in creating health problems and vulnerabilities in this way. The destructive effects of financial crisis, debt, and debt-based market discipline on health systems are now well known, not least of all because of the global crises that began to unfold in 2008. Thus, in the same year that the WHO Commission delivered its report on the Social Determinants of Health, global financial markets began simultaneously to provide an especially spectacular reminder of how market failure overshadows governmental financing for health systems and wider investments in public services that have known health benefits. The costs of bailing out banks and other market players such as AIG, the devastating global recession that followed the credit crunch in 2008, the increased burdens of unemployment, and the declining state revenues around the world all combined to make financial austerity and cutbacks in public services the new global policy norm. Coming together with other global market integration effects, including the complex ties between a falling dollar, rising oil prices, and rising global food prices, the result seemed to many to represent market failure at its most unhealthy. Margaret Chan, the Director of the WHO, spoke thus at the World Congress on Public Health in 2009, noting that the resulting costs and damage to the health sector were akin to an uncontrollable global disease epidemic. "Last year," she said,

> our imperfect world delivered, in short order, a fuel crisis, a food crisis, and a financial crisis. All of these events have global causes and global consequences, with serious implications for health. They are not random events. Instead, they are the result of massive failures in the international systems that govern the way nations and their populations interact. In short: they are the result of bad policies. Under the unique conditions of the 21st century, the consequences of faulty policies are highly contagious. This contagion shows no mercy and makes no exceptions on the basis of fair play. Even countries that managed their economies well, did not purchase toxic assets, and did not take excessive financial risks are suffering the consequences. The health sector, which had no say when these policy decisions were made, will bear the brunt of the consequences.[109]

Chan went on to say that: "The market does not solve social problems. Public health does." But as she called on global health leaders to provide a corrective to systemic market failure, her words were overshadowed by two obvious challenges. One of these she acknowledged: namely that market forces still dominate the terms of debate, forcing advocates of public health and social welfare investments to defend them in terms of increasing economic growth, security, and the development of human capital. The second challenge was the more material and broader market impact of the financial crisis around the world on the ability of governments to go on funding such "investments." Initial predictions provided to the WHO indicated that big cuts to health, social welfare, and aid budgets were all coming at the same time as tens of millions of people were losing jobs and being pushed into poverty as a result of the global recession.[110] Not only were exports falling and FDI flows diminishing, but remittances being sent back to poor countries by migrant workers were also plummeting, too. In this context, the IMF was gearing up to administer new rounds of austerity and social-welfare cutbacks on even relatively wealthy European countries such as Greece, Portugal, Ireland, and Spain. Meanwhile, in lower-income countries, the impacts not only looked worse but also looked all too familiar. This familiarity is confirmed by empirical studies across the Global South that have found a repeated pattern of financial crises being followed by both reduced health spending and deteriorating health outcomes, leading, for example in Southeast Asia after the 1997 financial crisis, to increased mortality (Korea), maternal malnutrition (Indonesia), and increases in crime and child prostitution coupled with widespread declines in public spending (a pattern found across Southeast Asia).[111]

Going back further, the long-term impact of financial crisis and post-crisis market discipline has been to repeatedly undermine public-service programs that improve health outcomes. Most notoriously, there remains the shocking case of Russia's rapid decline in average life expectancy (especially for men) following the imposition of neoliberal shock therapy in the 1990s.[112] More globally, it is the earlier debt crises of the 1980s and the structural adjustment programs that followed that have had the most systematic and lasting impact.[113] The reason why is that they completely undermined another more market-critical pathway towards global health that had been developing in the context of decolonization. The late 1970s had been a high-water mark in this respect, with government commitments around the world to improving health by building health systems focused on primary health care (PHC), an approach that combined low-cost investments in community health workers with action on social determinants of health such as education and housing. This "basic needs approach" was best exemplified and encoded in the 1978 Alma Ata Declaration: a declaration by 134 participating countries that reaffirmed the WHO's definition of health as "a state of complete physical, mental, and social well-being and not merely the absence of disease or infirmity" while also insisting that governments had a responsibility to work towards "health for all."[114] It was the ability of governments across the Global South to fulfill this declaration that was subsequently destroyed by the debt crises of the 1980s.

Instead of the new more equitable international economic order imagined by the participants at the Alma Ata conference, and instead of their critique of the "gross inequality" in health created by economic inequality, the debt crises led to an altogether more draconian and destructive economic order of financialized market discipline and public-service cutbacks. As a result, the PHC plans of the conference were effectively defunded on a global scale. Instead, and over time, the vision of improving health for all with action on social and economic injustice has come to be replaced by a much more biomedical and selective approach to health interventions focused on specific diseases and bio-tech solutions. Leading the way in this respect was the approach sponsored by the Rockefeller foundation that became known as "Selective Primary Health Care" (SPHC). Taken up at UNICEF and the WHO in the early 1980s, SPHC narrowed the agenda of PHC to a focus on child survival with programs such as UNICEF's GOBI (Growth monitoring, Oral rehydration, Breast feeding, and Immunization). As the debt crises hit, and market discipline started to bite, the limits of SPHC also became clear, but instead of leading back to Alma Ata and a radical critique of market failure, all sorts of new selective programs were added to address particular diseases such as AIDS (for which the WHO's Global AIDS program was started in 1986). And guiding this patchwork development of diverse disease-specific programs was the increasingly popular idea that the combined challenge of health crises and economic crises demanded a new kind of market foster care.

3. Neither market fundamentalist nor based on arguments that the market repeatedly fails when it comes to health, the market-foster care approach radically reverses the terms of debate over globalization and global health. Instead of saying wealthier is healthier, and instead of showing that creating wealth without redistribution undermines health, the increasingly dominant perspective that drives much of today's global health policy is that health is a prerequisite for wealth and that everyone everywhere ultimately ought to have both. This then is not a radical critique of global wealth creation leading to the structural violence that is embodied in illness, or even a liberal argument about market inequalities inhibiting the creation of health with wealth. Instead, it is an approach that understands market failure more in terms of failed connections to global markets, including the failure of markets to translate the health needs of the world's poor into what economists call "effective demand" for health services. Market foster-care advocates therefore imagine their work in terms of reconnecting disconnected populations by bringing in biomedical solutions that are developed and distributed using the external market incentives of multilateral aid and private philanthropy. It is this approach that leads to today's "vertical interventions" through disease-specific global health initiatives (GHIs), interventions that aim to correct and compensate for the macro failures of the global market while nevertheless deploying micro-market methods and metrics (such as grant competitions and cost-effectiveness analyses) to prioritize particular diseases and places for investment.

Notwithstanding the micro-neoliberalism involved in GHI implementation, the market foster-care approach still represents a significant revision of the old laissez-faire fundamentalism of macro-neoliberal reform. A good illustration of this revisionism is provided by the work of the economist-turned-global-health-activist, Jeffrey Sachs. A former advocate of neoliberal shock therapy (including the deadly prescription of market discipline for post-communist Russia), Sach's subsequent work as special advisor to the UN and WHO on the development of the Millennium Development Goals has made him one of the world's most influential advocates of the health-leads-to-wealth argument. "A large number of the extreme poor," he explains, "are caught in a poverty trap, unable on their own to escape from extreme material deprivation. They are trapped by disease, physical isolation, climate stress, environmental degradation, and by extreme poverty itself."[115] Sachs argues thus that new forms of foster-care intervention are necessary to enable those who are unable to help themselves climb out of the traps of poverty. He calls this correction of laissez-faire orthodoxy "Clinical Economics," and he deliberately models its diagnostic terminology and methodology on clinical medical practice. What this means in practice for Sachs involves treating individual countries like individual patients, abandoning the one-size-fits-all fundamentalism of the IMF and replacing it with a detailed "differential diagnosis" of each country's discrete national situation. And along with the detailed physical geography maps he recommends as a way of understanding global isolation, Sachs is also keen to stress that physical diseases need treating as a prerequisite for treating the economic disease of disconnection from the global economy. Adding a market-foster-care coda to his former free-market therapy, he therefore reflects: "It should have been possible to tend to the problems of closed trading systems and excessive nationalization of industry without ignoring the problems of malaria and AIDS, mountain geographies, and inadequate rainfall."[116]

The shift from market fundamentalism to market foster-care exemplified by Sachs may not be revolutionary, but it is widespread and has come to influence many different individuals and agencies with an interest in global health. For example, in an important textbook published by the American Medical Association as a primer on global health service for new physicians, Edward O'Neil uses all the same ideas in order to offer students "a map and compass through which many will find their way to service."[117] He encourages such service as an activist response to the legacies of laissez-faire orthodoxy, and is very critical of trickle-down development ideology, of structural adjustment policy and the one-size-fits-all neoliberalism of the traditional Washington Consensus. However, citing Sachs, he also assures his readers that the poor are not poor because the rich are rich and conceptualizes the need for global health service in terms of helping vulnerable populations out of poverty traps by giving them the health needed to generate wealth. As a result, both the problems of poor health and O'Neil's proffered solutions are presented as geographically discrete opportunities for intervention from afar.

In institutional settings, the same notion of using biomedical action to remedy poverty trap isolation has become common, too. Not surprisingly, with Sachs as chair, the WHO's 2003 *Commission on Macroeconomics and Health* came to consensus precisely through a new attention to the disease challenges of poverty traps.[118] "We found that the health crisis in Africa and other impoverished regions was indeed causing a poverty trap," explained Sachs.[119]

> Massive proportions of the poor are sick and dying, and sick people are unable to generate income and pay taxes. Without household incomes and with bankrupt governments, health systems have collapsed and epidemics are running unchecked. To break this vicious cycle, the rich countries would have to help."

Similarly, in its landmark 2007 Healthy Development strategy, the World Bank significantly replaced its earlier prioritization of growth first with a new concern for how health interventions may help with growth. While the older consensus policies were justified in terms of the "wealthier is healthier" mantra, the 2007 report instead portrayed good health as the very foundation for good economic growth.

> Health is often thought to be an outcome of economic growth. Increasingly, however, good health and sound health system policy have also been recognized as a major, inseparable contributor to economic growth. Advances in public health and medical technology, knowledge of nutrition, population policies, disease control, and the discovery of antibiotics and vaccines are widely viewed as catalysts to major strides in economic development, from the Industrial Revolution in 19th century-Britain to the economic miracles of Japan and East Asia in the 20th century.[120]

These ideas have in turn led the Bank to either develop or support a wide array of GHIs focused on particular diseases such as AIDS and specific global health challenges such as reproductive health.

Taken on its own – and therefore ignoring the difficulty of implementing new health investments in the context of ongoing insistence in World Bank Poverty Reduction Strategy Papers on paying off old debts – the new market foster-care philosophy of the Bank represents a notable revision to structural adjustment orthodoxy about user fees and increasing private provision. However, the changes have been contested internally, and it was actually NGO complaints about the pro-privatization emphases of earlier drafts that played a role in shaping the final 2007 report.[121] Instead and ironically, NGO leaders pushed the Bank to support more centralized governmental control over the multitudinous global scattering of non-governmental health interventions. This was ironic because it simultaneously revealed both the power and problems associated with NGO-influence within market foster-care approaches to global health. No longer is it just the Bretton Woods institutions, the WHO, and wealthy western governments that set the agenda. Instead, NGO involvement and hybrid public–private partnerships (PPPs) with business have added challenging new layers of complexity. As the World Bank report and many other observers of global health governance have noted, these additional layers create all sorts of institutional coordination problems on a global scale with national governments being repeatedly side-lined or reduced to the role of collecting health data for all the different NGOs, PPPs, and disease-specific grant competitions.[122] Nevertheless, running through all this complexity, the idea of targeted market foster-care interventions for particular diseases in particular places remains a common denominator, and as such it allows for new health-policy combinations in which powerful market players and market methods on the one side reconnect with enduring Alma Ata ideas about health as a human right on the other.

No institution better illustrates the market foster-care common denominator and combinations than the Seattle-based Bill and Melinda Gates foundation. Its motto, expressed in capital letters on the foundation's website, is that: ALL LIVES HAVE EQUAL VALUE, and both Bill and Melinda Gates frequently make clear their deep humanitarian belief in the equal worth of all human beings everywhere.[123] As much as this humanitarianism conflicts with the macroeconomic inequalities of the global marketplace, their foundation nevertheless deploys a comprehensive regime of market methods and market metrics to organize and assess its global health interventions. In this way, we are seeing the old Washington (DC) Consensus on wealth leading to health being replaced by a new form of Washington (state) Consensus, a consensus in which the world's wealthiest foundation is using its extraordinary market power to incentivize and organize a targeted biomedical approach to tackle specific diseases in specific places. Avoiding political and governmental entanglements wherever possible by focusing on interventions such as ARVs, vaccines, and bed nets, the foundation's approach effectively delinks the "health is a human right" idea from the PHC plans of Alma Ata and reconnects it to a much more market-friendly vision of PPP-led product development.[124] The resulting redefinition of market failure makes it seem more like a correctable error: not a systemic problem demanding a new economic order (the old Alma Ata diagnosis), but rather a technical problem that can be fixed with technical solutions.

The Gates foundation's redefinition of market failure has been well summarized by one of its former directors of global health policy, Joe Cerrell. In a 2007 speech entitled "Making Markets Work" that was published on the IMF's website, Cerrell offered both an indictment of market failure and an explanation of how he sees private-sector health funding as providing a compensatory form of market foster care.[125] Sometimes, he explained,

> markets need some scaffolding to function effectively . . . Influencing market dynamics related to global health can bring about a transformation similar to the one we have seen in developed countries.

Pointing to the poor who live outside developed countries, Cerrell then highlighted the massive inequalities in treatment that result from letting the market operate independently as the only guide for health delivery.

> Some of the greatest inequities in global health result from markets that are not structured to serve the poor. Every year, millions of people in developing countries die from diseases, including malaria and tuberculosis, that have been all but forgotten in rich countries. For these diseases, the economics of the marketplace are not sufficient to commercially justify the large-scale investment needed to develop and deliver vaccines and drugs.

And so we come to the Gates foundation's philosophy of providing the financial scaffolding for markets in order to correct these market failures.

> Through global advocacy, the Bill & Melinda Gates Foundation is working to address this market failure by promoting innovative health financing mechanisms that provide better incentives to the private sector to create global public goods.

While the biomedical humanitarianism of the Gates foundation illustrates how market foster-care ideas influence contemporary approaches to global health, they by no means completely dominate the field. Both market fundamentalists and critics of neoliberalism continue to contest the direction of global health policy-making. Thus, against the unabashed faith in economic incentivization expressed by neoliberal media such as *The Economist*, many global health leaders remain deeply skeptical about market-mediated solutions and all the attendant emphases on short-term grant competitions and cost-effectiveness analyses. Arguing that the micro-neoliberalism of the Gates foundation is unsustainable because it also fails to address all the ongoing health problems created by the political and economic context of macro-neoliberalism, global health activists such as the People's Health Movement call for a comprehensive restoration of PHC and the government commitments to health for all made at Alma Ata.[126] These sorts of demands have led many sponsors of GHIs, including the Gates foundation, to explore new ways to support health systems strengthening (HSS). Advocates of more mixed methods propose using GHI funding for HSS programming, and some global health leaders have thereby discussed "diagonalizing" the Global Fund for AIDS, Tuberculosis, and Malaria, and turning it into a Global Fund for Global Health that can reinvest globally in primary health care.[127] Whether this new HSS push will survive the economic austerity simultaneously sweeping the world in the context of a prolonged global recession remains to be seen (in November 2011, for example, it was announced that there was no money available for new Global Fund grants in 2012). And for the time being, most of the global health money continues to flow towards narrowly defined projects of biomedical intervention targeted at specific diseases in specific places.

For students, health workers, and governments who find their fates entangled with the ongoing controversies over global health policy, it remains a daunting challenge to keep up with the changing terms of debate, not to mention the different demands and metrics of all the distinct disease-specific grant programs. Sometimes, it seems as if time is being wasted when the real work of action and change is not being done. Certainly, the fact that millions of people die each year from completely preventable and treatable diseases remains a terrible indictment of our current world health systems (and lack thereof). And yet at the same time, the debates over globalization as they relate to global health are simultaneously encouraging because they show us that the intellectual disputes matter, that for good or ill they have consequences, and that they can over time lead to improvements in the ultimate measure of policy success: healthier and longer lives.[128] They remind us in this way that engaging with globalization intellectually can also lead to changing it practically, and by doing so they prompt us to turn to the theme of the next and final chapter of this whole book: the wider challenge of action in the context of increasing global interdependency.

Student Exercises

Individual:
1. This chapter identified four different ways in which the forms of body-counting associated with personal health-risk management (cholesterol counting, blood

sugar counting, T-cell counting, and so on) are tied to population-scale forms of life and death body-counting in poorer contexts. Beyond these ties of experimentation, surveillance, organ "donations," and health-worker movements, what other sorts of connections can you identify between the two worlds of body-counting? Hint: the global environmental changes outlined in Section 9.1 are integrally involved in creating such connections.

Group:
2. A *Financial Times* article on biohacking by a growing movement of so-called Quantified-Selfers indicates that the body-counting developments in molecular bio-medicine and biological citizenship are intimately intertwined with other ways in which everyday life is becoming financialized. "Footsteps, sweat, caffeine, memories, stress, even sex and dating habits – it's all quantified like a quarterly revenue statement. And if there isn't an app or a device for tracking it, one will probably appear in the next few years."[129]

In your group discuss the pros and cons of creating an app such as this. How might it be created in ways that actually help users think critically about what self-quantification includes, excludes, and thereby tends to privilege in terms of health.

Notes

1   Paul Crutzen and Eugene Stoermer, "The 'Anthropocene,'" *Global Change Newsletter* 41 (2000): 17–18.
2   Millennium Ecosystem Assessment, *Ecosystems and Human Well-Being: Synthesis* (Washington, DC: Island Press, 2005).
3   See Roy Porter, *The Greatest Benefit to Mankind: A Medical History of Humanity* (New York: Norton, 1997) chapter VIII.
4   Porter, *Greatest Benefit*, 166.
5   http://en.wikipedia.org/wiki/Treponema_pallidum.
6   Bruno Latour, *The Pasteurization of France* (Cambridge, MA: Harvard University Press, 1988), 142.
7   James Shreeve, *The Genome War: How Craig Venter Tried to Capture the Code of Life and Save the World* (New York: Alfred A. Knopf, 2004); Kaushik Sunder Rajan, *Biocapital: The Constitution of Postgenomic Life* (Durham, NC: Duke University Press, 2006).
8   Sidney W. *Mintz, Sweetness and Power: The Place of Sugar in Modern History* (New York: Viking, 1985).
9   CIA Factbook, http://www.cia.gov/library/publications/the-world-factbook/.
10   Anthony McMichael, *Human Frontiers, Environments and Disease: Past Patterns, Uncertain Futures* (Cambridge: Cambridge University Press, 2001).
11   Sharon Friel, Michael Marmot, Anthony J McMichael, Tord Kjellstrom, Denny Vågerö, "Global Health Equity and Climate Stabilisation: A Common Agenda," *Lancet* 372 (2008): 1677–83.
12   Intergovernmental Panel on Climate Change, *Climate Change 2007: Synthesis Report*, http://www.ipcc.ch/publications_and_data/publications_ipcc_fourth_assessment_report_synthesis_report.htm.

13   IPCC, *Climate Change*, 72.

14   See http://climate-debt.org/, including the declaration to the 2009 Copenhagen conference on climate change by the Summit of Heads of State and Government of the Bolivarian Alliance (ALBA), *The Sunrise of The Peoples*, Cochabamba, October 17, 2009, http://climate-debt.org/wp-content/uploads/2010/09/Finance-Assessment-31-August-2010.pdf.

15   Anne-Emanuelle Birn, Yogan Pillay, and Timothy H. Holtz, *Textbook of International Health: Global Health in a Dynamic World*, Third Edition (New York: Oxford University Press, 2009), chapter 10.

16   Christian Parenti, *Tropic of Chaos: Climate Change and the New Geography of Violence* (New York: Nation Books, 2011).

17   Oxfam, 2011, *Growing a Better Future: Food Justice in a Resource-Constrained World*, http://www.oxfam.org/en/policy/growing-better-future.

18   People's Health Movement, *Global Health Watch 2: An Alternative World Health Report* (Cairo: PHM, 2010), 103–11.

19   United Nations Development Program, *Fighting Climate Change: Human Solidarity in a Divided World* (New York: UNDP, 2007), http://undp.org/en/media/HDR_20072008_EN_Complete.pdf.

20   Desmond Tutu, "We Do Not Need Climate Change Apartheid in Adaptation," in United Nations Development Program, *Fighting Climate Change*, 166.

21   http://www.popoffsets.com/.

22   For the most recent data on progress towards the Kyoto targets (and lack thereof), see the website of the United Nations Framework Convention on Climate Change, http://unfccc.int/ghg_data/ghg_data_unfccc/items/4146.php.

23   Patrick Bond and Rehana Dada, eds, *Trouble in the Air: Global Warming and the Privatised Atmosphere, Centre for Civil Society* (Amsterdam: South Africa and Transnational Institute, 2005).

24   Melinda Cooper, "Turbulent Worlds: Financial Markets and Environmental Crisis," *Theory, Culture & Society* 27, no. 2–3 (2010): 167–90; and Michael Pryke, "Geomoney: An Option on Frost, Going Long on Clouds," *Geoforum* 38, no. 3 (2007): 576–88.

25   http://www.wfp.org/hunger/stats.

26   Birn et al., *International Health*, chapter 10.

27   See https://genographic.nationalgeographic.com/genographic/index.html.

28   Andrew Feinberg, "Epigenetics at the Epicenter of Modern Medicine," *Journal of the American Medical Association* 299, no. 11 (2008): 1345–50.

29   http://www.jcvi.org/cms/research/groups/synthetic-biology-bioenergy/.

30   Quoted in Hub Zwart, "The Adoration of a Map: Reflections on a Genome Metaphor," *Genomics, Society and Policy* 5, no. 3 (2009): 29–43.

31   http://www.genome.gov/10001772.

32   See Leah Ceccarelli, *At the Frontiers of Science: An American Rhetoric of Exploration and Exploitation in a Postcolonial Transnational Context*, forthcoming.

33   http://www.ipcb.org/issues/human_genetics/htmls/geno_pr.html. See also Leona Lone Dog, "Whose Genes are They? The Human Genome Diversity Project," *Journal of Health and Social Policy* 10, 4 (1999): 58; and Susan Hawthorne, "Land, Bodies, and Knowledge: Biocolonialism of Plants, Indigenous Peoples, Women, and People with Disabilities," *Signs: Journal of Women in Culture and Society* 32, no. 2 (2007): 318.

34   E. Marris, "The Genome of the American West," *Nature* 457 (2009): 950–52.

35 Francis Collins, Eric Green, Alan Guttmacher and Mark Guyer, "A Vision for the Future of Genomics Research," *Nature* 422 (2003): 835–47.

36 Quoted in Zwart, page 35.

37 Quoted in National Human Genome Research Institute, "International Human Genome Sequencing Consortium Describes Finished Human Genome Sequence," http://www. genome.gov/12513430.

38 Bruce Braun, "Biopolitics and the Molecularization of Life," *Cultural Geographies* 14, no. 1 (2008): 6–28.

39 Nikolas Rose, *The Politics of Life Itself: Biomedicine, Power, and Subjectivity in the Twenty-First Century* (Princeton, NJ: Princeton University Press, 2008); Nikolas Rose and Carlos Novas, "Biological Citizenship," in Aiwha Ong and Stephen Collier, eds., *Global Assemblages: Technology, Politics and Ethics As Anthropological Problems* (Oxford: Blackwell, 2005), 439–63.

40 This is the vision of Leroy Hood and his *Institute for Systems Biology*, http://www. systemsbiology.org/Intro_to_Systems_Biology/Predictive_Preventive_Personalized_ and_Participatory.

41 On the actuarial or investment-minded approach to self-management under neoliberalism, see Lauren Berlant, "Slow Death (Sovereignty, Obesity, Lateral Agency)," *Critical Inquiry* 33, no. 7 (2007): 754–80; Randy Martin, *Financialization of Daily Life* (Philadelphia: Temple University Press, 2002).

42 World Health Organization, 2008, *Closing the Gap in a Generation: Health Equity through Action on the Social Determinants of Health*, Report of the WHO Commission on the Social Determinants of Health (Geneva: WHO 2008), http://www.who.int/ social_determinants/thecommission/finalreport/en/index.html.

43 Rebecca Skloot, *The Immortal Life of Henrietta Lacks* (New York: Crown Publishers, 2010).

44 Melinda Cooper, "Experimental Labour – Offshoring Clinical Trials to China, East Asian Science," *Technology and Society: An International Journal* 2 (2008): 73–92; Adriana Petryna, "Clinical Trials Offshored: On Private Sector Science and Public Health," *BioSocieties* 2 (2007): 21–40.

45 Seth W. Glickman, et al., "Ethical and Scientific Implications of the Globalization of Clinical Research," *New England Journal of Medicine* 360 (2009): 816–23.

46 Kaushik Sunder Rajan, *Biocapital: The Constitution of Postgenomic Life* (Durham, NC: Duke University Press, 2006): 149.

47 Vinh-Kim Nguyen, *The Republic of Therapy: Triage and Sovereignty in West Africa's Time of AIDS* (Durham, NC: Duke University Press, 2010).

48 John Le Carré, *The Constant Gardener* (New York: Scribner, 2004; and Marcia Angell, "The Body Hunters," *The New York Review of Books*, October 6 (2005) http://www. nybooks.com/articles/archives/2005/oct/06/the-body-hunters/?page=1.

49 *World Medical Association*, Declaration of Helsinki: Ethical Principles for Medical Research Involving Human Subjects, http://www.wma.net/en/30publications/10policies/ b3/index.html.

50 Paul Farmer, *AIDS and Accusation: Haiti and the Geography of Blame* (Berkeley: University of California Press, 2009).

51 Farmer, *AIDS*, 8.

52 Mark Heywood, "Drug access, patents and global health: "chaffed and waxed sufficient." *Third World Quarterly* 23 (2000): 224.

53   Susan Craddock, "Market incentives, human lives, and AIDS vaccines," *Social Science & Medicine* 64, no. 5 (2007): 1042–1057.

54   Aids2031, *AIDS: Taking a Long-Term View* (Upper Saddle River, NJ: Pearson Education, 2011), 11–13.

55   Vinh-Kim Nguyen, *The Republic of Therapy: Triage and Sovereignty in West Africa's Time of AIDS* (Durham, NC: Duke University Press, 2010).

56   Ippolytos Andreas Kalofonos, "'All I Eat Is ARVs': The Paradox of AIDS Treatment Interventions in Central Mozambique," *Medical Anthropology Quarterly* 24, no. 3 (2010): 363–80.

57   Aids2031, Taking a long-term view, 40.

58   Michael Enserink, "Developing Countries to Get Some H1N1 Vaccine – But When?" *Science* November 6 (2009): 782; Lawrence Gostin, "Swine Flu Vaccine: What Is Fair?" *Hastings Center Report* 39, no. 5 (2009): 9–10.

59   Chan Khoon, "Equitable Access to Pandemic Flu Vaccines," *Third World Network* (2010), http://www.twnside.org.sg/title2/intellectual_property/info.service/2010/ipr.info.100311.htm.

60   Robert Wallace, "Breeding Influenza: The Political Virology of Offshore Farming," *Antipode* 41, no. 5 (2010): 916–51; Mike Davis, *The Monster At Our Door: The Global Threat of Avian Flu* (New York: Owl Books, 2005).

61   Andrew Lakoff, "Two Regimes of Global Health," *Humanity Fall* (2010): 59–79.

62   *Third World Network*, Agreement on influenza virus sharing and benefit sharing is a step forward but has some shortcomings, http://www.twnside.org.sg/title2/health.info/2011/health20110402.htm.

63   Scott Carney, *The Red Market: On the Trail of the World's Organ Brokers, Bone Thieves, Blood Farmers, and Child Traffickers* (New York: William Morrow, 2011).

64   Catherine Waldby and Robert Mitchell, *Tissue Economies: Blood, Organs and Cell Lines in Late Capitalism* (Durham, NC: Duke University Press, 2006).

65   Debra Budiani-Saberi and F. L. Delmonico, "Organ Trafficking and Transplant Tourism: A Commentary on the Global Realities," *American Journal of Transplantation* 8 (2008): 925–29.

66   Nancy Scheper-Hughes, "The Last Commodity: Post-Human Ethics and the Global Traffic in Fresh Organs," in Aiwha Ong and Stephen Collier, *Global Assemblages: Technology, Politics and Ethics as Anthropological Problems* (Oxford: Blackwell, 2005): 145–67.

67   Scheper-Hughes, *Last Commodity*, 150.

68   Scheper-Hughes, *Last Commodity*, 151.

69   Sallie Yea, "Trafficking in Part(s): The Commercial Kidney Market in a Manila Slum," *Global Social Policy December* 10 (2010), no. 3: 358–76.

70   Budiani-Saberi and Delmonico, Organ Trafficking.

71   Gamal I Serour, Healthcare Workers and the Brain Drain. *International Journal of Gynecology and Obstetrics* 106 (2009): 175–78.

72   Data from the WHO's Global Health Workforce Alliance, at http://www.who.int/workforcealliance/countries/en/.

73   The density metrics for physicians, nurses, and other health workers globally are all reported by the WHO (per 1000 population) at http://apps.who.int/ghodata/?vid=92100.

74   These data are from the OECD at http://www.oecd.org/document/24/0,3746,en_2649_33929_36506543_1_1_1_1,00.html.

75 Vikram Patel, "Recruiting Doctors from Poor Countries: the Great Brain Robbery?" *British Medical Journal* 327 (2003): 926–28; and Amy Hagopian et al. "The Migration of Physicians from Sub-Saharan Africa to the United States of America: Measures of the African Brain Drain," *Human Resources Health* 2 (2004): 17.

76 Edward Mills, "Should Active Recruitment of Health Workers from Sub-Saharan Africa Be Viewed As a Crime?," *The Lancet* 371 (2008): 685–88.

77 Martineau T, Decker K, Bundred P. "Brain drain" of health professionals: from rhetoric to responsible action," *Health Policy* 70 (2004): 1–10.

78 http://www.who.int/hrh/migration/code/practice/en/index.html.

79 Fitzhugh Mullan, "The Metrics of the Physician Brain Drain," *New England Journal of Medicine* 353 (2005): 1810–81.

80 WHO Global Code of Practice on the International Recruitment of Health Personnel accesed at http://www.who.int/hrh/migration/code/practice/en/index.html June 29, 2011.

81 Julio Frenk *et al.*, "Health Professionals for a New Century: Transforming Education to Strengthen Health Systems in an Interdependent World. *The Lancet* November 29 (2010), http://www.thelancet.com/journals/lancet/article/PIIS0140–6736%2810%2961854-5/fulltext?_eventId=login.

82 David Arnold, D. ed., *Warm climates and Western Medicine: The Emergence of Tropical Medicine, 1500–1900* (Atlanta, GA: Rodopi, 1996); and David Livingstone, 1999: "Tropical Climate and Moral Hygiene: The Anatomy of a Victorian Debate," *British Journal for the History of Science* 32: 93–110.

83 http://www.gapminder.org/videos/200-years-that-changed-the-world-bbc/.

84 Lant Pritchett and Larry Summers, "Wealthier is Healthier," *Journal of Human Resources* 31, no. 4 (1996): 841–68, 841.

85 Samuel Preston, "Causes and Consequences of Mortality Decline in Less Developed Countries in the Twentieth Century," in Richard Easterlin, ed., *Population and Economic Change in Developing Countries* (Chicago: Chicago University Press, 1980).

86 David Stuckler, Sanjay Basu, Martin McKee, "Budget Crises, Health, and Social Welfare Programmes," *British Medical Journal, June* 24, 341 (2010): 77–79.

87 Simon Szreter, "Rapid Economic Growth and 'the Four Ds' of Disruption, Deprivation, Disease and Death: Public Health Lessons from Nineteenth-Century Britain for Twenty-First Century China?" *Tropical Medicine and International Health* 4, no. 2 (1999): 146–52.

88 Howard Stein, *Beyond the World Bank Agenda: An Institutional Approach to Development* (Chicago: University of Chicago Press, 2008).

89 Ronald Labonté and Ted Schrecker, "Globalization and Social Determinants of Health: The Role of the Global Marketplace," *Globalization and Health* 3, no. 6 (2007): 1–17.

90 See Jim Yong Kim *et al.*, *Dying for Growth: Global Inequality and the Health of the Poor* (Monroe, ME: Common Courage Press, 2000); Meredith Fort, Mary Anne Mercer, and Oscar Gish, eds., *Sickness and Wealth: The Corporate Assault on Global Health* (Cambridge, MA: South End Press, 2004): 43–54; and Giovanni Cornia, Richard Jolly, Frances Stewart, eds., *Adjustment With a Human Face*, vol. 1: Protecting the Vulnerable and Promoting Growth (Oxford: Clarendon Press, 1987).

91 Rick Rowden, *The Deadly Ideas of Neoliberalism: How the IMF has Undermined Public Health and the Fight Against AIDS* (New York: Zed Press, 2009); and David Stuckler, Sanjay Basu, Martin McKee, 2011, "International Monetary Fund and Aid Displacement," *International Journal of Health Services* 41, no. 1 (2011): 67–76.

92   Ronald Labonté, Chantal Blouin and Lisa Forman, "Trade and Health," in Adrian Kay and Owain Williams, editors, *Global Health Governance: Transformations, Challenges and Opportunities Amidst Globalization* (New York: Palgrave Macmillan, 2009): 182–208; and Ed McGill, Poverty and Social Analysis of Trade Agreements: A More Coherent Approach? *Boston College International and Comparative Law Review* 27, no. 2 (2004): 371–427.

93   Matthew Sparke, *In the Space of Theory: Postfoundational Geographies of the Nation-State* (Minneapolis: University of Minnesota Press, 2005) chapter 3; and Roy Romanov, *Building on Values: The Future of Health Care in Canada*, Commission on the Future of Healthcare in Canada, Final Report, (Ottawa: 2002) http://publications.gc.ca/site/eng/237274/publication.html.

94   John Graham, Prescription Drug Prices in Cda & the US: Canadian Prescriptions for American Patients Are Not the Solution, *Public Policy Sources*, 70, (2003) http://www.fraserinstitute.org/research-news/display.aspx?id=13299.

95   Kim et al., 2000, Dying for growth; Paul Farmer, *Pathologies of Power: Health, Human Rights, and the New War on the Poor* (Berkeley: University of California Press, 2005); Fort *et al.*, *Sickness and Wealth*.

96   Vinh-Kim Nguyen and Karine Peschard, "Anthropology, Inequality, And Disease: A Review," *Annual Review of Anthropology* 32 (2003) 447–74; and Nancy Krieger, "Embodiment: A Conceptual Glossary for Epidemiology," *Journal of Epidemiology and Community Health* 59, no. 5 (2005): 350–55.

97   Data gathered from *World Economic Outlook Database – April 2011*, International Monetary Fund, *The World Factbook*, Central Intelligence Agency. The United States, continues to fall behind other low mortality countries, with recent research at the county level within the United States further underlining how much inequality manifests itself in worsening racial and economic disparities in longevity, Sandeep Kulkarni, Alison Levin-Rector, Majid Ezzati, Christopher Murray, "Falling Behind: Life Expectancy in US Counties from 2000 to 2007 in an International Context," *Population Health Metrics* 9, no. 16 (2011), doi: 10.1186/1478-7954-9-16.

98   Richard Wilkinson and Kate Pickett, *The Spirit Level: Why Greater Equality Makes Societies Stronger* (New York: Bloomsbury Press, 2009). See also http://www.equalitytrust.org.uk/.

99   David Stuckler, Sanjay Basu, Martin McKee, "Budget Crises, Health, and Social Welfare Programmes," *British Medical Journal* 24, no. 341, (2010): 77–79.

100 G. Rose and Michael Marmot, "Social Class and Coronary Heart Disease," *British Heart Journal* 45, no. 1 (1981): 13–19; and Michael Marmot and Richard Wilkinson, *Social Determinants of Health* (New York: Oxford University Press, 2006).

101 Ichiro Kawachi, "Social Capital, Income Inequality, and Mortality," *American Journal of Public Health*, 87, no. 9 (1997): 1491–98.

102 Vincente Navarro, ed., *Neoliberalism, Globalization and Inequalities: Consequences for Health and Quality of Life* (Amityville, NY: Baywood Publishing Company, 2007).

103 WHO, *Closing the Gap in a Generation: Health Equity through Action on the Social Determinants of Health*, The Report of the Commission on the Social Determinants of Health, WHO: Geneva, 2008, http://www.who.int/social_determinants/thecommission/finalreport/en/index.html.

104 Paul Farmer, *Infections and Inequalities: The Modern Plagues* (University of California Press, London, 1999); and Mike Davis, *Late Victorian Holocausts: El Niño Famines and the Making of the Third World* (New York: Verso, 2001).

105 Paul Farmer, "An Anthropology of Structural Violence," *Current Anthropology* 45 (2004): 305–25.
106 Quoted in Howard Waitzkin, "One and a Half Centuries of Forgetting and Rediscovering: Virchow's Lasting Contributions to Social Medicine," *Social Medicine* 1 (2006): 5–10. Barbara Starfield, "Politics, Primary Health Care and Health: Was Virchow Right?" *Journal of Epidemiological Community Health* 65, no. (2011): 653–55.
107 Wallace, Breeding Influenza, 924.
108 Ronald Labonte, Katia S Mohindra Raphael Lencucha, "Framing International Trade and Chronic Disease, *Globalization and Health* 7, no. 2 (2011) doi:10.1186./1744-8603-7-21; Anne Marie Thow, Corinna Hawkes, "The Implications of Trade Liberalization for Diet and Health: A Case Study From Central America", *Globalization and Health* 5 (2009): 5, doi: 10.1186/1744-8603-5-5.
109 Margaret Chan, "Steadfast in the midst of perils," Keynote address at the 12th World Congress on Public Health Istanbul, Turkey, April 27 2009, http://www.who.int/dg/speeches/2009/steadfast_midst_perils_20090428/en/index.html.
110 Andrew Steer, "Financial Crisis and Global Health," remarks to the 2009 WHO consultation, http://www.who.int/mediacentre/events/meetings/financial_crisis_steer_20090119/en/index.html.
111 Ted Schrecker, "The Power of Money: Global Financial Markets, National Politics, and Social Determinants of Health," in Adrian Kay and Owain Williams, editors, *Global Health Governance: Transformations, Challenges and Opportunities Amidst Globalization* (New York: Palgrave Macmillan: 2009): 160–81.
112 Mark Field, David M. Kotz, and Gene Bukhman, "Neoliberal Economic Policy, "State Desertion," and the Russian Health Crisis," in *Dying for Growth: Global Inequality and the Health of the Poor*, ed. Kim et al. (Boston: Common Courage Press, 2000): 119–137.
113 See, for example, Steve Gloyd, "Sapping the Poor: The Impact of Structural Adjustment Programs," in Fort *et al., Sickness and Wealth*, 43–54; and Anna Skosireva and Bonnie Holaday, Bonnie, "Revisiting Structural Adjustment Programs in Sub-Saharan Africa: A Long-Lasting Impact on Child Health," *World Medical & Health Policy*, 2, no. 3 (2010), http://www.psocommons.org/wmhp/vol2/iss3/art5.
114 The text of the Alma Ata Declaration is available from the WHO at http://www.who.int/hpr/NPH/docs/declaration_almaata.pdf.
115 Jeffrey Sachs, *The End of Poverty: Economic Possibilities for Our Time* (New York: Penguin Press, 2005), 19.
116 Sachs, *End of Poverty*, 82. For more of his maps of disconnection and disease, see Jeffrey Sachs, *Common Wealth: Economics for a Crowded Planet* (New York: Penguin Press, 2008).
117 O'Neil Edward, *Awakening Hippocrates: A Primer on Health, Poverty and Global Service* (Chicago: American Medical Association, 2006).
118 http://www.who.int/macrohealth/en/.
119 Jeffrey Sachs, "A Simple Plan to Save the World", *Esquire* 141, no. 5 (2004): 125–32.
120 World Bank, 2007: *Healthy Development: The World Bank Strategy for Health, Nutrition, and Population Results*, available online at the time of writing at http://siteresources.worldbank.org/HEALTHNUTRITIONANDPOPULATION/Resources/281627-1154048816360/HNPStrategyFINALApril302007.pdf at page 20.
121 David McCoy, "The World Bank's New Health Strategy: Reason for Alarm?" *The Lancet* 369 (2007): 1499–501.

122   Adrian Kay and Owain Williams, editors, *Global Health Governance: Transformations, Challenges and Opportunities Amidst Globalization* (New York: Palgrave Macmillan, 2009); and Ilona Kickbusch, Mapping the Future of Public Health: Action on Global Health. *Canadian Journal of Public Health* 97, no. 1 (2006): 6–8.

123   http://www.gatesfoundation.org/Pages/home.aspx.

124   Andrew Jack, "Remedies for drug development," *Financial Times* July 21 (2011): 10.

125   Joe Cerrell, "Making markets work," IMF (2007) http://www.imf.org/external/pubs/ft/fandd/2007/12/view.htm.

126   http://www.phmovement.org/.

127   Gorik Ooms, Wim Van Damme, Brook K Baker, Paul Zeitz and Ted Schrecker, "The 'Diagonal' Approach to Global Fund Financing: a Cure for the Broader Malaise of Health Systems?," *Globalization and Health* 4 (2008): 6; and James Pfeiffer and Mark Nichter, "What Can Critical Medical Anthropology Contribute to Global Health? A Health Systems Perspective," *Medical Anthropology Quarterly* 22, no. 4 (2008): 410–15.

128   Ursula Casabonne and Charles Kenny, *The Best Things in Life are (Nearly) Free: Technology, Knowledge, and Global Health*, Center for Global Development, Working Paper 252, May 2011, www.cgdev.org; and Charles Kenny, *Getting Better: Why Global Development Is Succeeding: And How We Can Improve the World Even More* (New York: Basic Books, 2011).

129   April Dembosky, "Invasion of the Body Trackers," *Financial Times*, June 11, 2011: Life and Arts, 19.

10

Responses

Chapter Contents

Chapter Concepts

1. Responses to the interdependencies of globalization are affected by divergent discourses about Globalization.
2. Responses range from rightist and hyper-nationalistic reactions to mainstream concerns with personal resilience to leftist resistance based on global solidarity.
3. Leftist resistance demands radical reforms of the 10 neoliberal policy norms and the globalization of global justice versus the inequalities of the global market.
4. Rightist reactions reject global solidarity and international collaboration, offering national self-assertion as the answer to transnational market rule.
5. Universities now position themselves as centers for global education.
6. The goals of global education tend to range from entrepreneurial training for global competition to teaching and learning for global solidarity and justice.

Key Concept

Our responses to globalization rest in turn on whether and how we see our ethical responsibilities. Conservatives generally tend to see these more in terms of protecting national and local communities from global forces that look like foreign threats

Introducing Globalization: Ties, Tensions, and Uneven Integration, First Edition. Matthew Sparke.
© 2013 Matthew Sparke. Published 2013 by Blackwell Publishing Ltd.

to cherished traditions and institutions. Market-oriented mainstream responses tend instead to focus on individualistic acts of integration, innovation, and self-improvement within the existing world system. And more radical leftist alternatives imagine and work globally towards freedom from this market-dominated system, rethinking our global responsibilities as the basis of our response-abilities and thus our capacity to struggle globally for a better world.

10.1   Globalization and the Three "R"s: Reaction, Resilience, and Resistance

Responses to globalization clearly come in many different forms, with divergent discourses about capital "G" Globalization repeatedly reshaping the ways communities respond to increasing global interdependencies. There are extreme right-wing anti-Globalization responses that tend to be ultra-nationalistic and *reactionary*, that blame global elites and foreigners for all the problems produced by global change, and push for various sorts of repression and reprisal against the perceived threats. There are more moderate mainstream responses that focus on *resilience*, using global, national, and local coping strategies that also turn at times to relief in individualistic self-investment, entertainment, enclaving, and escapism. And then there are diverse forms of active and collective *resistance*, some of which look a little like twentieth century national revolutions (as in a number of Latin American countries in the last decade), but which more commonly today seek global justice by linking local challenges to **neoliberalism** (such as the Occupy movement) with "alter-globalization" ideas and initiatives aimed to increase the globalization of global justice, global human rights, and global health through varied forms of transnational solidarity.

Examples of the diversity of possible responses have already been highlighted throughout this book. In Chapters 4 and 9, for instance, we noted the ways in which reactionaries blame migrants as sources of economic insecurity and illness, and in Chapter 8, reactionary forms of geopolitics were discussed, too. In Chapter 9, we examined how biomedical responses to climate change are conceptualized in terms of building resilience for the anthropocene. And also on resilience, in Chapter 5 on market hedges against financial crisis, and in Chapter 8 on enclaving, we considered other privileged investments in personal risk management, as well as the more desperate coping strategies adopted by slum dwellers in the face of environmental and urban change. Elsewhere, meanwhile, in Chapters 2, 4, and 7, we noted how global activists, unions, environmentalists, feminists, and groups representing the poor and landless have gone beyond the reworking strategies of resilience to focus instead on how to resist neoliberalism with transnational meetings, organizing, and advocacy.

Along the way, we have also addressed some of the most influential global responses to the challenges of poverty, including the development targets of the UN's Millennium Development Goals and the rise (and more recent fall) of micro-finance as a popular neoliberal strategy targeted both trans-nationally *and* sub-nationally at nurturing resilient entrepreneurs among the poor through individualized lending and monitoring. Finally, in Chapter 9, we examined how similarly targeted global health interventions have developed as another micro-reworking of traditional "Washington Consensus" macro-neoliberalism: a new kind of compensatory market foster care that responds to the market failures indicated by ill health with new market-mediated investments in disease-specific biomedical responses. Being pioneered by the Gates Foundation in Washington state, this compensatory innovation in neoliberalism can be usefully called the "New Washington Consensus." But dependent as it is on philanthropic efforts to correct market failures, its development as a consensus among private philanthropists also indexes public dissensus over the old consensual claims concerning the inevitable benefits and leveling effects of market-based globalization.

Clearly, questions can be asked about the degree to which all the diverse responses to globalization challenge or rework the traditional neoliberal discourse of big "G" Globalization, including its appeals to historical newness, political inevitability, and socio-geographical leveling. Section 10.2 here therefore examines how leftist alter-globalization alternatives contrast with rightist reactions in the way they consciously reflect on neoliberal discourse: questioning its monopoly on the truth about globalization by rethinking the ways in which global ties can be made more just and fair. Unlike extreme rightists, these alter-globalization activists therefore tend to acknowledge the real-world interdependencies that Globalization discourse reflects, but they do so in order to advance counter-arguments that, in the words of the World Social Forum, "another world is possible." Rightist reactions to Globalization instead tend to insist on national sovereignty in ways that block collaborative international approaches to addressing problems such as global warming and hyper-exploitation. Section 10.2 also highlights how rightist responses to globalization therefore end up supporting some neoliberal norms – such as property rights, minimalist government, and anti-tax ideas – even as they rage against the unemployment, lost local control, and other economic insecurities introduced by global market competition.

Finally, in Section 10.3 we turn the focus onto the sorts of response being developed in venues where textbooks like this one are read: namely, universities. In rich countries at least, political radicalism has been relatively muted over the last two decades in these privileged spaces of higher education. This may now be changing as the economic aspirations of university students hit the economic wall of a deep planetary recession. In 2011 in the context of the deepening global crises, budget cuts for higher education provoked broad anti-austerity protests on college campuses, along with more radical alliances between students and the Occupy movement. Yet despite the spiraling costs of higher education created by neoliberal cutbacks, fees, and tuition hikes, despite the increasing unemployment among college graduates, and even despite more desperate demands for free food pantries and emergency shelter on poorer college campuses, extreme suffering and economic despair remain rare for most university students. Instead, university education still tends to increase connections and economic opportunities, while cultivating diverse technological and humanitarian hopes about building a better collective future. Even quite conservative students are therefore enabled to think and act beyond narrow "hometown" concerns of upholding tradition, cherishing old rituals, and defending property and privilege. And thus, instead of advancing rightist reactions, typical student-led responses to globalization and its challenges – responses such as social entrepreneurship programs, global health volunteerism, and anti-sweatshop campaigns – tend to fall along a continuum between building resilience and resistance. We will conclude the book by considering these two categories in turn: addressing the globalized university as a venue for building new global futures with strategies that range from entrepreneurial and distinctly neoliberal investments in resilience to radically anti-neoliberal struggles of resistance.

Before we head into these final sections, though, some clarifications need to be made about the categories being used. At a theoretical level, all three "r" words being considered here – reaction, resilience, and resistance – make for useful organizing categories. However, as we proceed, we must remember that out in the world at large, the tidy distinctions between the words do not mesh perfectly with the messy middle grounds where economic imperatives, collective organization, personal interests, and conflicting visions of alternative futures all come together to shape responses. University-based reflections on globalization, particularly those that are critical of mainstream or hegemonic commonsense about neoliberalism, can sometimes seem utopian and overly idealistic when considered from this real-world perspective. However, on this point about utopianism, it is also worth remembering that neoliberalism depends on a kind of utopian visioning of the future itself, a belief that the self-regulating efficiencies of the market will eventually correct for all the social and economic problems unleashed by market forces and create a perfect world. This is important to note because it further helps us understand why so much of contemporary popular culture is preoccupied with imagining and building neoliberal utopias. These, too, are responses to globalization in so far as they promise escapes for all those who can pay and play away from the downsides of liberalized market forces. Holiday resorts, cruise liners, private shopping malls, gated communities, luxury SUVs, and many of the other enclaved spaces discussed in Chapter 8 are illustrative of neoliberal utopianism in this way. So, too, are onscreen and online getaways such as *The Biggest Loser* and *Second Life*. These and many other examples from so-called Reality TV and online gaming present us with high-definition but unreal realities where competition and money-making are celebrated at the same time as the promises of new looks, new prosperity, or new e-scapes are offered as alternatives to flesh and blood worlds of obesity, economic distress, ruined landscapes, and loneliness.

Much of the popular culture that presents us with onscreen vistas of entrepreneurial opportunity does little to make us think critically about the utopianism and escapism involved. And, given the huge profits to be made in the sale of products such as video games (the global market for which was worth about $56 billion in 2011), this is not surprising. However, there are also now a long list of dystopian movies and TV shows that do seek to prick the utopian bubbles and explore the fake realities created by the commercialized cultural universe of neoliberal globalization. *The Matrix* trilogy, *Surrogates*, *The Truman Show*, *Pleasantville*, *Inception*, and *WALL-E*, for example, all address widespread unease with the superficiality and unreality of everyday life in a world dominated by commercial media and capitalist interests, while other movies and shows such as *Avatar, Babel, Bladerunner, Minority Report*, and *The Wire* force audiences to consider forms of violence occurring on the frontier between hyper-mediated life-worlds and the real deaths that the high-tech mediations hide but yet support. Taking a cue from this kind of critical questioning of commercial commonsense, the next section outlines how the utopian promise of neoliberal Globalization has been addressed (or not) in responses to globalization. Of notable interest here, of course, are the responses to the TINA-tout argument we examined in Chapter 2. Taking on big G Globalization myth-making, anti-neoliberal activists argue thus that there are a whole suite of alternatives to neoliberal reform and the inequalities, asymmetries, and exclusions it has produced.

10.2   Reaction and Resistance to Global Neoliberalization

To begin with, it is useful to remember the 10 neoliberal norms or "commandments" that we originally examined in Chapter 1. Each one has provoked divergent responses. Table 10.1 shows thus how for each main neoliberal norm there are both alter-globalization resistance responses and anti-globalization reactionary responses, too. The alter-globalization responses are anti-neoliberal and thus propose alternative approaches to globalization contrary to the TINA-tout myths about Globalization. By contrast, the reactionary responses tend to be opposed to all new forms of global interdependency, and, while they are anti-liberal in its liberal welfarist sense, they are not necessarily anti-neoliberal. Indeed, libertarian and extreme far-right responses can, depending on the national context, sometimes share and concur with neoliberal ideas about the benefits of letting markets self-regulate. For the same reason, they do not generally use the term neoliberalism as a focus for criticism and organizing.

At the outset it should be clear that the lists of positions described in Table 10.1 are only approximate guides to where political allegiances lie and how responses to globalization are organized. Due to their generally nationalistic nature, reactionary responses tend to adopt very specific local characteristics and xenophobic attitudes that often divide them from one country to the next. For the same reason, the list of anti-globalization reactionary responses suggests more unity across borders than is actually felt by rightist groups themselves who often define their reactionary projects by emphasizing national differences and demanding the buildup of border defenses. Witness in Europe, for example, the contrasts between the True Finns in Finland with their mix of social conservativism and welfarist ideals, the Austrian Freedom Party with their neo-Nazi linkages, and the British National Front, which points with pride to Britain's historic victories over European enemies in the past,

Table 10.1   Neoliberal norms and responses from left and right

Neoliberal norms	Alter-globalization resistance responses	Anti-globalization reactionary responses
1 Trade liberalization	Fair trade with worker rights	Nationalistic protectionism
2 Privatize public services	Protect public services and spaces	Limit migrant access to services
3 Deregulate business	Re-regulate business globally	Subsidize national business, farms, and weapons industries
4 Cut public spending	Increase spending on education, health, and social services	Cap spending and reduce public debt as if it were family debt
5 Reduce and flatten taxes	Redistribute wealth with taxes	Only tax to fund law and military
6 Entice foreign investment	Tax Forex markets to fund debt relief, aid, and global health	Blame foreigners and stop immigration
7 De-unionize and increase labor market flexibility	Link global worker solidarity with social-justice campaigns	Fight socialism and maintain traditional social hierarchies
8 Encourage export-led growth	Foster local food security and environmental sustainability	Control protected environments for energy independence
9 Reduce inflation	Develop debt relief and local economic bartering systems	Punish debtors and return to gold standard for money
10 Enforce property rights with patents and titling of land	Promote open-source, shared science on global priorities	Defend property with weapons and criticize global science

with the Front National in France and the Italian neo-fascists who themselves do not agree on much except getting rid of Roma gypsies, which in turn puts them at odds with Romanian rightists, except on the issue of keeping moslems out of Europe! Meanwhile, hard-line Islamic reactionaries in countries such as Saudi Arabia oppose the freedoms women have won amidst global capitalism, even as they use global networks and money from the global capitalist demand for oil to spread their conservative (but quite newly refurbished) traditions of Wahhabism internationally.

More generally, due to their particularistic historical concerns with preserving cultural, ethnic, and religious traditions, reactionary responses to globalization tend to be more context contingent and contradictory: varying much more than the global justice movement from one nation-state to the next, and sometimes actually supporting neoliberal policies (such as anti-unionism and privatization) at the same time as condemning the demise of tradition and the loss of national economic control. It is partly as a result of all these idiosyncrasies that rightist anti-globalization discourse tends not to talk about neoliberalism or critique its dominance in policy-making. The implication instead is that global interdependencies can be ignored, or at least re-conquered, even when all the proud displays of national flags and patriotic clothing bear the "Made in China" hallmarks of globalized commodity chains. By targeting outsiders, reactionary responses prefer to pin blame for social and economic problems on foreigners or the cultural globalism of Hollywood or the corporate cosmopolitanism of "liberal" elites, all the while they resubmit themselves to market forces by insisting on forms of national sovereignty that (as we saw in Chapter 7) repeatedly block transnational efforts to regulate the global marketplace.

Some of the complexity of reactionary responses to neoliberalism is well illustrated by the US "Tea Party" movement that developed in response to the global financial crisis in 2008. With its name and old-fashioned costumes, this conservative movement deliberately recalls the American revolution against an old global empire in order to connect popular US discontent over global financial crisis management with the traditional arguments of US conservatives – including anti-tax arguments – that have more normally tended from Reagan onwards to be aligned quite effectively with the interests of global financial elites and their support for neoliberal norms. Tea Partiers, as they have come to be called in the United States, worry a great deal about the loss of US economic power and particularly about the decline of the dollar as a *de facto* global reserve currency. After 2008, they linked these concerns with complaints about Federal Reserve monetary accommodation and government spending on the post-crisis bail-out of banks, including foreign banks and other global financial interests. And they have called at times for new forms of economic nationalism, too, with Tea Party-affiliated blogs sometimes decrying the threats posed to US economic sovereignty by free-trade agreements and globalization.

Ironically, their nationalistic position has nevertheless led the Tea Party leaders to push for forms of US debt reduction, austerity, and anti-inflationary policy at the Federal Reserve that put the Tea Party in the same hard-line neoliberal position as some of the financial markets' most cosmopolitan and globalized investors: namely Asian owners of US treasury bonds. Thus, even as their movement feeds on popular US discontent surrounding banks, declining property values, mortgage foreclosures, unemployment, and all the suffering associated with widespread personal bankruptcies, Tea Partiers just like global bankers tend to be against any kind of debt forgiveness, and most decidedly opposed to federal stimulus through deficit spending. Perhaps most ironically of all, these same positions led the Tea Party in the summer of 2011 to force through big budget-cutting measures in the US Congress, the political struggle around which in turn precipitated one of the big ratings agencies to downgrade US debt and thereby generate yet further financial crisis for the United States and the rest of the world. Anti-neoliberal critics see such patterns as a sign of the wider global crisis of neoliberal capitalism itself, particularly its overreliance on credit and its resulting dependency on an extraordinarily powerful global financial industry. But Tea Partiers do not talk about neoliberalism, and prefer instead to blame so-called liberals in the US government for America's declining economic fortunes.

Meanwhile, far-right reactionaries in the British National Party wrap themselves in the flag that the original Boston Tea Party turned against in order to turn against immigrants to the United Kingdom, European bureaucrats, and the economic threats of global competition that they see as undermining British sovereignty. In these arguments, the royal family and associated flag-wrapped rituals of war and remembrance also loom large as national traditions that are perceived as threatened by globalization and corporate control, including foreign control of the British media by companies such as Rupert Murdoch's *News International*. "The indignation with which the controlled media have covered the news that Royal wreaths commemorating Britain's war dead are now made in China," noted the British National Party website in a typical complaint about foreign threats, "illustrates precisely how little they know about the dangers of globalisation – and how correct the British National Party is."[1] The anti-Islamic attitudes of the British National Party are also a disturbingly powerful example of the way in which moslem immigrants in particular have been targeted by western reactionaries as the most dangerous examples of globalization. However, this widespread far-right reaction should not obscure the fact that Islamic extremists themselves also engage in anti-globalization rhetoric. Most notoriously, after the 9/11 terrorist attacks on the United States, Osama bin Laden himself described al-Qaeda's strike on the World Trade Center as an attack on the towers of global economic power. This in turn has led many commentators to note the obvious contradiction between al-Qaeda's opposition to globalization and its own extensive global networks of communication and terrorist training, as well as its use of a notably globalizing technology – commercial jets – to carry out the 9/11 attacks. But such contradictions are just as apparent in the West itself, with extreme white supremacist nationalists such as the Norwegian Anders Behring Breivik drawing heavily on the transnational influence of anti-Islam, anti-multicultural, and anti-Marxist bloggers in the United States.[2]

In contrast to the convolutions we see in reactionary responses, the global alter-globalization movement shares a common set of critiques of neoliberalization and a common agenda for radically re-regulating global capitalism (although there is obviously disagreement between reformers and those who see themselves as committed anti-capitalists). Participants from different parts of the world still respond to unique local experiences of dispossession and distress. And yet, much of what unites the global justice movement is a collective demand for repossession (hence the Occupy movement's interest in retaking public space) and a collective sense of grievance against dispossession. Accumulating a long list of such grievances, left-leaning alter-globalization activists often talk explicitly about the global dominance of neoliberalism as a shared global narrative linking local stories of loss and suffering. As well as responding to what the activists critique as its ideological lies, the global justice movement is thus also a response focused on the global ties created by the global expansion and entrenchment of neoliberal governance.

Alter-globalization organizing is for all the above reasons knowingly based upon a critical awareness of the processes of neoliberalization. Directly addressing the inequalities and asymmetries that define these processes and their outcomes, these forms of resistance are at the same time advanced in opposition to the myth-making surrounding "big G" Globalization. And yet, it is obviously not by any means opposed to the "little g" globalization of solidarity and protest against neoliberalization. Instead, it tends to be deliberately organized across borders using global networks and meetings to develop a shared agenda of global alternatives to neoliberal policy-making norms and assumptions. Even though Korean workers, American anti-sweatshop activists, Mexican peasants, English environmentalists, and Indian opponents of dam-building may not share many of the same experiences of globalization, they see the political, economic, and ecological ties that bind their lives together as the basis for shared struggle against neoliberal policies. For the same reason, alter-globalization events such as the World Social Forums have tended in turn to be as unified in opposition to neoliberal governance as events such as the Davos-based World Economic Forum are consistently in agreement on neoliberalism's benefits.[3] Thus, for each of the 10 neoliberal commandments, there are anti-neoliberal alternatives, although as we shall now see, some of them remain refracted through particular local experiences of global interdependency, and all of them tend in turn to be opposed in reactionary responses to globalization.

10.2.1   "Fair trade" versus "free trade"

In proposing plans for "fair trade," alter-globalization activism generally begins by responding to the actual effects of free-trade agreements, including their legal harmonization effects. In response to this response, TINA-touts and other advocates of neoliberal norms usually seek to defend free trade by turning to abstract economic models of comparative advantage and the gains from trade. But for most activists, these theoretical models are beside the point, because they do not address the messy reality in which trade agreements operate to advance the interests of particular countries at particular times in ways that also impose all sorts of new quasi-constitutional regulations on signatory governments. As we saw in Chapter 6, the empirical effects of free-trade agreements are generally better understood as re-regulative rather than simply de-regulative. They only approximate slowly and unevenly to classical economic ideas about liberalizing trade from all tariff and non-tariff barriers. This means that demands for fair trade have generally taken two different forms based on where critics of traditional Washington Consensus policies find themselves.

First, the more radical anti-neoliberal approach involves forms of fair trade designed to resist and reverse "race to the bottom" tendencies. Proposals of this kind include ideas about protecting workers from sweatshop conditions, allowing union organizing, preventing child labor, improving environmental impacts, and guaranteeing a basic living wage and health protections for workers all the way along global commodity and outsourcing chains. Sometimes, these proposals envision using the power of trade agreements themselves to force a new race up from the bottom (or at least a steady march towards incremental improvements), and to a very small extent this is what unions organizing in the EU have been able to achieve with their transnational works councils and other networking efforts.

More commonly, fair-trade goals of "upward harmonization" are consumer-driven. They involve efforts to create third-party fair-trade certification schemes that enable consumers to leverage their buying power to benefit the workers and communities producing the commodities that are consumed at the end of global commodity chains. These sorts of certified fair-trade sourcing programs have been especially successful for food items favored by wealthy consumers, and thus it is now relatively easy to find fair-trade chocolate, fair-trade coffee, fair-trade olive oil, and certain fair-trade fruits (such as bananas) in rich-country superstores. However, many staple foods such as wheat, corn, rice, and soya seem to be beyond the reach of fair-trade certification (even when third-party certifiers such as Fair Trade USA relax their rules – as they did in 2011 – in the name of scaling up their impact). Moreover, as was noted in Chapter 9, for other common consumer items such as petroleum, non-recycled plastics, and beef burgers consumer-based fair trade simply seems a contradiction in terms.

The second approach to fair trade is actually much more relevant to the global trading of staple agricultural goods. It is in fact a neoliberal response to the unevenness and re-regulative effects of actual trade agreements, but it still reflects a dissenting response from the Global South to the way in which **Washington Consensus** neoliberalism has worked in practice. In short, this second sort of appeal to fair trade has come from big staples-exporting countries such as India and Brazil that have complained about the unfair subsidies and other trade protections that still exist for rich-country farmers. Whether it is in regards to EU support for the common agriculture policy subsidies to rural parts of EU member states, or US support for American farmers of corn, cotton, soy, and sugar, or Japan's support for its rice farmers, the main complaint made by the staples-exporting countries is that rich countries need to play fair and practice the actual free trade that they are always pushing when it comes to other more high-tech goods and pharmaceuticals.

Although the two main forms of fair trade are quite distinct in their positions on neoliberalism, they have nevertheless been often tied together in practice in venues where neoliberalism has also been simultaneously questioned. Thus, although India and Brazil led neoliberal calls for fairer free trade at the ill-fated 1999 meetings in Seattle, and although the protestors outside in the streets demanded anti-neoliberal fair trade based on the upwards harmonization of global working conditions and environmental protections, the two sorts of demands effectively came together to represent a significant dissensus with Washington Consensus neoliberalism at the **WTO**. For the same reason, the subsequent Doha round of WTO trade negotiations have led to more and more questioning of US and western dominance, and American negotiators have become increasingly unable to push the agenda of Washington DC. This is one of the main reasons why, in turn, the United States has instead tended over the last decade to pursue narrow bilateral deals with countries such as Singapore and South Korea. Nevertheless, as well as marking the impact of fair-trade opposition to traditional free trade, these developments index the growing reaction against multilateral trade agreements from the right, too, with Tea Party affiliated Republicans in particular expressing hostility towards trade liberalization to pollsters.

Indeed, one Pew Research Center poll after the elections of 2010 found that 54% of Republican voters thought that trade agreements like **NAFTA** and the policies of the WTO were "bad for the US" (compared with only 35% of Democrat voters).[4] And given that multilateral free-trade agreements look set over the long haul to undermine the national protections enjoyed by wealthy farmers in North America, Japan, and Europe, it is not hard to understand why rural conservatives in these regions are tending towards anti-free trade positions, too.

10.2.2   Protecting the public versus privatization

In contrast to conservative right-wing concerns about lost economic sovereignty and diminishing influence, another underlying alter-globalization concern with trade agreements is the way in which they have helped to lock in the neoliberal privatization of public services. When left-leaning governments return to power after public assets, and agencies have been sold off, they frequently find that trade agreements prevent them from moving what has been privatized back into the public realm. To do so, as Canadian governments have found out the hard way, risks being accused in the language of NAFTA's **Chapter 11** of actions "tantamount to expropriation." More generally, any effort by governments to provide public services risks being labeled protectionist. Universal public services in particular are considered non-tariff barriers to trade if they undercut private-sector competition and thereby deprive private companies of market access. However, considered from the perspective of protecting the public – say, for example, by providing free nursing care, free schooling, universal auto-insurance, or nationally sponsored media that retains locally relevant content – the protectionism involved is not about trade and markets at all. Instead, it's about protecting public health, welfare, and democracy. From the perspective of anti-neoliberal critics, public service, public education, public health, and public spaces of democratic deliberation should not even be considered commodities in the first place. They should be protected as part of the commons and for the common good.

In reactionary responses to declining public services in Europe and North America, the more dominant concern is with how these services are being used by immigrants and others deemed unworthy of national protection. Particularistic notions of national identity that encode racial, ethnic, sexual, and class-based stereotypes in a vision of the ideal national citizen – for example, the straight, white, Christian man of property in the United States or the upper-caste male Hindu in India – are thereby put to work in arguments about who truly deserves to benefit from services funded by national taxpayers. Meanwhile, in the name of defending their particular nation's tax base, conservative protectionists in turn try to support national businesses in the name of the nation, too. Protecting free health care or free schools is not the issue for them. Instead, they urge consumers to "Buy British" or "Buy American" as a way of supporting national businesses and a territorially defined vision of national capitalism.

In contrast to nationalistic conservatives, the fact that anti-neoliberal protectionism is about protecting the commons and not about protecting national businesses also explains why it is often transnational, too. Protecting the global climate, and all the oceans, forests, and other ecosystems that cross national borders is thus just as much part of the alter-globalization movement as protecting national and local public services such as health care and libraries. Indeed, while defending high-quality public services from privatization is obviously only an anti-neoliberal issue in wealthy contexts where the services exist in the first place, protecting public ecosystems and common lands is a much more universal and thus unifying alter-globalization concern in the Global South. This is why some of the same protestors and activists who have organized at the World Social Forum and against the G8 have also turned their energies in recent years to action on global climate change, using their anti-neoliberal arguments to contest the limits of corporate sustainability plans at the unsuccessful "COP15" Copenhagen meetings in 2009 along with the follow-up failure in Durban in 2011.

In turn, it is their related commitment to protecting public spaces for free speech and democratic protest that also led many in the global justice movement to see common cause in the 2011 uprisings against Middle Eastern autocrats as well as in the almost simultaneous street protests in Greece, Spain, and Portugal against IMF austerity measures. These same commonalities traveled transnationally still further in the subsequent development of the Occupy movement in the U.S in the second half of 2001. Indeed, the original call to bring a tent to Wall Street on September 17, 2011 (itself coming across the border from *Adbusters* in Canada) invoked the inspiration of preceding global protests by referring back to the "Arab Spring" in Egypt and asking: "Are you ready for another Tahrir moment?" Taking this transnationalizing trajectory forward, the Occupy movement subsequently went global itself, with more and more occupations of other centers of neoliberal calculation all around the world. And amidst all of these efforts to repossess public space in the face of neoliberal privatization, the Occupy movement has also highlighted global commonalities among the world's 99%: in short, a shared sense of grievance against the global 1% capitalist class and its efforts to liberalize business and investors from democratic accountability.

10.2.3   Re-regulating versus deregulating business

While they criticize the imposition of neoliberal regulations by the IMF in moments of financial crisis, alter-globalization activists also argue that these moments come about in the first place because of the ways other neoliberal reforms have deregulated global business, giving free rein to finance in particular. In response, they argue that global finance and transnational capitalism more generally should be much better regulated. However, rather than argue for re-regulation on the national level, the broader goals of the global justice movement involve promoting global laws and codes of conduct aimed to create new global protections for the vulnerable and an upward harmonization of labor and environmental standards across international borders. Going global in this regulatory way is not about undermining national democracy, argue the activists, but rather about matching economic globalization with a much more inclusive and democratically accountable political form of globalization, too. In other words, it is imagined as a way of bringing global political accountability to the global economic accountancy of the market.

One minimal political demand that alter-globalization activists share with many mainstream commentators is for more than just trade ministers to be party to trade negotiations. They argue thus that policy-makers and stakeholders with responsibility for other issues of international importance should be there, too. It is hoped that this will allow negotiations on trade to accommodate a wider political awareness of their implications for all the supposedly non-trade issues – the environment, health, education, and labor rights – that are nevertheless profoundly affected by trade, and which often enjoy widespread international support for protection. If, for example, an environment minister with national support for upholding international agreements on protecting endangered species was part of trade negotiations, those negotiations and resulting regulations and arbitrations might do much more to balance economic interests with environmental interests. More radically, global justice campaigns are conceptualized around the hope that regulatory protections for many other supposedly non-trade issues can be expanded globally as a political counterweight to the neoliberal norms enabled and enforced by trade agreements.

As we saw in Chapter 7, while neoliberal national reforms are entrenched by trade agreements and structural adjustment plans, non-neoliberal laws tend to be systematically blocked in the name of recognizing and protecting national administrative autonomy. This is often where nationalistic reactionary responses come in handy for global businesses. Any time talk turns to raising global labor standards or taxing polluters and global financiers, conservative calls for respecting national sovereignty can be used to slow down and stop the reform process. It is precisely this selective sovereignty that alter-globalization activists seek to challenge by proposing parallel transnational laws to protect workers, citizens, and the environment. Meanwhile, conservatives themselves reject the accusation that they are supporting global neoliberalism and insist on more nationalistic protection and subsidies for domestic businesses, especially agricultural and, in the United States and the United Kingdom at least, weapons-making industries, too.

10.2.4   Spending on education, health, and social services versus austerity

Challenging the law-like effects of global financial discipline, structural adjustment plans, and free-trade agreements, the alter-globalization movement also makes the case repeatedly for spending the world's riches to alleviate the suffering of the world's poor and dispossessed. For welfare-state liberals and Keynesian-minded economists, such departures from strict neoliberal market discipline are justified in the name of keeping capitalism going for the long haul. They argue that less punitive approaches to policing debt ultimately pay back bigger dividends to lenders because they allow for the deficit spending and demand creation necessary for regenerating capitalist growth. They also argue that without aid for education, welfare, and health, countries will remain mired in poverty and sickness, becoming politically unstable threats to the rest of the world system. By contrast, for more radical global justice activists, such debt relief is merely the start of paying back debts that should more generally flow the other way: in other words, the debts the west owes the rest for slavery and colonization; the debts owed to sweatshop factory workers for their exploitation; and the debts owed to countries with ruined environments for all the wars and resource-extraction projects they have endured from the years of empire onwards. Activists demanding such radical responses argue that economic austerity is itself a form of domination against which strategic defaults and other more radical acts of disobedience are entirely justified. And in making such arguments, they also tend to condemn neoliberalism as an immoral form of political control concealed behind the abstract formulae and cost–benefit calculations of economic management.

By contrast, rightist responses appeal to home truths about personal responsibility, frugality, and hard work to argue that deficit-spending by governments on public services is the real moral hazard. Orthodox neoliberals also complain about the moral hazard of the debts created by expensive public services. But while this is a matter of economic returns on investment for neoliberal lenders and their lawyers, for more conservative advocates of austerity the issue really is one of moral probity, of making individuals properly accountable for their own choices whether they are good or bad, and of reducing government as much as possible to the role of providing law, order, and security. Balancing the national budget is also commonly reduced in rightist reactions to a family-scale morality tale about living within one's means. Economic arguments about nation-states being different from individual families are thereby ignored, while Keynesian calls for deficit-spending and pump-priming by governments are described as socialist and traitorous, even when they are put forward in the name of saving capitalism from its own cyclical crises. Instead, whether deliberately or not, conservatives recall the original Greek word for economy: that is *οἰκονόμος*, meaning roughly "rules of a household" (a composite derived from *οἶκος* [oikos] "house," and *νόμος* [nomos] "law or custom"). Their concern with the virtues of the private home come together with their suspicions of public corruption to shape negative conservative reactions to public spending in general. They argue that giving government the right to borrow and implement demand management always invites corruption and the misallocation of resources. And these concerns with government corruption only become more heightened for conservatives when they hear global calls for redistribution. Yet this is exactly what many alter-globalization activists demand.

10.2.5   Wealth redistribution versus tax cuts

Everywhere neoliberal norms have been implemented, in-country levels of inequality have increased. To pay for tax cuts for the wealthy and corporations, public services are reduced and public assets privatized in ways that further reduce resources available to the poor. In response, workers strike, activists agitate, and protestors march demanding wealth redistribution, and while police repression is common in countries as different as the United Kingdom and China, recent democratic revolutions in Latin American countries such as Bolivia and Ecuador show that the anti-neoliberal calls can nevertheless prevail, leading to electoral success and real redistributive changes, too. The key according to scholars of global resistance is for anti-neoliberal campaigns to connect the concerns with economic inequality with wider forms of dispossession affecting people's everyday lives in the context of neoliberal privatization and austerity.[5] In other words, struggles against global class injustice are more effective when linked with local campaigns addressing place-specific forms of loss, suffering, and survival. This is what the Occupy movement was seeking to do in the United States by juxtaposing the wealth of the 1% against the economic insecurity of the 99%. Rightist responses to this movement have been quick to associate it with delinquency and social disorder. They see Occupiers not as part of a global resistance movement but rather as the rise of an un-American mob scene, a specter of socialist unrest that somehow looks foreign in the eyes of hard-right American exceptionalists. Accordingly, they are willing for tax-dollars to be raised and spent on policing and the military to keep this and other foreign threats at bay.

In contrast to conservatives, calls for taxation and economic redistribution have been rearticulated as part of the broad public interest by Occupy activists. By including so many in the so-called 99% – a percentage that is increasingly seen to refer to a global as well as a national citizenry – the movement has been charged with being overly vague and overly generalizing. But it is precisely the inclusivist aspect of 99% arguments that has allowed the Occupy movement to highlight all the many different sorts of communities that have been hard hit by Wall Street-led neoliberalism. Whether it is families who have seen their homes foreclosed on by banks, students who have seen the cost of college become impossible to afford, the swelling ranks of the unemployed trapped in wageless lives, or union workers who have had their pensions and benefits slashed, people have started to see the common thread of dispossession. Moreover, whether or not they have actually started camping or joining protest marches themselves, many ordinary Americans identify with the protestors' discontent and agree with calls for more taxes on the top 1%. They report feeling disenfranchised by a political process that is heavily influenced by financiers and other monied interests, and, having seen their democracy become increasingly financialized, they have no hesitation in supporting the re-democratization of finance and thus the occupation of Wall Street and other financial centers.

10.2.6   Tax Forex markets versus chasing foreign investment

One particular demand of Occupy Wall Street that has resonated globally and been taken up as a meaningful policy alternative to neoliberal globalization is the idea of taxing global financial transfers in the foreign-exchange (Forex) markets. This idea needs to be understood in turn as a direct response to the TINA-tout argument that Globalization makes it imperative for governments to entice foreign investment by deregulating capital markets. In a globalized world, they say, any attempt at controlling and taxing capital will scare off foreign investment and end wealth generation altogether. The extraordinarily footloose mobility of money movements around the world is a key concern in this respect, as are the multiple ways in which such movements discipline governments worried about a sudden loss of standing among foreign investors. Yet it is precisely in response to this anxiety about footloose capital that global activists recommend implementing a so-called Robin Hood tax on the speculative flows of "hot money" moving around the planet through Forex markets.

Debate continues over what size such a Forex currency-exchange tax would have to be to slow down speculative flows, but the basic idea initiated by the Nobel laureate economist James Tobin in the early 1970s was for a relatively low rate of about 0.5% per currency transaction. Tobin himself has subsequently complained about his ideas being "hijacked" by the alter-globalization movement.[6] Like most neoliberal economists, he insists he is in favor of free trade and that he supports the work of the international financial institutions such as the World Bank and IMF. Nevertheless, led by the Jubilee debt-forgiveness organization in the United Kingdom and by ATTAC in France, alter-globalization groups argue that Tobin's taxation ideas actually present an alternative to IMF and World Bank austerity measures. With the revenue generated by such a Robin Hood tax, they believe a globally accountable organization or development agency at the UN could administrate real debt relief and fund new aid and global health programs, too.

Going forward, it is clear that one of the big challenges facing any effort to establish a tax on Forex exchanges is that of making it a truly global tax. Currency centers that are not included would immediately become the staging ground for a way around the tax by globally mobile financial players. This kind of financial diversion problem became especially clear in 2011, when EU leaders began to discuss French government proposals that a financial transaction tax be imposed across the EU. While this was clearly transnational, the fact that it was not a global proposal also immediately raised concerns that it would have only negative repercussions for EU member countries. European banking capitals would lose business to Wall Street and other centers of global finance in Asia, it was feared, and meanwhile the anxieties of the financial industry in the City of London made it clear that the United Kingdom would never approve of the French initiatives. The British anxieties were forcibly articulated by the Prime Minister David Cameron, who was also able to present his position as consistent with a conservative brand of Britons-first nationalism. And this in turn provided further evidence of the ways in which assertions of national sovereignty from the right continue to do global service in protecting the interests of transnational capitalists, providing a persistent block against leftist attempts at transnational re-regulation and anti-neoliberal redistribution.

10.2.7 Global worker solidarity and social justice versus de-unionization

Notwithstanding all the nationalistic obstacles, another alter-globalization alternative to neoliberalism norms is solidarity with workers and support for transnational union organizing. As we saw in Chapter 4, old nineteenth-century ideas about workers of the world uniting are being rearticulated in the twenty-first century by new union efforts to organize globally. While Marx and Engels had said that workers of the world had "nothing to lose but their chains," today's neoliberal chains of downward harmonization are raising consciousness among unions that nationally focused strategies alone will not win them the world. In the face of "race to the bottom" whipsawing and the use of offshoring to undermine established worker benefits, unions have seen quite clearly the practical need for transnational solidarity. This has led not only to the revitalization of older international union organizations such as ICFTU and the Global Union Federations described in Chapter 4, but also notably to new grassroots solidarity efforts, including collaborations with non-union community organizers in global social justice movements such as the World Social Forum, as well as to all sorts of new global city "living wage" campaigns.[7] The results, though still very vulnerable to transnational whipsawing and nationalistic competition, have led to concerted and explicitly anti-neoliberal efforts to promote the upward harmonization of labor rights, pay, and protection on a global scale. And it is this same focus on redefining protectionism in terms of protecting people and communities transnationally that has allowed such efforts to be articulated with the broader global justice movement.

Linkages between union organizing and broader community activism do not by any means always go smoothly. For example, in December 2011, efforts by Occupy organizers to shut down west coast ports in the United States and Canada led to union complaints that the strike actions and blockades were being called without a proper democratic consultation process with workers. Robert McEllrath, President of the International Longshore and Warehouse Union (ILWU), issued a statement warning thus that: "Support is one thing. Organizing from outside groups attempting to co-opt our struggle in order to advance a broader agenda is quite another."[8] The ILWU therefore refused to officially endorse the port shutdown. However, such efforts to distance unions from more militant anti-neoliberal organizing do not do much to raise respect for unionization among conservatives. Instead whether it is an informal blockade or a union-sanctioned strike, any use of consequential economic actions tends to be criticized by right wing populists as a "socialist" attack on the economic freedom of ordinary citizens. And notwithstanding the long history of internationalist unionism in the United States – a history that actually includes west coast port organizing by the International Workers of the World (IWW) in the early twentieth century – such socialist internationalism is also repeatedly depicted by conservatives as unpatriotic and un-American.

10.2.8   Local food and environmental security verusus export-led development

One area where alter-globalization activists are much more likely to find common cause with conservatives is over protecting local food systems and the conservation of the natural environment, or at least particularly cherished national landscapes and landmarks. Many traditions of conservative thought, including some hard-right forms of hyper-patriotism, see food security and environmental security in terms of protecting national soil, national farming, and the national environment as the natural foundation of the nation. This was a dominant theme, for example, in Italian fascism. And while German Nazis brought disrepute to the idea of expanding a national fatherland militarily, various visions of preserving and protecting national landscapes as part of honoring national sovereignty persist as a classic feature of purist conservative thought. Nevertheless, as Table 10.1 highlights, other more recent reactionary responses to globalization emphasize national control of nature in the cause of "energy independence." Such positions can clearly lead policy-makers far away from the cause of environmental conservation. In the United States, for example, debate over drilling for oil in the Arctic National Wildlife Refuge has led the old conservative idea of protecting national wilderness areas to give way to new interests in developing oil reserves that might reduce American dependency on foreign oil. So, while some conservatives are conservationists when it comes to nature, others are not, and the result is a rather mixed set of political responses.

Another reason why conservative positions are mixed is more immediately economic. Agricultural fixed capital is especially fixed in place in the form of farmland, and so the normal business pressures to go global and find cheaper production opportunities overseas tend not to apply so much to farming. To put it graphically, it is much more difficult to "offshore" a mid-west corn-field than it is to move a car plant overseas. Of course, there are many exceptions. These range from European and American **agribusinesses** growing fruits and vegetables in the Global South to the recent land grabs in Africa by Middle Eastern and Asian countries who are buying vast tracts of prime farmland in attempts to hedge against looming global food-supply shortages. But more generally, historic fixed investments in creating and maintaining farmland make the opportunity costs of offshoring agriculture high. Thus, as the everyday business of protecting Japanese rice farms, European vineyards, and American cotton fields illustrates, the reaction of many agricultural capitalists to globalization is to demand ongoing forms of old-fashioned economic protectionism. Pro-business conservatives who on other issues demand more trade liberalization therefore also adopt calls for subsidizing and defending domestic agriculture, and this is one reason why American and European trade negotiators have found it hard to move forward, as we saw in Chapter 6, with efforts to reach agreement on a development round of trade liberalization with big agricultural exporters such as Brazil and India.

By contrast, anti-neoliberal advocates of agricultural "localization" and environmental sustainability are concerned with a much more global kind of protection.[9]

Table 10.2   Alter-globalization protection vs. global corporate agriculture (after Hines[10])

Neoliberal global agriculture	*Alter-globalization alternatives*
Long commodity chains/high food miles	Local sourcing/low food miles
Import–export approach to food security	Food from local community and lands
Market monopolies and concentration	Multiple agents and diverse producers
Monoculture and mega-scale farming	Biodiversity and small-scale farming
Petro-chemical inputs and toxic waste	Organic inputs and re-used outputs
Factory farms with rural depopulation	Small-scale farms and rural/urban partnering
Hypermarkets	Farmers' markets
Created wants (advertizing)	Healthy wants (education)
Fast food	Slow food
Dependency culture	Local community self reliance
Social polarization	Social inclusion
Citizen treated as consumer	Consumer treated as citizen
Top-down control	Bottom-up empowerment
Commodification and patenting of nature	Socially shared science

They promote national or local food security as the basis for protecting communities from famine and malnutrition. They demand national food system autonomy or sovereignty with the goal of protecting communal farming traditions and the communities that depend on them for food. They refuse patent monopolies in the interests of protecting non-commercial seed-sharing and the livelihood of farmers who cannot afford patented seeds and the pesticides with which they are often designed to be used. And they demand environmental sustainability with a view to protecting a common global future for humanity on the planet. For every farming trend driven by neoliberal globalization, they therefore propose alternatives based on forms of protection for local food systems (Table 10.2). These forms of protection of food systems and food security also in turn have important implications for environmental sustainability. The emphasis on reducing food miles and petro-chemical inputs has the benefit of reducing carbon emissions, too. The concern with re-using outputs as inputs reduces harmful environmental externalities from farming. And the aim of moving beyond an export–import approach to food security promises to build more sustainable, bottom-up approaches to environmental management and control.

10.2.9   Debt relief and local bartering versus anti-inflationary monetarism

Another aspect of alter-globalization approaches to developing local food sustainability involves the use of bartering and local trading systems that avoid traditional monetary exchange. This is as much a product of pragmatic need as idealistic post-capitalist experimentation, and oftentimes such bartering has developed in desperate contexts shaped by spiraling inflation and other sorts of currency crisis (e.g. Zimbabwe in recent years). By allowing traders to avoid some of the perils of rapidly rising (or falling) prices, it also represents a quite radical bottom-up alternative to neoliberal orthodoxy about using central bank control over interest rates to control prices via the money supply. In this respect though, there are many other alter-globalization alternatives on offer, too: including the forms of debt relief and aid discussed in Chapters 5 and 7 as alternatives to the neoliberal **conditionalities** of SAPs and PRSPs. However, the relatively small amounts of capital that would have been needed to help poor countries out of their debt traps are now being jeopardized as a result of the increasingly huge and globalized debt crisis: the crisis that started with the US subprime mortgage repayment problems and the collapse of Lehman brothers in 2008, but which by 2011 was metastasizing into a European debt crisis, and thus a Euro crisis, and thus a global trade crisis, and thus into the all-encompassing planetary vortex of a global depression.

Although it is rarely noted in the financial press, the problems with neoliberal orthodoxy highlighted by anti-neoliberal activists continue to be illustrated by the global financial crisis. But now the disciplinary damage of **debt** has returned to wreak economic havoc on rich countries, too. When Milton Friedman said that **inflation** "is always and everywhere a monetary phenomenon," he not only helped establish the market-fundamentalist faith in "supply side" monetarism but also set the scene for the orthodox neoliberal approach to disciplining debtor countries. Keynesian deficit-spending for the purposes of reducing national unemployment was thereby replaced by the new focus on balanced budgets, austerity, and a reliance on central-bank interest-rate setting to manage the money supply. As we noted in Chapter 5, Friedman's emphasis on central bank monetary policy has now been eclipsed by the global money movements that his parallel emphasis on deregulating finance helped advance. But even amidst the recent crises of deregulated global finance, the neoliberal orthodoxy on austerity and money supply management that Friedman and the Chicago School helped fashion still remains dominant. Obviously, alter-globalization alternatives demanding debt relief for poor countries are especially vulnerable in this context, as, too, are efforts to promote aid and global health initiatives. Thus, in a sign of the depressed economic times in December 2011, the Global Fund to Fight AIDS, Tuberculosis, and Malaria announced that it would replace a previously planned "Round 11" of full proposal funding with a more limited transitional funding mechanism. "We are living in uncertain economic times and budgets are strapped," explained the Global Fund's top manager. "It would have been irresponsible to continue promising opportunities for additional funding when we are not sure we will have the money needed."[11]

With wealthy countries in economic crisis themselves, the global recession has caused foreign aid budgets to fall more generally. Far from following the alter-globalization calls for debt relief, in late 2011 neoliberal debt discipline was therefore expanding globally, moving on to new targets in Europe. Greece, Portugal, Ireland, Italy, Spain, and even France saw their government bond ratings downgraded like a set of falling dominoes. Their treasury ministries in turn started to play host to visits from the IMF. As a result, and rather ironically, some former targets of IMF attention such as Brazil could now join China and lecture rich countries on the neo-liberal need to balance budgets and meet debt-repayment deadlines on time. Perhaps most ironically of all, however, they were also joined in this respect by more reac-tionary conservative critics in the countries in crisis: critics who insisted along with the foreign bondholders that debts must always be paid back no matter what the damage to national economies and citizenry.

According to reactionary supporters of debt repayment and neoliberal crisis-management, only good discipline will restore market confidence and the value of money. They do not even approve therefore of the solution proposed by Friedman and his followers for dealing with deflationary crises: namely ultra-low interest rates and other forms of central bank monetary easing (i.e. "printing money") that inflate away debts (i.e. reducing debts by reducing the value of the money in which they are denominated). Instead, they believe in protecting the value of national currencies (and thus savings saved in these currencies) before all else. Whether or not they are owners of capital, conservative defenders of national currencies tend also to be espe-cially anxious about the threat of inflation. As a result, audiences of rightist radio and TV shows in countries such as the United States are regularly targeted by trad-ing firms as eager buyers of gold, silver, and other more complex hedge investments against inflation. Right-wing "strong currency" reactions to the global financial crisis thereby end up supporting the very same global financial industry players that so much conservative and nationalistic anger was directed against in the first place.

10.2.10   Promote open-source shared science on global priorities versus patents

Extending from the protection of monetary value and the protection of savings to the protection of private property more generally, conservatives also tend to agree with neoliberals on the need to protect intellectual property, too. They may at times have religious reservations about the patenting of human DNA and genomic modi-fication mechanisms or the patenting and private control of other life forms, too. But the general principle of protecting private property runs deep in conservative thought, including support for turning formerly public resources and common property into private property through forms of legal enclosure and titling. For this reason, the main concerns about intellectual property we examined in Chapter 6 in relation to the WTO's TRIPS rules and monopolization have come from anti-neoliberal critics. As was explained further in Chapter 9, one of the main concerns in this respect is the limitation on access to life-saving medicines created by the patenting and licensing of pharmaceutical innovation. Added to this, there are other ethical concerns raised by critics of IP law related to the ways in which patent regimes restrict the global sharing of scientific discovery. Instead of disseminating and building on one another's findings, patent law and the kind of funding mechanisms it promotes instead tend to push scientists towards the privatization of their data and discoveries. In response to this new form of scientific enclosure, alternatives are already being developed. Government support for compulsory licenses for essential medicines, for example, and the government-sponsored development of generic drugs both aim to overcome the exclusionary impacts of patents. However, there are also more "upstream" approaches that aim to foster greater sharing and access to the discovery process itself. And here is a case where alternatives to neoliberal norms are already alive and well in established global practices.

As we noted in Chapter 9, science is itself a form of globalized human endeavor, and its global interdependencies have depended from the start (and from long before capitalism) on the long-distance global sharing of new findings and claims. Philosophers continue to debate the different mechanisms through which science develops and through which new discoveries are tested and then established and accepted as scientific facts, but we know enough about the processes involved to understand that the open sharing of data and discovery processes is vital to scientific advancement. Scientists have to be able to test other scientists' results and reproduce them, and for the same reason they have to make their own results public and open for investigation by others. It is precisely this openness that patent regimes tend to inhibit. In response, therefore, a number of alternatives to patents and licenses have been developed to reward scientists for innovation in ways that do not limit access to life-saving benefits. Instead of giving innovators the ability to charge monopoly rents on patented discoveries, other ideas include establishing Nobel-like prizes as rewards for new innovations, creating open-access "patent pools," and offering compensation directly indexed to the life-saving impact of the medicines that result.

Some critics worry that prize schemes are half-way measures that still buy into the idea of using economic incentives to motivate scientists (rather than appeal, say, to the idea that having a lab and a chance to make discoveries that help humanity is a reward itself). Another concern is that such programs may even create limitations on the development of generics and inhibit governments from exercising their rights under the Doha Declaration to issue compulsory licenses. But a key principle that the prize schemes do at least support is the idea that science develops better when it is seen as an open, collaborative, and global project of shared study and experimentation. This may sound utopian to some, and yet, as such, it is a defining utopian ideal at the very heart of global research universities. It is to these institutions, and how we can best work within in them to advance global learning and education that we now turn in the final section.

10.3　Resilience and Resistance in the Global University

Debate over the implications of intellectual property illustrates how universities often find themselves today at the center of global controversies. These controversies indicate in turn the degree to which universities are being remade in the era of neoliberal globalization. Whether it is the commercialization of innovations coming

Figure 10.1   Signs of the global university. Photo by Matthew Sparke.

out of university labs, the global sourcing of university-licensed apparel, the use of corporate vendors with bad global records on labor rights, or the training of new knowledge workers and managers, the issues involved underline the ways universities are deeply entwined with globalization. They therefore make the old image of the university as an ivory tower utopia seem as out of sync with today's global realities as the old ivory tower inhabitants were supposed to have been out of touch with ordinary everyday life. In response, however, universities have for the most part embraced their new worldliness with gusto. Gone for the most part is the traditional idea of the university as a non-commercial place where students are tutored in the liberal arts and science of being responsible national citizens. Instead, we generally find ourselves as professors and students alike in rapidly corporatizing institutions that tend because of neoliberal norms to depict their educational and research endeavors as being all about delivering global education and global benefits for a global community. And whether it is a foreign business internship aimed to build corporate leadership skills or a global health study abroad program advertised with a global justice agenda, or a Peace Corps opportunity being marketed as a way of training for the global job market, the resulting emphasis on moving away from the old ivory tower idea of the university (and oftentimes going away from the physical campus) is impossible to ignore (Figure 10.1).

It is hard to find a university website in any country in the world today that does not somewhere somehow make the case that it offers a global or so-called world-class education to its students. Beyond the obviously competitive and neoliberal concerns of moving up and down different global rankings of the world's most "global" universities, something more interestingly ambivalent and bifurcated has happened to the old utopian ideals embedded in the idea of the university as a place set aside to help imagine and develop new and better futures for national citizens. On the one hand, these utopian imaginings have morphed into calls on universities to take the lead in managing neoliberal globalization by training resilient global entrepreneurs. On the other hand, they have led to equally utopian demands that universities develop forms of global knowledge and global education that support new forms of global citizenship. In short, as well as opening up a tension with older traditions of training for national citizenship, the new global education discourses divide between emphases on global entrepreneurship and an evolving form of global civics.[12]

Too often, these bifurcated approaches to globalizing university education are assumed to be somehow aligned or overlapping. In the dominant discourse of most US university presidents, it is therefore assumed that training global entrepreneurs and cultivating global citizens are one and the same project, or that at least the two endeavors can be happily made to coincide. Here, however, for the sake of analytical clarity, Figure 10.2 seeks to make the distinction clearer than it normally is, and by doing so the aim is to list some notable differences in the two resulting visions of "global education." In the middle are listed in turn all the many different forms of university teaching and learning that are now increasingly used to deliver on the promise of "global education." These include a set of common skills (such as lan-guage learning and the study of different parts of the worlds) and a set of common teaching practices (such as study abroad and, yes, lecture classes and textbooks on globalization). These skills and practices both reflect and reproduce the different visions of global education (hence the four arrows). But what is most significant about these shared skills and teaching practices, though, is the type of global edu-cation that they actually help to provide, and this is where the contrasting ideals of the global entrepreneur and the global citizen come into play.

The vision of the global entrepreneur is certainly the more dominant "ideal type" and as such represents a distinctly neoliberal idealization of the sort of global subject global education should be preparing for the world. The global entrepreneur is most definitely not a provincial or hyper-nationalistic reactionary. Rather he or she is enabled by university education to develop **cosmopolitan** cross-cultural communi-cation skills, instrumentally useful global knowledge, and an ability to fly anywhere, work anywhere, and thus get along and make business deals anywhere. Upon gradu-ation, the successful global entrepreneur has been prepared to be highly flexible and mobile, someone who has the skills to remain a life-long learner, and thus someone who can remain resilient and personally successful in a world of global labor market competition.

By contrast, a very different "ideal type" is represented in terms of training the caring global citizen. This is more of an alter-globalization or global justice vision of global education, and, although its advocates generally have fewer resources and influence within the corporatized university, it, too, has its supporters among

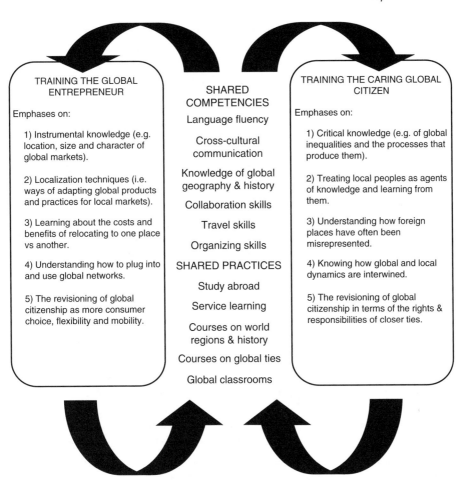

Figure 10.2 Two approaches to global education in the contemporary university.

students, professors, and administrators. In this vision, global education is thought of in far less instrumental terms and is not so focused on building individual personalized forms of resiliency. It is much more attuned to the possibilities for collective resistance to neoliberal norms, and to the lessons that can be learned from other communities and places in the world that are already engaged in such resistance. Thus, in contrast to a concern with knowing about other places for the sake of making use of the place-specific opportunities they present, students of caring global citizenship are more concerned with the processes of uneven development that lead to differential space-specific experiences of globalization. Instead of learning about localization techniques, the goal is more about learning to learn from other people and places for what they can teach about globalization and its inequalities. Instead of discovering how to assess the costs and benefits of different places like a global manager, a training for global citizenship teaches students how various different modes of representing foreign places – including the econometric calculus of cost/benefit analysis itself – reflect particular interests and perspectives leading to a long history of misrepresentation, too. And instead of turning global citizenship into the entrepreneurial stuff of self-investment and personal choice maximization, the hope underpinning this vision of global education is an ideal type of global citizen who cares about the responsibilities that spring from global interdependency.

As Figure 10.2 also suggests, the two visions of global education can both be equally supported by and influential on today's most common forms of global teaching practice. The point that they are idealizations of global education is therefore an important one. In reality, what most students experience, and indeed what most professors provide – whether they mean to or not – is much more of a mix. Moreover, the increasing unemployment problems facing contemporary college graduates in the context of the global recession are making this mix even more complicated and messy. Students who feel pulled to be more resistant global citizens concerned with global justice are increasingly anxious about being able to find work when they leave university, and this increases the pressure on them to make personal investments in their own capacity for labor market resilience. They may care deeply about worker solidarity, social justice, and organizing. They may join organizations like USAS (University Students Against Sweatshops) or their local Occupy movement or marches to contest tuition raises. But they also know that finding a job in the global marketplace makes resilience a necessity alongside resistance. Meanwhile, other students who may be pulled more towards the managerial model of the global entrepreneur are nevertheless increasingly interested today in the sorts of global social entrepreneurship programs being run by university business schools and global health programs. They may also want to add a stint of global service to their résumés. And they also often see ways in which they can harness the lessons of instrumental education in business to philanthropic aid and global health work (e.g. using supply-chain management models to help set up cold chains to deliver life-saving medicines in underserved areas).

Hovering over all of today's students, however, is another kind of global education altogether: the globally regulative and behavior-transforming force of student debt. Universities everywhere are raising tuition as state support dwindles, and the competition for university places is increasingly joined by students from countries such as India and China whose middle-class parents often attach much prestige and acclaim to a foreign education. As a result, more and more students are taking out huge college loans that will leave them in debt for decades to come. This in turn will discipline their post-graduate career choices, steering them into more money-making professions in order to pay off the loans. More than this, increasing debt also looks set to discipline students when they are in university, too, making intellectual risk-taking and critical questions about the limits of knowledge, democracy, and citizenship that much more difficult to ask. At the same time, though, the debts and discipline are now becoming so obvious that many students are taking the risks and asking big critical questions about the influence of global market power over their lives.

For all those who want to ask these questions, the contemporary university still offers enormous inspiration and resources. Having written all of the chapters of this book in the passive voice without ever saying directly what "I" personally think or see as the best response to globalization, let me therefore end this final chapter by indicating in an active voice that I hope my writing may be of some use in this critical and caring way, too. While I have tried to chart the global ties and tensions of globalization in a style that is accessible to all, and while I see this therefore as a contribution to global education in all its multiple forms, I am sure by now that it is clear that I care deeply about the need to contest the inequalities, asymmetries, and suffering caused by global neoliberalization. Globalization with a big G may continue to hide these problems and their connections to global market rule, and many may continue to suggest, as Margaret Thatcher did when I was a child growing up in England, that there is no alternative to market-led and market-dominated global governance. Nevertheless, it is my concluding hope that this book has helped sow doubts about the TINA-touts. I hope it has at least enabled you to become more open to analysis and critique by all those who rethink the responsibilities of globalization as response-abilities for resistance. The world and all our global connections both invite and enable such solidaristic responses, I think, but beyond understanding the connections and capacities, action is what turns the responsibility into real response-ability, and how you yourself use your university education to respond remains – notwithstanding all your student debts – up to you.

Student Exercises

Individual and Group: Take a moment to write down your own personal vision of good global citizenship. Then, work in small groups to discuss how each individual's personal sense of responsibility might be turned into a form of collective response-ability and action.

Notes

1 http://www.bnp.org.uk/news/bnp%E2%80%99s-warnings-globalisation-dangers-echoed-furore-over-prince-charles%E2%80%99s-poppy-wreath.
2 http://www.democracynow.org/2011/7/27/norwegian_shooting_suspects_views_echo_xenophobia.
3 See Jai Sen, Madhuresh Kumar, Patrick Bond, and Peter Waterman, eds, *Political Programme for the World Social Forum? Democracy, Substance and Debate in the Bamako Appeal and the Global Justice Movements*, Indian Institute for Critical Action: Centre in Movement (CACIM), New Delhi, India & the University of KwaZulu-Natal Centre for Civil Society (CCS), Durban, South Africa, http://www.cacim.net/bareader/home.html; and Matthew Sparke, Liz Brown, Dominic Corva, Heather Day, Caroline Faria, Tony Sparks, and Kirsten Varg, "The World Social Forum and the Lessons for Economic Geography," *Economic Geography*, 81 (2005): 359–80.
4 http://rodrik.typepad.com/.a/6a00d8341c891753ef013488d85d61970c-pi.
5 David McNally, Global Slump: *The Economics and Politics of Crisis and Resistance* (Oakland, CA: PM Press, 2011).

6   James Tobin, "The Antiglobalisation Movement Has Highjacked My Name," 2001, *Der Spiegel*, reprinted on the website of Jubilee2000 at http://web.archive.org/web/20050306201839/http://www.jubilee2000uk.org/worldnews/lamerica/james_tobin_030901_english.htm.

7   See Kavita Datta, Yara Evans, Joanna Herbert, Jon May, Cathy McIlwaine, and Jane Wills, *Global Cities at Work: New Migrant Divisions of Labour* (London: Pluto, 2010); and Peter Waterman, "The Forward March of Labour (and Unions?) Recommenced: Reflections on an Emancipatory Labour Internationalism and International Labor Studies", *Antipode*, 37, no. 2 (2005): 208–18.

8   Mallia Wollen and Steven Greenhouse, "With Port Actions, Occupy Oakland Tests Labor Leaders," *New York Times*, December 13, 2011, accessed at: http://www.nytimes.com/2011/12/14/us/occupy-oakland-angers-labor-leaders.html.

9   Colin Hines, *Localization: A Global Manifesto* (London: Earthscan, 2000).

10   This chart is adapted from Hines, *Localization*, 214.

11   http://www.theglobalfund.org/en/mediacenter/announcements/2011-12-01_The_Global_Fund_is_alive_and_well_But_Global_Health_Progress_is_in_Peril_by_Simon_Bland_the_Chair_of_the_Board_of_the_Global_Fund/.

12   For a useful review (and grid) of these bifurcations and tensions as they also play out in schools as well as universities, see Walter Parker and Steven Camicia, "Cognitive Praxis in Today's 'International Education' Movement: A Case Study of Intents and Affinities," *Theory & Research in Social Education*, 37, no. 1 (2009): 21–48. For more on the neoliberalization of universities, see Thomas Docherty, *For the University* (New York: Bloomsbury Academic, 2011); Gaye Tuchman, *Wannabe U: Inside the Corporate University* (Chicago: University of Chicago Press, 2009); Christopher Newfield, *Unmaking the Public University* (Cambridge, MA: Harvard University Press, 2008); Marc Bousquet, *How the University Works* (New York: New York University Press, 2008); and most excellent in its prescience about the fall of training for national citizenship, Bill Readings, *The University in Ruins* (Cambridge, MA: Harvard University Press, 1996).

Keywords

agribusiness	debt	Washington Consensus
Chapter 11	inflation	WTO
conditionalities	NAFTA	
cosmopolitan	neoliberalism	

Glossary

Many of the definitions of key terms in this glossary use other key terms that also
have their own definitions. All these terms are shown in **bold**. Thus, while you can
just read individual definitions, another way of using the glossary is to follow the
links between terms shown in bold on whatever global journey they take you.

AAA "Triple A" is the highest credit rating given by **credit rating agencies** to issuers
of **bonds**. It indicates that the issuer is considered to have an extremely strong
capacity to meet the financial commitments of the loans it is taking out by selling
bonds. Wealthy sovereign governments and other issuers with the prized AAA
rating typically find it easy to auction their bonds with very low interest rates. This
is because their borrowing is considered almost risk-free from the point of view of
the bond traders. However, if their risks of default go up, and the high ratings go
down, then (as has happened to a number of European countries amidst the financial
crises following the "sub-prime" crash of 2008) increasingly large interest rate "risk
premiums" are attached to the bonds in global market trading. As the interest rates
on the bonds go up, it costs much more for governments to borrow and service their
existing debts, and this can unleash a damaging spiral of further financial crises. The
threat that this might happen is also often used to discipline policy-makers that
consider adopting alternative policies to the low inflation, pro-market norms of
neoliberalism (Sinclair, 2005). And despite the fact that the credit ratings agencies
mistakenly gave high ratings to the mortgage-backed securities at the heart of the
sub-prime fiasco, their ratings still continue to regulate how governments are
disciplined by global market rankings.

Introducing Globalization: Ties, Tensions, and Uneven Integration, First Edition. Matthew Sparke.
© 2013 Matthew Sparke. Published 2013 by Blackwell Publishing Ltd.

Reference

Timothy Sinclair, *The New Masters of Capital: American Bond Rating Agencies and the Politics of Creditworthiness* (Ithaca, NY: Cornell University Press, 2005).

AFL-CIO The American Federation of Labor and Confederation of Industrial Organizations is the main umbrella organization representing unions at a national level in the United States. Faced with the challenges of anti-unionism and global **outsourcing** in the context of **neoliberalism**, the AFL-CIO has been attempting to move away from the model of nationalistic organization it developed in the context of **Fordism**. "Global companies begat global problems for workers," explained the AFL-CIO secretary treasurer, Richard Trumka, in 2006. "Global problems begat the need for global unions – and if global unions want to truly match the might and power of global corporations, we have to undertake global research and global campaigns. (quoted in Bronfenbrenner, 2007: 1). Such calls for global organizing continue to intensify in the US union movement, and the AFL-CIO now seeks to work more closely with global union organizations such as **ICFTU** to develop transnational labor solidarity. These efforts are also in turn increasingly tied to moves away from old fashioned business unionism (Moody, 1997), and to the rise of what some refer to as "social movement unionism" (Walsh, 2012) that includes community-based organizing and other outreach efforts to migrant worker communities in global cities (Wills et al., 2009), as well as corporate campaigns focused on labor rights across the global **commodity chain** networks of **TNCs** (Herod, 2009).

References

Kate Bronfenbrenner, *Global Unions: Challenging Transnational Capital through Cross-Border Campaigns* (Ithaca, NY: Cornell University, 2007).

Andrew Herod, *Geographies of Globalization: A Critical Introduction* (Oxford: Wiley-Blackwell, 2009).

Kim Moody, *Workers in a Lean World: Unions in the International Economy* (London: Verso, 1997).

Jane Walsh, "A 'New' Social Movement: US Labor and the Trends of Social Movement Unionism," *Sociology Compass*, 6, no. 2 (2012): 192–204.

Jane Wills, Kavita Datta, Yara Evans, Joanna Herbert, Jon May, and Cathy McIlwaine, *Global Cities at Work: New Migrant Divisions of Labour* (London: Pluto Press, 2009).

Agribusiness A name for any kind of commercialized agriculture run using business principles and profit-making goals to manage both upstream inputs and downstream food processing and marketing. Agribusinesses are key agents of economic globalization in so far as they tend to market their products transnationally as well as rely upon global suppliers of synthetic pesticides, herbicides, and fertilizers for inputs. Typically agribusiness involves either highly mechanized monocropping (e.g. Brazilian soybeans) or labor-intensive work using transnational workers (e.g. Californian strawberries). It includes the production of both non-food and food products from farms (beverages, ethanol, tobacco, paper, textiles, and leather, for example) as well as highly processed products – such as high-fructose corn syrup, ketchup, and hydrogenated oils – that are hard to classify. One of the problematic features of pro-market globalization from the perspective of critics has been the increasing global encroachment of agribusiness on more traditional forms of farming for local consumption. *Via Campesina* and other organizations advocating for farming communities organize in this way against the loss of local food sovereignty (http://viacampesina.org/en/). Such loss has been dramatized recently in the form of massive land grabs for agribusiness in poor countries, including the plains of eastern Africa, the paddy fields of Southeast Asia, the jungles of South America, and even the prairies of Eastern Europe (Pearce, 2012).

At a general level, the global encroachments of agribusiness are undeniable. They include not just the buying-up of public lands and family farms, but also micro-practices such as the use of more commercial pesticides and genetically modified seeds. On closer inspection, investigations of such changing farming practices make it increasingly hard to distinguish between traditional farming and agribusiness. In one way or another, farmers throughout the world have become interdependently linked to commercial farming processes whether it is in terms of the inputs they use for farming (the seeds, fertilizers, and equipment) or the ways in which they market their produce or their labor practices. Even organic farming, which is generally understood as an alternative to agribusiness, is part of a larger global trend towards the commercialization of agriculture, just as "fresh" food has continued to be commodified and packaged in ways that obscure its agribusiness basis (Jarosz, 2008; Freidberg, 2009). In this respect, it should be remembered that when organic farmers avoid all commercial inputs on the production side, they still rely on the sales side on access to very small niche markets (such as wealthy educated urban consumers) that exist only because of highly developed consumer education that is responding to agribusiness.

References

Susanne Freidberg, *Fresh: A Perishable History* (Cambridge, MA: Belknap Press of Harvard University Press, 2009).

Lucy Jarosz, "The City in the Country: Growing Alternative Food Networks in Metropolitan Areas," *The Journal of Rural Studies* 24 (2008): 231–44.

Fred Pearce, *The Land Grabbers: The New Fight over Who Owns the Earth* (Boston: Beacon Press, 2012).

Aid Aid to the world's poor countries and communities or **Global South** has gone through a number of stages of transformation since the era of imperialism.

Initially, it was a way in which wealthier western countries sought to exercise influence over the post-colonial states that had previously been their colonies. Over the course of the twentieth century, it became a more complex phenomenon with some aid (especially medical aid) being given for humanitarian reasons, while other interventions (such as food aid) took the form more of crisis-management and yet others, the majority in terms of the value of supplies and equipment (including military equipment), being injected into countries as part of a Cold War struggle between the so-called First World (the United States and western Europe) and the Second World (the Soviet system) over control of the Third World. In the wake of the fall of Soviet communism after 1990, aid has become yet more complex. Private philanthropies (such as the Bill and Melinda Gates Foundation) have come to be as important as government spending on aid by rich countries (which has on average declined as a share of GDP), and a vast variety of NGOs, universities, and celebrities (such as Bono) are involved in highlighting aid needs, raising aid money, and debating its best forms of distribution. Useful websites such as *Humanosphere* and *Aidsource* provide daily briefings on aid news and debates for aid workers. And even the category "aid worker" reflects the professionalization of aid as a form of global career path. Indeed, with the rise of social entrepreneurship and other business-based approaches to development, aid work has sometimes been turned into a form of self-improving investment in **cosmopolitanism** identity by global elites.

In the wider context of **neoliberalism**, there is much talk of "trade not aid" and a parallel tendency to emphasize Victorian ideas of self-help or, as the **World Bank** likes to call it, "help for self-help." Some hard-line neoliberal advocates such as William Easterly (2006) argue that aid is generally counter-productive or, as an African economist Dambise Moyo (2009) put it in the title of her polemical book, aid is really just "Dead Aid." But at the same time, the globalization of communications has meant that knowledge of ongoing suffering in other parts of the world has increased (except in places where the news has been turned into a form of infotainment). This means that when ordinary citizens are polled about their feelings towards aid, they remain very keen to support publicly funded assistance programs in the Global South.

References

Tom DeHerdt and Johan Bastiensen, "Aid As an Encounter at the Interface: The Complexity of the Global Fight Against Poverty," *Third World Quarterly* 25, no. 5 (2004): 871–85.

William Easterly, *The White Man's Burden: Why the West's Efforts to Aid the Rest Have Done So Much Ill and So Little Good* (New York: Penguin Press, 2006).

Julio Godoy, "Development: Report Reveals Drop In Aid To Poor Countries," *Global Information Network*, May 16, 2002: 1.

Dambisa Moyo, *Dead Aid: Why Aid Is Not Working and How There Is a Better Way for Africa* (New York: Farrar, Straus, and Giroux, 2009).

AIDS see **HIV/AIDS**

Anti-globalization A term generally used by pro-market commentators and advocates of **neoliberalism** to describe the outlook of their critics. The term is quite
misleading because most of the activists, NGOs, and other groups involved in the
struggles against neoliberal policies and ideas remain nevertheless committed to
forging global links of resistance (George, 2004). Developments such as the World
Social Forum are testament to this, as too are all the globalized ties on the Internet
that critics use to organize public protests such as the Battle in Seattle or, more
recently, the Occupy and *Indignado* encampments. What such critics demand is a
different, more democratic, more environmentally sustainable, and much more
socially just kind of globalization. In this respect, the term *alter-mondialisation*
used by French activist groups such as **ATTAC** is more appropriate because most of
the critics seek to develop alternative forms of globalization (ATTAC, 2006). It is
important to remember though that from the perspective of advocates of neoliberalism, such critics still seem to be "anti-globalization" because the only kind of
globalization that neoliberals can conceive of is one organized by markets and
pro-business regulation. For this reason, they tend to see all critics as supporters of
national economic protectionism and find it hard to conceive of a different kind of
globalized protectionism based on a vision of protecting the global environment,
workers, and global standards of social and economic justice. It is true, however,
that some critics of neoliberal globalization are protectionist in a simple economic
sense. Both reactionary right-wing critics of free trade such as Patrick Buchanan in
the United States and Le Pen in France, and a few traditionalist union groups sub-
scribe to a defensive nationalism based on protecting national jobs. Yet this kind of
nationalist protectionism is increasingly rare on the left. Even among American
unions and the **AFL-CIO**, where a nationalist outlook was quite longstanding,
there is now a strong movement towards creating a transnational and therefore
much more globalized network of resistance against neoliberalism. For this reason,
the simple binary of globalization vs. anti-globalization is increasingly unstable
(Held and McGrew, 2002).

References

ATTAC, *Le Petit Alter: Dictionnaire altermondialiste* (Paris: Mille et une nuits Parution, 2006).
Susan George, *Another World is Possible If . . .* (New York: Verso, 2004).
David Held and Anthony McGrew, *Globalization/Anti-Globalization* (Malden, MA: Blackwell Publishers, 2002).

APEC Headquartered in Singapore, the Asia Pacific Economic Cooperation
organization was founded in 1989 as a pro-free-trade coordinating body for
Pacific Rim countries. By the later 1990s, APEC included 21 members: Australia,

Brunei, Canada, Chile, China, Hong Kong, Indonesia, Japan, South Korea, Malaysia, Mexico, New Zealand, Papua New Guinea, Peru, the Philippines, Russia, Singapore, Taiwan, Thailand, the United States, and Vietnam. APEC's decisions require consensus among all member nations. In 1994, the organization planned to create a Free Trade Area of the Asia-Pacific (FTAAP) by 2010. Thus far, little progress has been made towards these ambitious goals, but new initiatives in 2011–2012 such as the Trans Pacific Partnership indicate that the underlying effort at liberalizing trade and investment flows across the Pacific continues unabated.

Arbitrage A term usually used to describe stock-market practices such as daytrading that involve the rapid trading of currencies, equities, bonds, and derivatives in the hopes of buying low, selling high, and making a quick profit.

ASEAN The Association of Southeast Asian Nations was established by the governments of Indonesia, Malaysia, the Philippines, Singapore, and Thailand in 1967, with the goal of increasing economic growth and promoting peace and security in Southeast Asia. Subsequently, Brunei, Vietnam, Laos, Myanmar, and Cambodia have all joined. The major focus of the association has been promoting free trade among the member countries, and in 1992 the members signed a free-trade pact that reduced intraregional tariffs and eased restrictions on interregional foreign investment flows.

ATTAC A French group organized to contest global neoliberalism and offer alternatives. Its acronym stands for **A**ssociation pour la **T**axation des **T**ransactions financières pour l'**A**ide aux **C**itoyens (Association for a Tax on Financial Transactions in order to Aid Citizens). Having dedicated itself from the start (in the 1990s) to the development of some sort of global Tobin tax (or Robin Hood tax) on financial transactions, and having simultaneously sought to develop plans for aiding citizens of the world, ATTAC has become critically involved in all kinds of global struggles against neoliberalism (George, 2002) . It played an important role, for example, in leading the fight against the Multilateral Agreement on Investments (MAI) in the 1990s, and having succeeded in scuttling this initial attempt to entrench the rights of corporations to sue democratically elected governments, ATTAC has continued to be a voice of protest against similar Trade Related Investment Measures (TRIMs) within the **WTO** (Ancelovici, 2002). The organization has also more recently dedicated itself to the struggle against genetically modified (GM) foods. On the global stage, one of ATTAC's leaders, Bernard Cassen (2003), has also been centrally involved in bringing French involvement into the creation and development of the World Social Forum. It is through these sorts of transnational engagements that ATTAC is seeking to develop a clearer picture of what aid for global citizens might look like.

References

Marcos Ancelovici, "Organizing Against Globalization: The Case of ATTAC in France," *Politics & Society* 303 (2002): 427–63.
Bernard Cassen, "On the Attack," *New Left Review* 19 (2003): 41–60.
Susan George, "ATTAC: A Citizens' Movement for Global Justice Responds to September 11th," *Development* 45, no. 2 (2002): 97–98.

Austerity see **Fiscal austerity**

Autarchic An economy that is turned inwards and which therefore has low levels of trade and investment flows across its borders. In economic models, autarchy is often defined as the technical opposite of completely open international free trade. In reality, it is better understood as a tendency away from open trading, and as such was a major feature of many national economies in the period that followed World War II. In the context of contemporary globalization, the complete economic self-sufficiency implied by the Greek origins of the word cannot be found in any country on the planet.

Balance of payments A term used to describe the total financial transactions between the residents of one country and the rest of the world. The balance of payments "accounts" are divided into a "capital account" (which includes the sum of flows of capital assets such as stocks, **bonds**, and **derivatives**) and a "current account" (which includes all the flows of goods and services). As a simple equation of all these types of flows, the balance of payments is always in "balance." However, the big concerns about "balance of payments deficits" relate to disequilibria between the "capital account" and "current account." For example, the "current account deficit" that has been a growing feature of the US economy since the mid 1970s has been paralleled by a big "capital account surplus" (Brenner, 2002). In other words, the United States has been importing more goods and services than it has been exporting (the current account deficit), and to pay for these unbalanced import flows, it has also had to borrow money from abroad (the capital account surplus). This is a concern for the United States because ultimately it makes the country dependent on the ongoing supply of capital from foreign lenders (i.e. foreign investors into the United States). When these lenders develop concerns about the likely future value of US capital assets (for example, when they think the dollar will no longer hold its value), they are likely to be less inclined to invest in the United States, which will reduce the demand for US assets (including US treasury bonds and mortgage-backed securities), which will eventually increase interest rates in the United States (because of the need to attract new lenders by paying out greater rates of interest). For the same reasons, the disequilibrium for the foreign countries with current account surpluses and capital account deficits also creates concerns (Wolf, 2010). Countries like Japan and China are investing their profits back into US capital markets, but they risk losing the value they have invested in these assets if the dollar starts to fall or if the US government refuses to pay the interest payments on US treasury bonds.

References

Robert Brenner, *The Boom and the Bubble: The US in the World Economy* (New York: Verso, 2002).

Martin Wolf, *Fixing Global Finance (Baltimore*, MD: Johns Hopkins University Press, 2010).

Bonds These are contracts to pay back borrowed money with interest. They are sold by governments and corporations to investors who, by buying bond contracts, become lenders. Bonds usually provide fixed-income yields (interest payments) to bond-holders, assuring them of a set of repayments over a set time period. The price of a bond reflects market demand from investors. The more demand there is, the higher the price, and, reciprocally, less demand for a bond means it is priced lower. Also, reflecting demand and supply, bonds are auctioned with an **interest** rate as well as a price, and the interest rate or "yield" is generally seen by investors as an indication of the level of risk associated with the bond. More risky bonds have higher yields, and less risky bonds have lower yields. This is because bigger risks have to be compensated for by larger yields in order to persuade investors that buying the bond is worth the risk (a risk premium above the so-called risk-free bonds that receive **AAA** ratings). In 2007 and 2008, it became clear that a great many complex bond instruments sold as collateralized debt obligations (CDOs) with low-risk premiums were based on mortgage-backed securities (MBSs) that included extremely risky subprime loans to American home buyers. When these buyers began to default on their mortgage payments, the real risks became clear, and it set off a global financial crisis. Many global investors who had purchased the CDOs thinking that they were low risk lost money, and suddenly risk premiums spiked globally on a wide range of bond contracts. The increased borrowing costs caused by the decreased demand for high-risk bonds globally went to affect what were previously seen as the "risk-free" bonds issued by sovereign governments. Most notably in 2011–2012, the low demand, low prices, and high yields on European sovereign debt, and on Greek, Spanish, Irish, and Portuguese government bonds in particular, led to deeper economic crises in all the affected countries. Throughout the crisis, US and Japanese bonds have generally benefitted from enduring market demand, fetching higher prices and lower yields despite historically high levels of national debt to GDP. Whether these government bonds will continue to enjoy this "risk-free" status in the future nevertheless remains a matter of great controversy in the context of "quantitative-easing" (i.e. money creation) by the US Federal Reserve and the Japanese central bank.

What is not in doubt, however, is that the spectre of the globalized bond-trading system will continue to be used to discipline political leaders who stray from the norms of **neoliberalism**. When he was told about this by advisors, President Bill Clinton asked a very good question about the binding power of the bond market: "You mean to tell me that the success of [my economic] program and my re-election hinges on the Federal Reserve and a bunch of fucking bond traders?" (quoted in Peck, 2010: 237). Answers to this sort of question look set to remain affirmative until and unless deeper questions can be asked about how bonds bind everyday life right across the planet (Konings, 2009).

References

Jamie Peck, *Constructions of Neoliberal Reason* (Oxford: Oxford University Press, 2010).
Martijn Konings, "Rethinking Neoliberalism and the Subprime Crisis: Beyond the Re-regulation Agenda," *Competition and Change* 13, no. 2 (2009): 108–27.

Capital flight A term used to describe the very rapid removal of investments from a particular country or region. The money that leaves quickest tends to take the form of investments in highly liquid stock and bond funds. However, capital flight can also take the form of sell-offs of residential and commercial property. Sometimes the governments of countries experiencing capital flight seek to slow or block the herd-like rush to disinvest by closing certain markets temporarily and reducing the ability of financial institutions to move currency in and out of the country. This is what the Malaysian government did during the 1997–1998 Asian financial crisis. Other countries in the region fell victim to ongoing capital flight because they followed IMF advice about keeping the markets open. Malaysia, by contrast, refused the IMF rulings and retained a degree of control over the crisis. As a result, it suffered much less damage than neighboring Indonesia and Thailand, and enjoyed one of the quickest economic recoveries in the region (Stiglitz, 2002).

Reference

Joseph Stiglitz, *Globalization and Its Discontents* (New York: W.W. Norton, 2002).

Chapter 11 Not to be confused with the Chapter 11 bankruptcy protection for US firms who seek "reorganization" by a bankruptcy court, Chapter 11 is more famous in globalization debates as a key chapter dealing with foreign investment in the **NAFTA** free-trade agreement. The provisions of Chapter 11 were primarily designed to protect US and Canadian corporations who feared that future Mexican governments might want to roll back **neoliberalism** in Mexico and nationalize (i.e. transfer back to public ownership) things such as water supply and public land that were privatized in the 1980s and 1990s. The business lobbyists demanded legal protections that would mean that governments would have to compensate corporations who suffered lost profits as a result of government intervention. This is what Chapter 11 provided. However, it was written using terminology that has allowed for extraordinarily far-reaching corporate lawsuits against a wide array of democratic efforts at regulation. Under Chapter 11, the signatory nations are prevented from "directly or indirectly nationaliz[ing] an investment" or taking measures "tantamount to nationalization or expropriation," and it is with the latter phrase in particular that the door has been opened to the direct attacks on regulation by democratically elected governments. Most infamously, there have been two cases involving carcinogenic gasoline (petrol) additives. In 1997, a US company, the Ethyl Corporation, sued the Canadian government under Chapter 11 demanding damages because the Canadian authorities had implemented a ban on an Ethyl product, the gasoline additive methylcyclopentadienyl manganese tricarbonyl (MMT). The NAFTA arbitration tribunal hearing the case found for Ethyl, and Canada was forced to pay the company US$13 million and subsequently had to withdraw its ban of MMT. Such cases show that NAFTA created a new set of rights for corporations that enable them not only to side-step government regulations by moving factories but also, through Chapter 11, to actually enable corporate challenges to the legislative authority of democratically elected governments. For an up-to-date critical analysis of these corporate efforts to sue governments, see the *Public Citizen* Trade Watch website at http://www.citizen.org/trade/.

Commodification The transformation of something that is not necessarily bought and sold into a commodity that has a price in a market. It is often used in conjunction with criticisms of the **privatization** of public space, public assets, and common property: turning water from rivers, for example, into something that is bottled and bought and sold for money (Barlow, 2008; Shiva, 2002). The commodification of social goods such as health care, water provision, and transportation has been accelerated globally by the policy-making norms of **neoliberalism**. Justified in the name of market rationality and profit-making, such commodification has nevertheless prompted critics to wonder what the profits really look like. Arundhati Roy puts these concerns in the form of a critical question.

> When all the rivers and valleys and forests and hills of the world have been priced, packaged, bar-coded, and stacked in the local supermarket, when all the hay and coal and earth and wood and water have been turned to gold, what shall we do with all the gold? (Roy, 2001: 42)

Two years later, she answered her own question with a still more bleak portrait of the lost values that seem to come with rampant commodification:

> Meanwhile down at the mall there's a midseason sale, Everything's discounted – oceans, rivers, oil, gene pools, fig wasps, flowers, childhoods, aluminum factories, phone companies, wisdom, wilderness, civil rights, ecosystems, air – all 4.6 billion years of

evolution. Its packed, sealed, tagged, valued, and available off the rack (no returns). As for justice, I'm told its on offer, too. You can get the best that money can buy. (Roy, 2003: 73–74)

References

Maude Barlow, *Blue Covenant: The Global Water Crisis and the Coming Battle for the Right to Water* (New York: New Press: Distributed by W.W. Norton, 2008).
Arundhati Roy, *Power Politics* (Cambridge, MA: South End Press, 2001).
Arundhati Roy, *War Talk* (Cambridge, MA: South End Press, 2003).
Vandana Shiva, *Water Wars: Privatization, Pollution, and Profit* (Cambridge, MA: South End Press, 2002).

Commodity chains A commodity chain (or "value chain" as it is sometimes described) is the name for the overall production process of commodities from the initial collection of raw materials through basic production and assembly through to transportation, retailing, sales, and consumption. Geographers have been at the forefront of theorizing and mapping commodity chains globally (e.g. Coe *et al.*, 2008). However, perhaps the most well-known theorist of commodity chains is the economic sociologist, Gary Gereffi, who introduced the distinction discussed here in Chapter 3 between "Producer-driven commodity chains" and "Market-driven commodity chains." More recent collaborative contributions to this analytical project have introduced a typology of five commodity chains sub-types (Gereffi *et al.*, 2005). Between the one extreme of producer-driven chains and the other extreme of market-mediated chains (which the three scholars rename "hierarchical" and "market" chains, respectively), the new account allows for the formulation of three other sub-types called "captive," "relational," and "modular."

Beyond economic sociology, there is also now a larger and still-growing collection of work that uses particular commodities as a lens through which to explore globalization more generally. Sugar, chocolate, coffee, tea, water, tobacco, marijuana, cotton, oil, coal, diamonds, and even the potato have in this way become the basis of studies of how commodities both connect and divide us globally (see the references listed below). Using commodity histories to examine global geographies of trade, these studies often aim at exploring where everyday commodities come from and who they connect through global networks of production and distribution. In this sense, they offer a critique of **commodity fetishism**, and at their best, they thereby also follow the path-breaking example of Sydney Mintz (1985), whose work on sugar sourced from Caribbean slave plantations documented global power relations of domination and exploitation, too. But, as the literary critic, Bruce Robbins, argues in an excellent essay on commodity histories as a genre, the authors of these works can sometimes claim so much world historical significance for their particular commodity chain that they also in some sense re-fetishize the commodities (Robbins, 2005). The focus on goods at the center of global commodity chains may in this way also unfortunately obscure the bads of global injustice.

References

Neil Coe, Peter Dicken, and Martin Hess, "Global Production Networks: Realizing the Potential," *Journal of Economic Geography* 8 (2008): 271–95.

Sophie Coe and Michael Coe, *The True History of Chocolate* (London: Thames and Hudson, 1996).

Barbara Freese, *Coal: A Human History* (Cambridge, MA: Perseus Books, 2003).

Iain Gately, *Tobacco: A Cultural History of How an Exotic Plant Seduced Civilization* (New York: Grove Press, 2001).

Gary Gereffi, Tim Sturgeon, and John Humphrey, "The Governance of Global Value Chains," *Review of International Political Economy* 12, no. 1 (2005): 78–104.

Alan Macfarlane and Iris Macfarlane, *Green Gold: The Empire of Tea* (London: Ebury Press, 2003).

Sidney Mintz, *Sweetness and Power: The Place of Sugar in Modern History* (New York: Viking Penguin, 1985).

Priti Ramamurthy, "The Cotton Commodity Chain, Women, Work and Agency in India and Japan: The Case for Feminist Agro-Food Systems Research," *World Development* 28 (2000): 551–78.

Bruce Robbins, "Commodity Histories," *PMLA* 120, no. 2 (2005): 454–63.

Larry Zuckerman, *The Potato: How the Humble Spud Rescued the Western World* (New York: North Point Press, 1998).

Commodity fetishism This is what happens in capitalism when products for sale on the market become invested by consumers with the same sorts of hopes, desires, and dreams normally reserved for religious symbols and gods. For Marxist theorists, the concept remains a way of coming to terms with how capitalism makes the symbolic and monetary values of commodities seem so important that they obscure all the social and economic relations (including diverse globe-spanning **commodity chains**) that go into producing commodities in the first place (Marx, 1965, chapter 1). A main aim of global justice movement activists in recent years has been to make this critique of commodity fetishism meaningful in the context of **neoliberalism**. Groups such as *Behind the Label* (http://behindthelabel.net) and *United Students Against Sweatshops* (www.studentsagainstsweatshops.org/) have sought in this way to investigate the working conditions of workers producing commodities for big brand firms and retailers, revealing in this way the degree to which **consumerism** in places such as malls is commonly dependent on exploitation in other places such as EPZs on the other side of the world.

In theoretical debates over psychoanalysis and post-colonialism, another rather different global re-framing of fetishism has been developed as a result of work by the American critical theorist, Anne McClintock (1995). While Marx had been drawing on a secular critique of religious fetishism in order to strip away the mystifying meanings of commodities in capitalism, Sigmund Freud was famously interested in the sexual meanings and drives connected to fetishism. McClintock examines all these interpretations vis-à-vis imperial attitudes about the colonies that were common during the times in which Marx and Freud were writing: attitudes that dismissed native religious icons as fetishistic while simultaneously propagating commodity fetishism and propagating Christian icons, statuary, and beliefs along the way. McClintock's approach not only takes us beyond one of Freud's sexist errors (i.e. explaining sexual fetishes solely in relation to the so-called "castration anxieties" of men) but also interestingly opens questions about the degree to which Marx's critique might have contained (albeit in an unexamined way) an awareness of the non-economic gender and racial power relations underpinning commodity production in the colonies.

References

Karl Marx, *Capital, Volume 1* (Moscow: Progress Publishers, 1965).
Anne McClintock, *Imperial Leather: Race, Gender, and Sexuality in the Colonial Conquest* (New York: Routledge, 1995).

Comparative advantage David Ricardo reportedly became interested in economics after reading Adam Smith's *The Wealth of Nations* while on holiday at the English spa town of Bath in 1799. Subsequently, his theory of comparative advantage sought to explain how trade could increase the wealth of nations by allowing specialization. The basic argument is very simple: namely that even if country "x" can produce everything more efficiently than country "y," both countries can still reap economic gains when country x specializes in what it is best at producing and trading freely – without tariffs – with country "y." While this theory is still widely taught in economics classes around the world and on the website of the World Bank, it is less often noted that there was a historical context that made Ricardo's arguments make sense to him and the leaders of British industry in the nineteenth century (but see Hobsbawm, 1964). They wanted to open new markets for the commodities being made in their new factories. Likewise, they had an economic interest in food being cheaper for their workers (so they did not have to pay them so much to feed themselves). As a result of these two major economic imperatives, they wanted Britain to have free trade with other countries by repealing the Corn Laws that imposed import tariffs on cheap foreign grain. From the perspective of Ricardo and the business class to whom his arguments appealed, these Corn Laws were economically irrational because they only increased the profits of British landowners – an older feudal class of aristocratic elites – who "wasted" their wealth on personal extravagances that did little to expand the industrial economy. Ricardo died in 1823, and it was not until 23 years later that the Anti Corn Law League finally succeeded in having the import tariffs repealed with the 1846 Importation Act (in the mean time, the League had also founded *The Economist* magazine in 1843 as a way of popularizing its pro-free-trade arguments). Too late for Ricardo himself, the repeal of the Corn Laws nevertheless went on to have many of the effects that he and Britain's business leaders had envisioned. It made it possible to import cheap foreign grain, allowing, among other things, for the importation via steamboat of the new and especially cheap American prairie corn. It moved Britain's governing elites towards a wider commitment to free trade. And along the way, it had another useful economic effect in that it made farming more marginal land in Britain unprofitable, leading to increasing unemployment of the agricultural labor force and their steady migration to the industrial cities where their demand for work helped to keep wages down and profits up for business.

Reference

Eric Hobsbawm, *The Age of Revolution, 1789–1848* (New York: New American Library, 1964).

Conditionalities Conditionalities are another name for the structural reforms generally demanded of indebted countries by the **IMF**, **World Bank**, and other lenders as the conditions for new loans, debt rescheduling, debt relief, and **aid**. As such, conditionalities generally consist of the **Washington Consensus** policy norms of **neoliberalism**: including, most notably, budget-balancing austerity, price stability, public-sector wage controls, privatization, trade liberalization, and financial deregulation. Although conditionalities have also hit the headlines in recent years due to anti-austerity protests in Greece and other parts of southern Europe, and while the practice of imposing neoliberalism this way goes back to the IMF's dictates to the United Kingdom in the 1970s, it has been the structural adjustment programs (**SAPs**) imposed by the IMF and World Bank on the **Global South** in the 1980s and 1990s that have spread neoliberal conditionalities most forcefully and globally (Corbridge, 1992; Payer, 1974; Peet, 2003). As a result of the widespread suffering and criticism generated by these policies – illustrated very well in the brilliant film *Life and Debt* (directed by Stephanie Black) – there has been increasing disagreement between the World Bank and IMF over the merits of traditional SAP conditionalities (Stiglitz, 2002). This Washington dissensus means that while the IMF continues with the old "one-size-fits-all" structural reform orthodoxy, World Bank programs tend instead to emphasize more tailored programs of country-specific conditions, some of them also being increasingly focused on individuals rather than governments through so-called conditional cash transfers (CCTs). The latter programs seek to change personal behavior by incentivizing individuals with direct cash transfers. They may still rely on neoliberal nostrums about the social coordination capacity of market forces, but they also represent a response in many cases to the market failures and social neglect associated with traditional SAPs. In examples such as *Oportunidades* in Mexico and *Bolsa Família* in Brazil, we therefore see new conditionalities focused on encouraging poor families to enrol their children in education and health programs. Applauded and emulated as they may be in the United States, these kinds of conditionalized programs are clearly quite different to the original Washington Consensus conditionalities that ended up closing down schools and imposing user fees for health services in poor countries in the 1980s and 1990s (Peck and Theodore, 2010).

References

Stuart Corbridge, "Discipline and Punish: The New Right and the Policing of the International Debt Crisis," *Geoforum*, 23, no. 3 (1992): 285–301.

Cheryl Payer, *The Debt Trap: The International Monetary Fund and the Third World* (New York: Monthly Review Press, 1974).

Jamie Peck and Nick Theodore, "Recombinant Workfare, Across the Americas: Transnationalizing 'Fast' Social Policy," *Geoforum* 41 (2010): 195–208.

Richard Peet, *Unholy Trinity: The IMF, World Bank and WTO* (London: Zed Books, 2003).

Joseph Stiglitz, *Globalization and its Discontents* (New York: W.W. Norton, 2002).

Consumerism A way of living that is so dominated by commercialized consumption that people's primary feelings and desires are overtaken by a preoccupation with buying and displaying everything that they can possibly purchase. This is a way of life in which the symbolic values of commodities (including their function as status symbols) come to dominate over their practical use value. Consumerism is in this sense a cultural and social phenomenon as well as a basic economic necessity of continued capitalist growth (Cohen and Kennedy, 2000). But it remains an ongoing capitalist necessity, too, and as such it is commonly viewed as one of the most notable and most homogenizing cultural and social phenomena to have been extended globally in the era of **neoliberalism**. The business need to find and cultivate consumers has led not only to the opening up of new markets through **free trade** but also to the relentless recruitment of new consumers through the worldwide expansion of advertising. Such advertising has become so omnipresent around the world that it has entrenched what critics view as a dominant "culture-ideology" of consumerism. Free-market globalization has thus taken the basic human need to consume food, clothing, and shelter, and created a new and evermore global common denominator based on **commodity fetishism** and the resulting **commodification** of everything from love to politics itself. The result to many critics represents the wholesale make-over of diverse global cultures in the simplified and homogenous image of the capitalist market. This so-called **McDonaldization** of social life (Ritzer, 2004) has of course also been matched by the global spread of fast-food consumption itself, a development in consumerism that is also tied in turn to the rise in obesity around the world (Kearney, 2010).

References

Robin Cohen and Paul Kennedy, *Global Sociology* (London: Macmillan, 2000).

John Kearney, "Food Consumption Trends and Drivers," *Philosophical Transactions of the Royal Society B* 365, no. 1554 (2010): 2793–807. doi:10.1098/rstb.2010.0149.

George Ritzer, *The McDonaldization of Society* (Thousand Oaks, CA: Pine Forge Press, 2004).

Leslie Sklair, *Sociology of the Global System* (London: Prentice-Hall, 1995).

Cosmopolitanism The outcome of increased commitments to being "cosmopolitan," which is to say worldly and transnationally oriented as opposed to parochial and nationally restricted. Back in the mid-nineteenth century, the new transnational ties being developed by capitalist merchants and industrialists were often perceived to be leading to more feelings of cosmopolitanism. Karl Marx and Frederick Engels (2008) waxed lyrical over these changes with some of their highest praise for capitalism. The business class, they famously argued in the *Communist Manifesto*, "has through its exploitation of the world market given a cosmopolitan character to production and consumption in every country." Marx and Engels saw in this cosmopolitanism the demise of older national forms of social organization and the rise of new consciousness about global interdependency. "All old-established national industries have been destroyed or are daily being destroyed," they said. "In place of the old local and national seclusion and self-sufficiency, we have intercourse in every direction, universal interdependence of nations." For Marx and Engels, this eclipse of older traditional and national modes of being was something to celebrate because they saw it as a prelude to the spread of socialism globally. Capitalism would in this vision wipe away all the old fixed traditions and, by creating transnational ties of free trade, prepare the way for transnational solidarities of workers. However, as the development of capitalism since the mid-nineteenth century has shown, local traditions have not so much been eclipsed as transformed by global economic interdependency. This has led more contemporary scholars to rethink what exactly cosmopolitanism might mean. If it is not the complete eclipse of local feelings by global feelings, what is it?

Many commentators argue that we need to think instead about increasingly hybrid feelings and commitments, some of them re-worked by progressive movements such as environmentalism and feminism, and others transformed by other more traditionalist kinds of transnational identity including the bonds across borders created by religious systems (Cheah and Robbins, 1998). In either case, however, the transnationalizing imperatives of capitalism – the **consumerism** it breeds, the instabilities it unleashes, and the shared fates it creates between workers and consumers everywhere – all contribute to the ongoing destabilization of the nation-state as the principal container of political and ethical belonging. In response to such destabilization, some more idealistic scholars have argued for newly inclusive kinds of cosmopolitan democracy and constitutionalism on a world scale. Such utopian initiatives, however, would seem to be vulnerable to at least two countervailing characteristics of actually existing cosmopolitanism. On the one side, today's dominant cosmopolitan spaces – multicultural business boardrooms, international food courts, frequent flier lounges, and so on – are so overwhelmingly shaped by capitalist forces that they tend to uphold and enforce norms of competitive individualism that are likely to block any more substantive articulations of collective social rights and social justice at a global level (Sparke, 2006). On the other side, the fact that these capitalist constructions of cosmopolitanism are also interwoven with the creation of so many subordinated cosmopolitans (prisoners subject to extraordinary rendition, for example, or sex workers smuggled across borders) means that too many people are simply excluded from the possibility of cosmopolitan democracy, even as they experience high-speed cross-border movement. Despite its long existence in world cities and market centers going back to Greek and Roman times, and notwithstanding a long lineage in philosophical thought, cosmopolitanism as a singular global constitutional project would therefore seem to face a bleak future. However, considered in a less idealistic and more critical way (Harvey, 2009), the restrictions on actually existing cosmopolitanism can be better considered as spurs to examine what constituencies and identities are left out of institutions of global governance – organizations such as the **IMF, World Bank, WTO** – institutions that could all be much more inclusively cosmopolitan than they actually are.

References

Pheng Cheah and Bruce Robbins, eds, *Cosmopolitics: Thinking and Feeling Beyond the Nation* (Minneapolis: University of Minnesota Press, 1998).
David Harvey, *Cosmopolitanism and the Geographies of Freedom* (New York: Columbia University Press, 2009).
Karl Marx and Frederick Engels, *The Communist Manifesto* (London: Pluto Press, 2008).
Matthew Sparke, "A Neoliberal Nexus: Citizenship, Security and the Future of the Border," *Political Geography* 25, no. 2 (2006): 151–80.

Credit rating agencies There are three main international credit rating agencies that are recognized worldwide: Standard & Poor's, Moody's Investor Service, and Fitch Ratings. Historically, the main business of these private US-based companies was to provide financial information about American corporations. Over the course of the twentieth century, they grew into huge globally active ratings agencies, assessing risk and assigning ratings not just to corporate debt but also to governmental debt ranging from US municipal bonds to the incredibly varied loans and securities used by sovereign governments around the world (Sinclair, 2005; Hackworth, 2007). Such ratings relate, or at least should relate, to the fundamental question of whether the borrowers being assessed (i.e. the corporations, cities, or national governments) are in a position to make reliable ongoing payments on their debts. Those that are seen as very low risk then win **AAA** ratings. However, because of the huge stakes involved, because a low rating can destroy the ability of a company or city or country to acquire loans at competitive rates, and because the agencies are private for-profit corporations, there have been increasing questions about the objectivity of ratings. These have intensified still more amidst the 2008–2012 crisis with various European governments as well as the US government asking ever-more urgent questions about the enormous influence but often flawed analysis of the ratings of everything from mortgage-backed securities to Greek, French, Irish, Spanish, and Italian sovereign debt. Meanwhile, in business, universities, and city administration buildings all over the world, credit rating agencies continue to exert disciplinary control in ways that expand and entrench neoliberalism.

References

Jason Hackworth, *The Neoliberal City: Governance, Ideology, and Development in American Urbanism* (Ithaca, NY: Cornell University Press, 2007).

Timothy Sinclair, *The New Masters of Capital: American Bond Rating Agencies and the Politics of Creditworthiness* (Ithaca, NY: Cornell University Press, 2005).

Debt In its simplest sense, debt is just **money** that is owed. However, in the world of finance, it comes in a wide array of increasingly complex forms including credit card borrowing, bank loans, mortgages, diverse **bonds**, swaps, options, swaptions, and many other still more complex **derivatives**. All these forms of debt represent value, but like money itself, they are not a source of value. Instead, they represent a capitalist bet on the likely production of new profits from new investments. Such bets effectively put a monetary valuation on future value generation before it has happened. They therefore also represent a monetary valuation of the risks involved in securing ongoing capitalist processes of profit generation. This means that risk assessment lies at the core of most financial dealings over debt. Loans to supposedly stable financial entities such as large companies or governments are often termed "risk-free" or "low risk" and made at a so-called "risk-free interest rate." This is because the debt and interest are expected to be repaid without fail. This does not always happen, of course, and other risks also affect the value of debt, including the risk that the currency in which the debt is owed loses value. Given these uncertainties, lenders often rely on **credit rating agencies** as well as a number of international institutions to anticipate and manage the risks involved. Alongside the **IMF**, a key institution in this regard is the Bank for International Settlements, which sets rules to define what loans qualify as "risk-free" or not.

   In absolute terms, the United States owes more than any other country in the world. However, because of the historic importance of the dollar as a global currency of last result, and because of the dependency of producers in Japan, China, and Europe on the ongoing capacity of Americans to consume their exports, lenders continue to lend money to the United States by buying US government and corporate **bonds**. Some commentators believe that this lending and the cheap credit it provides for American companies and consumers are likely to become increasingly harder to maintain as lenders come to terms with the declining value of the dollar. However, for the moment, the United States continues to be able to borrow more, and the countries who are suffering the most from indebtedness are countries in the **Global South** (and increasingly southern Europe) where debt causes a vast array of problems ranging from malnutrition and miserable educational services to widespread political instability. While, in 1997, the United Nations Development Programme (UNDP) stated that 21 million children's lives could be saved if the money used for debt service was put into health and education, in 2002 the same agency reported that among 50 African countries, 29 spent more on debt service than on health. These kinds of debt crises have led to a huge political effort to reduce and relieve the debt of the 41 states that are classified as heavily indebted poor countries (**HIPCs**). The main objective of the HIPC initiative is to reduce debt in these countries to a sustainable level, thereby releasing extra budgetary resources for poverty-reducing expenditure, including expenditure on health. However, the politics and economics of debt forgiveness are complex and commonly rely on the governments of wealthy countries taking over the risks of the remaining loans from the private commercial banks that saddled the HIPCs with the huge debts in the first place.

Derivatives A derivative is a financial instrument that *derives* its value from the trading and price movements of other underlying assets. It is traded in a way that puts a market price on the financial risk associated with the future price fluctuation of these other underlying financial instruments (including stocks, **bonds**, currencies, and commodities). The main three types of derivatives are called *futures*, *options*, and *swaps*, and collectively they are used to put prices on the risks associated with the future values of various traded instruments ranging from currencies and basic commodities such as coffee and pork bellies, to ordinary stocks and bonds, to much more complex instruments with exotic names like "dual currency bonds" and "synthetic noncallable debt." Whether simple or complex, the way derivatives put a price on risk enables market agents to either speculate on risk (e.g. bet that the price of coffee next year will be much higher) or conduct risk management by effectively selling risk to speculators (e.g. fix a price of a future delivery of coffee despite not knowing what climatological and transportation challenges may be faced in the year ahead). Interestingly, from the perspective of the history of globalization, the development of futures, options, and swaps can be examined in terms of how they have enabled capitalists to deal with the risks of doing business at a distance (Leyshon and Thrift, 1997). Futures, for example, can be traced to the opening of the Chicago Board of Trade in 1848 when traders established forward contract calls for the exchange of certain commodities (such as cattle) at a future date for cash. Buyers and sellers could thereby use the futures market to manage all the risks associated with the colonization of the American west, with communicating long distance by telegraph and railway, with moving cattle vast distances and turning them into refrigerated meat, with transforming the prairies into gigantic grain-growing farms, and with dispossessing the native inhabitants (Cronon, 1991). Options perhaps go back even further as simple agreements between individual market actors to reserve a choice to buy or sell in the future. However, the development of institutionalized option exchanges represents a much more recent revolution in financial affairs, and allows securitized long-distance risk trading between parties that are often on opposite sides of the world. It has created two types of options: put options and call options. The latter give their owners the right to *buy* an underlying financial instrument (e.g. a bond) at a specific price until a specific date. Reciprocally, put options allow their owners to reserve the right to *sell* a financial instrument at a specific price up to a specific date. These rights are then traded by options traders who offer them at a price (while retaining a premium for the service). Swaps are a still more complex kind of derivative that have come to be associated with the speculation and risk management generated by global trading in currencies and bonds between parts of the world with varied interest rates. Swaps take the form of an agreement between the trading counterparties to exchange certain sequences of cash flow over a specified future period. Commonly, for example, swaps are used to trade fixed rates of interest for floating rates of interest. Such swaps allow the sellers to speculate that future interest rates will generate higher payments while allowing the buyers of the fixed rate payments to reduce their exposure to the risks associated with interest-rate volatility. More exotic "accreting swaps," "amortizing swaps," "seasonal swaps," "roller coaster swaps," "off-market swaps," "yield curve swaps," "rate differential swaps," "flavored currency swaps," "CIRCUS swaps," and so-called "swaptions" allow market players to hedge all kinds of additional risk factors in financial markets (Kolb, 2000). An ironic outcome of the related explosion of hedge-fund trading in derivatives in recent years, however, has been the increasing system-wide risks and instabilities associated with trading risk – the 2008–2012 global financial crisis and risk bankers being a case in point (Tett, 2009). Even if one thinks such risks are exaggerated, there can be no doubt that derivative trading has become a defining feature of today's global financial system: a system that has swapped monetary control by individual nation-states for a kind of transnational "phantom state" whose unending money movements continue 24 h a day, 7 days a week, shaping life right across the planet.

References

William Cronon, *Nature's Metropolis: Chicago and the Great West* (New York: W. W. Norton, 1991).

Robert Kolb, *Futures, Options and Swaps*, third edition (Oxford: Blackwell, 2000).

Andrew Leyshon and Nigel Thrift, *Money/Space: Geographies of Monetary Transformation* (New York: Routledge, 1997).

Gillian Tett, *Fool's Gold: How the Bold Dream of a Small Tribe at J.P. Morgan Was Corrupted by Wall Street Greed and Unleashed a Catastrophe* (New York: Free Press, 2009).

Downward harmonization This is the process whereby wages, environmental standards, and health and safety standards are systematically reduced to the lowest common denominator in a **free-trade** area or system. For proponents of **neoliberalism**, such a process is merely about producing a so-called **level-playing field** for business. However, for ordinary workers and consumers, the actual experience of downward harmonization is better understood as a **race to the bottom** that enforces neoliberalism through competition. Real regulatory reforms are thereby imposed through market forces because countries and communities are so eager to avoid losing footloose business. The outcome of downward harmonization is therefore best understood thus as a form of "disciplinary neoliberalism" (Gill, 1995).

Reference

Stephen Gill, "Globalisation, Market Civilisation, and Disciplinary Neoliberalism." *Millennium: Journal of International Studies* 24, no. 3 (1995): 399–423.

FDI Foreign direct investment is what happens when a company invests abroad by building a new plant or directly acquiring new facilities and operations. It is distinguished from foreign portfolio investment (FPI) in which companies, fund managers, and individuals purchase the stock of foreign companies. There are two main types of FDI. The first involves establishing brand new factories or retail facilities on the ground. The second involves buying-up, merging with, or otherwise acquiring a foreign company. These two types are known respectively as *Greenfield* FDI and *Mergers and Acquisitions* FDI. Greenfield investment simply means new investment in new facilities, infrastructure, and equipment. It does not have to happen literally in a green field, and can take place in sites as varied as former housing zones and former rainforests. *Mergers and Acquisitions* can be very varied too, but they are all usually investments made specifically with the purpose of exercising executive control over foreign companies.

Fiscal austerity A term used to describe governmental policies that are deliberately designed to cut budgets and reduce government spending. These policies generally lead to cuts in public services, including everything from education, libraries, and health care to the provision of clean water. As such, fiscal austerity goes against conventional Keynesianism that argues governments need to manage demand during downturns in the business cycle by pump-priming economies, creating new job opportunities and providing a boost for business by serving as the consumer of last resort. "Supply siders" and other advocates of **neoliberalism** in institutions like the **IMF** disagree with such deficit-spending demand management. They argue that the supposedly short-term pain caused by fiscal austerity allows for long-term gain because it will (again supposedly) create business confidence. It is supposed to do this by preventing governments from overborrowing and from thereby creating high **inflation** and the associated risks for business and owners of large amounts of money (inflation effectively representing a fall in the value of money). Against this, it is now clear in the context of global financial crisis that even when governments such as Argentina, Ireland, Greece, and Spain follow the neoliberal rule book and reduce spending by imposing fiscal austerity, business confidence can still plummet. The countries can still fall into inflationary cycles of fast rising prices and all the attendant economic instabilities. Meanwhile, even if they do not suffer the total financial meltdown that Argentina went through in 2002–2003 or that Greece experienced in 2011–2012, fiscal austerity still reduces the capacity of governments to make the kinds of investments in education and health care that ensure the long-run survival and recovery of ordinary citizens. Such disinvestment leads not surprisingly to widespread social upheaval. In the 1980s and 1990s, many other parts of the world that had had fiscal austerity forced on them by the IMF and World Bank as one of the main **conditionalities** of new loans experienced "austerity protests." These often started with riots over foods prices but usually also extended into broader campaigns against wage cuts, the privatization of public services, and the general decline of social infrastructure. Recent forms of Occupy activism have repeated this pattern, decrying particular kinds of austerity and inequality but extending into broader critiques of neoliberalism more generally.

Fiscal policy A bracket term for government budget policies and associated approaches to government spending and borrowing. It is generally used in juxtaposition with the term **monetary policy**.

Fordism/Post-Fordism These terms are used by political theorists to distinguish between the general organization of capitalist societies in the mid-twentieth century (Fordism) and the later period, from the early 1970s to today (post-Fordism). The theory is that these periods have been characterized by distinctive *regimes* (systems) of capitalist regulation in which different kinds of political, economic, and societal ordering come together in distinctive ways. Following Antonio Gramsci's pioneering discussion of Henry Ford's concerns with his workers' ability to consume and buy his cars, regulation theorists argue that Fordism was characterized by the macro-economic balancing of mass production and mass consumption (Gramsci, 1992). Taking Gramsci's attention to Ford's labor practices further, the regulation theorists also argue that Fordism as a general, society-wide system was also characterized by careful attention by political elites to the management of sociological crises (Ford had instituted social worker visits at his big factory complex in Dearborn Michigan in order to make sure his workers were not distracted by non-economic pressures in their homes). At a society-wide level, these social aspects of Fordism included government investment in national welfare, health care, and education systems; the idea being that looking after workers in downturns, making sure that they remain healthy and educated, became a way for the state to ensure that the workers would be ready and willing to return to work after a business cycle started up again.

Of course, another contextual factor that enabled the development of Fordism in this way was the existence of an alternative to capitalism in the Communist bloc countries. Perhaps still more important, though, was the firm belief among governing elites that national governments had a strong role to play in maintaining economic stability. This kind of commitment also led to the widespread adoption of Keynesianism, and the common involvement by governments in attempting to arbitrate industrial disputes between workers' unions and business owners. All of these modes of governance – developing a social safety net, deficit spending for pump-priming, balancing mass-production and mass-consumption within national economies, etc. – constituted the regime called Fordism, and all of them started to become challenged and weakened in the context of post-Fordism after the mid 1970s. Post-Fordism is characterized fundamentally by a breakdown in the balancing of national mass-consumption with national mass production.

What might once have been good for General Motors is no longer necessarily good for America. General Motors and many other TNCs no longer depend on either producing goods domestically or just selling them domestically. They employ people all over the planet and sell products everywhere, too. Thus, their Fordist self-interest in maintaining a specifically national pool of decently paid workers who can also double as customers has been destroyed. They seek out customers wherever they can find them. Equally, they use labor of different sorts (educated for R & D in some places, ill-paid, ill-educated, and oftentimes just plain ill in other places for the low-skill labor-intensive parts of their **commodity chains**). In this context, TNCs have great flexibility, and so some writers, like David Harvey (1989), have described post-Fordism as the era of "Flexible Accumulation." Post-Fordism has also witnessed the erosive impact of **neoliberalism** on national government capacity for macro-economic management, and this has led other scholars to refer to the period as "The End of Organized Capitalism" (Lash and Urry, 1987). Yet another feature noted by regulation theorists themselves is that post-Fordism has seen the fast erosion of national welfare systems and the end, as President Clinton called it in the United States, of "welfare as we know it." The replacement vision of a "workfare state" has been spread around the richer countries as the new model for the post-Fordist period, and while during the 1990s it reduced welfare rolls, it did nothing to reduce poverty and related forms of suffering (Peck, 2002).

References

Antonio Gramsci, *Prison Notebooks* (New York: Columbia University Press, 1992).
David Harvey, *The Condition of Post-Modernity* (Oxford: Blackwell, 1989).
Scott Lash and John Urry, *The End of Organized Capitalism* (Madison, WI: University of Wisconsin Press, 1987).
Jamie Peck, *Workfare States* (New York: Guilford, 2002).

G8 Officially established in 1985 as the G7 or Group of Seven, The Group of Eight now includes Russia and continues to function as an international governance forum that provides a venue for dialogue over economic policy among its member nations. Historically, it has been dominated by the United States, but the other nation-state members that belong are Canada, France, Germany, the United Kingdom, Italy, and Japan. Whether with eight members or seven, the organization has proved ineffective at pursuing any common policies except the free-market reforms of **neoliberalism**. Non-western leaders have asked why a country such as Canada is a member when much bigger economies such as China and India are not. The G8 is nevertheless presented by its leaders and the media as a global leadership group, its very narrow version (and vision) of globalization notwithstanding. The Indian social and environmental activist, Vandana Shiva, uses the G7 in this way to exemplify that the "global" is ultimately a political construction in which a dominant "local" seeks global control, stating:

The "global" does not represent any universal human interest; it represents a particular local and parochial interest that has been globalized through its reach and control. The Group of Seven most powerful countries may dictate global affairs, but they remain narrow, local and parochial in the interests that guide them. (Shiva, 2004: 196)

Reference

Vandana Shiva, "Conflicts of Global Ecology: Environmental Activism in a Period of Global Reach," *Alternatives* 19, no. 2 (2004): 195–207.

GATS The **WTO**'s General Agreement on Trade in Services was designed to liberalize global trade in services the same way the **GATT** worked through the 1970s, 1980s and 1990s to liberalize trade in goods. Its implications are enormous, threatening to privatize wide areas of human activity related to service industries. GATS applies to trade in four key service areas: telecommunications, financial services, air transport, and maritime transport. Under GATS, WTO members are obliged to allow foreign companies to: (1) establish a commercial presence, (2) provide services from one country to another, and (3) engage in travel between countries to supply services. Services were brought under GATT rules after intense lobbying by the United States, which is the world's largest exporter of services. Poor countries fear that GATS will allow foreign **TNCs** to overwhelm smaller, local companies. They also fear that a future, more comprehensive GATS agreement would give **TNCs** the kinds of rights they have under **Chapter 11** of **NAFTA**, including rights to sue governments for policies that limit a TNC's ability to sell services.

GATT The General Agreement on Tariffs and Trade was one of the three main institutional legacies of the Bretton Woods Agreement and was meant to coordinate global trade rules. Unlike the **IMF** and the **World Bank**, however, the GATT was never transformed into an International Trade Organization with a permanent office because the dominant world powers in the 1950s and 1960s could not agree to making coordinated cuts in tariffs. Instead, the GATT became the name for a set of ongoing and never finalized conferences, thereby living up to the nickname "The General Agreement to Talk and Talk." This pattern changed in the 1970s as commitments to neoliberal free-trade policies gained in support, and national economies around the world became less self-enclosed and autarchic. Building on the increasing momentum for free trade, the Uruguay Round of GATT talks led finally in 1995 to the formation of the **WTO**.

Global Compact The Global Compact was first launched by Kofi Annan, the Secretary General of the **UN**, at the annual World Economic Forum in Davos in January 1999. He asked business to be socially responsible by "demonstrating good global citizenship wherever it operates." The compact invites business in this way to uphold 10 basic principles, derived from the Universal Declaration of Human Rights, the International Labor Organization Declaration on Fundamental Principles and Rights at Work, the 1995 Copenhagen Social Summit, and the Rio Declaration of the Earth summit. See http://www.unglobalcompact.org/aboutthegc/thetenprinciples/index.html

These 10 principles are listed as:

1. Support and respect the protection of international human rights within their sphere of influence.
2. Make sure their own corporations are not complicit in human-rights abuses.
3. Freedom of association and the effective recognition of the right to collective bargaining.
4. The elimination of all forms of forced and compulsory labour.
5. The effective abolition of child labour.
6. The elimination of discrimination in respect of employment and occupation.
7. Support a precautionary approach to environmental challenges.
8. Undertake initiatives to promote greater environmental responsibility.
9. Encourage the development and diffusion of environmentally friendly technologies.
10. Businesses should work against corruption in all its forms, including extortion and bribery.

Despite the good intentions of the compact, it remains like other codes of corporate social responsibility (CSR) an entirely voluntary system, and there is no way in which the UN, the ILO, or any other body can at present oblige **TNCs** to follow its principles.

Global South A term used as a kind of catch-all to describe all the countries and communities of the world that are poorer than the richer countries of the so-called "North." The Global South is thus generally said to include all of Africa, South, and Southeast Asia, Latin America, and Central America. The Global South and the North are effectively successors to the terms "Less Developed World" and "Developed World," and, before these, "Third World" and "First World." A common set of problems of assumption and overgeneralization tend to haunt all these meta-geographical categories. Obviously, there are many poor people living in rich countries like the United Kingdom, Australia, and the United States. Equally there are many wealthy elites in poorer countries such as India. Historically, there were problems with the terminology of Less Developed and Developed because it tended to support the inaccurate assumption that all aspects of life (including cultural life and ethical norms) were less developed in poor countries. In a different way, the terminology of the Third World and First World also seemed to rest on assumptions about the rich western countries moving first and fastest up some singular road to progress. This was despite the fact that the "Third World" idea was actually fashioned in the Cold War by post-colonial countries that did not want to become aligned with either the Soviets (the supposed "Second World") or the US-led capitalist countries. Now the Cold War is over, "Third World" has lost much of that "non-aligned" resonance. So in its place has come the Global South – although it by no means captures many other post-colonial remappings of the world that persist (Young, 2001).

A clear geographical problem with the Global South as a term is that many of the poorest countries globally are actually in the northern hemisphere. At the same time, there are some very wealthy countries in the Southern Hemisphere. Nevertheless, many commentators still find the categories useful. For example, the geographers Eric Sheppard and Richa Nagar (2004) define the global north as "constituted through a network of political and economic elites spanning privileged localities across the globe," and proceed from this dislocated definition to argue that the global South is similarly "to be found everywhere: foraging the forests of South Asia, undertaking the double burden of house and paid work, toiling in sweatshops within the United States, and living in urban quasi-ghettoes worldwide." This does not mean the end of geography at all, as a key aspect behind efforts to articulate the Global South has been to offer a counter-mapping of globalization that, unlike flat-world and borderless-world visions, is attuned to uneven development and inequality (Sparke, 2007).

References

Eric Sheppard and Richa Nagar, "From East–West to North–South," *Antipode* 36, no. 4 (2004): 557–63.

Matthew Sparke, "Everywhere but Always Somewhere: Critical Geographies of the Global South," *The Global South* 1, no. 1 (2007): 117–26.

Robert Young, *Postcolonialism: An Historical Introduction* (Oxford: Blackwell Publishers, 2001).

Global Union Federations Until recently known as "International Trade Secretariats" or ITSs, these were the original pioneers of international cooperation among individual unions in particular economic sectors. In conjunction with **ICFTU**, federations such as UNI (Union Network International) have established dialogue with a number of **TNCs** in their sectors. These discussions have led to various "framework agreements." Each of these agreements is negotiated between a global union federation and a TNC, and concerns the conflict management in the international activities of the company. For more information on the GUFs and global framework agreements, see www.global-unions.org/.

Globalism A term that is generally used critically to describe the instrumental use of "Globalization" rhetoric to justify policy changes that lead in the direction of **neoliberalism**. Sometimes, globalism is used in the media to describe a more humanitarian kind of global vision and **cosmopolitanism** embodied in a figure such as Nelson

Mandela. John Lennon's lyrical appeal to "imagine all the people" might also be seen as an example of this more pacific and humanitarian kind of globalism. For the most part, though, globalism is associated with the hard-edge advocacy of neoliberalism by the likes of Thomas Friedman (himself a self-declared "globalist").

Glocalization There are two dominant uses of this awkward term. The first is as a name for business strategies in **TNCs** that seek to adapt their corporate activity and products for particular national clients and markets (Svensson, 2001). Whether it is selling vegetarian Big Macs in India or, to pick a more egregious recent example, Google's willingness to let Chinese authorities censor Internet searches in the PRC, illustrations of such corporate glocalization are increasingly obvious everywhere. At a superficial level, such market adaptation practices counteract myths about globalization creating a flat homogeneous world. But in another sense, they merely exemplify the reductive "nothing is sacred" imperatives of the capitalist search for markets (Ritzer, 2003). In either case, geography itself is imagined by writers on business glocalization in static terms as a generic map of market differentiation. By contrast, the second use of glocalization by geographers themselves works with a much more productive and dynamic sense of geography. In this way, the term is employed to describe the reciprocal spatio-temporal processes through which globalization both shapes and gets shaped by local geographies. For Erik Swyngedouw (2004), it serves thus as a way of underlining how simultaneously the local exists in the global and the global in the local. With the "local in the global," Swyngedouw seeks to underline how the global capitalism both reflects and depends upon specific local bases and mediations (e.g. the role of financial centers such as New York, London, and Tokyo as command and control centers of global finance). By the "global in the local," he refers to the ways in which global forces always in some way shape local developments whether they are agricultural practices, regional growth initiatives, or urban landscapes. Taking this argument further forward and foregrounding the implications for embodied personal geographies, Cindy Katz (2001) has argued that we need thus to understand the local as "constitutively global."

References

Cindi Katz, "On the Grounds of Globalization: A Topography for Feminist Political Engagement," *Signs: Journal of Women in Culture and Society* 26, no. 4 (2001): 1213–34.

George Ritzer, "Rethinking Globalization: Glocalization/Grobalization and Something/Nothing," *Sociological Theory* 21, no. 3 (2003): 193–209.

Roland Robertson, "Glocalization: Time–Space and Homogeneity–Heterogeneity," in *Global Modernities*, eds M. Featherstone, S. Lash, and R. Robertson (London: Sage Publications, 1995), 25–44.

Goran Svensson, "Glocalization of Business Activities: A "Glocal Strategy" Approach," *Management Decision* 39, no. 1 (2001): 6–18.

Erik Swyngedouw, "Globalisation or Glocalisation? Networks, Territories and Rescaling," *Cambridge Review of International Affairs* 17, no. 1 (2004): 25–48.

HIV/AIDS Human immunodeficiency virus (HIV) is a virus that attacks the human immune system. This weakened immunity leaves the body open to attack from infections, eventually leading to the development of acquired immune deficiency syndrome (AIDS). Over 25 million people have died from AIDS globally, and about 34 million more live with the disease (AIDS Consortium, 2011). For some of these survivors, AIDS has become a "life sentence" rather than a "death sentence," thanks to the remarkable success of treatment using anti-retroviral drugs (ARVs). These drugs have also been shown to have a considerable capacity to slow the spread of the disease, but, despite such successes, more than 7000 people become newly infected with HIV everyday. Moreover, while HIV/AIDS affects every country in the world, and while it is clearly a global disease that reflects a common human vulnerability, access to ARVs in many countries is still limited because of the prohibitive cost created by drug-patent monopolies. The impact of HIV/AIDS is therefore extremely uneven, being powerfully skewed by economic inequalities and disproportionately effecting heavily indebted poor countries in sub-Saharan Africa (Craddock et al., 2004). Thanks to the treatment access campaigns that started in South Africa in the late 1990s, the **WTO's** global patent regime has been challenged and reformed with the so-called Doha Declaration providing for exceptions from TRIPS rules in cases of health emergencies (Heywood, 2002). However, despite these reforms and the impressive intervention efforts of agencies such as the *Global Fund to Fight AIDS, TB and Malaria*, treatment still tends to be spatially selective and inaccessible to many poor communities globally (Hunter, 2010).

References

AIDS Consortium, *AIDS: Taking a Long-Term View* (Upper Saddle River, NJ: Pearson Education, 2011).

Susan Craddock, Ezekiel Kalipeni, Joseph Oppong, and Jayati Ghosh, *HIV and AIDS in Africa: Beyond Epidemiology* (Oxford: Blackwell, 2004).

Mark Heywood, "Drug Access, Patents and Global Health: 'Chaffed and Waxed Sufficient',", *Third World Quarterly*, 23, no. 2 (2002): 217–31.

Mark Hunter, *Love in the Time of AIDS: Inequality, Gender and Rights in South Africa* (Bloomington: Indiana University Press, 2010).

Horizontal integration A term used to describe a high level of market intermediation of commodity chains; in other words, commodity chains where production, distribution, and sales are tied together more through market mechanisms such as **outsourcing** and **subcontracting** than by vertical organization and internalization within a single company. An extreme example of a commodity chain that is horizontally integrated is the production, distribution, and sales process for sportswear marketed under the Nike brand: sportswear that is made by networks of subcontrators, distributed by various independent shippers and logistics firms and yet sold under a brand name that is developed and maintained by a small staff of white collar workers at Nike's headquarters in Beaverton, Oregon.

Human Development Index This is a measure developed by the United National Development Program in order to rank national development based on measures of life expectancy at birth, educational attainment, and adjusted real per capita income. It is designed to give a more holistic view of a country's development status, compared to increases in GDP and per capita income (the measures used more commonly by mainstream political commentators and development advisors to rank countries). See http://hdr.undp.org/en/statistics/hdi/.

IBRD The International Bank for Reconstruction and Development was the original name for the **WORLD BANK** as it was conceived at Bretton Woods in 1944. Back then, as World War II was approaching its end, the chief target of the bank's investment efforts was envisioned in terms of reconstructing war-torn Europe.

ICC The International Criminal Court has developed out of a 50-year process of international human-rights law development that began most conspicuously with the Nuremberg war crimes trials after World War II. Up until the foundation of the ICC in 2002, international war-crimes tribunals were established in only an ad hoc fashion with uneven and far-from-global jurisdiction. The ICC is designed instead to be a permanent war-crimes tribunal with global jurisdiction. However, this planetary scope crucially depends on a process of nation-by-nation ratification through which individual governments sign on to the court's jurisdiction by ratifying the so-called "Rome Statute" (the ICC's founding charter). On April 11, 2002, there were 66 such ratifications, and by November 2004, there were 90. This expansion of the court's authority represented a major step towards creating a global legal regime for upholding the protection of human rights right around the world. However, over the course of this same time period, the United States has gone from being a major supporter of the ICC to one of its most active opponents. While in 2000 the United States signed the Rome Statute during the Clinton administration, in 2002 the Bush administration declared that the US signature was nullified. This turnaround took place during the so-called War on Terror. One of the main aims of the ICC, after all, is to prosecute individuals for war crimes, crimes against humanity, genocide, and crimes of aggression. Yet even before the much-publicized example of the use of cruel and unusual punishment at the Iraqi prison of Abu Ghraib, US critics of the ICC worried that the court might undermine American judicial sovereignty and lead to the prosecution of Americans. Against these concerns, US supporters of the ICC see it as a court of last resort, designed to prosecute individuals for genocide and crimes against humanity, but only when national courts have failed to do so themselves (Mayerfield, 2004). For more information on the ICC provided by students for students, visit the website of the US-based Independent Student Coalition for the International Criminal Court: http://www.isc-icc.org/aboutus.html.

Reference

Jamie Mayerfield, "The Democratic Legacy of the International Criminal Court," *Fletcher Forum of World Affairs* 28, no. 2 (2004): 147–56.

ICFTU The International Confederation of Free Trade Unions, which has its headquarters in Brussels, brings together workers from 221 national centers in 148 countries and territories. Collectively, 156 million members are represented (www.icftu.org/).

IDB The InterAmerican Development Bank is a regional version of the **World Bank**, providing loans for large infrastructure projects in the Americas. IDB is a key advisor to the trade negotiators working on the new FTAA.

IMF Headquartered in Washington DC, and connected to the **World Bank** by an underground tunnel, the International Monetary Fund or "Fund" is an international organization of 188 member countries. Along with the **IBRD**, it was set up at the Bretton Woods conference in 1944. At the time, it was charged with ensuring the stability of the world financial system and, in particular, with dealing with the short-term financing crises experienced by countries with big **balance of payments** imbalances. The Fund further claims on its website that it has a mission "to foster international monetary cooperation, secure financial stability, facilitate international trade, promote high employment and sustainable economic growth, and reduce poverty around the world" (www.imf.org/). From the beginning, however, its bias has been towards the protection of the world's big lenders (wealthy countries, big banks, and their shareholders). Over time it has also come to take on more and more of a managerial role in the world economic system, and since the 1970s has been an integral agent in expanding and entrenching the policies of **neoliberalism** globally. It exercises this managerial role most directly by defining the **conditionalities** countries should follow in order to secure loans or loan rescheduling arrangements. Due to the desperate financial emergencies that lead countries to seek such help with loans, the Fund has enormous leverage in imposing its conditions, and has therefore been very successful in enforcing structural adjustment programs (**SAPs**) of financial deregulation, privatization, and deflation around the world. Nevertheless, in the wake of the global financial crisis that erupted in 2008, these enduring aspects of IMF influence have come in for renewed criticism and revaluation – not least of all in Europe (from where the Fund's presidents have traditionally been recruited). Most notably, a report published by the IMF itself (but prepared by a watchdog agency charged with reviewing the performance of the Fund in the run-up to the financial crisis of 2008) was extremely critical (IEO, 2011). It highlighted how the IMF had continued to offer upbeat assessments for the global economy in the months preceding the crash. And it underlined the basic point that the IMF had failed to issue any meaningful warning about the systemic risks being created in the global financial system because of its market fundamentalist "groupthink" and "intellectual capture." This was a huge acknowledgment of institutional failure from within the institution, and confirmed what critics on the outside had been saying for decades (e.g. www.brettonwoodsproject.org/).

Reference

IEO, *IMF Performance in the Run-Up to the Financial and Economic Crisis* (Washington, DC: IMF, 2011).

Import substitution A policy of industrial and national economic development taken up by post-colonial countries after World War II. Newly independent countries such as India and Indonesia sought to substitute domestically manufactured goods for the imports formally foisted on them by the imperial powers. The hope was that such a policy would nurture a strong domestic industry and make the new nation-states economically independent. However, after the debt crises of the 1980s, the lender countries – the former colonial powers – used the pressure of debt-rescheduling negotiations through the **World Bank** and **IMF** to force **SAPs** on the debtor nations. Such structural economic changes centrally involved abandoning policies of import substitution and adopting new export-led development policies based on selling raw materials and manufactured goods on the world market. One notable problem with this new approach in addition to the growth in sweatshops, huge inequalities, and the eclipse of food sovereignty by **agribusiness** is that it has led to much more unbalanced and unpredictable national economic development patterns that are vulnerable to shocks from currency disturbances and changes in global market demand. It is true that some developing countries such as China have been able to continue import substitution policies much longer. As a result, China, like Singapore before it, is now well placed to create a more coordinated national development policy in conjunction with its export-led growth. Nevertheless, even China, as big as it is, remains vulnerable to external demand changes and consequently has spent much of its profits from exports on buying dollars in order to support the dollar and thereby protect as long as possible an American market for Chinese goods. This kind of financial intervention abroad would seem to represent the very opposite of the old domestically oriented import substitution policies that were widespread in the 1950s and 1960s.

Inflation Inflation is a condition of rising average prices within an economy. Rising prices equate directly with the falling value of money, but the actual causes of inflated prices and the falling value money are much more complex and contested. The economists most closely associated with **neoliberalism** such as Milton Friedman (1969) tend to explain inflation primarily in terms of money supply dynamics. This so-called monetarist explanation is based on the argument that inflation is primarily caused by governments that borrow or print too much money, pumping it into national economies in ways that create an oversupply and hence a falling value of money. For other economists including both Keynesians and Marxists, the causes of inflation are understood to run deeper than this. They generally focus instead on the increasing costs of factors of production including the cost of labor as an economy expands, and the supply of labor and other inputs has to be shared between more and more producers. In addition to these more demand-side explanations, non-neoliberal economists also tend to point more to geopolitical dynamics and exogenous price shocks such as the 1973 oil price rises (associated with the creation of OPEC) as further factors explaining inflationary increases in the costs of production. Monetarists have acknowledged such factors, too, but have preferred to focus on monetary interventions by governments as a target for reform (particularly because they also blame stagflation – rising prices and decreasing growth – on government infusions of money, too). Keynesians, by contrast, have viewed deflation (lowered prices, lack of demand, and an increase in the purchasing power of money) as a more debilitating economic problem than inflation because of its association with increased unemployment and economic depression. For the same reason, they have tended to view government demand management (and the government borrowing and increased money supply it created) as the lesser of two evils. Keynes himself put it like this: "Thus inflation is unjust and deflation is inexpedient. Of the two perhaps deflation is ... worse; because it is worse, in an impoverished world, to provoke unemployment than to disappoint the rentier" (Keynes, 1972: 75). Here, Keynes clearly expresses an ethical and political concern with workers facing unemployment. For neoliberal monetarists, it is instead the rentiers, the large owners and loaners of money, who take pride of place. By keeping prices stable and ensuring that the interest payments on loaned money do not therefore fall in value, monetarist policy-making ensures that banks, bond-holders, and other big lenders do not see falling returns on their loans. Instead of aiming at zero unemployment, neoliberal economists speak instead about maintaining something called NAIRU, the "Non-Accelerating Inflation Rate of Unemployment." They believe that trying to reduce unemployment below this level increases inflation and that therefore it is necessary to maintain a reserve workforce of unemployed workers in order to keep prices (especially labor costs) down. They also argue that free markets should set prices for all other commodities except money itself, which should be managed only in careful conjunction with market forces by independent central banks committed to price stability.

Ironically, with the entrenchment of neoliberalism globally and the related rise in influence of global financial markets over national governments, simple explanations of inflation that treat national economies in geographical isolation from one another are increasingly out of date (Corbridge, 1994). Considered from a more adequate transnational perspective, inflation is also caused by three other factors in addition to rising costs in a domestic economy. In the global arena, it is caused by: (a) forces that increase international prices (like a war in the Middle East increasing oil prices); (b) factors that reduce the value of a national currency vis-à-vis other currencies (such as national indebtedness); or (c) the so-called exporting of inflation from countries (most notably the United States) that create artificial levels of global demand based on precarious forms of credit. In

considering these complex factors, it is worth remembering that national currencies usually tend to be pushed *downwards* in value when countries operate a large
fiscal deficit or large **current account deficit**. Such downward movements in currency values in turn create rising prices. This is what has happened in many
indebted countries such as Nigeria, Mexico, Brazil, Argentina, and Indonesia in
the contexts of their various **debt crises**. In each case, steep spikes in inflation have
resulted, and massive devaluations of national currencies have ensued. Ever since
the great depression, the US dollar has been the big exception to this rule, however, and the United States in the late 1990s saw a strong dollar and low inflation
despite huge fiscal and trade deficits. This was the result of historical reasons that
made the dollar a global currency of last resort, and also because of contemporary
reasons associated with the needs of Japan and China to prop up the dollar (so that
Americans would keep being able to afford their exports) and the loss of other
seemingly safe places to put savings and reserves in global markets. When these
underpinnings of the strong dollar change (as they started to do in 2003 and after
2008), the United States also risks inducing inflation as the dollar declines in
value, and the costs of imports go up.

References

Milton Friedman, *The Optimum Quantity of Money and Other Essays* (Chicago: Aldine,
    1969).
Stuart Corbridge, "Plausible Worlds: Friedman, Keynes and the Geography of Inflation," in
    Stuart Corbridge, Ron Martin, and Nigel Thrift, eds, *Money, Power and Space* (Oxford:
    Blackwell, 1994), 63–90.
John Maynard Keynes, *Essays in Persuasion* (London: Macmillan, 1972).

Level playing field A favorite term among advocates of **neoliberalism**, the
metaphor of the "level playing field" is frequently used to represent the ways in
which globalization has torn down or needs to tear down barriers to business right
around world. The only players imagined as playing on this flattened field are businesses and their **CEO**s, plus occasionally, and in no particular order, nation-states,
consumers, and, if only as obstacles to be overcome, unions and other opponents
of neoliberal reform. There are three other key features that need to be noted about
the metaphor and the ways in which it functions as a discourse about the so-called
"economy" (Gibson-Graham, 1996). The first is that the level playing field clearly
represents some sort of omniscient god's eye view of the world. It is a view from a
position of mastery (Morris, 1992: 51), and it is therefore a view that also tends to
reduce all of the diversity of the world to the cost calculus of business. It follows
that the second key feature of the metaphor is that it is not just metaphorical, but
rather a discourse about the world that is directly linked to real practices such as
the implementation of free-trade agreements, the reduction in transportation
costs, and the development of the Internet, practices that in one way or another
reduce the friction of distance on business. The third feature of the level playing

field as discourse, however, is that despite its repeated use as a common-sense neo-liberal world view with world-shaping consequences, it is also a fundamentally misleading representation of economic geography. It is a view that hides the vast asymmetries of wealth, poverty, power, and vulnerability across the planet, and it is a view that, despite being developed in the United States, systematically conceals the dominance of the United States within the context of contemporary globalization (Sparke, 2003).

References

J. K. Gibson-Graham, *The End of Capitalism (As We Knew It): A Feminist Critique of Political Economy* (Oxford: Blackwell, 1996).

Meaghan Morris, *Ecstasy and Economics* (Sydney: Empress, 1992).

Matthew Sparke, "American Empire and Globalisation: Postcolonial Speculations on Neocolonial Enframing," *Singapore Journal of Tropical Geography* 24, no. 3 (2003): 373–89.

Liberalization The process of freeing up international trade and investments: including the removal of both **tariffs** and **non-tariff barriers** (NTBs). Liberalization is therefore only about liberty (its etymological root) in a very narrow economic sense of liberating the movement of **capital**. In terms of personal choice, liberalization is often not about freedom at all. Instead, it often involves both restrictions on the ability of democratic governments to make rules and the privatization of public goods such as clean water.

McDonaldization A term used by the sociologist George Ritzer (2000) to describe a wide array of production and consumption processes for which the Americanized, standardized, routinized, and franchised operations of the McDonalds fast-food chain serve as a model. In this sense, the model's defining concerns with *efficiency*, *calculability*, *predictability*, and *control* have spread from the restaurant business to many other areas of global life ranging from offices and factories to education, health care, and the family. Despite the advantages accruing to such an approach to management and governance in an age of **neoliberalism**, the irrationalities of McDonaldization (including its links with unhealthy diets and illness) have inspired all kinds of resistance (Smart, 1999).

References

George Ritzer, *The McDonaldization of Society* (Thousand Oaks, CA: Pine Forge Press, 2000).

Barry Smart, ed., *Resisting McDonaldization* (London: Sage, 1999).

Maquiladora Sometimes shortened in Spanish to *maquila*, the term was originally associated with the process of milling. However, in Mexico, it has since become the word for another kind of processing – the assembly of imported component parts for re-export. In 1965, the Mexican government started its Border Industrialization program, which allowed US companies to import unfinished goods into the northern border regions of Mexico for final assembly. The unfinished goods were given duty-free entry into the country, and once they had been assembled and packaged, they could then be exported back into the United States also without facing tariffs at the border. The result was the very rapid economic development of Mexico's border zone, a zone that basically became synonymous with maquiladora development. US companies flocked to the region attracted by the low wages of Mexican workers, the lack of enforcement of environmental regulations, and the low taxes. Since the peak period of growth in the 1980s, however, two main changes have taken place. First, in 1994, NAFTA effectively turned the whole of Mexico (and not just the border zone) into a giant maquiladora. US companies were now able to locate factories anywhere in Mexico and exploit still lower labor costs and other advantages of previously undeveloped regions. This has led to increased efforts by workers' rights groups – including the *Maquila Solidarity Network* or MSN en.maquilasolidarity.org/ – to reach out to workers more broadly (Bandy, 2004). Second, towards the end of the 1990s, cheap production possibilities in China (where many workers are paid even more poorly) began to pull the low skill manufacturing and assembly jobs away from Mexico. As a result of these developments, the maquiladora zone has suffered falling growth and increasing unemployment. These conditions, combined with the ongoing drug wars in Mexico, have made the Mexican maquiladora border zone an extraordinarily dangerous place to live, most especially for women workers (Wright, 2006).

References

Joe Bandy, "Paradoxes of Transnational Civil Societies under Neoliberalism: The Coalition for Justice in the Maquiladoras," *Social Problems* 51, no. 3 (2004): 410–31.
Melissa Wright, *Disposable Women and Other Myths of Global Capitalism* (New York: Routledge, 2006).

Market-driven commodity chains see **Commodity chains**

Market-access One of the main forces pushing companies to globalize is the need to reach and sell their products in larger markets. This need for market-access has sometimes (particularly in the 1950s and 1960s) forced companies into moving production sites, too, in order to obviate high tariffs. It has also forced them into joint ventures with local producers in foreign-market areas (e.g. Boeing's joint ventures with Chinese aircraft manufacturers in order to gain access to China's market). Other times, the need for market access simply means that **TNCs** lobby hard for free-trade agreements that reduce tariffs and enable them to export into foreign markets. Even then, however, considerable planning and investment still have to go into setting up supply chains, maintenance, and retailing operations in the foreign market.

Market failure Conservatively, market failures are understood as situations in which markets do not function properly due to causes such as imperfect information. Mainstream commentators tend to point to broad areas of poor service provision – such as providing affordable drugs to the world's poor – as market failures. More critically, however, global justice advocates tend to see the whole approach of using the free market as a development tool as a failure. Healthy water provision, and free access to education and primary health care, they argue should be considered basic human rights and not made subject to the hidden hand of the market. For the critics, in other words, the market approach itself is the failure, not the various moments in which markets do not perform adequately.

Mercosur Mercado Comun del Cono Sur (or the Common Market of the Southern Cone) is a free-trade block and customs union made up of Brazil, Argentina, Uruguay, and Paraguay. It was formed in 1991 as a regional common market agreement between Argentina, Brazil, Paraguay, and Uruguay with Chile and Bolivia as associate members. More like the European Union and less like NAFTA, Mercosur is a common market that includes consensus agreements on common immigration, labor, and other policies, as well as special trade and investment preferences.

MFN In trade jargon, "most favored nation" treatment means a country commits to offering all of its trade partners the same packages of preferential trade terms it provides to the most favored of them all. In other words, it is a policy of treating all countries that export into your own country in the same way. MFN is the core principle of WTO agreements, but the terminology is American in origin. Some US trade partners such as China traditionally received MFN treatment on a provisional annual basis only. However, during the congressional battle over eliminating China's annual reviews, the corporate trade lobby succeeded in persuading legislators in congress to change the term "most favored nation" into "normal trade relations" (NTR).

Monetarism see **Inflation**

Monetary policy is generally used to refer to national policies vis-à-vis interest rates and currency controls. "Strict" or "tight" or "hawkish" monetary policy is used to describe the approach of raising interest rates at the first signs of inflation. Financiers and other owners of capital tend as a rentier class to be very hawkish on monetary policy, as they do not like to see their money lose its value due to inflation. Nevertheless, when the overall economy stalls, and deflation threatens basic profit-making from investments, even rentiers can be in favor of more monetary stimulus. Thus, monetary easing or monetary accommodation in turn describes policies of low interest rates designed in such moments to promote more borrowing, investment, and economic growth.

Mutual funds These investment funds (which are called unit trusts in the United Kingdom) are set up by large investment companies who buy stocks and bonds, package them together as a single fund, and then sell units of the resulting fund to investors. The stocks and bonds may be extremely mixed, but more commonly they are selected based on a particular theme such as utilities stock, Asian stock, real-estate funds, or high-risk bonds, to name just a few of the thousands of varieties. By bundling investments in this way, mutual funds provide investors with a number of services: they hedge risk by investing in a number of different firms at once; they provide professional stock and bond-picking knowledge that cannot be easily duplicated by a single investor; and they allow investors to hand over the day-to-day management of their investments to institutions that are dedicated to financial management. For these services, however, investors have to pay some sort of fee, and as the number of investors who have entered into the financial markets through mutual funds has risen, so, too, have the profits of the investment firms that create them.

NAFTA The North American Free Trade Agreement between the United States, Canada, and Mexico was signed in 1992, ratified in 1993, and finally implemented in January 1994. It built upon the system of free-trade rules already agreed to by Canada and the United States in the form of the Canada United States Free trade Agreement (CUFTA) but extended the scope of the free-trade area to include Mexico. Canada had not initially been invited into the process, but Canadian trade ministers were worried about US dominance and demanded that they also become full members of the negotiation process. Like CUFTA, NAFTA basically represented an agreement to reduce tariffs on all goods entering the signatory countries from the other signatory countries. One key goal was to make it possible thereby for businesses to maximize **sourcing efficiency** by locating their production facilities based purely on market costs. It was now going to be possible, for example, to locate a large production plant in central Mexico, exploit low-paid labor and lax environmental regulation there, and yet still export the products tariff-free into the United States and Canada. In this sense, NAFTA can also be understood to have extended the prior **maquiladora** regime to the whole of Mexico. To do this, NAFTA was not so much deregulatory as re-regulatory. It introduced a whole new set of laws and codes in order to entrench **neoliberalism** across North America (McCarthy, 2004; Sparke, 2005). Relatedly, it also did more than CUFTA to reduce what trade negotiators call "non-tariff barriers to trade," meanwhile providing new rights to business investors to sue the governments of the signatory countries for any act of regulation deemed to be an infringement on their right to buy, own, and control property. These investor protection rights enshrined in **Chapter 11** of NAFTA have become hotly contested in more recent years as they have been used by businesses to sue local and national governments for actions ranging from the passage of a law to ban the use of toxic additives in gasoline to refusal to grant a permit to a company that sought to develop a toxic waste dump next to a community.

References

James McCarthy, "Privatizing Conditions of Production: Trade Agreements As Neoliberal Environmental Governance," *Geoforum*, 35, no. 3 (2004): 327–41.
Matthew Sparke, *In the Space of Theory: Postfoundational Geographies of the Nation-State* (Minneapolis: University of Minnesota Press, 2005).

Neocolonialism This is a name for the ways in which long-distance control and domination over the **Global South** have continued to be exercised by the world's wealthy societies since the formal end of imperialism and its associated colonial practices. Neocolonialism is distinct from colonialism in so far as it is usually considered to be market-mediated rather than military-mediated. As such, it tends to involve armies of accountants and bankers rather than soldiers. Organized through the hidden hand of the free market, it operates invisibly (more like radiation than old-fashioned colonial control) having profound effects that are nonetheless hard to see and track. Che Guevara, the Cuban revolutionary, once described neocolonialism in these ways, as "the most redoubtable form of imperialism – most redoubtable because of the disguises and deceits it involves" (quoted in Johnson, 2004: 30). Nonetheless, the continuities with traditional colonialism are there for those who care to notice. In this sense, perhaps the best description of neocolonialism in the last few years has come from the Indian writer, Arundhati Roy. "Our British colonizers stepped onto our shores a few centuries ago disguised as traders," she writes.

> We all remember the East India Company. This time around the colonizer does not even need a token white presence in the colonies. The CEOs and their men do not need to go to the trouble of tramping through the tropics, risking malaria, diarrhea, sunstroke, and an early death. They don't have to maintain an army or a police force, or worry about insurrections and mutinies. They can have their colonies and an easy conscience. "Creating a good investment climate" is the new euphemism for third world repression. Besides, the responsibility for implementation rests with the local administration. (Roy, 2001: 17)

References

Chalmers Johnson, *The Sorrows of Empire: Militarism, Secrecy and The End of the Republic* (New York: Metropolitan Books, 2004).
Arundhati Roy, *Power Politics* (Cambridge, MA: South End Press, 2001).

Neoliberalism Variously referred to as "market fundamentalism," "free-market capitalism" and the "**Washington Consensus**," neoliberalism names an approach to governing capitalism that emphasizes liberalizing markets and making market forces the basis of economic coordination, social distribution, and personal motivation. It recalls the eighteenth- and nineteenth-century liberal market ideals of economists such as Adam Smith and David Ricardo, as well as earlier French advocacy of "laissez-faire." And yet it is new – hence the "neo" – in so far as it comes after and actively repudiates the interventionist state and redistributive ideals of welfare-state liberalism in the twentieth century. Despite this clear historical rationale for referring to neoliberalism, it remains a confusing term, especially in the United States where (unlike in Europe and Latin America) the word "liberal" is widely assumed to refer to just welfare-state liberalism. For related reasons, references to neoliberalism tend to be made more often by its global critics, than by its American advocates: the latter generally preferring to use alternatives such as the "free market," "small government," or the "limited" or "minimalist" state.

   Whatever term is used to describe and prescribe neoliberalism, processes of *neoliberalization* have now been set in motion all over the globe – including in Europe, Asia, Africa, and Latin America as well as in the United States itself. Moreover, these processes have become so closely tied to globalized trade and finance that for many commentators, the all-in-one synonym and argument for neoliberalism is simply Globalization. In other words, because they believe big "G" Globalization is inevitable, they also think neoliberalization is necessary and natural as well. Liberalizing markets is vital, goes the argument, because it is the only way to adapt to the competitive borderless economy of Globalization. Making this case repeatedly in multiple countries, pro-market advocates have successfully expanded and entrenched the top 10 policies of neoliberalism right around the world. In the process, this disciplinary rule set for neoliberalism's market constitution has come to sound like a contemporary political equivalent of the biblical 10 commandments: (1) liberalize trade; (2) privatize public services; (3) deregulate business and finance; (4) shrink big government; (5) reduce taxes on business; (6) encourage foreign investment; (7) marginalize unions; (8) expand exports; (9) reduce inflation; and (10) enforce property rights. And so far, despite the obvious connections between these policies and the economic crises that have rocked the world from 2007 onwards, and despite the statements by various global leaders about the need to rein in markets, neoliberalism is showing no signs of dying soon (Crouch, 2011).

   Something that advocates of neoliberalism do not say so much about but something that is nevertheless betrayed by all their pro-market activism is the fact that none of the neoliberal policies are themselves either natural or inevitable. **TINA** touts may well argue that there is no alternative to neoliberalism amidst Globalization, but the very fact that they have to make the case so often reflects a global reality in which many alternatives exist and inspire communities (especially those that have already experienced the distress and dispossession of market rule). In the same way, neoliberalism is never automatic in practice either. The anti-state state requires all sorts of active pro-market re-regulation. Defining and defending the practical details of these regulations also remains a constant challenge, and whether they are actually implemented with sustained political support hinges in turn on historical and geographical circumstances. A good example of all this non-natural contextual contingency is the work of the Austrian, Friedrich Von Hayek.

Von Hayek published what many consider the original argument for neoliberalism – a polemic against state planning entitled *The Road to Serfdom* – back during World War II (Hayek, 1944). Despite his move to the United States, this was not a propitious time or space to promote neoliberal ideas. Instead, western policy-makers, including US leaders, considered welfare-state liberalism a common-sense capitalist alternative to communism and fascism. In the wake of the Great Depression, the European financial crises, and the subsequent war, Keynesian ideas about government demand management were also seen as a common-sense response to market volatility. Thus, Hayek's neoliberal arguments had no immediate influence on policy, and he was obliged instead to help foster intellectual institutions that would keep the ideas afloat to such a time that they might gain policy-making traction (Peck, 2010). He worked in this way to develop the Mont Pelerin Society and contribute to the pro-market theorizing of the Chicago School of Economics. But as successful and influential as these institutions have subsequently become as bastions of pro-market orthodoxy, it was not until the 1970s that their ideational work began to bear policy-making fruit. With simultaneous economic stagnation and inflation (so-called stagflation) creating a crisis of Keynesianism, **Fordism**, and the national balancing of national mass production with national mass consumption, the times had changed in the United States. The opportunity was now right for other Chicago intellectuals such as Milton Friedman to take-up the baton from Von Hayek, and help political leaders such as Ronald Reagan make the public case that government intervention in the economy was the problem, not the solution. Von Hayek had been saying similar things for decades (and in 1974, he finally received his Nobel prize for doing so), but it was the changed real-world circumstances that made all the difference in terms of the wider acceptance and translation of the ideas into policy (e.g. "Reaganomics") in the 1980s.

Global economic integration was undoubtedly the major backstory behind the crisis of welfare-state liberalism in the 1970s, and to this extent the argument that a form of **post-Fordist** globalization precipitated the implementation of neoliberalism is convincing (Harvey, 2005). But as David Harvey also emphasizes, the context-contingent rise and spread of neoliberalism has also meant that it is very uneven geographically. As a set of simple pro-market ideals, it inspires the one-size-fits-all edicts of the 10 neoliberal commandments. But as a set of real-world practices, it has been variegated and experimental, both in the original moments of implementation and in subsequent episodes of failure, correction, and adaptation (Peck, 2010). Sometimes it has been introduced with military force by far-right authoritarians – as happened in Chile in 1973 when the *coup d'état* of an army general, Augusto Pinochet, opened the door to a forced experiment in overnight neoliberalization led by Chicago-trained economists (Klein, 2007). But in other more privileged times and places, it has been developed as so-called social democratic or Third Way or New Labor policy by western political leaders pulling traditionally left-leaning and centrist parties in more conservative pro-market directions. Then again, in many poor countries in the 1980s and 1990s, it has been imposed from the outside through the policy **conditionalities** of **World Bank** and **IMF** structural adjustment programs. More recently still, it has been further globalized by two new sets of neoliberal experiments: the first involving the use of military force again, but this time in Iraq by the United States in the name of spreading freedom (Pieterse, 2005; Sparke, 2005, chapter 5); and the second, much more globally, by promoters of microfinance as a solution for global poverty (Roy, 2010).

What all the examples of implementation share is also something that microfinance makes most obvious, namely that the variegated experiments in neoliberalization also represent attempts to articulate transformations in macro-economic policy-making (including various re-mixes of the 10 commandments) with much more individualized approaches to inducing entrepreneurial behavior. Social theorists call this personal inculcation of market imperatives "neoliberal governmentality" (Dean, 2010). They suggest it involves forms of "responsibilization" in which individuals start to see their personal lives as investment projects in which they must act as accountable investors. However, given that the articulation of such micro neoliberal governmentality with macro neoliberal governance remains context contingent, and given that contemporary economic crises are undermining the ability of many people to invest in entrepreneurialism in this way, alternative responses – such as the 2011 Occupy movement – remain real possibilities, too. Thus, just as neoliberalism had to be kept alive intellectually before being implemented, thinking about alternatives remains a non-neoliberal response-ability for the twenty-first century.

References

Colin Crouch, *The Strange Non-Death of Neoliberalism* (Malden, MA: Polity Press, 2011).
Mitchell Dean, *Governmentality: Power and Rule in Modern Society*, 2nd edition (Los Angeles: Sage, 2010).
David Harvey, *A Brief History of Neoliberalism* (Oxford: Oxford University Press 2005).
Naomi Klein, *The Shock Doctrine: the Rise of Disaster Capitalism* (New York: Metropolitan Books/Henry Holt, 2007).
Jamie Peck, *Constructions of Neoliberal Reason* (Oxford: Oxford University Press 2010).
Jan Nederveen Pieterse, "Neoliberal Empire," *Theory Culture and Society* 21, no. 3 (2004): 119–40.
Ananya Roy, *Poverty Capital: Microfinance and the Making of Development* (London: Routledge, 2010).
Matthew Sparke, *In the Space of Theory: Postfoundational Geographies of the Nation-State* (Minneapolis: University of Minnesota Press, 2005).
Friedrich Von Hayek, *The Road to Serfdom* (Chicago: University of Chicago Press, 1944).

NIDL The New International Division of Labor was a name used by many scholars in the 1980s and 1990s to describe the ways in which old industrial areas of richer capitalist countries were becoming deindustrialized as low-wage employment moved increasingly to poorer parts of the **Global South**. The process continues today, although after two decades it can hardly be called "new" any more. It has two distinctive consequences. First, it leads to the development of low-wage employment, often in sweatshops, and volatile, sometimes fast, sometimes slow, and sometimes nonexistent economic growth in the Global South. Second, it also leads at the same time to the expansion of the service sector as a predominant field of employment in the North. Such employment can be highly lucrative for the managerial class in such sectors as banking, business consulting, global logistics, and financial services. CEOs and others employed as decision-makers in these sectors extract a huge financial payout from working at the pinnacle of global business empires. However, the predominant form of service sector employment tends instead to be much less remunerative and much more insecure. Thus, temporary workers in the clerical sector or burger flippers in the "McJob" food-services sectors receive far less benefit from the exploitation of low-wage workers elsewhere. Economists point out that such workers at least enjoy access as consumers to the cheap products being made in distant sweatshops. Yet in so far as this access is itself dependent on easy credit, and in so far as this credit is vulnerable to shifts in interest rates, it too is very insecure. It is not, however, as insecure as the lives of sweatshop factory workers themselves. Their position in the new international division of labor is the most precarious of all. Poorly paid and frequently subject to terrible working conditions, such workers often feel nervous about organizing against employers because of the possibility that their jobs may be moved to yet lower wage areas. In this sense, new iterations of the international division of labor continue to discipline workers and perpetuate a global **race to the bottom**.

NTBs Non-tariff barriers This is how **NAFTA** and **WTO** legalese characterizes any policy or government regulation that is not a tariff but has the effect of limiting trade. Many of these laws are designed to protect the environment, workers, and consumers, but this does not stop the trade lawyers from calling them protectionist in terms of trade. For instance, a law that prohibits imports of strawberries containing carcinogenic pesticide residues could be considered a *non-tariff barrier* to trade, as it restricts trade in strawberries. The WTO and NAFTA set very narrow rules for which non-tariff barriers are permitted, and this is how trade law can end up trumping national and state laws.

Offshoring A colloquial phrase used to describe the process in which both **TNCs** and smaller companies seek **sourcing efficiency** by moving production facilities out of high-cost countries and into regions where labor and other costs of production are cheaper. Some of this offshoring is also simultaneously **outsourcing**, as in all the external supply chains providing commodities from overseas to big US retailers such as Wal-Mart and Costco. But just as often, offshored production is conducted within factories that are still actually owned by the big brand-name TNCs (e.g. Sony-owned factories in Indonesia, and GE-owned factories in Mexico). In the United States, in 2004, as George Bush faced the challenge of John Kerry for the presidency, offshoring became one of the big issues of the campaign year. Magazines and newspapers were full of articles and cartoons about the number of jobs, many of them in the service sector, being offshored to places such as India and China. "Everybody's talking about offshoring and plenty of companies are doing it," noted an article in *American Airlines* magazine, "but hype has swallowed a few key facts" (McGarvey, 2004). The author of the article went on to caution business managers (the presumed readership of the inflight magazine) about the risks of offshoring:

> Number one: It's no panacea. Number two: It doesn't always deliver the promised cost savings and efficiencies. Number three. If you're the manager in charge of work that's headed offshore, get some asbestos-soled shoes, because your feet will be held to the fire.

By 2004, offshoring had developed to such an extent that there were a large number of business consultants available for an author like McGarvey to interview about the costs and benefits of sending the work overseas. By 2012, the issue was still a hot topic in the presidential race between Mitt Romney and Barack Obama, but by this time the whole offshoring support industry was also already changing again: this time to support TNCs interested anew in "in-shoring," or bringing back offshored work to factories in wealthy countries now made more cost-effective by the depressive effects of the global financial crisis on the price of labor, land, and infrastructure.

Reference

Robert McGarvey, "Offshoring 101," *American Way, August* 1 (2004): 28–31.

Outsourcing Sourcing components, sub-components, services, and other diverse commodities into a company's supply chain from external suppliers. These external suppliers need not necessarily be located overseas, and so outsourcing is not always the same as **offshoring**. Particularly in integrated regional economies, diverse forms of outsourcing account for the close ties between firms that co-locate in the same area. Nevertheless, in many cases offshoring and outsourcing do come together and, as such, are commonly seen as the most marketized form of **commodity-chain** globalization.

Post-Fordism see **Fordism**

Privatization This is the process by which assets or institutions that were formerly publicly owned by governments in the name of their citizens are sold to corporations and individuals. It has been one of the cornerstone policies of **neoliberalism** and has often allowed neoliberal governments to follow their other policies of balanced budgets and fiscal conservatism by providing them with one-time windfall profits. The problem is that having softened the initial impacts of tax cuts and revenue reductions with such short-term strategies, neoliberal politicians do not have to explain that in the long term much deeper cuts in government services will be required because of the lack of any further windfall privatization profits. Meanwhile, the actual consequences of privatization have been uneven at best and, more often, devastating. In rich countries, the disaster of rail privatization in the United Kingdom stands as a powerful example of the deaths, delays, and knock-on economic drag that privatization can have on an economy. And in the Global South, the example of the privatization of water in countries such as Bolivia has not only led to shortages, but also led to death, disease, and widespread chaos. Here is how the writer, Arundhati Roy, describes the more general problem:

> What does privatization mean? Essentially, it is the transfer of productive public assets from the state to private companies. Productive assets include natural resources. Earth, forest, water, air. These are assets that the state holds in trust for the people it represents. In a country like India, seventy per cent of the population lives in rural areas. That's seven hundred million people. Their lives depend directly on access to natural resources. To snatch these away and sell them as stock to private companies is a process of barbaric dispossession on a scale that has no parallel in history. (Roy, 2001: 43)

Reference

Arundhati Roy, *Power Politics*, (Cambridge MA: South End Press, 2001).

Race to the bottom A term often used by critics of **neoliberalism** to describe the net effect of new free-trade regimes such as **NAFTA**. When countries enter into free-trade agreements with one another and begin to reduce **tariffs**, it becomes easier for **TNCs** to produce goods in locations that provide for the maximum degree of **sourcing efficiency**. They can move to any of the signatory countries that have joined the free-trade agreement, and yet they can still export back their products to their original "home" markets. They can therefore freely move to a country where workers are paid much less, or to a country where environmental regulations are much lower, or to a country where workers are not protected by health and safety rights. Once a company has moved to such a country, it can still export back its produce to its former markets because the free-trade agreement eliminates any tariffs on imported goods from countries that have signed on. As more and more companies move production to such low-cost areas, the net result is a widespread competition to cut costs. This forces companies who remain behind in better-paying and better-protected areas to consider how they, too, can cut costs. Sometimes they will do so by moving. But in other cases, they stay and force wage and other concessions from their workers by arguing that they cannot otherwise compete. The free-trade agreement allows businesses to threaten to move, even if they do not actually do so. As a result, workers and their unions often give in because they want to retain their jobs. The net result of all these tendencies is the race to the bottom as wages, protections, and regulations all fall to the lowest common denominator. A less polemical term for the same process is **downward harmonization**.

SAPS Structural adjustment programs are the main way that **neoliberalism** that has been imposed by the **World Bank** and the **IMF** on poor countries. They consist of neoliberal reforms packaged and presented as the **conditionalities** for new loans or debt rescheduling. The supposed purpose of such programs is to make states more "competitive" and therefore better able to pay off their **debt** with the revenue generated by economic growth. Being more "competitive" in this neoliberal sense also means sharply cutting various social programs, including all kinds of investments in education, health systems, and even the infrastructural development of roads, running water, and sewage treatment. In practice, this kind of overnight **austerity** has tended to undermine long-term economic performance. All of the indebted countries have remained deeply indebted, with 41 of them now considered as **HIPCs** (Heavily Indebted Poor Countries).

Services Services consist of every type of commodity that can be bought and sold in the market but which you cannot drop on your foot. In other words, services include all the intangible products from accounting, banking, and insurance as well as the output of more obviously service-oriented sectors such as nursing, cleaning, and car repair. All of these services produce things that capitalism needs in order for traditional industrial production to proceed. Amidst such diversity in the services sector, it is useful to make a distinction between *business services* (such as banking and management consultancy) and what can be broadly defined as the *human services* (such as hair-cutting and nursing care) that enable everyday social life to continue. Considered as a whole, though, services can be understood as creating, supporting, and reproducing the enabling contexts in which capitalist production, distribution, and consumption can be successfully reproduced.

As a consequence of the new international division of labor (**NIDL**) that led to the increasing deindustrialization of richer economies, services have come to represent by far the largest area of employment in most wealthy countries. Achieving such a services-dependent economy has been regarded as a way of finding economic security in the context of globalization. Originally, this was partly because services were less prone to **offshoring**. No one, for example, has yet found a way to offshore haircuts. However, economic globalization is now beginning to transform services employment in much the same way as it has already changed industrial employment patterns. For business services in particular, the Internet has been especially important in enabling new forms of **outsourcing** that also enable offshoring, too. While in the past, business services such as call-center development and accounting have been seen as so-called "non-tradables," they are now, courtesy of real-time e-based connectivity, extremely tradable. More and more business services, including increasingly high-value-added services such as programming, engineering design, and data-management services, can be transferred anywhere instantaneously to places where pay and benefits are less expensive for TNCs. The most-discussed outcome of this trend has been the development of India's IT-enabled services sector. It has become one of the fastest-growing economic developments of the last few years. The impact on rich countries is still evolving but will likely include more "job-less recoveries" in which business productivity and profits for TNCs are increased, but with no parallel expansion in employment in formerly rich countries.

Sourcing efficiency This term is used in the project descriptions in this book as a catch-all term to describe all the ways in which TNCs attempt to reduce the costs of production. It therefore includes all the practices that lead to the downward pressures on wages and environmental standards such as finding cheaper labor inputs, less rigorous, or less rigorously enforced environmental standards, and less expensive taxation regimes. But at the same time, sourcing efficiency can include more organizational sorts of cost cutting such as maintaining a particularly well-synchronized network of subcomponent producers. Thinking about the organization of global capitalism in terms of efficiency is a useful way of putting yourself in the shoes of managers and imagining how they think. It therefore makes it possible to see how business leaders often act in inhuman ways (e.g. by driving wages down below the poverty line) without necessarily seeing their inhuman consequences. Instead of pollution, ill-health, hunger, stress, and overwork, they see bottom-line efficiency.

Structual adjustment see **SAPs**

Tariffs Tariffs are the duty or tax usually paid by exporters in order to move their products across a national border into a foreign market. One of the central goals of the push for free trade around the world has been to reduce and eventually eliminate such tariffs. The reasons why governments impose tariffs on foreign-made imports are multiple. They may be designed to protect domestic producers from foreign competition, or to correct a trade deficit, or to give preference to imports from certain countries over others, or, contrarily, to retaliate against another country's preferential tariff regime. Preferential tariffs designed to privilege or punish particular exporting countries have a history that goes back to imperial trading practices that tended to be organized within networks of imperial preference. But it was also in the context of nineteenth-century imperialism that the rhetorical inflation of free trade and the political struggle to reduce tariffs began. British industrialists at the time wanted to be able to export their products to foreign as well as domestic markets, and meanwhile, they also saw the benefits of having foreign-made foodstuffs enter Britain tariff-free so that their workers could be fed and therefore maintained more cheaply. Early economists such as David Ricardo helped the industrialists make their case with academic arguments about the so-called gains from trade, and until the 1930s the cause of free trade and tariff reduction advanced around the world, albeit within limits created by inter-imperial struggles (including the immense upheaval of World War I). During the Great Depression, however, as governments rushed to protect their domestic capitalists from the global crisis, steep tariffs were imposed on foreign imports creating "tariff walls" that drastically reduced world trade. These walls created much more self-contained national economies, and it was this territorialization of something called "the economy" that set the geographical pattern for the distinctively national **Fordism** that characterized the mid twentieth century.

The Fordist pattern of economic nationalization was also influenced by global politics, the rise of communism, and, most notably, the national mobilizations forced by World War II. However, it was also as the war drew to a close that the cause of free trade was launched again with the American-led meetings at Bretton Woods. The United States had emerged from the war with its economy unscathed and eager to expand markets for its products worldwide. American negotiators pushed for a more open global free-trade system that could absorb the US trade surplus, and slowly but surely they prevailed; the crowning achievement being the establishment of the WTO in 1994. However, by the 1990s, the US trade surplus had turned into a large and fast-growing deficit, and thus in the years since its inception, the WTO has had to deal with increasing complaints by developing countries that the United States is abandoning free trade and, ironically, albeit unsurprisingly, imposing tariffs on foreign products.

TINA An acronym based on the UK Prime Minister Margaret Thatcher's claim "There Is No Alternative" and her associated argument that the reforms of **neoliberalism** were demanded by global economic necessity. Repeated in various other venues throughout the 1980s and 1990s by various other TINA touts, the argument has served to naturalize a single market-based discourse about Globalization while simultaneously normalizing neoliberalism as the politically correct policy response.

TNC A transnational corporation is a company that has the power to coordinate and control operations in more than one country, even if it does not own the foreign factories and pay the foreign workers directly. Some commentators have a narrower definition that contrasts TNCs with MNCs or Multi-National Corporations. The slight terminological difference is meant to recognize how, for a certain time in the mid twentieth century, many large companies operated in multiple countries yet without functionally integrating their whole sourcing and production system on a global scale. In other words, they operated *multi-nationally*, but not by creating commodity chains *across* national boundaries: not, in other words, *trans-nationally*. Instead, the main aim of MNCs was to avoid high-tariff walls around big foreign markets by making goods *within* the countries that constituted the largest of such markets. With the rise today of companies that coordinate their global operations as a single whole, and with the rise of intracorporate transnational trade, the TNC term is increasingly more appropriate.

Trade deficit The condition that exists when a country is importing *more* than it is exporting. One of the general tendencies that ensues as a result of a long-term trade deficit is that the country in question has to keep selling its currency (using it to buy the foreign money needed to pay foreign producers). This tends to push the value of the country's currency down, importing **inflation** into the country because of the increasing cost of imports. The United States is an exceptional case in this regard because it has been able to maintain a huge trade deficit since the 1990s without too much downward pressure on the US dollar. One reason for this is that the makers of all the goods that American consumers are buying (most notably the Chinese and Japanese) have been investing much of their profits in US-dollar-denominated savings, most especially US government and corporate debt. A significant result of these relations is that from the 1990s onwards, more and more of US debt has been owed to foreign investors. Technically, this is called a capital account surplus. It ensures a short-term balance of payments but remains precariously dependent on the willingness of foreign lenders to go on investing in an increasingly debt-burdened economy.

Trade liberalization Also sometimes known as **free trade**, trade liberalization involves opening up national markets to foreign trade. Generally, this involves the removal of both **tariffs** and non-tariff barriers to trade and thereby has consequences that stretch way beyond narrow questions of imports and exports to the overarching systems of governance through which economies are managed. It is for these sorts of reasons that trade liberalization is often seen by critics as a trojan horse of **neoliberalism**.

Vertical integration A term used to describe a hierarchical, top-down approach to managing **commodity chains** and a correspondingly low-level of market intermediation. In other words, commodity chains where production, distribution, and sales are all organized and managed internally by one, usually, large company.

Washington Consensus The Washington Consensus (henceforth WC) was an early 1990s name for **neoliberalism** that usefully (albeit unintentionally) underlined the connections between the promotion of pro-market reforms and the confluence of interests linking the Federal Reserve, US Treasury, Wall Street lobbyists, the **IMF**, and the **World Bank** in Washington DC. The term remains a useful complement to neoliberalism in so far as it draws attention to how these Washington-based agencies have a hegemonic influence over and amidst market-based globalization. However, the initial articulation of the WC owed less to critics of American hegemony and more to pro-market academics operating within the "Beltway" in Washington, DC. John Williamson, the economist who originally coined the term, has subsequently come to regret the way it has become a synonym for neoliberalism. He also says that the last thing he meant to do was attract attacks on the specific policies he was recommending by linking them with hegemonic US interests. Instead, his own goal, he argues, was simply to recommend "10 specific policy reforms that most influential people in a certain city [DC] agreed would be good for a specific region of the world [Latin America] at a certain date in history [1990]" (Williamson, 2003). Nevertheless, reviewing those 10 specific reforms, it is not hard to see multiple overlaps with the "10 commandments" of neoliberalism more generally. Williamson's 1990 wish list was as follows:

1. Introduce fiscal discipline
2. Redirect public spending
3. Broaden the tax base
4. Let markets set interest rates
5. Let markets set exchange rates
6. Liberalize trade
7. Encourage foreign direct investment
8. Privatize state enterprises
9. Deregulate business
10. Establish legal security for property rights

The only reform on Williamson's list that is slightly anomalous with other neoliberal wish-lists is number 2: namely the call to redirect public spending into funding for primary education and primary health care (and away from subsidies to industry). This may, as he argues, distinguish Williamson's WC reforms from the more austere "anti-public-spending" and minimalist government ideals of Von Hayek, Friedman, and the Mont Pelerin purists. But this one item does not differentiate the list all that much, and Williamson's post hoc attempt to distinguish himself from what he calls "the ideology" of neoliberalism ignores the ways in which Von Hayek and Friedman themselves urged pragmatism over purism in their promotion of neoliberal ideals.

Given the cracks in the consensus that subsequently emerged in the 1990s, it is easy to understand why Williamson may have wanted to nuance his earlier position. Most notably, splits between the World Bank and the IMF over how to handle the Asian financial crises of 1997–1998 started to index disagreement between hardliners and pragmatists rather than consensus. While the Bank increasingly noted the need for local "ownership" and the tailoring of reform to longer-term local needs, the IMF tended to stick with more draconian demands for more deregulation and more austerity with no concern about long-term sustainability and developmental stability. Gillian Hart notes thus that:

> As the financial crisis deepened, there were key defections from the WC. For example, Jeffrey Sachs (until then, a prominent IMF consultant) alleged that "instead of dousing the flames, the IMF screamed fire in the theater." At around the same time, Joseph Stiglitz (then senior vice president and chief economist at the World Bank) delivered his famous "post-Washington consensus" speech to the World Institute for Development Economics Research in Helsinki in which he asserted that financial market liberalization had contributed to instability, and called for a reversal of neoliberal orthodoxy. (Hart, 2001: 653)

Thus, by 2000, the crisis had developed so far that *The Economist* magazine even spoke of a "Washington *Dissensus*." Subsequently, Joseph Stiglitz's book, *Globalization and its Discontents*, took the argument further and made a case for a post-Washington consensus (Stiglitz, 2002). But it is not yet clear whether one is forming – at least not in Washington DC. Clearly, the World Bank is making many more noises about the need for social investment, state aid, global health, and sustainable development. But the IMF continues with the old WC rules, even after the financial problems that started in 2007 brought its new (and more pragmatic) European director, Christine Lagarde, face to face with debt crises back in Europe.

Potentially, the Geneva-based **WTO** holds some potential for fostering a post-Washington consensus in so far as it is has proved an important venue for poor-country complaints about US farm subsidies. These complaints may yet have some affect in displacing Washington's ability to uphold huge global asymmetries in world trade. But even if they do, the new consensus will still be neoliberal, and many of its leading thinkers and promoters will still be based in Washington. A new Washington State consensus may also be emerging as a novel suite of responses to **market failure** led by the philanthropic experiments of the Bill and Melinda Gates Foundation in Seattle. If so, it, too, is still also broadly pro-business in practice, even if it has moved on from the macroeconomics of the WC to a series of micro-interventions (micro-biological research, microsavings, and so on) in global health and development. Meanwhile, outside of the United States, where there is talk of a Bangladesh Consensus (on microfinance), a Kerala Consensus (on socialist investment in education and health), and a Mumbai Consensus (on Asian-centered globalization), bigger breaks with the old WC seem possible. But all of them still have to be created in a world that has been remade on the basis of the 10 (or so) policies at the heart of the old consensus.

References

Gillian Hart, "Development critiques in the 1990s: culs de sac and promising paths," *Progress in Human Geography* 25, no. 4 (2001): 649–58.

Joseph Stiglitz, *Globalization and Its Discontents* (New York: W. W. Norton, 2002).

John Williamson, "What Washington Means by Policy Reform," in John Williamson, ed., *Latin American Adjustment: How Much Has Happened?* (Washington, DC: Institute for International Economics, 1990), online at http://www.iie.com/publications/papers/paper.cfm?researchid=486

John Williamson, "Democracy and the Washington Consensus," *World Development* 21, no. 8 (1993): 1329–36.

John Williamson, "Did the Washington Consensus Fail?," Outline of speech at the Center for Strategic & International Studies, Washington, DC, November 6, 2002, online at http://www.iie.com/publications/papers/paper.cfm?researchid=488

John Williamson, "Our Agenda and the Washington Consensus," in Pedro-Pablo Kuczynski and John Williamson, eds., *After the Washington Consensus* (Washington, DC: Institute for International Economics, 2003), 323–31.

World Bank Originally established in 1944 at Bretton Woods as the International Bank of Reconstruction and Development (**IBRD**), the World Bank has grown now to become a multi-faceted global governance institution of enormous influence.

Today, the IBRD is just one of the five agencies comprising what is formally known as the "World Bank Group" (www.worldbank.org/). The other four agencies are: the International Development Association (which focuses on credits and grants to world's poorest countries); the International Finance Corporation (which provides loans and consulting designed to stimulate private-sector investment in poor countries); the Multilateral Investment Guarantee Agency (which offers insurance against losses caused by non-commercial risks to investors in poor countries); and the International Centre for Settlement of Investment Disputes (which works to arbitrate international investment disputes). Together, the five agencies are governed by Boards of Directors drawn from member countries. While this allows for multi-country representation, the directors can only vote using a weighted system based on bank capital share quotas, and these quotas are in turn based on the size of a country's capital subscription to the **IMF**. All 188 countries that have qualified for World Bank membership (and who are therefore able to participate in its programs) are thus also obliged to have already joined the IMF as a condition of membership.

The membership and voting quota arrangement is just one example of how the two agencies were set up jointly by US leaders at Bretton Woods to work in tandem to enforce a post-war peace based on American leadership and market interests. Back in 1944, the United States was the owner of much of the world's capital, was the biggest global lender, and thus held the majority quotas. The World Bank, like the IMF, has effectively institutionalized this historic US hegemony and allowed it to persist into the present. In these US-centric arrangements, the IMF was designed to address short-term balance of payments emergencies, while what became the World Bank was envisioned as an agency that would deal with longer-term developmental challenges. The underlying idea was that the two agencies would help secure cooperative global economic integration and crisis management on US-centric and pro-market terms. This enduring US influence continues to be marked in other ways, too: including very practically in the location of the World Bank head quarters (on H Street in Washington DC), and in the tradition of always appointing an American to serve as the World Bank President, as well as in the less obvious ways through which the Bank's practices of hiring, rule-making, and even data collection remain tied to American academic institutions and pro-market paradigms (Wade, 2002; Broad, 2006). However, one of the big questions being raised today by China, India, and other fast-developing countries concerns whether the United States should continue to wield so much influence in and through the World Bank when it has become the world's biggest borrower.

Back at Bretton Woods, the World Bank was principally designed to address the needs of post-war reconstruction in Europe. Up until the 1970s, its developmental efforts were therefore largely concentrated on countries that were rebuilding war-torn economies rather than initiating postcolonial economic recovery. The focus of the World Bank really only switched to development in the **Global South** after the austere **conditionalities** it imposed on the United Kingdom in 1976. These scared off other wealthier western countries, and shortly thereafter the debt crises of the 1980s suddenly brought many poor countries to the doors of the Bank instead. It was in negotiating the debt rescheduling for these countries (i.e. paying off private lenders and making new loans to be paid back over longer periods of time) that the World Bank worked in conjunction with the IMF to impose structural adjustment programs (**SAPs**). It has been chiefly through these programs, including all the associated "technical advice" and "surveillance," that the World Bank has been able to impose **neoliberalism** on poor countries. The advice is always to immediately adopt the same set of policy reforms recommended by neoliberal economists, and the surveillance is always about subjecting this reform process and its economic outcomes to rigorous scrutiny (constantly monitoring everything from interest rates and tax codes to whether or not bank demands to liberalize trade and deregulate capital flows have been met). More recently, as a result of criticism of this "one-size-fits-all" approach to imposing neoliberalism, there has been much more talk at the World Bank about the need for tailoring programs to local contingencies such as health problems and allowing for so-called country ownership. But even this economic language of "ownership" illustrates the way in which banking principles continue to structure the replacement programs for SAPs. These replacement programs are now known as Poverty Reduction Strategy Papers (PRSPs), and they are supposed to be authored by individual countries themselves. However, most PRSPs look just the same as each other, and this means that the local ownership largely amounts to each country dutifully writing its own timetable for the same old neoliberal reforms (Weber, 2006; Joseph, 2010). Thus, while there has been much talk about the so-called **Washington Consensus** breaking down – with the IMF upholding more traditional neoliberal austerity and the World Bank supposedly adopting newer more pro-poor policies – many of the Bank's day-to-day practices continue to end up imposing neoliberalism and simply modifying its modes of enforcement and accountability (Ruckert, 2006).

Given the immense policy-making influence and oversight exercised through SAPs and PRSPs, it is sometimes hard to understand how the World Bank has come to have so much power. Why do sovereign governments submit themselves to the Bank's demands for neoliberalization? The answer is that they have few other choices. Facing sovereign debt crises and major cash flow problems, they have to turn somewhere for new money when private lenders stop lending (or charge exorbitant interest rates). It is therefore market forces that make governments go to the World Bank in the first place. And in the same way, it is also market forces that then set the conditionalities of the new loans. The World Bank's SAPs and PRSP conditions thereby effectively turn financial market pressures into political and governmental pressures. In short, they transform the economic force of debt into the political enforcement of neoliberaism, and the result has been a remarkably consistent top-down global application of pro-market policy reforms (Peet, 2003). It is crucial, therefore, to understand that the bank is not an aid agency, development fund, or philanthropy – even though many of these other sorts of organization now follow the Bank's neoliberal approach to imagining and implementing new development initiatives (Fine, 2009). The World Bank remains a bank. While the webpage slogan reads "Working for a World Free of Poverty," this slogan still only appears in small type under the larger font and all capitals name: "THE WORLD BANK." It is much easier to understand the way the Bank works, then, if one remembers that it was designed to function as a bank using banking principles. From the start, it was set up in a way that made it dependent on Wall Street and market lending to raise capital for its loans. This meant that right from the beginning, it also functioned as an institution that relayed market pressures, issuing the regulatory requirements of market discipline at the same time as issuing loans for development (Benjamin, 2007). Rather than an aid organization, it has always entered into the business of aid (where "business" is increasingly the operative term thanks to the Bank) as a market intermediary.

At least within the global market of ideas, the World Bank's disciplinary vision of neoliberalism has been subject to criticism. From "Spank the Bank" protests in DC in 2000 to brilliant intellectual decodings of World Bank literature, its influence on both popular debate and expert knowledge about global governance has faced tough opposition (Kumar, 2003; Goldman, 2005; Lawson, 2010; Watts, 2012). Critical websites such as the *Bretton Woods Project* (www.brettonwoodsproject.org/) and the *Whirled Bank* (www.whirledbank.org/) also continue to scrutinize and satirize the online outpourings of official World Bank analysis. This is important because the Bank itself remains a moving target. Most recently, Barack Obama's appointment of Jim Yong Kim as the new president has given hope that a new and genuinely caring commitment to social justice will start to reshape the Bank's pro-growth agenda, not least of all because Kim once co-edited a book (entitled *Dying for Growth*) that was very critical of the impact of neoliberalism on health (Kim, 2000). Unlike Robert Zoellick and Paul Wolfowitz (the neoconservatives who immediately preceded Kim and who had previously pushed for the Iraq war), and also unlike Robert McNamara (who is commonly thought to have seen his 1970s work at the Bank as a form of expiation for his preceding role in the Vietnam war), Kim comes to the job as a physician famous for prior work with Paul Farmer in establishing *Partners in Health*. But early signs nevertheless suggest that the Bank will shape Kim more than the other way round (Bond, 2012). And if this turns out to be the case, it will reflect the way in which the Bank continues to function as an intermediary that turns market forces into innovations in political influence that in turn expand and entrench market forces globally.

References

Bret Benjamin, *Invested Interests: Capital, Culture and the World Bank* (Minneapolis: University of Minnesota Press, 2007).

Patrick Bond, "Why Jim Kim Should Resign From the World Bank," *Counterpunch* April 16, 2012, online at http://www.counterpunch.org/2012/04/16/why-jim-kim-should-resign-from-the-world-bank/

Robin Broad, "Research, Knowledge and the Art of 'Paradigm Maintenance': World Bank's Development Economics Vice-Presidency (DEC)," *Review of International Political Economy* 13, no. 3 (2006): 387–419.

Ben Fine, "Development as Zombieconomics in the Age of Neoliberalism," *Third World Quarterly* 30, no. 5 (2009): 885–904.

Michael Goldman, Imperial Nature: *The World Bank and Struggles for Justice in the Age of Globalization* (New Haven, CT: Yale University Press, 2005).

Jonathan Joseph, "Poverty Reduction and the New Global Governmentality," *Alternatives* 35 (2010): 29–51.

Jim Yong Kim, ed., *Dying for Growth: Global Inequality and the Health of the Poor* (Monroe, ME: Common Courage Press, 2000).

Amitava Kumar, ed., *World Bank Literature* (Minneapolis: University of Minnesota Press, 2003).

Victoria Lawson, "Reshaping Economic Geography? Producing Spaces of Inclusive Development," *Economic Geography* 86, no. 4 (2010): 351–60.

Richard Peet, *Unholy Trinity: The IMF, World Bank and WTO* (New York: Zed Books, 2003).

Arne Ruckert, "Towards an Inclusive-Neoliberal Regime of Development: From the Washington to the Post-Washington Consensus," *Labour, Capital & Society* 39, no. 1 (2006): 34–67.

Robert Wade, "United States Hegemony and the World Bank: The Fight over People and Ideas," *Review of International Political Economy* 9, no. 2 (2002): 201–29.

Michael Watts, "Economies of Violence: Reflections on the World Development Report 2011," *Humanity: An International Journal of Human Rights, Humanitarianism, and Development* 3, no. 1 (2012): 115–30.

Heloise Weber, "A Political Analysis of the PRSP Initiative: Social Struggles and the Organization of Persistent Relations of Inequality," *Globalizations* 3, no. 2 (2006): 187–206.

WTO Although the idea of an international trade organization was formulated in 1944 at Bretton Woods, today's World Trade Organization was only founded in 1994 at the close of the Uruguay Round (1986–1994) of the GATT talks in Marakesh. Its purpose is to liberalize international trade by enforcing free-trade rules, arbitrating international trade disputes, and working to forge new global agreements on the removal of **tariffs** and so-called non-tariff barriers to trade (the latter including all sorts of national rules on health and environmental protections). Unlike the **IMF** and the **World Bank** – which were set up at Bretton Woods to run on a "one dollar, one vote" principle – the WTO operates on an ostensibly more inclusive model in which the voices of individual member states are all meant to count. However, because the ground rules for inclusion are fixed as free-trade rules, because the basic goal of the organization is to remove frictions on the movement of commodities, and because the organization's dispute-resolution mechanism works on the assumption that it is intrinsically good to reduce both tariff and non-tariff barriers to trade, the WTO serves institutionally to expand and entrench **neoliberalism** on a global scale (Peet, 2003; Harvey, 2005).

Everywhere its rules apply, the WTO enables the privatization of formerly public goods and common property resources, whether they be medicines, government-provided health services, shared forests, or clean water. WTO rules also simultaneously undercut democratic governance in so far as they provide a powerful lever through which businesses can reduce or eliminate democratic law-making (including, for example, legislation banning carcinogenic chemicals and pesticides) by coding the resulting public interest laws as non-tariff barriers to trade (Wallach and Woodall, 2004). Another neoliberal aspect of the WTO is that there is very little possibility under its free-trade rules to permit non-neoliberal development strategies such as the production of cheap generic drugs or state assistance to new industries facing competition from developed producers elsewhere. As a result, the WTO has been criticized for "pulling up the ladder" for the world's poorer countries, preventing them from following a path once taken by countries such as the United States and Japan that used industrial protectionism in their early approach to development. It has been this basic injustice, combined with the WTO's democracy-eroding complicity in processes of dispossession, that has led so many critics to take to the streets from Seattle in 1999 through to Hong Kong in 2006. Ironically, however, it has been yet another injustice noted by the protestors that has ultimately proved most damaging to the WTO's own attempts to expand free trade since the "Battle in Seattle." This additional injustice is the disproportionate power still wielded by the US government in negotiations because of the importance of the US market in global trade. The irony is that because the United States has been unwilling to fully implement free trade itself, and, most notably, because (like the EU) it has been unwilling to give up the huge subsidies given each year to domestic **agribusiness**, US officials have been moving increasingly away from the mulitalteralism of WTO negotiations where they face growing demands from developing countries to eliminate such practices and actually implement free trade in farmed goods. As a result, American trade negotiators have preferred more recently to develop bilateral trade deals with particular countries such as Singapore, and, meanwhile, the WTO's failing attempts to expand free trade remain an important reminder that globalization is not so inevitable after all.

References

D. Harvey, *A Brief History of Neoliberalism* (Oxford: Oxford University Press, 2005).

Richard Peet, *Unholy Trinity: The IMF, World Bank and WTO* (London: Zed Books, 2003).

L. Wallach and P. Woodall, *Whose Trade Organization: A Comprehensive Guide to the WTO?* (New York: The New Press, 2004).

Index

Please note that page numbers in italics refer to figures or tables. Page numbers in bold refer to the glossary definition.

Introducing Globalization: Ties, Tensions, and Uneven Integration, First Edition. Matthew Sparke.
© 2013 Matthew Sparke. Published 2013 by Blackwell Publishing Ltd.

class divisions, 116–22
climate change, 341, 343–9, 400
Clinton, Bill
  CUFTA expansion, 242
  end of welfare, 439
  financial policies, 156, 160, 425
  genomics, 350, 351, 353
  globalization, 32
  inevitability argument, 35
Cold War, 64, 153, 166, 246, 264
collateralized debt obligations
    (CDOs), 155, 424
Collins, Francis, 350, 351, 352
commodification, 59, **426–7**
  of nature, 59, 70, 338, 426
  pharmaceutical and medical
    knowledge, 200
  of social relations, 142
  World Social Forum (WSF), 50–1, 53
commodities
  data collection, 58–9
  defined, 58
  interdependencies of, 12–13, 57–95
  see also trade
commodity chains, 69–82, **427–8**
  captive-supplier model, 77, 79–80, 88, 91
  defined, 13, 59
  functional integration, 71
  global management development, 76–82
  horizontal integration, 77, 79, 80, 444–5
  in-house model, 77–9, 77, 82, 88, 91
  intellectual property (IP), 77, 79
  intermediation, 76, 79
  "market efficiency" rationale, 187
  market mediation, 77–82
  marketized model, 77, 81–2, 88, 91
  modular model, 77, 80, 82, 91
  production phase, 69–70, 72, 74, 84
  relational model, 77, 81, 82, 88, 91
  stages and inputs, 70–1, 71
  three main parts of, 69–70, 72, 74
  ties to workers, 14
  turnover time, 72–3
  vertical integration, 77–9, 83, 464
  vulnerability to union action, 132–3
  see also TNCs (transnational
    corporations)

commodity fetishism, **428–9**
communication technologies, 12, 72–5,
    263, 268–9
Communism, 8–9, 63, 85–6
comparative advantage, 112–14, 188, 397,
    429–30
competition
  global emergence of, 75–6
  trade agreements, 186–9
  see also monopolization
competitive ranking systems, 271–4
conditionalities, **430–1**
  IMF, 169, 171, 172, 255–8, 260–1,
    430, 446
  World Bank, 169, 255–8, 259,
    260–1, 430
  see also fiscal austerity
consumerism, **431**
copyright, 196–7
Corporate Social Responsibility
    (CSR), 219, 441
cosmopolitanism, 121, 298, 395, **432–3**
credit default swaps (CDSs), 155, 156–7
credit-ratings agencies, 38, 148, 252, 272–4,
    305, 306, 417, **433–4**
crises *see* debt crises; financial crises
    (2008–); financial crisis (1997), Asia
Cuba, 9, 194, 371
currencies
  supply-and-demand relation, 141,
    146, 147
  see also US dollar
currency speculators, 144–5, 146, 155, 161

Davis, Mike, 313, 323–4, 331–2, 372
de-unionization, 405
  neoliberal norm, 6, 229, 394, 455
debt, **434–5**
  American, 17, 141, 144, 148, 159–65, 434
  HIPC program, 172, 173, 174, 435
debt crises
  development of, 141, 165–7
  and dispossession, 167–8
  Euro-zone countries, 143, 144, 158, 163,
    261, 272, 273, 375, 400, 408–9, 424
  Global South, 17, 165–77, 256,
    375–6, 434